PLANNING

PLANNING LANDSCAPE

DIMENSIONS, ELEMENTS, TYPOLOGIES

ASTRID ZIMMERMANN

Birkhäuser
Basel

PLANNING LANDSCAPE

1 Introduction

Planning processes must take into account a multitude of demands and desires. In addition to design concerns and conceptual considerations, dimensional specifications and parameters often become part of the design task. These can be a source of inspiration – a starting point for how to particularize a design – and can also be integrated, through an assessment process, in the intended concept. In both cases, an interplay of necessity and exclusion, of logical consequences and inevitable contradictions comes about. Compensating these and finding the optimal balance is the task of the planner.

Some practical requirements, such as ensuring effective drainage of rainwater from the surfaces of paths and roads, can place constraints on design freedom. But with the backdrop of climate changes and an increasing occurrence of heavy rainfall events, planners cannot do without taking measures to create a generously dimensioned stormwater management system that will also suffice in extreme situations, so as to ensure the usability of an outdoor facility over the long term.

Savings cannot be achieved solely with a purely economic approach, such as by selecting inexpensive materials or utilizing a specifically customized means of construction. Giving consideration to sociocultural aspects also affects long-term economic sustainability. By considering the needs of as many potential user groups as possible or by ensuring that a site is adaptable to future use requirements, an outdoor facility remains interesting and attractive for different user groups that may develop even long after it has fulfilled its initial use. That leads to greater acceptance and appreciation, and consequently, to less vandalism and less need for reconstruction in the future.

"Design for all" is what is called for here, going well beyond the requirements of barrier-free accessibility. It deals with the needs of all people. Of course, a focus of attention must certainly also be to ensure access to places for people with special needs. Besides wheelchair users, this group includes pregnant women, people with impaired mobility, hearing, or sight, and adults accompanied by young children or pushing strollers. But even for cyclists, elements like stairs can represent unacceptable and insurmountable barriers. That is why the requirements of different groups of people – those that go beyond the measures prescribed by building codes and regulations – should be given full consideration and complied with when feasible.

Conversely, this implies that in cases where only specific user groups are anticipated, no comprehensive measures must be taken. Thus benches without backrests or armrests are sufficient for a skate park, for example. On a playground for small children, by contrast, it can be expected that older people, who have a need for comfortable seating, may be attending to or accompanying some of the children.

Accessibility and sustainability in outdoor facilities target not only locomotion and access but also versatile usability. The goal of a design should not be to create uniform open spaces, but a differentiated perception of people's diversity, which is duly taken into account by weighing all the influencing factors. The general advice given by the European Concept for Accessibility (ECA), which supports universal design to create environments that are open to everyone, can be of assistance in the planning process.

The environmental objectives of sustainable planning should also be considered at an initial stage of design, so that the way is paved early for the conservation of resources and the minimization of environmental impacts. The fundamentally positive impact of green spaces (such as binding the greenhouse gas

Table 1.1 Recommendations for accessibility, from: ECA for Administrations, 2008 (EuCAN – European Concept for Accessibility Network)

Thus an accessible environment has to be:

1. Respectful: It should respect the diversity of users; nobody should feel marginalized and everybody should be able to get to it.	**5. Comprehensible:** All users should be able to orient themselves without difficulty within a given space, and therefore the following are essential: (1) information must be clear; and (2) the spatial distribution must be coherent. Clear information means using icons that are common to different countries and avoiding the use of words or abbreviations from the local language which may lead to confusion; for example, using the letter *C* on taps, which suggests *cold* in English but *caliente* (meaning "hot" – exactly the opposite) in Spanish. Spatial distribution should be coherent and functional, rather than segregating and exclusive.
2. Safe: It should be free of risks to all users; therefore, all those elements which form part of an environment have to be designed with safety in mind (slippery floors, parts jutting out, dimensions, etc.).	
3. Healthy: It should not be a health risk or cause problems to those who suffer from certain illnesses or allergies.	
4. Functional: It should be designed in such a way that it can carry out, without any problems or difficulties, the function for which it was intended.	**6. Aesthetic:** The result should be aesthetically pleasing, as this will make it more likely to be accepted by everybody (the previous five points always being borne in mind).

CO_2, climatic moderation through a reduction of the temperature in overheated urban areas by means of evaporative cooling, or the dust-capturing capability of the leaf surfaces of trees and shrubs) should not be counteracted by unnecessary changes to the natural grade or a high degree of sealing.

Choosing durable materials and considering their potential options for reusability, recyclability, or safe disposal are also important aspects for sustainable construction. Depending on how building materials are used, their durability can vary significantly – and this must be taken into account. In the interests of the client, a proper relationship between the investment costs and the expected or desired life span of the construction project should be maintained in the process.

So the task of the planner is to identify and explore the leeway between local conditions, subjective interests, and functional requirements as well as between the legal and safety-related requirements, the design ideas, and economic aspects. Timely consideration of as many requirements as possible promotes an optimal planning process and, inasmuch as it is constructed as planned, leads to an outdoor facility that is sustainable in every sense of the word. The term *sustainability* is fully justified with respect to a landscape architecture design when, in addition to responding to design concerns and economic issues, both ecological and sociocultural aspects are also integrated and their quality is lastingly secured. Almost every design process is accompanied by a multitude of dimensional specifications and parameters. These frequently have an undeniable impact on the spatial or formative design. And for the subsequent use of an outdoor facility, they ensure it will be functional and safe. The sooner that relevant aspects are included in the planning process, the better they can be integrated into a design idea. Subsequent efforts to make modifications can be avoided that way, as can planning deficiencies.

Planning Landscape is conceived as a tool and aid for planning that provides assistance in the process of landscape architecture design. Consequently, this book presents planners and designers with a well-conceived planning instrument that is divided into two main parts: "Elements" and "Typologies," between which the reader can freely switch back and forth, depending on the scale being considered. All the pertinent planning information is put into context and explained clearly and in detail with text and illustrations: the relevant dimensional specifications, physical dimensions, characteristics, parameters, and guidelines. Accessibility issues and age-specific regulations are addressed in the applicable chapters and in respect to specific subjects.

In the *Elements* section, fundamental factors such as climate and grading are assembled, together with generally applicable dimensions and standard sizes of such open space elements as paths, parking spaces, trees and shrubs, and boundary enclosures, which are relevant to a great many open-space typologies. In the *Typologies* section, the various open-space typologies and the specific requirements that go beyond generally applicable limits and minimum standards (for playgrounds and preschools, for example) are described and the characteristics and dimensions of special areas such as sports or recreational facilities are presented.

These two main sections are flanked by the introductory section *Human Measure*, which details human proportions and basic dimensions, portrays aspects of human perception in the environment, and presents the sizes required for outdoor facilities in residential contexts, and by the *Reference Guide* section at the end of the book, which contains basic information about systems of units, angular dimensions, aesthetic benchmarks, and urban design parameters, supplemented by bibliographic references, information on relevant regulations, and a list of suggested further reading.

Inasmuch as pertinent governmental regulations exist, the data presented is based on the applicable European or international regulations. For topics that are subject to varied regulations at a national level, German standards and legislation are taken as the basis. In individual cases, these are supplemented by the regulations of other countries.

Since stipulations can also differ at the regional or local level, it is not always possible to make generally applicable statements. In such cases, the information presented here should be taken as guidelines.

The use of plants, which is an extensive field of study in itself, can only receive limited treatment within the framework of this book. An emphasis is given here to woody plants and to the use of plants in relation to built structures.

2 Human Measure
2.1 Basic Human Measurements

2.1 Basic Human Measurements

Almost every design project addressed by planners is based in some way on human measure. This can pertain to people and their proportions – human scale – as well as the aspects of sensory and social perception. Whereas human dimensions modulate the form of the individual object, the parameters of visual and auditory perception constitute a basis for the formation of space.

Human Proportions and Basic Measurements

Scores of scientists, artists, architects, engineers, philosophers, and educators – often united in the same person – have already engaged with anthropometry, the study of human measurements and proportions. Vitruvius, Leonardo da Vinci, Albrecht Dürer, Le Corbusier, and Adolf Zeising have all explored the natural or divine principles of the human body. They found these principles by studying the human body in relationship to geometric forms and by examining the individual limbs of a person and their relationships to each other with reference to the golden section. Throughout the cultural history of the human race, efforts have been made to transfer these principles to architecture and thus to find a harmonious measure that is also functionally attuned to human proportions. One of the best-known studies of proportion is Le Corbusier's Modulor, which is based on the proportions of the human body and the golden section. With it, Le Corbusier sought to give architecture a mathematical order that is oriented around the measurements of people. Functional and aesthetic considerations fused together to form a whole and established the creative starting point for Le Corbusier's work. (→ Chapter 5 Reference Guide – Dimensions and Units)

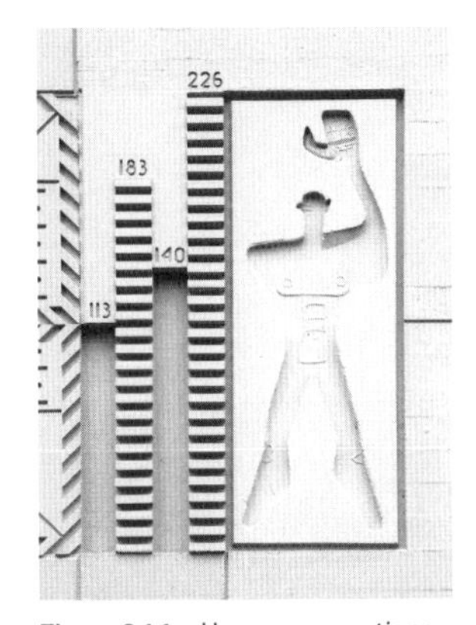

Figure 2.1.1 Human proportions as exemplified by Le Corbusier's Modulor (relief on the facade of a building in Berlin-Westend)

Nonetheless, a person cannot represent a rigid point of reference. Certain principles and proportions are indeed discernable and reappear time and again, but just the same, individual studies also repeatedly attest to deviations from the norm. This is even already evident in the diversity of people due to their age, their gender, or their origin. A worldwide comparison reveals that today there are deviations of 15 to 25 cm in average body height, and the average difference between men and women is about 10 cm. It can make sense to take this into account in a specific context, and it is also relevant in today's context of global design and planning activity. The idea of "Design for All" (DfA) also takes into consideration human diversity in all of its manifestations and seeks to make the (built) environment accessible – and thus convenient, comfortable, and safe – for everyone. Because the basic measurements that serve as an initial aid for planning can only express average values for human dimensions and other measures, they should also be applied creatively and consciously. For the dimensioning of spaces for play and physical activity or the design of seating, these measurements represent basic standard values for reference, which can be modified as needed by taking the expected use into account. → Figures 2.1.2 and 2.1.4

Defining a standard seat height, for instance, constitutes a compromise between practicability and functionality. Although it is sufficient as a general rule, deviations from such a standard are needed to meet specific requirements for use. Occasionally providing benches with a lower, nonstandard seat height of 0.3 m for use by people of short stature is one example, and in the context of diverse efforts to give equal treatment to everyone, this will increasingly become the rule rather than the exception. (Compare draft standard DIN 18040-3.)

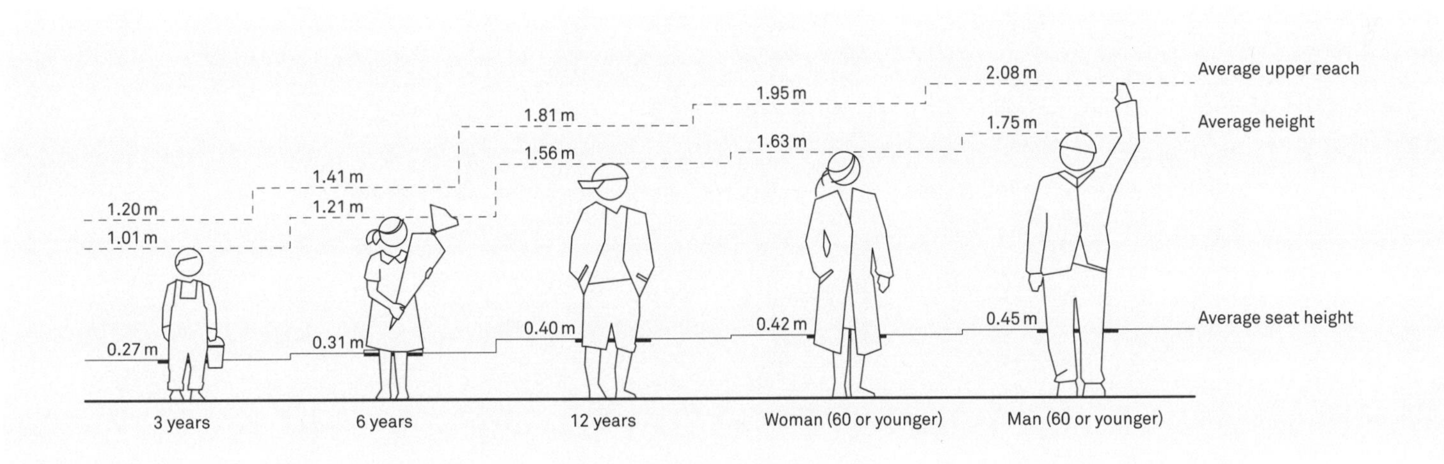

Figure 2.1.2 Human scale – heights of different age groups

Figure 2.1.3 "Generational bench" with different sitting heights

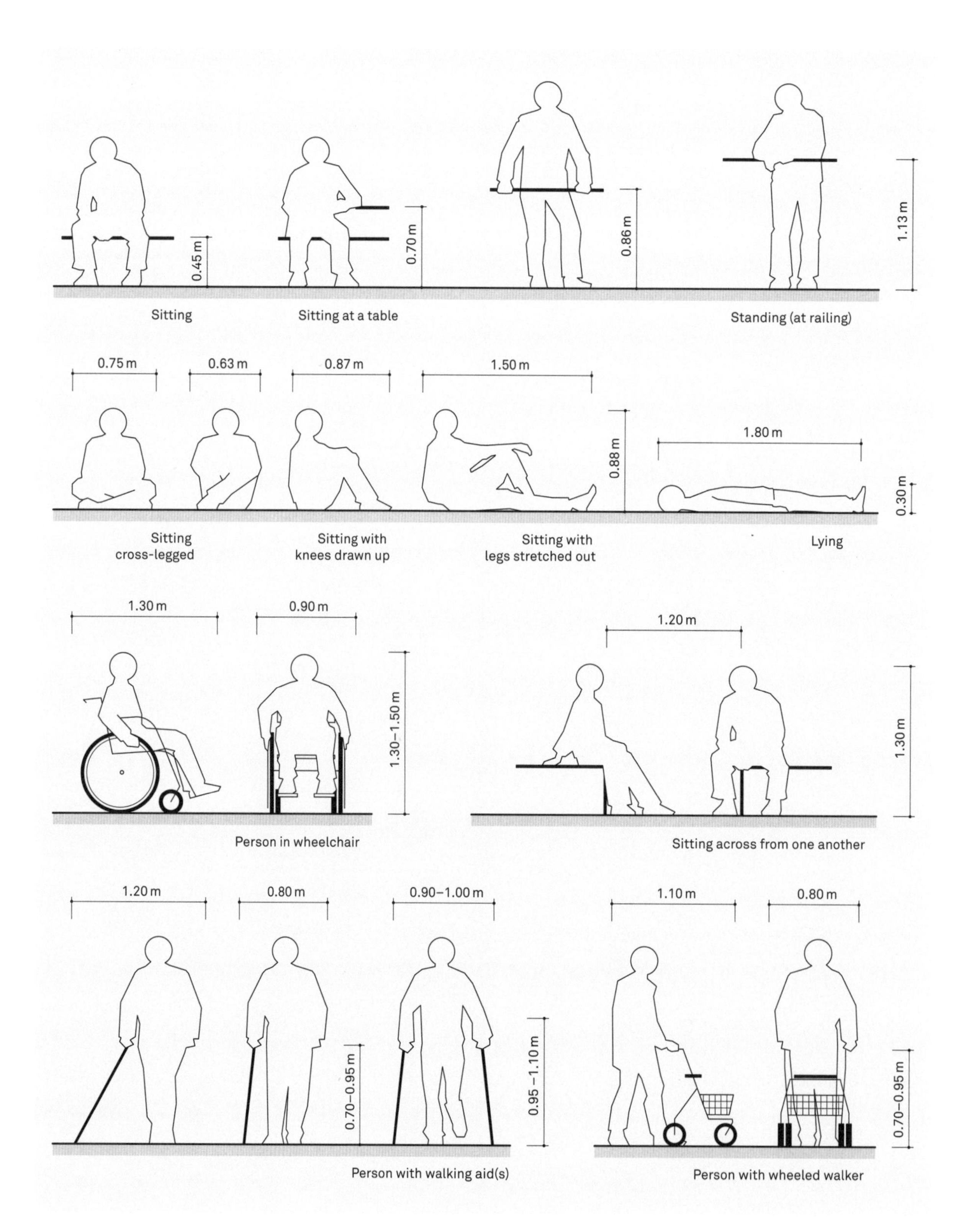

Figure 2.1.4 Human scale – dimensions while sitting and standing

Distances of Perception

Human vision and hearing regulates the coexistence between people and their interaction in space. With increasing distance, visual details are perceived less well, just as sounds or spoken words are harder to understand. This "range of the senses" comprises distances of perception that are important parameters for the spatial design of outdoor spaces, because they help determine the arrangement of functional areas and the spacing needed between them. In his book *Life Between Buildings*, Jan Gehl describes in detail how these distances work in an urban context and their meaning for public space. → Figures 2.1.5 and 2.1.6

Verbal communication requires a certain proximity to each other. Conversation distance – the space of direct communication between two individuals – extends up to 7 meters. It can, however, be strongly affected by noise sources. Difficulties in conducting verbal communication begin to arise when background noises reach a level of 55 dB(A). Furthermore, health-related impairments can arise from exposure to the prolonged emission of sounds with levels higher than 65 dB(A). If such noise pollution can be expected, certain minimum clearances around the source of the noise must be observed or appropriate noise abatement measures (→ Chapter 3.6) must be taken. → Figures 2.1.7 and 2.1.8

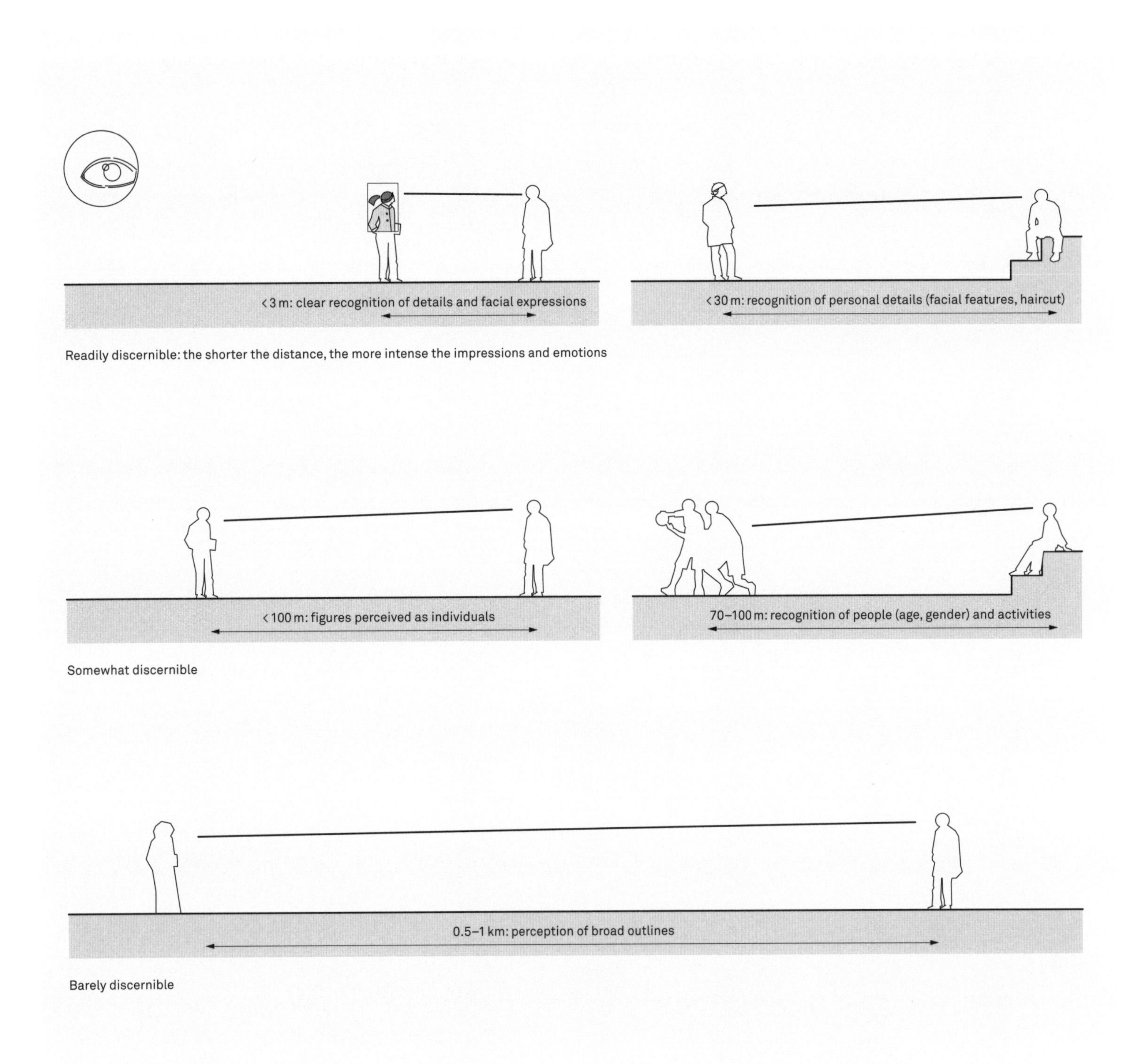

Figure 2.1.5 Distance of perception – vision
(Source: Jan Gehl, *Life Between Buildings*, 1987)

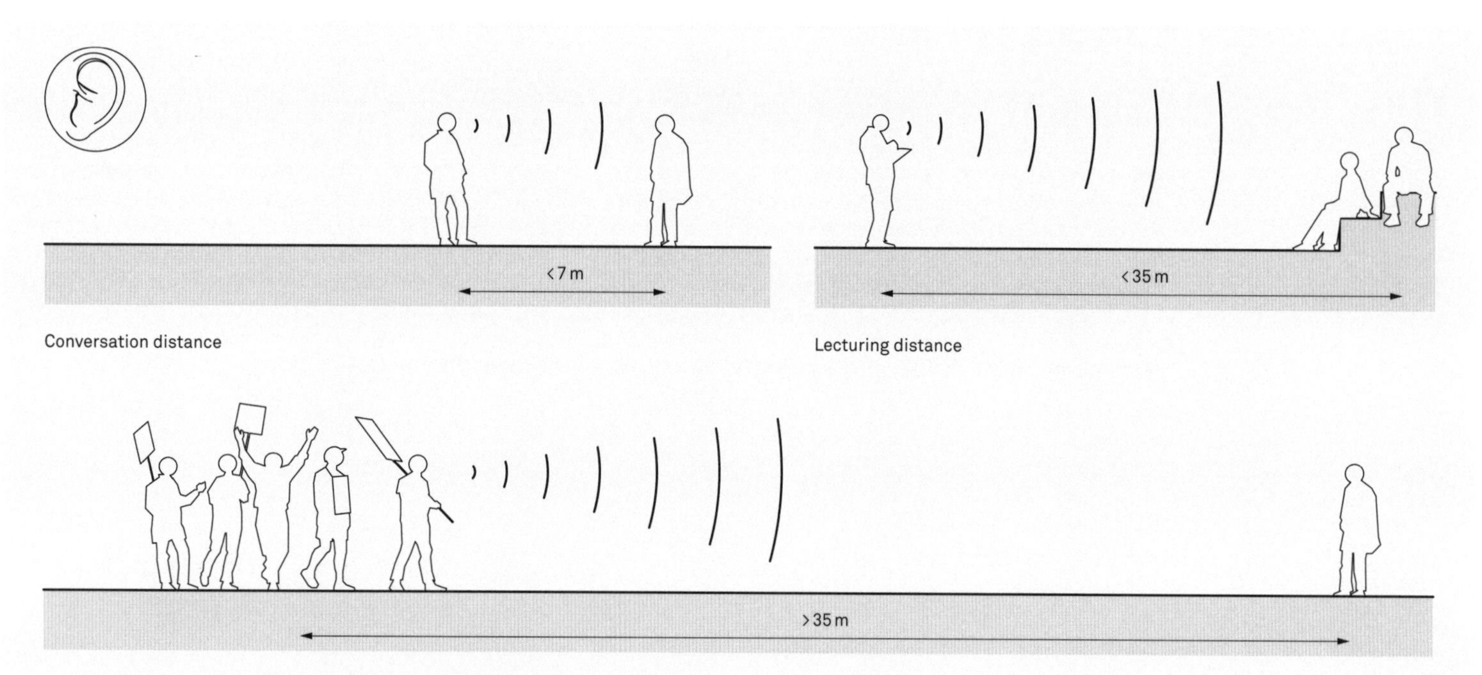

Figure 2.1.6 Distance of perception – hearing (Source: Jan Gehl, *Life Between Buildings,* 1987)

Perception	Limits	Effect	Loudness in dB(A)	Noise source
Painful		≥ 120 dB(A) Pain threshold, hearing impairment possible within a short time	130	Jet airplane
			120	Waterfall
Intolerable			110	
			108	Outdoor pools (800–1,000 people)
			100	
				Skate park (halfpipe/bowl), skater passing by on asphalt
		≥85 dB(A) Injury possible; risk to hearing according to workplace regulations (8 hours/day)	95	Lawn mower / string trimmer / leaf blower (statutory upper limit)
			90	Activity on soccer field, truck passing at a distance of 5 m, passing train
			85	Lawn mower / string trimmer / leaf blower (eco-friendly)
Loud	65 dB(A) Limit value for commercial areas 55 dB(A) Limit value for residential areas (daytime)*		80	Motorcycle, screaming, children's noise
			75	Bicycle bell (standardized minimum loudness)
			70	Car driving past at a distance of 10 m
		≥65 dB(A) Increased risk of cardiovascular disease	65	Major road at night
			60	Frog croaking, normal speech
		Disruptions to communication	55	
Quiet			50	Light rain, birds twittering, background noise in the city
			40	Quiet residential street
			30	Whispering
			25	
			20	Rustling of leaves
			10	Extreme silence, not experienced in cities
Silent		0 dB = Threshold of hearing	0	

Data corresponds to average values; sound pressure level is dependent on the distance from the source of the sound
* per Technical Instructions on Noise Abatement (TA Lärm) and DIN 18005-1 supplementary sheet 1

Figure 2.1.7 Sources of noise and their impacts

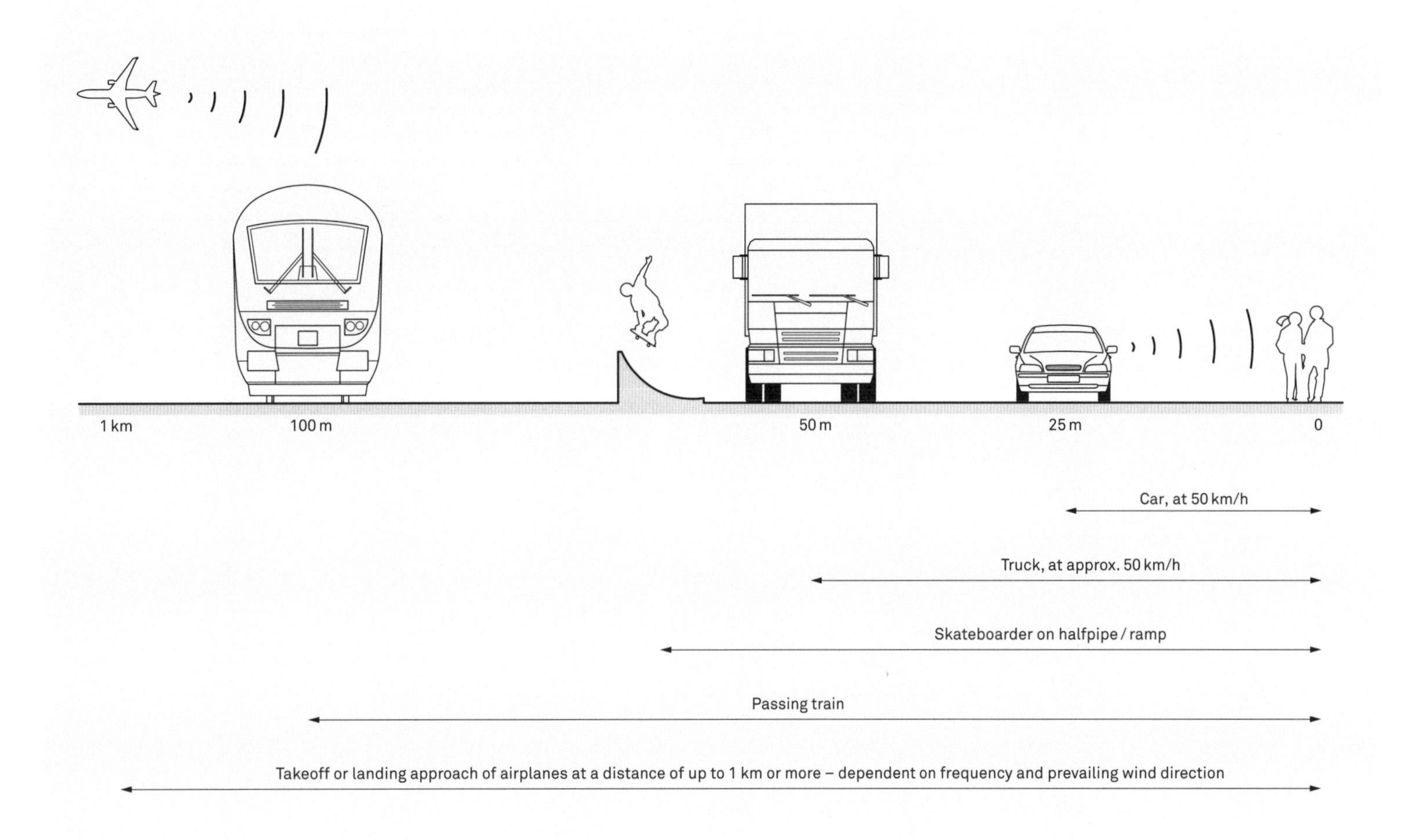

Figure 2.1.8 Distance of perception – conversation disrupted by noise emissions (threshold for communication disruptions = 55 dB(A))

Distance Zones

The term *social distance* is used in psychology to refer to the subjectively experienced distance (remoteness) from a person or group. It is influenced by gender and cultural or social background (see, among others, Bogardus). Edward T. Hall used the term to describe a specific spatial distance between people holding a conversation. In his 1966 book *The Hidden Dimension*, he defined four "distance zones." These comprise intimate, personal, social, and public distance. An intimate distance is only assumed by people who share a great amount of familiarity. The personal zone also typically presupposes a degree of familiarity or at least a warranted interest, such as in the context of social events. This distance is also tolerated in public transit, in the movie theater, or sitting in a stadium. Social distance is a distance that is maintained in communication between individuals who are compelled to come into contact or who are still unfamiliar with each other. Such confrontations commonly occur when conducting business transactions or while formalizing a chance encounter. Finally, we assume a public distance toward strangers and unfamiliar groups. These distance zones must also be viewed in the context of the personal or cultural background of a person or a group or of a specific situation, thus the distances they formulate vary accordingly. → **Figure 2.1.9**

Aside from the distance zone, spatial factors can promote or hinder social contacts. The arrangement of elements in outdoor space and the design of the topography bring about or even promote social contacts and encounters. → **Figure 2.1.10**

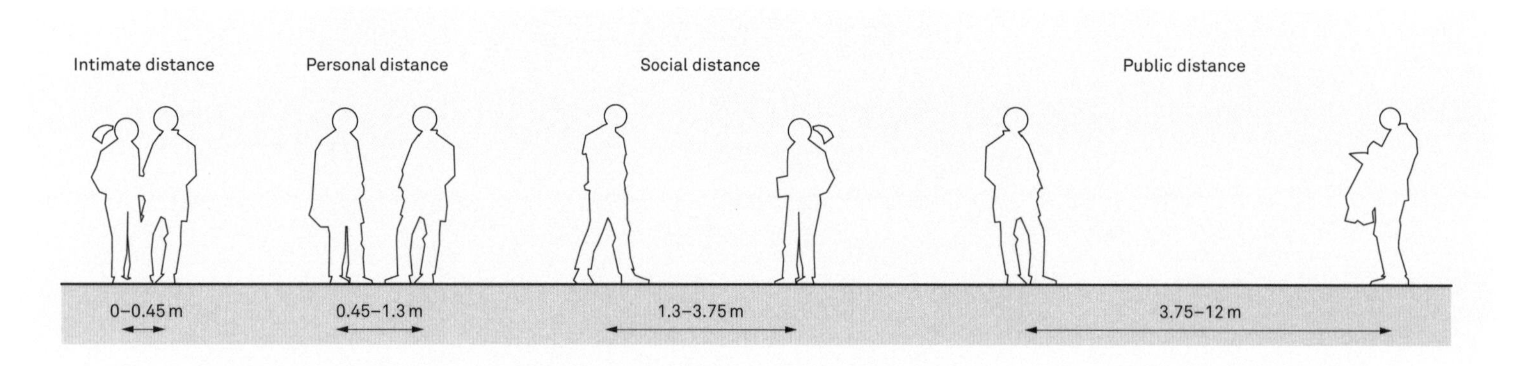

Figure 2.1.9 Distance zones (Source: Edward T. Hall, *The Hidden Dimension*, 1969)

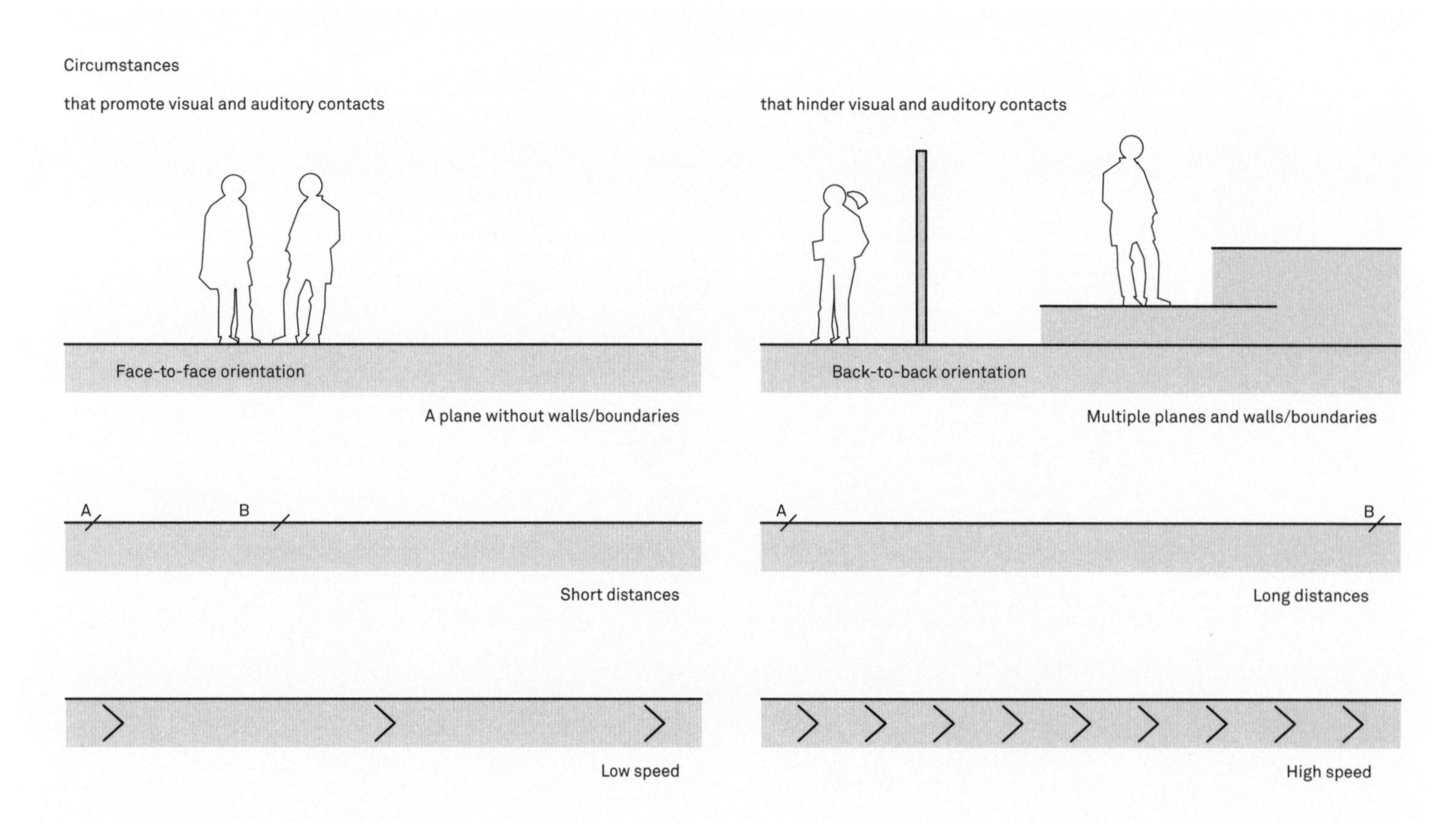

Figure 2.1.10 Spatial perception – influence of different circumstances on visual and auditory contacts (Source: Jan Gehl, *Life Between Buildings*, 1987)

Orientation and Vision

Another important reference value with relevance to planning is a person's visual field and their field of view. The visual field describes the space detectable by the human eye. It is an important parameter for orientation in space and therefore it should be taken into consideration for spatial planning.

The field of view is the area in which sharp vision is possible. With the greatest possible ocular movement and no movement of the head, a person's vision is sharp within an area extending about 120° horizontally and 60° vertically. → Figure 2.1.11

Signage of all kinds should be designed, positioned, and installed in a way that makes it clear and easy to read. The signage must have sufficient contrast, and a character height of adequate size should be used for any text. When positioning signage, the eye level of the relevant target audience must be taken into account. For standing adults (of average stature), this is at a height of approximately 1.6 m, and for wheelchair users it is approximately 1.2 m. → Figure 2.1.12 and Table 2.1.1

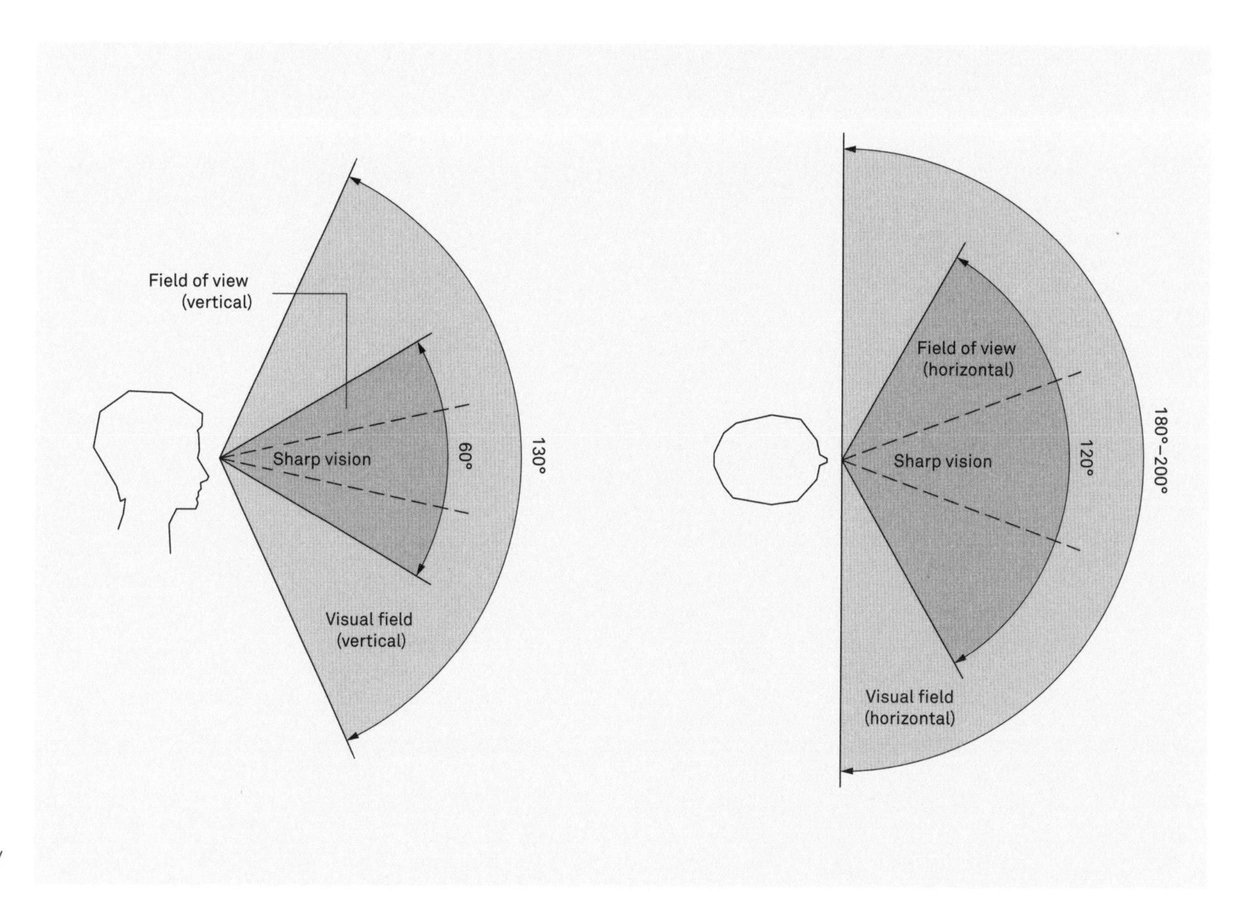

Figure 2.1.11 Human visual field / human field of view

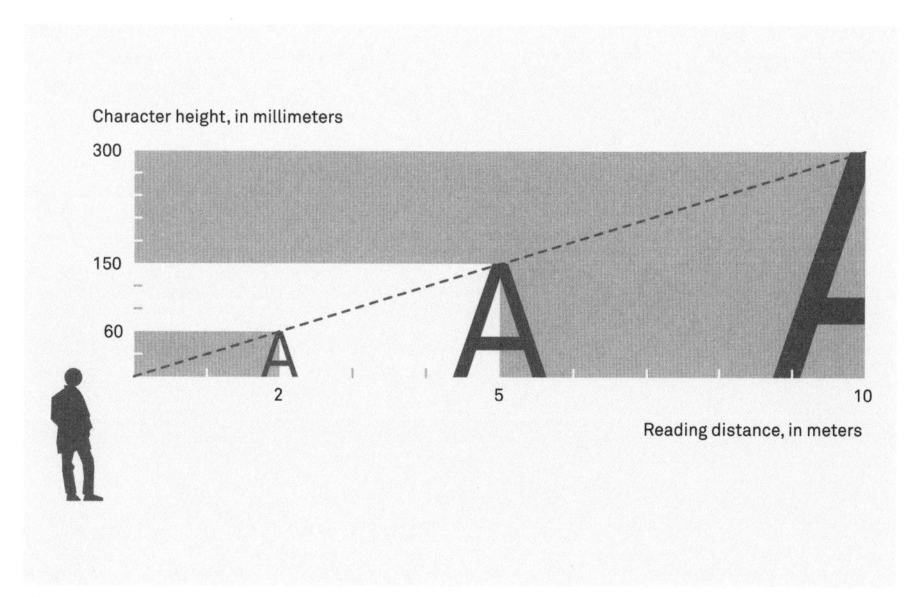

Figure 2.1.12 Text size as a function of reading distance (Source: *Barrierefreies Bauen für alle* [Barrier-free building for all], City of Graz, 2006)

Distance from which the text should remain legible	Character height at 1° to 2° visual angle
30 m	52–104 cm
25 m	44–87 cm
20 m	35–70 cm
15 m	26–52 cm
10 m	17–35 cm
5 m	9–18 cm
2 m	3.5–7 cm
1 m	1.8–13.5 cm
0.3 m	0.5–1 cm
0.25 m	0.4–0.9 cm

Table 2.1.1 Recommended text sizes for use in public spaces (Source: *Verbesserung von visuellen Informationen im öffentlichen Raum* [Improvement of visual information in public spaces], Bundesministerium für Gesundheit, 1996)

2 Human Measure
2.2 Quantifying Need

2.2 Quantifying Need

Urban Open Spaces

For the planning of open spaces, there are no high-level statutory requirements for the size and quantity of particular green spaces. However, standard values (recommended values) and minimum sizes are specified to some extent at the state or municipal level.

These values are to be adapted to the local conditions so that they are appropriate to the site's context within its surroundings and the type and frequency of use. Generally accepted requirements for playgrounds and sports areas are exceptions.

While also taking into account any possible local regulations, the following requirement figures can be used as recommended standard values.

Figure 2.2.1 How much open space does a person need? Standard values can offer guidance when planning, but they can seldom replace a precise determination of requirements.

Open space / reference value	Standard value / requirements	Minimum size	Remarks
Generally accessible public open spaces			
Parks / green spaces Local (serves nearby residents)	6 m²/resident [a] 3.5–4 m²/resident [b]	1 ha 2,000 m² 5,000 m² (Berlin)	• Maximum 500 m walking distance
Serves entire residential area	3–6 m²/resident [b]	10,000 m²	• Small parks, urban green spaces, youth playgrounds • Especially children's playgrounds, open spaces in apartment complexes, and tenant gardens
Neighborhood	7 m²/resident	10 ha	• Community park, 1,000 m walking distance
District-level	7–8 m²/resident [b]	5 ha	• District parks, parts of green corridors
Regional	7 m²/resident	75 ha	• District park, up to 5 km away via public transit
Parks	6–7 m²/resident [c] 8 m²/resident for 0.2 FAR ≤ 15 m²/resident for 1 FAR	2–25 ha [b] (*urban greenery* 0.5 ha; *urban garden* 0.1–0.2 ha)	
Purpose-related public open spaces			
Total requirement for play and sports areas • Up to 2,500 residents • 2,500–10,000 residents • Over 10,000 residents • District-level	4 m²/resident (D) 3.5 m²/resident (A) 5 m²/resident 3.5 m²/resident 2.5 m²/resident 3.5 m²/resident [b]	6 ha	• Net area = area usable for sports • District sports facility (example)
Sports fields	6 m²/resident (gross area) [a]		• Relative to the entire metropolitan area; sports areas excluding gymnasiums
Gymnasiums (indoor facilities)	0.2 m²/resident (net area) [c]		
Outdoor swimming pools / bathing waters	1 m²/resident [a] or 0.05–0.15 m² water surface per resident [c]		• Relative to the entire metropolitan area; public and private pools
Play areas in general (DIN 18034) • Local, within detached development • Local, within attached development • Neighborhood • Regional		500 m² 5,000 m² For large-scale, near-natural areas up to 10,000 m² 10,000 m²	• Areas usually comprise multiple play areas
Play areas for children to age 5 or 6	Minimum 30 m² [b] 0.75 m²/resident 0.5 m²/resident (net area) 60–225 m² gross area 40–50 m² usable play area [c]		
Play areas for children from ages 6 to 12	Minimum 500 m² [b] 0.75 m²/resident 0.5 m²/resident (net area) [c] 675–1,200 m² gross area		
Play areas for youth age 12 and older	0.75 m²/resident 0.5 m²/resident (net area) 800–3,750 m² gross area 1 m²/resident (average) [c]		
Play areas for adults	1.5 m²/resident		
Cemetery areas	5 m²/resident 3.5–5 m²/resident		• Relative to the entire metropolitan area; public and sectarian cemeteries
Parking	1 parking space per 1.1–1.2 dwellings		

Open space / reference value	Standard value / requirements	Minimum size	Remarks
Semipublic and semiprivate open spaces			
Schoolyards	5 m²/student (excluding sports areas)	–	–
Preschools, daycare centers, orphanages	Minimum 600 m² usable area; grass-covered area min. 300 m² hard-surfaced playing area min. 200 m² 10 m²/ child [(b)]		• Boundary enclosure 1.5 m high
Retirement homes	0.45–0.5 m²/resident [(c)]		
Hospitals	0.8–1.2 m²/resident or 80–150 m² per bed 1–1.7 m²/resident [(c)]		
Allotment gardens	1 allotment garden for each 7–10 dwelling units with no garden of their own 1 allotment garden per 7 dwelling units for apartments 2.8 m²/resident for 0.2 FAR, up to 15 m²/resident for 1 FAR; 10–17 m²/resident [(c)]	320 m²; Facility: 1.8–4.5 ha	• Maximum size: 400 m² (D) 650 m² (A)
Gross residential land	70–150 m²/resident		
Net residential land	45–75 m²/resident		
Children's play and recreation areas on residential lots			
Playgrounds for small children (to age 5)	2 m²/dwelling [a]	30 m²	As per Hamburg building code (HBauO) for buildings with 3–5 dwelling units on the premises
Children's play and recreation areas	10 m²/dwelling [a]	150 m²	As per Hamburg building code (HBauO) for buildings with more than 5 dwelling units on the premises; incl. playground for small children (30 m²), on the property or nearby

Table 2.2.1 Standard values for urban open spaces (per area, resident, or dwelling unit) (Sources: [a] Landschaftsprogramm HH [Hamburg landscape program], 1997 [b] Gälzer 2001/ City of Vienna [c] Richter 1981)

Green Connections and Green Corridors

Regardless of its overall size, the usability of an outdoor area is dependent in part on its width. This has a considerable impact on the design options that are feasible and in the layout of different functional zones.

Standard width [m]	Options for use & design
3–5 m	Path
5–10 m	Path + planting
10–30 m	Path + road + planting; path + grass; path + seating; ball court (lengthwise) + planting; promenade + trees
30–100 m	Children's playground, lawn for play and sunbathing, small sports facility, possibly an allotment garden site
100–500 m	Play and sports facility, allotment garden site, cemetery, urban gardens of all types, green corridors with recreation facilities
500–1,000 m	Sports stadium, cemetery, amusement park, public park, bodies of water, woods, orchards, open-air gardening, and special facilities, e.g., equestrian sports, zoo
>1,000 m	Horticulture, arable fields and pastures, woods, recreational areas(landscape portions)

Table 2.2.2 Standard widths of green connections and green corridors (Source: Gälzer, 2001)

Radius of Action

Planning should always strive to enable the age-appropriate use of open space by all segments of the population in equal measure. In connection with the planning of public open spaces – and above all, of those open spaces that are close to housing – the potential radius of action of the various demographic groups constitutes an important point of reference.

Demographic groups	Radius of action / freedom of movement
Small children up to 5 or 6 years	≤ 100–200 m
Children between 5 or 6 and 12 years plus families	≤400 m
Children over 12 years/ adolescents	>400–1,000 m
Adults	≥ 1000 m
Seniors	Decreasing, with reduced mobility ≥ 400 m

Table 2.2.3 Accessibility of open spaces and play areas by age group (Source: City of Hamburg, 1997; DIN 18034)

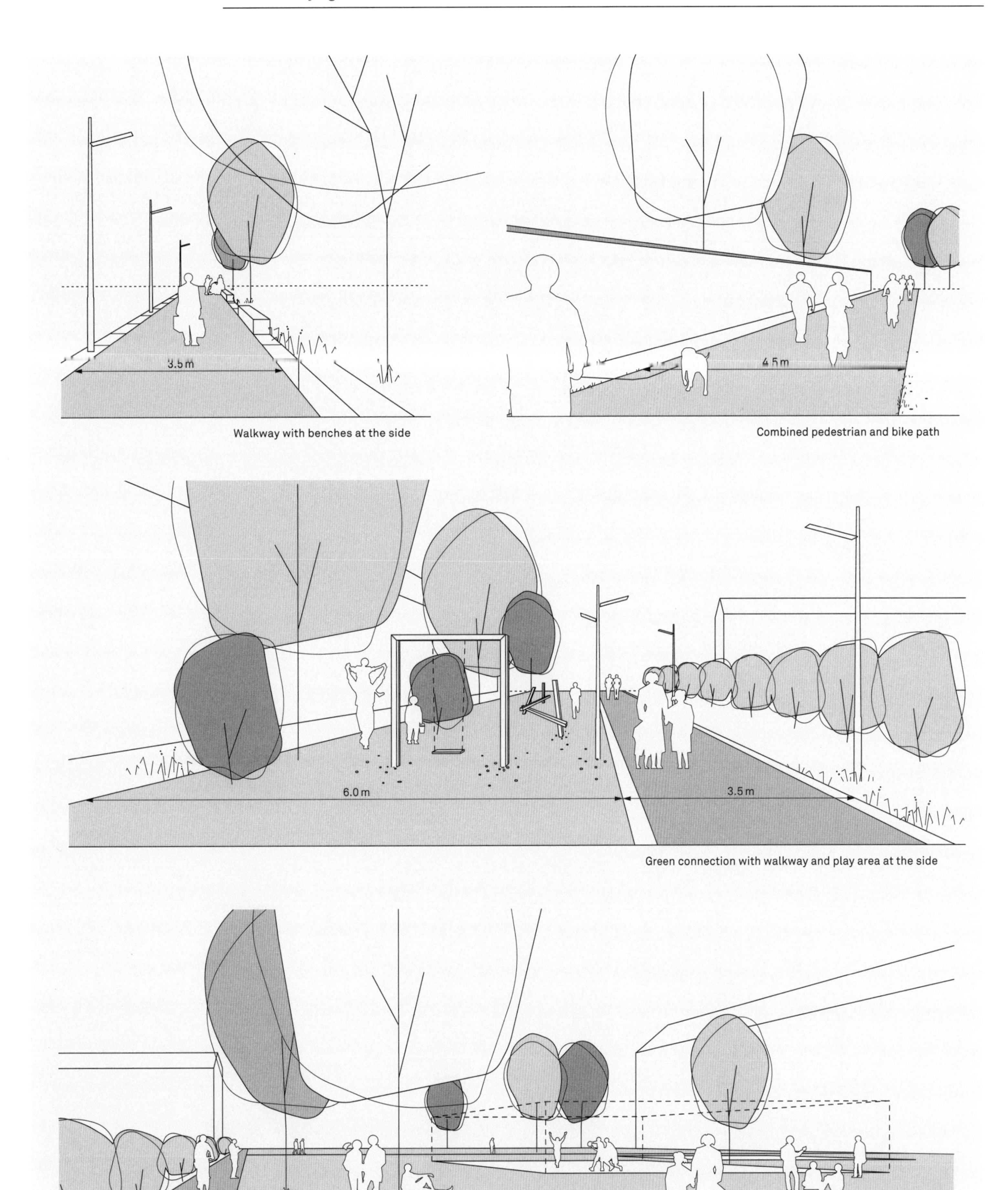

Figure 2.2.2 Exemplary widths of green connections

3 Elements
3.1 Climate and Exposure

3.1 Climate and Exposure

Climate is a basic aspect affecting the selection of plants for an outdoor area. Beyond the fundamental categorization in terms of regions such as corresponding winter hardiness zones, however, there are other factors that can also result in microclimatic idiosyncrasies at a local level. Outflows of cold air, a site located on a mountain or in a valley, or exposure to the windward or leeward side all have an effect on the microclimate, which has relevance for many plants. Likewise, these parameters should be given consideration when designing an outdoor area, for instance through conscious use of protected areas for occupiable areas or the purposeful use of walls as a protective measure.

The same pertains to whether a site faces the side toward or away from the sun or the wind. Slopes or the presence of buildings or tall trees in the immediate vicinity can yield particularly intense sunny or – conversely – shady locations and affect the availability of water.

The limit of cultivation of some crop plants that are also used in gardens and parks provides a good illustration of plants' possible ecological amplitude.

The limits for the (agriculturally relevant) cultivation of wine grapes, olives, and dates are much further south than the actual extent of growth of these plants. By taking advantage of differences in microclimate and by using resilient species or varieties, growing areas in northern regions beyond the intrinsic ecological amplitude are also possible.

Europe's northernmost wine-growing areas are in Hablingbo on the island of Gotland in Sweden and in the town of Sabile in Latvia. Germany's northernmost olive grove is found near Cologne. The comparatively mild climate in Great Britain also allows for the successful cultivation of olive trees, which thrive there – particularly in the southern and western regions, on the coast, and in urban surroundings. Agricultural use of the date in North Africa is augmented by its use of the tree along streets and in parks throughout the Mediterranean region and in mild areas of Great Britain. → Figure 3.1.1

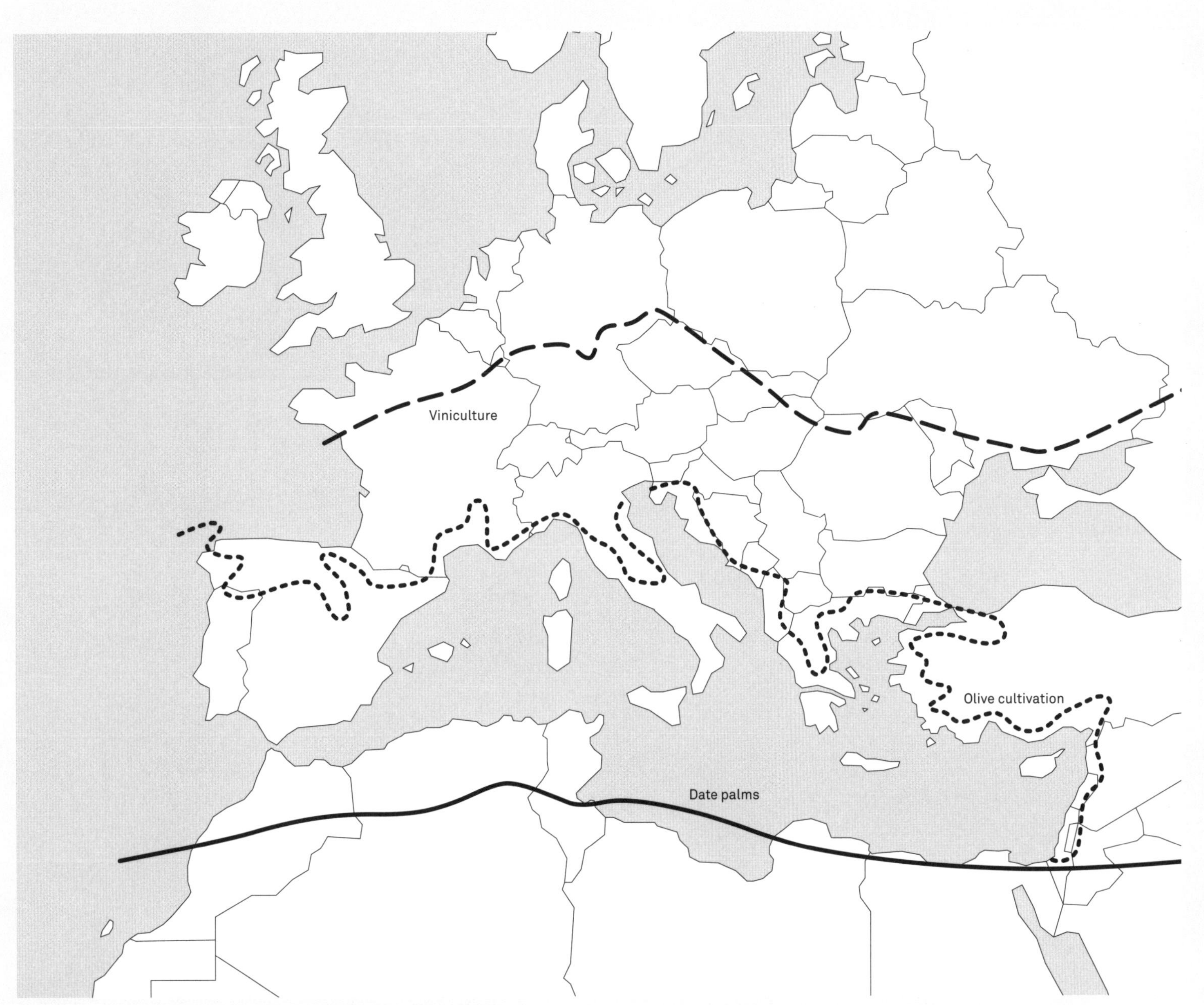

Figure 3.1.1 Northern limits of the cultivation of wine grapes, olive trees, and date palms – all these species are also found much further north, mainly as ornamental plants, in protected locations or areas with sufficient sun exposure.

Location

Winter Hardiness Zones

In regard to climatic conditions, the ecological amplitude of many plants, especially trees and shrubs, often covers a very broad area. This circumstance is intensified still further when the plants grow in a well-maintained green space where they are not as exposed to competitive pressure from other plants, as would be the case in their natural habitat. In addition to precipitation, groundwater, and soil conditions, the temperature conditions constitute a significant limiting factor. Figure 3.1.2 presents an initial survey of an overall classification of regions into winter hardiness zones.

Winter hardiness zones and their ranges of average annual minimum temperatures ($t_{\overline{min Y}}$)

Zone	°F	°C
1	< −50	< −45.5
2	−50 to −40	−45.5 to −40.1
3	−40 to −30	−40.0 to −34.5
4	−30 to −20	−34.4 to −28.9
5	−20 to −10	−28.8 to −23.4
6	−10 to 0	−23.2 to −17.8
7	0 to 10	−17.7 to −12.3
8	10 to 20	−12.2 to −6.7
9	20 to 30	−6.6 to −1.2
10	30 to 40	−1.1 to 4.4
11	>40	>4.4

Figure 3.1.2 European winter hardiness zones (based on W. Heinze and D. Schreiber 1984)

Cold Air Drainage

Due to specific local circumstances, small areas of very different climate conditions can develop. In a hillside situation, cold air drainage causes many very different temperature conditions within a confined area. Cold air ordinarily flows downward and accumulates in the valley. This can lead to temperature differences of several degrees Celsius between the higher slopes and the valley area. Valley floors are thus often subject to frost in late spring. In hollows and other depressions, cold air seeps out in layers, making quite large temperature differences possible there. Because of barriers in the form of garden walls, buildings, or dense windbreak hedges, cold air may accumulate on the hillside, forming small islands of cold air with a greater danger of late spring frost. → **Figure 3.1.3** At the same time, the areas behind remain protected. At the micro scale, protected sites thus emerge for sensitive plants. → **Figure 3.1.4**

In valleys located within the inner city, by contrast, cold air drainage will frequently have a positive impact through its effects. This is particularly true if the processes of air exchange are stimulated and inner-city locations are cooled down as a result.

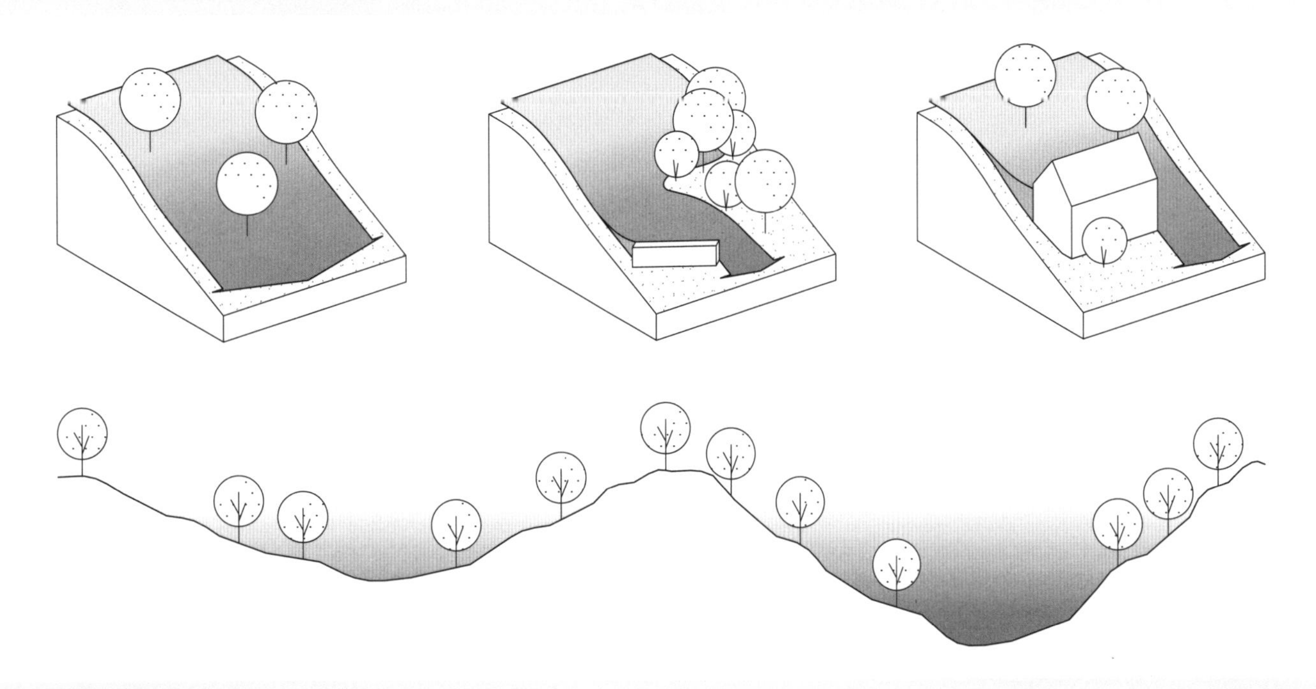

Figure 3.1.3 Drainage and accumulation of cold air at obstacles and in the valley (based on Häckel)

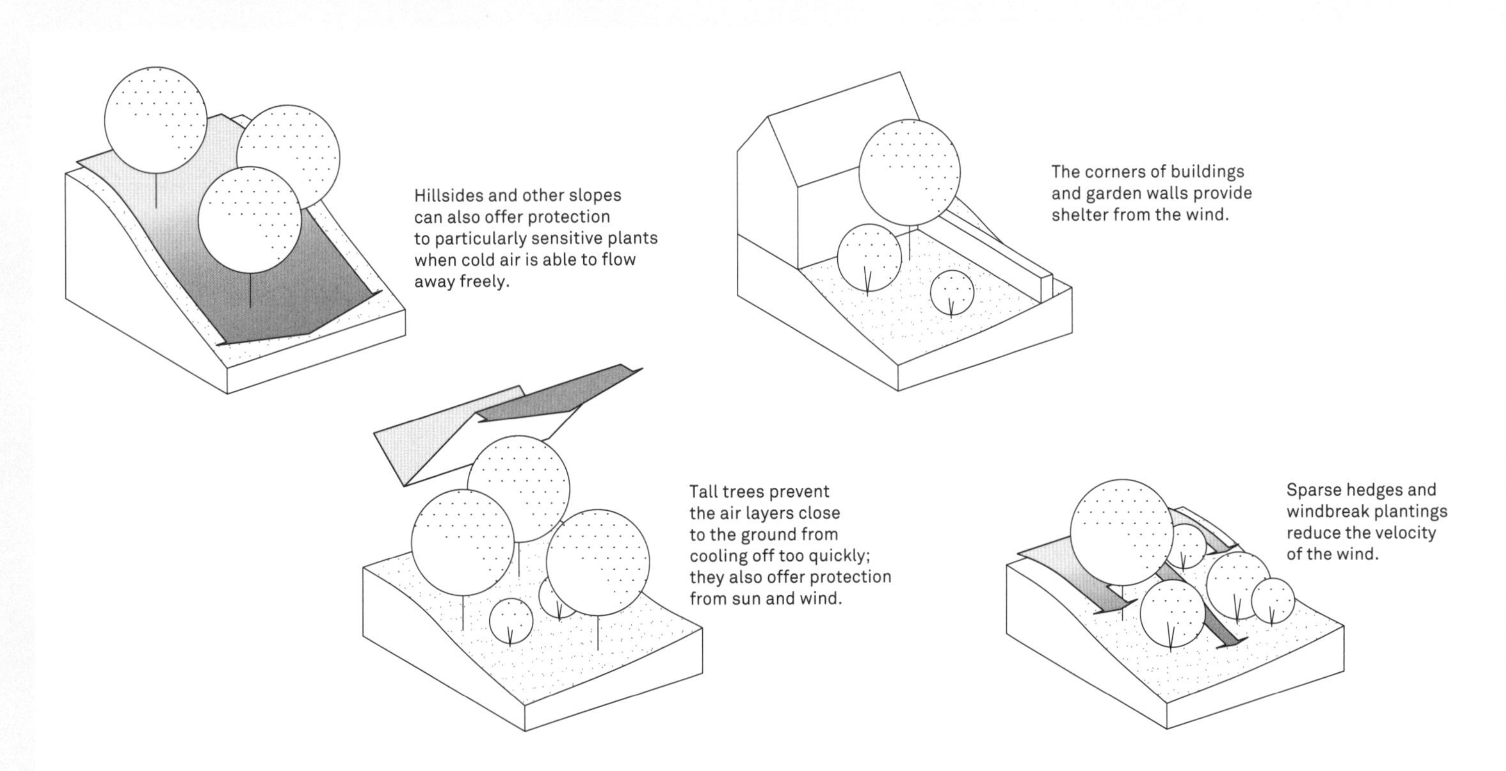

Hillsides and other slopes can also offer protection to particularly sensitive plants when cold air is able to flow away freely.
The corners of buildings and garden walls provide shelter from the wind.
Tall trees prevent the air layers close to the ground from cooling off too quickly; they also offer protection from sun and wind.
Sparse hedges and windbreak plantings reduce the velocity of the wind.

Figure 3.1.4 Conditions and sites protected from cold air and wind

Wind Exposure

For built structures and for groups of woody plants, the orientation of a surface in relation to the wind direction affects the microclimate in different ways: In addition to having a protective function as a shield against cold air, a wind shadow always brings with it a scarcity of water, which can actually be a significant benefit in rainy locations. On the windward side, this results in an increased demand for water drainage. A carefully considered selection of plants can yield a sensible response to a water scarcity (or surplus). → **Figure 3.1.5**

Wind speed and wind circulation are affected by the topography and the disposition and height of buildings. Whereas an increased wind velocity can be expected on hilltops, valleys are characterized by reduced wind speeds in comparison with level conditions. → **Figure 3.1.6**

In an urban context, the average wind speed drops by as much as 20 % – sporadically even by 30 % – in comparison to an open landscape due to the "roughness" of the overall surface texture, which manifests itself most notably in an increased area of still wind. A negative consequence of this effect, however, can be reduced air exchange. Yet another negative consequence can come about in the vicinity of tall buildings through the formation of vortexes or from channeling effects in urban street canyons. Both lead to the occurrence of drafts, which make for less agreeable surroundings in open spaces and can even result in the need to restrict certain uses.

Lower and denser development can minimize vortex formation. → **Figure 3.1.7**

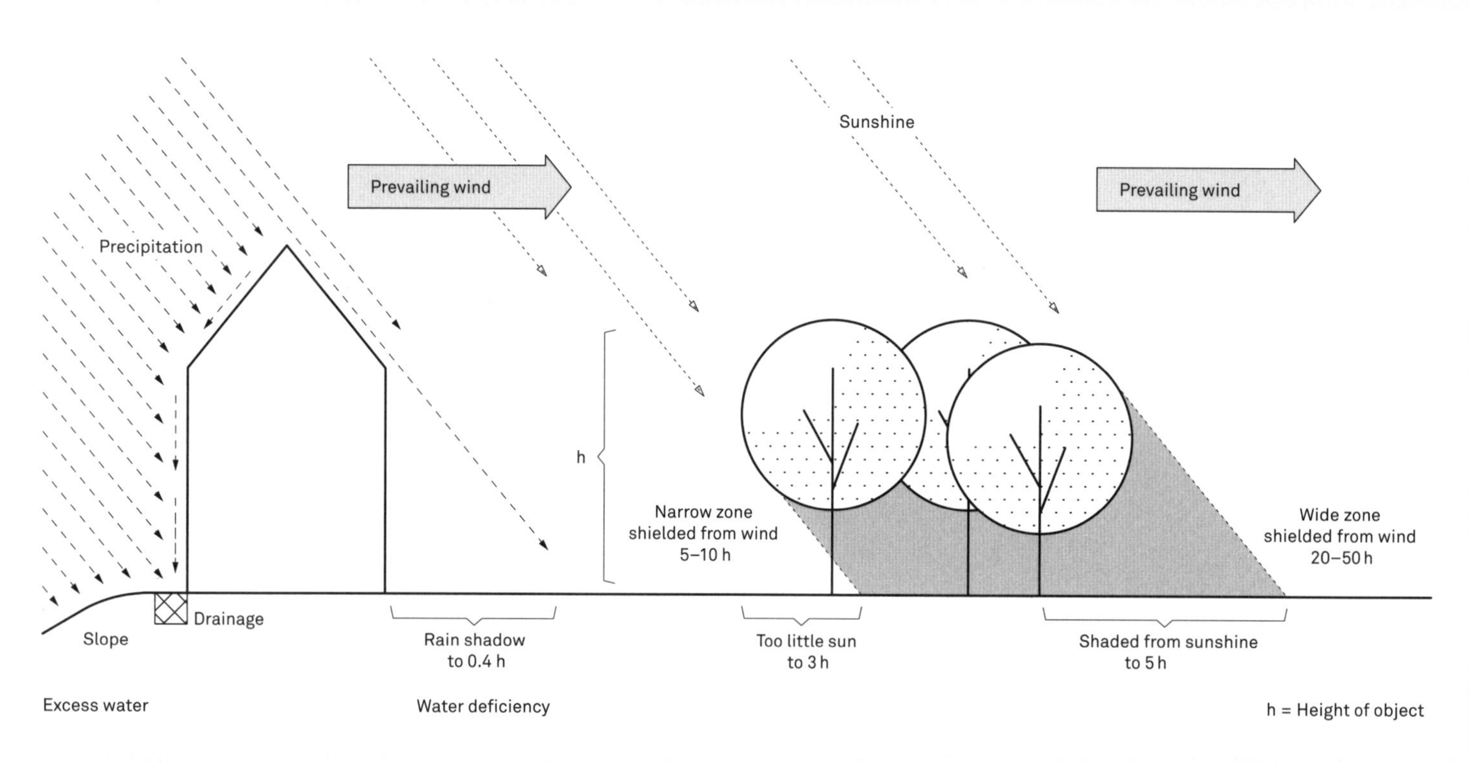

Figure 3.1.5 Impact of wind exposure and solar radiation on the microclimate of buildings and groups of trees

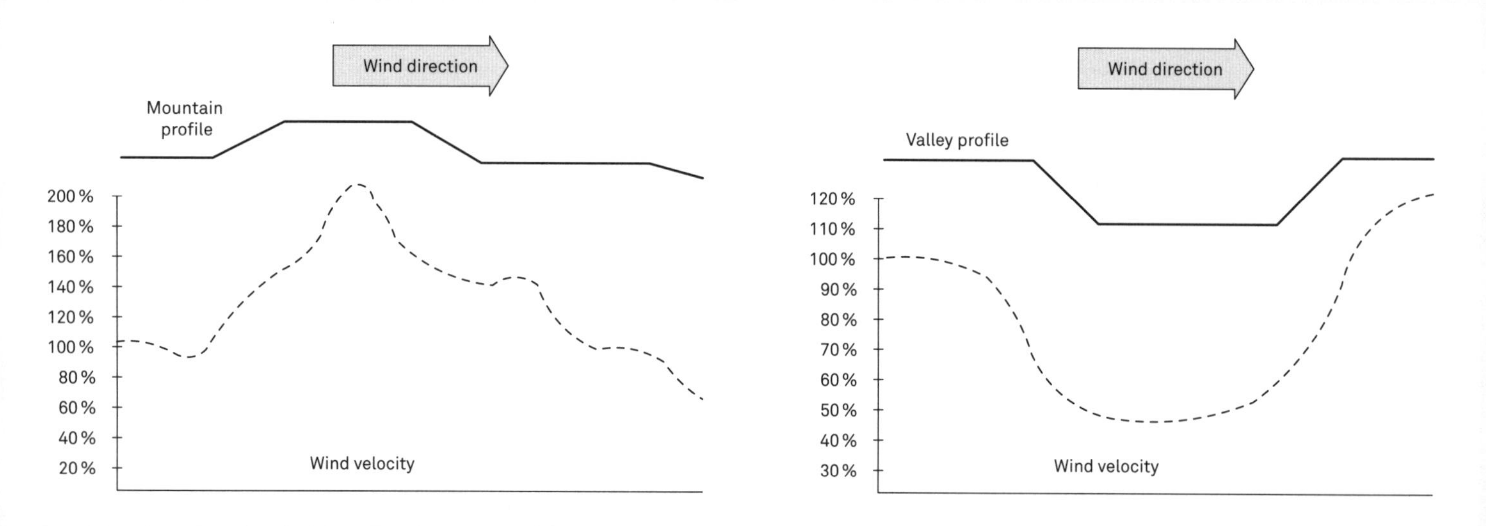

Figure 3.1.6 Impact of topography on wind speed, 100 % = wind velocity unaffected by topography (based on Flemming)

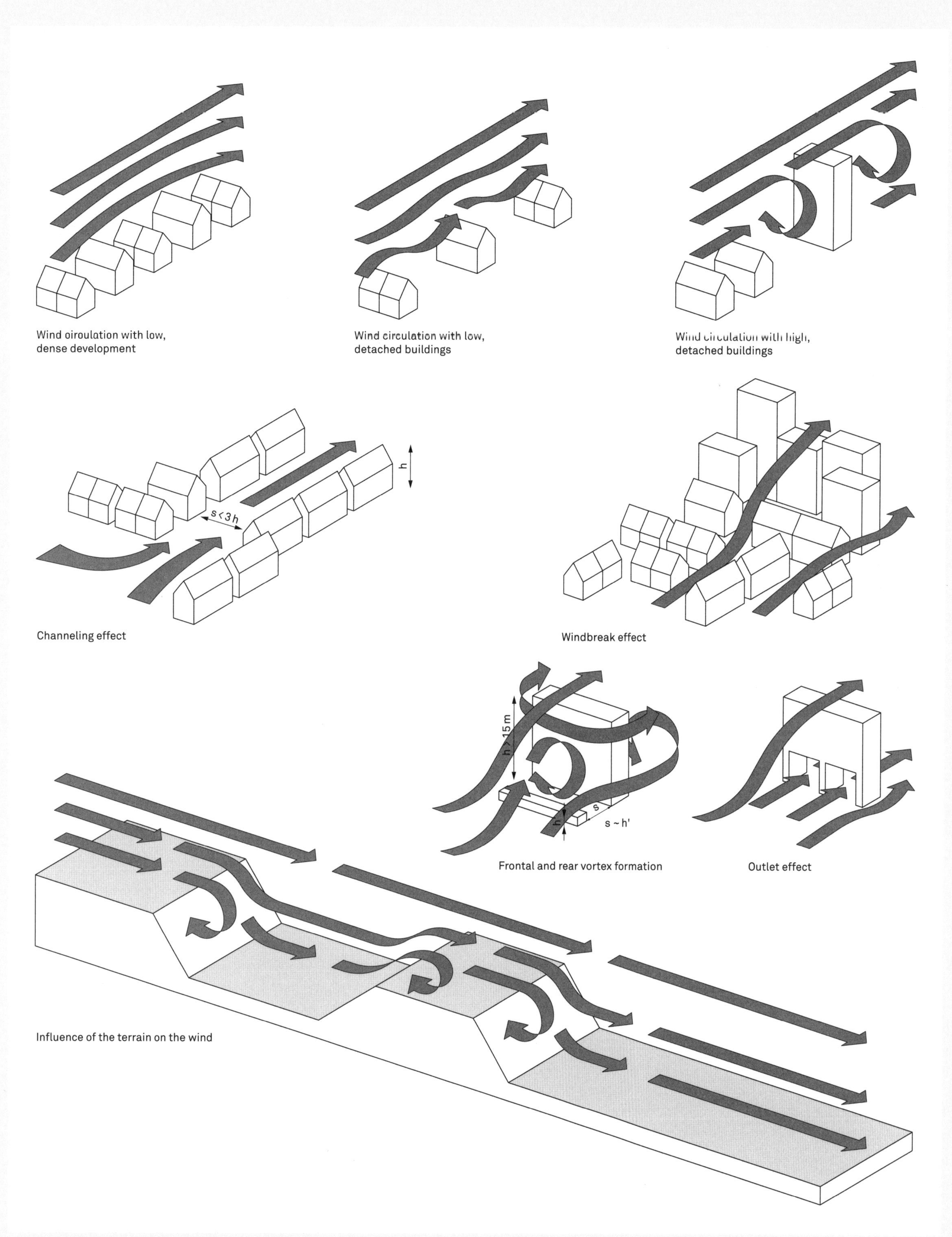

Figure 3.1.7 Influence of height and disposition of buildings on wind circulation

Solar Radiation

By utilizing the greater solar radiation intensity on a slope or a wall, the development of optimal conditions for some plants is fostered, because they benefit from the increased thermal radiation there, especially in spring and autumn. The reduced angle of incidence of the sun in the transitional period is compensated for by the inclination of the slope or by a vertical wall, thus enabling the thermal radiation to be optimally utilized. This principle finds expression in the planting of vineyards on hillsides or the positioning of fruit trellises and other facade planting on walls with good exposure.

Thermal Radiation

In the immediate vicinity of buildings, trees, and slopes, radiative heat transfer results, which is due to the surface of the body radiating more heat in contrast to the weaker radiating sky. The greater the proportion of radiating surface area in relation to the surface of the sky, the greater the effect. → **Table 3.1.1** In the immediate vicinity of walls or trees, the temperature is higher as a result – and, for example, the formation of frost is reduced or snow melt is accelerated. The effect is reduced with an overcast sky, because cloud droplets send more thermal radiation to the earth than does a cloudless sky.

Figure 3.1.8 Solar radiation (based on Häckel)

Table 3.1.1 Influence of the surroundings on radiative heat transfer (based on Häckel)

	Elevation angle of the surroundings					
	10°	20°	30°	45°	60°	90°
	> Greater object surface with decreasing sky surface					
Depression	2%	8%	21%	45%	60%	90%
Slope	1%	5%	10%	20%	33%	50%
Building wall, forest edge, garden wall	1%	2%	5%	12%	23%	40%
Street along a building	14%	26%	38%	55%	70%	100%

Reflectivity of Surfaces

When solar radiation meets a body, it is absorbed and warms the surface. The reflectivity of a surface is measured by a ratio designated by the term *albedo*. Dark surfaces such as asphalt reflect back less heat and therefore heat up more than, for instance, light concrete surfaces. The same is true for soil: whereas sandy soils reflect 20–40 %, the value for heavy humus soils is only 5–20 % – that is, "dark" soils warm up faster than light-colored soils.

The reflective property of light surfaces is also useful for protecting trees: In late winter, solar radiation can cause dark bark to heat up intensely. Large temperature differences arise compared to the colder, shaded side of the trunk, and this can lead to the development of enormous stresses. A consequence is the formation of cracks in the bark, which can lastingly damage the tree. By whitewashing the tree trunks, reflection from the trunk surface is increased and the effects of heating can be minimized, thus avoiding excessive stresses. Furthermore, by reducing excessive heating, blossoms are hindered from budding too early and hence late frost damage is averted.

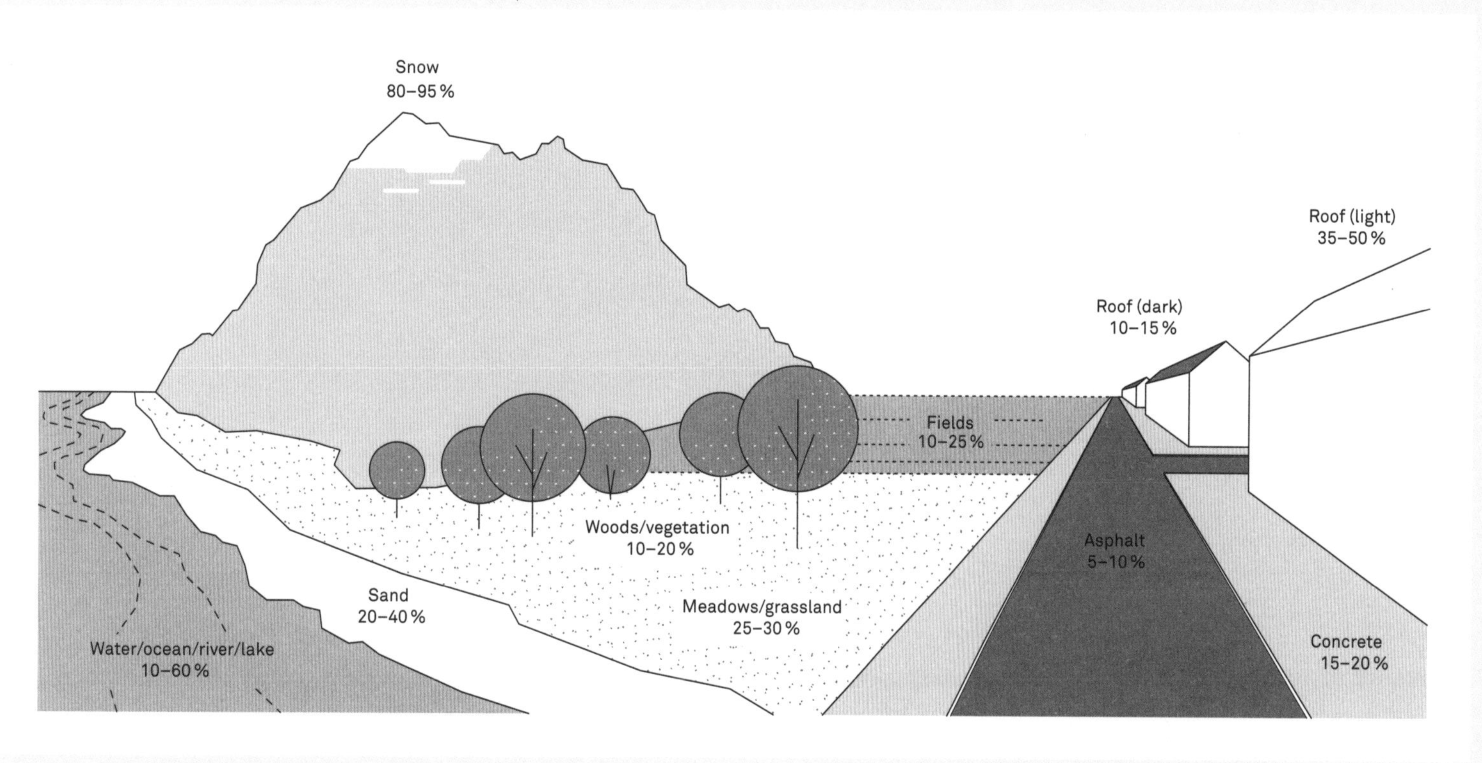

Figure 3.1.9 Albedo effect of diverse surfaces

Sunlit and Shaded Areas

Depending on the climate zone, season, or time of day, either sunlit or shaded areas offer the preferred place for people to gather. This makes it necessary for certain functions to be located in certain areas and it simultaneously offers the opportunity to govern the use of the open space with areas of sun and shade. For occupiable outdoor spaces, both sunny as well as shady locations should normally be provided. Especially at midday in the summer, areas that receive full sun can only be used to a limited extent. The characteristics of the shade itself can be modulated with shade-giving roofs of varied opacity and trees with shadow-casting crowns that are more or less dense.

Knowledge about which areas of an outdoor facility are cast in shade over the course of the day and year provides important information for zoning the site and selecting the right plants. Depending on the design task at hand as well as the use of an outdoor area and its relation to any surrounding built structures, the need for a shadow study must be determined and, if applicable, its scope defined. To be able to assess the different effects of shadows in different seasons, it is generally useful to determine the shadows cast at different times at both the summer and winter solstice (June 21 and December 21) as well as for the spring and autumn equinox (March 21 and September 23).

There are different methods for creating a shadow study. In principle, cast shadows are calculated using trigonometry, with the aid of the cotangent. The calculation is simplified by using prepared shadow-casting diagrams or by using a CAD program that determines solar altitude as part of its 3D rendering function.

For determining the orientation and length of the cast shadow, what is basically required are the location of the site (latitude – and also longitude if needed), the time of day or the sun's angle of incidence, and the height of the shadow-casting object.

The values for the highest (corner) points of a built structure or other object are always determined. For a house with a rectangular plan and a gable roof, six points must be calculated, whereas for a flagpole, by contrast, only one point is needed. → See also Figure 3.1.17 and 3.1.16 For each different time and different season, a new calculation must be made.

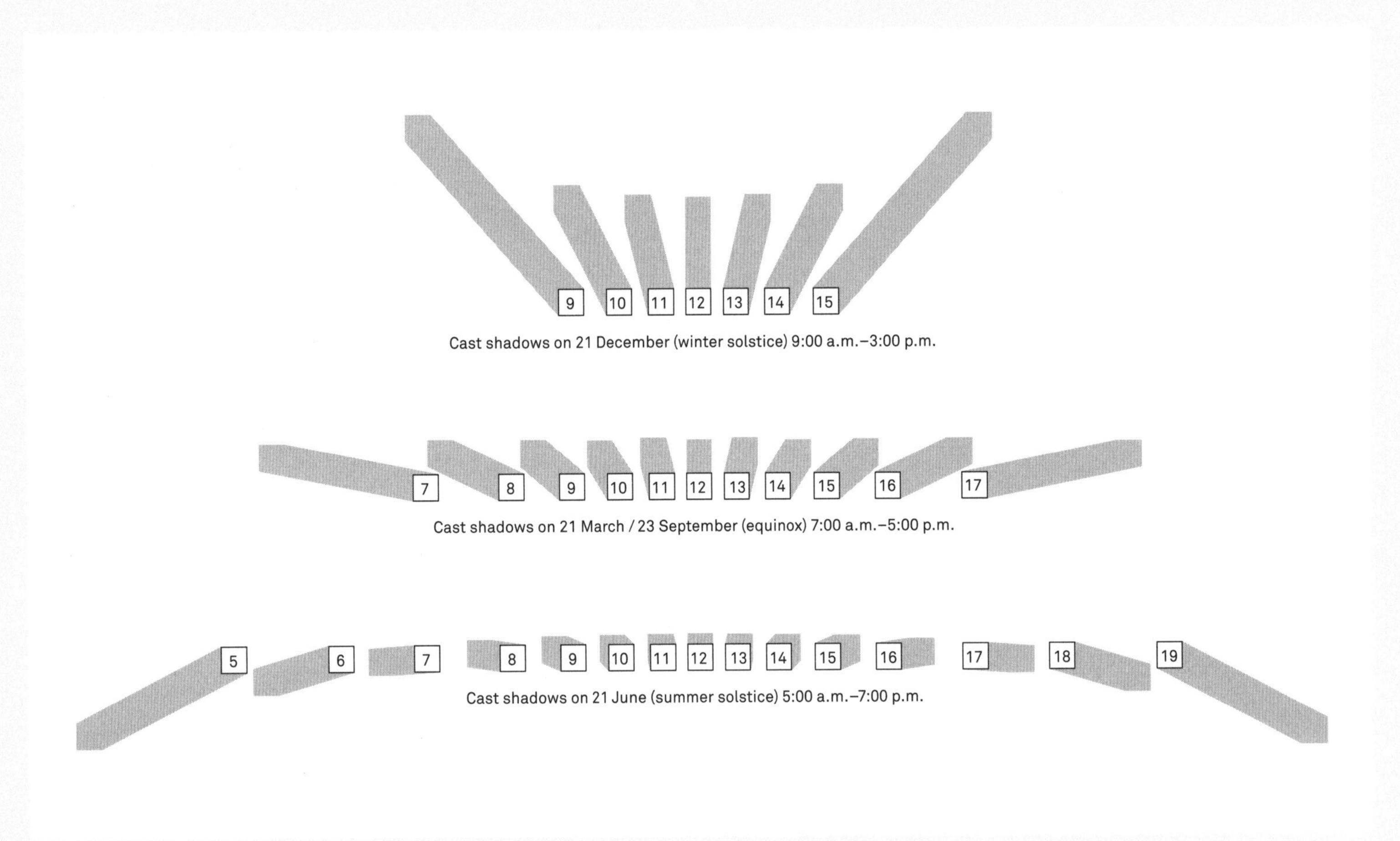

Figure 3.1.10 Shadow diagram of a cubic form measuring 2 × 2 × 2 m: representation of the cast shadows on June 21 and December 21 as well as on March 21 and September 23 in Central Europe

Calculating Shadow Length by Means of Cotangent

The shadow length can be computed by using the formula for calculating the ratio of the sides of a right-angled triangle. The shadow length **s** (adjacent side b) is equal to the cotangent of the solar altitude **cot α** multiplied by the height of the object **h** (opposite side). → Figure 3.1.11

To determine the value of s, what is needed is the height of the object together with the height of the sun (solar altitude), in other words, the angle at which the rays of the sun will meet the ground. This can be calculated or – for simplicity – read from tables.

The sun reaches its highest point in the sky when it is exactly in the south at 12 o'clock noon (although the deviation between daylight saving time and standard time must be taken into account). It is very easy to calculate this noontime angle:

Date	Calculation for solar altitude (angle of elevation or angle of incidence)
Mar. 21 and Sept. 23	90° – Latitude
June 21	90° – Latitude + 23.5°
Dec. 21	90° – Latitude – 23.5°

Shadows are particularly long early in the morning and late in the afternoon, so a shadow diagram is particularly interesting for these times.

The azimuth angle indicates the deviation from absolute south → Figure 3.1.12, so western positions of the sun (in the afternoon hours) are given as positive values and the eastern positions (in the morning hours) are given as negative values.

The tables → Figure 3.1.2 show the solar angle of incidence (solar altitude = H) and the deviation from the north-south axis at different times of day for different latitudes.

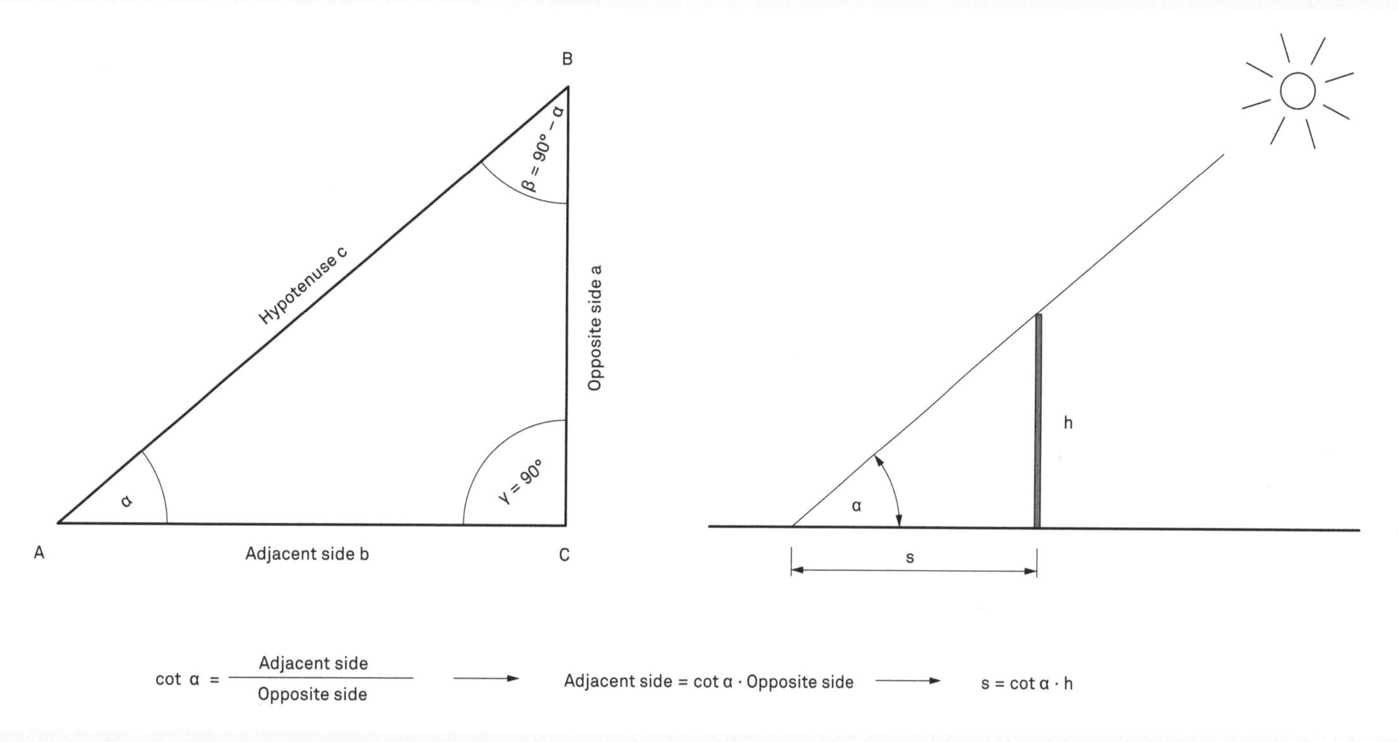

Figure 3.1.11 Right-angled triangle and formula for determining the adjacent side as the basis for determining the shadow length using the cotangent

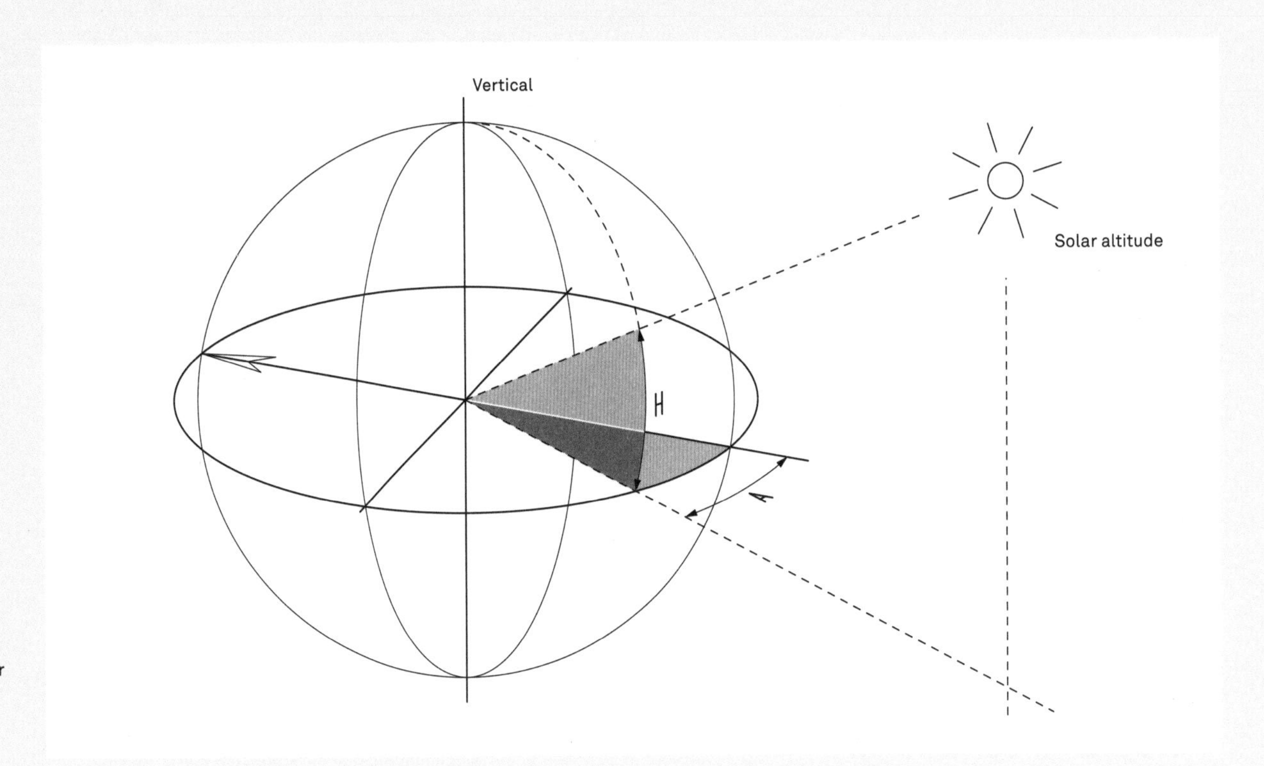

Figure 3.1.12 Azimuth and solar altitude: A (azimuth) = deviation of the sun's position from the north-south axis, H = angle of elevation (solar altitude)

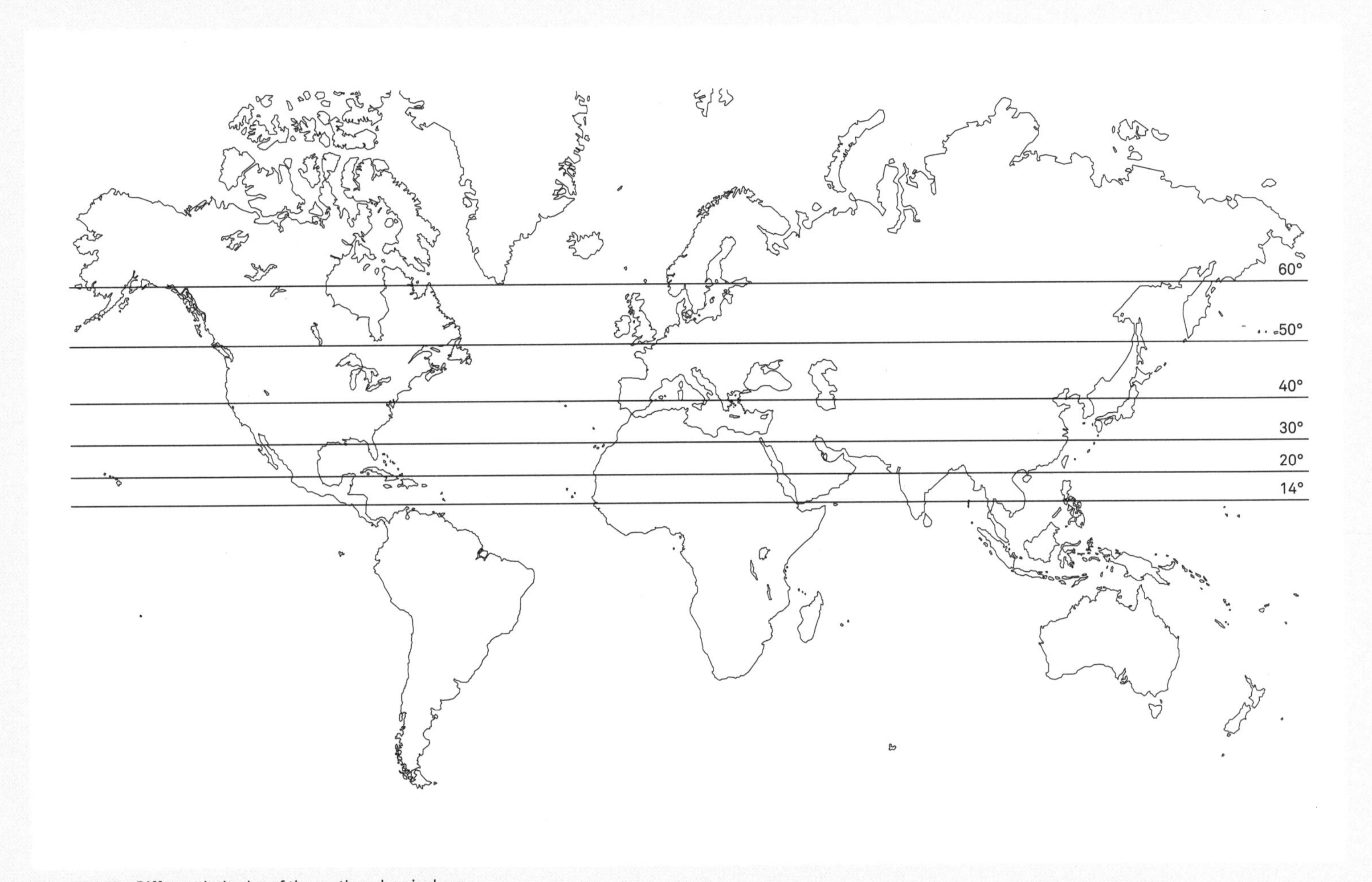

Figure 3.1.13 Different latitudes of the northern hemisphere

Latitude		Azimuths and solar altitudes on March 21 and September 21				Azimuths and solar altitudes on June 21				Azimuths and solar altitudes on December 21			
		6 a.m. 6 p.m.	8 a.m. 4 p.m.	9 a.m. 3 p.m.	12 noon	6 a.m. 6 p.m.	8 a.m. 4 p.m.	9 a.m. 3 p.m.	12 noon	6 a.m. 6 p.m.	8 a.m. 4 p.m.	9 a.m. 3 p.m.	12 noon
14°	A	±90.0	±81.8	76.3	0.0	±112.9	±109.1	±109.5	180.0	*	±58.0	±50.0	0.0
	H	0.0	29.0	43.3	76.0	5.5	32.8	46.5	80.6		20.4	32.2	52.6
20°	A	±90.0	±78.7	±71.0	0.0	±112.2	±105.1	±103.2	180.0	*	±56.3	±47.4	0.0
	H	0.0	28.4	41.6	70.0	7.8	34.6	48.2	86.6		17.2	28.3	46.6
24°	A	±90.0	±76.7	±67.7	0.0	±111.7	±102.6	±99.3	0.0	*	±55.3	±45.9	0.0
	H	0.0	27.2	40.2	66.0	9.3	35.5	48.9	89.4		14.9	25.5	42.6
30°	A	±90.0	±74.0	±63.3	0.0	±110.6	±98.0	±92.7	0.0	*	±54.1	±44.1	0.0
	H	0.0	25.7	37.7	60.0	11.5	36.0	49.5	83.0		11.4	21.2	36.6
32°	A	±90.0	±73.0	±62.1	0.0	±110.2	±96.5	±90.0	0.0	*	±53.8	±43.6	0.0
	H	0.0	25.1	36.9	58.0	12.2	36.9	49.6	81.4		10.3	19.8	34.6
34°	A	±90.0	±72.1	±60.8	0.0	±109.8	±95.8	±87.5	0.0	*	±53.6	±43.1	0.0
	H	0.0	24.5	35.9	56.0	12.8	37.0	49.5	79.4		9.1	18.4	32.6
36°	A	±90.0	±71.3	±59.5	0.0	±109.4	±94.1	±85.6	0.0	*	±53.4	±42.7	0.0
	H	0.0	23.9	34.9	54.0	13.5	37.2	49.4	77.4		7.9	16.9	30.6
38°	A	±90.0	±70.5	±58.4	0.0	±108.8	±92.6	±82.2	0.0	*	±53.1	±42.3	0.0
	H	0.0	23.2	33.9	52.0	14.2	37.3	49.1	75.4		6.7	15.4	28.6
40°	A	±90.0	±69.6	±57.3	0.0	±108.3	±90.0	±80.0	0.0	*	±53.0	±41.9	0.0
	H	0.0	22.5	32.8	50.0	14.8	37.4	48.8	73.4		5.5	13.9	26.6
42°	A	±90.0	±68.8	±56.2	0.0	±108.0	±90.0	±77.8	0.0	*	±52.8	±41.6	0.0
	H	0.0	21.8	31.7	48.0	15.4	37.4	48.4	71.4		4.3	12.5	24.6
44°	A	±90.0	±68.2	±55.1	0.0	±107.4	±87.4	±75.4	0.0	*	±52.7	±41.4	0.0
	H	0.0	21.1	30.5	46.0	16.0	37.3	47.9	69.4		3.1	11.0	22.6
46°	A	±90.0	±67.4	±54.1	0.0	±106.9	±85.9	±73.4	0.0	*	±52.6	±41.1	0.0
	H	0.0	20.3	29.4	44.0	16.6	37.2	47.4	67.4		1.9	9.5	20.6
48°	A	±90.0	±66.7	±53.3	0.0	±106.2	±84.9	±71.6	0.0	*	±52.6	±40.9	0.0
	H	0.0	19.5	28.2	42.0	17.2	37.1	46.9	65.4		0.6	7.9	18.6
50°	A	±90.0	±66.1	±52.5	0.0	±105.6	±83.6	±69.8	0.0	*	*	±40.7	0.0
	H	0.0	18.8	27.0	40.0	17.8	36.9	46.2	63.4			6.4	16.6
52°	A	±90.0	±65.5	±51.8	0.0	±105.0	±82.0	±67.9	0.0	*	*	±40.6	0.0
	H	0.0	17.9	25.8	38.0	18.3	36.6	45.5	61.4			4.9	14.6
54°	A	±90.0	±64.9	±50.9	0.0	±104.5	±80.4	±65.9	0.0	*	*	±40.5	0.0
	H	0.0	17.1	24.6	36.0	18.8	36.3	44.7	59.4			3.4	12.6
56°	A	±90.0	±64.4	±50.3	0.0	±103.7	±78.8	±64.0	0.0	*	*	±40.5	0.0
	H	0.0	16.2	23.3	34.0	19.3	35.9	43.8	57.4			1.9	10.6
58°	A	±90.0	±63.9	±49.7	0.0	±103.0	±77.1	±62.3	0.0	*	*	±40.4	0.0
	H	0.0	15.4	22.0	32.0	19.7	35.4	42.9	55.4			0.4	8.6
60°	A	±90.0	±63.5	±49.1	0.0	±114.5	±75.9	±61.0	0.0	*	*	*	0.0
	H	0.0	14.5	20.7	30.0	13.1	35.0	42.1	53.4				6.6

* no cast shadows, because the defined point in time is before sunrise or after sunset at the specified location

Table 3.1.2 Azimuth (A) and solar altitude (H) at various times of year and day, according to latitude

Time Zones and Actual Position of the Sun

Since the sun reaches its zenith, or highest point, at different times depending on the longitude, but the time of day itself is linked to a certain time zone, the values taken from tables and graphic charts are always related to the meridian (line of longitude) defined for the pertinent time zone. Thus the sun at a location that is not situated directly along the meridian will actually reach its zenith slightly earlier or later. Central European Time is centered on the 15th meridian, which, among other places, runs through the cities of

- Motala in Sweden
- Gudhjem on Bornholm in Denmark
- Görlitz/Zgorzelec in Germany and Poland
- Jindřichův Hradec in the Czech Republic
- Gmünd in Austria
- Catania in Sicily

Thus in Munich, for instance, the deviation is about 20 minutes.

A time zone difference of one hour results from a deviation of 15° longitude.

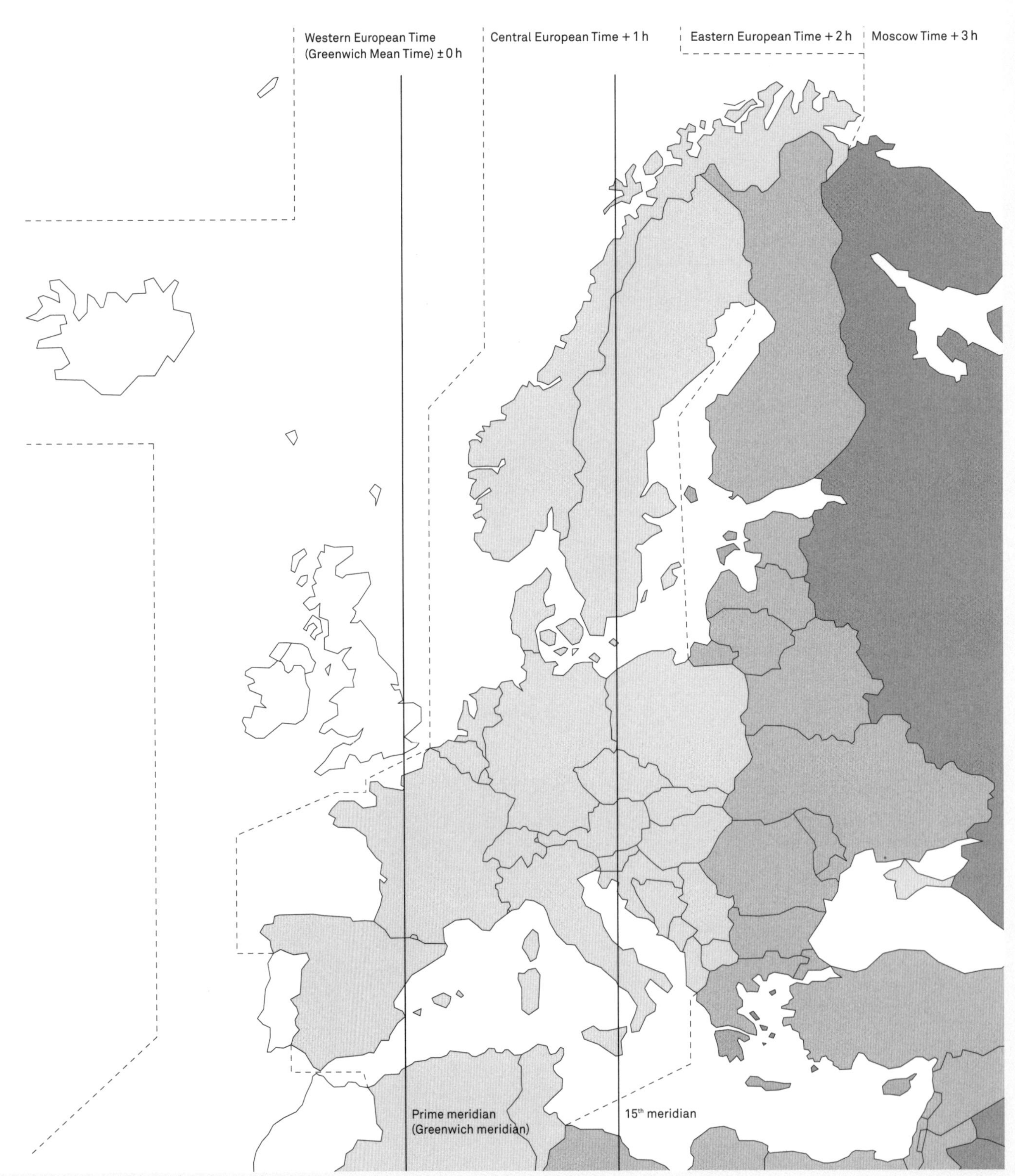

Figure 3.1.14 Time zones in Europe and their position relative to the prime meridian (Greenwich meridian) and the 15th meridian

Calculating Shadow Length by Means of Diagram

With the aid of a special shadow diagram, shadow lengths can be determined simply. For this purpose, Häckel created a diagram whose point of reference is the city of Mainz, at 50° north latitude. For specific dates, the diagram makes it possible to relatively easily read the parameters that are needed, such as the time of day, the multiplication factor for calculating the shadow length, and the direction in which the shadow is cast.

The diagram also illustrates the areas that are never impacted by shadows at any time of the year (hatched areas above and below). The light gray area, on the contrary, lies "in shadow at some time during the year." The region affected by shadows is bounded by the solar paths on December 20 (approximate winter solstice) and June 20 (approximate summer solstice).

The basis for calculating a point is an (imaginary) pole that needs to be pictured in the center of the diagram. The concentric circles (1 to 10) represent the multiplication factor for calculating the length of the shadow. Seven solar paths enable the user to establish the direction and length of the shadow over the course of the year for each full hour. The degree values noted at the outer edge of the chart show the shadow's orientation.

Using Figure 3.1.16, the shadow cast by a flagpole at 8:00 a.m., for example, is the result of a combination of the center point and the intersection of the solar path with the time scale. The intersection point in this case lies exactly on circle 2, meaning that the shadow at 8:00 a.m. is exactly twice as long as the original object casting it.

As a final step, by extending the construction line to the outer edge of the chart, the shadow's orientation – the direction in which it is cast – can be ascertained.

Following the construction scheme, on April 20 at 8:00 a.m. a 4-meter-high flagpole casts an 8-meter-long shadow in the direction west-northwest (~290°), at 1:00 p.m. it casts a shadow about 3.2 m long toward the north-northeast (~20°) and at 5:00 p.m. it casts a shadow about 13.6 m long toward the east, or more precisely, east by north (~85°).

For depicting shadows of solid objects, such as buildings, for example, the pole assumed at the center represents the building's edges or its corners. As a final step, by connecting the individual shadow points, the outline of the full shadow is created.

In order to utilize the contents of this chart for casting various shadows easier in practice, Table 3.1.3 provides the necessary parameters at a glance.

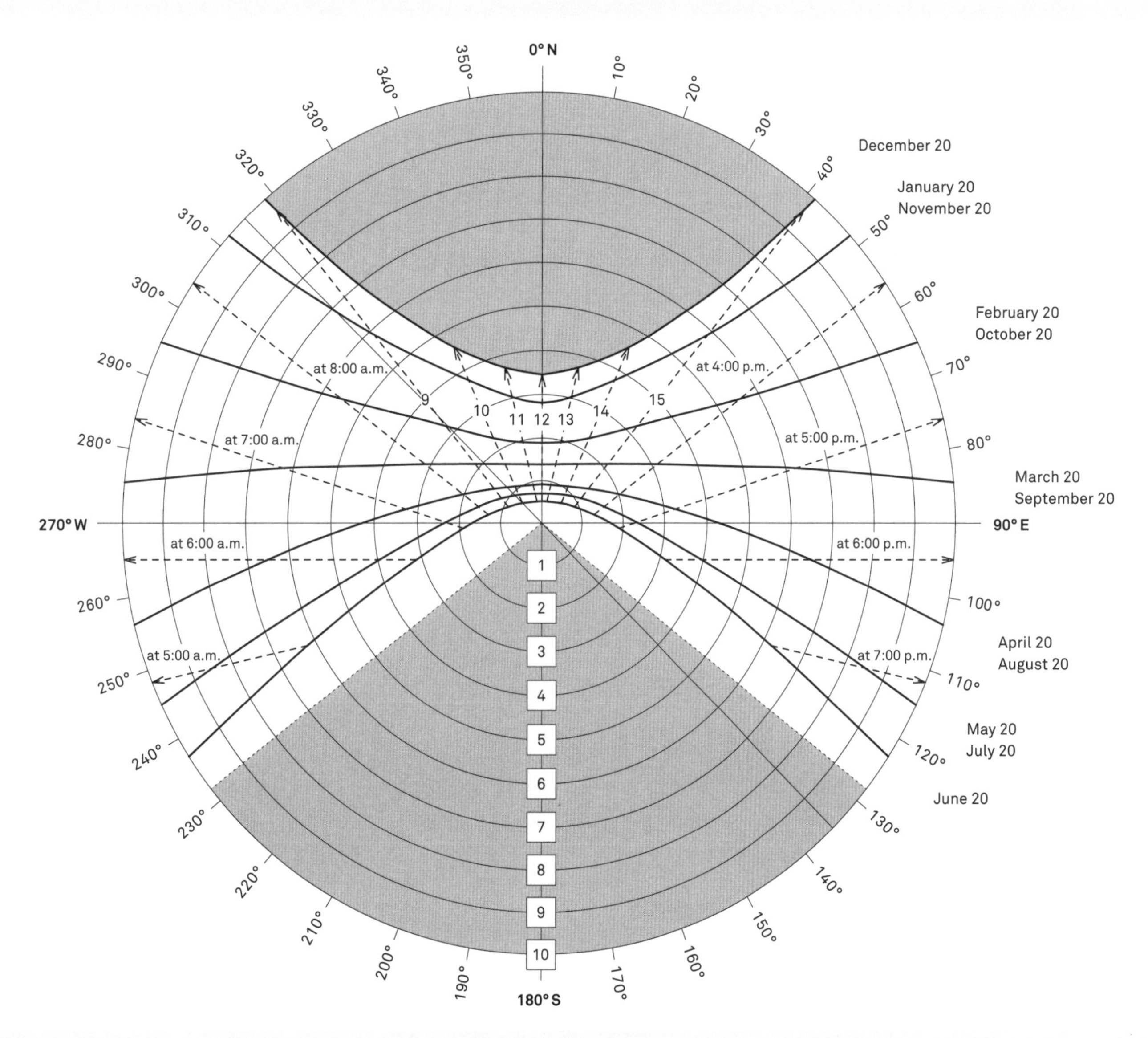

Figure 3.1.15 Shadow diagram

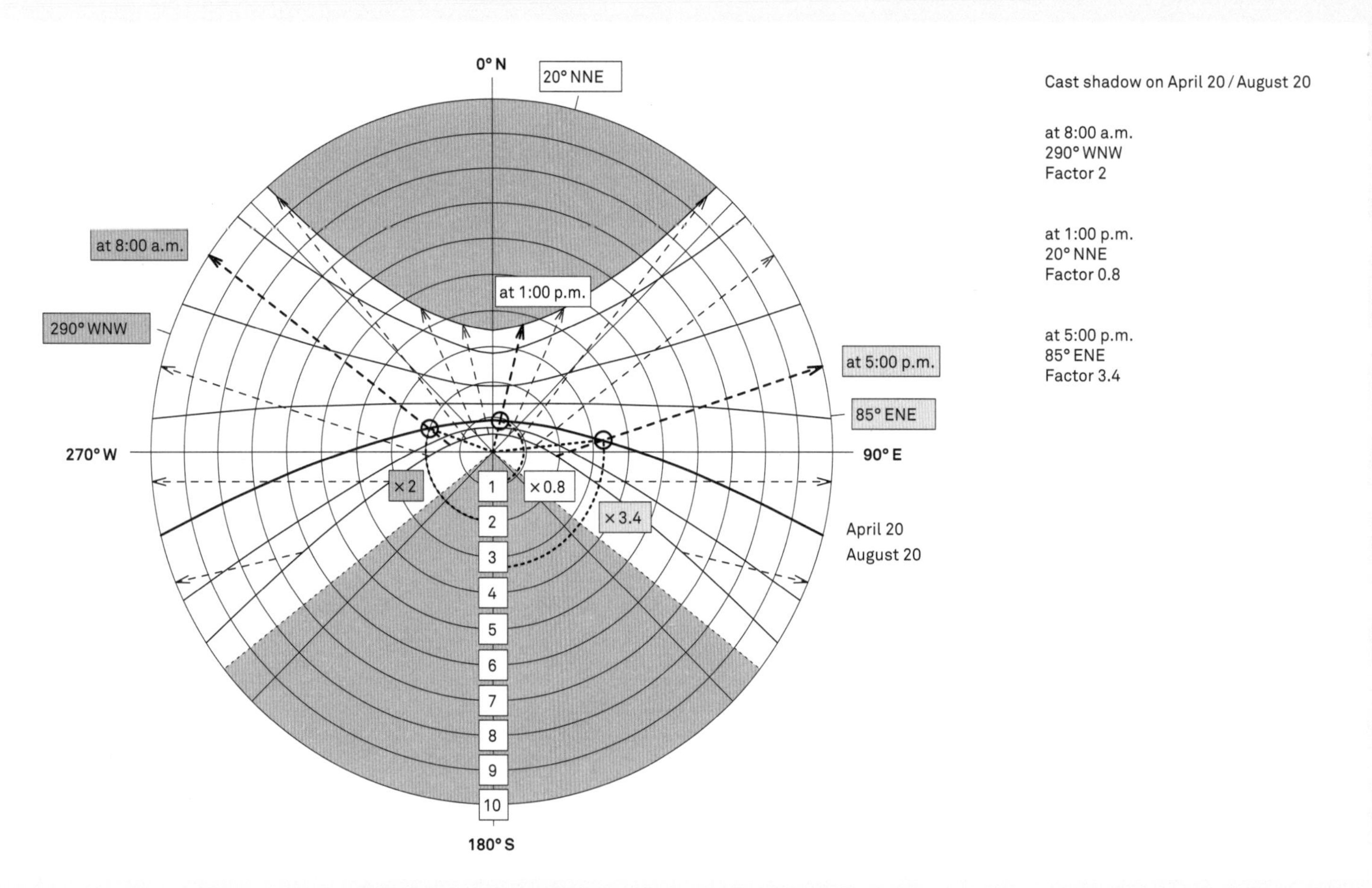

Figure 3.1.16 Exemplary cast shadows from a 4 m high flagpole on April 20 at 8:00 a.m., 1:00 p.m., and 5:00 p.m. (each of these times of day is marked by a small circle)

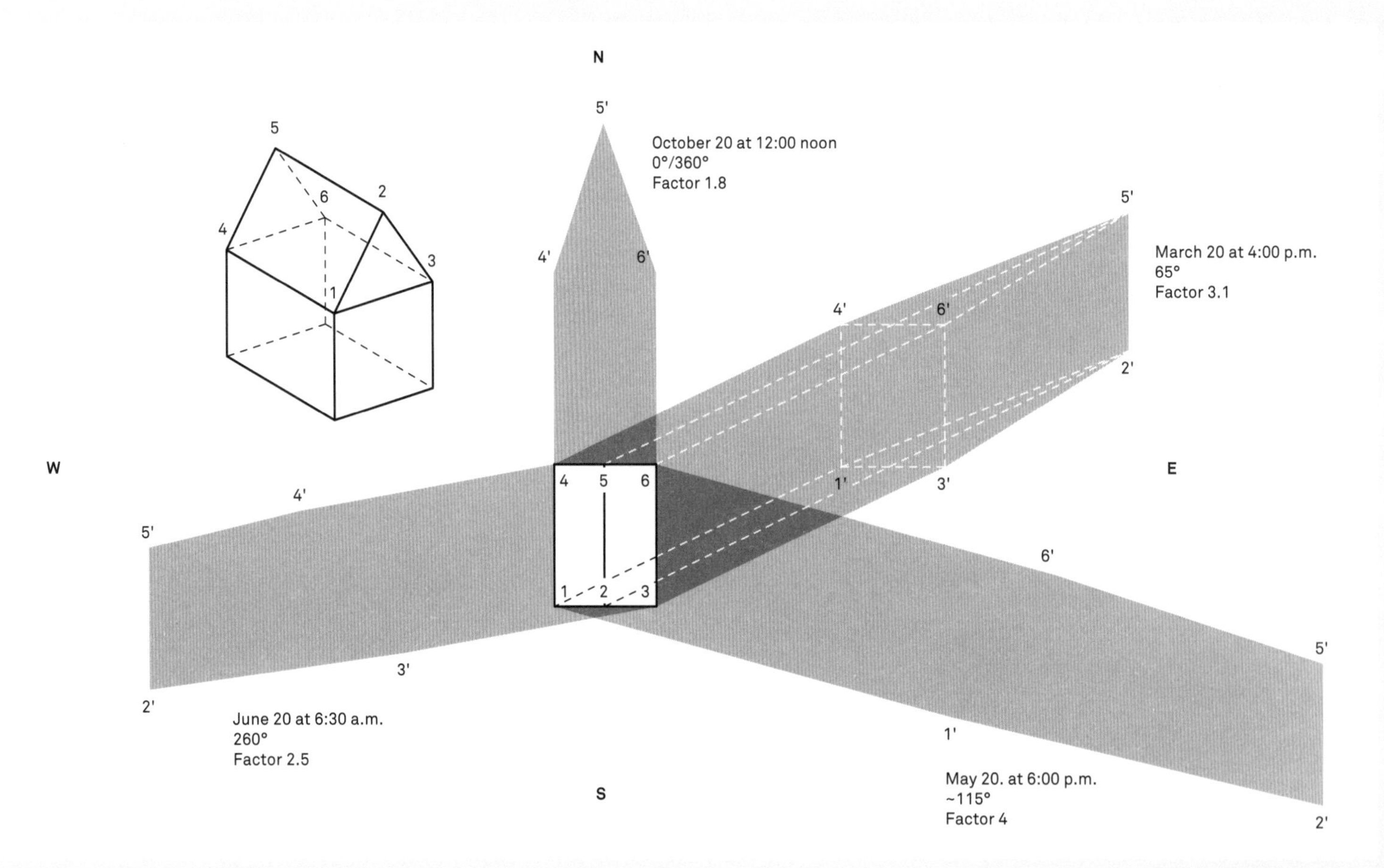

Figure 3.1.17 Exemplary shadows cast by a building at different times of day and year, indicating the direction and factor for use in calculating the shadow length (based on Häckel)

Date/time	Multiplication factor	Orientation	Multiplication factor	Orientation	Multiplication factor	Orientation
	Solar path on June 20		Solar path on March 20 / September 20		Solar path on December 20	
5:00 a.m.	6.4	243°				
6:00 a.m.	3.1	254°				
7:00 a.m.	1.8	266°	6.2	281°		
8:00 a.m.	1.3	278°	3.1	295°		
9:00 a.m.	0.8	293°	2	310°	9	318°
10:00 a.m.	0.5	315°	1.5	327°	4.5	332°
11:00 a.m.	0.4	346°	1.4	346°	3.7	346°
12:00 noon	0.4	0°/360°	1.3	0°/360°	3.5	0°/360°
1:00 p.m.	0.4	14°	1.4	14°	3.7	14°
2:00 p.m.	0.5	45°	1.5	33°	4.5	28°
3:00 p.m.	0.8	67°	2	50°	9	42°
4:00 p.m.	1.3	82°	3.1	65°		
5:00 p.m.	1.8	94°	6.2	79°		
6:00 p.m.	3.1	106°				
7:00 p.m.	6.4	117°				

Table 3.1.3 Parameters needed for creating a shadow diagram for selected times and dates for a location at 50° N latitude: Mainz (Germany), Lizard Point (Southern England), Portage la Prairie (Canada), Ulaangom (Mongolia), Kharkiv (Ukraine)

3 Elements
3.2 Grading, Stairs, and Ramps

3.2 Grading, Stairs, and Ramps

The basis for every design in landscape architecture is an engagement with the existing elevations on the site. Even on flat ground, slight variations in the grading can be required to ensure adequate drainage. Often, greater differences in elevation require further grading measures that include the creation of walls, stairs, and/or ramps and which can ultimately involve more extensive earthworks.

With earth as a building material, landscape architecture has at its disposal an extremely manipulable material that can be employed for implementing a design. Yet for reasons of soil conservation, interventions in intact soil structures should be kept as minimal as possible so as not to impair proper functioning of the soil. The goal of sustainable planning is therefore to avoid – as far as possible – damage to the soil structure that would be caused by moving and compacting earth. Thus any changes in grade should optimally be made in a way that takes advantage of and develops the existing topography.

The addition or removal of large amounts of soil represents a substantial economic aspect of any grading work. For this reason, a balance between the cutting and filling of soil should be sought in all construction projects.

In addition to addressing design concerns, the grading concept must also address functional concerns from an early point in time, so that all the uses anticipated within the area of concern are taken into account and – to the extent required – accessible site circulation is established and integrated into the formal language of the design. To ensure that places with substantial differences in elevation can be traversed by all persons, whether driving or walking, such sites must be made accessible through the use of ramps, stepped paths, and/or stairs, thus necessitating the development of a detailed grading plan.

The nature and extent of the measures are dependent on the function and location of the open space. If no legal requirements exist, such as those for assuring access to public buildings or event venues, there should always be an evaluation process to determine, based on the anticipated user groups, specifically how access should be provided.

Minimal interventions that adequately take into account the topographic conditions are an expression of economically and ecologically prudent treatment of the land. This can be the symbol of a sustainable and likewise creative design process.

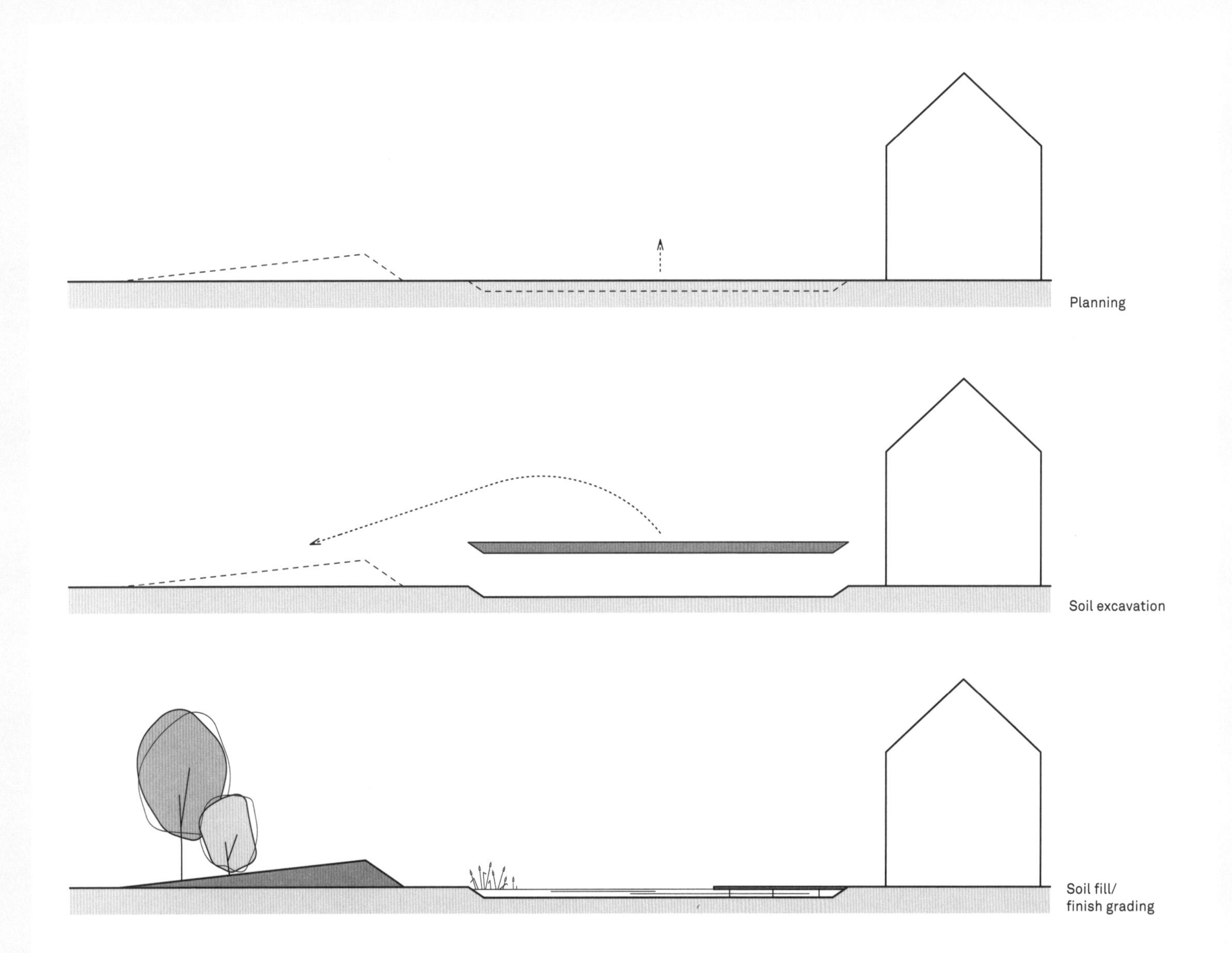

Figure 3.2.1 Resource- and cost-saving grading through a balance of cut and fill

Location

Reference Levels

Heights are indicated in meters as spot elevations. A height reference system provides a common basis for ground elevations that are nationally uniform. The point of origin (PO) is defined in most countries by the mean sea level at a specified location. → Table 3.2.1

The reference point for height measurements on a site is a benchmark. In built-up areas, these are usually to be found at intervals of 300–500 meters at easily accessible locations such as on building bases, and they establish the starting point for surveyors' field measurements of heights.

Survey plans that show the existing elevations thus determined ordinarily constitute the basis for working on a building project. If no such primary survey data are available and the building project is relatively small, a datum (reference elevation) can also be defined by the planner himself. Any static element can serve as a datum, but it should be an immutable, distinctive, and easily accessible point, such as the step of a stair, a manhole cover, or the ground-floor level of an existing building. To avoid negative values in relation to the datum, this unique reference point is assigned a higher positive value instead of a value of zero. This is particularly true when reference is made to building construction. In that case, the finished floor level of the ground floor is, as a basic principle, defined as the zero level for the planning. → Figure 3.2.2

Country	Designation	Abbreviation	Gauge datum as reference value	Zero level in relation to DHHN92
Germany (DHHN92)	Meter über Normalhöhennull* [meters above normal height null]	m. ü. HNH	Amsterdam	0
Austria	Meter über Adria [meters above Adriatic Sea]	m. ü. Adria	Trieste 1875	−34 cm
Switzerland, Liechtenstein (LN02)	Meter über Meer [meters above sea level]	m. ü. M.	Derived from the tide gauge at Marseille > Datum is a rock outcrop in Lake Geneva known as the Repère Pierre du Niton (373.6 m above the tide gauge at Marseille)	−32 cm
Belgium	meter boven Oostends Peil [meters above Ostend ordnance datum]	m O.P.	Ostend	−32 cm
Denmark				−2 cm
France (NGF-IGN69)	mètres au-dessus du niveau de la mer [meters above sea level]	m	Marseille	−50 cm
Great Britain	meters above sea level	MASL/m.a.s.l.	Newlyn	
Italy	metri sul livello del mare [meters above sea level]	m s. l. m.	Genoa	−35 cm
Luxembourg				+1 cm
Netherlands	meter boven/onder NAP [meters above/below Amsterdam Ordnance Datum]	m NAP	Amsterdam	−1 cm
Poland	metry nad poziomem morza [meters above sea level]	m n. p. m.	Braşov	+14 cm
Spain	metros sobre el nivel del mar [meters above sea level]	msnm	Alicante	−39 cm
Czech Republic	metrů nad mořem [meters above sea level]	m n. m.		+13 cm

* Introduced throughout Germany in 1993 in the course of reunification; before: DHHN12/m ü. TBD (West Germany) and SNN76/m ü. HN (East Germany)

Table 3.2.1 Official height reference systems in Europe

Existing and Proposed Finished Elevations

The basis for all grading decisions is an exact knowledge of the topographic circumstances. For this purpose, corresponding plans of the existing conditions should be consulted when available.

Existing elevations at specific locations that cannot be modified are restrictions that can affect the planning. These include:

- Elevations within the root zone of existing trees
- Defined elevations along adjacent properties and roads
- Existing and finished elevations of adjacent buildings and other structures
- Minimum coverages for existing pipes/ducts as needed (e.g., protection from frost or excessive loading)

To illustrate the particular topographic situation (existing condition or planned design) – especially in hilly or undulating terrain – a contour plan, contour model, or digital terrain model can be made based on the existing surveyor heights or the finished elevations.

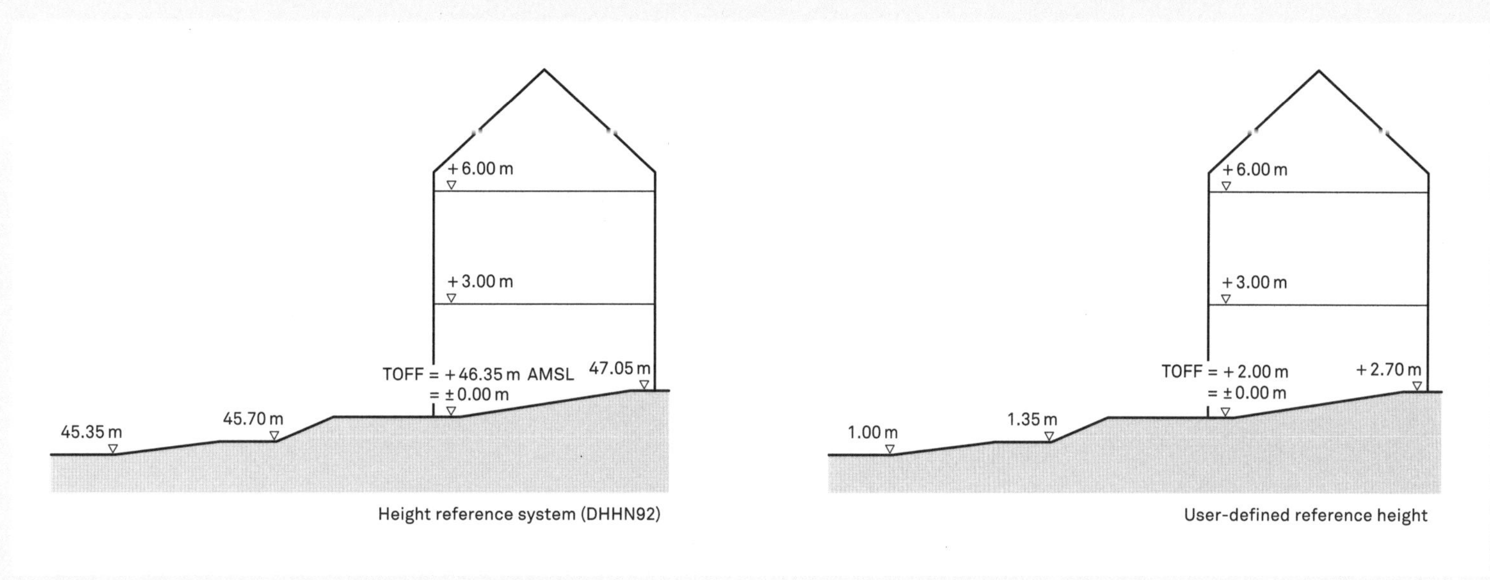

Figure 3.2.2 Finished elevations based on a height reference system and user-defined datum

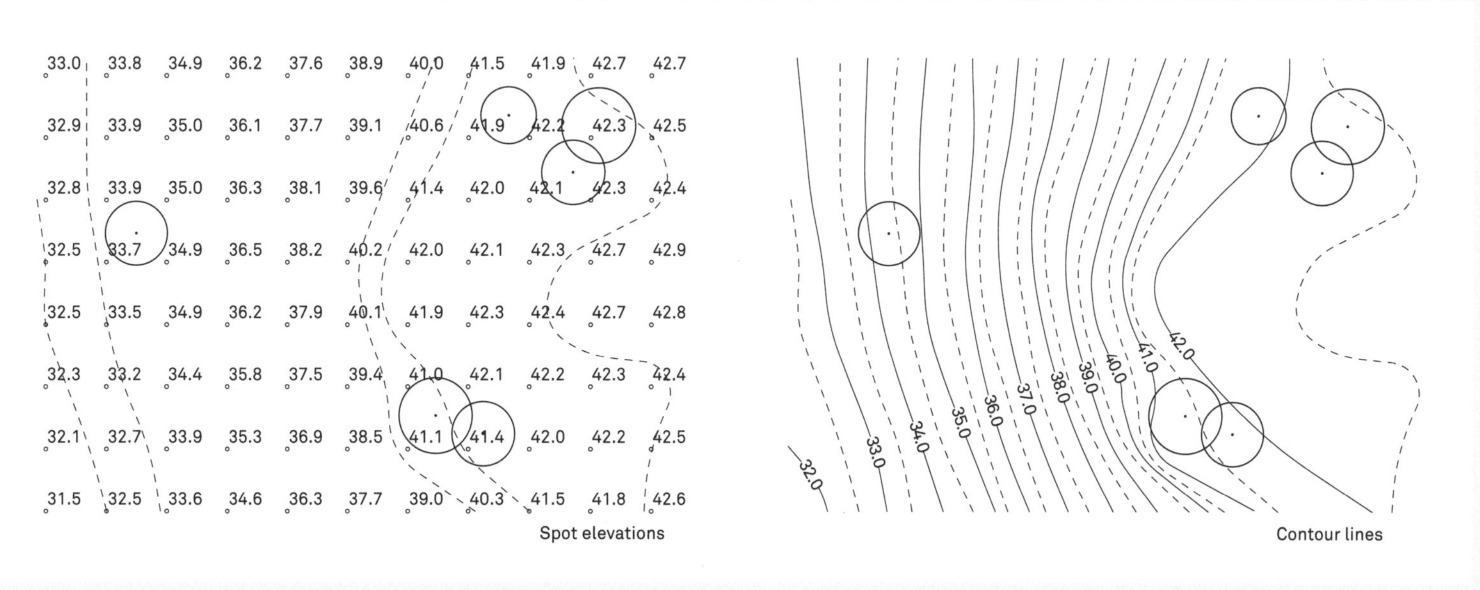

Figure 3.2.3 Representation of the terrain conditions using spot elevations, contour lines, and a contour model

Drainage

An essential aspect of grading design is the drainage of surface water from the site. Water naturally seeks the shortest path downward and then collects at the lowest point of a natural ground surface. In nature, this results in watercourses and, at low points and where there are impermeable soil layers, wetlands and bodies of water. Accordingly, drainage gutters, point drains, swales, or stormwater retention ponds must be situated at the low points of outdoor facilities to collect and conduct away the flows of stormwater in optimal fashion. Grading work can effectively regulate water runoff.

Paved surfaces in particular must be designed for direct drainage of stormwater in order to ensure that they can be used safely regardless of the weather and to prevent damage from occurring to existing buildings due to water infiltration. On hilly as well as flat terrain, this circumstance places high demands on the planning, hence it should be taken into account from the very beginning.

The goal of drainage planning is to drain stormwater away from path surfaces as quickly as possible and to divert it away from buildings. As a rule, water may not be directed onto adjacent roads or adjoining properties. In addition, many communities stipulate that precipitation must infiltrate the ground on the property, or failing that, a stormwater fee becomes payable. Therefore appropriate infiltration facilities must be planned (→ **Chapter 3.9, Table 3.9.2 and 3.9.6**). The minimum and maximum slopes (→ **Table 3.2.2**) are taken into account when planning the drainage, and specific requirements pertain for sports fields (→ **Figures 3.2.5 and 3.2.2**).

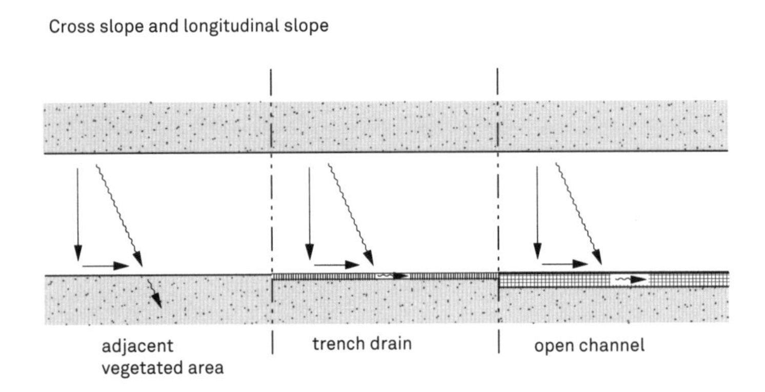

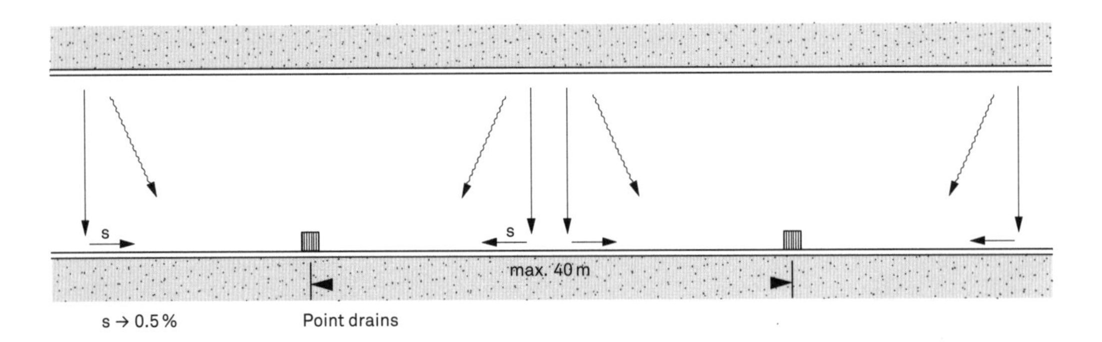

Figure 3.2.4 Examples of linear drainage

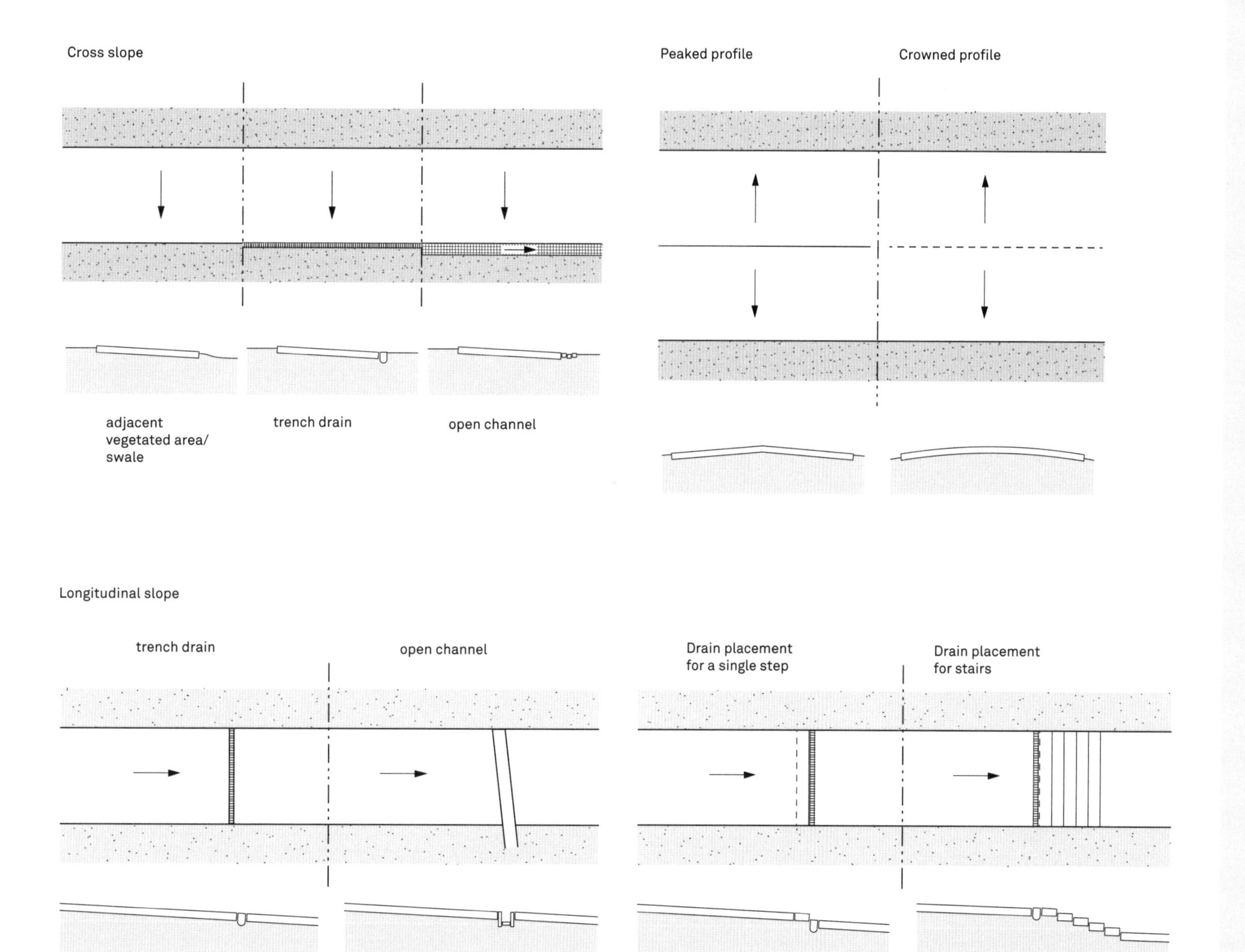
Cross slope
adjacent vegetated area/ swale
trench drain
open channel
Peaked profile
Crowned profile
Longitudinal slope
trench drain
open channel
Drain placement for a single step
Drain placement for stairs

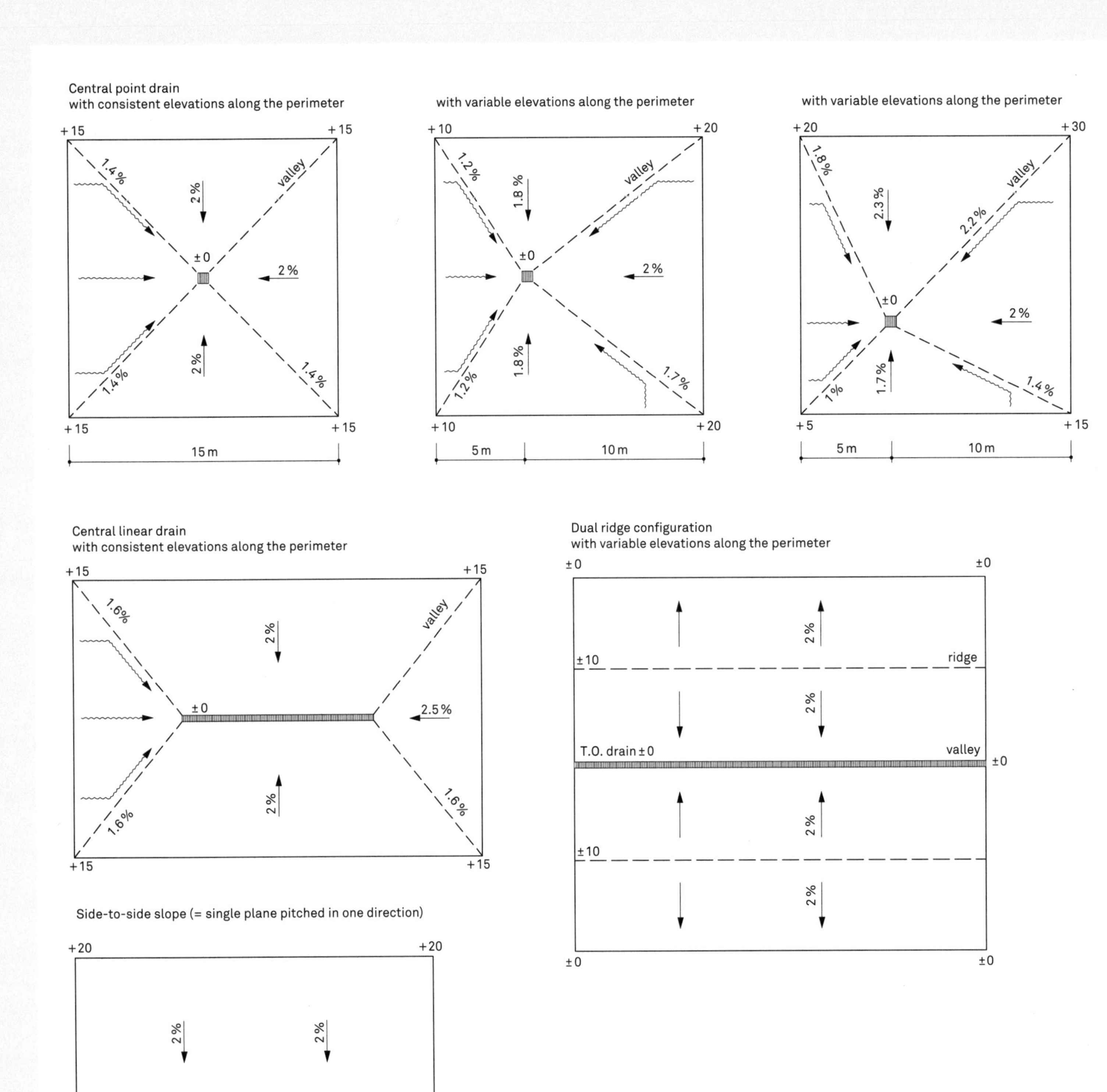

Figure 3.2.5 Exemplary drainage patterns for plazas and sports fields

Hipped configuration
with consistent elevations along the perimeter

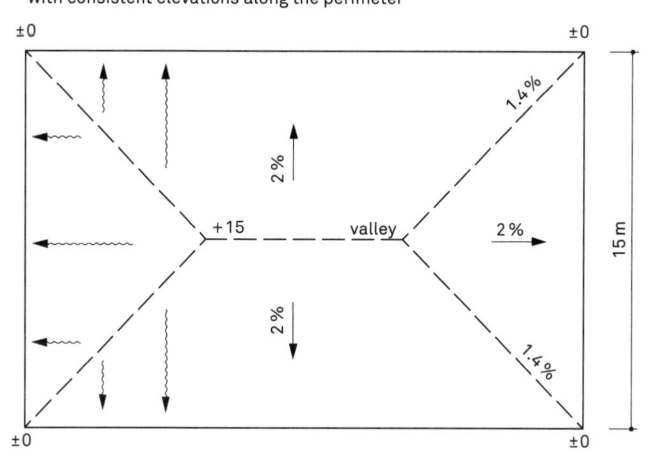

with variable elevations along the perimeter

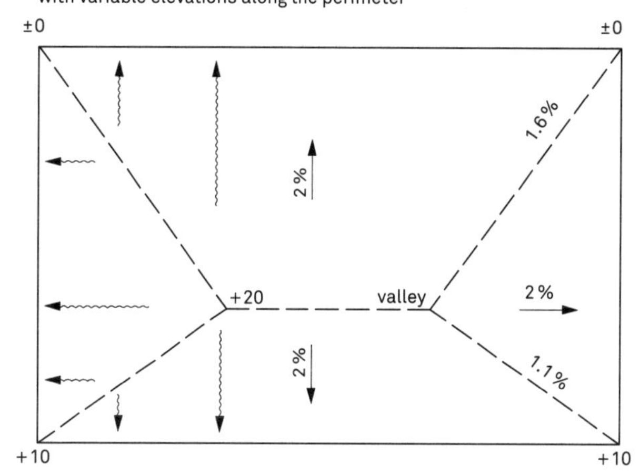

Football pitch with hipped configuration

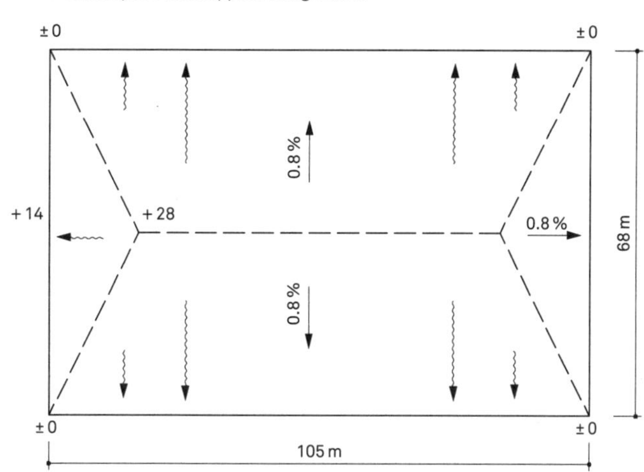

Grass soccer field with traditional central (longitudinal) crown

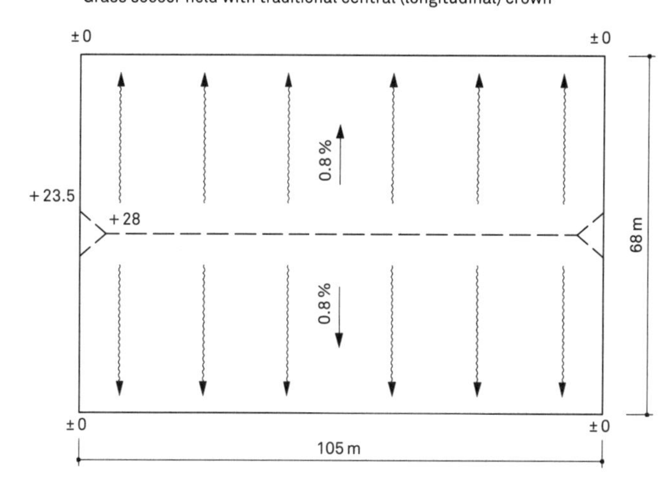

Tennis court, treshing floor with side-to-side slope

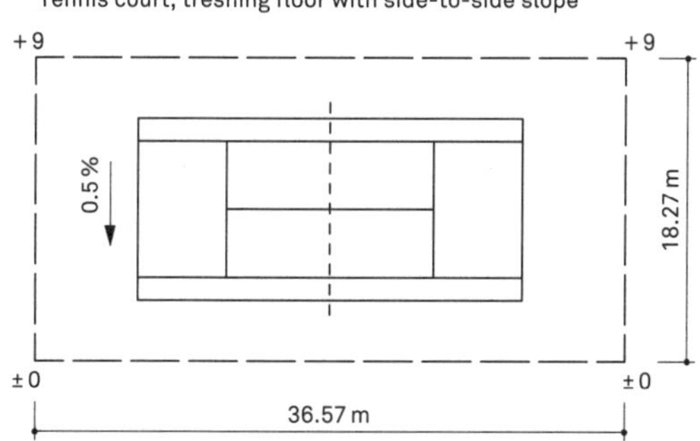

Dimensions and Characteristics

Embankments

Varied slopes of an embankment yield different possibilities for use and options or rather requirements for surface stabilization of the soil. → **Figure 3.2.5**

Slope and Ground Incline

Depending on the surface and intended use, there are different threshold values for the slope on paths and paved spaces as well as on lawns for both sports and recreation. In order to ensure prompt drainage of the water and thus assure traffic safety, a minimum slope must be established on all surfaces subject to pedestrian or vehicular traffic. This depends primarily on the type of groundcover. The maximum slope, on the other hand, is more a function of the use: An excessive cross slope on roads and paths, for instance, can have a negative impact on those driving or walking past, and the maximum slope of a grass embankment is limited by the intensity of its potential use and a possible necessity to use machines for maintenance.

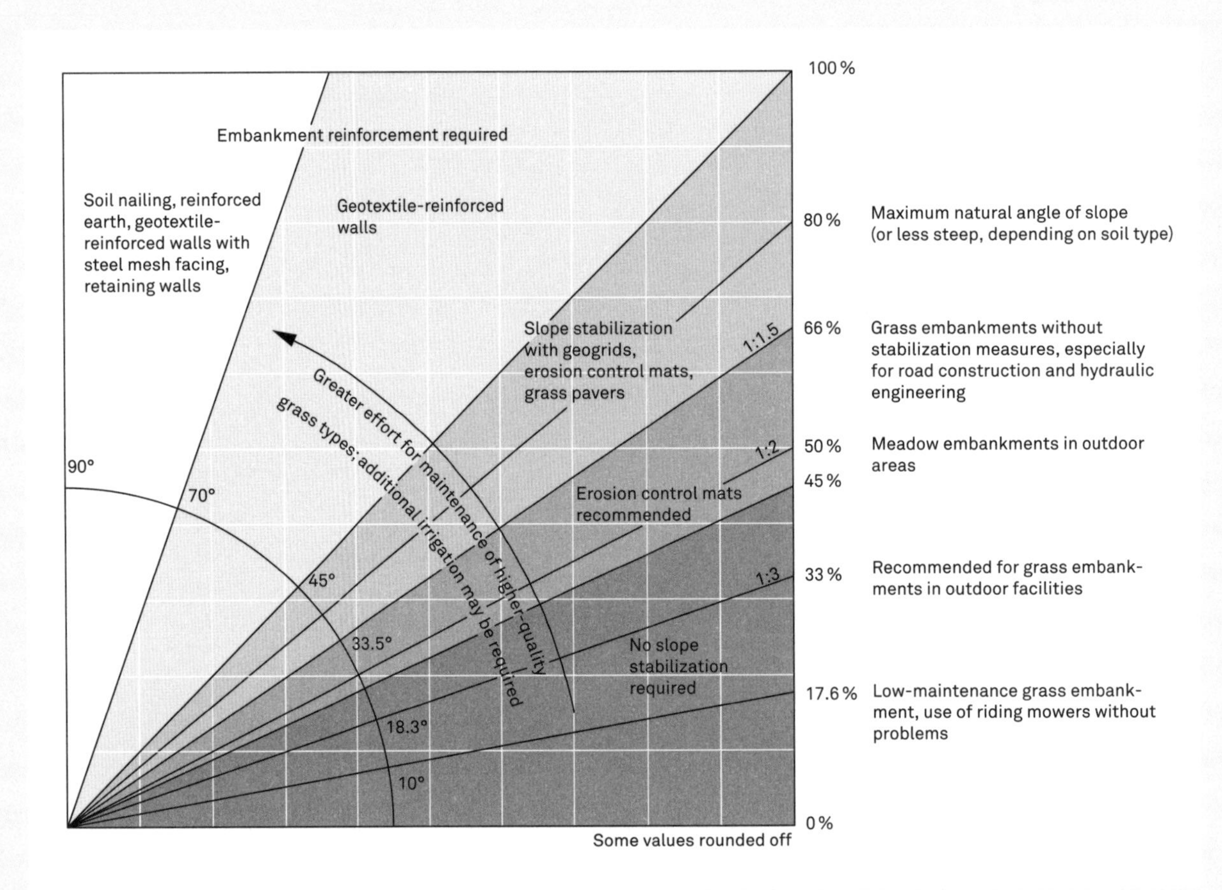

Figure 3.2.6 Types of use and attachment methods as a function of the embankment slope

Wear surface/type of use	Minimum slope	Maximum slope	Remarks	Guidelines
Categorized by surface				
Concrete and asphalt pavement	1.5%		≥2.5% for roads	
Pavers of precast concrete or fired brick	2.5%		Cross slope	DIN 18318
Cobblestones and other natural stone paving blocks	3%	–		
Slabs of concrete or natural stone	2%			
Water-bound and other unbound paving	3% (2%)	5%		
Permeable paving (pavers with gravel or grass joints, grass paving blocks, etc.)	1%	5%		FLL guideline "begrünbare Flächenbefestigungen" [Greenable surface pavements]
Categorized by use				
Public access roads, longitudinal slopes (streets lined with buildings, maximum 50 km/h)	–	8% (12%)		RASt 06
• at road intersections	–	4%		
Cross slope of public roadways				
Concrete and asphalt pavements	2.5%	Typically 5%	If cross slope cannot be maintained: drainage gradient ≥2%	RAS-Ew*
Stone paving	3%		If cross slope cannot be maintained: drainage gradient ≥3%	
Ramps and approaches to garages and parking spaces	–	15% (short ramps maximum 20%)	At changes in slope with a difference of 8% or more, a flat or curved transition is required → Figure 3.2.16 Ramp cross slopes should be avoided (maximum 2% for drainage)	EAR 05
Walkways, longitudinal slope	–	12% (15%)	On short sections: 15%, maximum 20%; alternatively or in addition: ramp stairs	
Walkways, cross slope	–	Typically 2.5%		EFA 02
Bikeways, longitudinal slope	–	6% (5% for wear surfaces without binding agents)	Greater width needed; with more than 3% slope, an asymmetric division of the cross section is expedient	ERA 10
Bikeways, cross slope	2.5%	≤4%	With low planarity, e.g., water-bound paving, the cross slope of 2.5% should be increased to 3%	ERA 10
Paths for inline skaters, longitudinal slope	–	12%	Longer distances with slopes ≥3% will already limit the performance of inexperienced skaters	Deutsche Verkehrswacht e.V.
Accessible paths and paved spaces, longitudinal slope	–	≤3%	≤8% is also possible on short segments	DIN 18040-1
		≤4%	4% over maximum length	DIN 18040-1
		≤6%	One intermediate landing with maximum 3% slope at least every 10 m	DIN 18040-1
Accessible paths, cross slope	–	≤2%	Acc. to DIN 18040-1 ≤2.5%; maximum 6% at driveway approaches to lots; no cross slope on ramp runs	DIN 18024-1 & 18040-1
Seating areas, esp. with tables (e.g., terraces)	1%	2%		
Sports fields	0.5%	1%	With clay/artificial turf surfacing ≥0.8%	DIN 18035-4
Tennis courts	0.5%	0.5%		DIN 18035-5
Grass playing fields	1%	5%		
Lawns	1%	–		
Grass embankments in outdoor facilities	–	33%		

* ERA: *Empfehlungen für Radverkehrsanlagen* [Recommendations for cycling facilities]; RAS-Ew: *Richtlinie für die Anlage von Straßen – Teil: Entwässerung* [Directive for the construction of roads: Drainage]

Table 3.2.2 Recommended minimum and maximum slopes on paths, paved spaces, and utility lawns, as functions of surface and use

Figure 3.2.7 A combination of stepped paths and ramps allows a choice between a ramp without steps – for use by someone with a bicycle or stroller, for example – and the less arduous option of alternating steps and landings

Ramps and Stairs

When a ramp would have a slope of about 18 % or more, it should be replaced by stairs. Since even an incline of 10 % or more can prove to be difficult on longer stretches, stepped paths can be used in such cases. These offer lots of flexibility in their design, since both the step height and the slope of the connecting landings can vary. For accessible use by wheelchair users or people with baby carriages or walkers, the installation of ramps is nevertheless essential. → Figures 3.2.7 and 3.2.8, and Table 3.2.3

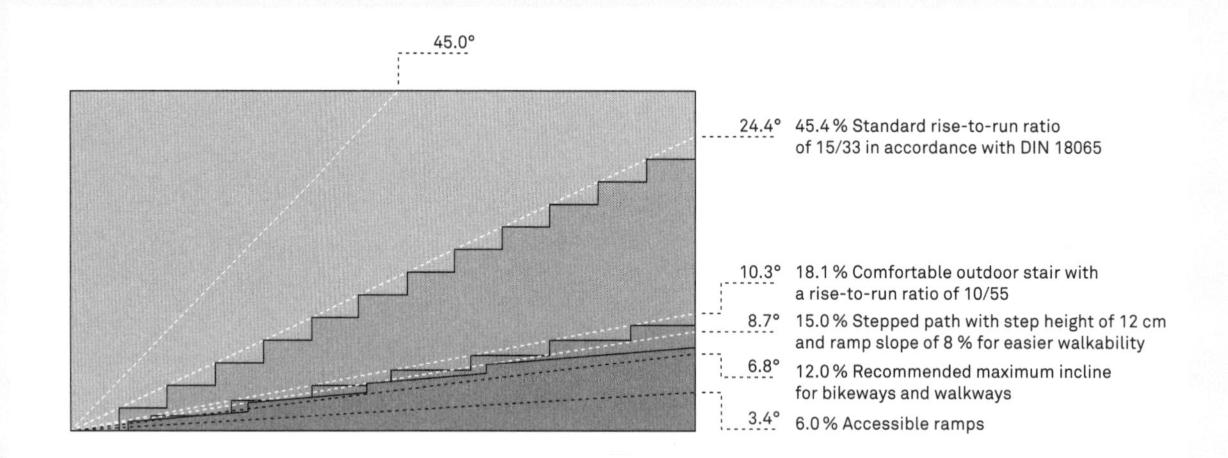

Figure 3.2.8 Selected inclines of ramps and stairs

Stride	Ground slope	Slope of intermediate landing	Length of landing	Riser height
One intermediate step on each second landing	26 % 24 % 22 %	12 % 11 % 10 %	83 cm 85 cm 89 cm	12 cm 11 cm 11 cm
2 intermediate steps on each landing	20 % 19 % 17 % 15 % 13 %	12 % 11 % 10 % 8 % 7.5 %	175 cm 180 cm 185 cm 190 cm 200 cm	14 cm 14 cm 13 cm 12 cm 11 cm

Table 3.2.3 Dimensions of stepped paths (Source: Mader 2004)

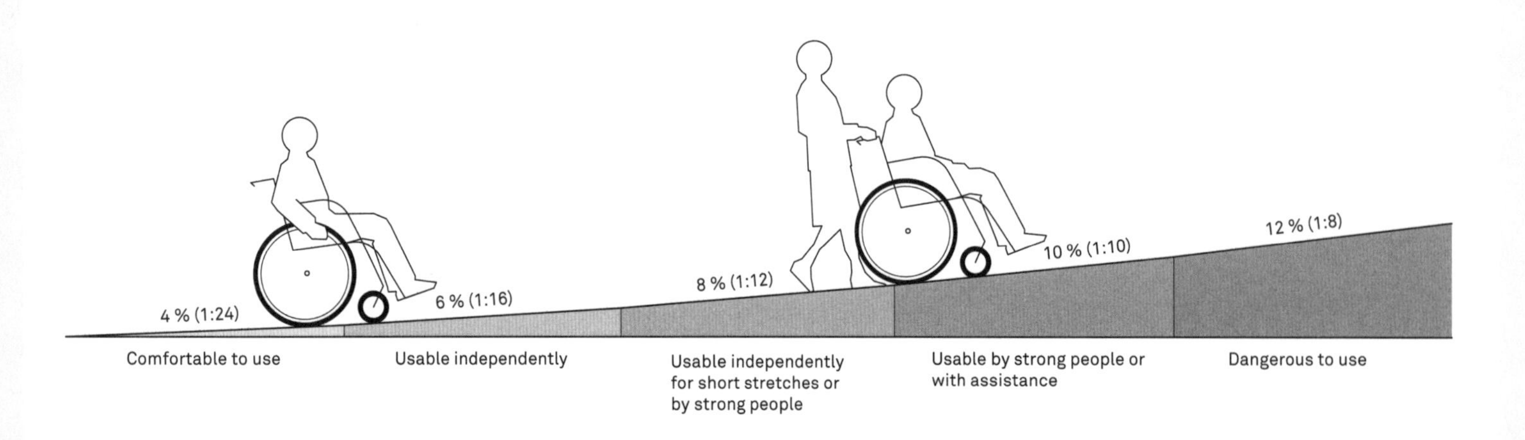

Figure 3.2.9 Usability of various ramp slopes by wheelchair users

Stair Types

Three or more steps constitute a flight. Individual flights are separated by landings. Flights are also sometimes called runs (e.g., double flight or double-run). Stair flights can also be arranged at angles to one another. Straight stairs are considered accessible for visually impaired people.

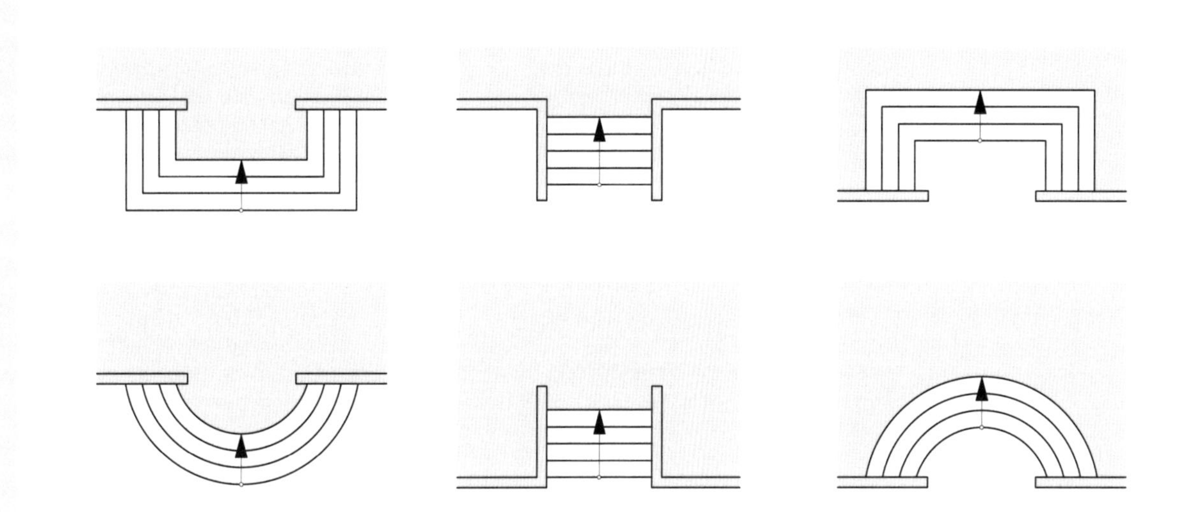

Figure 3.2.10 Protruding and recessed steps

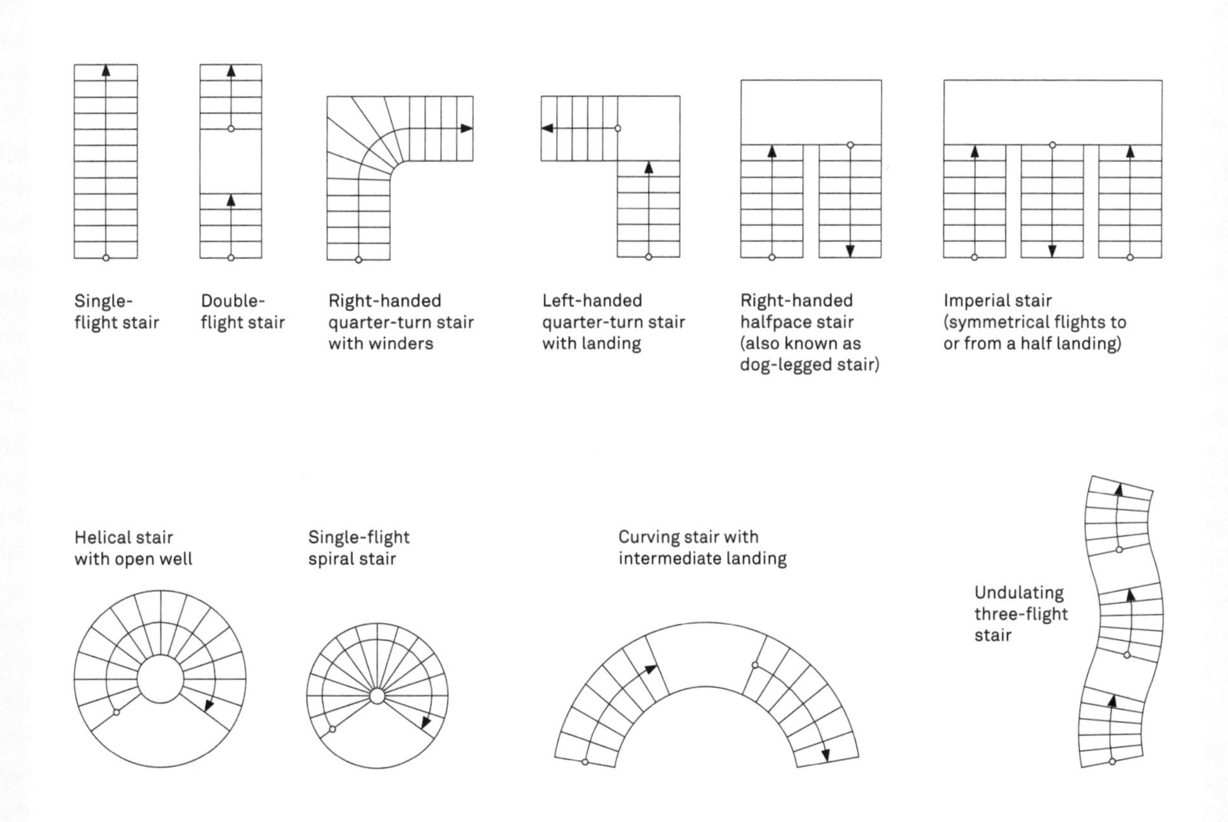

Figure 3.2.11 Stair configurations

Stair Treads

The step dimensions needed for a particular stair are the result of a combination of factors: first, the slope of the ground and second, the riser height (unit rise) and tread depth (unit tread), which are defined in relation to a person's stride length. As the incline, or pitch, increases, however, a person's stride shortens and, vice versa, it gets longer as the pitch decreases. This results in a variable basis for the design of steps. For stairs in and adjacent to buildings, however, the standards used in some countries stipulate a mandatory formula with a constant stride length as the basis for calculation. → **Table 3.2.4** The applicable formulas differ mainly in variations of the basic stride length, which is always the result of an interplay between rise (r) and tread (t):

Stride length = 2r + t

The length of a landing between two stair runs is calculated by using the determined tread depth and a variable number of strides, as follows:

Length of landing (l) = t + n × 63 cm

In Germany, there is a binding requirement to use a riser height of 14–19 cm for legally essential stairs in and around public buildings. Whereas the common standards for stairs in and adjoining buildings treat the stride length as a constant value of 59–65 cm independent of the stair's pitch, flatter pitches with a longer stride length are more suitable for outdoor stairs. The results of relevant studies and the recommendations of Seifert and Mader are presented in **Table 3.2.5** together with corresponding values based on the stride length formula.

Exterior stairs that are situated independently on a site and which do not serve as a means of access for a building can be freely designed without regard for the provisions of the DIN standard for building stairs. This way, stairs can be fitted more easily into the local topography and the pitch can also be optimized for more comfortable use. An extended, shallow incline enables strides to be taken with greater ease, thus making the ascent seem less difficult. Steep steps, by contrast, enable large differences in height to be surmounted along shorter distances, although long stair runs can quickly become arduous. → **Figure 3.2.8** For circular stairs, attention should be given to ensure that the steps have a depth of at least 10 cm at their narrowest point along the inside edge of the stair.

Steps and intermediate landings on stairs that are not roofed over or made with a permeable surface (e.g., metal grating) must be constructed with an inherent slope. For this purpose, a slope of 1–2 % should be provided, which must be included in the unit rise.

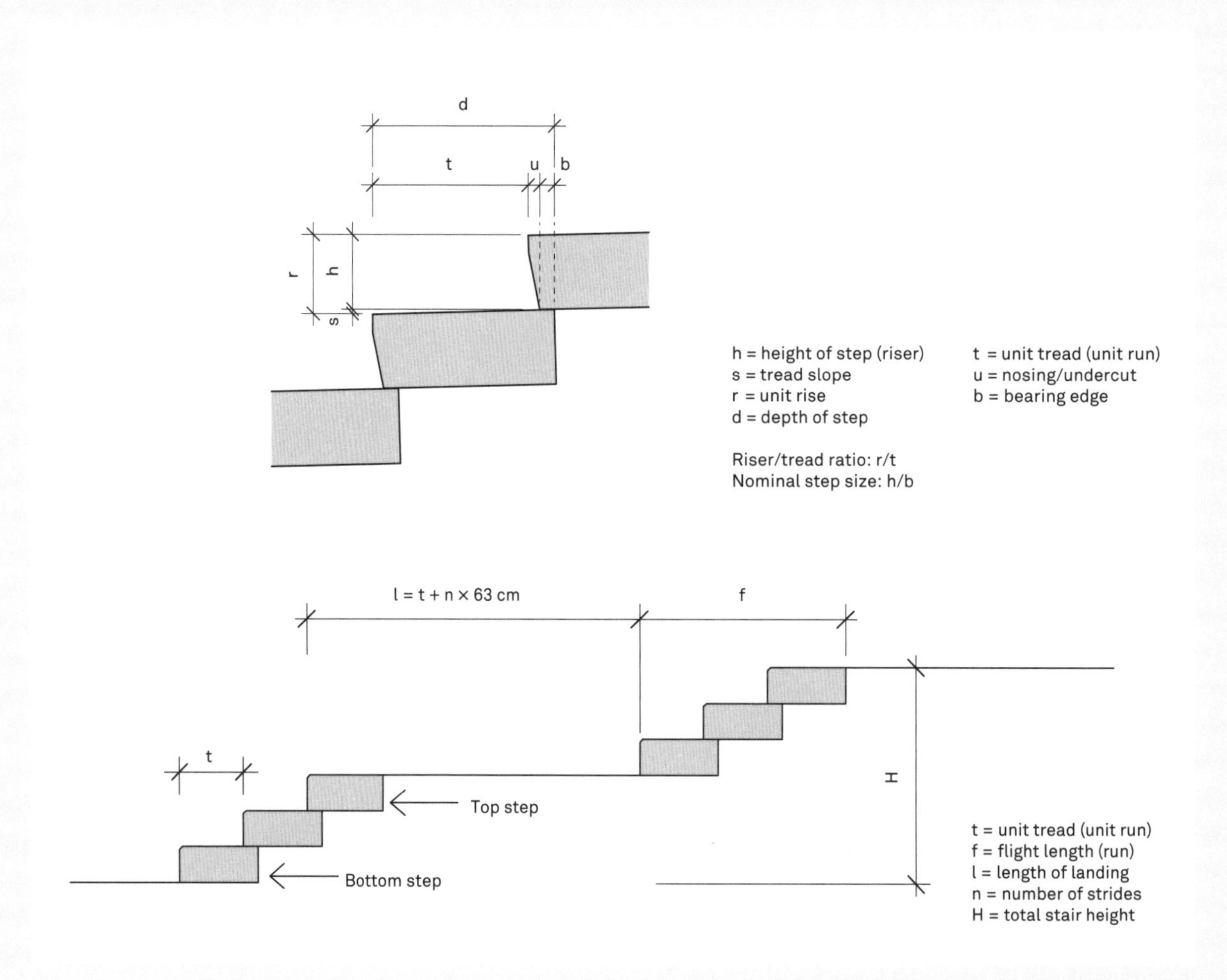

Figure 3.2.12 Calculating step and landing dimensions

Country	Formula	Applicability	Source
Germany	2r + t = 59–65 cm	At buildings (entrance area and access paths)	DIN 18065
Austria	2r + t = 59–65 cm	At buildings (entrance area and access paths)	ÖNORM B 5371
Switzerland	2r + t = 62–64 cm	At buildings, exterior: risers 13–18 cm and treads 28–35 cm, intermediate landings after 9–12 steps	bfu
France	2r + t = 59–64 cm		Ministère de l'équipement, du Logement, des Transport et du Tourisme
Spain	54 cm ≤ 2r + t ≤ 70 cm	Risers of 10–15 cm are recommended for outdoor grounds	Documento Básico de Seguridad de Utilización (DB-SU)
USA	2r + t = 65–67.5 cm (26–27 inches)	Outdoor premises	Time-Saver Standards

Table 3.2.4 Stride length formulas for calculating step dimensions

	According to stride length formula for stairs in and adjoining buildings		**Stride length and stride length formulas for outdoor stairs**			
	As per DIN 18065-1		**Recommendation according to Alwin Seifert for r < 17**		**Recommendation according to Günter Mader**	
r	Tread (t)	Stride length 2r + t	Tread t = 94 – 4r	Stride length 2r + t	Tread (t)	Stride length 2r + t
9	Not permitted in and adjoining* buildings as per DIN 18065-1		58 cm	76 cm		
10			54 cm	74 cm	50–63 cm	70–83 cm
11			50 cm	72 cm	45–58 cm	67–80 cm
12			46 cm	70 cm	41–53 cm	65–77 cm
13			42 cm	68 cm	38–48 cm	64–74 cm
14	31–37 cm		38 cm	66 cm	36–43 cm	64–71 cm
15	29–35 cm	59–65 cm	34 cm	64 cm	34–39 cm	64–69 cm
16	27–33 cm		30 cm	62 cm	32–35 cm	64–67 cm
17	25–31 cm		–	–	29–32 cm	63–66 cm
18	23–29 cm		–	–	27–30 cm	63–66 cm
19	21–27 cm		–	–	–	–
20**	21–25 cm		–	–	–	–
21 **	21–23 cm		–	–	–	–

* stairs serving as a means of access for a building
** only stairs that are not legally necessary (not part of a rescue route); 20 cm also permitted for residential buildings with max. 2 dwellings

Table 3.2.5 Rise-to-run ratio of steps

Stair Width

The required stair width is dependent on the use, and applicable guidelines must be taken into account for certain uses, such as for assuring access to public buildings or event venues. For legally essential stairs, a minimum width of 100 cm must be maintained (as per DIN 18065-1). Building stairs located outside shall be designed with a minimum width of 120 cm (as per Ö Norm B 5371).

Accessible Stairs

Stairs are considered to be accessible for use by people with limited mobility restrictions or visual impairments when they have closed risers, handrails → Chapter 3.6, and suitable aids for orientation along a straight run.

The line of travel (walking line) must be orthogonal to the leading edges of the stair's steps. Curved flights may also be used if the circular stair has an open well with an inside diameter ≥ 200 cm.

Treads that project beyond the risers are to be avoided, but nosings of up to 2 cm are permitted.

Due to their limited visibility, paired or single steps are, as a basic principle, to be clearly identified and distinguished from the surrounding terrain. Flights of stairs with up to three steps must have markings on each step, consisting of a 50–80 mm wide contrasting stripe across the entire tread width, and flights with more than three steps must have the same markings on at least the first and last steps. Furthermore, DIN 32984 specifies that attention fields which contrast with adjacent surfacing should be positioned in front of stair runs. → Figures 3.2.13 and 3.2.14

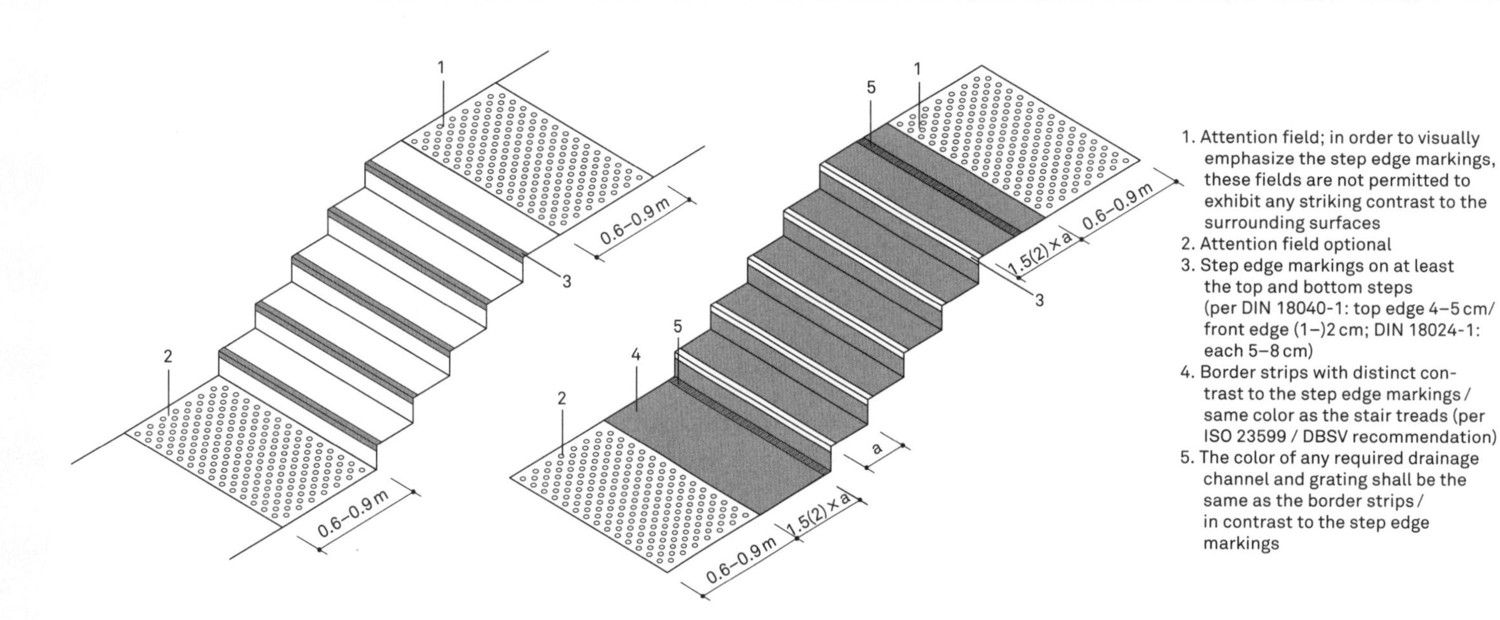

1. Attention field; in order to visually emphasize the step edge markings, these fields are not permitted to exhibit any striking contrast to the surrounding surfaces
2. Attention field optional
3. Step edge markings on at least the top and bottom steps (per DIN 18040-1: top edge 4–5 cm/ front edge (1–)2 cm; DIN 18024-1: each 5–8 cm)
4. Border strips with distinct contrast to the step edge markings / same color as the stair treads (per ISO 23599 / DBSV recommendation)
5. The color of any required drainage channel and grating shall be the same as the border strips / in contrast to the step edge markings

Figure 3.2.13 Attention fields in front of a stair

Figure 3.2.14 The contrasting front edges help to better identify the steps and simultaneously serve as a design element, Berlin Wall Memorial visitor center

Accessible Circulation Along Sloping Paths and Ramps

Walkways and traffic areas must be solid and even and should generally have a maximum longitudinal slope of 3%. If this limit cannot be maintained, ramps can be incorporated with a maximum slope of 6% and intermediate landings placed 6m apart. At access areas and entrances, ramps may not exceed 4%, and landings must then be located with a spacing of not more than 10m.

Platforms must have a usable length of at least 150cm and can have a maximum longitudinal slope of 3%. A width of at least 120cm shall be provided.

The maximum cross slope for accessible paths should not exceed 2%, and ramps are generally to be constructed without any cross slope, as this would jeopardize braking safety.

If a ramp is not bounded by a wall at the side, wheel deflector curbs with a height of 10cm and handrails at 85 to 90cm above the top of the ramped surfaces and the landings are to be provided (→ **Chapter 3.6 Boundary Enclosures and Railings**)

	Accessible as per DIN 18024-1	User-friendly/functional	Optimized (e.g., for additional use by bicycles)
Maximum longitudinal slope	4–6% (ramps)	3%–4%	3%
Maximum cross slope for surfaces/on ramps	2% (6% at driveway approaches to lots)/0%	1%/0%	0%
Width	1.2m	1.5m	≥1.8m
Maneuvering space/ landings at ramps	1.5m	2.0–3.0m	≥4.0m
Spacing of landings along ramps	Maximum 10m	Maximum 10m	

Table 3.2.6 Accessible design of inclined surfaces and ramps (Source: Design for All, supplemented)

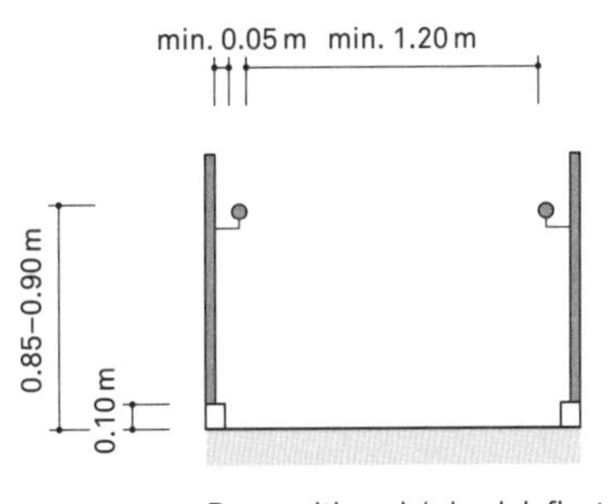

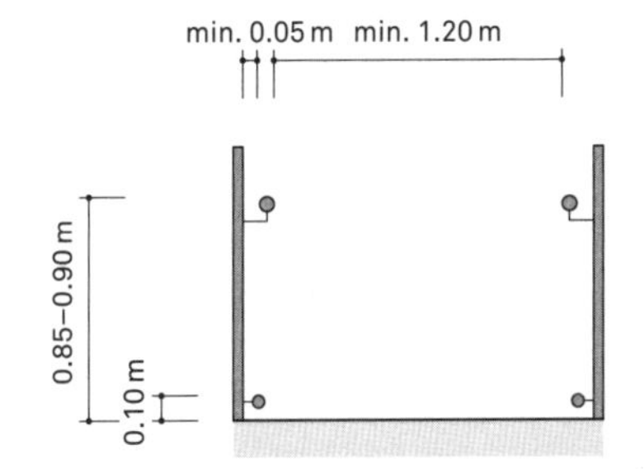

Figure 3.2.15 Ramp cross sections as per DIN 18040-1

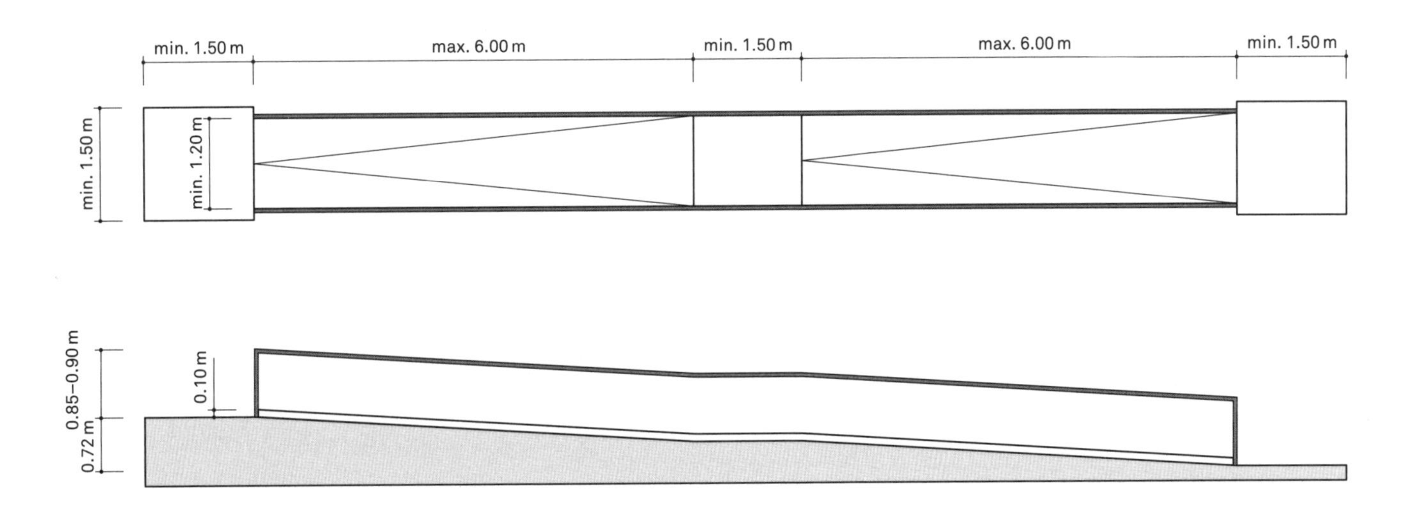

Figure 3.2.16 Requirements for ramp runs and landings as per DIN 18040-1

Wheeling Ramps

If, due to lack of sufficient space, it is not possible to provide a ramp that can be used by bicyclists without dismounting their bikes, a wheeling ramp (push ramp) should be integrated into the stairway. Wheeling ramps can be formed as either flat or grooved ramps, and the latter are known as wheeling channels or troughs. Flat wheeling ramps can be built into the stairs as solid concrete or natural stone elements, or they can be installed as surface-mounted metal ramps on top of or alongside the steps. Wheeling channels can also be integrated into the ramp, in order to make it easier to guide the wheels. At the side, a space of at least 30 cm from any obstacles (wall, handrail, railing, etc.) must be maintained to provide sufficient space for the handlebars and pedals as well as for luggage. If the stair will also be used by bicycles with trailers, a second ramp with steps in-between must be provided.

The ramp should be constructed asymmetrically – with a wider part on the outer side – so that the bicycle and one wheel of the trailer have sufficient space on the wider side. Since trailers are often made with a drawbar on the left side, the wider ramp should be on the outer left side when traveling upward on the ramp → **Figure 3.2.17** (see ADFC NRW: Empfehlungen zur Planung von Radwegen auf ehemaligen Bahntrassen [Recommendations for the planning of bicycle routes along former railroad lines], 2008).

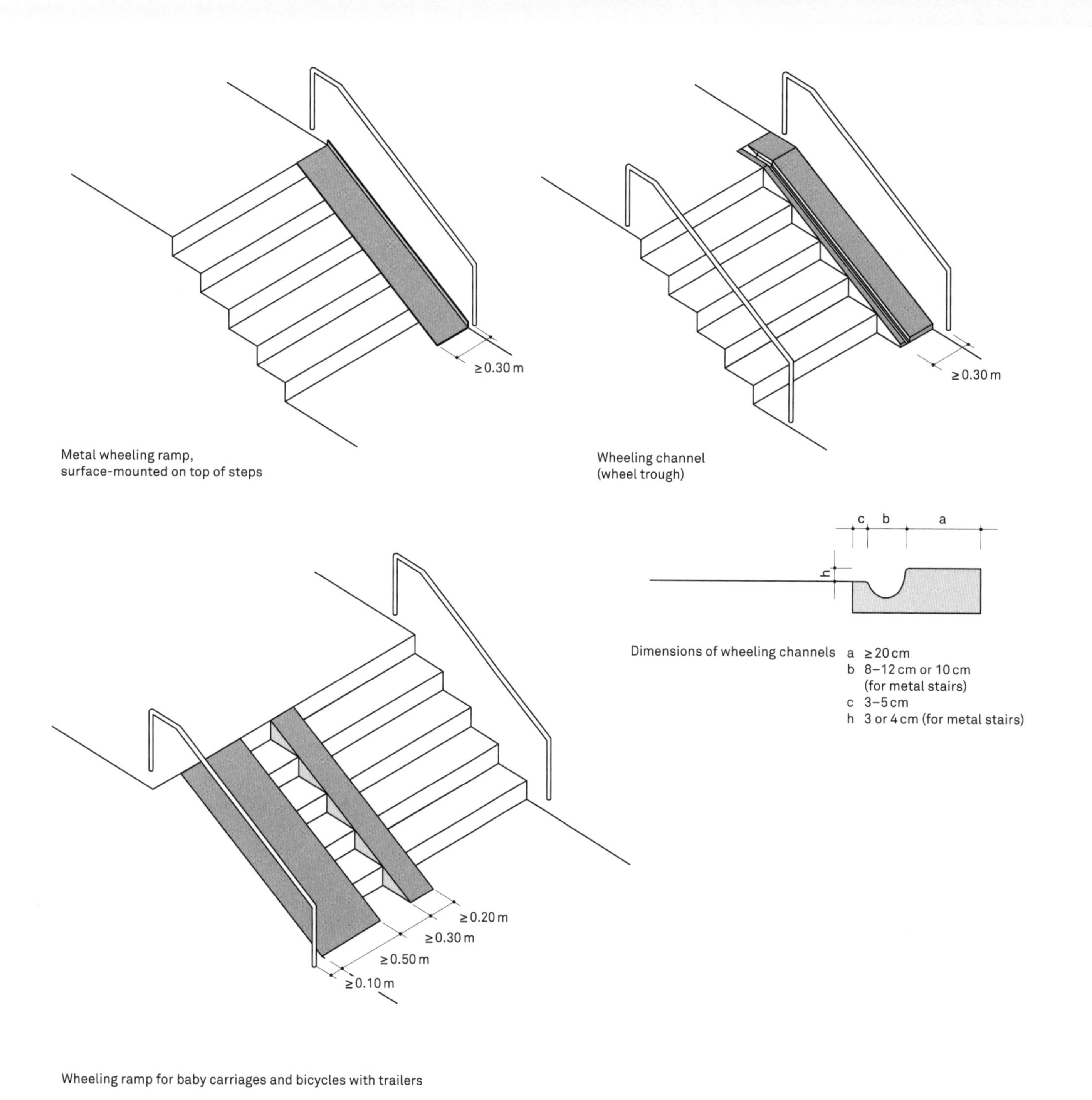

Abb. 3.2.17 Examples of wheeling ramps

Crest and Sag Curves

At changes in grade along roadways and on approach ramps leading up or down to garages or parking areas, a transition is made by either rounding off or flattening out the crests and sags in the course of the roadway in order to prevent the vehicle from bottoming out.

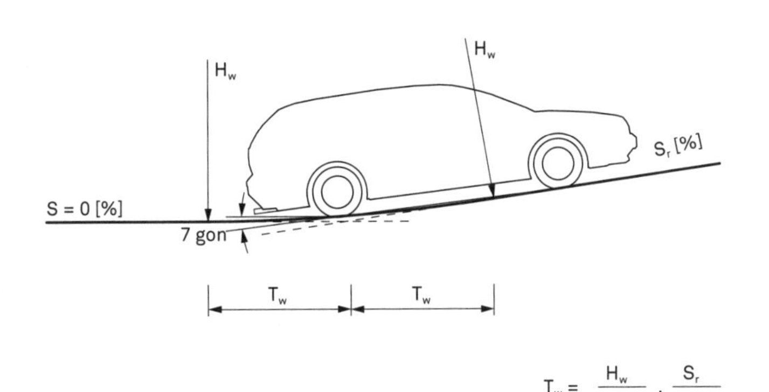

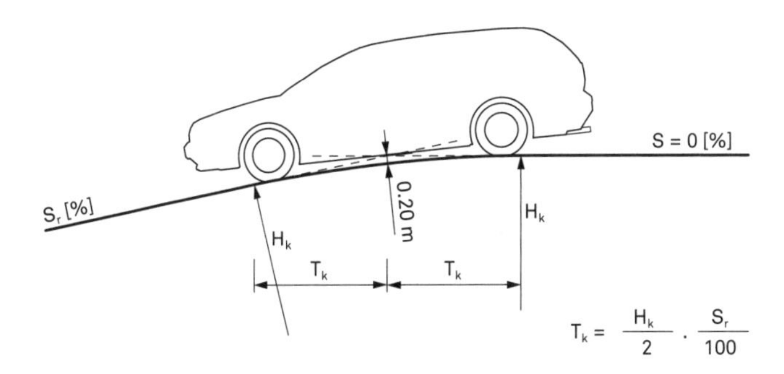

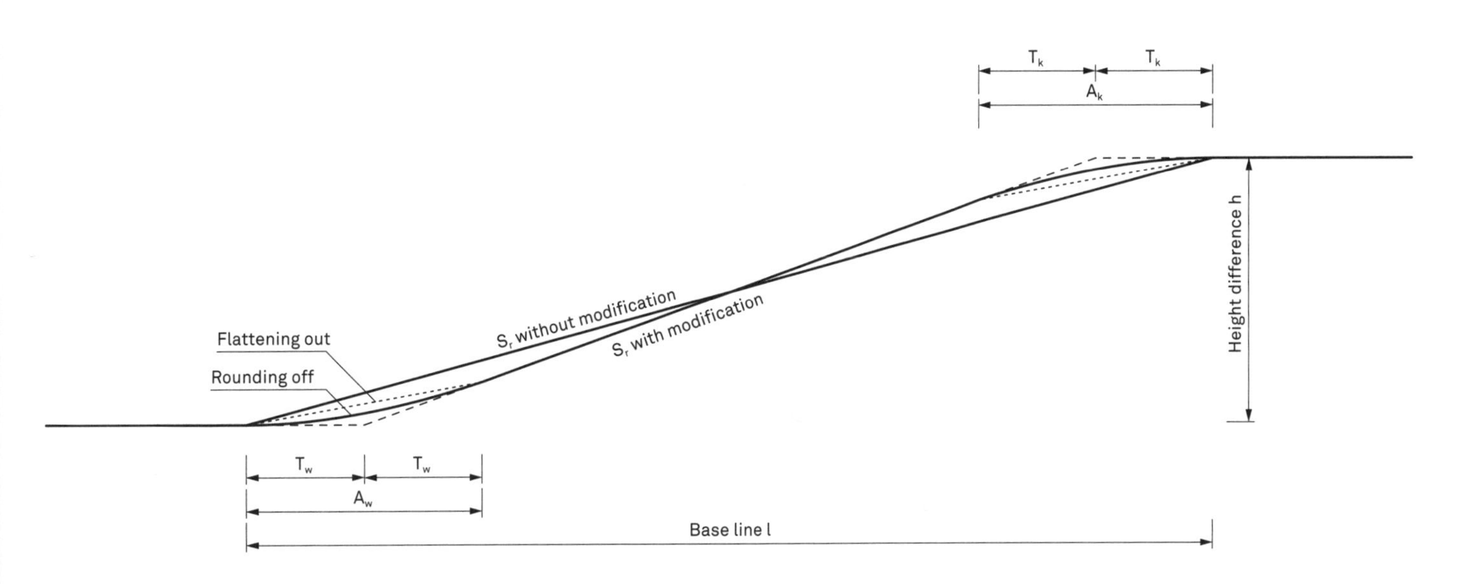

Figure 3.2.18 Rounding off and flattening out the roadway at gradient changes on crests and sags

Remarks on Building Law and Regulatory Approval

On public property, the guidelines and legal requirements for barrier-free construction must be observed. If full compliance is not possible, particularly due to spatially constricted conditions, different solutions are also possible upon application for approval.

For certain temporary uses, such as the outdoor facilities for event venues and the like, the building regulations foresee different provisions in some cases.

Handrails Along Stairs
→ 3.6 Boundary Enclosures and Railings

3 Elements
3.3 Paths and Roads

3.3 Paths and Roads

Requirements for paths and circulation areas are derived from the nature and frequency of their use and must, in addition, be adapted to their specific location, whether in a garden, park, supra-regional green corridor, or alongside public roadways. When planning public open spaces, it is particularly important to take into account the needs of pedestrian and bicycle traffic, including people with reduced mobility. Inline skaters or horseback riders must also be given due consideration where appropriate. In public spaces, on private access roads, and in parking lots, motorized traffic poses unique demands that must be accommodated through functional design that also pays regard to pertinent regulations (including road traffic regulations such as Germany's Road Traffic Ordinance, the StVO).

For roads, prime importance is given to the functional separation of lanes for different means of transport, such as pedestrian, bicycle, and private motor vehicle traffic as well as public transit, with parallel areas that jointly constitute the traffic space (separation principle) and which are subject to strong regulation. On secondary roads and residential streets and in places with special uses (e.g., pedestrian zones), the different means of transport can be combined, yielding mixed traffic areas.

Walkways and bikeways enjoy the greatest design freedom when laid out as independently routed paths in public parks and the open landscape. Generously dimensioned paths offer the greatest possible comfort, particularly when oncoming traffic is encountered and when multiple means of transport share the path. In the interests of ecological and economic sustainability, however, the space-saving planning of paths based on minimum values is equally desirable. The basis for this is the space occupied by all of the traffic participants. → Table 3.3.12 When setting the dimensions for areas in outdoor facilities, consideration should always be given to the use of footpaths by maintenance vehicles and – to the extent necessary – emergency vehicles.

Figure 3.3.1 In places where paths are shared, sufficient width must be provided.

Location

Surfacing

Depending on how they will be used, different surface properties are required for paths and other thoroughfares. Table 3.3.1 identifies specific properties that pertain to various functions and lists corresponding suitable surfacing materials.

For use in workplaces, in wet barefoot areas, and generally in all public facilities, regulations pertaining to slip resistance and the corresponding identification of floor coverings with nonslip properties are to be seen as obligatory stipulations. But additionally, they should also be taken into account for other design tasks and applied similarly.

In Germany, for shoe areas, the slip resistance classes R9–R13 as per DIN 51130 (Testing of floor coverings) and BGR 181 occupational safety regulations apply. In Swit-

Application	Required properties	Suitable surfacing materials
Walkway	Nonslip, even	Water-bound pavements, unit pavers of natural stone, concrete, and fired brick, natural stone and concrete slabs with a rough finish, cast-in-place concrete, asphalt, synthetic surfacing, wood decking **Conditionally suitable:** Metal grating (choose cross-bar spacing appropriate to use), metal plates (with adequate skid resistance), flagstones, slabs and pavers with grass joints, cobblestones and gravel paving, bark mulch and grass paths (garden paths and secondary paths)
Barrier-free access (wheelchair or walking aid)	Nonslip, even, good for wheeled devices / little rolling resistance	Tightly jointed brick, concrete, or natural stone paving blocks (preferably saw-cut finish), natural stone and concrete slabs with a rough finish, cast-in-place concrete, asphalt, hard-wearing synthetic surfacing **Conditionally suitable:** as an enhancement / in limited areas: Tightly jointed wood decking, grating with maximum grid size of 12 × 12 mm (better: 8 × 8 mm), water-bound pavements with a sanded surface of fine flint gravel (limited use under wet conditions)
Barrier-free access (visually impaired and blind persons)	Nonslip, even, tactile, contrast-rich, good water drainage	Water-bound pavements, tightly jointed brick, concrete, or natural stone paving blocks (preferably saw-cut finish), natural stone and concrete slabs with a rough finish, cast-in-place concrete, asphalt, hard-wearing synthetic surfacing **Conditionally suitable:** as an enhancement / in limited areas: Tightly jointed wood decking, grating with maximum grid size of 12 × 12 mm (better: 8 × 8 mm)
People with baby carriages	Nonslip, even, good for wheeled devices	Water-bound pavements, tightly jointed slabs and unit pavers of natural stone, brick, or concrete, cast-in-place concrete, asphalt, hard-wearing synthetic surfacing **Conditionally suitable:** as an enhancement / in limited areas: Tightly jointed wood decking, grating with maximum grid size of 12 × 12 mm (better: 8 × 8 mm)
Inline skaters	Even, sufficient static friction(grip), very good water drainage	(fine-grained) asphalt **Conditionally suitable:** Cast-in-place concrete (with sealed joints or narrow contraction joints)
Bikeway	Permanently smooth finish, little rolling resistance, antiskid, low-dust, very good water drainage	Asphalt, concrete unit pavers and slabs with a rough finish (higher rolling resistance than asphalt), cast-in-place concrete Conditionally suitable: Natural stone paving blocks and slabs, water-bound pavements with a sanded surface of fine flint gravel (in rural areas and for paths with infrequent use)
Riding paths	Elastic, good traction, low-dust, may not silt up or freeze, moisture storing, water-permeable	(Quartz) sand, organic materials (wood chips), vegetated surfaces / turf, in riding arenas also synthetic surfaces (e.g., shredded polyester, polypropylene fibers, or mineral gel) or sand mixtures
Motorcycles, cars and other motor vehicles	Even, antiskid, nonslip, very good water drainage, low-noise	Cast-in-place concrete, asphalt **Conditionally suitable:** Concrete, natural stone or brick unit pavers in limited areas, on approaches, in traffic-calmed areas, and in streets without special loading conditions (> up to construction classification III–VI as per RStO 01); Due to the high noise levels that result, sett paving is only conditionally suitable as road surfacing
Parking spaces for motor vehicles	Even, load-bearing, good water drainage	Concrete, asphalt, precast concrete unit pavers, interlocking concrete pavers, sett paving **Conditionally suitable:** for automobile parking spaces and seldom-used traffic aisles: also grass paving blocks, pavers with crushed stone or grass joints, and crushed aggregate lawns
Emergency vehicles	Even, load-bearing, nonslip, good water drainage or permeable	Crushed aggregate lawn, grass paving blocks, unit pavers of natural stone, brick, or precast concrete, asphalt, cast-in-place concrete

Table 3.3.1 Suitable surfacing materials for paths and paved open spaces

zerland, classification is made according to the Anforderungsliste für Bodenbeläge [List of requirements for floor coverings] issued by the Swiss Council for Accident Prevention (bfu). The R9 rating denotes the lowest antislip properties, and R13 the highest. Since the provisions pertain to workplaces (and thus primarily to indoor spaces), corresponding identification of exterior paving materials is not obligatory, but is nevertheless done with increasing frequency.

For wet barefoot areas, a distinction is made between the assessment groups A, B, and C as per GUV-I 8527 – Bodenbeläge für nassbelastete Barfußbereiche [Flooring for wet barefoot areas].

Area of application	Assessment group / slip-resistance class	
	DIN 51130 / BGR 181	bfu
Covered forecourts, entrance areas, and exterior stairs	R11	GS2
Open (unroofed) forecourts and exterior stairs	R12	GS3
Covered ramps up to maximum 6% slope	R11	GS2
Covered ramps with more than 6% slope	R12	GS3
Open ramps up to maximum 6% slope	R12	GS3
Open ramps with more than 6% slope	R13	GS4
Covered terraces and balconies	R10	GS1
Open terraces and balconies	R11	GS2
Schoolyard recess areas	R11	GS2
Pedestrian path	R11 or R10 V4	GS2 or GS1 V4
Loading ramps, covered	R11 or R10 V4	GS2 or GS1 V4
Loading ramps, open	R12 V4	GS3
Paved public spaces	R11 or R10 V4	GS2 or GS1 V4
Outdoor parking areas	R11 or R10 V4	GS2 or GS1 V4

Table 3.3.2 Necessary slip-resistance class according to area of application

Assessment group	Areas
A	• Barefoot passages (mostly dry) • Individual and common changing rooms • Pool floors in nonswimmer areas, if the water depth is more than 80 cm in the entire area
B	• Barefoot passages when not otherwise classified in group A • Shower rooms • Area of disinfecting spray facilities • Pool decks • Pool floors in nonswimmer areas, if the water depth is less than 80 cm in certain areas • Pool floors in nonswimmer areas of wave pools • Movable floors • Wading pools • Ladders leading into the water • Stairs leading into the water with a maximum width of 1 m and handrails on both sides • Ladders and stairs outside the pool area
C	• Stairs leading into the water, when not otherwise classified in group B • Walk-through foot baths • Sloped pool edges

Table 3.3.3 Assessment groups for slip resistance for wet barefoot areas per GUV-I 8527

Dimensions and Characteristics

Dimensions of Traffic Participants

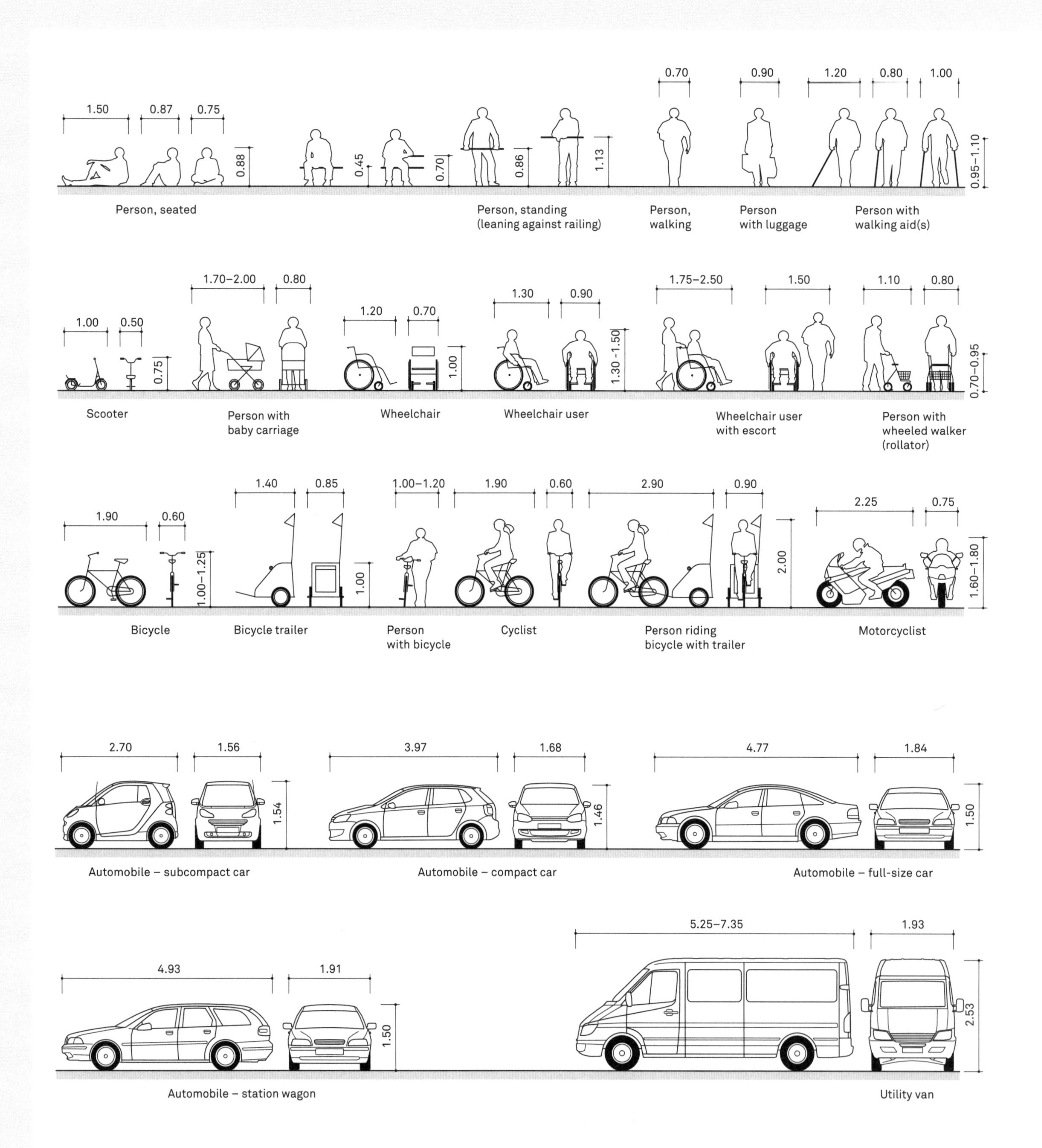

Figure 3.3.2 Dimensions of traffic participants (without maneuvering space)

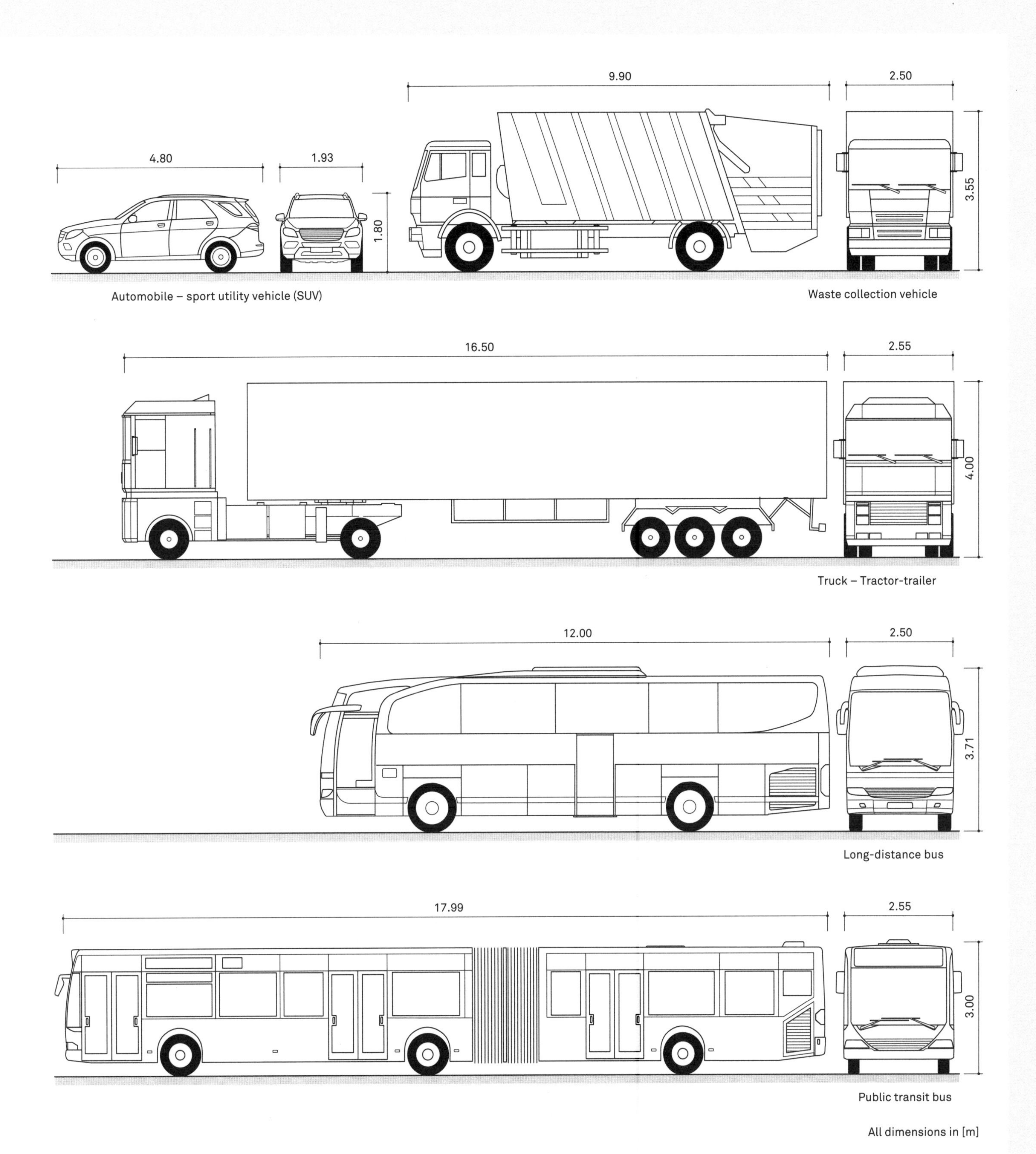

Automobile – sport utility vehicle (SUV)

Waste collection vehicle

Truck – Tractor-trailer

Long-distance bus

Public transit bus

All dimensions in [m]

Walk- and Bikeways

Pedestrian Traffic

When designing pedestrian paths that give access to parks and green spaces, many different path widths can result from varied functions and the anticipated frequency of use. In contrast to strictly regulated street spaces, relatively few specific directives exist for park trails and paths in gardens. As elsewhere, the path widths in these cases are always dependent on the density of the path network and on design considerations.

Specific requirements apply to sidewalks that are adjacent to roadways. As facilities for pedestrian traffic located directly in the roadside space, the dimensions are determined, according to RASt 06, by the traffic space and safety clearances for pedestrians. The standard width is 2.50 m, which includes a safety clearance of 0.50 m alongside the street and a safety clearance of 0.20 m on the side away from the street.

In addition to its use as a maneuvering area, roadside space can have additional requirements and functions that make it necessary to expand the space either linearly or at selective locations in accordance with the additional spatial requirements listed in **Table 3.3.5**.

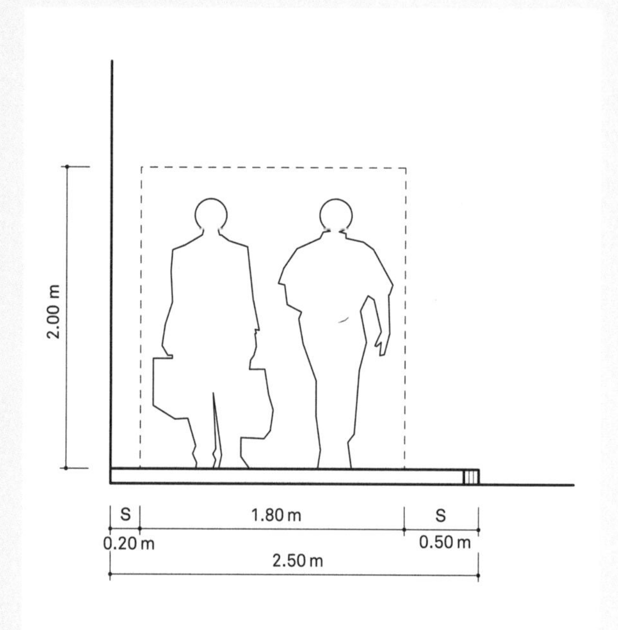

Figure 3.3.3 Standard width of a roadside space (as per RASt 06)

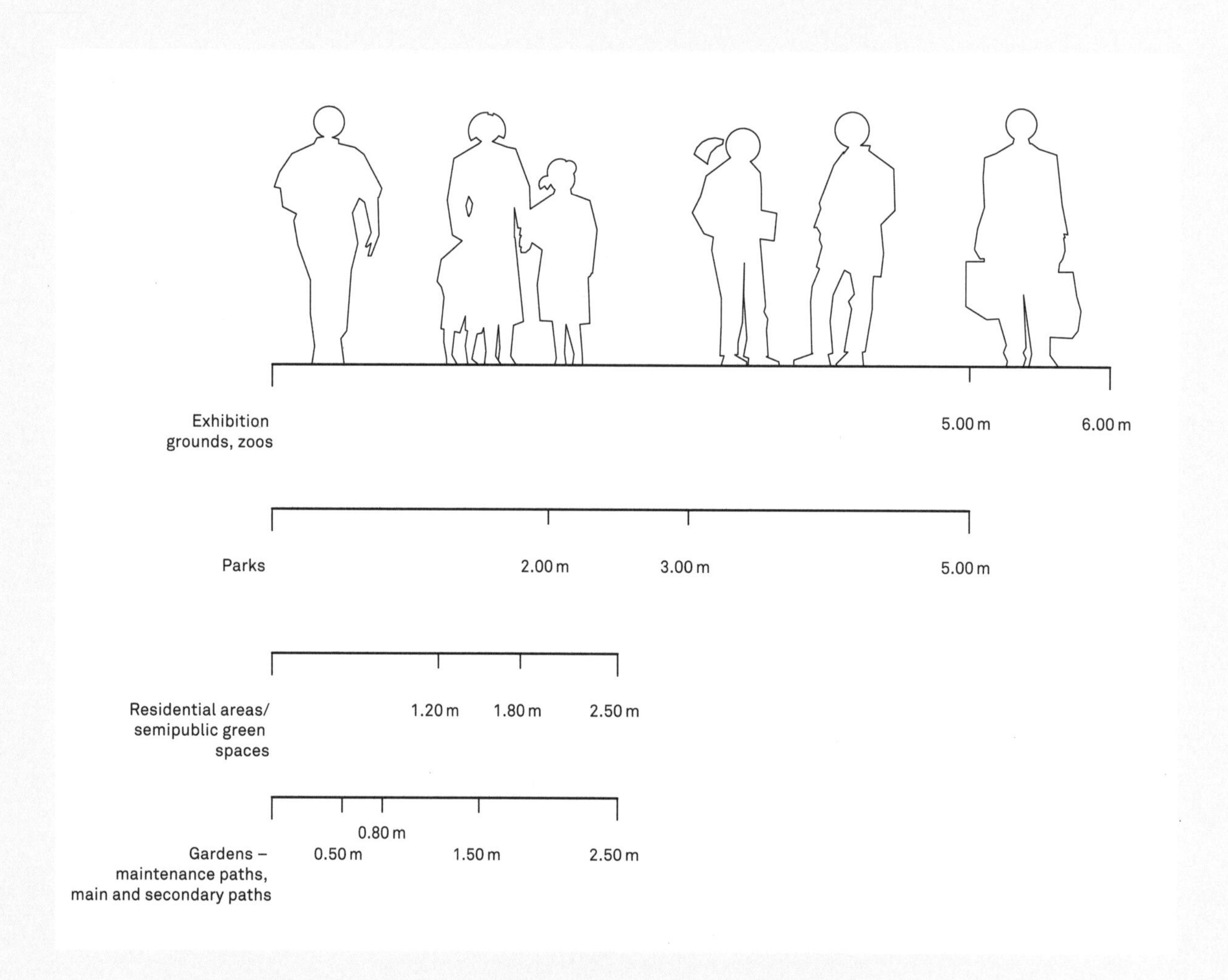

Figure 3.3.4 Space requirements for walkways

Category/function	Width (standard values)
Gardens	
Main paths	1.5–2.5 m
Secondary paths	0.8–1.5 m
Maintenance paths, not barrier-free	0.5 m
Access to public and semipublic buildings / semipublic green spaces / residential areas	
Main paths	1.8–2.5 m
Secondary paths	1.2–1.8 m
Parks	
Main paths (including shared use by bicycle traffic)	3–5 m
Secondary paths	2–3 m
Exhibition grounds, zoos	
Main paths	5–6 m

Table 3.3.4 Guideline values for path widths in outdoor facilities

Roadside space requirements	Space required
Standard width for walkways	2.5 m
plus...	+
Areas for children's play	≥2 m
Spaces for lingering in front of store windows	≥1 m
Median strip without trees	≥1 m
Median strip with trees	≥2–2.5 m
Benches	≥1 m
Waiting areas at bus stops	≥2.5 m
Display shelves in front of stores	1.5 m
Parking spaces for two-wheeled vehicles Parking angle 90°/100 gon Parking angle 45°/50 gon	 2 m 1.5 m
Vehicle overhang with rows of perpendicular or angled parking	0.7 m

Table 3.3.5 Standard values for the additional space required in roadside space due to special requirements and uses (as per RASt 06)

Barrier-Free Access

The accessible design of walkways encompasses diverse measures. To facilitate a person's orientation along their path, tactile paving surfaces in contrasting colors should be used to structure the walkway. Additionally, the main circulation route must be designed to be free of obstacles. Street furnishings such as street lights, utility cabinets, mailboxes, or benches are to be located along the edges of the sidewalk or in supplemental occupiable areas. → **Figures 3.3.5 and 3.3.3** In addition, the design of pedestrian crossings with depressed curbs and tactile paving surface indicators is of major importance. Separated crossing points take advantage of differentiated curb heights.

Curb heights of 6 cm and more constitute a clear boundary between sidewalk and roadway. For blind and visually impaired persons, the height difference is discernible by touch when using a cane and provides a warning signal that is clearly perceptible when crossing the curb. By also providing a flush curb, however, it is easier for people who are reliant on wheelchairs and rollators to cross the roadway. The spatial separation of the crossing areas and the judicious use of tactile paving surfaces significantly increases the aspect of safety for blind and visually impaired people. → **Figures 3.3.7–3.3.9** For the suitability of various curb heights for different types of users, see also **Table 3.3.4**.

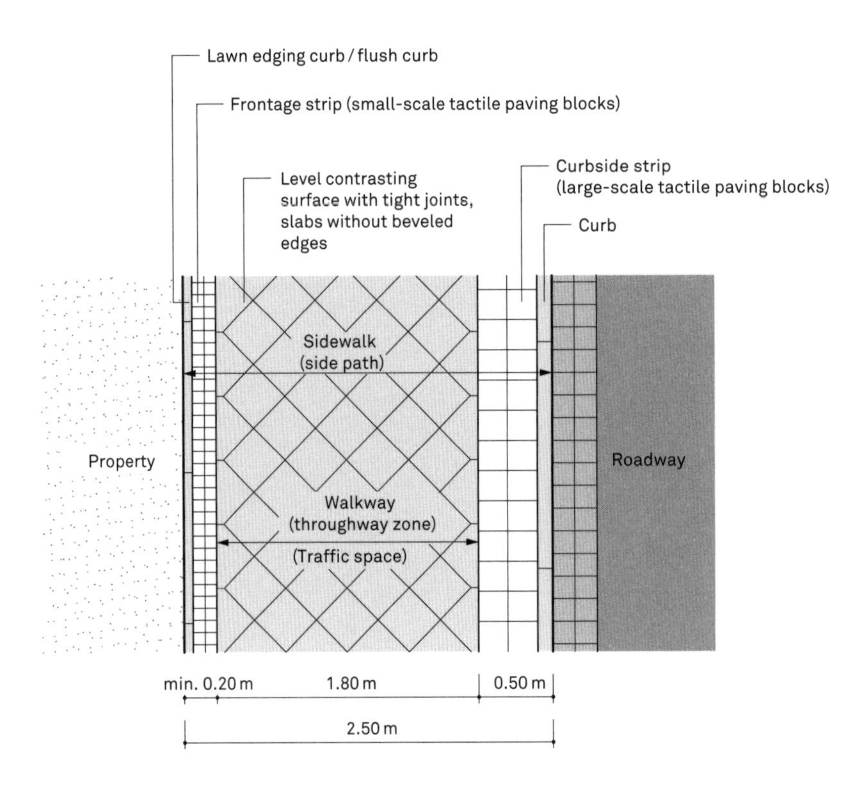

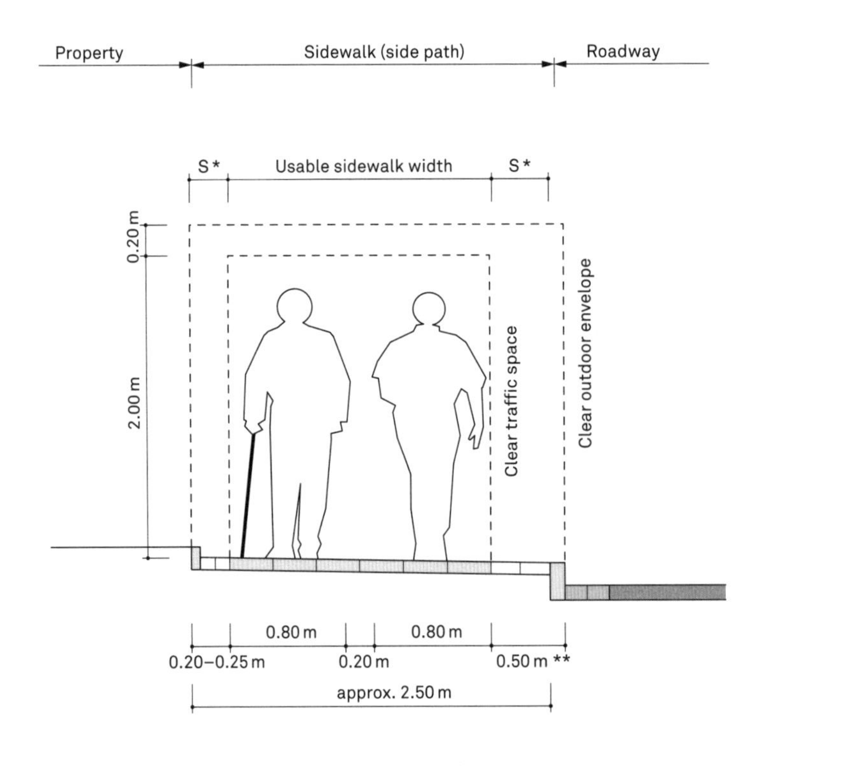

* S = Safety clearance
** Clearance as per EFA (Recommendations for pedestrian traffic facilities): minimum 30 cm with little heavy traffic

Figure 3.3.5 Tactile and visually tangible sidewalks

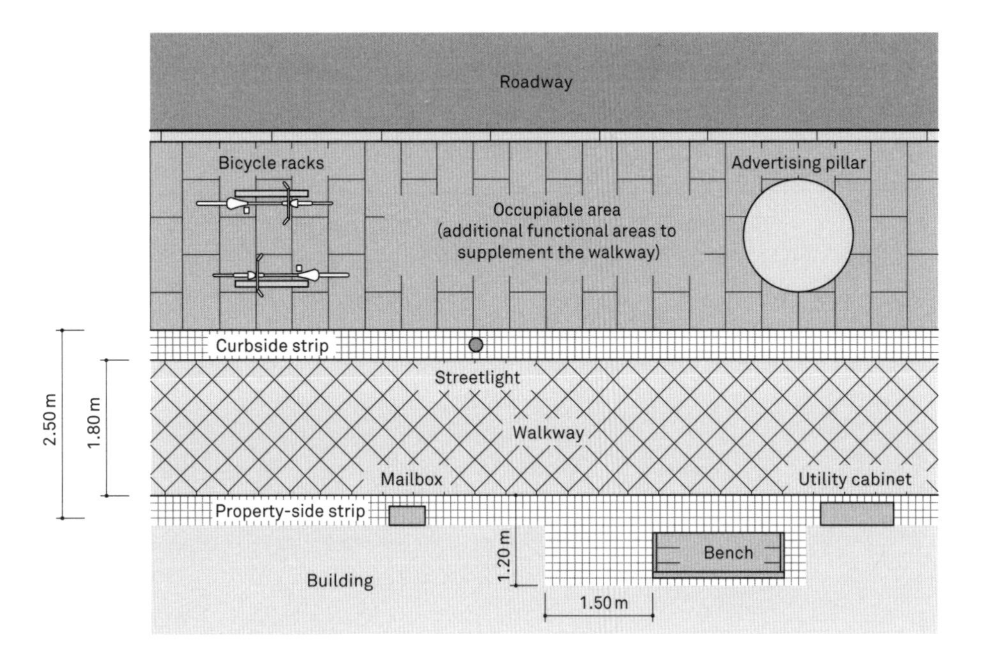

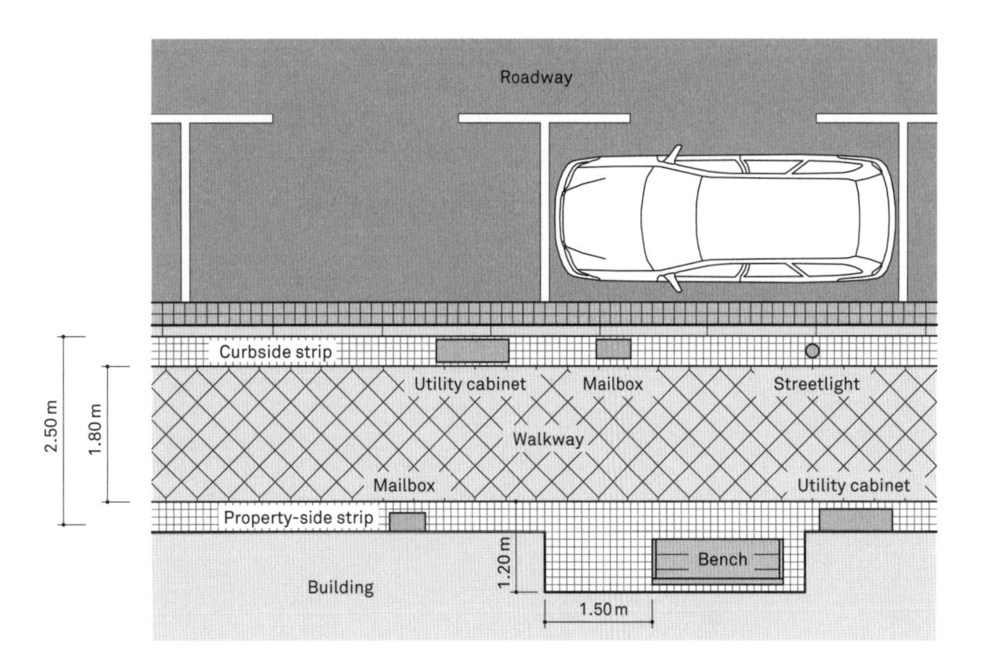

Figure 3.3.6 Obstacle-free design of sidewalks

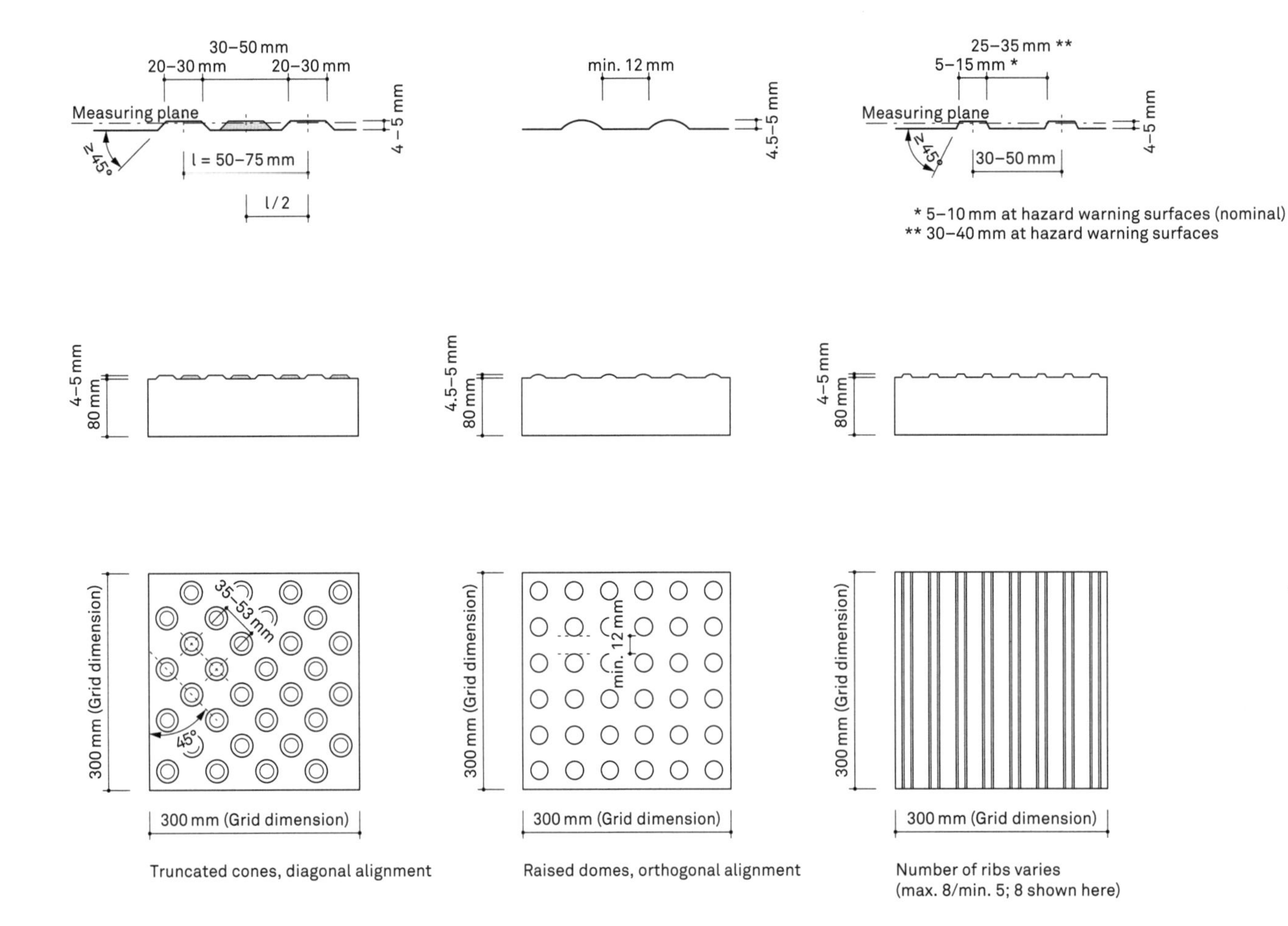

Dome surface pattern – attention and search

- Attention fields in front of stairs (diagonal alignment of domes)
- Attention fields in front of obstacles and hazardous areas within the maneuvering area or projecting into it more by than 20 cm (diagonal alignment of domes)
- Attention surfaces at junctures, as decision points in a guidance system (diagonal alignment of domes)
- Information surfaces at pedestrian crossings (orthogonal alignment of domes)

Ribbed surface pattern (corduroy) – orientation and direction

- Guidance path surfaces along pathways
- Direction fields indicating the direction of pedestrian travel, e.g. at pedestrian crossings
- Information surfaces indicating general target destinations off to the side of the walkway, e.g. bus stops, entries, or information elements (excluding crossing points)
- Information surfaces indicating the start and end of guidance systems for the blind (combined with a junction field where joined to the guidance system)
- Boarding areas at bus stops
- Hazard warning surfaces at crossing points with flush curbs

Figure 3.3.7 Paving surface indicators (tactile guidance elements) – patterns and functions

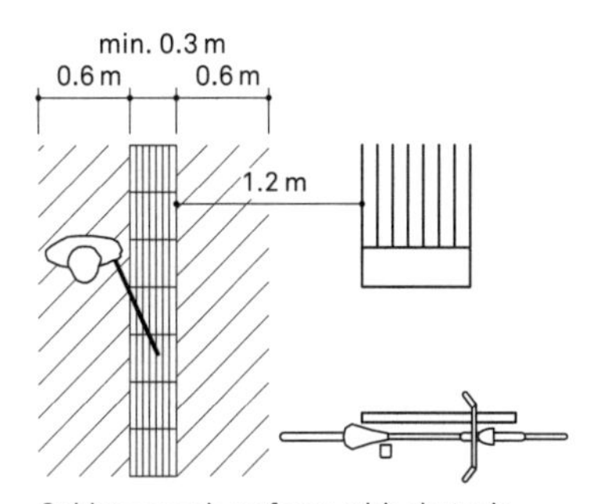

Guidance path surfaces with obstacle-free zones on both sides and clearance to street furniture *)

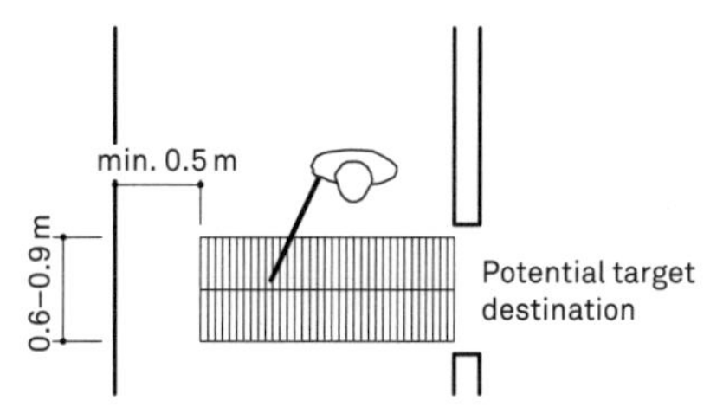

Information surface indicating general target destinations located off to the side *)

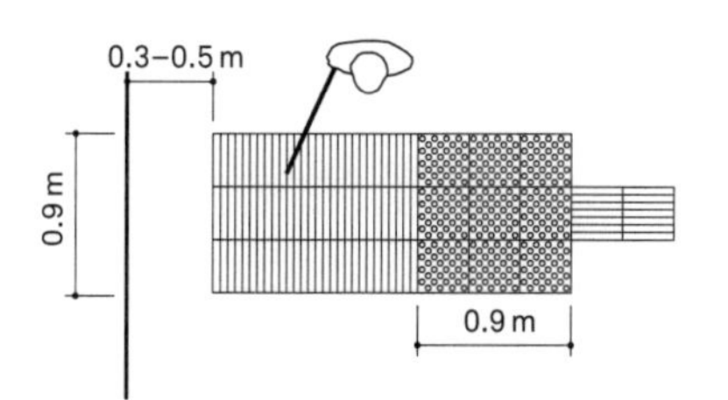

Information surface indicating the start and end of guidance systems for the blind (combined with a junction field) *)

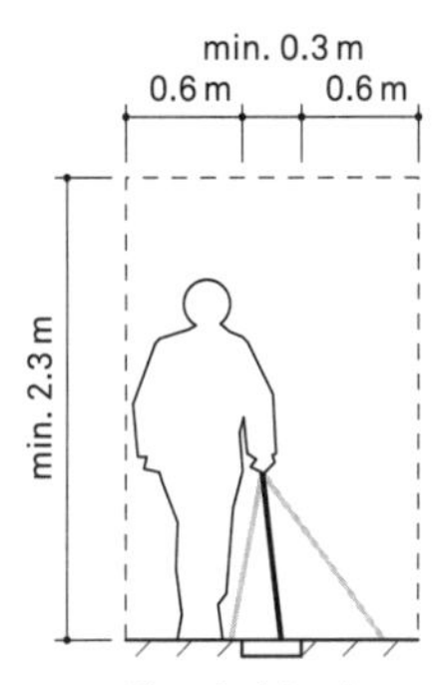

Clear height above guidance path surface and clear area on both sides *)

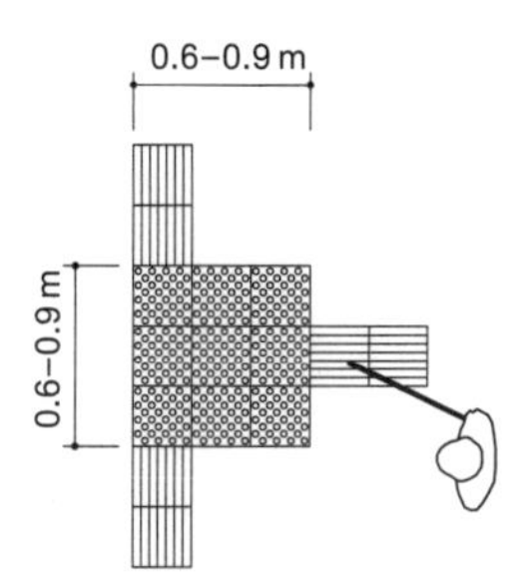

Junction field as decision point in a guidance system *)

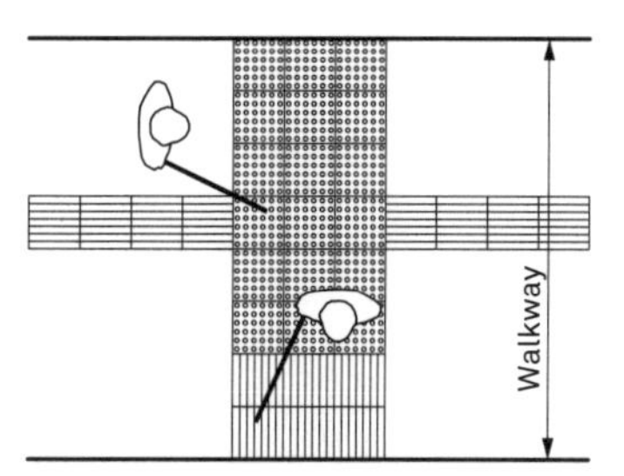

Information surface with adjoining direction field at pedestrian crossings *)

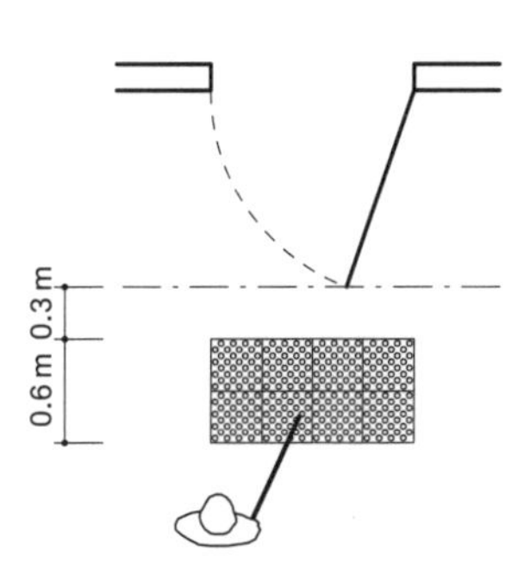

Attention field in front of obstacles and hazardous areas, e.g. automatic swing doors *)

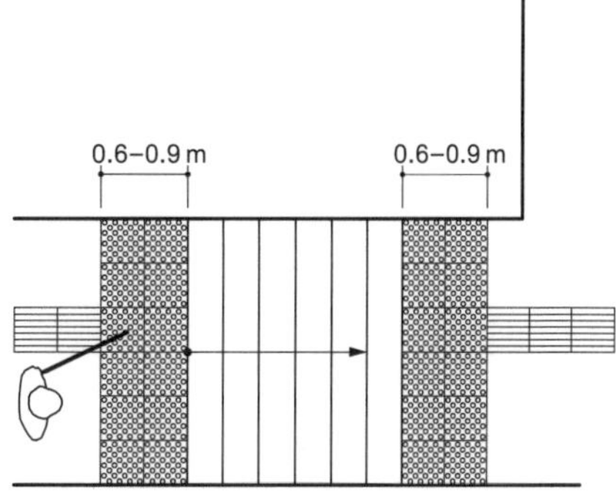

Attention field in front of stairs **)

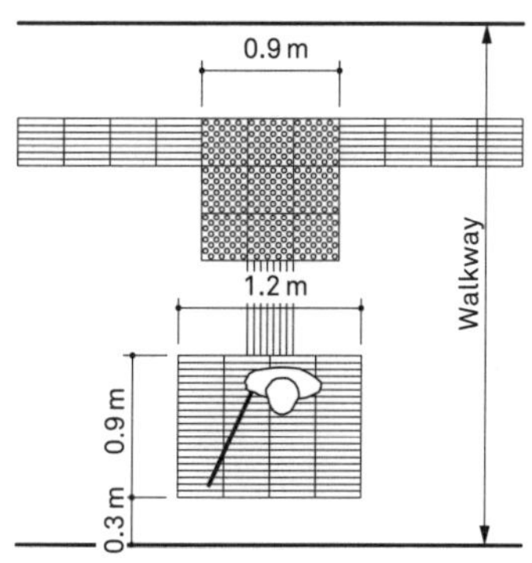

Indication in the guidance system of a bus stop, with boarding area set back 0.3 m from the roadway *)

*) If the tactile and/or visual contrast between the tactile paving surfaces and the surrounding pavement is poor, contrasting border strips or bordering surfaces should be installed on both sides.

**) Attention fields at stairs, individual steps, and ramps are not permitted to have any striking visual contrast with the surrounding surfacing.

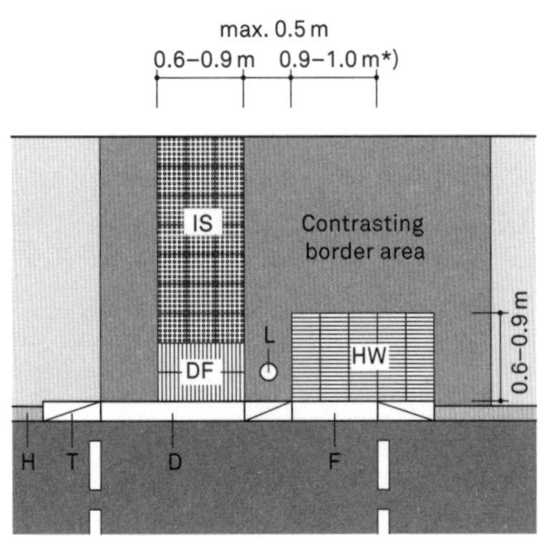

Controlled pedestrian crossing with traffic signal

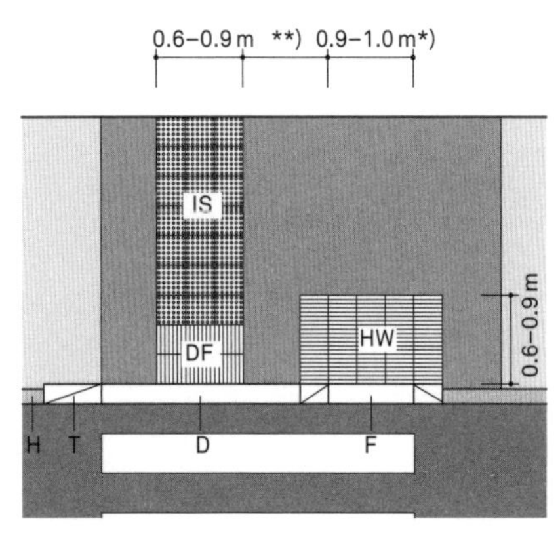

Controlled pedestrian crossing at crosswalk (zebra crossing)

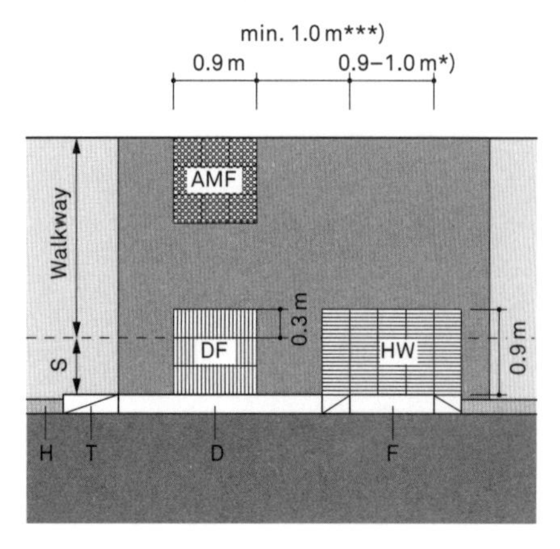

Uncontrolled pedestrian crossing at side streets

H: High curb (12 cm high)
T: Tapered curb
D: Detectable curb (6 cm high)
F: Flush curb at road level

L: Traffic signal light / Traffic signal for the blind
IS: Information surface (dome surface, aligned orthogonally)
DF: : Direction field (ribbed surface, aligned perpendicular to curb)
HW: Hazard warning surface (ribs)

AMF: Attention field (dome surface, aligned diagonally) No attention field shall be provided for sidewalk widths <5 m
S: Safety strip

*) Flush curbs >1 m wide can be hazardous areas for blind and visually impaired persons because the border between sidewalk and roadway cannot be identified by touch. For people with wheelchairs, rollators, and baby carriages, however, a minimum width of 0.9 m shall be provided.
**) The distance between the crossing areas should be maximized.
***) With depressed curbs of less than 3 cm, a minimum distance of 1 m is to be maintained between the crossing areas.

Figure 3.3.8 Separated crossing points with differentiated curb heights

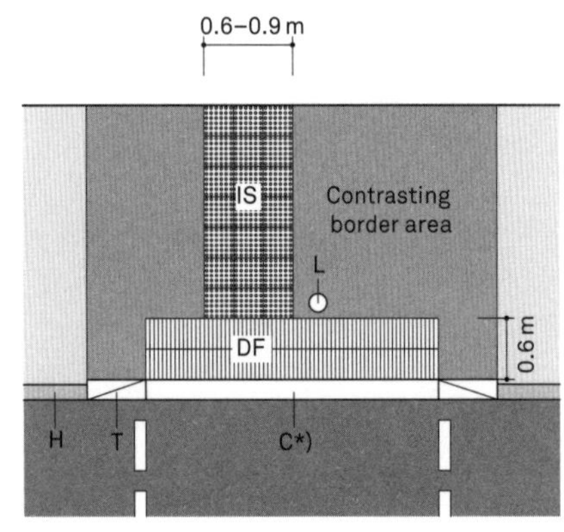

Controlled crossing point with traffic signal light

H: High curb (12 cm high)
T: Tapered curb
C: Curb (3 cm high)
L: Traffic signal light / Traffic signal for the blind
IS: Information surface (dome surface, aligned orthogonally)
DF: Direction field (ribbed surface, aligned perpendicular to curb)

*) Curb heights of 3 cm constitute a compromise; they are not ideal for people using wheelchairs or rollators or for blind and visually impaired persons.

Where there are common crossing points with uniform curb heights, the curb edges may be rounded off by no more than 10 mm (see RASt 06).

Figure 3.3.9 Shared crossing point with uniform curb height

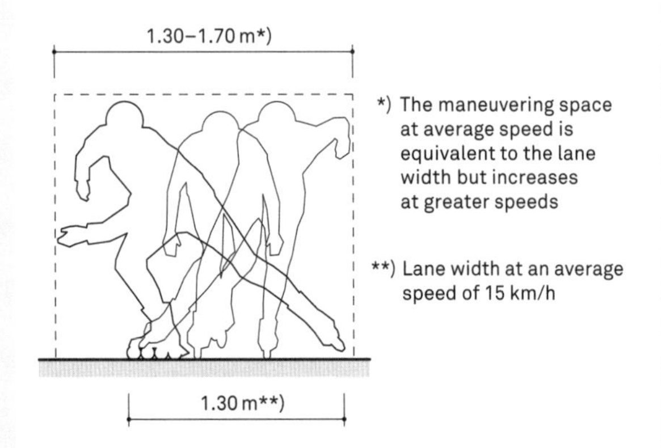

*) The maneuvering space at average speed is equivalent to the lane width but increases at greater speeds

**) Lane width at an average speed of 15 km/h

Figure 3.3.10 Space required by inline skaters

Inline Skaters

Paths for inline skaters should be designed to match the capabilities of their potential users. Especially over longer distances, the performance limit of novice inline skaters is reached on inclined stretches with uphill or downhill slopes of more than 3 %. For more experienced skaters, by contrast, gradients of up to 12 % are ordinarily easily negotiated.

Because certain braking maneuvers and other actions cannot be executed within a narrow space, a path width of at least 3 m is advisable. Path widths of 2 m should only be considered in exceptional cases or for use primarily by advanced inline skaters. Wider paths should be provided to accommodate simultaneous use by pedestrians and cyclists, or for higher frequencies of use.

Bicycle Traffic

When designing bikeways, a distinction is made between on-road bikeways, which follow the roadway, and off-road bikeways (e.g., separately routed in parks or as bike trails, and also running parallel to the road but separated from it by a median). The path width is determined by two factors: whether the path carries one- or two-way traffic; and its frequency of use.

When the route for bicycle traffic follows that of the road, it can be accommodated either on the roadway itself or in the roadside space, depending on the traffic volume of the other traffic participants: with 500 motor vehicles/hour on roadway widths up to 6 m or with 800–1,000 motor vehicles/hour on roadways that are 7 m wide, bicycle traffic can be accommodated directly on the roadway. On two-lane roads, however, designated advisory bike lanes should be incorporated for bicycle traffic according to Figure 3.3.11 (lane as separately marked area of the roadway).

When bikeways are situated in the roadside space, they are to be distinctly differentiated from the walkway by means of 0.3 m wide delineator strips (with tactile and visual contrast). → Figure 3.3.12 Due to an increased risk of falls, demarcating these by designing the bikeways and walkways to be at different levels is only to be considered when a minimum bikeway width of 2 m can be provided.

Bikeways adjacent to the roadway are preferably designed for one-way traffic. Two-way traffic is still a possibility in individual cases, however.

Any design must take into account the dimensions for standard widths and dividing strips that are found in Table 3.3.6 and the safety clearances for cycling facilities listed in Table 3.3.7.

The safety clearances presented in Table 3.3.7 can also be applied analogously to pedestrian traffic. The safety clearances for pedestrians and cyclists can overlap.

The Guideline for Rural Road Construction (RLW 75/88) specifies a minimum width of 1 m for bikeways, and 1.6 m with two-way traffic. For high-traffic bike trails, widths from 2 m to 2.5 m must be chosen to establish a balance of comfort, safety, and minimal disturbance of the traffic participants.

When designing bikeways, it is important to ensure that curves are formed with sufficiently large radii and that sharp bends are avoided. Especially outside urban areas, larger radii should be chosen wherever higher speeds can be expected. For bikeways outside urban areas, the radii should not be less than 10 m (except junctions). With water-bound paving, a slightly larger curve radius should be selected.

At tight curves with poor visibility, it is necessary to widen the bikeway by about 0.5 m.

Bikeway gradients should be as suitable as possible for the capabilities of inexperienced cyclists. Large differences in height should be overcome over very long distances with low gradients, although large gradients are possible over short distances. → Table 3.3.10

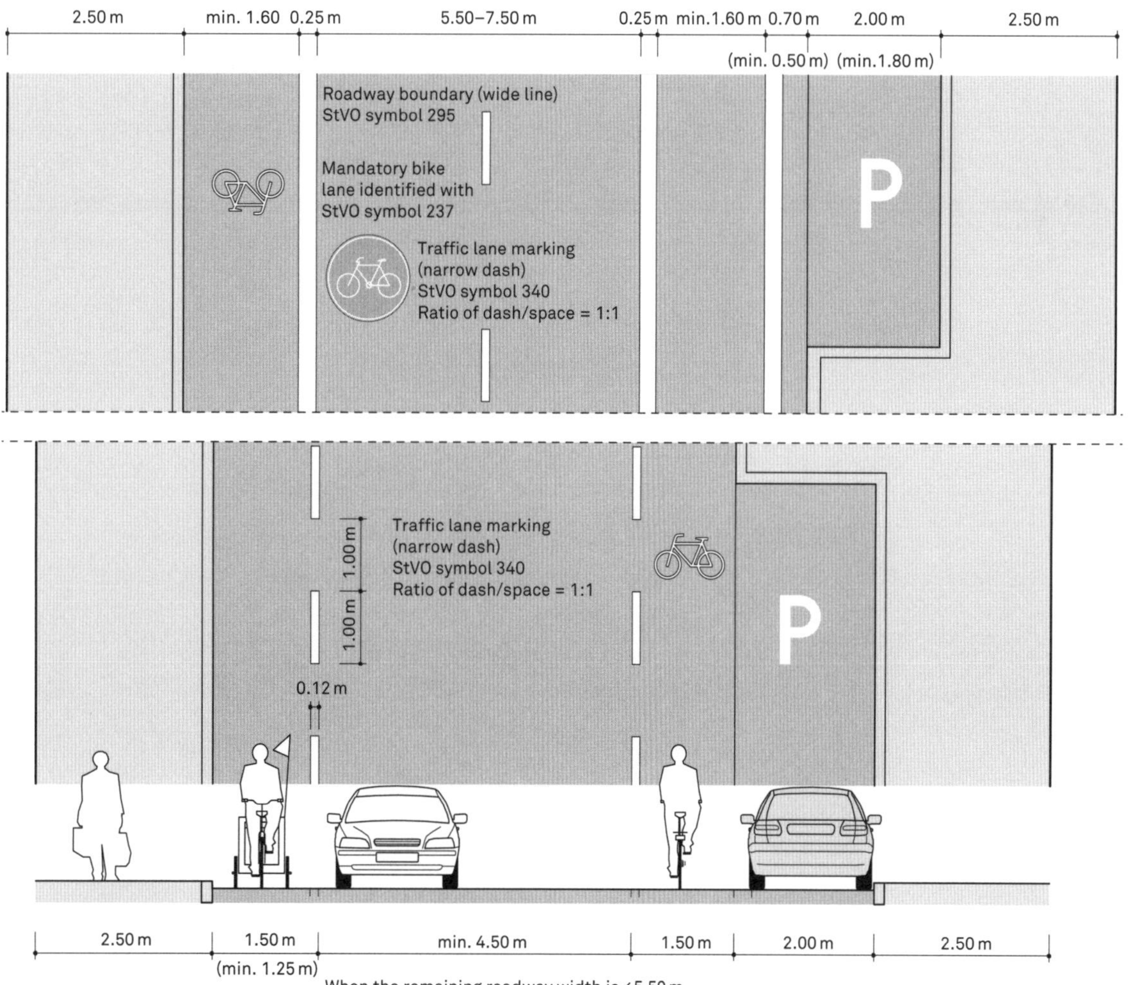

Figure 3.3.11 Arrangement of advisory bike lanes (multipurpose lanes in Austria) and mandatory bike lanes for bicycle traffic on the roadway

Facility type	Path width	Width of dividing strip		
		Along roadway	Along parallel parking spaces	Along angled/perpendi-cular parking spaces
On the roadway				
Advisory bike lane	1.50 m (minimum 1.25 m)	–	Safety clearance: 0.25–0.50 m (no markings required)	Safety clearance: 0.75 m
Mandatory bike lane	1.85 m (incl. markings)	–	0.50–0.75 m (marked as continuous strip)	0.75 m (marked as contin-uous strip)
Adjacent to the roadway				
One-way bikeway	2.00 m (1.60 m*)	0.50 m (can include overhang strip)	0.75 m	1.10 m (can include overhang strip)
Two-way bikeways on both sides	2.50 m (2.00 m*)	0.75 m (at permanent fixtures or with high traffic volume)		
Two-way bikeway on one side	3.00 m (2.50 m*)			
Shared pedestrian and cycle path (within built-up areas)	≥2.50 m (dependent on pedestrian and bicycle traffic volume, see → Figure 3.3.10)			
Shared pedestrian and cycle path (outside built-up areas)	2.50 m		1.75 m on rural roads	

* for low bicycle traffic volume

Table 3.3.6 Dimensions of bikeways accompanying roads (per RASt 06)

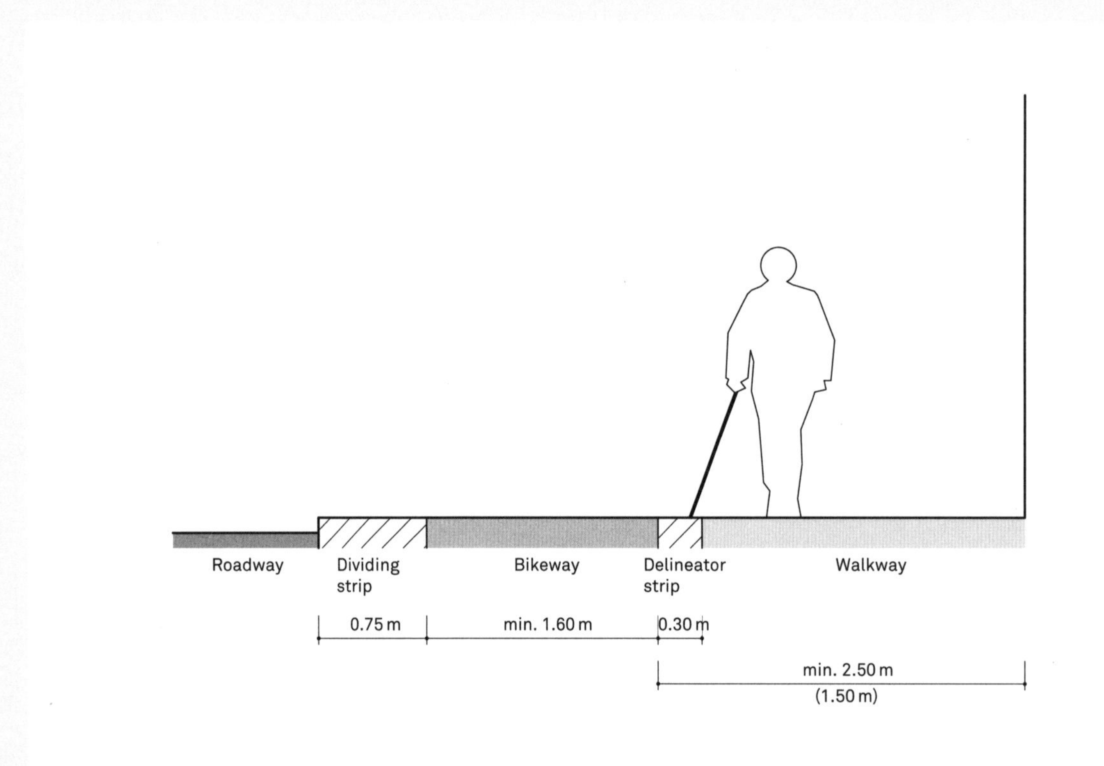

Figure 3.3.12 Delineator strip between bikeway and walkway

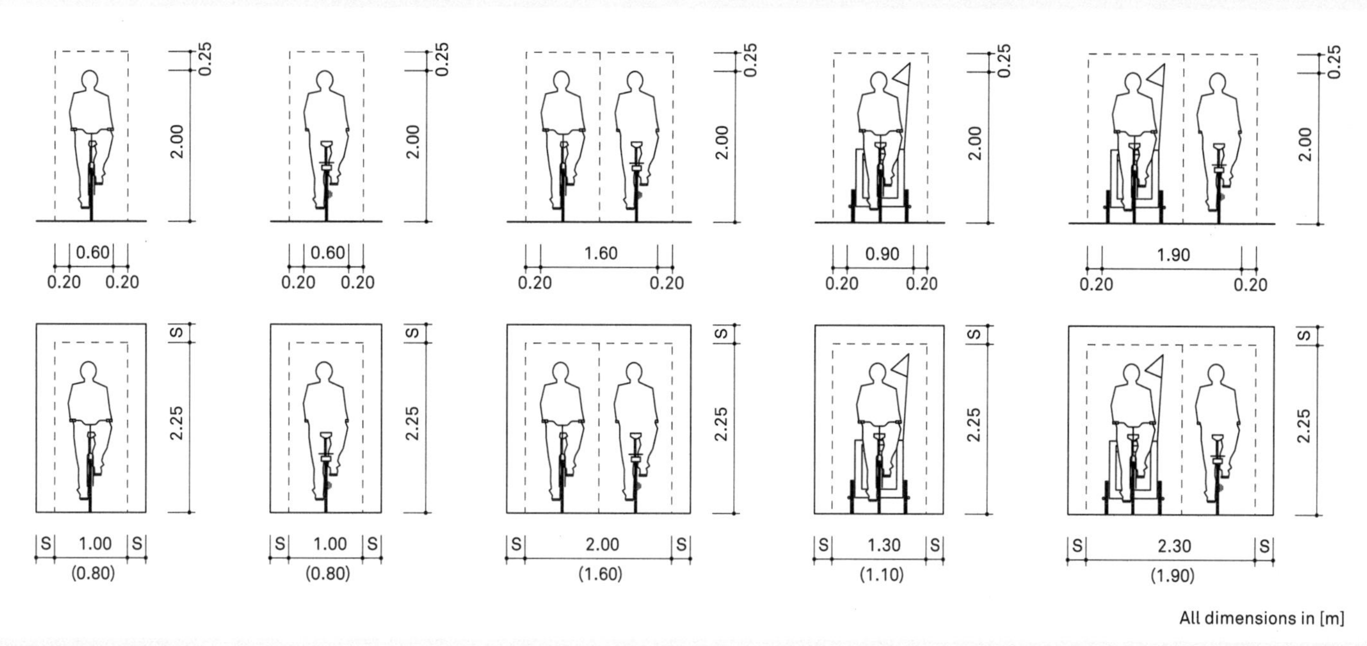

Figure 3.3.13 Space requirements for bicycle traffic with and without safety clearance (S)

Table 3.3.7 Dimensions of independently routed bikeways (per RLW 75/88)

Bikeway	Independently routed bikeways (per RLW 75/88) Minimum width	Safety clearance
One-way bikeway	1.00 m	Min. 0.25 m to obstacles on each side
Two-way bikeway	1.60 m; for heavily-used routes: 2.00 m and more	Min. 0.25 m to obstacles on each side

Table 3.3.8 Necessary minimum curve radii for bikeways with a cross slope of 2.5 % as a function of speed

Minimum curve radius Asphalt/ interlocking concrete pavers [in m]	2.5	5	10	15	20	30
Speed (km/h)	10	16	24	28	32	40

Table 3.3.9 Radii and stopping distances as a function of speed for the layout of off-road bikeways

Speed [km/h]	Minimum curve radius [m] Asphalt/interlocking concrete pavers	Unbound paving	Crest radius min H_K [m]	Sag radius min H_W [m]	Stopping distance with wet surface
20	10	15	40	25	15
30	20	35	80	50	25
40	30	70	150	100	40

Table 3.3.10 Acceptable lengths of ascending slopes for bikeways (per ERA 10, supplemented)

Slope [%]	Max. length of ascending slope	Height difference
12	8.00 m	0.96 m
10	20.00 m	2.00 m
6	65.00 m	3.90 m
5	120.00 m	6.00 m
4	250.00 m	10.00 m
3	>250.00 m	10.00 m

Combined Walkway/Bikeways

Table 3.3.11 and Figure 3.3.14 clarify the minimum requirements for shared facilities for pedestrian and bicycle traffic. In addition to a low traffic load (no intensive commuter use or public transit waiting areas), adequate path widths and a low slope are the prerequisites for deploying shared pedestrian and cycle paths.

Maximum roadside traffic at peak hours*	Necessary width aside from dividing strip
70 (P + C) / h	≥2.5–3 m
100 (P + C) / h	≥3–4 m
150 (P + C) / h	≥4 m

* The number of cyclists should not exceed one-third of the total traffic load.

Table 3.3.11 Shared pedestrian and cycle paths along streets (Source: RASt 06)

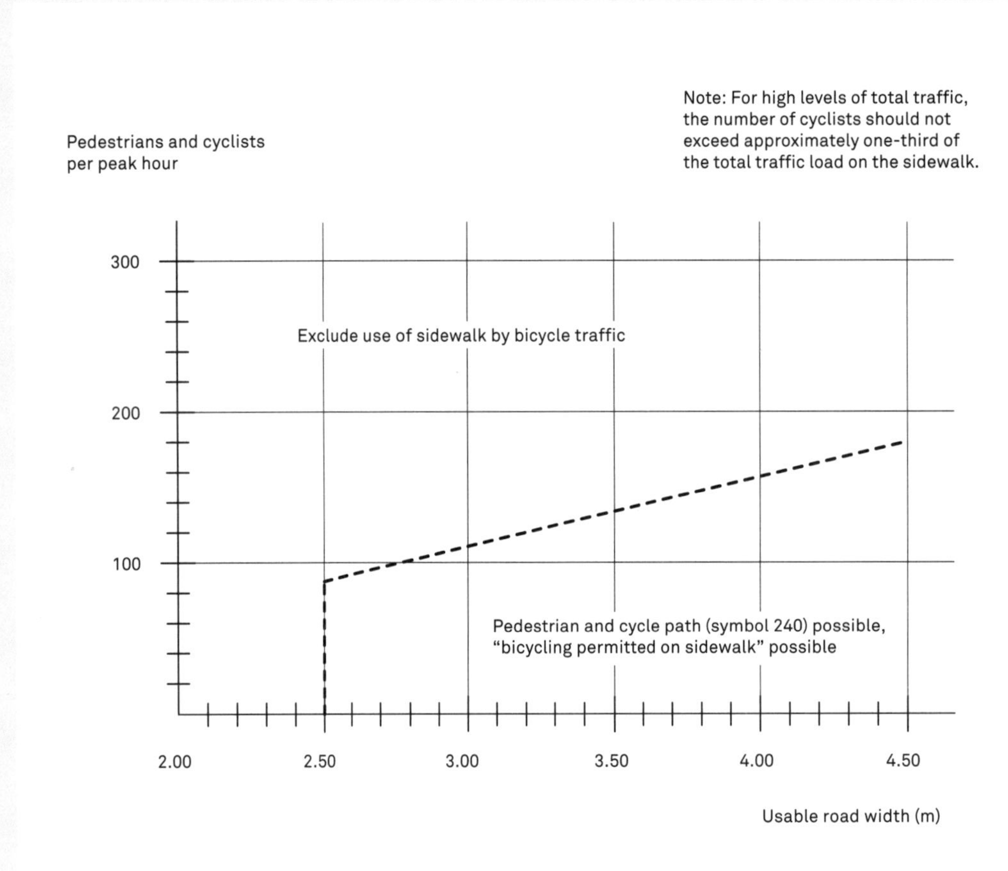

Figure 3.3.14 Application limits for implementing off-road shared paths for pedestrians and cyclists, in accordance with ERA-R2 recommendations for bicycle facilities

Maneuvering Spaces in Front of Obstacles
Sufficient space must be provided in front of doors and gates to enable wheelchair users or persons with baby carriages to maneuver without any problems. → **Figure 3.3.15** At cycle barriers in off-road shared paths for pedestrians and cyclists, at train and tram crossings, for example, a minimum clearance of 3 m shall be maintained from the edge of the road or track. → **Figure 3.3.16**

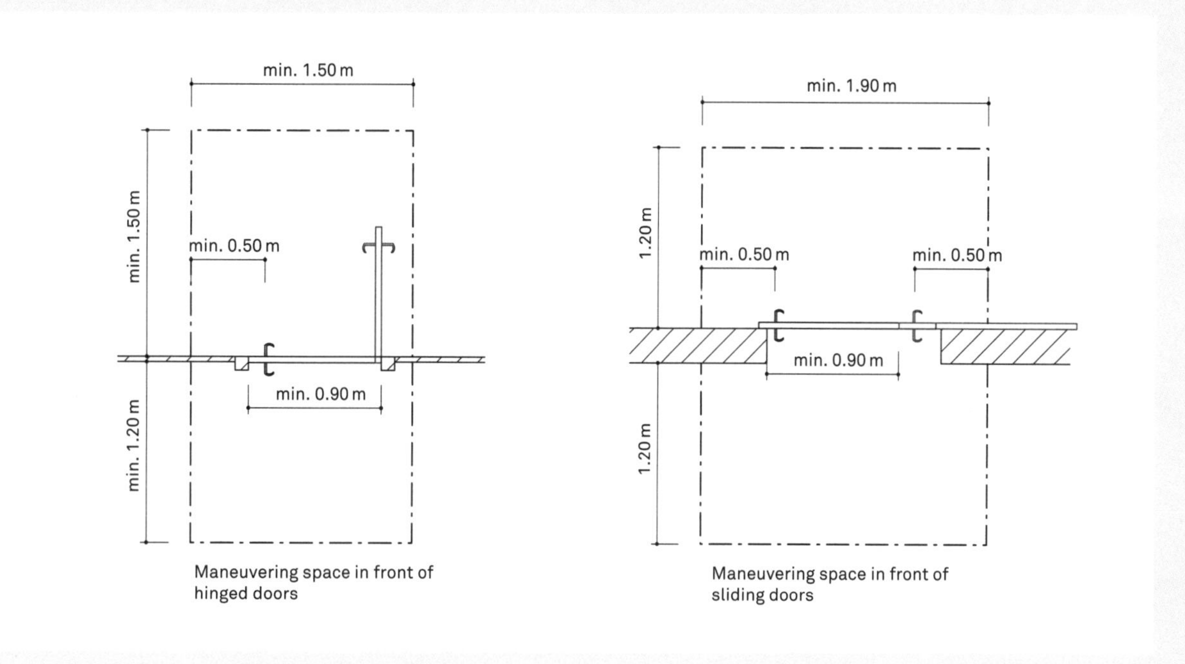

Figure 3.3.15 Maneuvering spaces in front of doors and gates

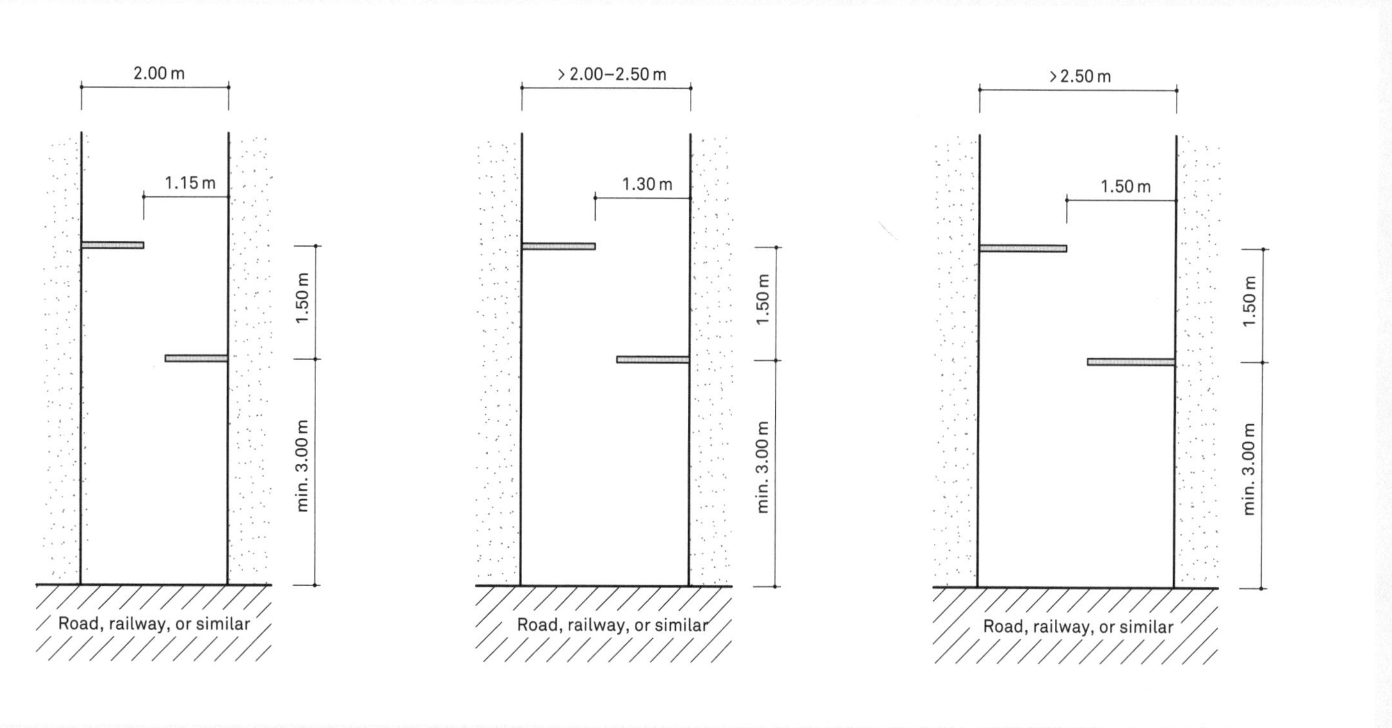

Figure 3.3.16 Cycle barriers in off-road pedestrian and cycle paths

Street Spaces

Traffic Areas

The traffic areas listed below for individual traffic participants are used to determine the expected space requirements when planning and establishing the necessary widths of roads and paths. A basic distinction is made between the standard dimensions of a traffic participant (W), in other words their average size, and maneuvering space (B) that accounts for movement during travel as well as safety clearances (S1, S2, and S3). Safety clearances specify the required distance from oncoming traffic (S1), to obstacles at the sides (S2), and upward (S3). Figure 3.3.17 illustrates the composition of the space required by traffic participants.

The traffic space values listed in Table 3.3.12 form the basis for calculating the space needed by traffic participants, which naturally varies depending on the type of travel. For most vehicles, a maneuvering space of 0.25 m (0.3 m for streetcars) is stipulated by RASt 06, but no maneuvering space is generally specified for people who are not operating a motor vehicle. Adding the specific safety clearance S1 to this amount yields the space required by traffic participants for oncoming and side-by-side traffic. In general, the average safety clearance S1 is taken to have a width of 25 cm. Exceptions include public transit buses and trams with a safety clearance of 40 cm and cyclists with a clearance of 75 cm from the traffic space. In Figure 3.3.18, the space required is portrayed with the addition of safety clearances S2 and S3. This is equatable with the clear space that is to be kept free for traffic participants. The standard width of the lateral safety clearance S2 is 50 cm (25 cm with restricted maneuvering space), and the vertical safety clearance is always 30 cm.

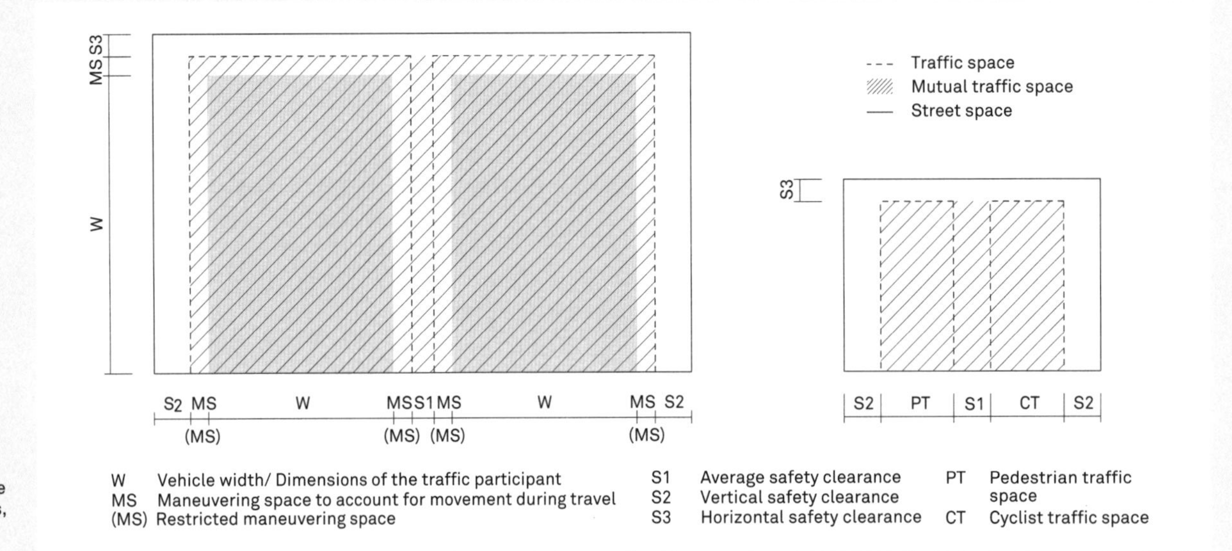

Figure 3.3.17 Composition of the space required for motor vehicles, pedestrians, and cyclists, per RASt 06

Traffic participant	Dimensions – average values (W) in cm		Maneuvering space in cm		Traffic space in cm	
	Width	Height	MS	(MS)	Width	Height
Pedestrian*	100 (80)	200	–	–	100 (80)	200
Wheelchair user, without change of direction*	110	–	–	–	110	–
Person with white cane*	120	200	–	–	120	200
Person with baby carriage*	100	200	–	–	100	200
Inline skater	180	210	–	–	180	210
Bicyclist*	100 (80)	225	–	–	100 (80)	225
Bicyclist with trailer*	130 (110)	225	20	10	130 (110)	225
Horseback rider	130	270	≥20	–	170	290
Motorcyclist	90**	180	20***	–	130	200
Car*	175**	150	25	15	225 (205)	200
Truck*	255**	400	25	20	305 (295)	450
Public transit bus*	255**	300	25	20	305 (295)	350
Streetcar (tram)*	265**	(420–) 500	30	(420–) 500	325	560

* as per RASt 06 ** without side mirrors *** disregarding tilted position while taking curves

Table 3.3.12 Traffic spaces of individual traffic participants, including their maneuvering space B and restricted maneuvering space (B)

If it can be assumed that a road has minor importance in terms of providing access and hence that the traffic flow and composition of motorized traffic can be adjusted correspondingly, it is possible to apply restricted maneuvering spaces and to partially omit safety clearances when determining the required cross section. In general, however, that requires a speed limit of ≤40 km/h and cautious driving as well as a suitable design and traffic regulation devices for visual support. Thus, for example, the average safety clearance S1 can be excluded for oncoming motor vehicle traffic (albeit not with bicycle traffic). In the case of side-by-side or passing traffic, however, an average safety clearance of 25 cm must still be observed, even with restricted maneuvering space.

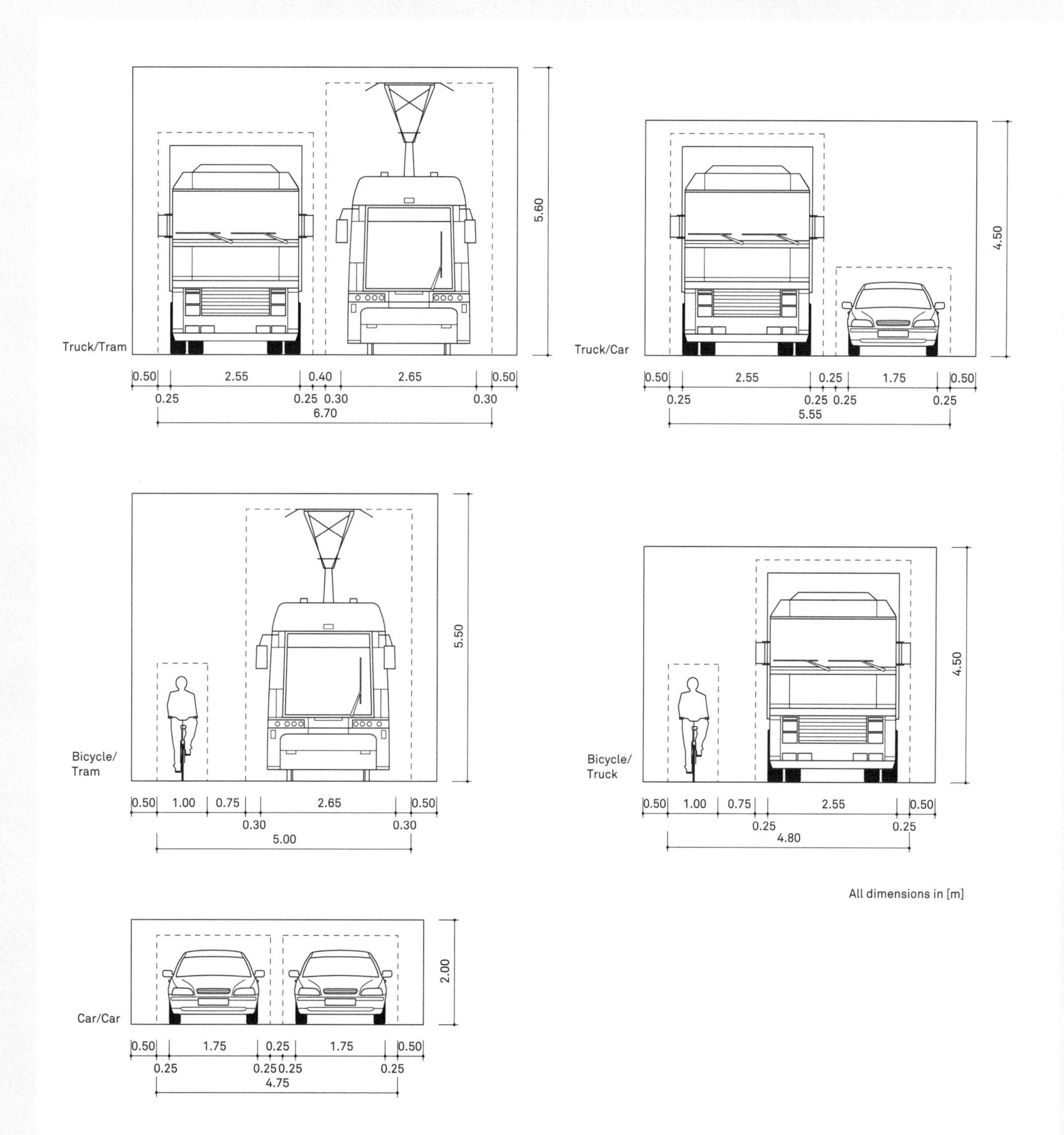

Figure 3.3.18 Composition of traffic spaces and clear spaces for oncoming, side-by-side, and passing traffic (as per RASt 06)

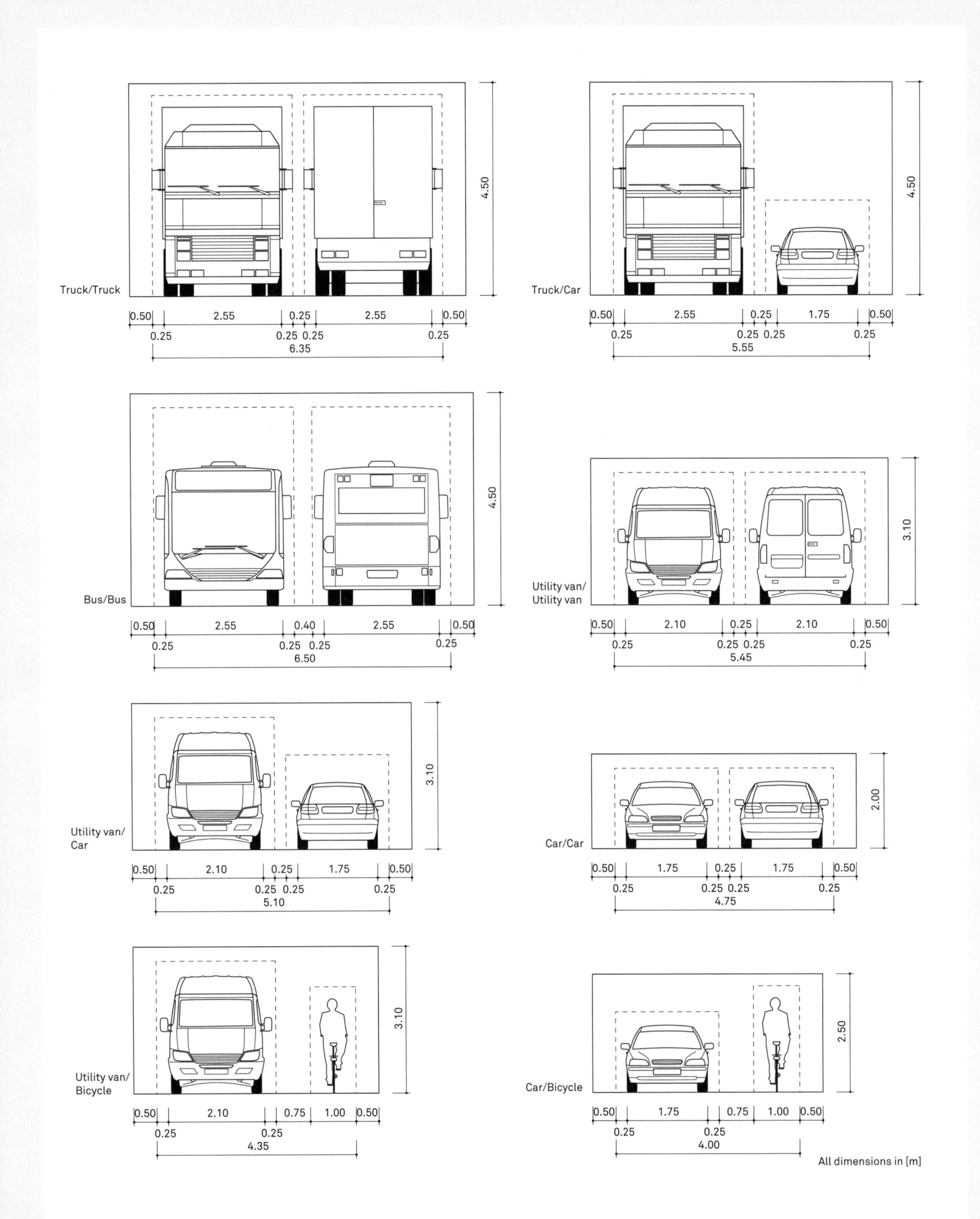

Figure 3.3.18 Composition of traffic spaces and clear spaces for oncoming, side-by-side, and passing traffic (as per RASt 06)

Roadway Types

When designing roads for motorized traffic, a distinction is made between the principles of separation and mixture. When the lanes are physically segregated, one can speak of a separation principle. If, on the other hand, multiple means of transport come together on one and the same roadway surface, one can speak of a mixing principle (→ **Shared Traffic Space, page 92**).

How and in what form the roadway is laid out depends on the traffic volume, any additional presence of public transportation, the routing of bicycle traffic, and functional requirements arising from how the road is used. The dimensioning of the roadway is based upon the traffic spaces and clear spaces of the traffic participants. In Germany, the width of the roadway that is needed is determined in accordance with the "Richtlinien für die Anlage von Stadtstraßen" (RASt 06) [Guidelines for urban road design]. The two-lane roadway covers a wide range of potential motor vehicle traffic volumes. **→ Table 3.3.13**

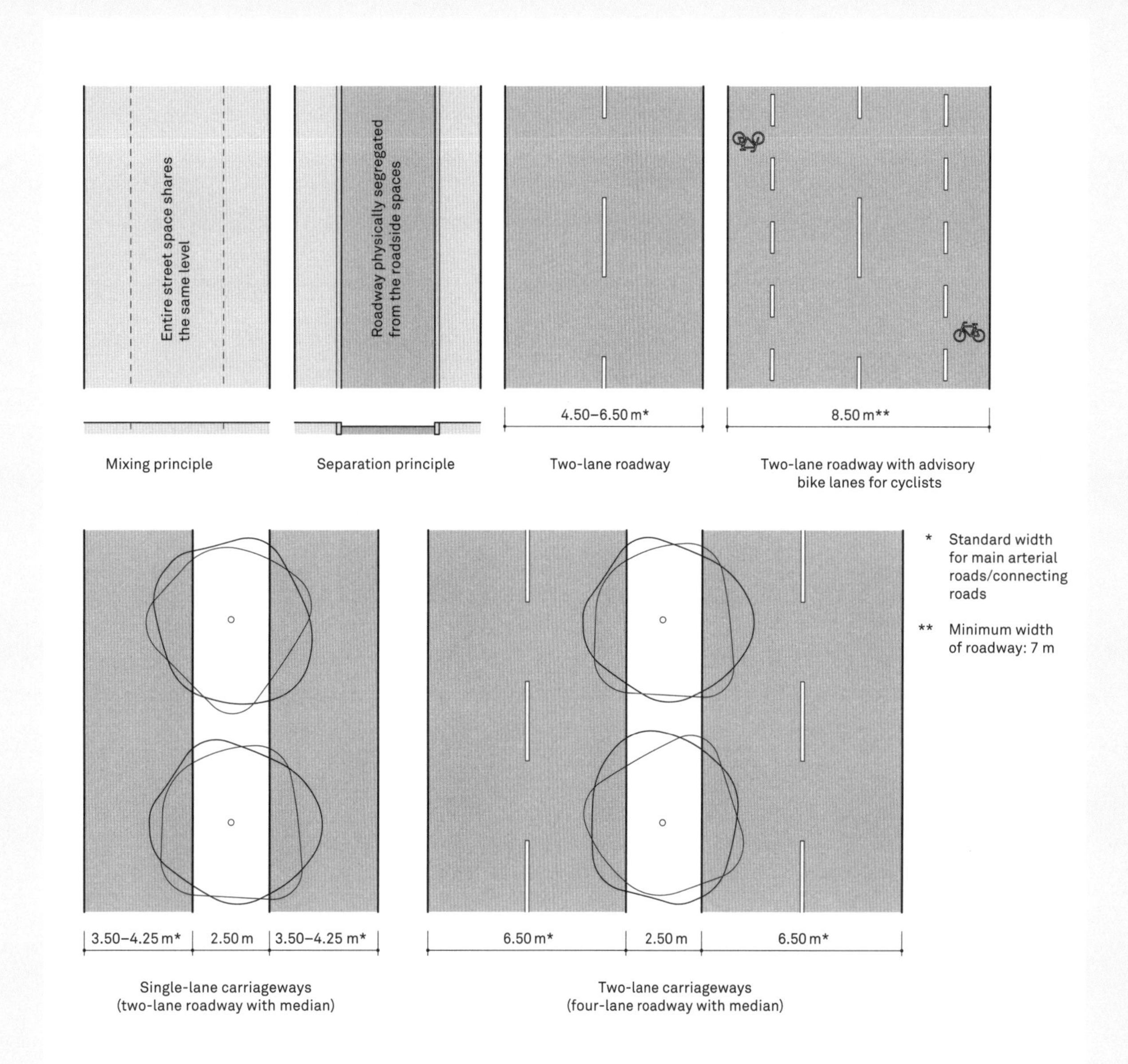

Figure 3.3.19 Roadway types

Application	Roadway width, main arterial road	Roadway width, connecting road
Single-lane carriageway / one-way street		
Typical case (with cyclists using the roadway)	4.25 m (where available space is limited: 3 m)	3.5 m (where available space is limited: 3 m)*
Bicycle traffic on roadway in opposed direction	Not applicable	3.5 m (3 m with sufficient turnout opportunities)
Roadway with advisory bike lane	3.75 m (2.25–1.5 m) with minor truck traffic	Does not generally occur
Two-lane roadway		
Typical case	6.5 m **	4.5–5.5 m
With public transit bus service	6.5 m **	6.5 m
Limited public transit bus service and minor use requirements***	6 m	6 m
Low frequency of encounters with truck traffic	5.5 m (at reduced speed)	–
High frequency of encounters with bus and truck traffic	7 m	–
With advisory bike lanes for cyclists	7.5 m with 1.5 m advisory bike lanes on both sides 7.5 m with 1.25 m advisory bike lanes on both sides in confined conditions****	
Two-lane carriageway	**Roadway width**	
Typical case	6.5 m	
Low frequency of bus or truck traffic	6 m (with limited available space: 5.5 m)	
Bus or truck traffic dominates	7 m (only in cases where continuous side-by-side travel should be ensured)	
Local residential streets and alleys		
Local residential street (Separation principle)	4.75 m (delivery vehicles permitted)	
Local residential alley (Mixed principle)	3 m (delivery vehicles and parking in adjacent areas permitted)	

* Requirements stemming from winter maintenance shall be checked individually ** With this dimension, obligatory mandatory cycling facilities are ordinarily to be provided *** For example, solely provides access **** Not adjacent to frequently used parking lanes

Table 3.3.13 Dimensions for one- and two-lane roadways as well as divided carriageways, local residential streets and local residential alleys, as per RASt 06

Abb. 3.3.20 Sidewalk with wheelchair-accessible curb ramp from 3 to 0 cm, information surface, and direction field at a shared crossing point for wheelchair users as well as blind and visually impaired persons

Curbs and Edging

Within municipal limits, the separation between roadway and side paths is usually made by a clearly recognizable curb, which can take the form of a high, half-height, or low curb. In accordance with the RASt 06 guidelines for urban road design, each of these configurations have different applications according to the particular road use. → Table 3.3.15

To ensure accessibility, curbs are lowered accordingly in the vicinity of driveways and bicycle crossings. At bikeways and for wheelchair users, a curb that drops down to the road level is desirable. For barrier-free accessibility in the interests of an environment designed to also be experienced through touch, a curb height of 6 cm is considered optimal because it is indisputably tactile for visually impaired and blind persons using canes. Curb heights of less than 3 cm should be safeguarded with a tactile warning surface to assist blind and visually impaired persons. (→ Figures 3.3.7 and 3.3.8)

Configuration	Height	Function	Areas of application
High curb	10–14 cm (maximum 20 cm)	Separation of roadway/walkway (roadside bikeway)	Non built-up main arterial roads, built-up four- and multilane main arterial roads
	8–12 cm	Division of roadway or parking lane from walkway (roadside bikeway)	Two-lane main arterial roads, connecting roads
Half-height curb	4–8 cm	Division of roadway from walkway (roadside bikeway) or roadway from parking lane	Two-lane main arterial roads, connecting roads
Low curb	0–4 cm	Division of roadway from walkway (roadside bikeway) or from parking lane	Two-lane main arterial roads with low traffic volumes, connecting roads, depressed curb at crossing points for pedestrians, wheelchair users (≤3 cm), cyclists*

* For cyclists, a flush curb represents the optimal alternative; deviations are only permitted in exceptional cases. Along segregated bikeways, a flush curb shall always be provided.

Table 3.3.14 Areas of application of varied curb heights

User group	Type of edging					
	<3 cm curb height (across entire width of crossing)	Ramp (across entire width of crossing)	≥3 cm curb height (across entire width of crossing)	Precast flush transitional curb unit ("Rollbord") + 6 cm curb height (segregated crossing)	Narrow ramp with central crossing (with lateral transitional curbs)	Narrow ramp with central crossing (ramp perpendicular to curb)
Suitable for pedestrians						
Conditionally suitable for pedestrians						
Suitable for wheelchair users						
Conditionally suitable for wheelchair users						
Suitable for persons with impaired mobility						
Conditionally suitable for persons with impaired mobility						
Suitable for blind and visually impaired persons						
Not suitable for blind and visually impaired persons						
Ensures safety						
Accessible in terms of "Design for all"						

Table 3.3.15 Suitability criteria of edging for various types of users of sidewalks – the variant with a separate crossing using a flush transitional curb unit ("Rollbord") next to a 6 cm high curb represents the optimal crossing solution in terms of "design for all"

Street Cross Sections

Depending on the requirements for use and the traffic volume, a combination of the traffic spaces of the various traffic participants, the necessary safety clearances (→ **Table 3.3.12 and Figure 3.3.18**) and the roadside spaces (→ **Table 3.3.5**) result in different cross sections for the street space.

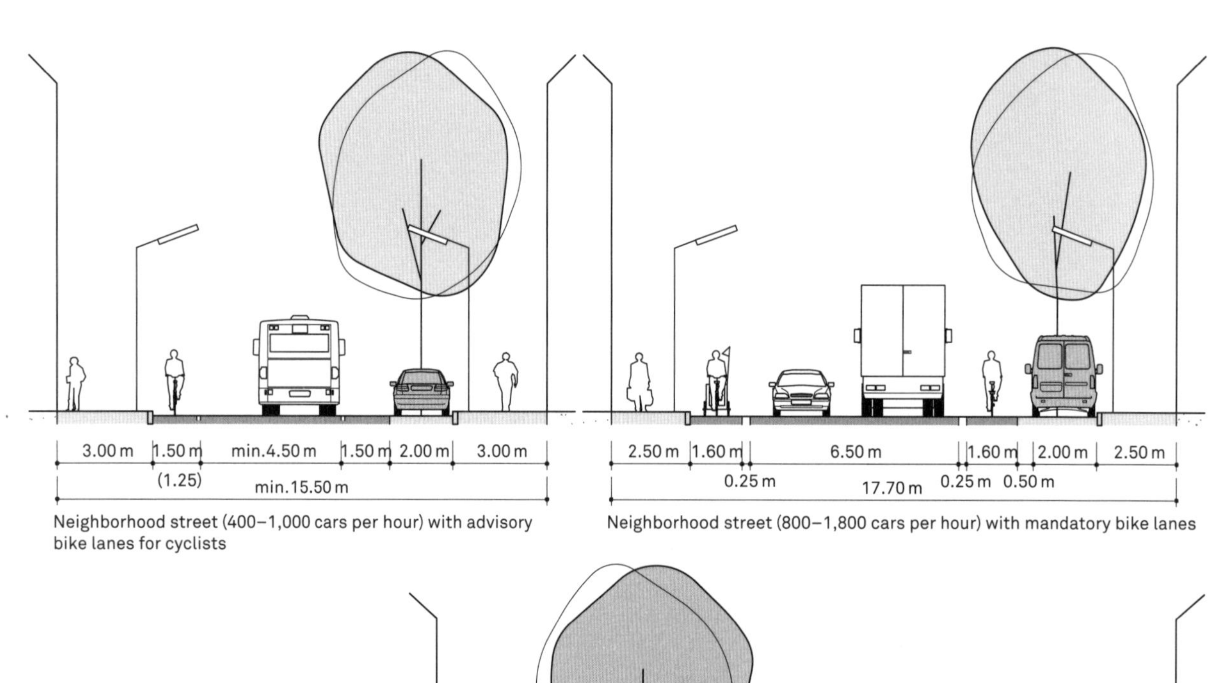

Neighborhood street (400–1,000 cars per hour) with advisory bike lanes for cyclists

Neighborhood street (800–1,800 cars per hour) with mandatory bike lanes

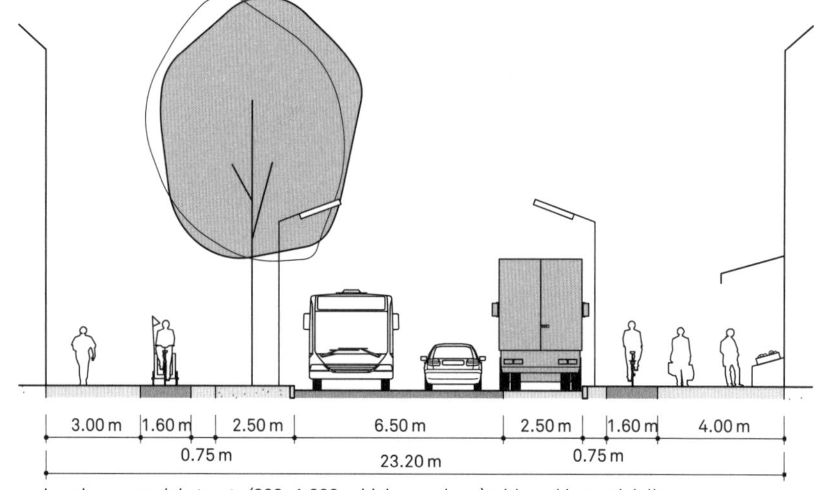

Local commercial streets (800–1,800 vehicles per hour) with parking and delivery, public transport, and accompanying roadside bikeway

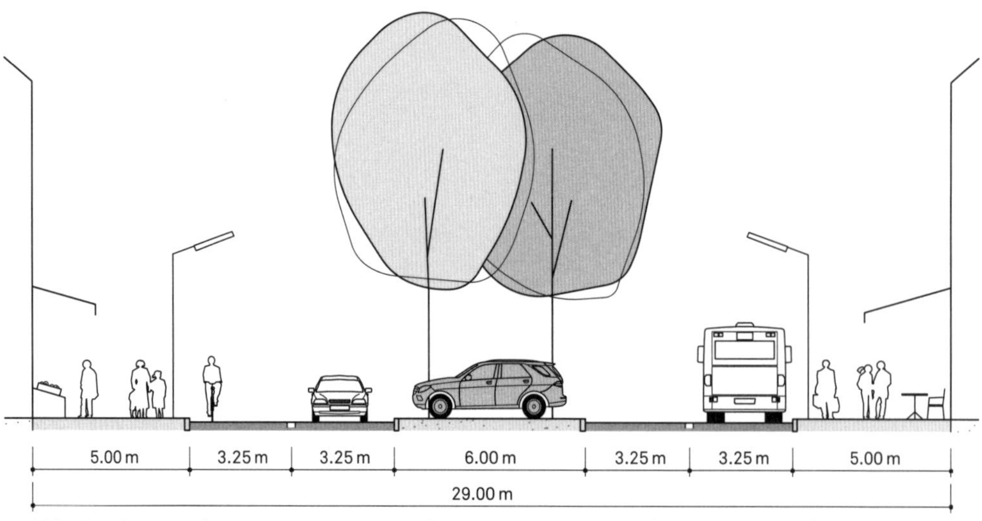

All dimensions in [m]

Main shopping street (800–1,800 vehicles per hour) with designated bus lanes (bicycling permitted) and median strip

Figure 3.3.21 Street space cross-sections for different usage requirements

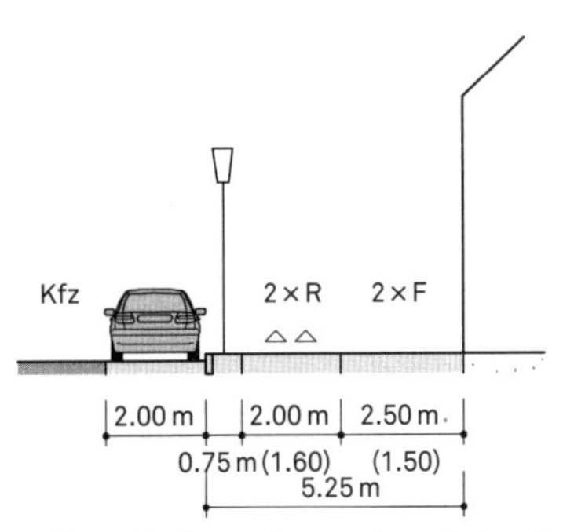

Bikeway adjacent to the roadway and parallel parking

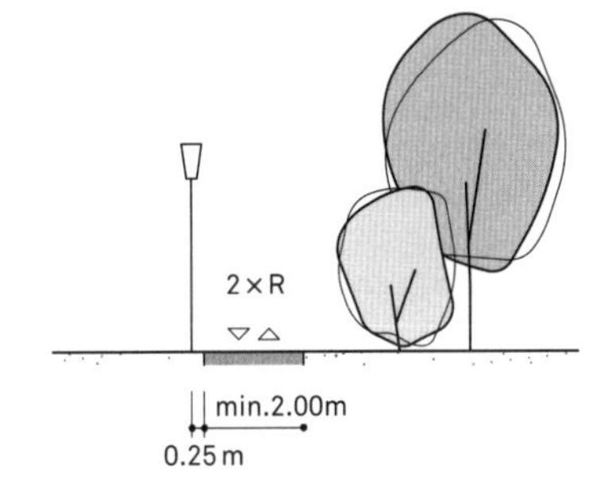

Independently routed two-way bikeway

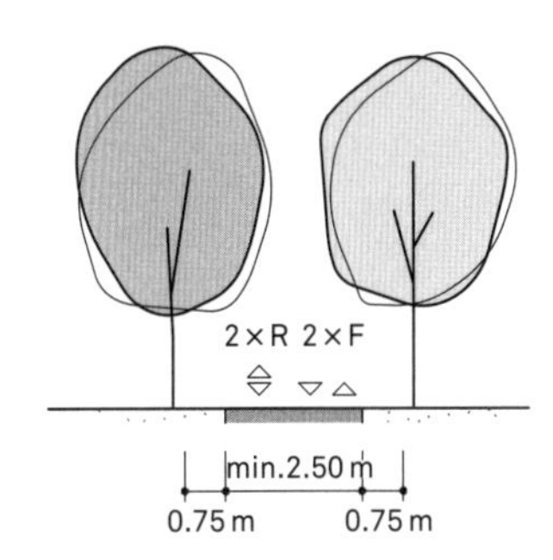

Combined pedestrian and bike path

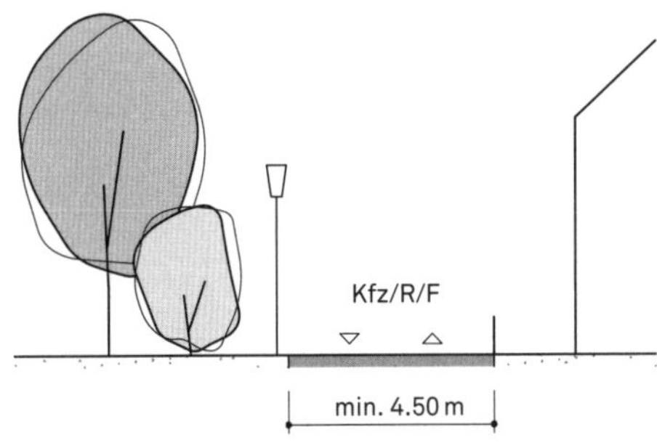
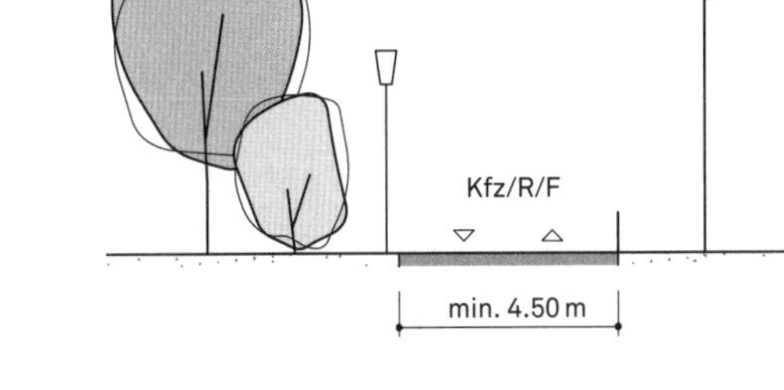

Residential lane (< 400 vehicles per hour) used as gathering place, mixed principle

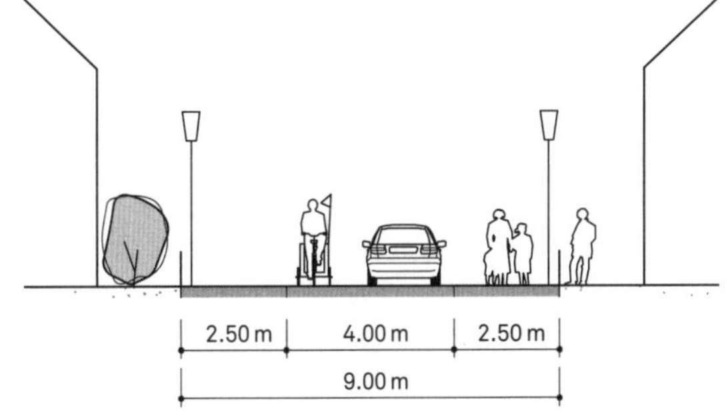

Residential lane (< 400 vehicles per hour) used as gathering place, mixed principle

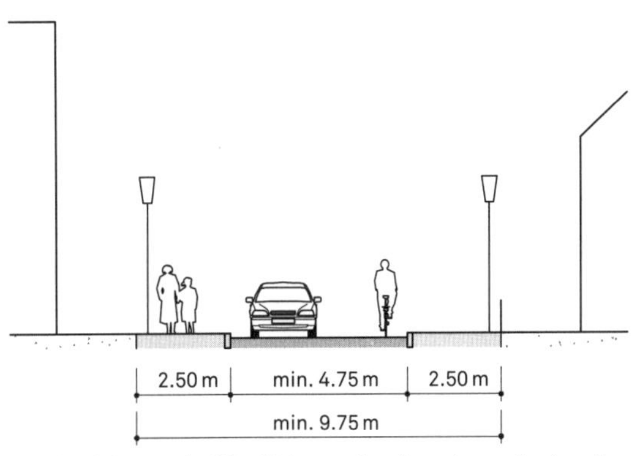

Residential street (< 400 vehicles per hour) used as gathering place, separation principle

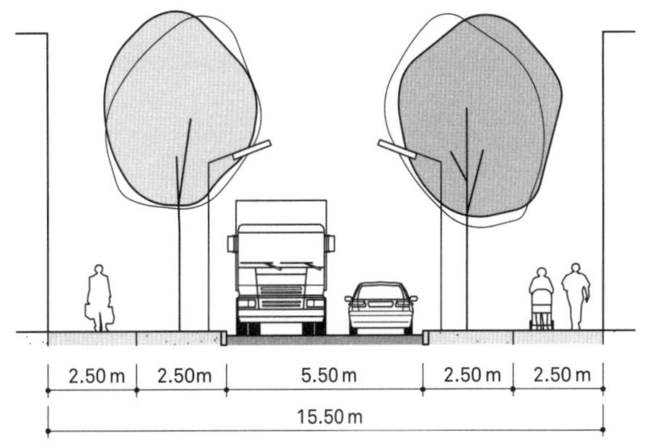

Residential street (< 400 vehicles per hour) with roadside vegetation strip, separation principle

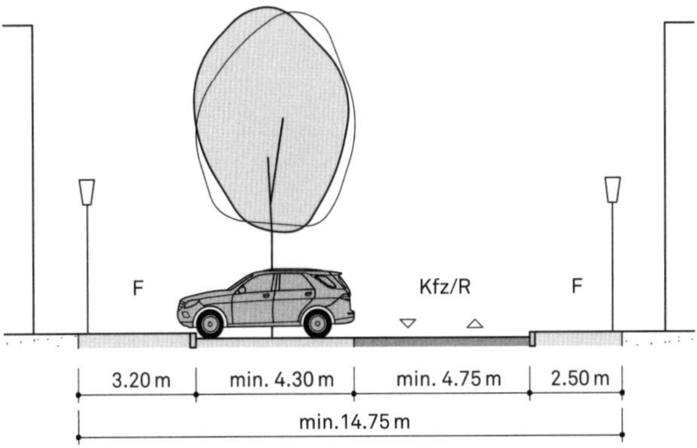

Residential street (< 400 vehicles per hour) with perpendicular parking, separation principle

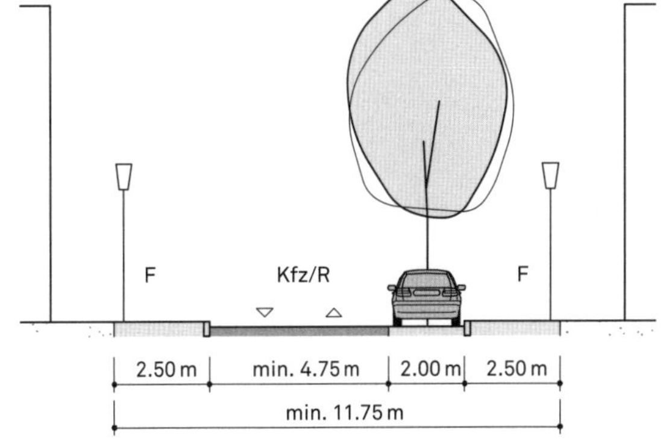

Residential street (< 400 vehicles per hour) with parallel parking, separation principle

Shared Traffic Space

Behind the concepts for shared traffic spaces, there is always the basic idea of supporting the equitable use of roads, paths, or plazas by different traffic participants – or to enable privileged use by weaker groups of traffic participants, thus improving the qualities that encourage people to congregate in those public spaces. Consequently, they are generally in contrast to the results of ordinary traffic planning, where motorized vehicles dominate the street space. Some of the concepts are specific to a certain country and are only used locally, or they require special regulations that are not necessarily compatible with the traffic laws of another country. For example: in contrast to the "traffic-calmed area" [*verkehrsberuhigter Bereich*], which is anchored in German traffic law, the "shared space" concept is not. In order to implement the shared-space principle in Hamburg, a pilot project was initiated with special regard to the metropolitan conditions existing there. → Table 3.3.16

Under the shared-space idea, the equal use of the traffic space is based on mutual consideration, thereby conferring greater responsibility to the individual. In contrast to shared space, which is established above all on central urban squares and plazas, on inner-city streets, and at traffic intersections, the traffic-calmed area is intended for streets with (predominantly) residential use, where the function as a gathering place dominates and very little motorized traffic is encountered.

A variant of the traffic-calmed area is the traffic-calmed commercial zone [*verkehrsberuhigter Geschäftsbereich*], which has a speed limit of 10 or 20 km/h. In this case, although there is a functional separation between roadway and walkways, the areas are not separated by differences in height. Furthermore, cyclists and motorists share the entire roadway, which has no designated bike lanes.

The "encounter zone" [*Begegnungszone*] is a version of traffic calming that was approved for use in Switzerland on January 1, 2002. In the encounter zone, pedestrians take precedence over vehicular traffic. They can cross the road anytime and anywhere, but may not unnecessarily impede the vehicles. Parking is permitted only at locations identified by signs or markings. Encounter zones may be established in side streets within residential and/or commercial areas.

Figure 3.3.22 Public space used collectively by pedestrian, bicycle, and tram traffic, Alexanderplatz, Berlin

Type/designation	Geographic scope / legal basis	Area of application	Features
Shared space	EU-wide design philosophy	Roads in commercial and residential areas, key segments of main shopping streets, local commercial streets, or rural main roads, comparatively large amount of pedestrian and/or bicycle traffic, 8,000–14,000 vehicles/day Bremen: 15,000 vehicles/day (approximately 1,200 to 1,500 vehicles/peak hour) should not be exceeded	• The three functions of connection, access, and congregation should be superimposed in a (traffic) space that remains undivided wherever possible and is designed in a manner characteristic for the area. Here, the mixing principle is employed largely without using traffic controls (traffic lights or signs). Because it is a design philosophy and not a concept regulated by traffic laws, an individual solution that must be brought into harmony with local traffic law is always needed.
l'aire piètonne (F) [pedestrian zone]	Worldwide, especially in Europe	Shopping streets	• Commercial street reserved for pedestrian traffic and deliveries, where pedestrians have priority and delivery vehicles are permitted, usually restricted to certain times. Bicycle traffic can be permitted, but is occasionally restricted to certain times.
Gemeinschafts-straßen [shared streets]	Hamburg	Pilot project that further develops the shared-space principle, giving attention to the metropolitan conditions of the Free and Hanseatic City of Hamburg, including streets and squares with traffic loads of < 20,000 vehicles/day and average to low public transit bus service	• Definition of certain preconditions and requirements for appropriate implementation pursuant to an expert review process: Limited to a segment length of a maximum 400 m, mostly all at one level. • "Right before left" rule at intersections and small traffic circles, public transit bus service with priority right of way, legal designation as traffic-calmed areas or traffic-calmed commercial zones.
Verkehrsberuhigter Bereich [traffic-calmed area]	D (signs: 325/326 StVO) "mixed areas"	Streets in residential and commercial areas, and individual streets or areas with very low traffic levels where the function as gathering place predominates	• Pedestrians are allowed to use the entire width of the street. • Children are allowed to play everywhere. • Vehicles may only travel at walking speed, pedestrians may not be impeded. • Pedestrian traffic has legal priority before vehicles in signed mixed traffic areas like these. • Pedestrians may not unnecessarily impede vehicular traffic. • Parking is not permitted outside of the specially marked areas, except for entering or leaving the vehicle and loading or unloading.
Verkehrsberuhigter Geschäftsbereich [traffic-calmed commercial zone] (Tempo 10/20 zone)	D	Shopping streets	• Separation of the street space into roadway and side paths is maintained. • Pedestrians can cross the roadway more easily due to the reduced speed of the vehicles.
Begegnungszone, Zone de rencontre (F) [encounter zone]	CH, F, B: Comparable to a traffic-calmed area with regard to traffic law, and similar to shared space in terms of design; D: Currently being tested in pilot projects (e.g., in Berlin), identified there as a "traffic-calmed commercial zone" with 20 km/h speed limit	Side streets in residential and commercial areas	• Pedestrians are allowed to use the entire traffic surface. • Pedestrians take precedence over vehicular traffic (may not always apply in D). • Parking is permitted only at identified locations. • 20 km/h speed limit. • Play is not permitted on the roadway.

Table 3.3.16 Systems of traffic calming and shared-space models in comparison (Source: Interreg IIIB North Sea, inter alia)

Bus Stops

For public transit buses, separate bus bays or curbside bus stops are to be provided along the path of the road. If bus shelters are envisaged on the sidewalk, certain clearances are required. → Figures 3.3.23 and 3.3.24

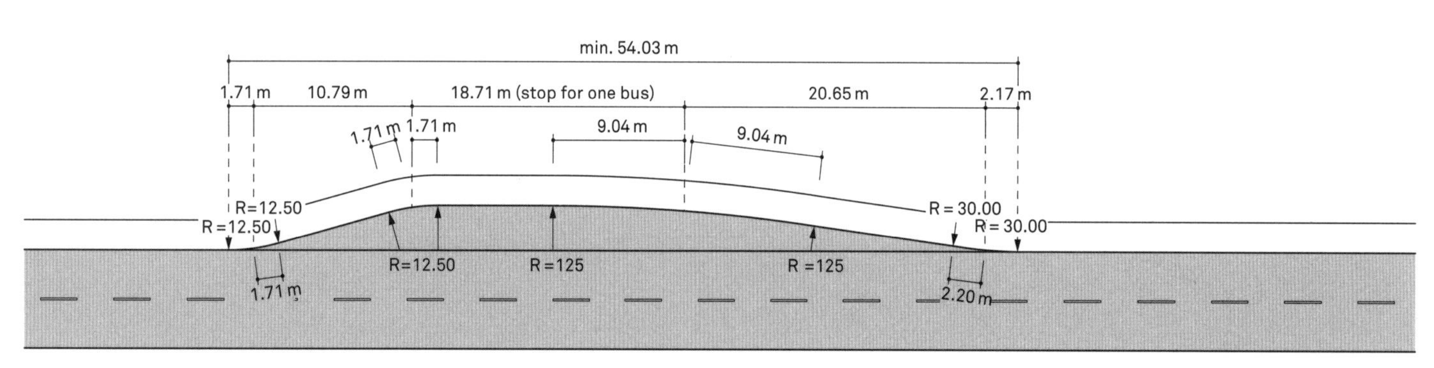

Bus bay, stop for one bus

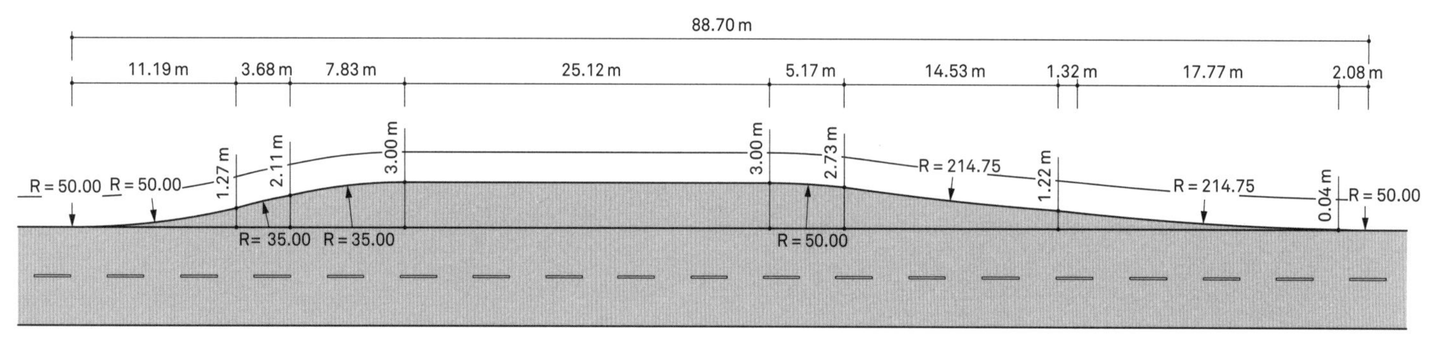

Bus bay with barrier-free accessibility for boarding and exiting by enabling the bus to pull up parallel to the curb

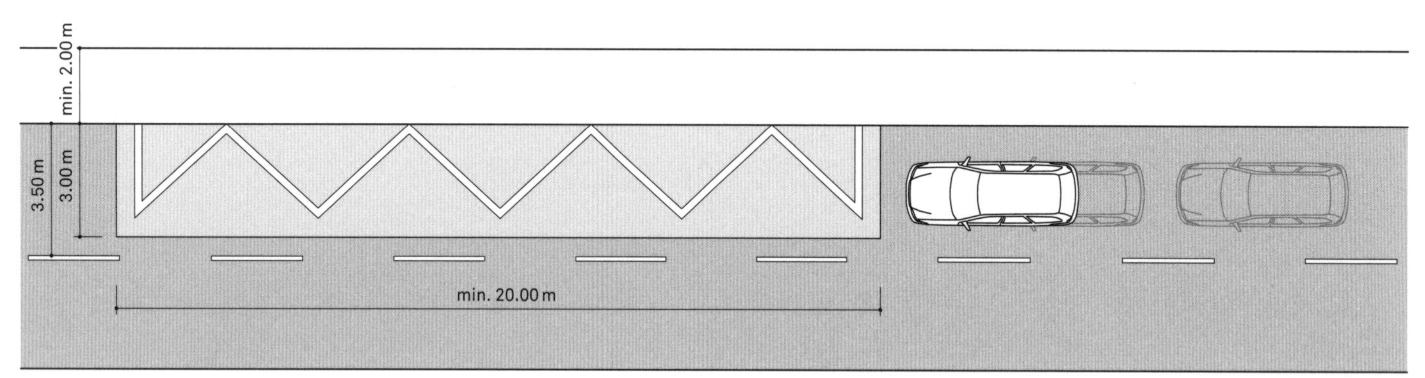

Curbside bus stop in a traffic lane

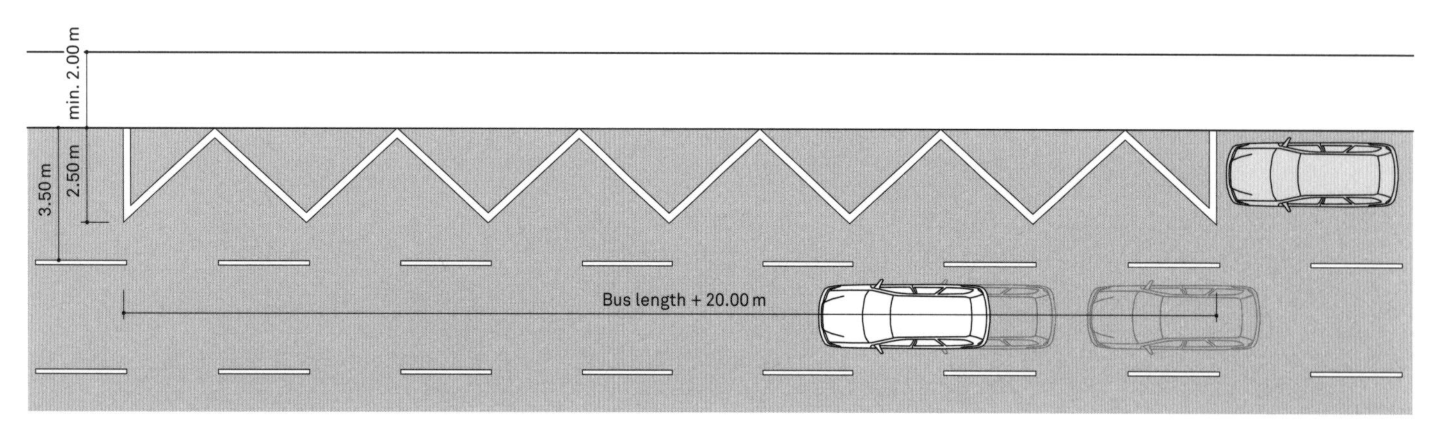

Curbside bus stop within parallel parking lane

Figure 3.3.23 Dimensions of bus bays and curbside bus stops

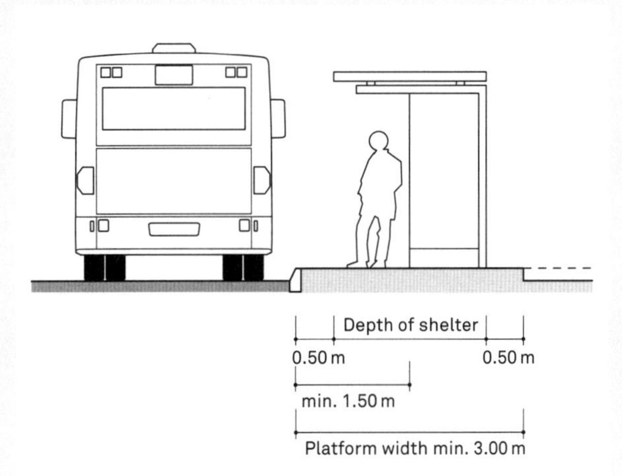

Figure 3.3.24 Dimensions of waiting areas and islands with shelters

Turnarounds

In dead-end streets and on many individual lots, it can be necessary to make space available for turning vehicles around. Depending on the vehicles to be accommodated, a hammerhead turning area or turnaround loop can be provided. One important consideration is whether it is desirable or even possible to drive the vehicle in reverse.

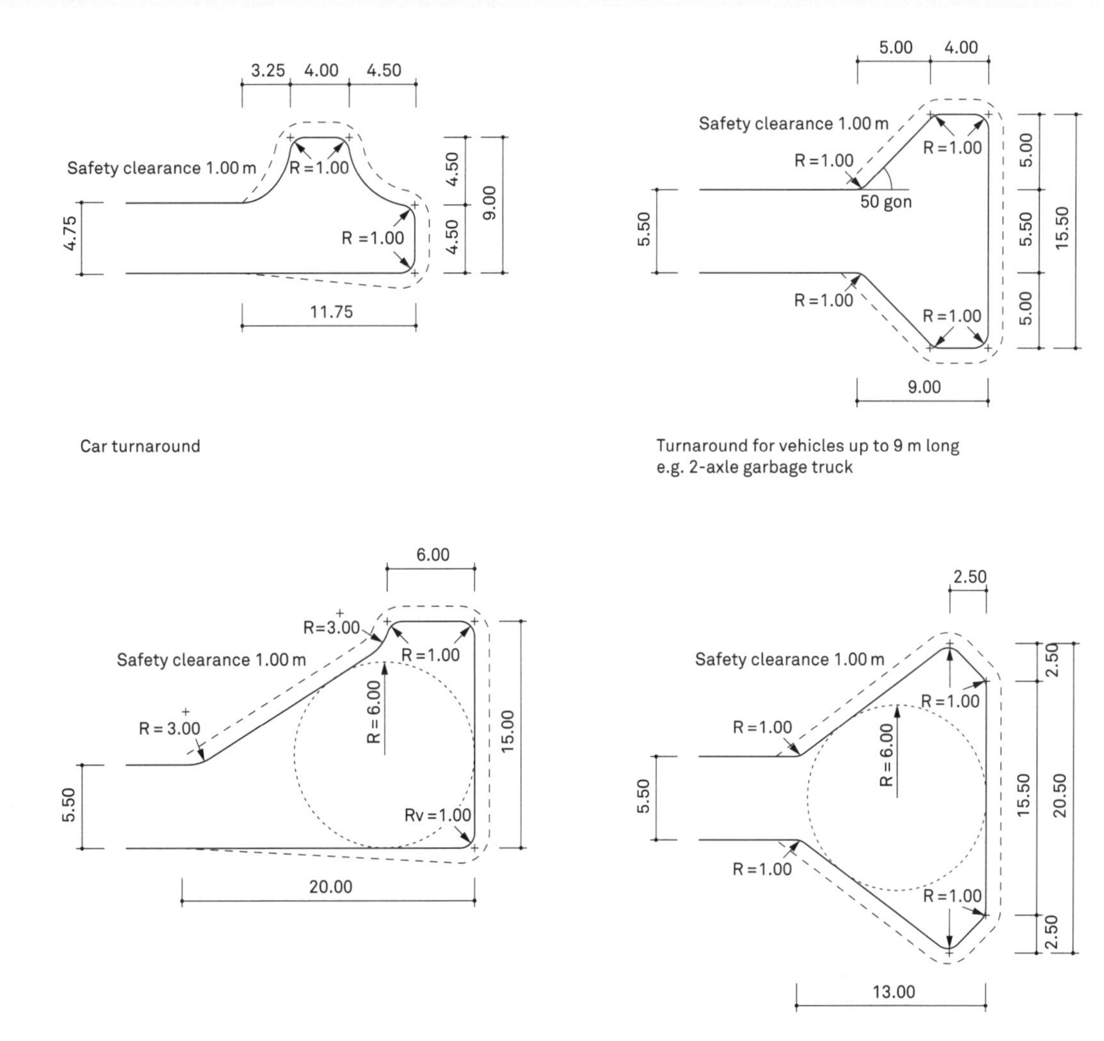

Figure 3.3.25 Hammerhead turning areas and turning circles for cars and trucks

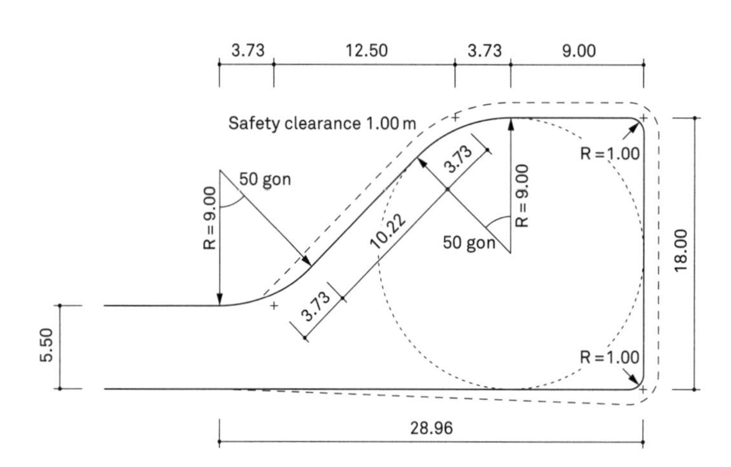

Turning circle for 2-axle garbage truck

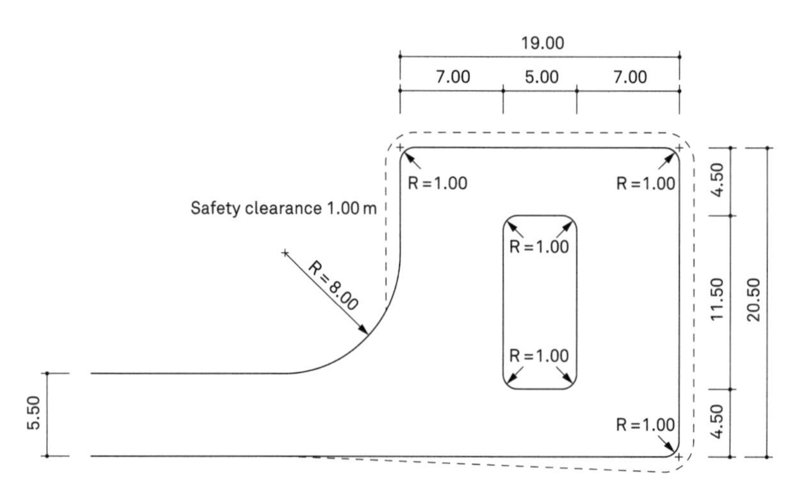

Turning circle for 3-axle garbage truck

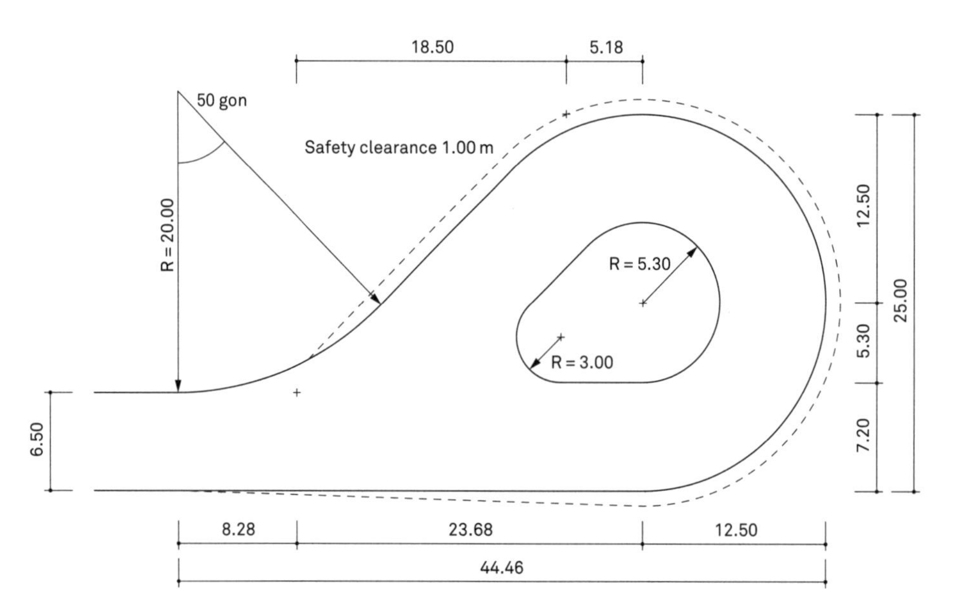

Turnaround loop for tractor-trailers

All dimensions in [m]

Figure 3.3.26 Turning circles and loops for garbage trucks and tractor-trailers

Escape Routes

For expeditious and safe firefighting and rescue of people and animals, maneuvering and deployment areas for the fire department must be provided near buildings. These areas are to be located in close proximity to the areas of the building that can be reached by ladders and have been identified for potential rescue efforts, such as balconies, windows, or other openings (second escape route) and – depending on the building height – can be accessed via driveways and/or passages from public thoroughfares.

Escape routes must, to the extent required, also be established for large parks and promenades as well as other outdoor facilities, in which case paths of adequate width and with suitable paving must be provided.

For fire lanes, there is a legal obligation to label them according to the provisions adopted by the responsible state or municipal authority.

The dimensioning of the necessary access route is dependent upon the location of the deployment areas on the property and the building height(s). For low-rise buildings (windowsills ≤8 m above grade) escape routes can be reached using portable ladders, so no access routes or deployment areas for vehicles are required. (→ Figures 3.3.27 and 3.3.28) For taller buildings, the regulations governing fire lanes and maneuvering and deployment areas for aerial rescue vehicles apply. If there are two stairways or at least one protected firefighting stair, neither areas for setting up ladders nor deployment areas for aerial rescue vehicles are required adjacent to the building. If buildings or parts of buildings are more than 50 m from a public road, access routes for emergency vehicles may be required even for low buildings.

Most of the requirements pertaining to areas for the fire department are determined by the respective states or municipalities. In Germany, the fundamental rules are stipulated in DIN 14090.

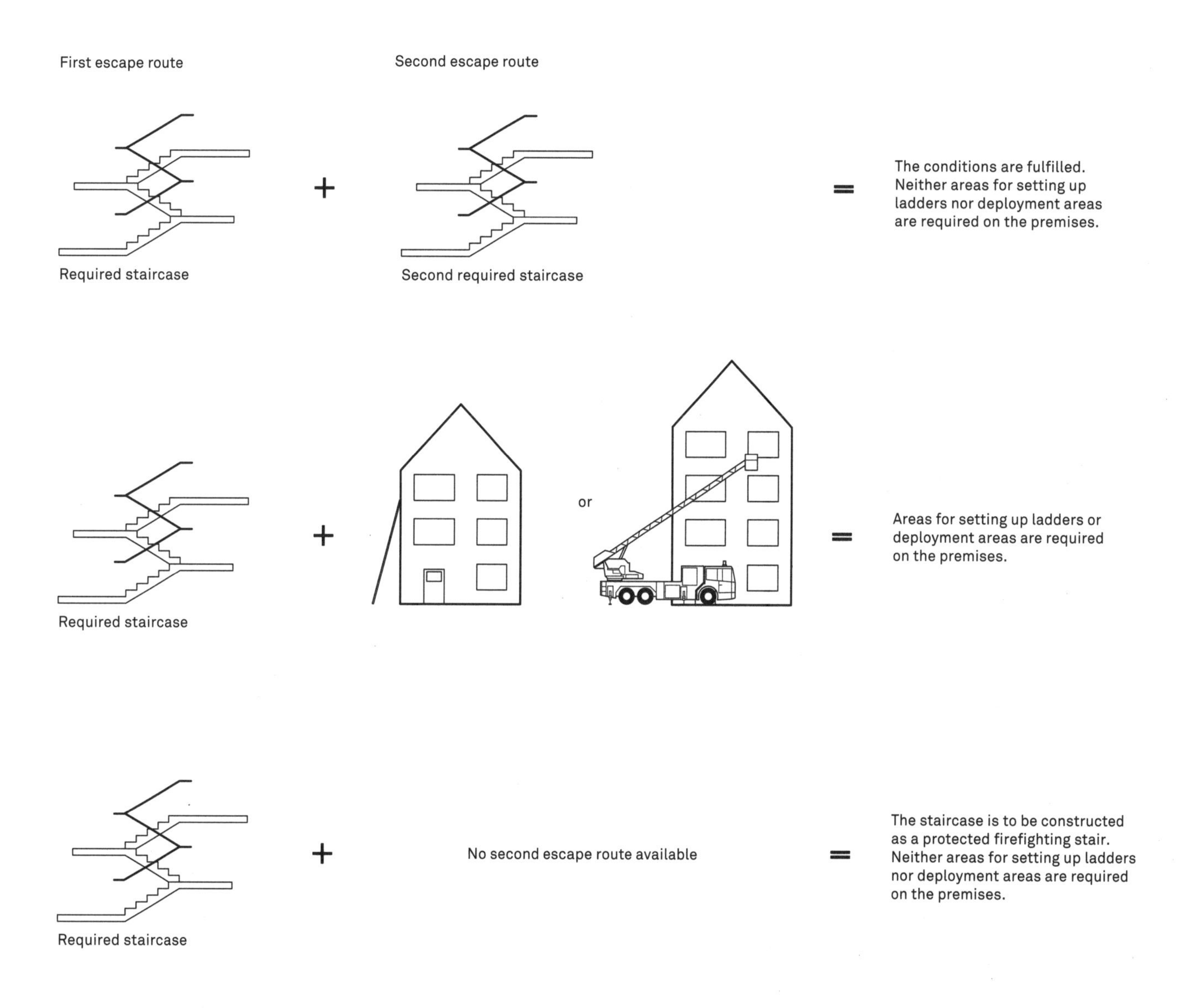

Figure 3.3.27 Need for deployment areas as a function of the type and quantity of stairs

Firefighter Access

Passages and paths providing access by foot shall comprise a route that is at least 1.25 m wide and as straight as possible. Where access is gained through a building, the passage must be constructed with a minimum of 2.2 m clear height (2 m headroom at doors).

Fire Lanes/Passages

The minimum width for vehicular access is 3 m. When both sides are bounded by constructive elements such as walls or piers over a distance of 12 m, the width shall be expanded to a minimum of 3.5 m. Access roads may consist of wheel tracks, provided that each track is at least 1.1 m wide and they are spaced 0.8 m apart. The route shall have a gradient that does not exceed 10 %. Transitions between sloping and level surfaces are to be rounded off with a radius of 15 m.

Steps and thresholds may not be higher than 8 cm and must be spaced a minimum of 10 m apart.

If it is not possible to establish the access route in a straight line due to local conditions, the outer radii of all curves shall determine minimum widths that must be maintained in those areas. → Table 3.3.17

Before and after curves, transitions of 11 m length are to be maintained to traffic lanes and/or passages. (→ Figure 3.3.29)

At passages through a building, a clear height of at least 3.5 m must be maintained. Within a distance of 8 m before and after such a passage, no gradient changes or steps are permissible.

Access controls such as barriers, stanchions, or chains must be openable by the fire department at all times and must therefore have appropriate locking mechanisms.

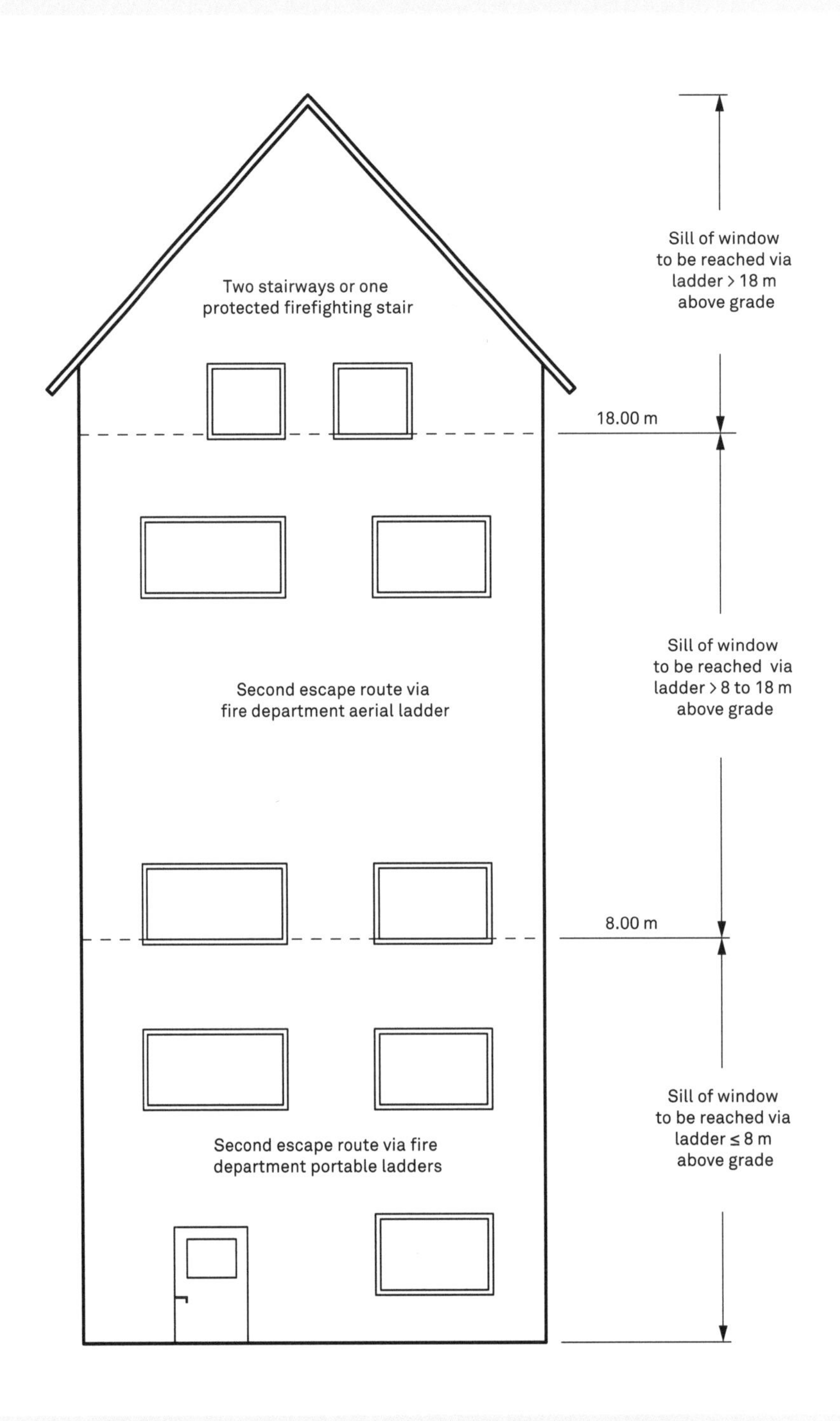

Figure 3.3.28 Use of rescue equipment on buildings

Outer radius of the curve	Minimum width
10.5 to 12 m	5 m
≥ 12 to 15	4.5 m
≥ 15 to 20	4 m
≥ 20 to 40	3.5 m
≥40 to 70	3.2 m
≥70	3 m

Table 3.3.17 Outer radii and minimum widths of curves

Maneuvering Areas for the Fire Department

Maneuvering areas provide space to park fire trucks, set up the extinguishing water supply, and prepare and organize the firefighting operations. For each fire truck to be accommodated, an area of at least 7 m wide and 12 m long shall be provided. To ensure unobstructed passing of vehicles when necessary, maneuvering areas are to be laid out separately from the access route, as turn-outs with 4-meter-long transition zones on both sides in cases where the access route continues. (→ **Figure 3.2.29**) Maneuvering areas can also be located on public property.

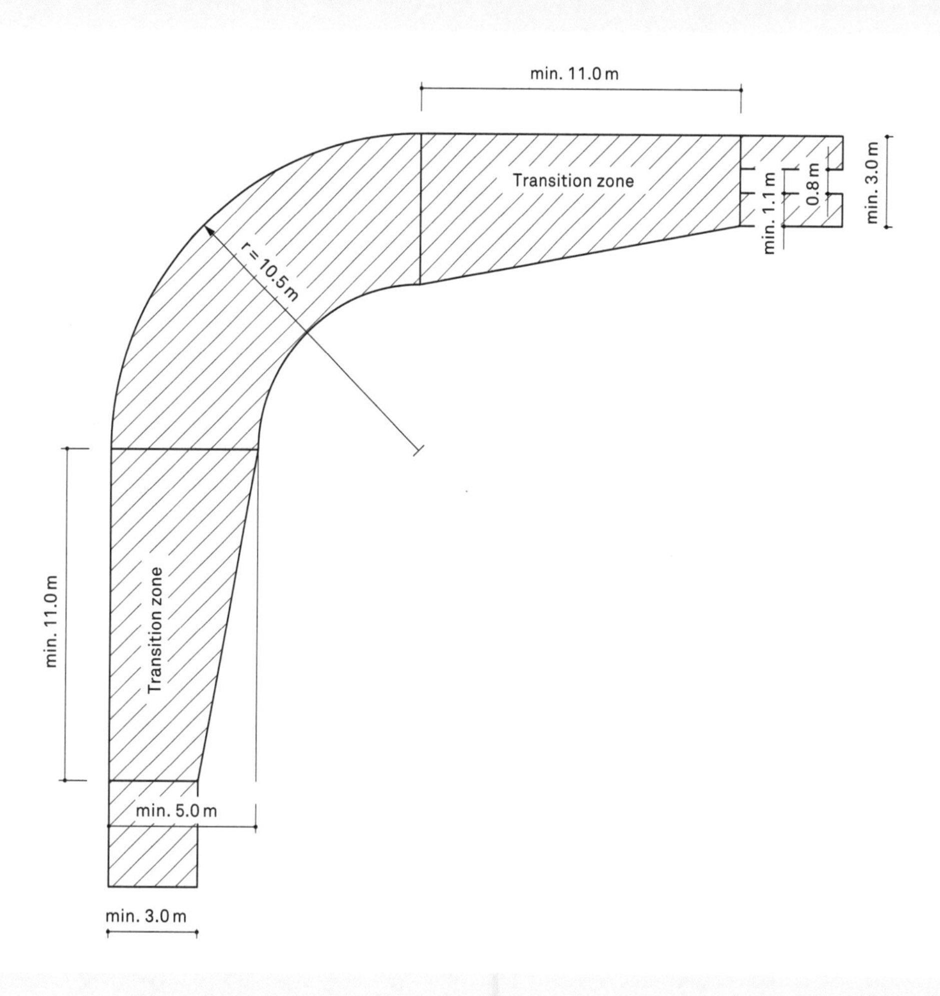

Figure 3.3.29 Curve radii and track and lane widths for fire lanes

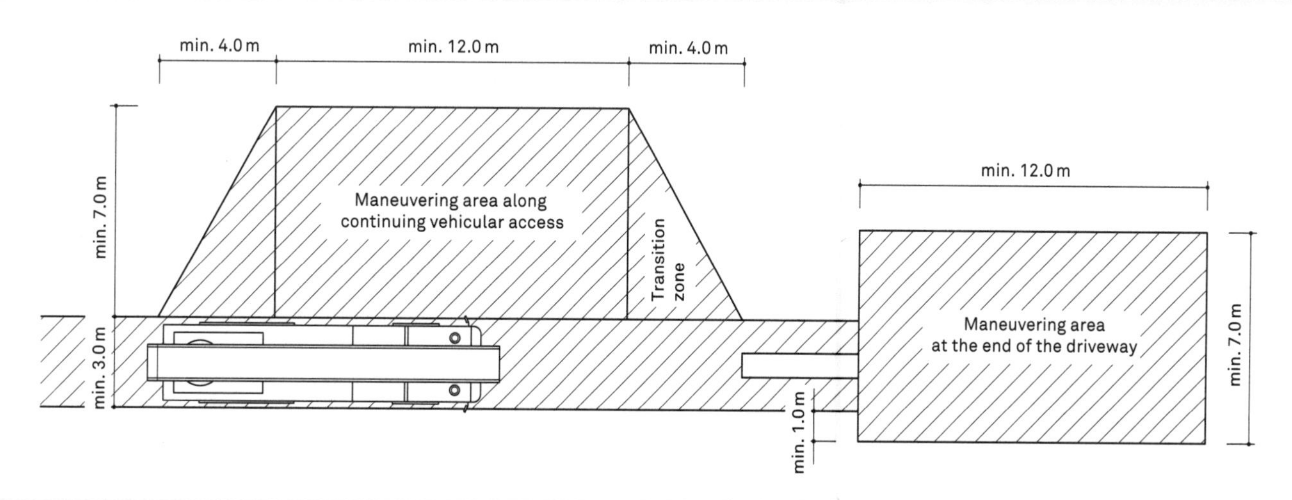

Figure 3.3.30 Dimensions of maneuvering areas

Deployment Areas for the Fire Department

For securing and safeguarding the second escape route, unobstructed deployment areas for aerial rescue vehicles shall be designated when a specific building height or windowsill height is exceeded. A deployment area can be established perpendicular or parallel to the building. The deployment area must be laid out such that all windows or other openings serving as escape routes can be reached with the ladder equipment.

The maximum slope of all deployment areas is 5%. Trees and building parts that could restrict the work in the area where the ladder will be in use should be avoided.

Deployment areas with stable surfacing must also be provided for using portable ladders. Trees or large shrubs that could cause obstructions should be avoided in such areas.

The quantity and precise locations of the maneuvering areas for escape routes should be coordinated with the responsible fire protection authority.

Vehicular Access Requirements and Areas for the Fire Department

All maneuvering and deployment areas as well as driveways and passages must be constructed to support an axle load of up to 10 tons and a total weight up to 16 tons. Deployment areas must support a bearing pressure of at least 800 kN/m². Impermeable paving is not mandatory, so various surfacing options, including crushed aggregate lawn, can be used in these areas.

Areas with underground construction that will be driven upon only by rescue vehicles in the case of fire shall be constructed in accordance with bridge class 16/16 as per DIN 1072/DIN 1055.

Walls and ceilings of passages are to be constructed with fire-resistance class F 90 and essential parts shall be made of noncombustible materials (F-90 AB).

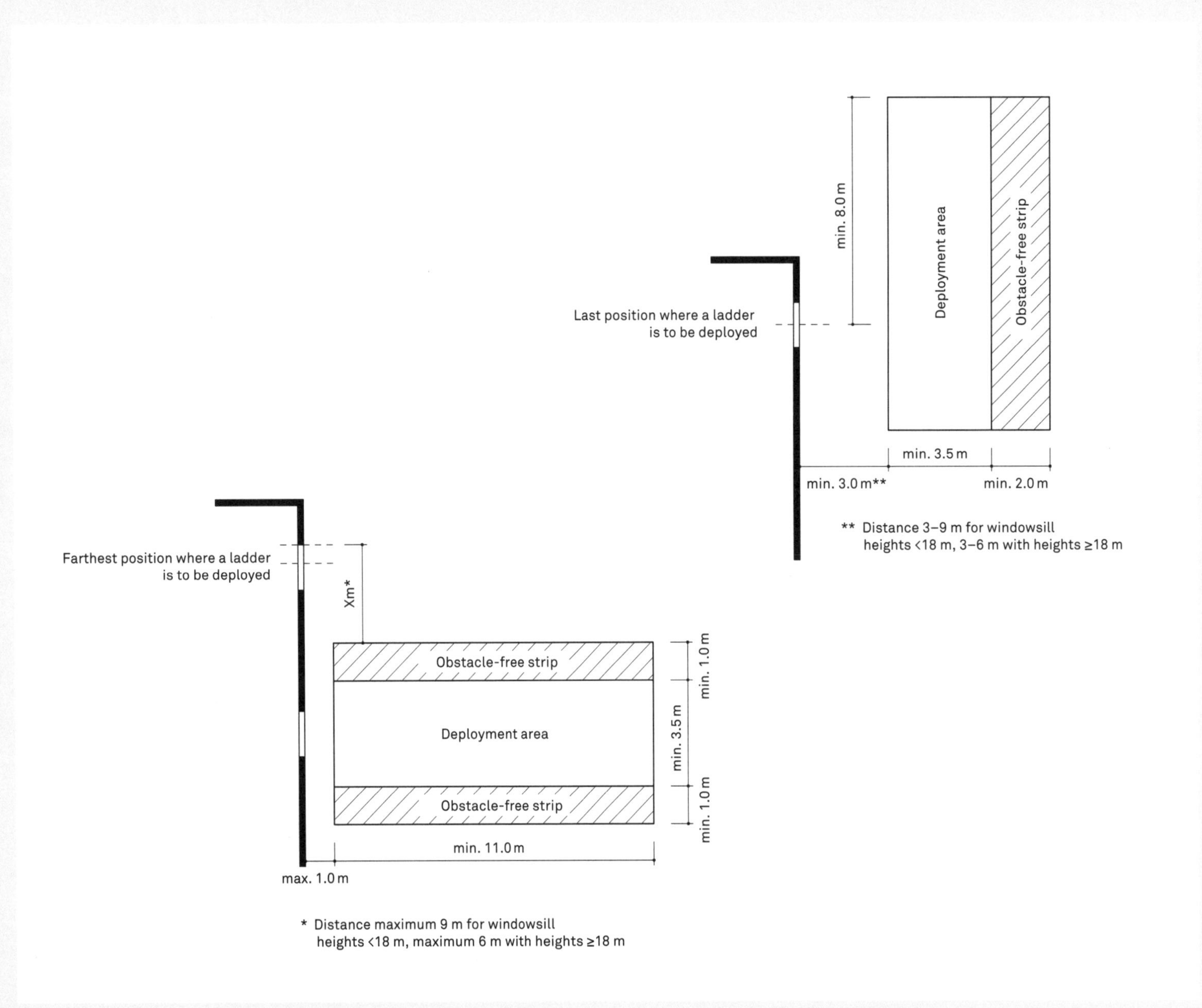

Figure 3.3.31 Dimensions and orientation of deployment areas

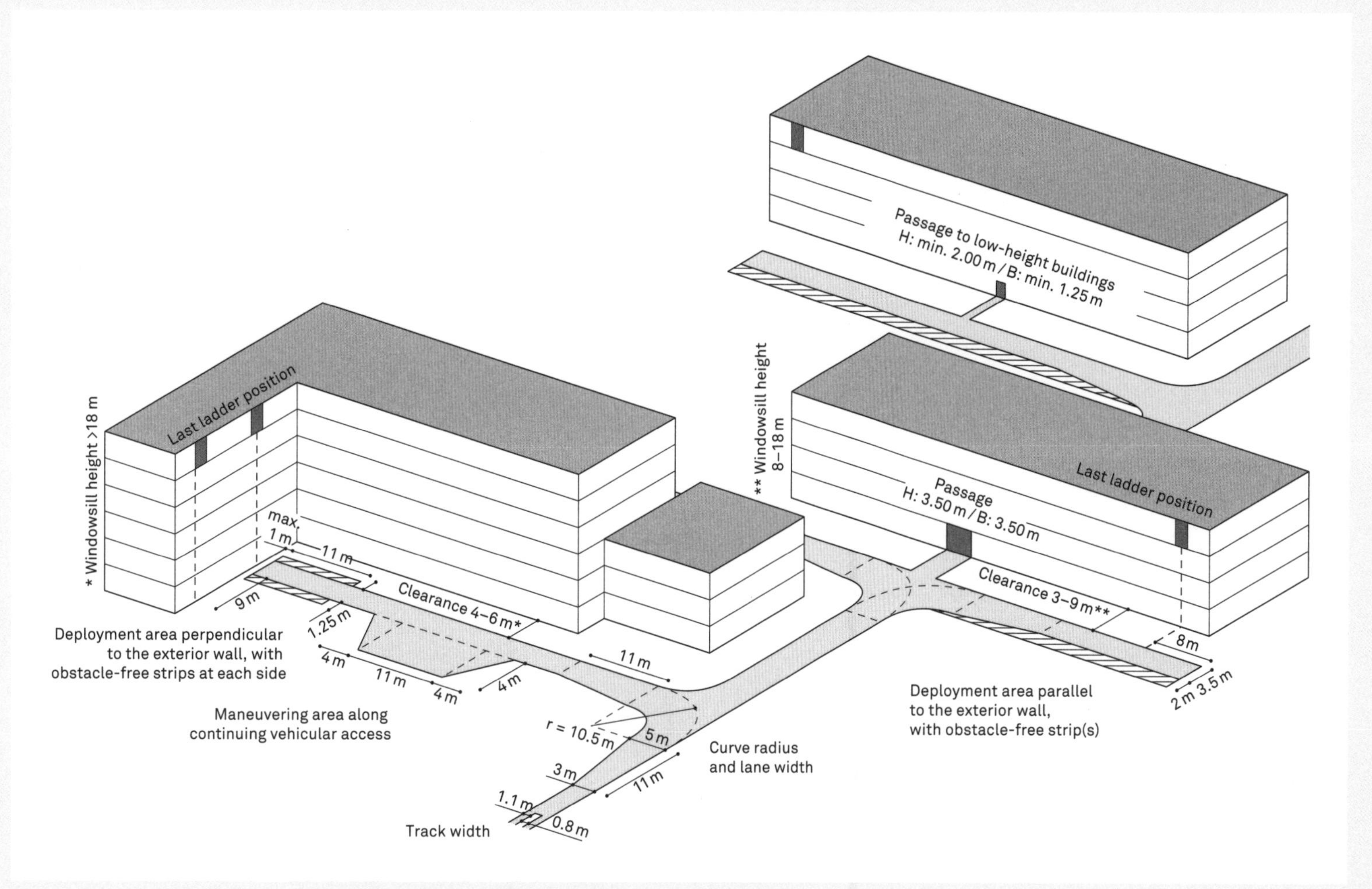

Figure 3.3.32 Overview – access to properties for the fire department

Stairs and Ramps
→ 3.2 Grading, Stairs, and Ramps

Handrails Along Stairs
→ 3.6 Boundary Enclosures and Railings

Drainage of Thoroughfares
→ 3.2 Grading, Stairs, and Ramps

3 Elements
3.4 Parking Lots for Motor Vehicles and Bicycles

3.4 Parking Lots for Motor Vehicles and Bicycles

For buildings and other built structures where vehicular traffic is to be expected, automobile parking spaces and bicycle parking spaces of a suitable character are to be provided in sufficient quantity and size, under consideration of the local traffic conditions and available public transit alternatives. Your design should enable their safe and convenient use.

There are no uniform building code requirements for certifying the adequacy of such facilities for new buildings, however. And many state building codes in Germany no longer have any regulations on required parking spaces. In that case it is incumbent upon the municipalities to adopt their own parking statutes as needed, and where appropriate, to mandate the obligation to certify the provision of automobile and/or bicycle parking spaces. Municipal legislative sovereignty makes it possible to react in a more targeted way to local needs and circumstances and to pursue specific transport policy objectives. In this context, legal standards increasingly require a minimum number of bicycle parking spaces for new buildings and changes of use.

The situation is similar in Austria: provisions that go beyond the building codes or state-specific legal standards are subject to municipal autonomy.

Location

Location of Bicycle Parking Spaces

Parking spaces for bicycles should ideally be laid out close to the destination. By locating the bicycle parking spaces in close proximity to the place of destination, people can be motivated to use bicycles more often as their means of transport. In addition, parking spaces in the immediate surroundings can help to contain chaotic parking habits.

Bicycle parking spaces should be established in the public street space at all destinations important for cyclists. The parking facility itself and the routes to reach it must not hinder or endanger pedestrian traffic. The parking facilities can be located near the roadway or off to the side and can be made as open or covered areas or lockable, enclosed bike boxes. The type of bicycle parking facility and its features are also determined by the length of time spent at the destination. → Figure 3.4.1

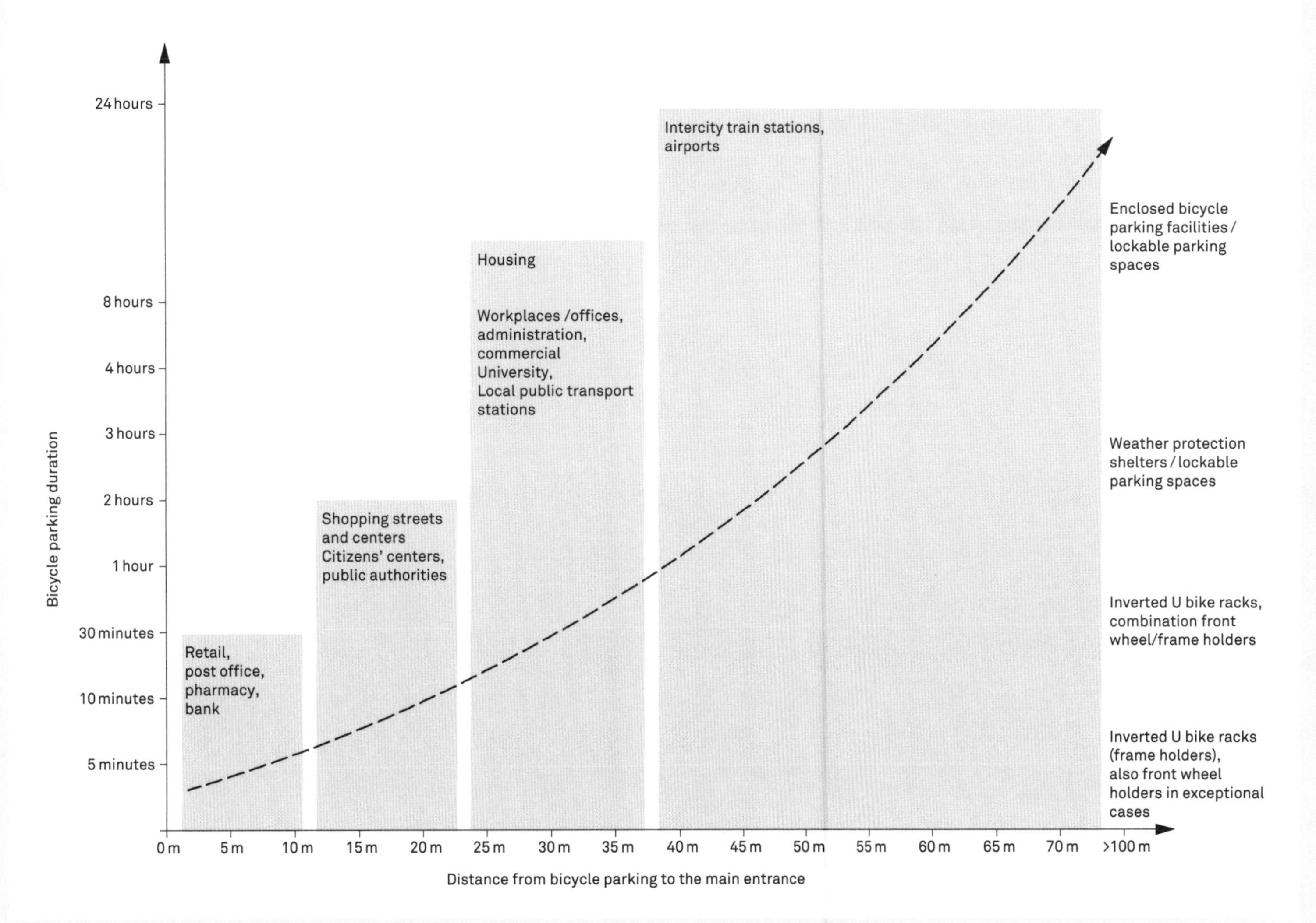

Figure 3.4.1 Recommended values for the distance from bicycle parking spaces to places of destination and their features (Source: Danish Cyclists Federation: Bicycle Parking Manual, adapted)

Paving of Parking Spaces for Automobiles and Bicycles

The area where bicycles are parked should be paved and at ground level. A permeable surface is desirable. Depending on the intensity of use, bicycle parking spaces can also be located on crushed aggregate lawn areas.

Depending on the frequency of use, automobile parking spaces can also have a permeable surface. With a very low intensity of use, this also applies to the traffic aisle. → **Table 3.4.1 and Figure 3.4.4** When using grass pavers or other unit pavers with large joints, paving strips without grass or gravel joints can be built between the parking spaces for better ease of access.

	Low-intensity use (Residential areas, employee parking lots in business parks, at schools, hospitals, etc.)	**High-intensity use** (Public parking lots, customer parking areas in business parks, at train stations, supermarkets, banks, etc.)
<10–20 parking spaces	Aisle with partially permeable pavement over entire width; for better pedestrian accessibility, an impermeably paved walkway can be laid out, with partially permeable parking spaces	Aisle with impermeable pavement over entire width (6 m); partially permeable parking spaces are acceptable if vegetation (grass joints, grass paving blocks) is omitted
>10–20 parking spaces	Aisle with impermeable pavement for 3 m width and partially permeable pavement for 3 m width, with partially permeable parking spaces	

Table 3.4.1 Permeability of paving for automobile parking lots with differing intensity of use

Figure 3.4.2 Combination front wheel/frame holder bike racks on a crushed aggregate lawn

Figure 3.4.3 Parking lot with impermeable pavement for traffic aisle and partially permeable grass parking spaces

< 10–20 Parking spaces

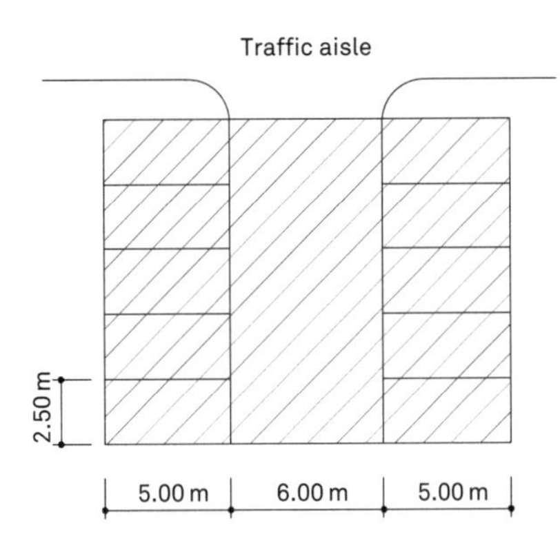

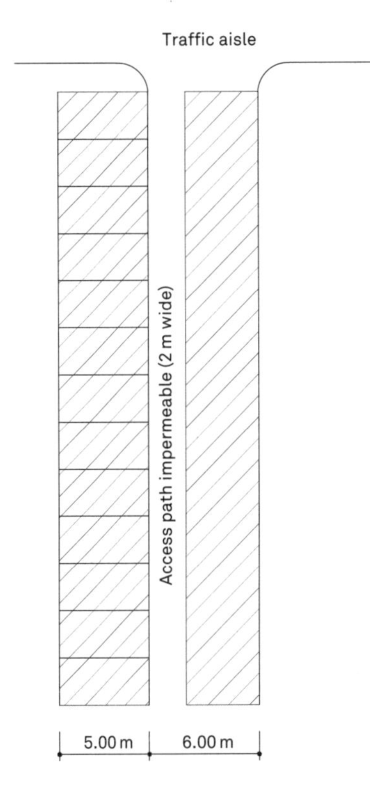

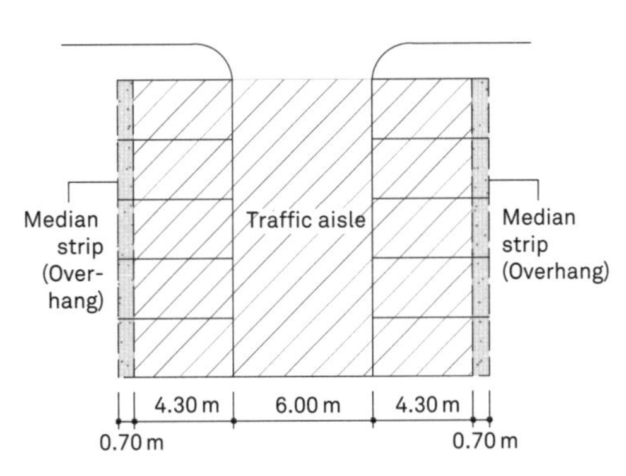

> 10–20 Parking spaces

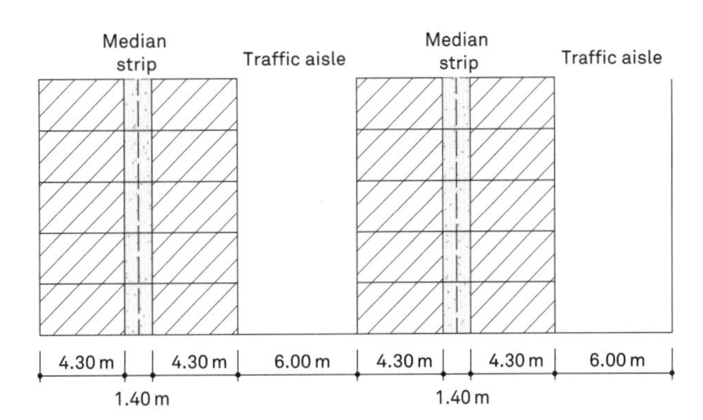

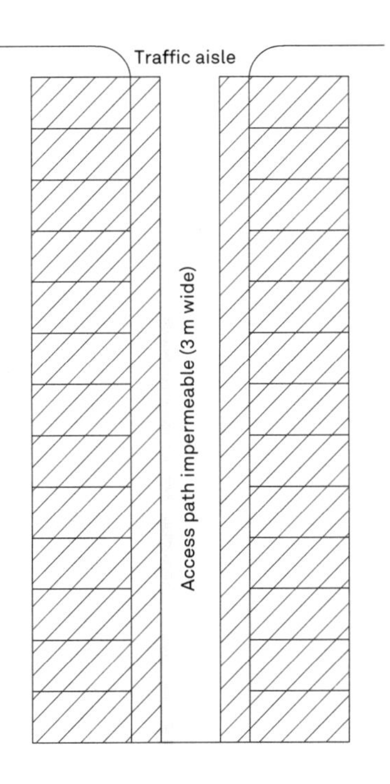

Overhang strip (vehicle overhang) permeable, (e.g. grass, infiltration swale)

Partially permeable (e.g. grass/gravel joints, grass pavers)

Impermeable

Figure 3.4.4 Greening potential for parking areas

Dimensions and Characteristics

Requirements for Bicycle and Automobile Parking Spaces

Whereas quantitative specifications for automobile parking spaces are increasingly absent from the legal standards, the provision of bicycle parking and of automobile parking for people with disabilities has gained special emphasis.

The required number of parking spaces generally results from the type of use and size of a facility, where the reference value is the usable area or number of users. Some regulations take other factors into account and provide for exemptions: thus, the required number of parking spaces can be minimized by the accessibility and timing of public transit (e.g., in Baden-Württemberg) or when the employer provides employees with job tickets for using local public transit. For the train station area in the city of Dornbirn (A), which is well-served by public transit, a ceiling on the number of parking spaces was even set for the first time (see Vorarlberg parking regulations). Requirements for facilities serving single-track motor vehicles (motorcycles, etc.) are seldom stipulated and are therefore typically to be calculated according to anticipated demand. Stipulations for motorcycle parking spaces in individual cases give one parking space per five dwellings as a benchmark for multifamily houses or residential developments.

If there are no building code requirements for bicycle and automobile parking spaces, the requirements in Table 3.4.3 can serve as a guide for planning.

Facility type	Quantity		
	Bicycle spaces	Car spaces	Accessible parking spaces*
Residential buildings			
Apartments	1 per 30 m² total living area or 2 per apartment	1 per apartment < 160 m², 2 per apartment ≥ 160 m²	Minimum 1, when apartments must be accessible
Multifamily houses with more than ten apartments		0.8 per apartment	
Weekend and vacation houses	1 per apartment	1 per apartment	
Children's residences and youth homes	0.5 to 1 per bed or 10 per 15 residents	0.6 to 1 per 15 beds	
Student dormitory	0.5 to 1 per bed or 0.7 per resident	1 per 3 beds or 0.2 per resident	
Dormitories for caregivers	1 per 2 beds or 0.7 per resident	1 per 4 beds or 0.2 per resident	
Employee dormitory	1 per 2 beds or 0.7 per resident	1 per 3 beds or 0.2 per resident	
Retirement home, assisted living facility	1 per 10 beds 0.7 per resident 1 per 5 apartments	1 per 10 beds 0.2 per resident	
Visitors to private apartments	1 per 200 m² total living area		
Office and administration buildings, doctors' offices, workplaces			
Offices and administration	1 per 60 m² usable area 0.7 per 40 m² usable area 1 per 100 m² GFA >4,000 m² office floor area → 1 per 200 m² GFA 1 per 70 m² usable area	1 per 40 m² usable area	
Spaces with substantial visitor traffic (customer service desks, dispatch rooms, consultancies, doctors' offices, etc.)	1 per 40 (50) m² usable area	1 per 25 m² usable area	
Offices, workshops, and manufacturing plants (per EAR 05)	0.3 per workstation		
Sales areas in sales outlets			
Retail stores, commercial buildings	For <400 m² → 1 per 50 m² sales area For >400 m²–800 m² → 1 per m² sales area min. 4 parking spaces For >800 m² → 1 per 100 m² sales area, min. 10 parking spaces	1 per 40 (100) m² sales area	
Shopping centers	1 per 80 (100) m² sales area	1 per 15 (100) m² sales area	

* Unless indicated otherwise, at least 1%–3%, but at least two, of the required total number of parking spaces shall be accessible spaces, and where possible, stalls that allow rear exit from the vehicle should be provided.

Table 3.4.2 Requirements for bicycle and automobile parking spaces, with guideline and average values as determined from various parking statutes (relevant valid building regulations must be observed!)

Facility type	Quantity		
	Bicycle spaces	Car spaces	Accessible parking spaces*
Places of assembly (except sports facilities) and churches			
Places of assembly (theaters, concert halls, movie theaters, etc.)	1 per 15 (20) attendees or movie theater, auditorium: 1 per 10 seats theater, concert hall: 1 per 50 seats	1 per 7 (10) visitors/seats	1 per 200 seats, minimum 1 per facility
Churches	1 per 20 attendees or 1 per 50 seats	1 per 30 visitors/seats	1 per 200 seats, minimum 1 per facility
Sports facilities			
Sports venues without spectator seating with spectator seating	1 per 250 m² sports area plus 1 per 30 spectator seats or 1.5 per 400 m² sports area plus 1 per 15 spectator seats or 1 per 20 spectators (local), 1 per 50 spectators (supra-local, e.g., stadium)	1 per 800 m² sports area plus 1 per 30 spectator seats or 1 per 400 m² sports area plus 1 per 15 spectator seats	1 per 200 spectators, but min. 1 (for minimum 100 spectators)
Multipurpose gyms without spectator seating with spectator seating	1 per 30 m² floor area; plus 1 per 15 spectator seats or 2 per 200 m² sports area plus 1 per 15 spectator seats Without: 1 per 250 m² sports area With: 1 per 10 spectator seats	1 per 80 m² floor area; plus 1 per 15 spectator seats or 1 per 200 m² sports area plus 1 per 15 spectator seats	1 per 200 spectators, but minimum 1 (for minimum 100 spectators)
Outdoor swimming pools	2 per 200–300 m² lot area or 1 per 50 m² lot area	1 per 200–300 m² lot area	
Indoor swimming pools without spectator seating with spectator seating	 1 per 7 lockers 1 per 10 spectator seats 2 per 10 lockers	 1 per 10 lockers 1 per 15 spectator seats	
Tennis courts, squash facilities without spectator seating with spectator seating	2 per court; plus 1 per 10 spectator seats	2 per court; plus 1 per 15 spectator seats	
Dance schools, fitness centers, saunas, solariums, etc.	1 per 50 m² usable area or 1 per 5 lockers	1 per 5 lockers	
Miniature golf courses	4 per miniature golf course 10 per facility	6 per miniature golf course	
Bowling alleys	2–3 per lane	2 per lane	
Boat berths in the water and/or in boathouses Solely winter storage	1 per 4–10 boat berths	1 per 3–10 boat berths	
Restaurants and lodging establishments			
Snack stands without seating	1 per 15 m² usable area	1 per 20 m² usable area	1 per 200 patron seats, but a minimum of 1 (for a minimum of 100 patrons)
Beer garden	1 per 2 seats or 1 per 20 m² usable area		
Restaurants of local significance	1 per 7–10 seats or 1 per 20 m² usable area		
Restaurants of regional significance	1 per 18 m² usable area	1 per 9 m² usable area	
Hotels, pensions, sanatoriums, etc.	1 per 3 lodging rooms; for attendant restaurant operation additional 1 per 15 m² usable area (full-serve restaurant) or 1 per 20 m² usable area (snack outlet without seating) or 1 per 20 beds	1 per 10 lodging rooms; for attendant restaurant operation additional 1 per 12 m² usable area (full-serve restaurant) or 1 per 15 m² usable area (snack outlet without seating)	1 per 200 beds, but a minimum of 1 (for a minimum 100 beds)
Youth hostels	1 per 4–5 beds	1 per 10 beds	

* Unless indicated otherwise, at least 1%–3%, but at least two, of the required total number of parking spaces shall be accessible spaces, and where possible, stalls that allow rear exit from the vehicle should be provided.

Facility type	Quantity		
	Bicycle spaces	Car spaces	Accessible parking spaces*
Medical institutions			
Hospitals, private clinics	1 per 20 beds	1 per 4 (5) beds	1 per 200 beds, but min. 1 (for min. 100 bodc)
Elderly nursing home	1 per 40 beds 0.5 per 12 beds 1 per 30 beds	1 per 8 beds 1 per 12 beds	
Schools, youth training centers			
Elementary schools	1 per 3 students 5 per 20 student slots 1 per 5 students 0.1 per student	1 per 50 students 1 per 20 student slots	1 per 200 seats/student slots, but a minimum of 1 per facility
Other general education schools, vocational schools	1 per student	1 per 40 students, plus 1 per 10 students over 18 yrs. old	
Special needs schools (for people with disabilities)	1 per 15 students	1 per 30 students	
Colleges and universities	1 per 5 students 3 per 10 student slots 0.6 per student	1 per 6 students 2 per 10 student slots	1 per 200 seats/student slots, but a minimum 1 per facility
Preschools, daycare centers, etc.	1 per 15 children (daycare spaces) or 1 per group/group room	1 per 30 children (daycare spaces) 1 per 30 visitors	
Youth clubs, etc.	1 per 3 visitors or 1 per 15 m² usable area	1 per 20 visitors	
Commercial facilities			
Trade shops and industrial businesses	1 per 70 (up to 200) m² usable area 0.4 per 2 workplaces 1 per 200 m² GFA 1 per 5 workers	1 per 70 m² usable area	
Warehouses, storage yards	1 per 150 m² usable area or 0.4 per 2 workplaces	1 per 150 m² usable area or 1 per 2 workplaces	
Auto repair shops	1 per 100 m² usable area	1 per 100 m² usable area	
Gasoline stations with self-service facilities	–	5 per self-service stall	
Automatic car wash	–	5 per car wash	
Car wash stalls for self-service	–	3 per washing station	
Other			
Allotment gardens	1 per 3 plots	1 per 30 plots	
Cemeteries	1 per 1,000 m² lot area 1 per 1,500 m² lot area	1 per 2,000 m² lot area, but min. 10	
Gaming centers and amusement arcades	1 per 20 m² useable area	1 per 20 m² useable area	

* Unless indicated otherwise, at least 1%–3%, but at least two, of the required total number of parking spaces shall be accessible spaces, and where possible, stalls that allow rear exit from the vehicle should be provided.

Table 3.4.2 Requirements for bicycle and automobile parking spaces, with standard and average values (differing legal requirements must be observed where applicable!)
Source: EAR 05 and regulations of various cities and municipalities

Bicycle Parking Spaces

Sufficient comfort of use is offered by bicycle parking spaces when they are easily accessible, a minimum distance between the bike stalls is maintained, the bicycle is given stable support, and it is possible to lock the bicycle securely, including the bike frame (e.g. with inverted U rack). Another relevant aspect that adds to the comfort is a roof covering the parking spaces.

The handlebar width of 0.6–0.7 m and bike length of about 1.9 m are decisive for the design of bicycle parking areas. The public space (access aisle) directly in front must be a minimum of 1.8 m and sufficient distance from walls and obstacles must be maintained.

Bicycle Racks

Inverted U bike racks (also known as Sheffield stands and "staple" racks) should have a height of 0.7–0.85 m. Such racks support bicycles leaned against them. An additional crosspiece at knee height (about 0.4 m above ground) enables more comfortable use with children's bikes. For providing stable support, the overall length should be at least 0.6 m, or preferably a minimum of 0.8 m. To enable comfortable use – even with a child safety seat, saddlebags, or a bicycle basket – the racks should be spaced 1.5 m apart, and this can be reduced to 1.20 m in confined situations where access from both sides is restricted. Thus a straightforward calculation of the space needed yields a width of 0.75 m (min. 0.60 m) per bicycle. → Figure 3.4.5

U-shaped racks with a front bend provide a secondary means of stabilizing the bicycle at the front, but can only be used from one side. Because they hold the front wheel, such racks can be lower in height than ordinary U-shaped racks. → Figure 3.4.6 U-shaped racks that also have a bracket for holding the front wheel use a similar principle. These are often available as units comprising multiple bike racks connected together. Such racks are usually designed primarily to grip the front wheel in a secure fashion. → Figure 3.4.7

If the bicycles are all at the same level, parking spaces should preferably be spaced 0.8 m apart (but not less than 0.7 m). With an alternating arrangement where the bicycles are offset vertically, the spacing can be reduced to 0.5 m. But sufficient comfort of use is only achieved when the rack can be reached from both sides.

Racks that only hold the front wheel should be avoided, because since the bicycle frame is not supported and the front tire is generally grasped inadequately, the bike can fall over and bend the rim. Exceptions should only be considered when the available space is very confined or when only short-term parking is needed, such as in front of shops.

A better alternative would be a bicycle railing, for example, mounted along a building with sufficient distance from the wall.

The design of bicycle parking spaces is based on an area requirement of approximately 1.5 m² (1.9 x 0.6 m) per bike without maneuvering and circulation areas. If the facility has a diagonal arrangement, the width of the access aisle and the length of the parking stalls should each be 1.5 m (lane up to 1.8 m). With such an arrangement, the lateral spacing is likewise reduced to 0.6–0.7 m, or even 0.4 m when the heights of the bicycles are staggered. The angle of installation is 45° (50 gon).

Figure 3.4.8 in combination with Table 3.4.3 shows various possibilities for parallel arrangements and their space requirements.

Bike Shelters

Covered parking provides additional protection from unfavorable weather conditions, but also from honeydew secretion under trees (especially from certain maple and linden species) or from bird droppings. For comprehensive protection, canopies should extend at least 0.6 m beyond the actual parking stalls. Bicycle parking for housing and school buildings as well as at places of work should provide covered shelters for a minimum of 50 % of the parking spaces. At train stations for local and long-distance travel, a higher percentage is desirable since it is expected that parking stays will be longer there. By using existing canopies, building projections, and other existing features, additional design effort and area costs can be forgone. Ideally, bicycle parking spaces for residents or employees are accommodated in the building and easily accessible (accessible at ground floor level or via ramps).

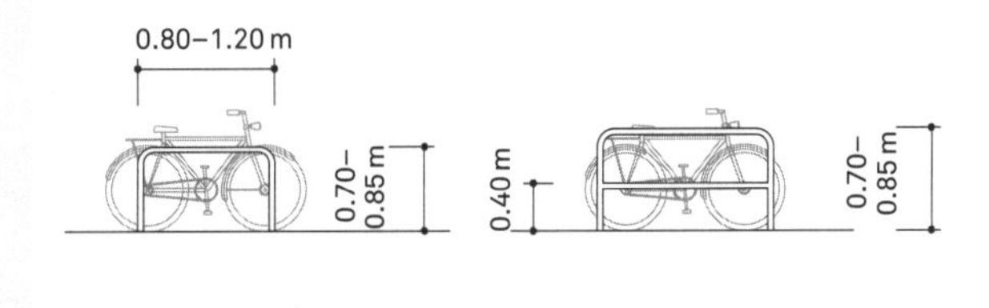

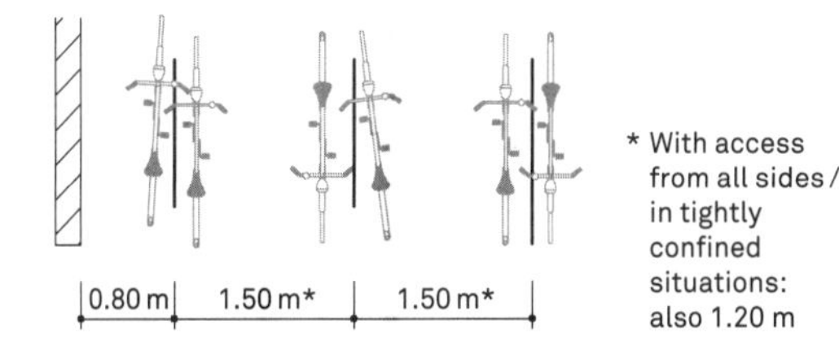

Figure 3.4.5 Dimensions and alignment of inverted U bike racks with/without crosspiece

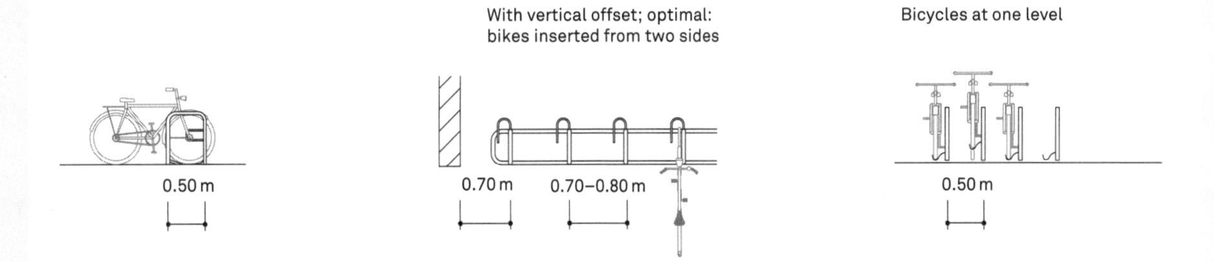

Figure 3.4.6 Dimensions and alignment of U-shaped racks with front wheel bracket, as multiple rack unit

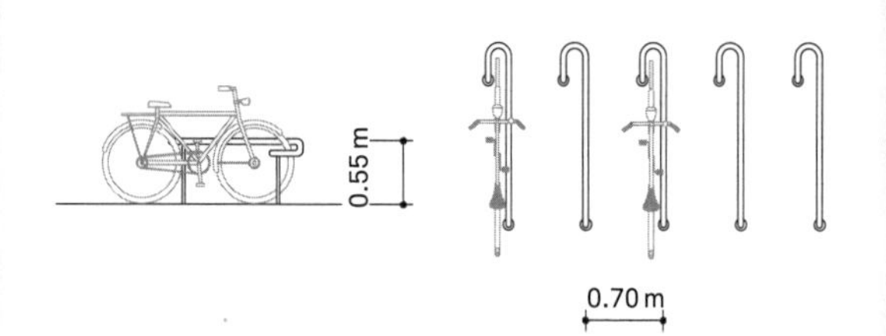

Figure 3.4.7 U-shaped racks with front bend

Table 3.4.3 Space requirements for bicycle parking spaces: inverted U bike racks with 1.5 m spacing

	Layout scheme	Area per rack (2 bicycles)	Area per bicycle
A	Perpendicular parking (90°), two rows	4.3 m²	2.15 m²
B	Perpendicular parking (90°), single row	5.2 m²	2.6 m²
C	Diagonal parking (45°), two rows, center aisle with two-way traffic	4.8 m²	2.4 m²
D	Diagonal parking (45°), two rows, center aisle with one-way traffic	4.3 m²	2.15 m²
E	Diagonal parking, single row, aisle with one-way traffic	5.6 m²	2.8 m²

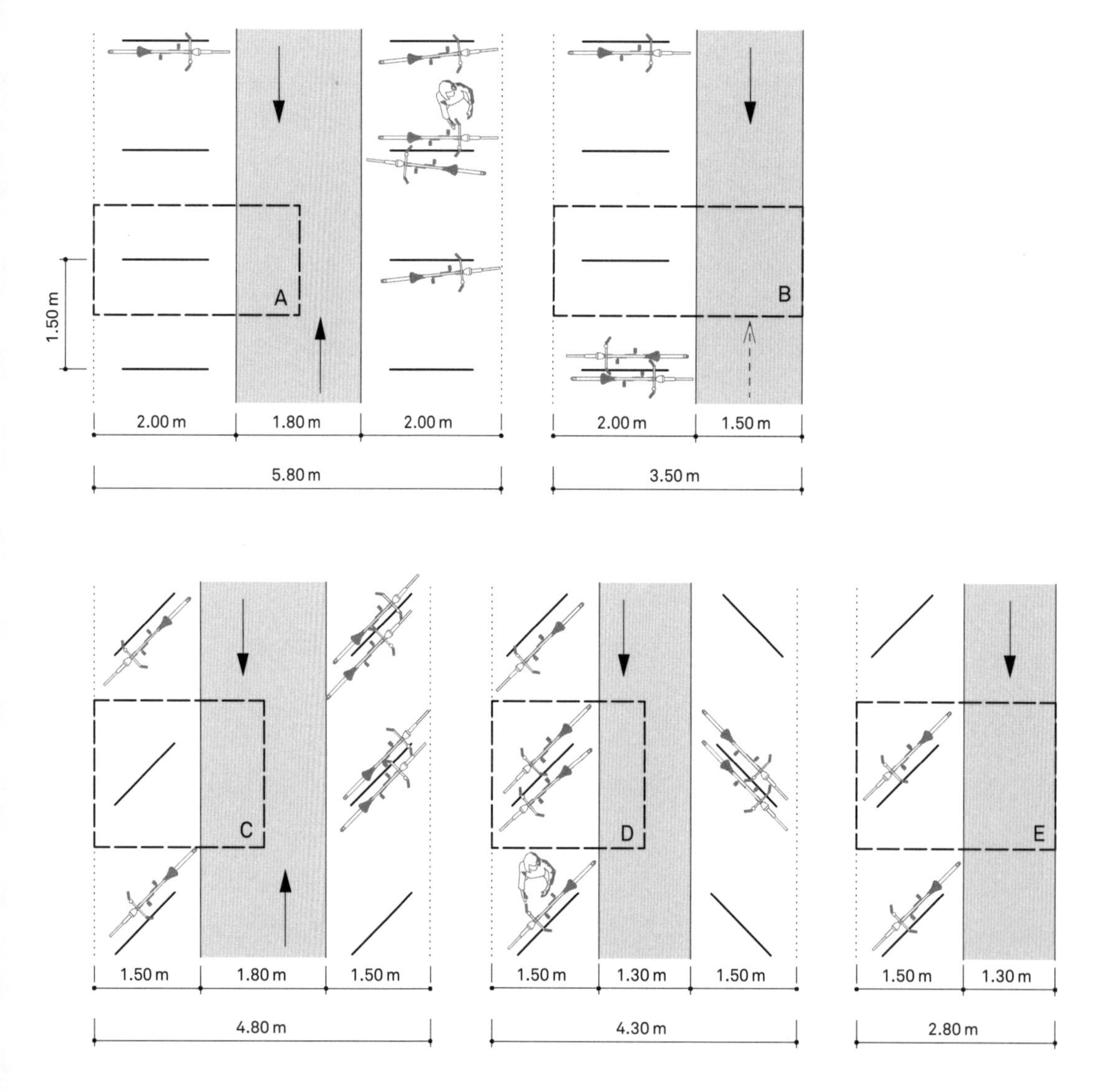

Figure 3.4.8 Widths of stalls and aisles for perpendicular and diagonal bicycle parking layouts

Parking Spaces for Motor Vehicles

The dimensioning of parking spaces is based on standard sizes of vehicles that are to be regarded as minimums. The generous dimensioning of parking spaces enables comfortable parking (including entering and exiting the car) and prevents both damage and injury as well as inconvenience. Nevertheless, since generously dimensioned facilities take up more space, a balance must be found. The basic dimensions for parking stalls are derived from the dimensions of the motor vehicles plus clearances and movement areas. In order to make optimum use of the space occupied by parking lots, residual areas can be laid out with stalls for compact or subcompact cars with shorter lengths than the standard. For the legal parking lot approval process, however, these are not included in the official count.

So it is more comfortable to enter and exit the car, a distance of 0.75 m should be planned between the parked vehicles and also to any boundaries at the sides. With a presumed vehicle width of 1.75 m and a vehicle length of 4.6 m, the resulting overall dimensions of the parking stall are 2.5 × 5 m, where the 5 m length comprises the depth from the lane edge plus the depth of the overhang strip.

Particularly in lots with multiple rows, the overhang strips can be designed as planted islands that promote infiltration of stormwater into the ground. For this purpose, the islands are usually formed as swales. Additionally, trees can be planted at a suitable spacing to shade the parking spaces.

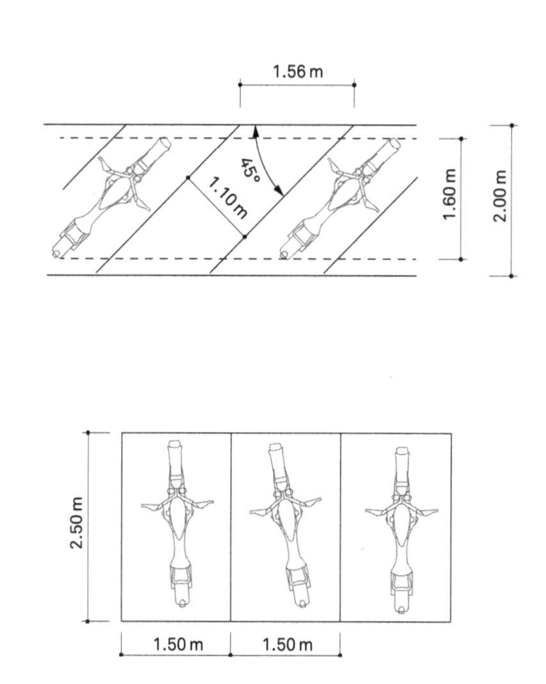

Figure 3.4.9 Basic dimensions for motorcycle parking

	Parking angle	Depth from lane edge	Width of overhang strip	Width of parking stall	Street frontage length l [m] needed while parking		Lane or roadway width g [m] needed while parking	
	α [gon]	t–ü	ü	b	Forward	Reverse	Forward	Reverse
Parallel parking	0			2.00 m	6.70 m [1]	5.70 m 5.20 m [2]	3.25 m	3.50 m
Angled parking	50 (45°)	4.15 m	0.70 m	2.50 m	3.54 m		3.00 m	
	60 (54°)	4.45 m	0.70 m	2.50 m	3.09 m		3.50 m	
	70 (63°)	4.60 m	0.70 m	2.50 m	2.81 m		4.00 m	
	80 (72°)	4.65 m	0.70 m	2.50 m	2.63 m		4.50 m	
	90 (81°)	4.55 m	0.70 m	2.50 m	2.53 m		5.25 m	
Perpendicular parking	100 (90°)	4.30 m	0.70 m	2.50 m	2.50 m	2.50 m	6.00 m	4.50 m

[1] Only applicable in special cases, for instance to avoid obstructions while reverse parking
[2] Average value without markings

Table 3.4.4 Dimensions of automobile parking spaces and aisles, for parallel, angled, and perpendicular parking

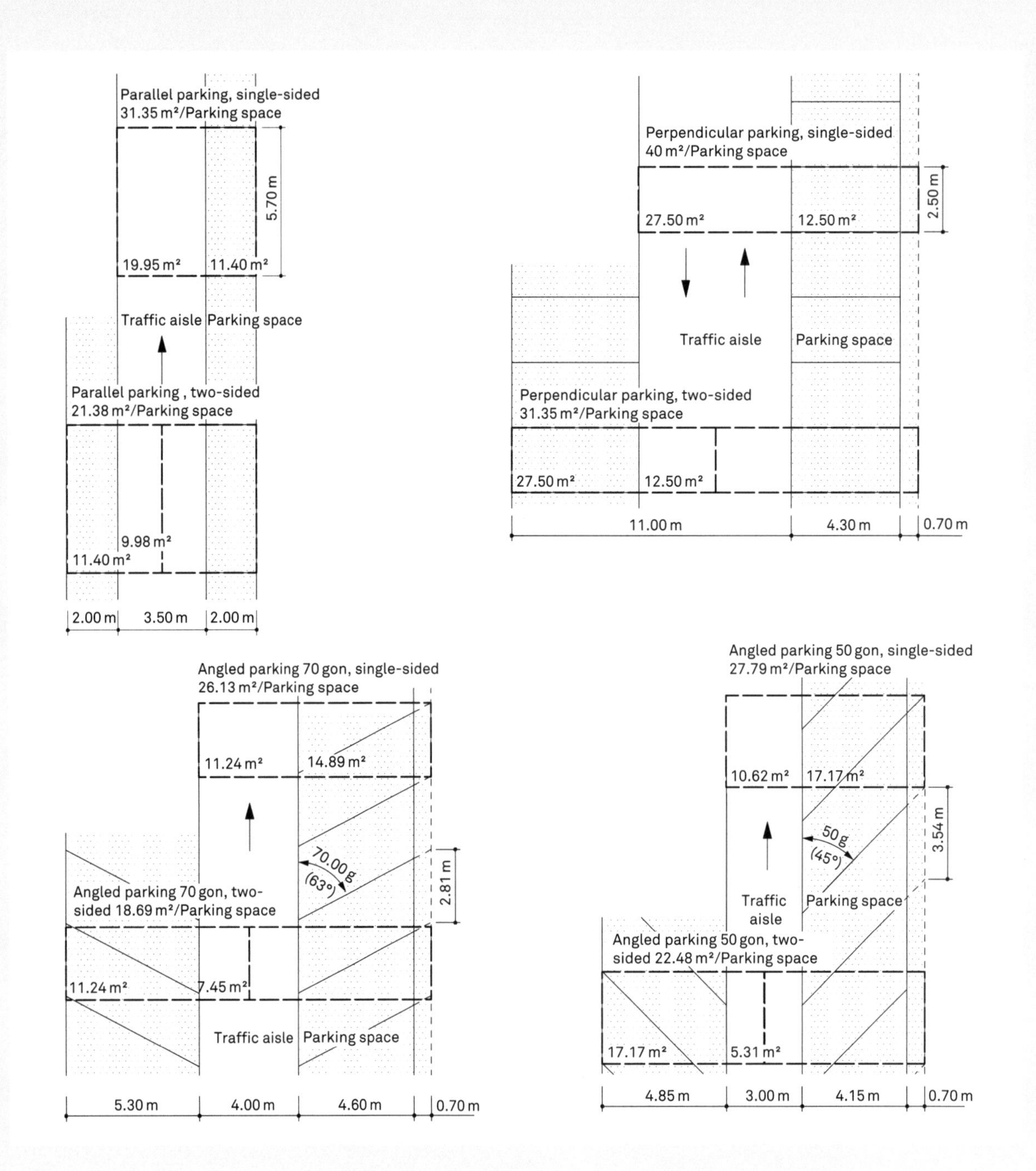

Figure 3.4.10 Dimensions of parking stalls and space requirements for automobiles in the street space as a function of the parking arrangement

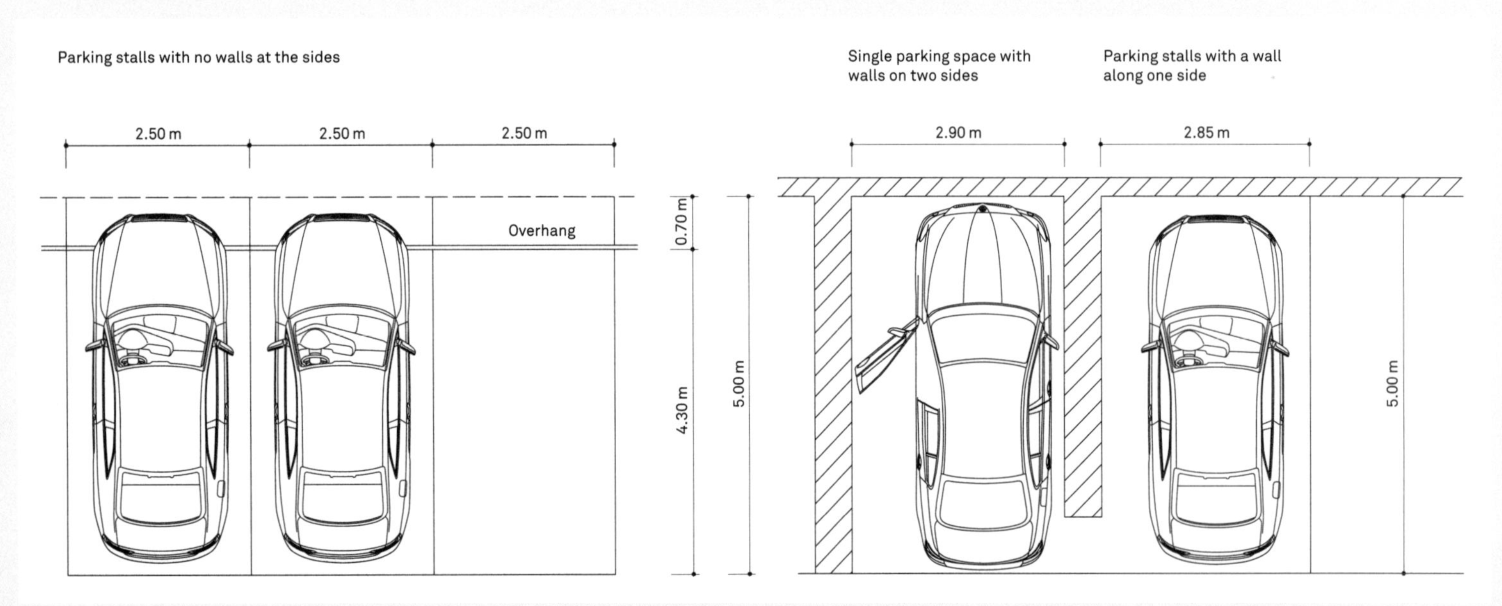

Figure 3.4.11 Exemplary layout of parking lots with perpendicular and angled parking

Automobile Parking Spaces for Wheelchair Users

When designing parking stalls for wheelchair users, attention must be given to ensure that (at least) one side has a clearance of 1.75 m and that there is direct barrier-free access to the walkway. The resulting minimum width of 3.5 m makes it possible to park as needed – perpendicularly or diagonally. → **Figure 3.4.12**

Parallel parking spaces are suitable for rear exit from the vehicle. Behind the usual stall length of 5 m, an additional maneuvering area of 2.5 m is to be kept free. Circulation space or pedestrian areas can share this area. For minivans, a minimum stall size of 3.5 × 7.5 m should be provided (see DIN 18040-1). In addition, a clear height of 2.5 m is needed. → **Figure 3.4.13**

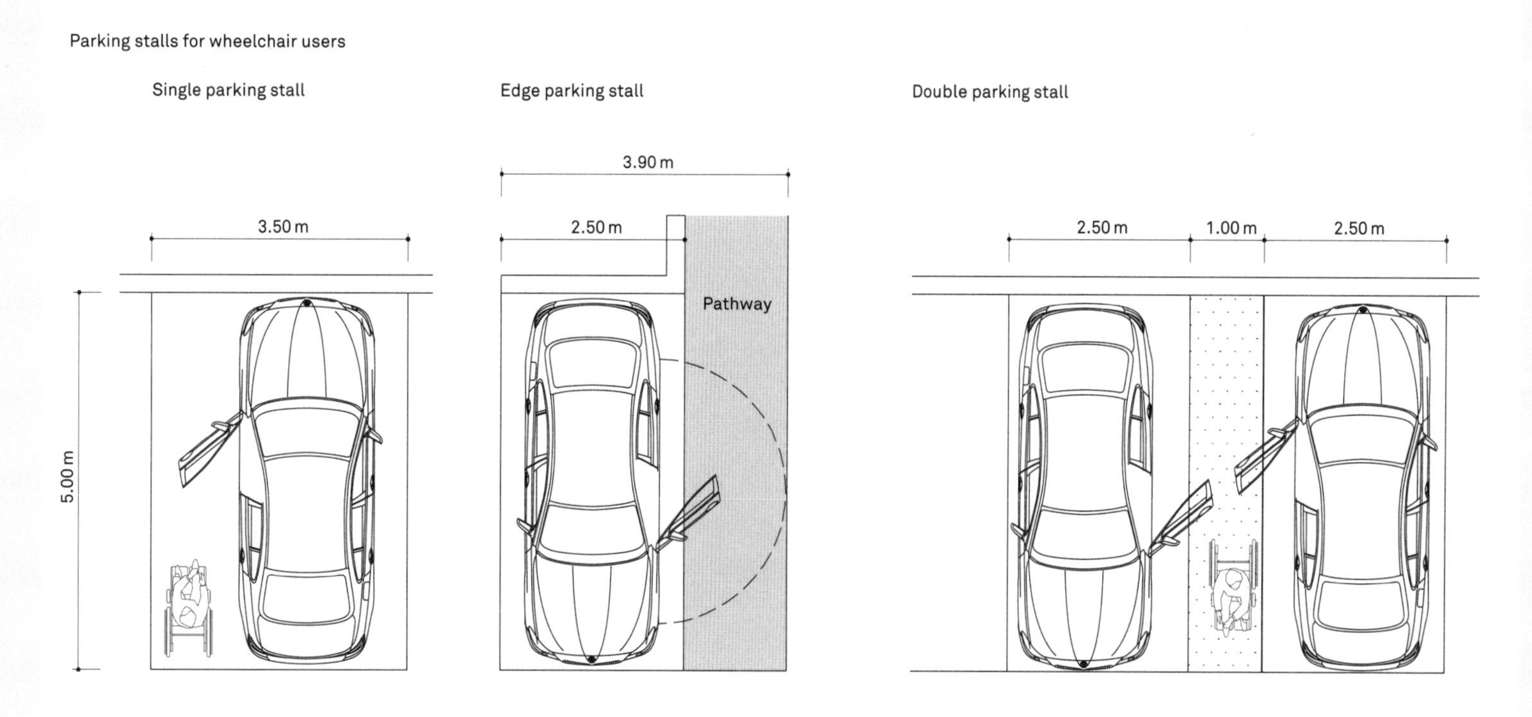

Figure 3.4.12 Dimensioning of parking stalls for wheelchair users – perpendicular parking

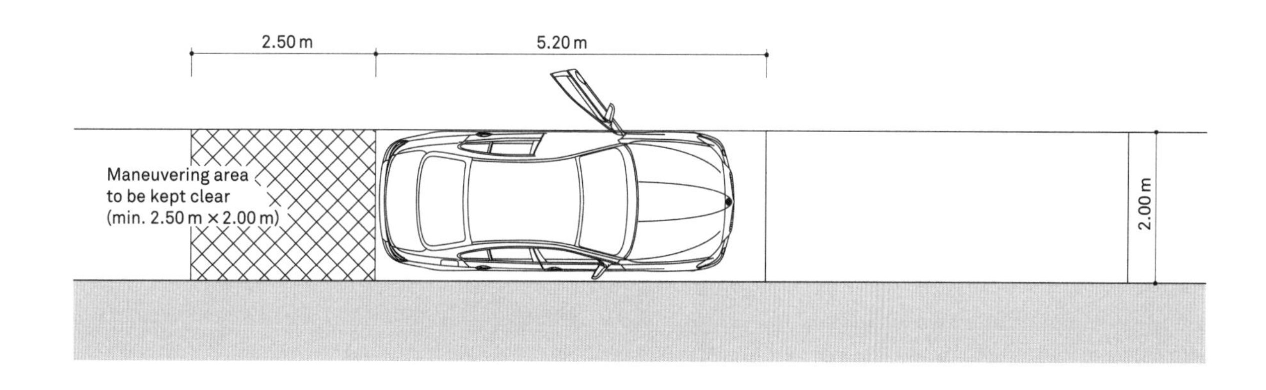

Figure 3.4.13 Dimensioning of parking stalls for wheelchair users – parallel parking

Parking Spaces for Trucks, Buses, and Motorhomes

Especially for larger vehicles, the layout of parking spaces results in an increased need to maneuver. This must be given special consideration when planning loading areas. In the vicinity of tourist destinations, consideration should be given to areas for parking intercity buses and recreational vehicles. For major arterial roads and highways, their use by trucks must also be considered and appropriate parking areas must be provided. These should be laid out so that the parking space is entered by turning to the left and exited by turning to the right (or exactly reversed for left-hand traffic, e.g. in UK). Parking spaces for trucks and buses should always be paved with an impermeable surface.

When determining the basic dimensions for motorhome parking spaces their use should be taken into account and provisions should be made for sufficient space to comfortably access the cabin. Hence individual bays measuring 10.00 m × 5.00 m are recommended. If the parking spaces are conceived for prolonged stays, more distance between the individual spaces can be provided for greater privacy.

When establishing spaces for recreational vehicles outside of camping sites, a useful addition is the provision of utility hookups (supply and disposal).

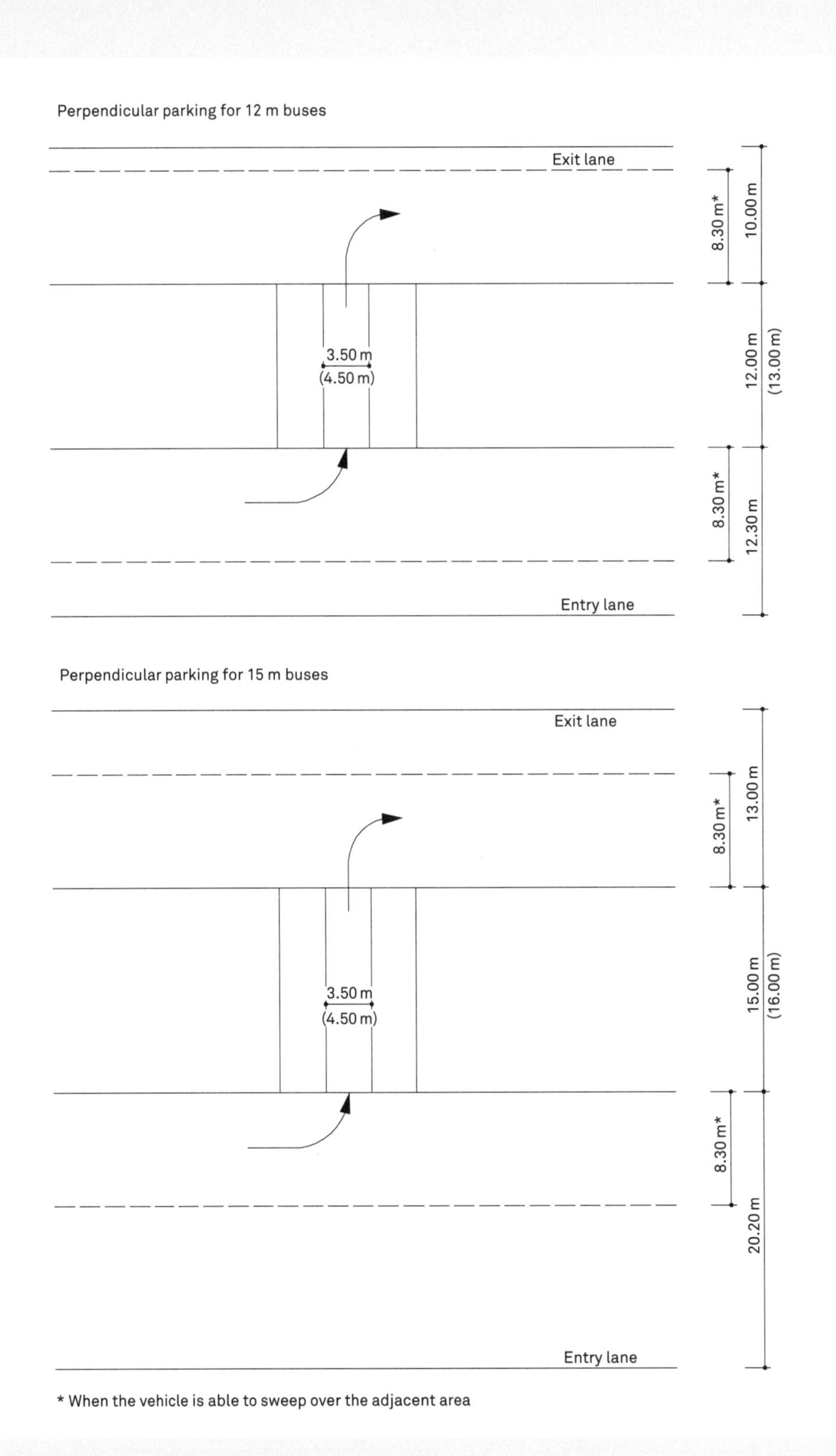

Figure 3.4.14 Basic dimensions for truck and bus parking – perpendicular spaces

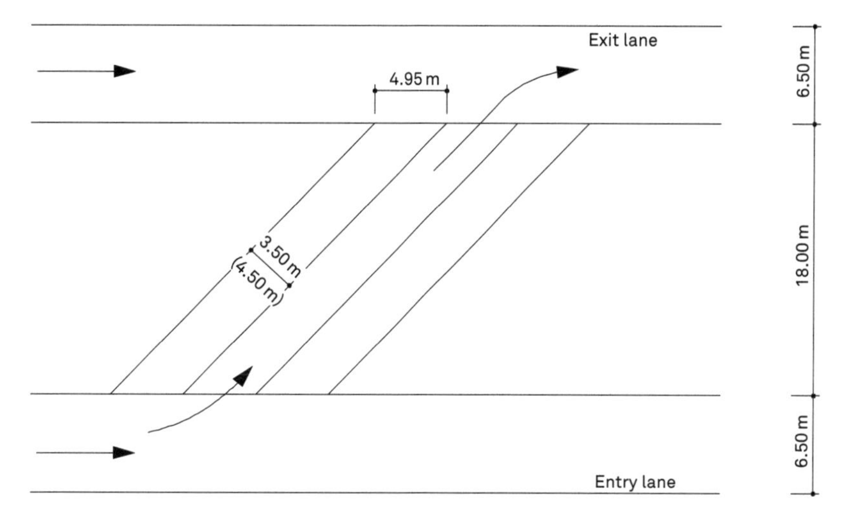

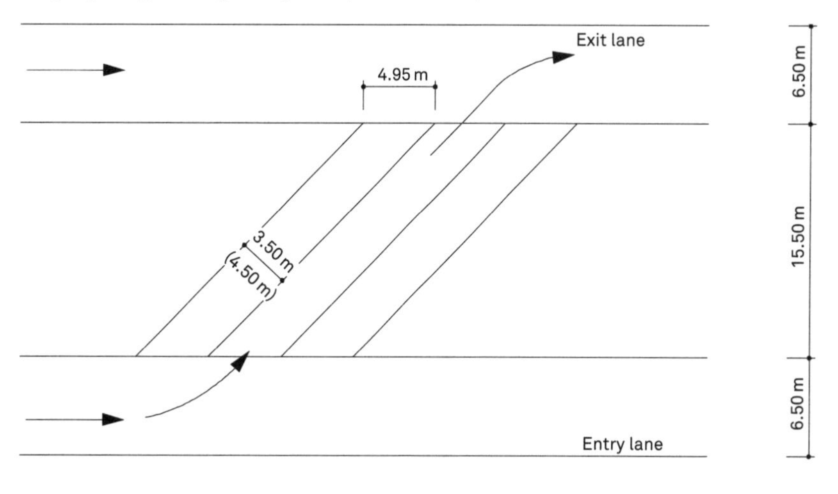

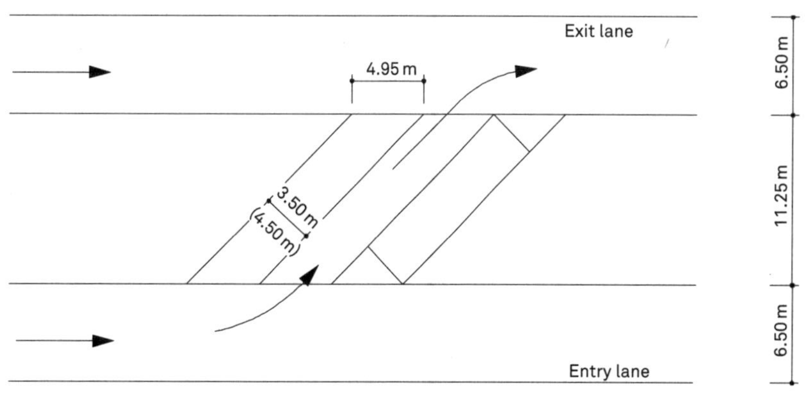

Figure 3.4.15 Basic dimensions for truck and bus parking – angled spaces

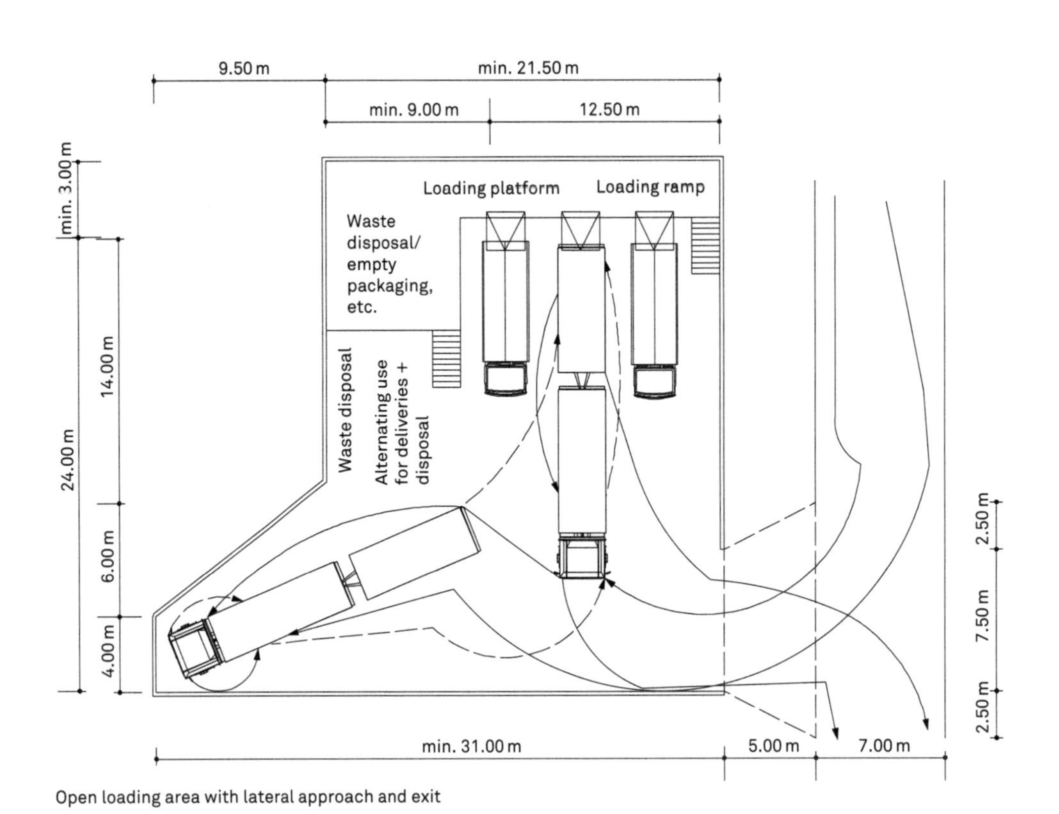

Open loading area with lateral approach and exit

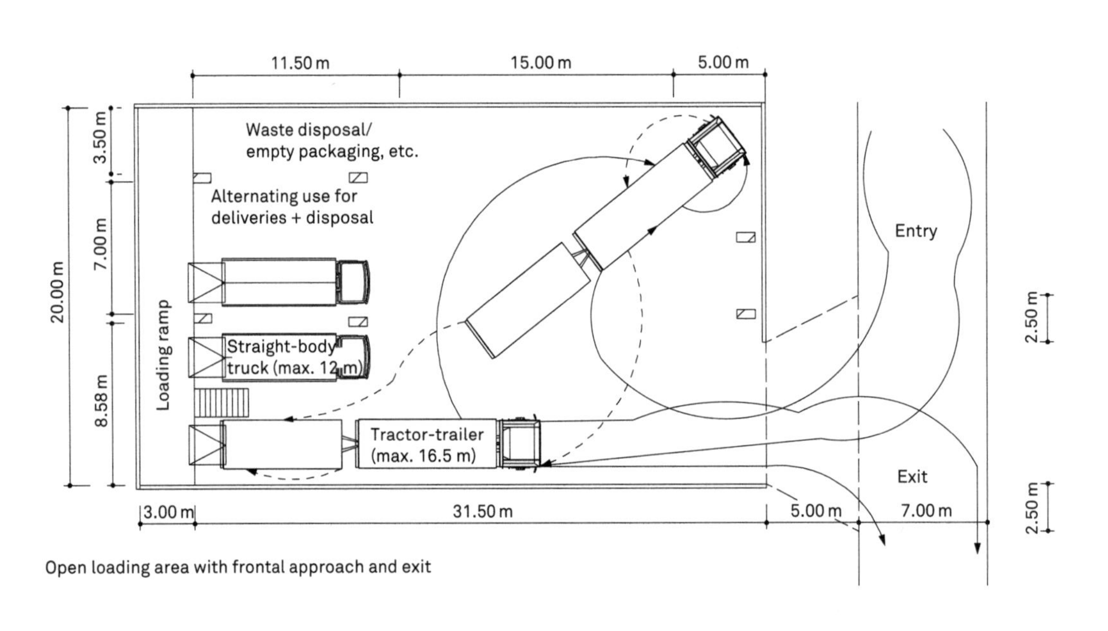

Open loading area with frontal approach and exit

Figure 3.4.16 Examples of loading areas

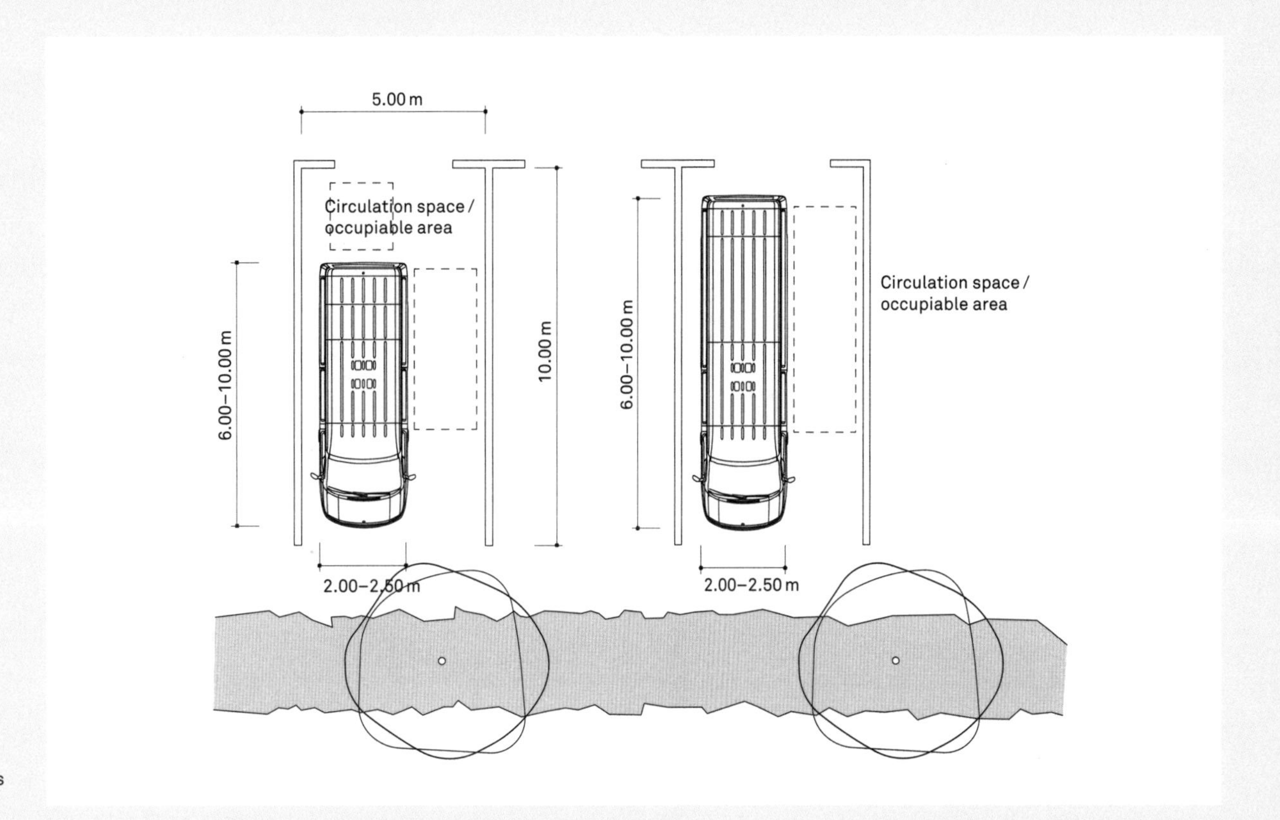

Figure 3.4.17 Basic dimensions for motorhome parking spaces

3 Elements
3.5 Waste Container Areas

3.5 Waste Container Areas

Waste disposal in outdoor facilities has significance in the public sphere mostly in the form of garbage baskets and other waste receptacles that are placed in green spaces and parks, along streets and sidewalks, or at playgrounds and sports fields. In addition, areas for collection containers for glass and other recyclable materials must be provided in the public street space. Finally, corresponding collection points for the temporary storage of household garbage or commercial waste must be provided at buildings.

In planning such waste container areas, attention must be given to their dimensioning, siting, and access. Conditions governing the container areas as well as characteristic and recommended values are found in the pertinent waste-management legislation, regulations, and guidelines, such as the following in Germany: VDI Guideline "Abfallsammlung in Gebäuden und auf Grundstücken" [Waste management in buildings and on grounds] and "Unfallverhütungsvorschrift: Müllbeseitigung" [Accident prevention regulations for waste disposal], from the German statutory accident insurer (DGUV). Detailed requirements for container sites, transport routes, and access paths are found in municipalities' waste statutes and/or they are governed by the local waste removal companies (terms of service). This results in site-specific differences, so the following information is based on minimum and maximum values.

The recyclable materials that are collected centrally or locally are also governed by location-specific rules, resulting in different requirements for garbage disposal at buildings.

The increasing separation of wastes and decentralization of garbage collection points leads to greater space needs in many municipalities, such that in places, independent of the amount of waste, six different containers are needed for organic waste, paper, glass, lightweight packaging, and recyclable materials as well as ordinary household garbage / residual waste.

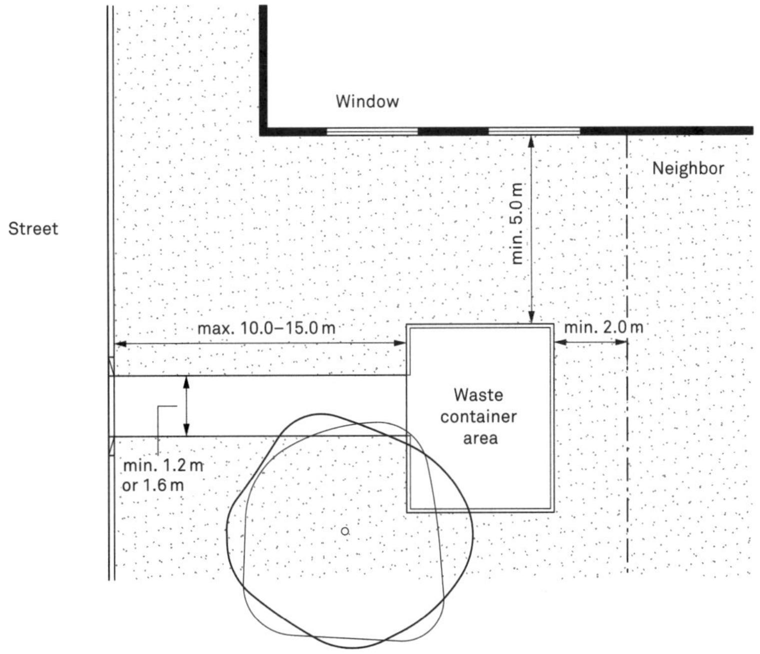

Figure 3.5.1 Position of the waste container area on the property

Location

Refuse Collection Points

A refuse collection point must be easily reachable and accessible at all times, both for the residents as well as for the waste removal companies. The container area should be adequately integrated into the overall site in such a way that the routes taken by individual parties are not too long. A location along the streetside property line is to be given fundamental preference. If this is not possible due to spatial limitations, a maximum distance must not be exceeded between the waste container area and the place where the collection vehicle stops. The length of the transport route should generally not exceed 10 to 15 m. In individual cases, the distances traveled across public thoroughfares can be ignored when calculating the transport route distance. In some cases it is necessary to place the waste containers a maximum of 2 m from public streets or on the front yard line. Exact details are governed by the pertinent waste disposal statutes.

A grade-level connection for the approach should be made whenever possible. When ramps are unavoidable, they shall not exceed a slope of 2 % – in exceptional cases up to a maximum of 6 % – and obstacles such as steps or channels are to be avoided; for large containers (i.e., Dumpsters) a dropped curb shall be provided.

A paved approach with a minimum width of 1.5 to 1.6 m is commonly provided. For containers up to a volume of 1,100 liters, a minimum width of 1.2 m is sufficient.

Particularly when storing hygienically sensitive refuse (organic waste), the containers should be kept at a distance of at least 5 m from occupied rooms and at least 2 m from property lines. Moreover, a well-ventilated location with as much shade as possible should be chosen.

Screening fences, hedges, trees, or climbing plants enable the container area to be integrated into the residential environment, but a possibility for the residents to maintain oversight should not be excluded.

The collection area and approach are to be illuminated sufficiently. The collection area should have a hard-wearing paved surface, such as concrete, asphalt, or paving blocks, that is suitably drained. → Table 3.5.1 Especially in and around preschools, a location beyond the reach of children is to be chosen for the waste containers.

	Berlin	Vienna	Zurich
Location	On private property; easily accessible; max. distance to street 10 to 15 m; minimum distance to occupied areas 5 m and to property lines 2 m	On private property; easily accessible; max. distance to street 10 m; minimum distance to occupied areas/ rooms 6 m	On private property (or, if space is insufficient, also on public property for a fee), avoid locating at underpasses, courtyard entrances, and courtyard passageways; placement of the containers at pickup location for waste removal
Paving	Hard-wearing pavement, e.g., concrete, asphalt, interlocking pavement blocks; load-bearing capacity of 2,000 N per wheel	Nonslip paving surface, e.g., concrete, asphalt, concrete pavers	Hard-wearing pavement (e.g., asphalt, slabs), curb approx. 10 cm high
Sunlight	Shady location	n/s	n/s
Lighting	Collection area and approach must be sufficiently illuminated	Must be sufficiently illuminated	n/s
Ventilation	Adequate fresh air supply for obstructed outdoor areas	Adequate fresh air supply for obstructed outdoor areas	n/s
Minimum size of area, per container	2 × 1.6 m for 1,100 L 2 × 1.2 m for 660 L 0.8 × 0.8 m for 60 to 240 L; 1 to 1.5 m wide path within the site; 20 cm space between containers and to any wall	2.1 × 1.5 m (+ 1.90 m) for 2,200 L containers 1.4 × 1.4 m (+ 1.40 m) for 1,100 L containers 1.4 × 1 m (+ 1.40 m) for 770 L containers 0.7 × 0.7 m (+ 1.20 m) for 240 L and 120 L containers; Space for maneuvering in front of the containers; 10 cm space between containers and wall, between containers max. 50 cm	0.4 m² for 140 L containers 0.7 m² for 240 L containers 1.7 m² for 770 L containers
Containers	Size and material in accordance with standard EN 840-1 to -6 for 60, 120, 240, 660 and 1,100 L containers	2,200 L, 1,100 L, 770 L, 240 L, and 120 L containers	Size and material in accordance with standard EN 840-1 to -6 for 140, 240, and 770 L containers
Approach	1.2–1.6 m wide paths, obstacle-free approach	1–2 m wide paths, 1–2 m clear width and 2 m clear height	No obstacles
Gradient	At ground level, max. 12.5 % slope (depending on container size) in exceptional cases	At ground level, max. 2 % slope (depending on container sizes);	At ground level, max. 5 % slope,
Access to container area	1.5 to 2 m clear width and 2 m clear height	1 to 2 m clear width and 2 m clear height (depending on max. container size)	
Guidelines	BSR: "Grundlagen für die Gestaltung von Standorten und Transportwegen für Abfallbehälter" [Basis for the design of locations and transport routes for waste containers], VDI Guideline "Waste Management in Buildings and on Ground," "Unfallverhütungsvorschrift: Müllbeseitigung" [Accident prevention regulations: Waste disposal] from the DGUV, waste statutes of the municipalities, terms of service of the waste removal companies	ÖNORM 2025, Bauordnung für Wien [Vienna building code], Wiener Abfallwirtschaftsgesetz (Wr. AWG) [Vienna waste management act]	Verordnung für die Abfallbewirtschaftung in der Stadt Zürich (VAZ) [Regulation for waste management in the city of Zurich], terms of service for ERZ Entsorgung + Recycling Zürich

Table 3.5.1 Requirements for garbage container areas, comparison of Berlin – Vienna – Zurich

Dimensions and Characteristics

Space Requirements for Waste Collection Vehicles

Streets used by waste collection vehicles (garbage trucks) should have the following dimensions: minimum width of 3.55 m (2.55 m + [2 × 0.5 m] safety clearance) for streets without oncoming traffic and minimum width of 4.75 m for streets with oncoming traffic. They should be designed for a vehicle with a permissible total weight of 28 metric tons. In the case of a cul-de-sac, turning facilities must be created; these should provide no less than a minimum diameter of 22 m or at least take into account the turning curves for the waste collection vehicles that will be used. → **Figure 3.5.2** The access road must be at least 5.5 m wide until the turnaround. A clear height of 4–4.2 m is required where trucks must drive through a passage. Passageways may not be obstructed by hanging branches or overhanging trees.

Driving in reverse with garbage trucks is generally not allowed (backing up while turning is not considered driving in reverse). Driving in reverse is only permitted when a qualified person instructs the driver (vehicle with min. two-man crew), the vehicle is equipped with a rear area monitoring system, or the area at risk is sufficiently visible in rearview mirrors. In turnarounds, it should be possible to reverse direction by backing up only one or at most two times. (See Berufsgenossenschaft für Fahrzeughaltungen, 2008) → **Figure 3.5.3**

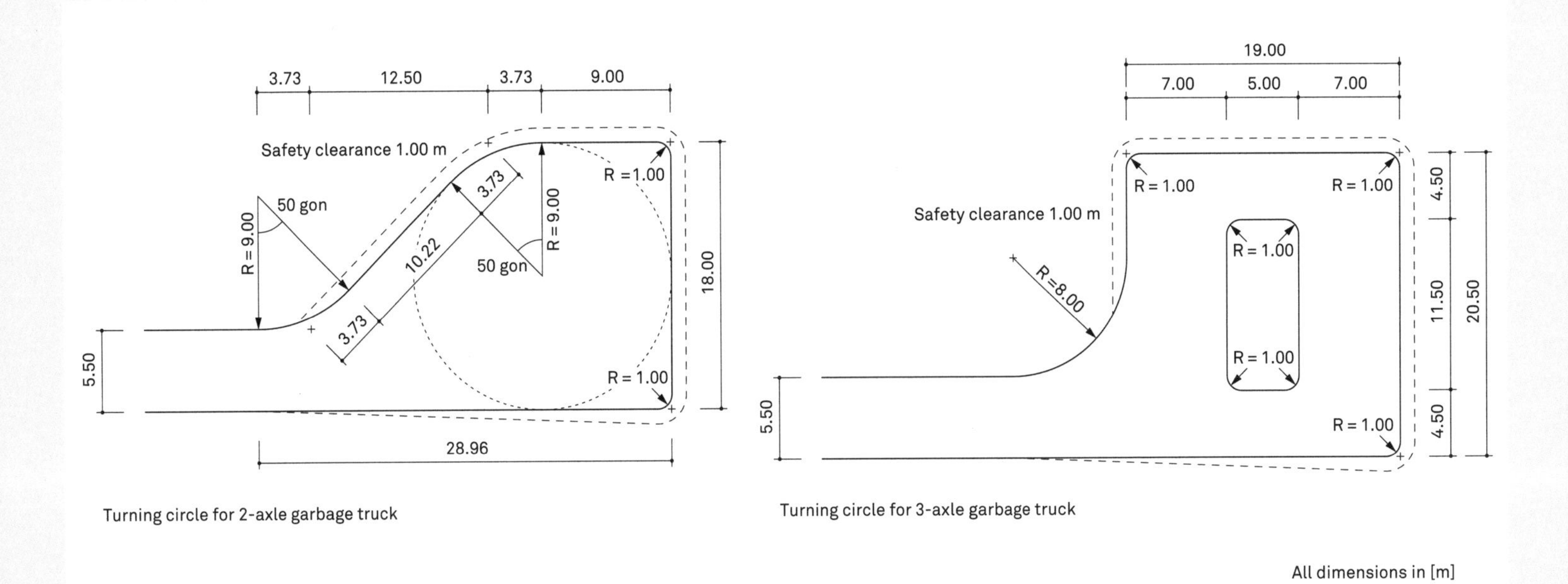

Figure 3.5.2 Space requirement for a turning circle for two- and three-axle garbage trucks (as per RASt 06)

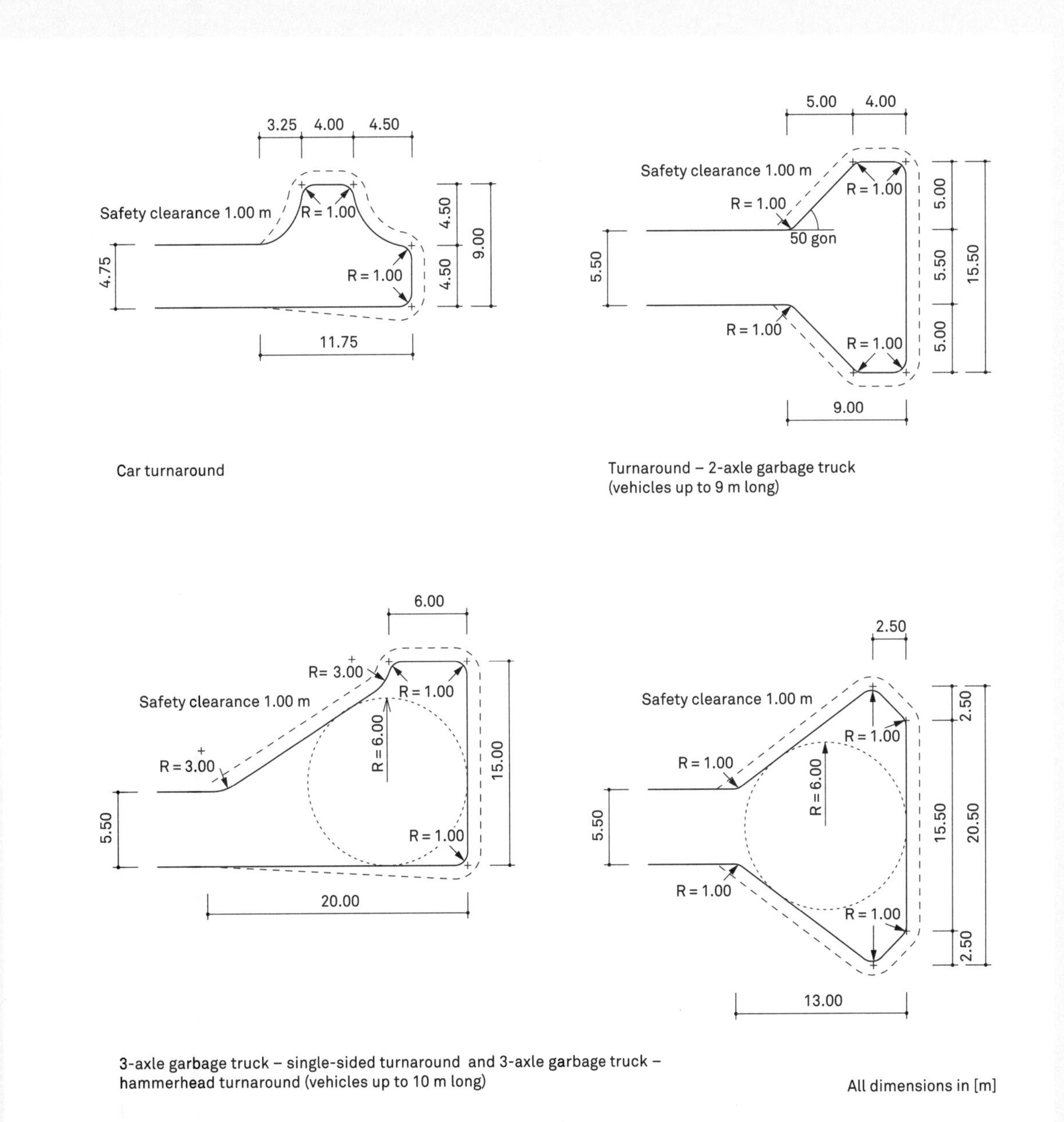

Figure 3.5.3 Turnarounds for two- and three-axle waste collection vehicles

Size of Waste Containers

The capacities of the receptacles in the waste container area are a consequence of the size of the housing complex or facility being served, the amount of waste generated per person per week, and the frequency of waste removal.

The following information from Munich's department of waste management, Abfallwirtschaftsbetrieb München (AWM), are based on empirical values established over many years and can be used to gain an initial estimate of the container quantities and sizes. → Table 3.5.2 and 3.5.3

Many waste removal companies offer individualized consultation as well as an online-calculator.

The size of the container area is determined by the quantities and sizes of the needed receptacles and by the applicable local technical requirements. So it is easier to fill and remove the receptacles, a 1–1.5 m wide lane should be provided within the container area.

Dumpsters with capacities of 1,100 L and 660 L require a minimum area of 2 × 1.6 m and 2 × 1.2 m respectively; 60 L to 240 L containers require a minimum area of 0.8 × 0.8 m → Table 3.4.3

The entrances to the container area should have a minimum width of 1.5 m and a height of 2 m. The clear height of roofed container areas may not be less than 2 m.

Number of persons	Residual waste container	Paper container	Organic waste container
3–4	1 × 120 L	1 × 120 L	1 × 120 L
7–8	1 × 240 L	1 × 240 L	1 × 120 L
20–25	1 × 770 L	3 × 240 L	1 × 120 L
30–35	1 × 1,100 L	1 × 110 L	1 × 240 L

Table 3.5.2 Orientation values for the quantity and size of residual waste and recycling containers for residential buildings (source: Recommendations of Abfallwirtschaftsbetrieb München [AWM], 2011)

Use	Amount/week						
	Residual waste	Paper	Organic	Food waste	Plastic	Metal	Glass
Office per employee	10 L	10 L	1–2 L	–	0.7 L	0.5 L	0.5 L
Daycare facility per 100 children	1,100 L	240 L	120 L	–	–	–	–
School per student	4 L	2 L	0.5 L	–	–	–	–
Nursing home/Hospital per bed	110 L	20 L	2 L	5 L	5 L	2 L	2 L
Restaurant per 100 meals	45 L	15 L	–	15 L	8 L	8 L	8 L
Bed and breakfast per bed	7.5 L	7 L	1 L	–	–	–	–
Hotel ****/***** per bed	85 L	20 L	2 L	5 L	5 L	2 L	2 L

Table 3.5.3 Orientation values for the waste generated in commercial establishments (Source: Recommendations of Abfallwirtschaftsbetrieb München (AWM), 2011)

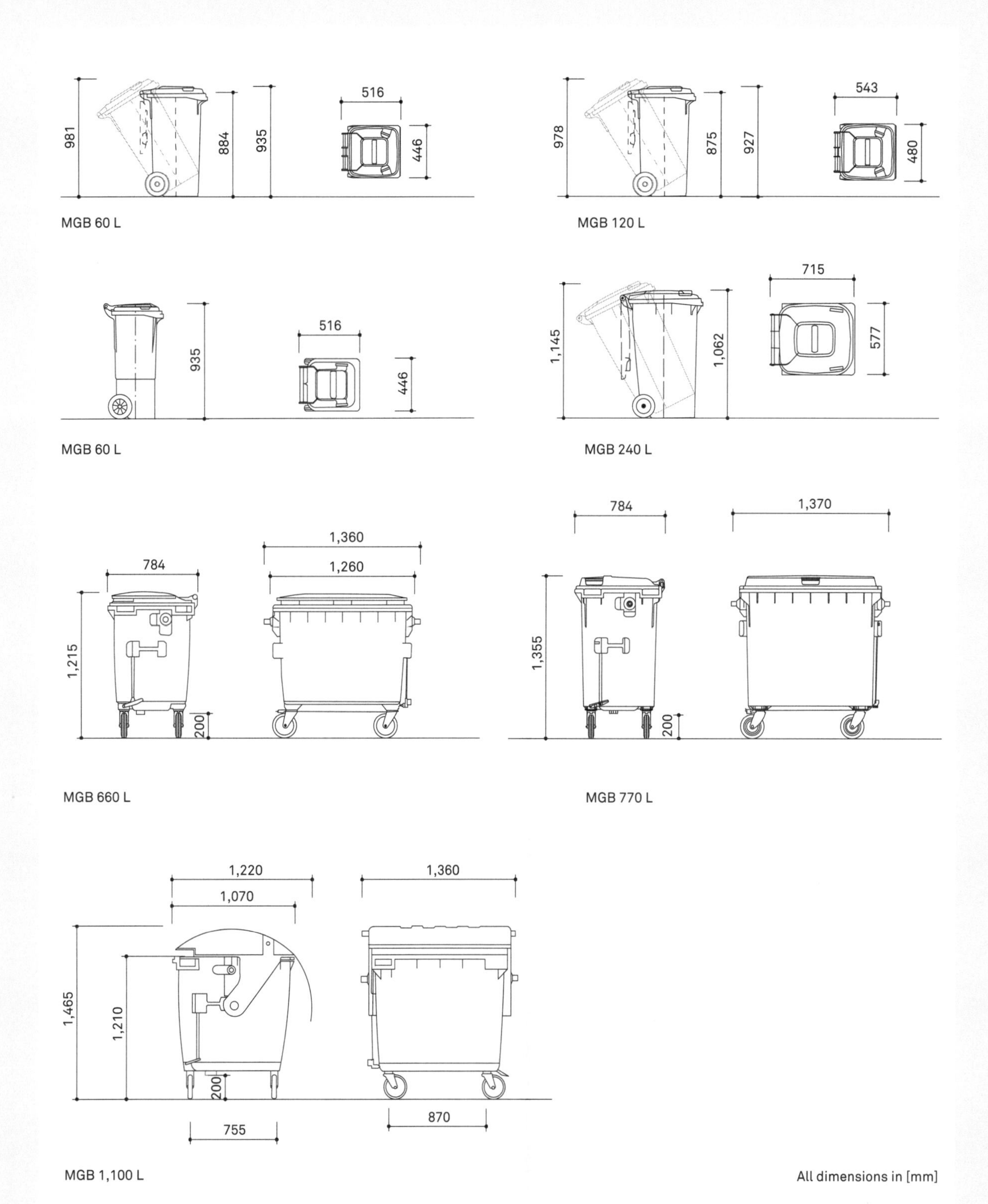

Figure 3.5.4 Common waste container sizes, in mm

Technical Devices

For safe transport of the collection containers, waste removal companies occasionally require hold-open devices on doors and gates used.

Building Codes and Regulatory Approval

Newly established or reconfigured waste container areas are subject to authorization and should be clarified in advance with the local waste removal company.

3 Elements
3.6 Boundary Enclosures and Railings

3.6 Boundary Enclosures and Railings

The construction of a boundary enclosure for a plot of land or a particular area can serve to identify property ownership or to prevent (unauthorized) entry or exit. Moreover, special functions are offered by noise barrier walls, privacy walls, and windbreaks.

In open spaces designed for specific purposes, use of a boundary enclosure – as a ball stop fence surrounding sports areas, for example – is of significant importance.

Fences, walls, hedges, trenches, berms, rows of trees, sunken areas, and raised areas all represent possible types of boundary enclosures. Depending on their permeability and height, they can have an impact on the microclimate both in front of and behind the enclosure, particularly in terms of temperature differences, cast shadows, and wind speed.

Railings and parapets serve as fall protection along paths, on plazas and squares, bridges, and stairs, and along bikeways. Depending on their design, they can also assume the functions of visual screening and wind protection. Parapets are primarily opaque constructions made of solid materials, for example masonry or concrete, whereas railings are open structures that might be made of metal or wood. Parapets with a railing as an upper termination are a common combination of both types.

Railings must always be provided with an infill, made of, for example, round or flat bars, nets, (punched) sheet metal, or safety glass. On stairs that are directly within or on a berm or which are flanked by a wall, a simple handrail (without infill) is sufficient.

For areas where a guard contradicts the intended use, no railing is required. This usually applies to docks, swimming pools, and ponds. A boundary enclosure may be necessary when, for example, a pond or a water basin is located in an area that is frequently visited by children.

Location

Enclosure Requirement

Boundary enclosures are generally always to be constructed on the property, or directly on the property line in the case of shared boundary enclosures.

In Germany, the enclosure requirement and setback rules as well as stipulations concerning the type, height, and design of the boundary enclosures are prescribed in the applicable building code, in the state laws concerning the respective interests of neighbors and/or by the binding land-use plan or other local building regulations. In general, the owners of built-up or commercially used properties within a built-up district are, upon request of the owner of the neighboring property, obligated to enclose their properties along shared borders with fences, hedges, or walls. In such instances, a customary boundary enclosure can be required. If there is no customary method or style identifiable in the boundary enclosures of the surrounding properties, an enclosure with a height of 1.2 m is normally required. In some countries and German federal states, each property owner must erect a boundary enclosure along the shared border with the neighboring property to the right, but elsewhere this is not an obligation.

For agricultural areas outside of a built-up district, a minimum setback distance must usually be observed. This is 0.5 m or more.

To protect the overall appearance of the landscape, the streetscape, and the townscape, design regulations are issued by some communities and federal states. For example, in Austria, the Styrian zoning ordinance provides that "boundary enclosures and living fences (...) are to be constructed or preserved in such a way that neither the streetscape, the townscape, nor the landscape will be affected nor will a danger to persons and property be effected. Boundary enclosures may not be constructed in front of the street frontage line."

Effectiveness of Boundary Enclosures

In addition to the impact of the type of construction on immediately adjacent sites (→ **Table 3.6.1**), the design should also take into consideration the functional effectiveness and spatial perception of a boundary enclosure. Heights up to 0.5 m (approximately knee height) can be climbed over easily and are therefore perceived by children and adults as the simple demarcation of an area more than as a boundary restricting access. Heights of up to 1.2/1.5 m (approximately chest height), however, clearly indicate the assertion of property rights or define another function, yet do not act as a deterrent. For children, this height already represents an unequivocal barrier.

Heights above eye level indicate a distinct separation of the areas. Walls and solid fences of this height also block views of the property. Depending on the height and thickness or the material choice itself, this type of boundary can appear forbidding and uninviting. An offset in height can also be perceived as a spatial separation and can replace a boundary enclosure under certain circumstances. → **Figure 3.6.1**

	Open	Solid
Protective Function	Limited protection	Visual privacy, wind protection, sun shading, noise abatement, emission control
Sunlight	Interesting play of shadows	100% shading with northern exposure
Air Circulation	Given	Air turbulence at the base
Soil Moisture	Rainwater can penetrate, low risk of drying out or excessive moisture	Areas sheltered from the wind often remain untouched by rain; southern exposures heat up and allow water to evaporate faster, whereas northern exposures suffer from continuous dampness (can also be an asset, depending on climatic conditions → water collection in dry areas)
Infill Planting	Conditions usually same as elsewhere on site	Can, in contrast to the surroundings, constitute a special location that is exceptionally warm → reflected radiation on walls), shady, or moist, depending on the particular exposure

Table 3.6.1 Influence of solid and open construction on the site

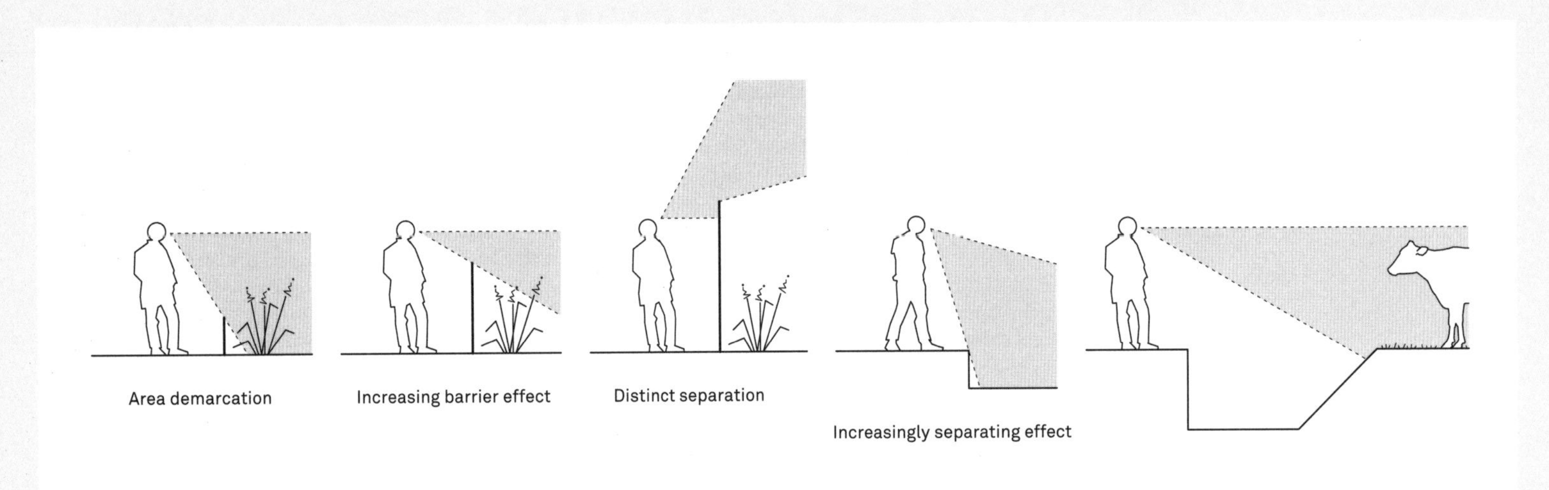

Figure 3.6.1 Impact of heights (and depths) and their barrier effect

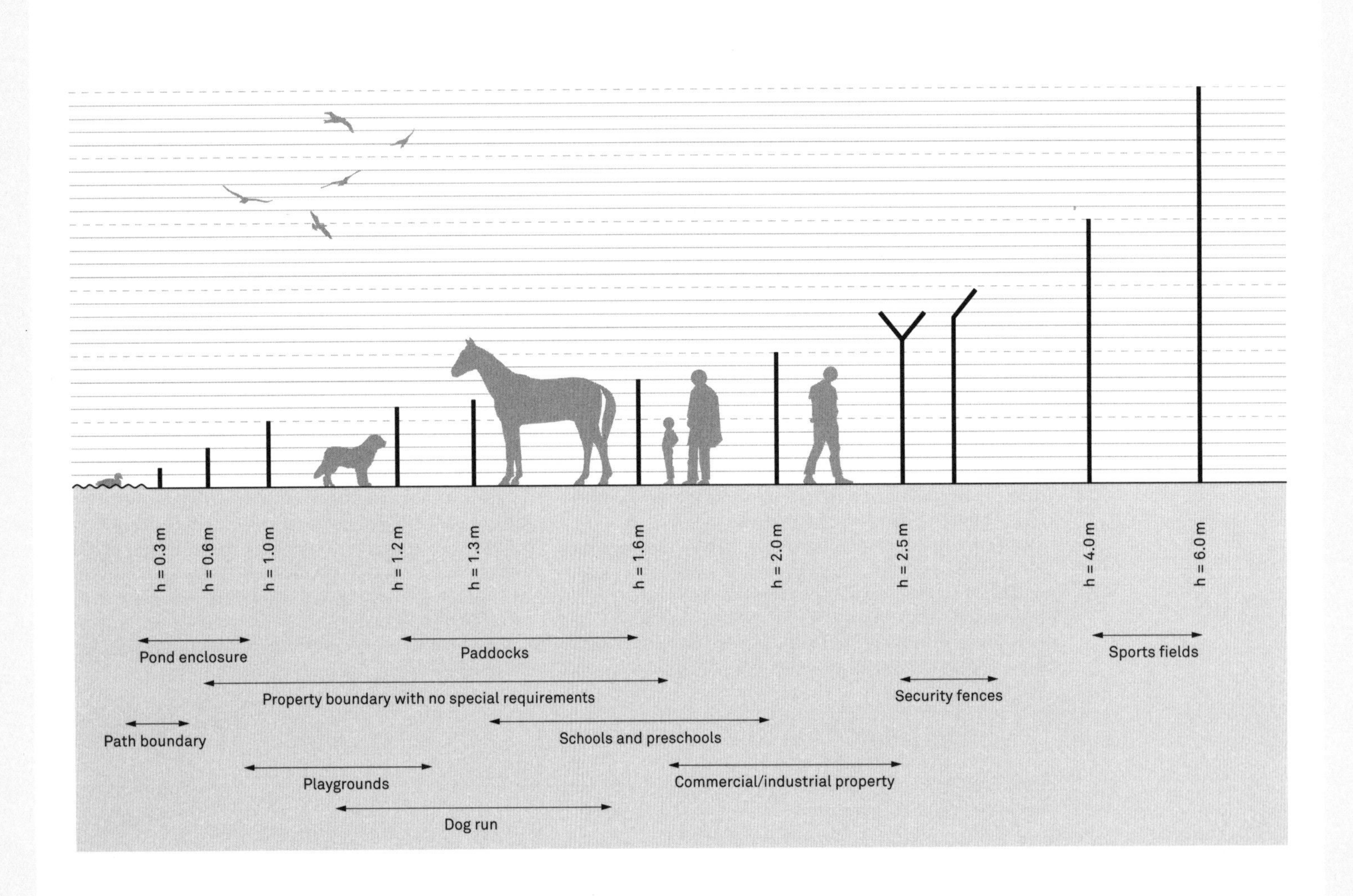

Figure 3.6.2 Heights (minimum/maximum) of boundary enclosures for specific purposes

Dimensions and Characteristics

Heights of Boundary Enclosures for Specific Purposes

Many areas require a boundary enclosure for a specific purpose. Fences surrounding ball sports areas, for instance, should be at least 3–4 m high, and areas used for dog runs should be enclosed with a fence at least 1 m high, preferably 1.2 m or higher. By contrast, playgrounds can, from a design standpoint, also be enclosed in other effective ways. According to DIN 18034 for playgrounds and outdoor play areas, the enclosure is effective only when ways of leaving the playing area are clearly perceptible for the children. For the purposes of social control, the boundary enclosures of playgrounds should be open and built to a height of 1 m.

Types of Construction for Boundary Enclosures

Depending on the location and use, there may be restrictions in the materials suitable for selection. Wire mesh fencing often represents the least expensive variant, but is comparatively unstable and can be easily trampled down. For sports fields and especially for areas used for ball sports as well as for dog runs, an advantageous type of construction is one that is simultaneously open and sturdy, such as welded wire fencing. Net-like ball stop systems can, however, also be used in individual cases. In addition, sports facilities require sound absorptive means of construction.

The size of openings and the spaces between the horizontal and vertical elements should be ≤ 12 cm or ≥ 23 cm in order to avoid creating a trapping hazard. For playgrounds and areas serving schools and preschools, the spacing should never exceed 12 cm. → **Table 3.6.2, chapter 4.2 and 4.3**

Privacy Screens

Privacy screens along the property line are, as a rule, permissible when certain dimensions and setback distances are observed. Setbacks of at least 0.5 m from the neighboring property and fence heights of up to 1.8 m represent average values for guidance. Depending on local laws concerning the respective interests of neighbors or the design statutes of individual communities, however, other requirements can apply. Furthermore, for duplex houses and townhouses, special provisions often permit privacy screens or terrace partitions with a height of up to 2 m directly on or along the property line.

Noise Abatement Walls and Noise Control Berms

To reduce acoustic emissions, noise control berms and noise barrier walls can be used. Plantable noise barriers facilitate integration of the design into their surroundings and offer an additional dampening effect. To achieve the required heights, designs with trapezoidal cross sections are often needed, so that widths of 1.5 to 2 m can be expected at the ground. Compared to noise barrier walls, pure noise control berms take up lots of space and therefore cannot be used everywhere. → **Figure 3.6.4** Cambered noise barrier walls are more effective than straight walls, so these can be designed to be shorter on the whole.

In general, one can presume a noise reduction of 15–20 dB(A) behind a protective berm or a barrier wall – depending on the location and height of the immission point (place of impact). The noise reduction achieved at the ground level is always considerably greater than, for example, on the second floor of a building. Hence the height of the immission point also determines the necessary height of the protective berm or barrier wall. → **Figure 3.6.5** Noise reduction by means of trees and shrubs requires disproportionately larger areas in comparison to walls or berms and can only be put to effective use in the open landscape, for parks and other large green spaces, or with a sufficiently dense stock of trees and shrubs. For new establishment, a development period of several years or even decades must be taken into account. → **Figure 3.6.6**

Use	Material	Construction method	Special characteristics
Generally-applicable		Size of openings and spaces between horizontal and vertical elements: max. 12 cm (France: 11 cm) or min. 23 cm	
Playgrounds	No restriction	Low or open construction that allows the grounds to be seen. Size of openings and spaces between horizontal and vertical elements: max. 12 cm (France: 11 cm)	Do not use pointed, sharp-edged, or protruding elements or barbed wire as an upper termination. Entries are to be designed so that they are lockable and, if there is nearby moving traffic, so that they cannot be opened by children's hands (for elementary schools and preschools).
Preschools and daycare facilities		Formation as visual screening can be sensible, depending on the situation. Size of openings and spaces between horizontal and vertical elements: max. 12 cm (France: 11 cm)	
School grounds			
Sports facilities for ball sports: tennis etc.	Polyethylene mesh, wire mesh, double wire panels (with noise abatement if applicable)	Recommended configurations for steel welded wire fences: • Up to 2 m high: grid size 50/200 mm • From 2 meters high onward: grid size 100/200 mm • Typical on-center spacing 2,520 mm (post spacing)	

Table 3.6.2 Fence materials and construction types

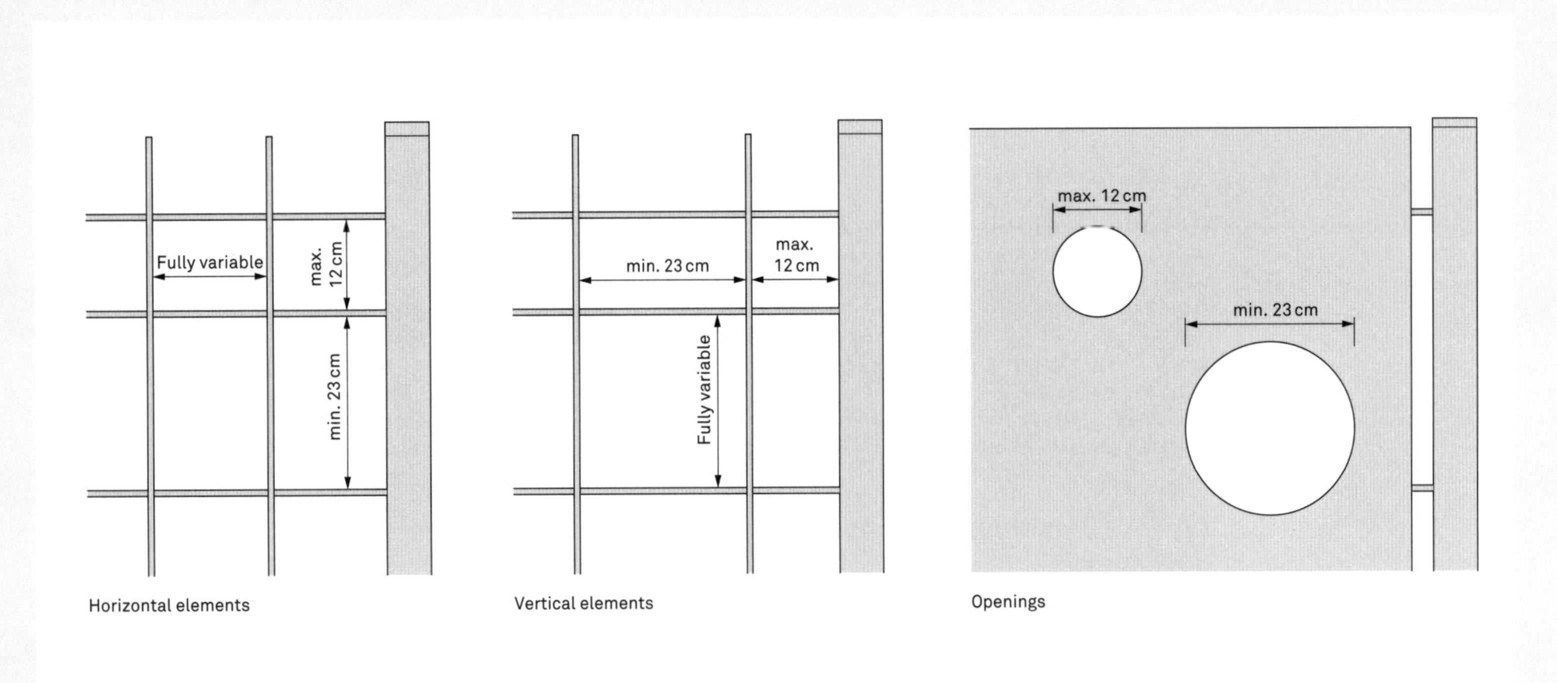

Figure 3.6.3 Mandatory sizes of openings and spaces between the horizontal and vertical elements of boundary enclosures

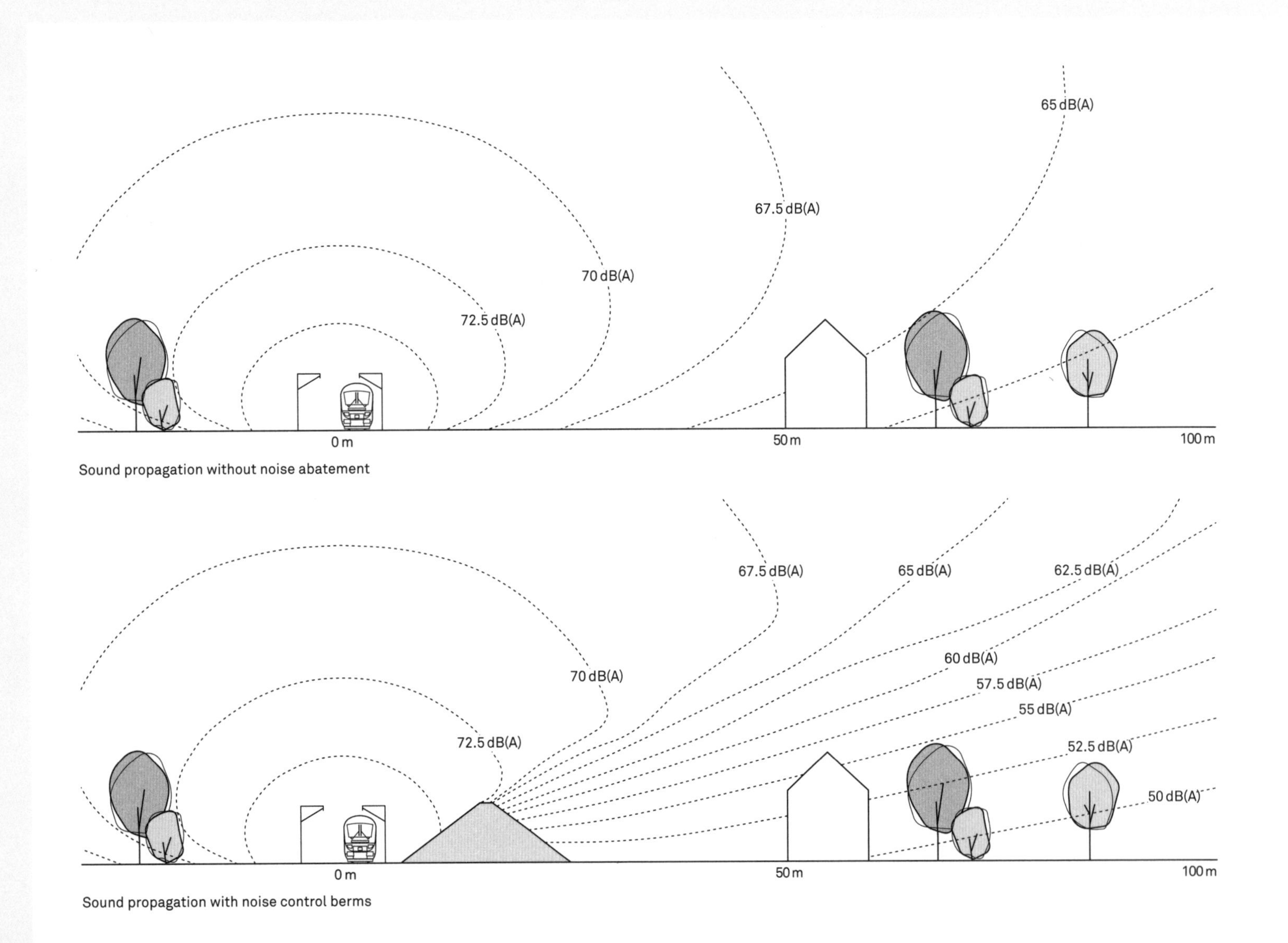

Figure 3.6.5 Behavior of sound propagation and acoustic shielding

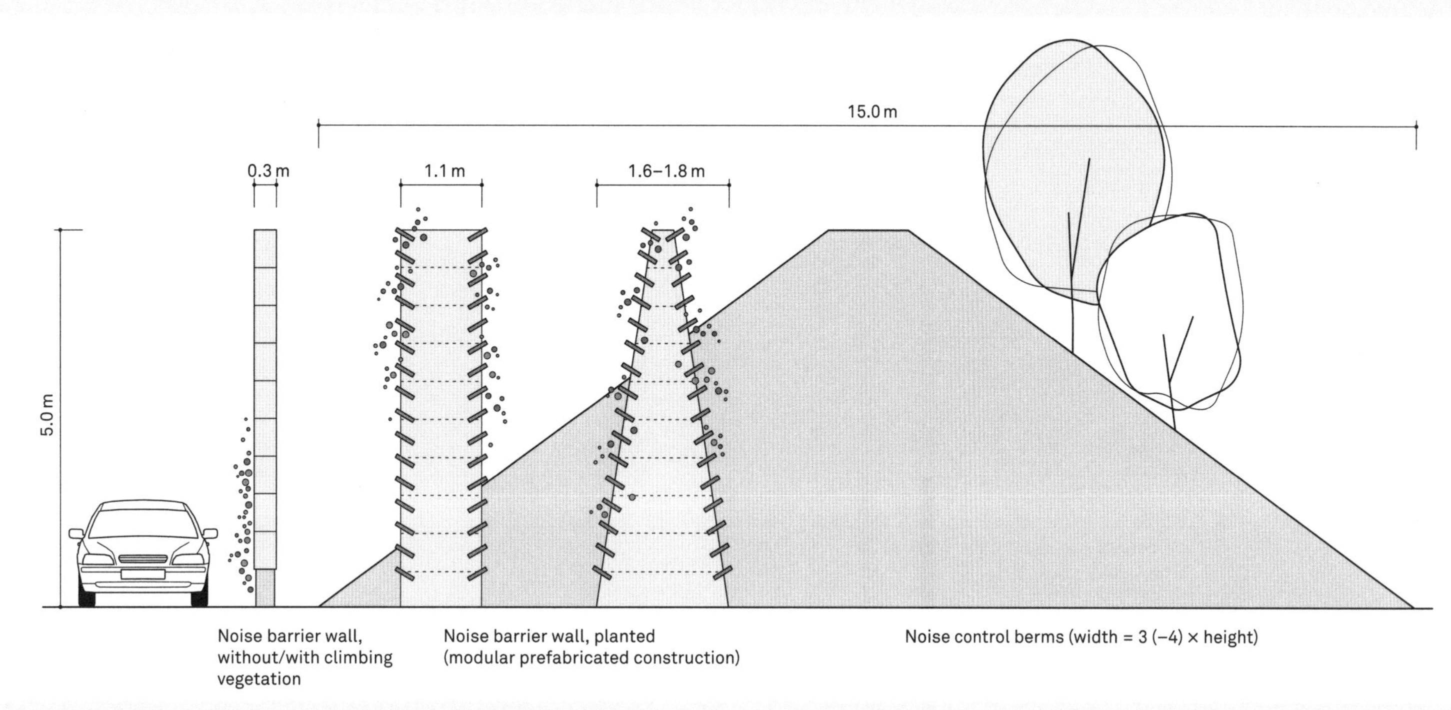

Figure 3.6.4 Exemplary space requirements for noise abatement measures

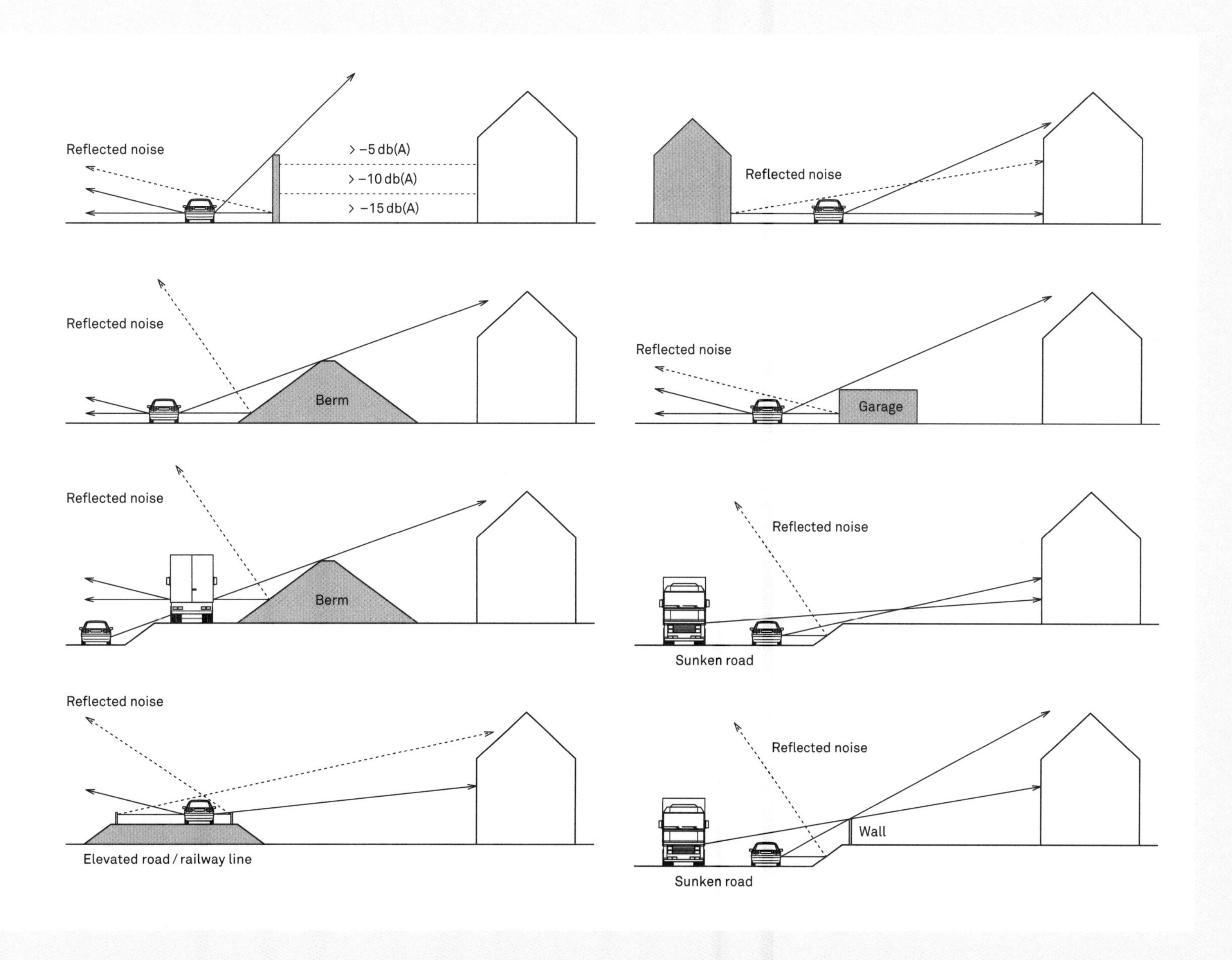

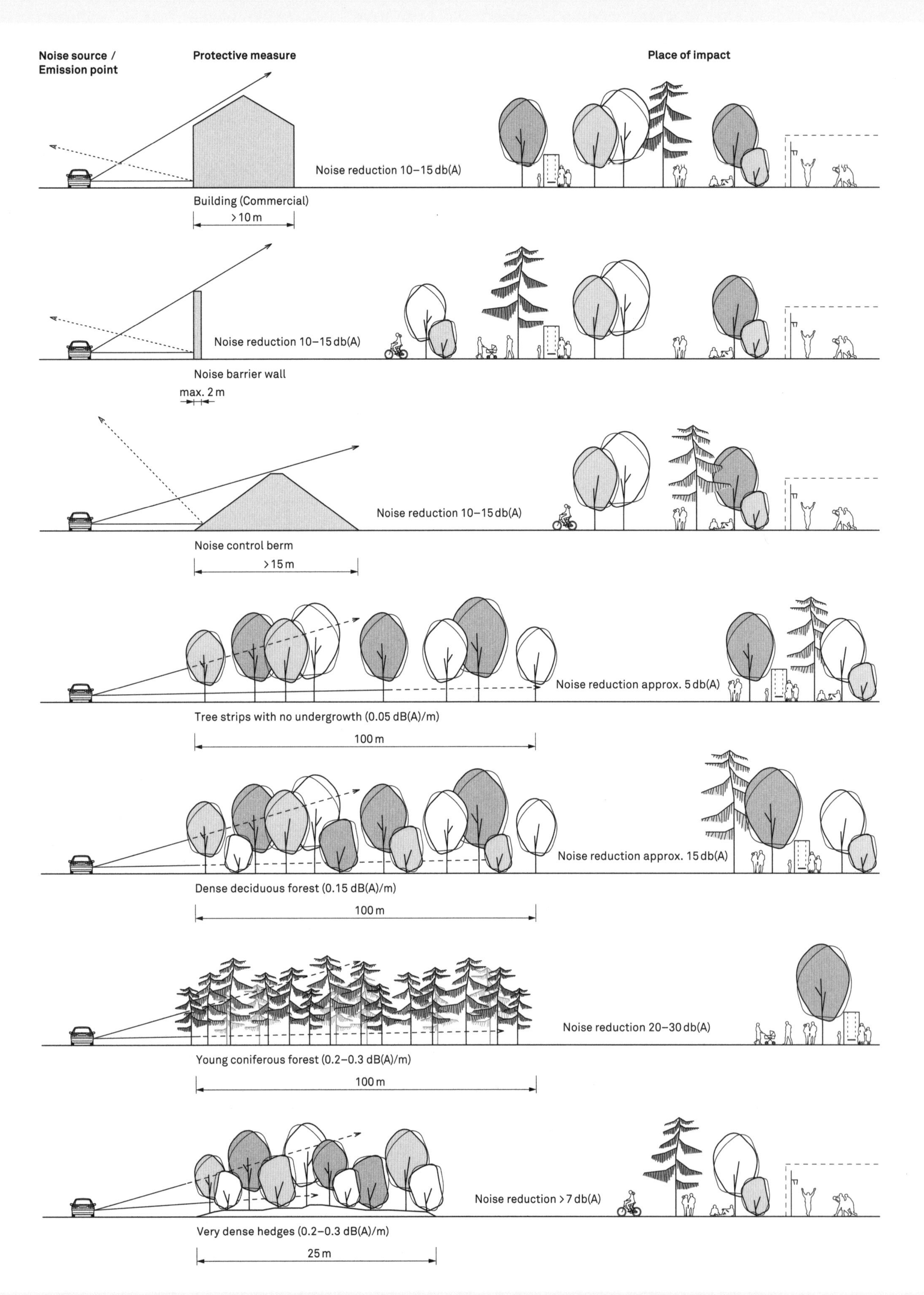

Figure 3.6.6 Effectiveness of different noise abatement measures

Heights and Setbacks of Boundary Enclosures

For demarcating a property from a neighboring property, the provisions of the laws concerning the respective interests of neighbors come to bear. In addition to the requirements of the building code, these determine setback distances and heights of hedges, fences, and walls. Additionally designated setbacks from neighboring properties must be accordingly maintained with regard to planting, especially for hedges. **Table 3.6.3** illustrates the differences between the individual German states. The permissible heights for permit-free construction of walls and fences on the border to the neighboring property also vary from country to country. → **Table 3.6.4**

State	Setbacks for hedge heights					
	Up to 100cm	101–120cm	121–150cm	151–180cm	181–200cm	>200cm
Baden-Württemberg	50cm	50cm	50cm	50cm	Hedge height minus 130 (180) cm	
Bavaria, North Rhine-Westphalia, Saxony	50cm	50cm	50cm	50cm	50cm	200cm
Berlin	50cm	50cm	50cm	50cm	50cm	100cm
Bremen, Hamburg, Mecklenburg-Vorpommern	No statutory regulation					
Brandenburg	One-third of the hedge height					
Hesse	25cm	25cm	50cm	50cm	50cm	75cm
Lower Saxony*	25cm	25cm	50cm	50cm	50cm	Up to h = 300cm: 75cm setback; up to h = 500cm: 125cm setback
Rhineland-Palatinate, Saarland	25cm	50cm	50cm	75cm	75cm	75cm
Thuringia	25cm	50cm	50cm	75cm	75cm	Hedge height minus 125cm
Saxony-Anhalt	50cm	50cm	50cm	100cm	100cm	Up to h = 300cm: 100cm setback; up to h = 500cm: 125cm setback
Schleswig-Holstein	50cm	50cm	One-third of the hedge height**			

* in built-up areas ** decisive here are the branches and not the leading shoot.

Table 3.6.3 Mandatory property line setbacks for hedges in the individual German states

State	Maximum heights of walls/solid boundary enclosures	Maximum heights of open boundary enclosures	Exceptions
Berlin	Up to 2m, with no height limit in commercial and industrial areas		In undeveloped open areas: open boundary fences with no base, on the premises of an agricultural or forestry operation or in areas used for agricultural purposes
Baden-Württemberg	Up to 1.5m	Up to 1.5m	Height of wire fences is not restricted
Bavaria	Up to 2m, except in undeveloped open areas; Mounds up to a height of 2m and a maximum area of 500m²	Up to 2m, except in undeveloped open areas	In undeveloped open areas: open boundary fences with no base, on the premises of an agricultural or forestry operation or in areas used for agricultural purposes
Brandenburg	Up to 1.5m high, except in undeveloped open areas	Up to 2m high, except in undeveloped open areas	In undeveloped open areas: open boundary fences up to 2m high, with no base, on the premises of an agricultural or forestry operation or in areas used for agricultural purposes
Hesse	Up to 2m, with no height limit in commercial and industrial areas		Open boundary fences in undeveloped open areas
Lower Saxony	Retaining walls and mounds up to a height of 1.5m	Up to a height of 2m, boundary enclosures may only be opaque above a height of 1.8m if the neighbor grants consent	Boundary fences up to a height of 3.5m when they enclose garden courtyards and the conditions of § 12 Par. 5 are fulfilled
North Rhine-Westphalia	Up to 2m high, along public thoroughfares up to 1m high above grade		In undeveloped open areas on built-up lots or when the construction is granted approval or on the premises of an agricultural or forestry operation or in areas used for agricultural purposes
Saxony	Up to 1.8m high, with no height limit in commercial and industrial areas		

Table 3.6.4 Permissible heights (permit-free construction) of boundary enclosures with no property line setbacks from the neighboring lot (selected examples, per respective building codes)

Handrails and Railings

Handrails must be affixed wherever there is an uninterrupted series of three steps (stair run; see DIN 18065). For barrier-free access, a handrail is required for two or more consecutive steps. For stair widths greater than 5 m, an additional center handrail shall be provided.

The height is measured vertically above the nosing and shall be 90 cm under normal circumstances. For workplaces, a minimum of 100 cm are required (see also height of railings). The handrail must be carried 30 cm (Austria: 40 cm) beyond the lowest and highest steps. For children, an additional handrail can be installed at a height of approximately 65 cm.

For the greatest possible barrier-free accessibility, the handrail forming the upper termination of the railing should have a round cross section with a diameter of 3.5–4 cm. → Figure 3.6.7

As a general rule, with a fall height (difference in elevation) of 1 m or more, railings or parapets are required as guards. This also pertains to embankments when these are very steep. The height of the railing or parapet shall in this case be min. 0.9 m (1 m in workplaces). In Switzerland, the guard can be replaced with planting of vegetation for fall heights of max. 1.5 m. For fall heights of 12 m or more, railings and parapets must be 1.1 m high. Deviating regulations exist, for instance in Bavaria, where a guard is required starting at 0.5 m.

Railings along bikeways or shared pedestrian and bicycle paths should generally be built 1.2 m high. The FGSV's "Empfehlungen für Radverkehrsanlagen" [Recommendations for cycling facilities] specify a height of 1.3 m.

For the protection of children, the distance between railing elements (in one direction) shall not be more than 12 cm. For adults, a distance of max. 30 cm provides sufficient protection against "falling through."

Horizontal elements are well suited as aids for climbing, and should therefore be avoided or placed particularly close together (max. 2 cm between crossbars). Apertures and the spacing of grids should be max. 4 cm when measured diagonally. Alternatively, a railing angled inward by at least 15 cm along the top (bent cross section) may be used, thus minimizing the ladder effect.

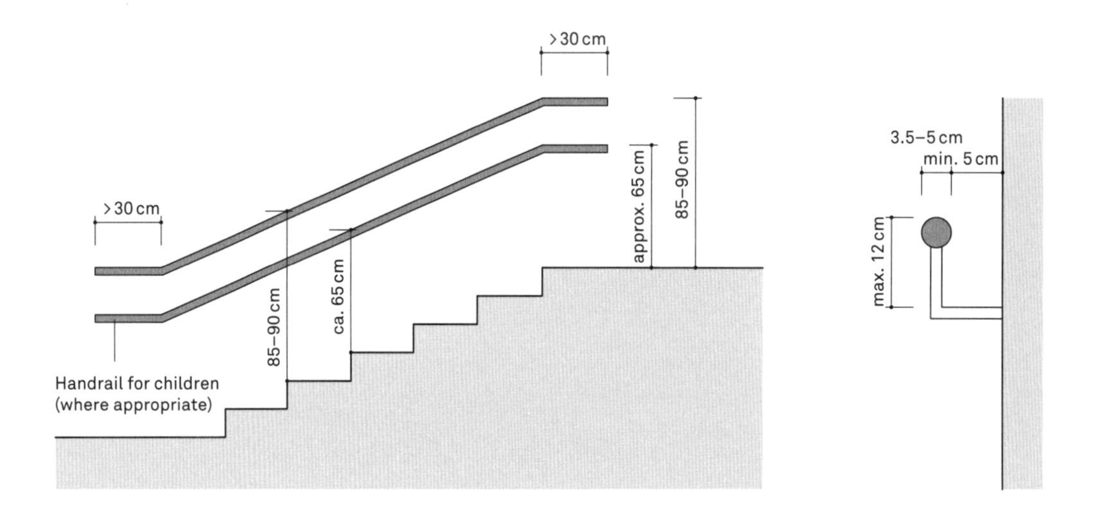

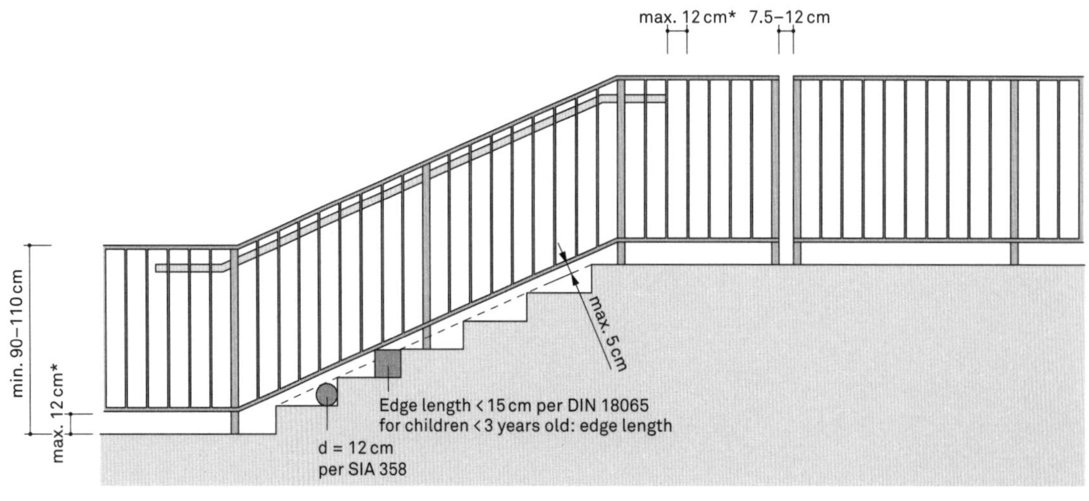

* in day care centers, max. 11 cm (children 3 years and older) or max. 8.9 cm (children under 3 years old)

Figure 3.6.7 Requirements for stair handrails

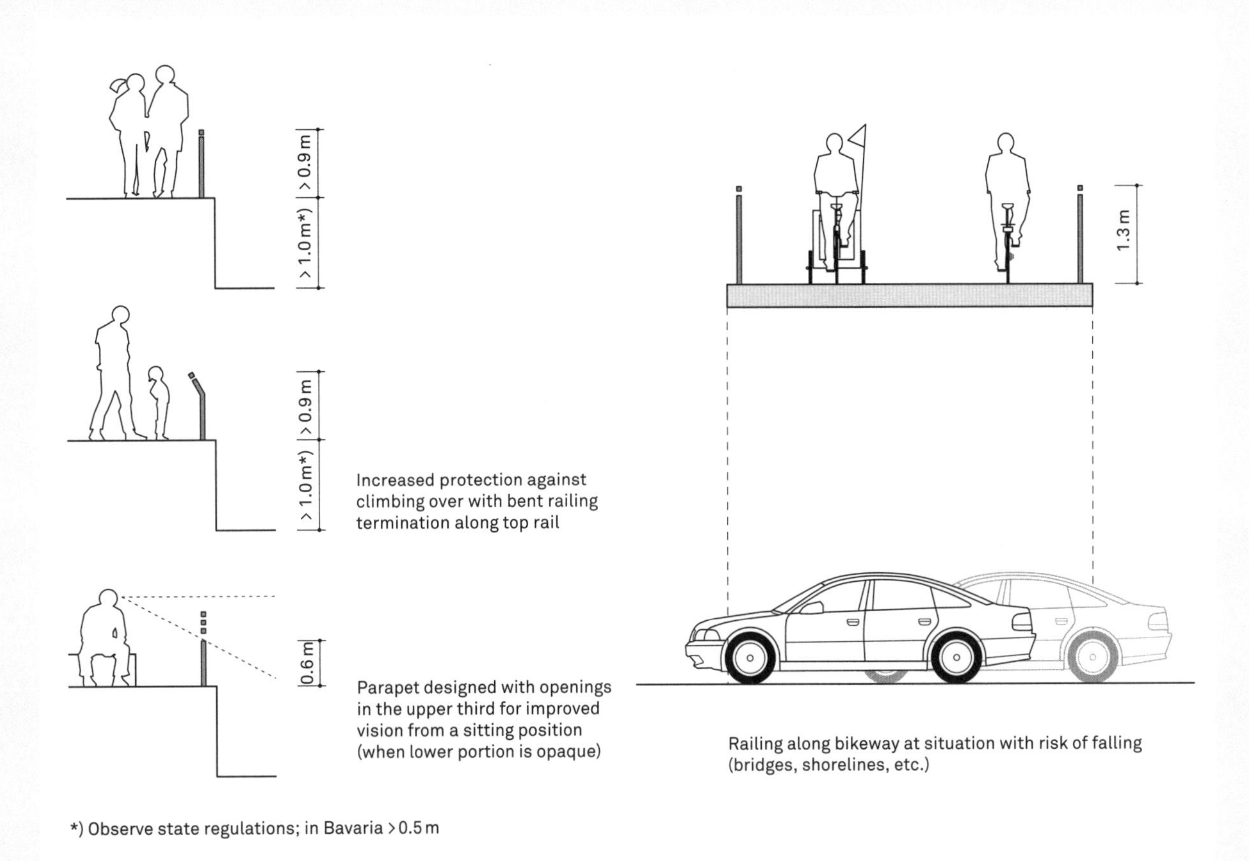

Figure 3.6.8 Requirements for railings and parapets

Remarks on Building Law and Regulatory Approval

Boundary enclosures, with the exception of hedges, are physical structures and thus subject to regulatory approval. Walls in development areas are generally permit-free up to a height of 2 m, as are open boundary fences for forestry and agriculture (see the pertinent building code).

In Austria there is an obligation to notify the authorities (see also model building code) for construction of or significant alterations to boundary enclosures greater than 1.5 m high.

Handrails on Ramps
→ 3.2 Grading, Stairs, and Ramps

Heights of Ball Stop Fencing
→ 4.4 Sports Facilities

3 Elements
3.7 Seating

3.7 Seating

Whether dimensioning patios and places to sit in gardens, picnic and seating areas in parks and other outdoor recreational facilities, or terraces for restaurants, the dimensions of benches, seating groups, and table arrangements as well as standards like the space requirements for eating establishments should be used as a basis. It is also important to take the solar orientation of the terraces into account during design and planning. Comfort naturally also plays a role when selecting seating elements, and various factors – the seat height as well as the inclination of the backrest, for instance – are dependent on the user group and the anticipated use.

Location

Seats and terraces must be provided with adequate slope to quickly drain away precipitation, especially from surfaces paved with slabs, unit pavers, or other materials with low water permeability. The slope should not be too considerable, however, particularly if tables are to be placed there. A slope of 1–2 % is appropriate for such cases.

The terrace should, as a rule, be laid out with a southwest orientation so that it optimally takes advantage of exposure to sunlight in the afternoon and early evening hours. If the terrace is used primarily in the morning or at lunchtime (e.g., in canteens or cafeterias), this should be taken into account, meaning that a different orientation might best be selected. For private gardens, a second terrace facing east (→ Chapter 4.1) is often a possibility. For eating establishments, the terrace areas are ideally oriented toward a park or other green space.

For people with health-related impairments, long distances can be an obstacle. Especially for people with impaired mobility or those with cardiovascular disease, for example, providing seating opportunities at short intervals therefore offers great relief. A maximum spacing of 100 m between seating elements is recommended.

Dimensions and Characteristics

Seating and Terraces

For adequate dimensioning of seating in outdoor facilities, the following dimensions of benches and seating groups can serve as guidelines. Because the designs of seating furniture, tables, and umbrellas are so highly diverse, manufacturer's data should be taken into account whenever appropriate. → Tables 3.7.1 and 3.7.2

For restaurant establishments, in addition to seating for the restaurant guests themselves, aisles between the seats and areas for storage and possibly for an outdoor counter should be taken into account as needed. For the seating at events above a certain size, specific recommended or prescribed values – subject to the applicable valid regulations – will apply (→ Chapter 4.7). For terraces of a smaller size, too, however, the specifications pertaining to larger events can still be used to set out minimum distances between rows of seating and between table groups. As a general rule, each table must be located on an aisle that leads to an exit. The distance from each seat to an aisle is often assessed differently, but typically a maximum of 5–10 m is stipulated. Between rows of chairs – or to be precise, between occupied chairs – a clear width of at least 0.45 m should be available for passage, or alternatively, a distance of at least 1.5 m should be provided between the tables. → Figure 3.7.3

When dimensioning and laying out aisles, the space needed for maneuvering wheelchairs must always be taken into consideration. For seating areas in parks, too, spaces measuring 1.5 × 1.5 m (incl. movement area) should be incorporated for wheelchairs. → Figure 3.7.4

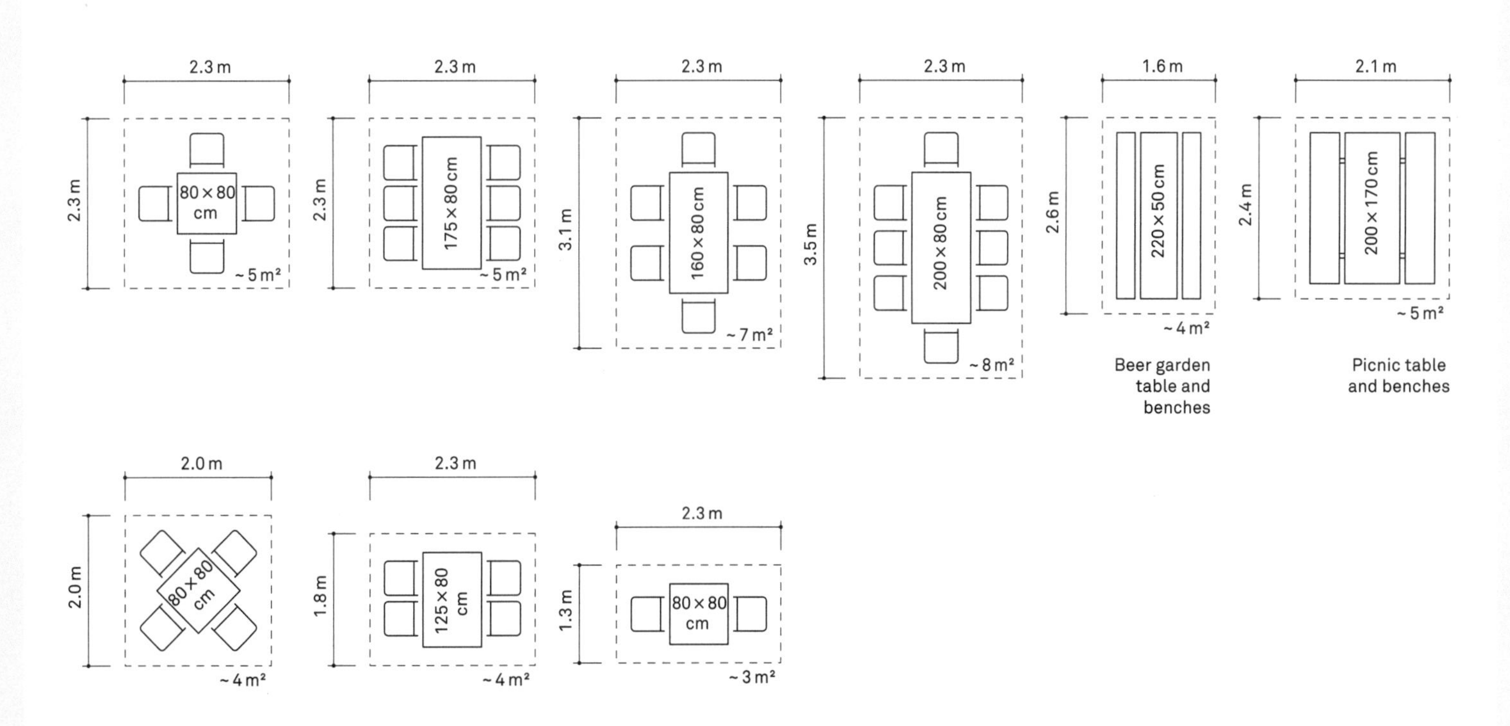

Figure 3.7.1 Space requirements for seating, including maneuvering space (minimum dimensions)

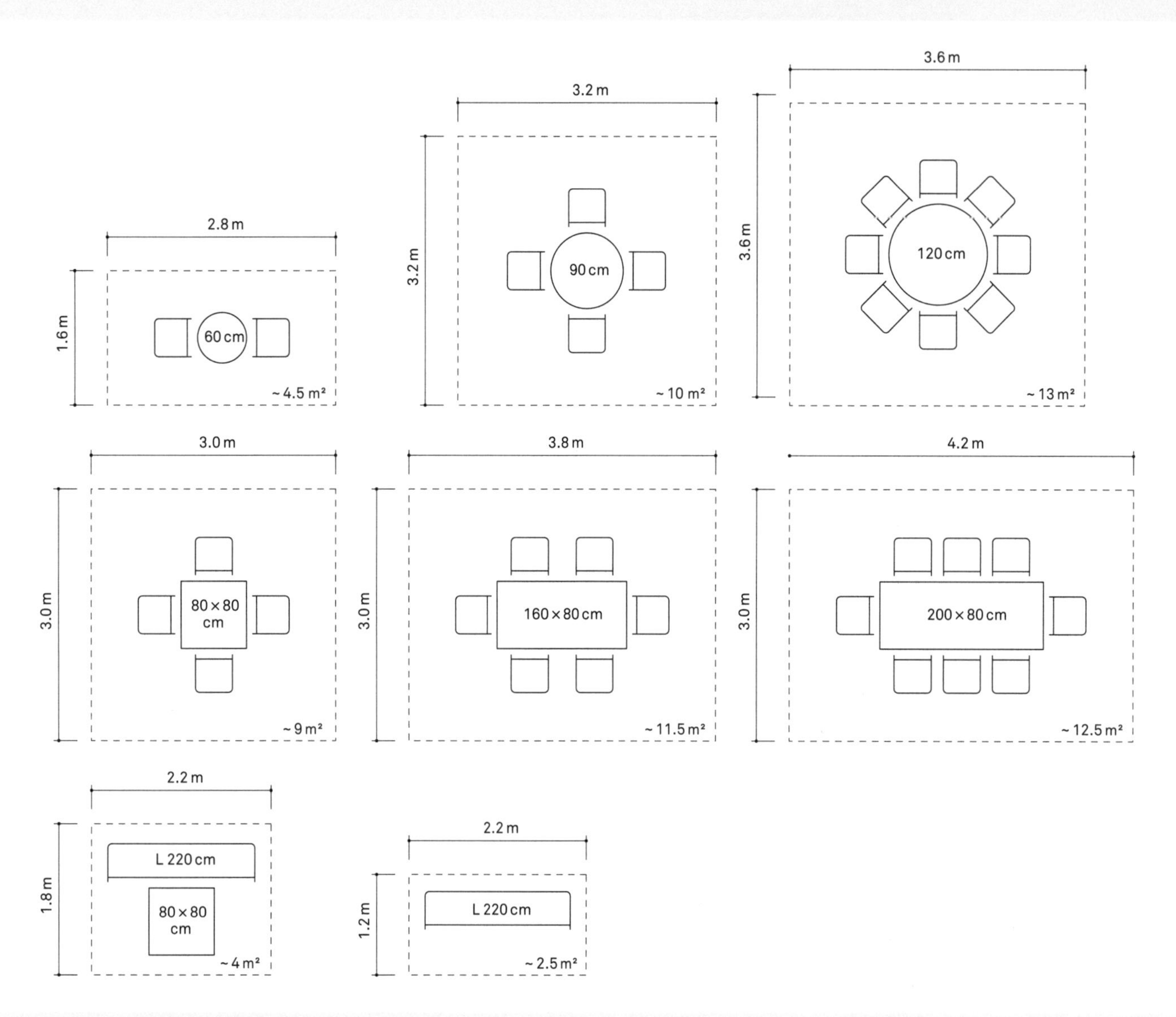

Figure 3.7.2 Space requirements for seating for solitary arrangement / on terraces

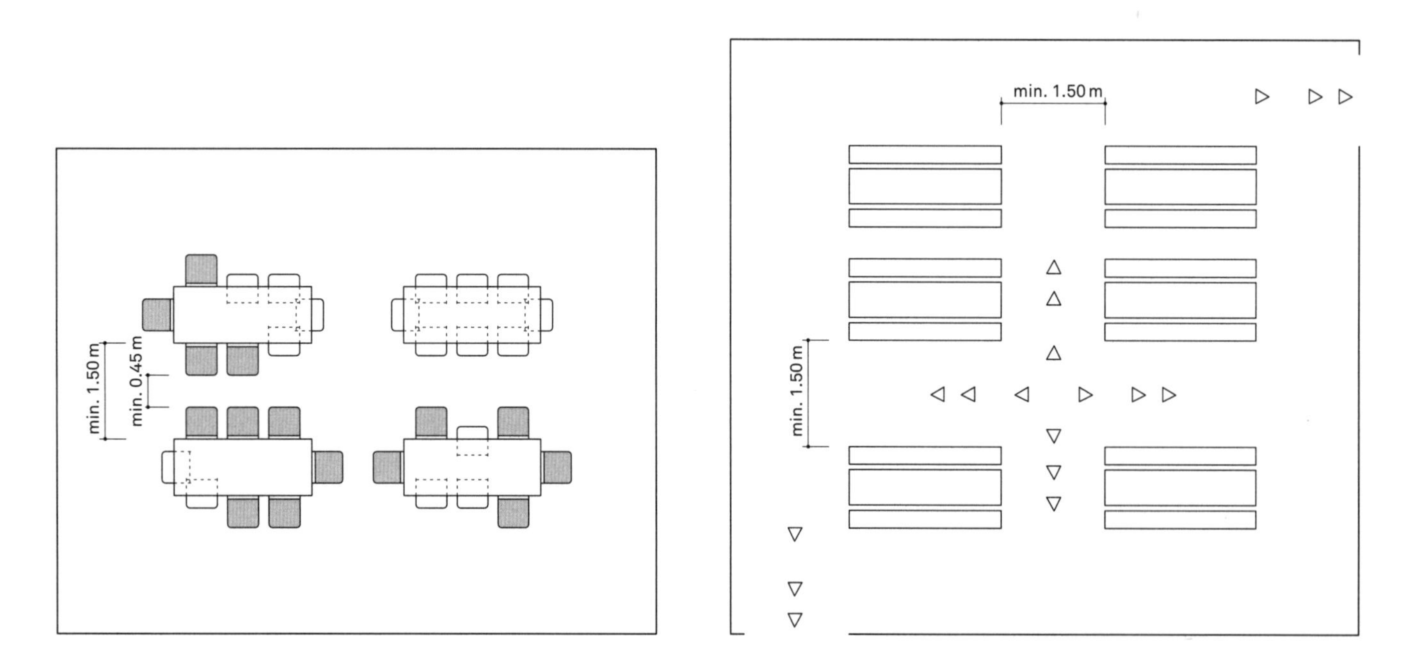

Figure. 3.7.3 Aisle widths and clearances for groups of chairs and tables with no specific egress requirements

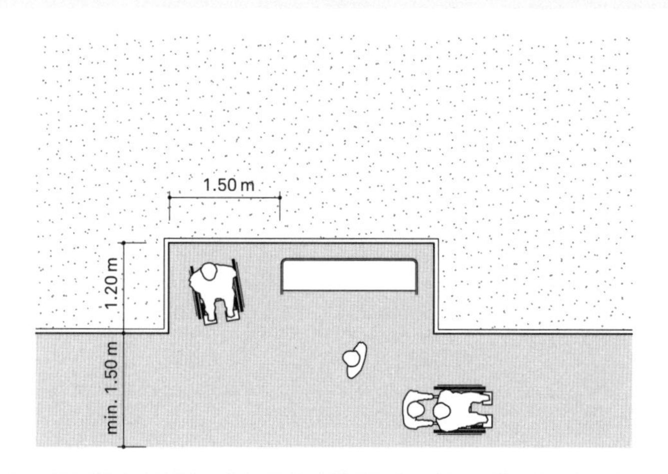

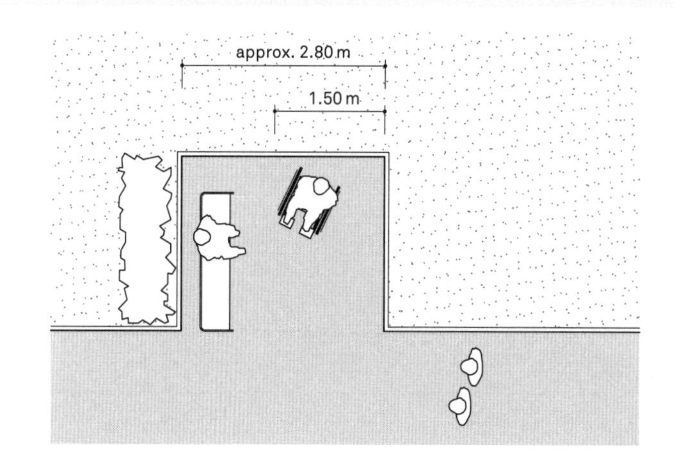

Figure 3.7.4 Space requirement for wheelchair spaces at benches in outdoor facilities

Table 3.7.1 Space requirements for seating

Type of seating	Space required	Total area
Individual dimensions		
Single chaise lounge	1.85 × 0.85 m	1.6 m²
Picnic table with benches (dimensions vary by manufacturer)	Length: approx. 2.00 m Width: approx. 1.70 m	3.4 m²
Beer garden table and benches	Large: table 2.20 × 0.50 m (0.80 m), bench 2.20 × 0.25 m Small: table 1.77 × 0.46 m, bench 1.77 × 0.23 m	2.2 m² (2.9 m²) 1.65 m²
Seating, including maneuvering space (minimum size)		
Seating with table (0.80 × 0.80 m) and 2 chairs	2.80 × 1.30 m	Approx. 3.7 m²
Seating with table (0.80 × 0.80 m) and 4 chairs	2.30 × 1.80 m to 2.30 × 2.30 m	Approx. 4 to 5 m²
Seating with table (1.60 × 0.80 m) and 6 chairs	2.30 × 2.30 m to 2.30 × 3.10 m	Approx. 5 to 7 m²
Seating with table (2.00 × 0.80 m) and 8 chairs	2.30 × 3.70 m	Approx. 8 m²
Picnic table with benches	2.40 × 2.10 m	Approx. 5 m²
Beer garden table and benches (2.2 m long)	2.60 × 1.6 m	Approx. 4 m²
Seating groups with tables, for solitary arrangements/on terraces		
Seating with round table (Ø 0.60 m) and 2 chairs	2.80 × 1.60 m	Approx. 4.5 m²
Seating with round table (Ø 0.90 m) and 4 chairs (+2)	3.20 × 3.20 m	Approx. 10 m²
Seating with table (0.80 × 0.80 m) and 4 chairs	3.00 × 3.00 m	Approx. 9 m²
Seating with table (1.60 × 0.80 m) and 6 chairs	3.00 × 3.80 m	Approx. 11.5 m²
Seating with table (2.00 × 0.80 m) and 8 chairs	4.00 × 3.00 m	Approx. 12.5 m²
Seating with round table (Ø 1.20 m) and 8 chairs	3.60 × 3.60 m	Approx. 13 m²
Seating with bench (length 1.80 m)	2.20 × 1.20 m	Approx. 2.6 m²
Seating with bench and table (0.80 × 0.80 m)	2.20 × 1.80 m	Approx. 4 m²
Seating with bench (length 1.80 m) and place for wheelchair	3.50 × 1.20 m	Approx. 4.2 m²
Recommended values for seating in restaurant facilities, per guest		
Fast food restaurant		1.2–1.5 m² per guest
System restaurant		1.3–1.6 m² per guest
Upscale restaurant		1.8–2.2 m² per guest

Type of umbrella	Length × width / diameter	Height when open	Clearance below	Height when closed
Small umbrella, round	Dia. = 2–3 m	2.60 m		
Large umbrellas, round	Dia. = 4 m	3.20 m		
	Dia. = 4.5 m	3.15 m	2.15–2.4 m	4.4 m
	Dia. = 5 m	3.15 m	2.15–2.4 m	4.3 m
	Dia. = 6 m	3.15 m	2.15–2.4 m	4.2 m
Large umbrellas, square	3 × 3 m	2.6 m		
	3.5 × 3.5 m	3.9 m		
	4 × 4 m			3.3 m
	5 × 5 m		2.15–2.4 m	3.35 m
	6 × 6 m	3.4 m	2.15–2.4 m	3.4 m
Large umbrellas, rectangular	6 × 4 m	3.4 m	2.15–2.4 m	3.4 m

Table 3.7.2 Exemplary dimensions of umbrellas

Seating Comfort

Unlike the absolute seat height that is calculated from an average person's body size (→ **Chapter 2.1**), the seat height for benches in outdoor spaces tends to be set slightly higher: the standard seat heights of benches are generally 45–48 cm, and 50 cm is increasingly also being offered.

One reason for this is comfort, since it is basically easier to get up from a slightly higher seat. Benches intended explicitly for seniors can even be designed with an elevated seat height of 52 cm. Other aspects make it easier to get up from a seated position are the presence of a (grippable) armrest and a seat that is slightly curved or angled slightly forward at the front.

The seating comfort is improved with a sufficiently high and slightly inclined backrest (inclination approx. 101°–108°) and a seating surface made of "warm" materials like wood or plastic. → **Figure 3.7.5**

Hammocks

In outdoor spaces, hammocks can be installed as fixed (play) elements and/or used for temporary attachment between trees or posts. Although dimensions vary depending on the manufacturer, the dimensions listed in **figure 3.7.6** enable a rough estimate of the space required for a fixed installation or the clearance needed to hang a portable hammock.

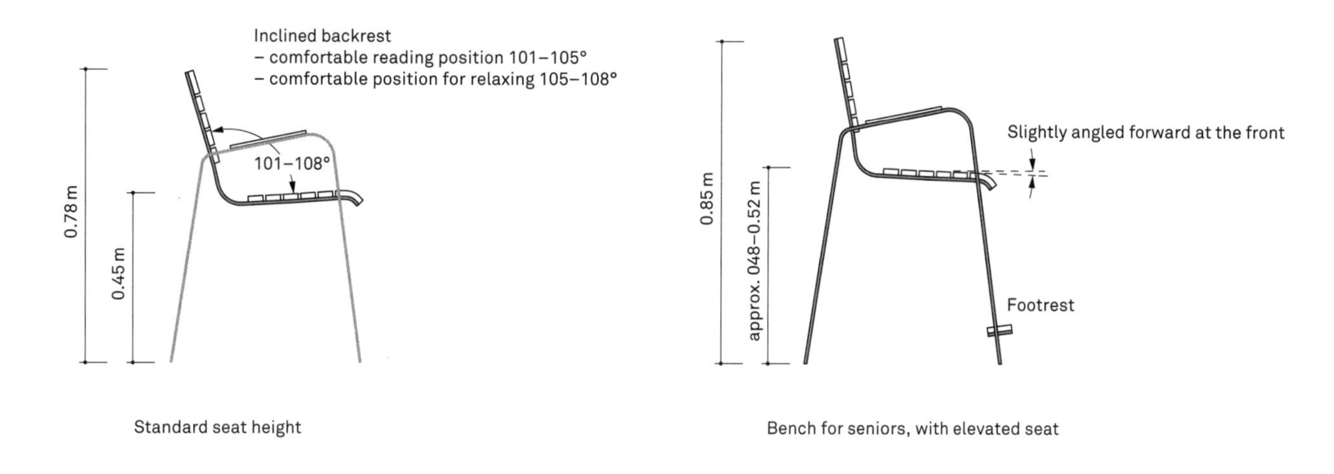

Figure 3.7.5 Seating comfort

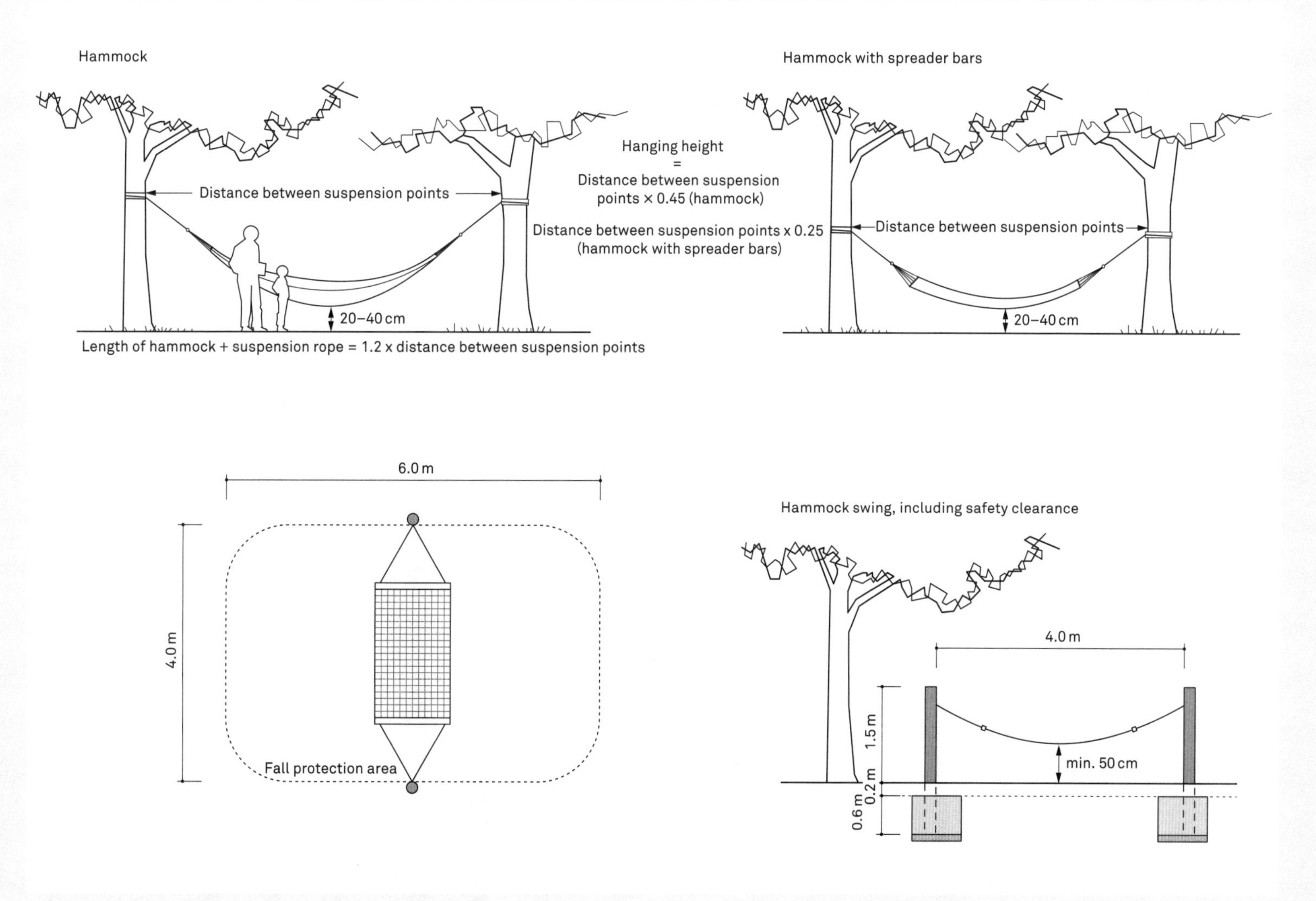

Figure 3.7.6 Dimensions and space requirements of hammocks, both portable and fixed in place

3 Elements
3.8 Lighting

3.8 Lighting

Outdoors, lighting provides orientation, contributes to safety, and also defines space. Depending on the design intent and function, different types of luminaires are used. → Table 3.8.2

Location

For the sake of sustainable planning, in addition to using energy-saving illuminants, attention should be given to reducing the lighting to the minimum needed. This could, for example, be a matter of minimizing the purely decorative lighting or limiting the hours of operation.

In any case, however, it is possible to exert influence on the choice of light source and the light can be directed in a targeted manner. This means preferably directing the light downward, with no unnecessary lateral scattering of light. This is to protect nocturnal insects, as is the preferred use of high-pressure sodium vapor lamps and compact fluorescent lamps as opposed to high-pressure mercury vapor lamps.

Term	Symbol	Definition
Illuminance	E	Quantity of light per unit area that falls on a surface (incident light), expressed in lux. As used in this guideline, illuminance is always the average level of light intensity that an apparatus continuously provides as a minimum (also known as average maintained illuminance), thus also defining when the lamp should be replaced and/or the apparatus should be cleaned.
Horizontal illuminance	Eh	The illuminance on a horizontal plane at the height of a surface
Vertical illuminance	EV	The illuminance on a vertical plane at a height of 1.5 m above a surface (oriented in the direction of a specific point)
Uniformity of illuminance	E_{min}/E_{max} E_{min}/E_{av}	Uniformity of light distribution across a surface; expressed by the ratios E_{min}/E_{max} and E_{min}/E_{av}.
Lamp/illuminant	–	The term *lamp* (or *illuminant*) refers to an engineered artificial light source. It converts electrical energy into light.
Luminaire	–	A luminaire – which is also imprecisely known colloquially as a *lamp* or *light* – is the entire lighting fixture with all the components needed for its attachment and operation as well as for protection of the lamp within. The luminaire protects the lamp and distributes and directs its light while limiting glare.
Illuminant		See Lamp
Light source height		The light source height identifies the height between the light source (= luminaire) and the target surface being illuminated.
Lux	lx	Unit of the illuminance that falls on a surface (lumens per square meter), 1 lux = 1 lm/m²
Lumen	lm	The spectral power distribution of a lamp, weighted by the luminous efficiency curve.
Mounting height	Hm	Mounting height of the luminaire in relation to a point on a surface. Hm = distance "d" + tan d
Color rendering index	Ra	The degree to which a specific light source reproduces a range of reference colors (Ra 8) when compared with the same colors under daylight conditions. This index (Ra) is measured on a scale of Ra 0 – Ra 100
Color temperature	Tk	The color appearance of the light emitted by a light source, in degrees Kelvin.
Maintained value	–	The maintained value represents the value for illuminance and luminance that is reached after a certain period of use. Thus it is below the original value and represents a minimum limit to be sustained.

Table 3.8.1 Terminology

Luminaire type	Image	Application
Floor lights	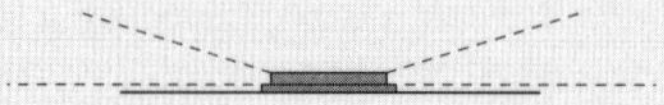	Orientation, building access
Bollard lights	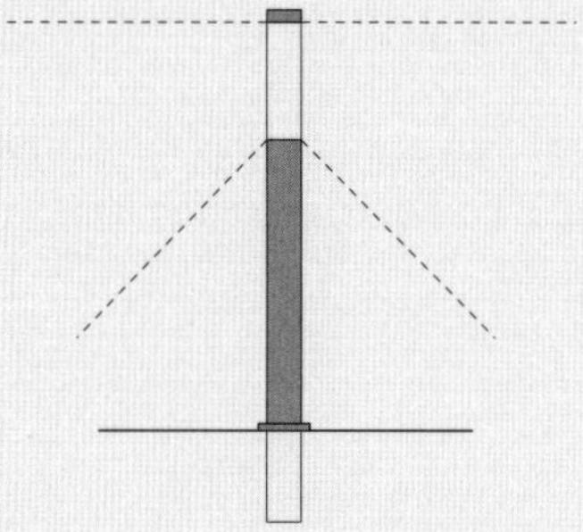	Orientation, building access, promenades
Floodlights	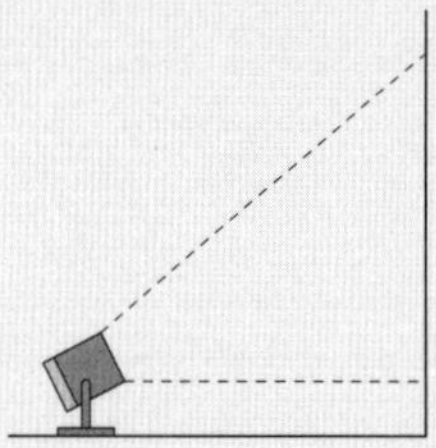	Lighting facades or objects, sports and area floodlighting
Wall-mounted luminaires Recessed wall luminaires	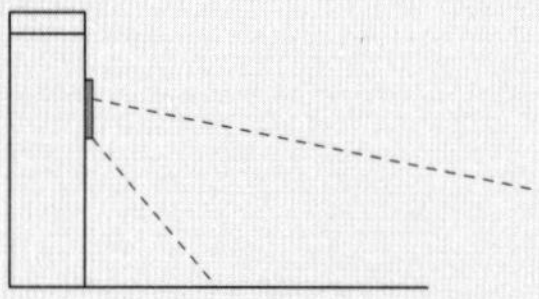	Stairs, building approach
Catenary suspended uminaires	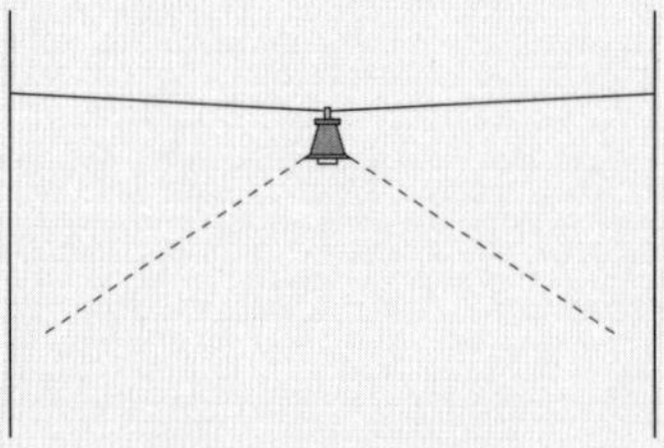	Streets and courtyards, especially between buildings
Mast lights with symmetric/ asymmetric light distribution	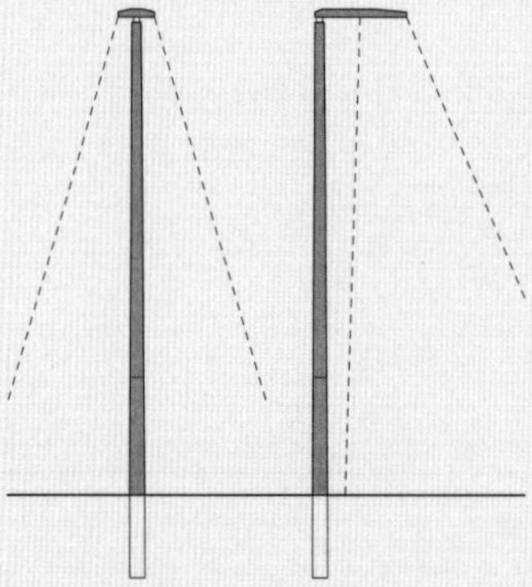	Road lighting, park paths, promenades

Table 3.8.2 Luminaire types and their applications

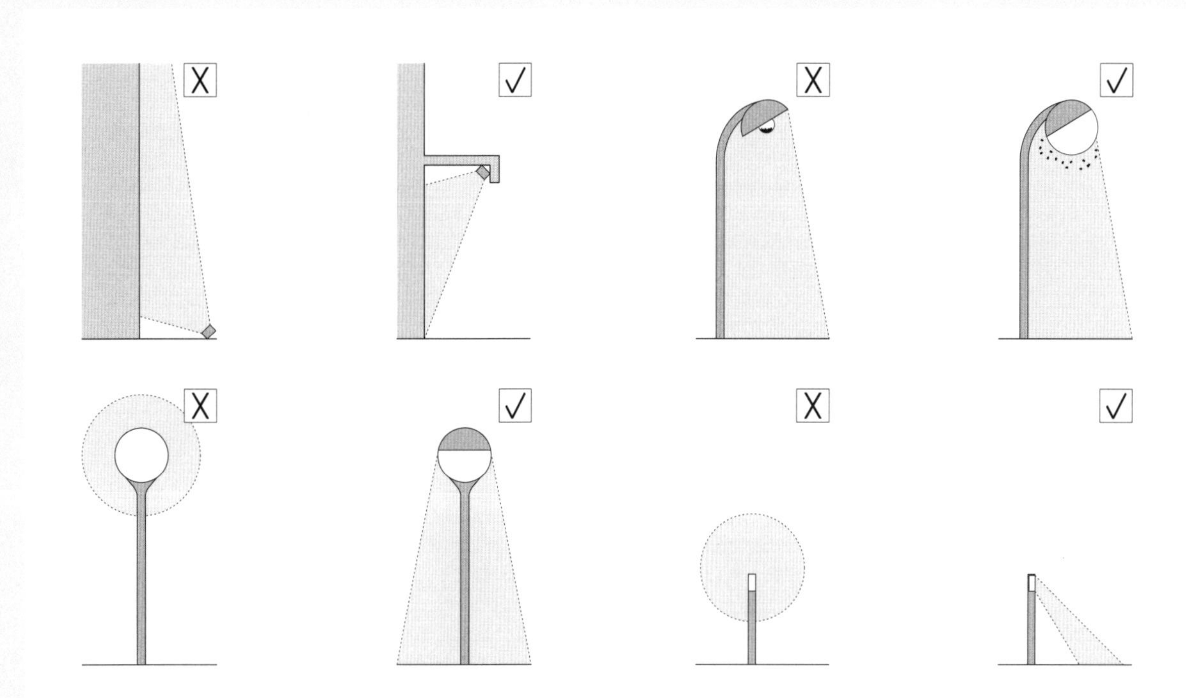

Figure 3.8.1 Sustainable use of luminaires outdoors: downward beam direction for general use and for illuminating facades, together with safeguards for nocturnal insects

Dimensions and Characteristics

Light source/lamp	Abbreviation	Luminous efficiency (approx.), in lumens/Watt	Life span (approx.), in hrs.	Light color	Negative effect on insects	Comments
Low-pressure sodium vapor lamps	SOX/LPS lamps	170–200	16,000	Orange-colored	<10%	Poor color fidelity, very insect-friendly, very efficient
High-pressure sodium vapor lamps	NA/HPS lamps	130–150	12,000–16,000	Warm white	10–20%	Insect-friendly
Incandescent bulbs (general-service tungsten-filament lamps)	A lamps	12	1,000	Warm white	10–15%	No longer state-of-the-art, inefficient
Halogen lamps	QT/QR lamps	25	5,000	Warm white	10–15%	
Compact fluorescent lamps ("energy-saving lamps" with integrated ballast)	TC lamps	60	8,000–15,000	White	20–25%	Only for low mounting heights
Linear fluorescent lamps (tubes)	T lamps	80	8,000–16,000	White	25–35%	
High-pressure metal halide discharge lamps	HCI/HSI lamps	85	8,000–12,000	White	30–55%	
High-pressure mercury vapor lamps	HPL/HPM lamps	50	12,000–16,000	White	100%	Obsolete, soon no longer available
Light-emitting diodes, electroluminescent diodes	LED	90	50,000	Warm white to neutral white	10–15%	Very efficient

Table 3.8.3 Characteristics of various lamps

Illuminance

Standard EN 13201-1 stipulates certain illuminance levels (lighting intensities) for street spaces based on the specific use. These are further defined by means of lighting situations and lighting classes. When selecting products, help can often be found in the pertinent manufacturers' data on the suitability of the luminaires for each lighting class and the corresponding required spacing of the fixtures. Standards D EN 13201-1 and ÖNORM EN 13201-1 are the national standards for Germany and Austria, respectively. The extent to which the illuminance levels are stipulated on the basis of Technical Report CEN / TR 13201-1, and thus analogously to these standards, must be examined individually for other EU countries.

To determine the illuminance, a classification of the lighting situation must first be made based on predefined user types and their typical speed (Motorized traffic, cyclists, or pedestrians). → Table 3.8.4 A lighting situation can then be attributed with lighting classes and performance requirements. → Table 3.8.5 and Table 3.8.6

Lastly, the lighting requirements for the lighting classes are differentiated according to various criteria through use of the basic and supplemental tables. → Table 3.8.7–Table 3.8.12

Whereas the basic tables factor in criteria such as traffic-calming measures, intersection density, difficulty of the visual task, and average traffic volume, the supplemental tables consider conflict areas, the complexity of the visual field, parked vehicles, luminance of the surrounding environment, crime risk, and facial recognition.

Lighting classes S1–S7 are used for pedestrian and cycling areas, parking and emergency lanes as well as other areas beyond the roadways, residential streets, pedestrian areas, footpaths, bikeways, parking areas, and schoolyards. The result is the required illuminance level. → Table 3.8.16

The necessary illuminance levels / maintained values for different types of use can be found in tables 3.8.13 through 3.8.17.

Typical speed of main user (km/h)	User types within a relevant area			Situations
	Main user	Other permitted users	Examples	
>60	Motorized traffic		Highways, divided roads, and bypasses	A1
		Slow-moving vehicles	Major and through roads	A2
		Slow-moving vehicles, cyclists, pedestrians	Major and through roads	A3
>30 and ≤60	Motorized traffic, slow-moving vehicles	Cyclists, pedestrians	Major, collector, local, and connecting roads	B1
	Motorized traffic, slow-moving vehicles, cyclists	Pedestrians	Major, collector, local, and connecting roads	B2
>5 and ≤30	Cyclists	Pedestrians	Motorized traffic, slow-moving vehicles	C1
	Motorized traffic, pedestrians		Sidewalks, footpaths, and bikeways	D1
		Slow-moving vehicles, cyclists	Taxi stands, train station forecourts, bus terminals	D2
	Motorized traffic, cyclists	Slow-moving vehicles, pedestrians	Local and residential roads	D3
	Motorized traffic, slow-moving vehicles, cyclists, pedestrians		Traffic-calmed zones, play streets, marketplaces	D4
Walking speed	Pedestrians		Pedestrian zones and shopping areas, bus stops, footpaths	E1
		Motorized traffic, slow-moving vehicles, cyclists	Factory roads, routes for loading and feeder traffic	E2

Table 3.8.4 Determination of the lighting situation. For pedestrian and cycling areas, the lighting situations C1, D4, E1, and E2 are possibilities.

Lighting situation	Lighting class	Performance requirements
A1, A2, A3	ME1–ME5	L_m, U_0, U_1, TI, SR
B1, B2	ME2–ME6	L_m, U_0, U_1, TI, SR
C1	S1–S6	E_m, E_{min}
D1, D2	CE2–CE5	E_m, U_0
D3, D4	S1–S6	E_m, E_{min}
E1	S1–S6, CE2	E_m, E_{min}
E2	S1–S5, CE2	E_m, E_{min}

Table 3.8.5 Allocation of lighting classes to lighting situations: higher numbers for lighting classes have lower requirements

Class	Allocation	Performance requirements	Application
ME, MEW	ME1–ME6 for dry roads with medium-to-high driving speeds, MEW1 to MEW2 for wet roads	Luminance assessment: L_m, U_0, U_1, TI, SR	Traffic routes with medium-to-high driving speeds
CE	CE0–CE5, similar to ME classes, but for streets with conflict areas, such as 4-way intersections, T-intersections, and traffic circles, with pedestrians and cyclists	Illuminance assessment: E_m, U_0	When a luminance assessment is not applicable
S	S1–S7 for pedestrian and cycling areas, parking and emergency lanes, neighborhood streets, pedestrian zones, bikeways	Illuminance assessment: E_m, E_{min}	For slow traffic flows in residential neighborhoods
A	A1–A6, similar to S classes but assessed with hemispherical (semispatial) illuminance	Hemispherical illuminance assessment: E_{hs}, U_0	For slow traffic flows in residential neighborhoods and in parking areas
ES	ES1–ES9 for areas with high crime risk, e.g., in pedestrian zones and in parking areas	Semicylindrical illuminance assessment: $E_{sc,min}$	With high crime risk, when facial recognition is necessary
EV	EV1–EV6 for special areas with vertical illuminance, such as tollbooths, transshipment and handling areas	Vertical illuminance assessment: $E_{v,min}$	When vertical illuminance levels are important

Table 3.8.6 Descriptions of the lighting classes

B2 basic table

Built measures for traffic calming	Quantity of intersections per km	Difficulty of navigational task	Traffic flow of vehicles <7,000 ◀	<7,000 ●	<7,000 ▶	≥7,000 ◀	≥7,000 ●	≥7,000 ▶
No	<3	Normal	ME5	ME5	ME4b	ME4b	ME4b	ME3C
		Higher than normal	ME4b	ME4b	ME3C	ME4b	ME4b	ME3C
	≥3	Normal	ME4b	ME3C	ME2	ME3C	ME3C	ME2
		Higher than normal	ME3C	ME3C	ME2	ME3C	ME3C	ME2
Yes			As above, but lighting class with one number lower, e.g., select class ME3b instead of ME4b.					

When assessment of luminance is not applicable as a design criterion, illuminance can be used. CE classes comparable to the recommended ME classes are specified in Table 3.8.12.

B2 supplemental table

Conflict area	Complexity of visual field	Parked vehicles	Ambient luminance Low – Traffic flow of cyclists Normal	Low – High	Average – Traffic flow of cyclists Normal	Average – High	High – Traffic flow of cyclists Normal	High – High
No	Normal	Not present	◀	●	◀	●	●	●
		Present	●	▶	●	▶	▶	▶
	High	Not present	●	●	●	●	●	●
		Present	●	●	▶	▶	▶	▶
Yes			▶					

In conflict areas, luminance is the recommended design criterion. The illuminance can be used as a criterion when the luminance cannot be assessed because viewing distances are too short or due to other factors. CE classes comparable to the recommended ME classes are specified in Table 3.8.12.

Table 3.8.7 Basic and supplemental tables for lighting situation B2

C1 basic table

Built measures for traffic calming	Crime risk	Facial recognition	Traffic flow of cyclists Normal ◀	Normal ●	Normal ▶	High ◀	High ●	High ▶
No	Normal	Not required	S6	S5	S4	S5	S4	S3
		Required	S5	S4	S3	S4	S3	S2
	Higher than normal	Required	S4	S3	S2	S3	S2	S1
Yes			S3	S2	S1	S3	S2	S1

Alternative A classes with lighting levels comparable to the recommended S classes are specified in Table 3.8.12. For ES and EV classes applicable in addition to the recommended S classes, see also Table 3.8.12.

C1 supplemental table

Ambient luminance Low	Average	High
◀	●	▶

Table 3.8.8 Basic and supplemental tables for lighting situation C1

D1/D2 basic table

Built measures for traffic calming	Crime risk	Facial recognition	Difficulty of navigational task	Traffic flow, cyclists					
				Normal			High		
				◄	●	►	◄	●	►
No	Normal	Not required	Normal	CE5	CE5	CE4	CE5	CE4	CE3
			Higher than normal	CE5	CE4	CE3	CE4	CE3	CE2
		Required	Normal	CE4	CE4	CE4	CE4	CE4	CE3
			Higher than normal	CE4	CE4	CE3	CE4	CE3	CE2
	Higher than Normal	Required	Normal	CE4	CE4	CE3	CE4	CE3	CE3
			Higher than normal	CE4	CE3	CE2	CE3	CE2	CE2
Yes			As above, but lighting class ≤ CE4, e.g., CE3						

D1/D2 supplemental table

Ambient luminance		
Low	Average	High
◄	●	►

Table 3.8.9 Basic and supplemental tables for lighting situations D1 and D2

D3/D4 basic table

Built measures for traffic calming	Parked vehicles	Difficulty of navigational task	Traffic flow, pedestrians and cyclists					
			Normal			High		
			◄	●	►	◄	●	►
No	Not Present	Normal	S6	S5	S4	S5	S4	S3
		Higher than normal	S5	S4	S3	S4	S3	S2
	Present	Normal	S5	S4	S3	S4	S3	S2
		Higher than normal	S4	S3	S2	S3	S2	S1
Yes			As above, but lighting class ≤ S4, e.g., S3					

Alternative A classes with lighting levels comparable to the recommended S classes are specified in Table 3.8.12. For ES and EV classes applicable in addition to the recommended S classes, see also Table 3.8.12.

D3/D4 supplemental table

Complexity of visual field	Crime risk	Facial recognition	Ambient luminance		
			Low	Medium	High
Normal	Normal	Not required	◄	●	●
		Required	◄	●	►
	Higher than normal	Required	●	►	►
High	Normal	Not required	●	●	●
		Required	●	►	►
	Higher than normal	Required	►	►	►

Table 3.8.10 Basic and supplemental tables for lighting situations D3 and D4

E1 basic table

Crime risk	Facial recognition	Traffic flow, pedestrians					
		Normal			High		
		◄	●	►	◄	●	►
Normal	Not required	S6	S5	S4	S5	S4	S3
	Required	S5	S4	S3	S4	S3	S2
Higher than normal	Required	S3	S2	S1	S2	S1	CE2

Alternative A classes with lighting levels comparable to the recommended S classes are specified in Table 3.8.12. For ES and EV classes applicable in addition to the recommended S classes, see also Table 3.8.12.

E2 basic table

Crime risk	Facial recognition	Traffic flow, pedestrians					
		Normal			High		
		◄	●	►	◄	●	►
Normal	Not required	S5	S4	S3	S4	S3	S2
	Required	S3	S2	S1	S3	S2	S1
Higher than normal	Required	S2	S1	CE2	S2	S1	CE2

Alternative A classes with lighting levels comparable to the recommended S classes are specified in Table 3.8.12. For ES and EV classes applicable in addition to the recommended S classes, see also Table 3.8.12.

E1/E2 supplemental table

Ambient luminance		
Low	Medium	High
◄	●	►

Table 3.8.11 Basic and supplemental tables for lighting situations E1 and E2

Lighting classes
Reduced lighting requirements →

	ME1	ME2	ME3	ME4	ME5	ME6		
CE0	CE1	CE2	CE3	CE4	CE5			
			S1	S2	S3	S4	S5	S6
				A1	A2	A3	A4	A5
ES1	ES2	ES3	ES4	ES5	ES6	ES7	ES8	ES9
	EV3	EV4	EV5					

Table 3.8.12 Comparable lighting classes and alternative additional classes (gray shading)

Parking Lots

	Maintained illuminance E_m in lx	Glare rating GR	Color rendering of the lamps R_a
Light traffic, e.g., parking lots for shops, schools, churches, and apartment buildings	5	55	20
Medium traffic, e.g., parking lots for department stores, office buildings, factories, and sports and multipurpose facilities	10	50	20
Heavy traffic, e.g., parking areas for large shopping centers, large sports and multipurpose facilities	20	50	20

Table 3.8.13 Minimum requirements for lighting parking areas per EN 12464-2

Bicycle and Pedestrian Areas

	Illuminance	Uniformity	Standards, guidelines
Bikeways with pedestrians and high traffic flow, depending on crime rate and other criteria	3 to 15	E_{min} = 1 lx to 5 lx	EN 13202-2 lighting situation D4
Bikeways with pedestrians and normal traffic flow, depending on crime rate and other criteria	2 to 10	E_{min} = 0.6 lx to 3 lx	
Traffic areas for slow-moving vehicles (max. 10 km/h), e.g., bicycles, trucks, excavators	10	g_1 = 0.40	EN 12464-2
Paths for bicycles near roads for automobile traffic with fixed illumination	–	E_{min} = 3 lx g_2 = 0.15	
Paths for bicycles near roads for automobile traffic with no fixed illumination	–	E_{min} = 3 lx g_2 = 0.3	FSGV values apply along the centerline of the bikeway
Paths for bicycles farther away than 8 m from roads for automobile traffic with no fixed illumination	–	E_{min} = 1.5 lx g_2 = 0.15	

Table 3.8.14 Minimum requirements for lighting bikeways

	Illuminance in lux	Uniformity	Semicylindrical illuminance, in lux	Standards, guidelines
Pedestrian paths, high traffic flow, depending on crime rate and other criteria	7.5 to 20	–	1.5 to 5	EN 13201-2 lighting situation E1
Pedestrian paths, normal traffic flow, depending on crime rate and other criteria	2 to 15	–	0.5 to 3	EN 13201-2 lighting situation E1
Walkways solely for pedestrians	5	g_1 = 0.25	–	EN 12464-2
Traffic areas for slow-moving vehicles (max. 10 km/h), e.g., bicycles, trucks, excavators	10	g_1 = 0.40	–	EN 12464-2
Walkways on factory premises	3	g_1 = 0.08	–	EN 12464-2
Walkways in parks and housing complexes	–	E_{min} = 1 lx	≥1	FSGV
Walkways with steps, unevenness, and other safety hazards	–	E_{min} = 5 lx	≥1	FSGV
Squares and entries	5	g_2 = 0.1	≥1	FSGV
Squares and entries with occasional high crowd density	10	g_2 = 0.1	≥1	FSGV
Inner-city pedestrian areas	≥5	E_{min} = 1 lx g_2 = 0.08	≥1	FSGV
Stairs, exterior	15	g_2 = 0.3	-	FSGV

Table 3.8.15 Minimum requirements for lighting pedestrian areas

Class	Horizontal illuminance	
	E_m in lx [minimum value, maintained level]	E_{min} in lx [maintained level]
S1	15	5
S2	10	3
S3	7.5	1.5
S4	5	1
S5	3	0.6
S6	2	0.6
S7	No requirements stipulated	No requirements stipulated

In order to ensure a certain uniformity, the actual value of the average illuminance may not exceed 1.5 times the minimum value designated for the class.

Table 3.8.16 Descriptions of the lighting classes S1 to S7 for pedestrian and cycling areas

Sports Facilities

For sports facilities, the athletes' requirements for sufficient illumination of the playing field are accompanied by spectators' requirements for good visibility of the events taking place and, in the case of television broadcasts, also heightened requirements for video recording. The basis for calculating the illuminance for sports facilities is EN 12193. Facilities are divided into lighting classes that correspond to different uses and thus different required illuminance levels:

Lighting class I:
Top-level sporting events (international and national competitions), high-performance training
Spectators: long viewing distance

Lighting class II:
Average-level sporting events, performance training
Spectators: medium viewing distance

Lighting class III:
Low-level competitions (usually no spectators), general training, general school and recreational sport

For venues that are primarily used for training, only minor requirements must be anticipated. Generally, training areas for soccer and tennis can be illuminated in compliance with the standards by using 4–6 masts with 8 floodlights and light source heights of 12–16 m. Depending on the sport, an illuminance between 70 and 200 lx is sufficient. For facilities where international competitions will be held, illuminance levels of up to 1,400 lx (UEFA stadium classification) in the direction of the camera can be required. The standard establishes no stipulations; recommendations and guidelines pertaining to the competitions in question should be consulted.

Sport	Lighting class	Horizontal illuminance	
		E_{av} lx	E_{min}/E_{av} (uniformity)
American football, Beach volleyball, Soccer, Rugby	I	500	0.7
	II	200	0.6
	III	75	0.5
Baseball	I	750	0.7
	II	500	0.7
	III	300	0.5
Basketball	I	500	0.7
	II	200	0.6
	III	75	0.5
Hockey	I	500	0.7
	II	200	0.7
	III	200	0.7
Track and field, Equestrian sports (jumping and dressage)	I	500	0.7
	II	200	0.5
	III	100	0.5
Tennis	I	500	0.7
	II	300	0.7
	III	200	0.6

Table 3.8.17 Requirements for horizontal illuminance by type of sport in outdoor facilities, as per DIN EN 12193

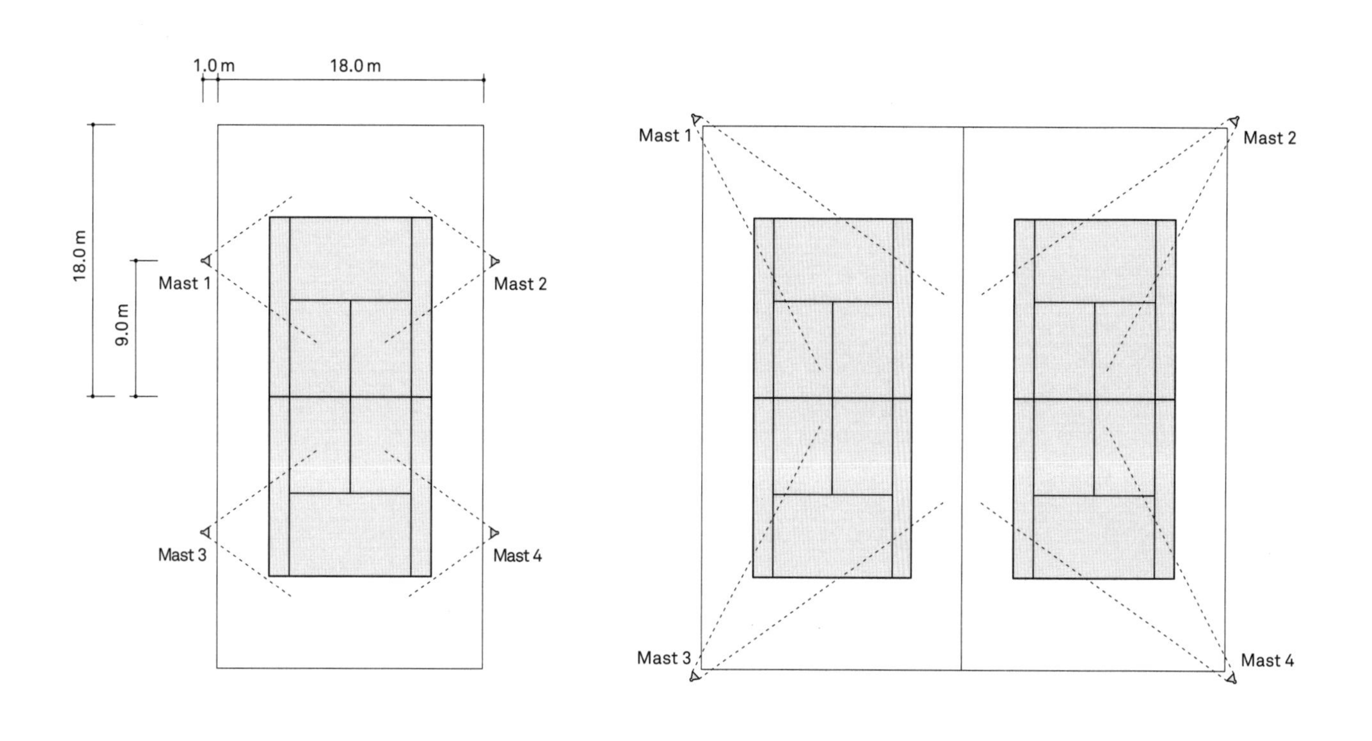

Figure 3.8.2 Example for lighting a tennis facility with a four-mast layout

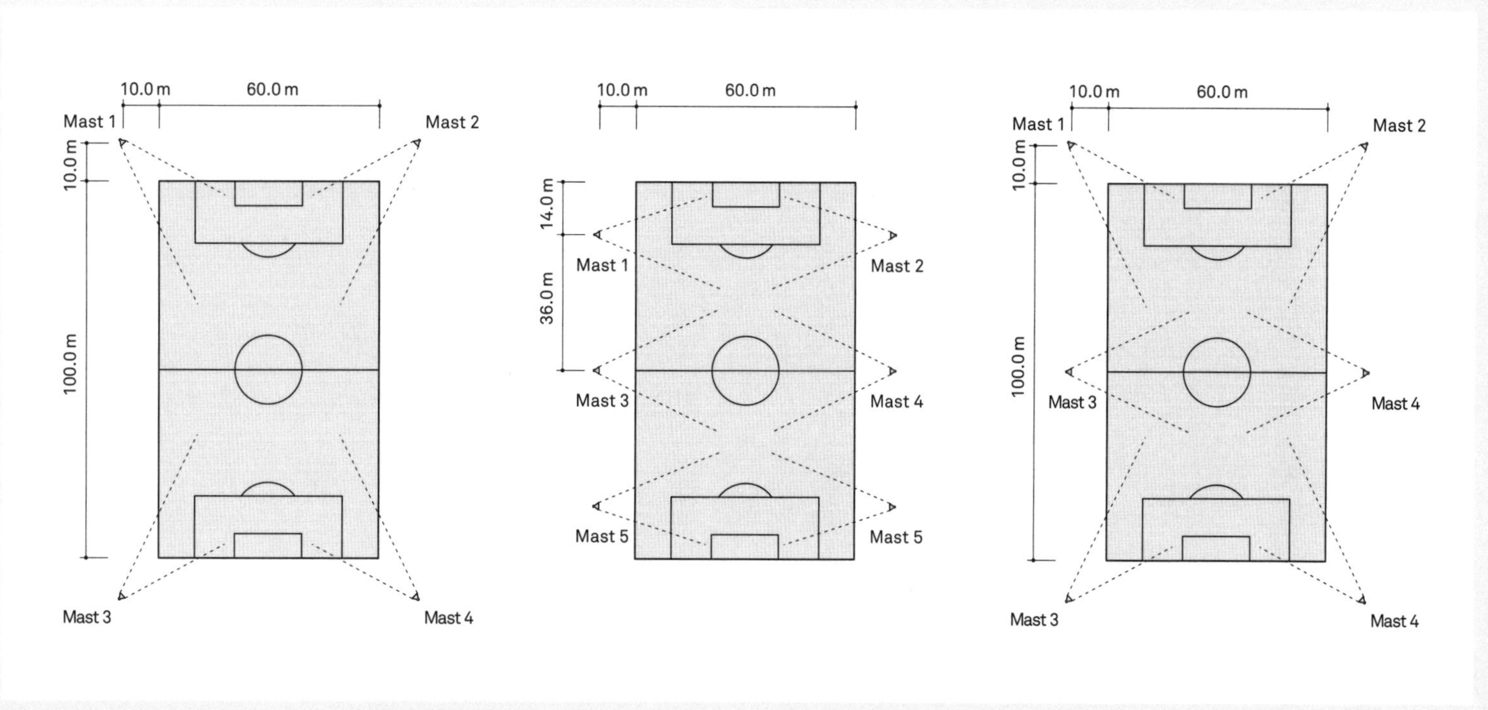

Figure 3.8.3 Example for lighting soccer fields: four-mast layout and six-mast layout

3 Elements
3.9 Water Features and Stormwater Infiltration

3.9 Water Features and Stormwater Infiltration

Water always flows to the lowest point and accumulates as soon as it reaches a depression. Thus natural ponds and lakes always fill an appropriate concave area, and the water surface traces the changing course along its edge, where it intersects the undulating terrain at a constant elevation. An artificially created pond seems most natural when it is sited to fit within the existing topography and is located at a low point in the terrain. If it is built using nonrigid construction – with membrane or clay seals, for example – not only is a seminatural character created that way, but the structural stability of the natural soil mass can be optimally utilized. No additional means of support are needed.

While still in the planning stage, choices should be made between nonrigid and rigid construction (concrete basin, masonry, prefabricated plastic basins), between a planted and an unplanted basin, and between facilities with standing or moving water (fountains, streams, etc.), in order to make allowances for the requirements that emerge regarding the site, the dimensions, and the technical equipment. This is important not in the least because these factors can significantly influence the functionality of a facility and the intensity of maintenance it requires.

Stormwater must be drained away from the surfaces of paths to allow their safe use and to prevent damage from occurring to built structures. To do so, appropriate measures must be planned together with any necessary changes to the grading, and all this should begin at an early stage in the planning process in order to integrate the necessary steps into the design of the outdoor facilities. → Chapter 3.2

In addition to rainwater that falls onto the ground surfaces, water from the roofs of any new buildings must also be taken into consideration. Green roofs always have positive impact in this regard, as they help minimize the volume of water discharge and retard water runoff.

The first choice for discharging stormwater is always decentralized infiltration directly on the property. This not only relieves the existing wastewater systems, but also contributes to groundwater enrichment. The options for on-site infiltration must be investigated and all the requirements under water law must be identified. In most municipalities, infiltration is, from the perspective of water law, already required for new construction as long as no hazard to the groundwater ensues.

If precipitation that falls onto paved areas cannot be directly discharged into adjacent green areas, then drainage gutters, yard drains, and/or street drains must be used to transport the water to the infiltration surfaces and facilities.

Intermediate storage and subsequent use of rainwater for irrigating the vegetated areas of the outdoor facility is another possibility.

Site

Exposure of Water Features

The right location for a water feature depends on its type and its intended function. The exposure plays a decisive role, particularly with respect to any planting. Most aquatic plants love conditions ranging from full sun to partial shade, so a location with full shade should be avoided. Too much direct sunlight, on the other hand, promotes the growth of algae and therefore a location in light partial shade is best. But partial shading can also be achieved through the use of plants with floating leaves. Six hours of sunshine are regarded as a minimum, but especially for lily hybrids, the optimum is closer to eight hours. As a general rule, direct sunlight in the mornings and the afternoons is preferable to midday.

In addition, minimizing the introduction of organic matter (e.g., from falling leaves, needles, pollen, or wind dispersed seeds) has a favorable effect on the ecological balance. Hence a proximity to larger trees and shrubs should be avoided.

Habitat of Aquatic Plants

Since the water level in ponds fluctuates under natural conditions, many plants along the bank and in the shallow water zone have a fairly high site amplitude with respect to the water depth. So many plants can colonize a fairly wide littoral zone in a pond that has a more or less constant water level. Floating-leaved plants and underwater plants often require a minimum depth of water. → Figure 3.9.2

Another factor to be considered is that some plants respond sensitively to moving water. This is especially true for water lilies, so fountains and similar features should be avoided in their vicinity.

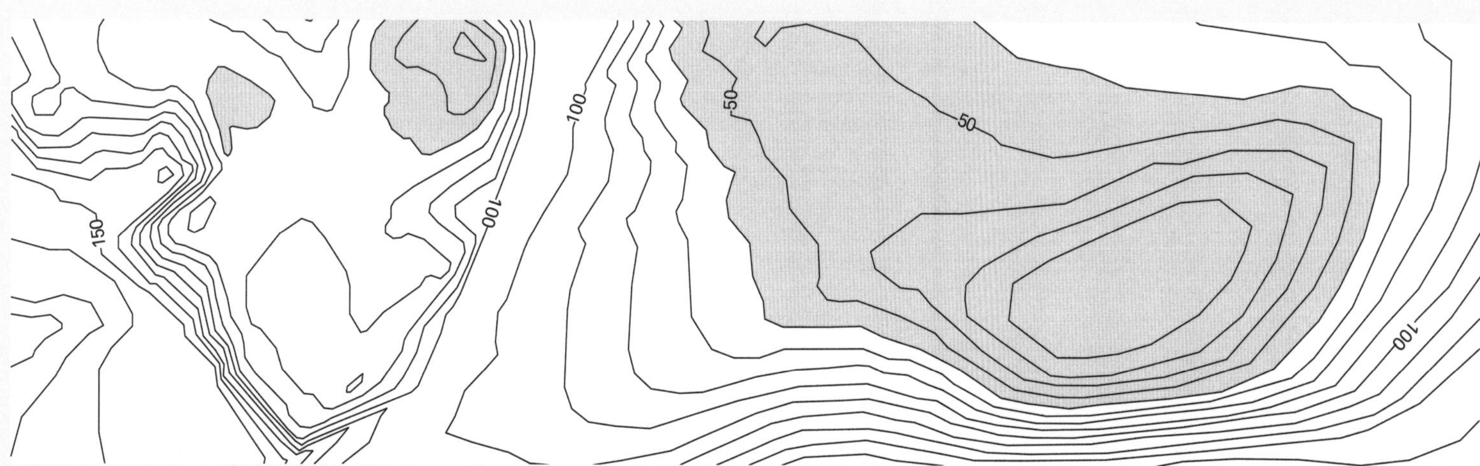

Figure 3.9.1 Natural course of the water level intersecting the topography

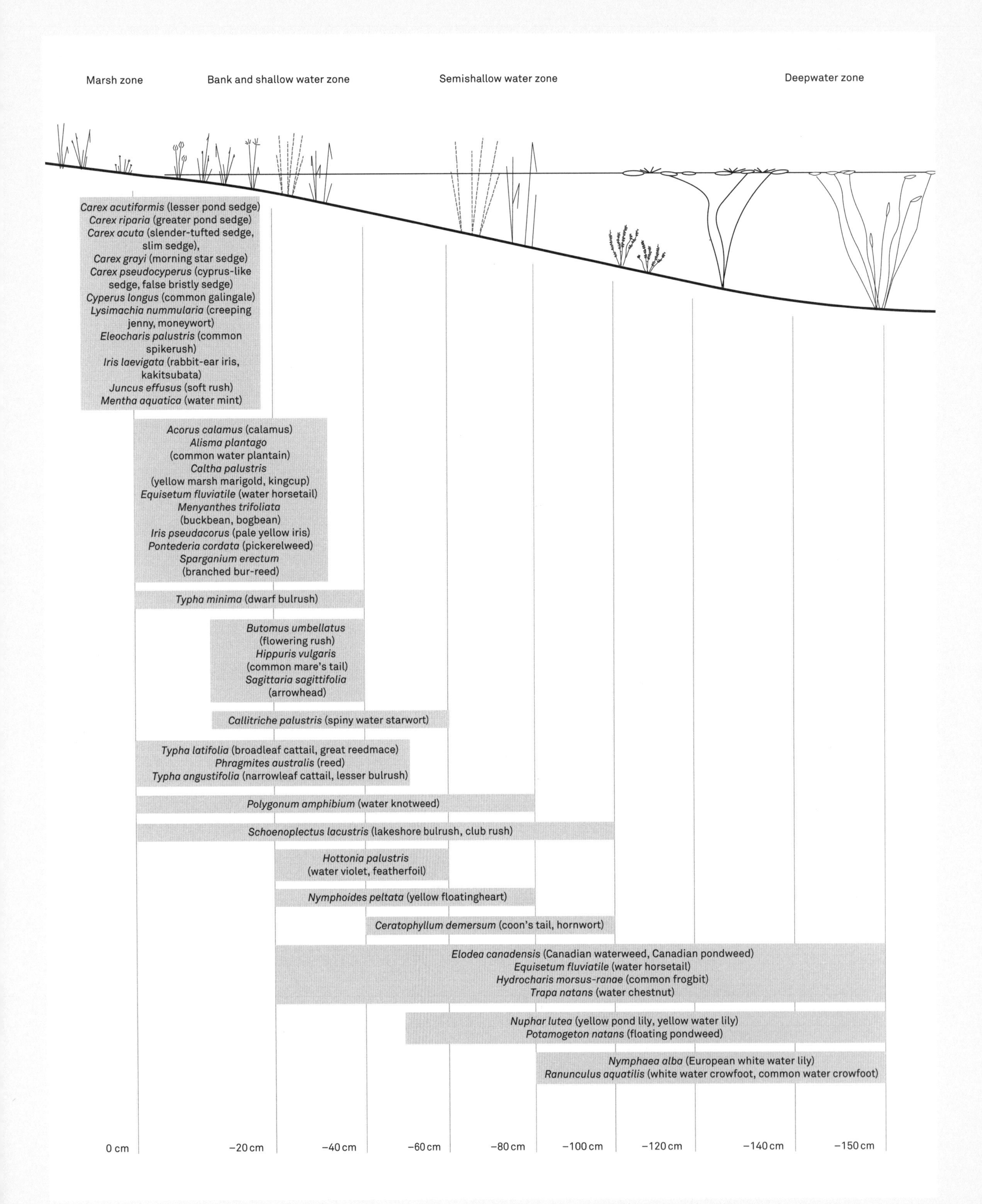

Marsh zone
Bank and shallow water zone
Semishallow water zone
Deepwater zone
Carex acutiformis (lesser pond sedge)
Carex riparia (greater pond sedge)
Carex acuta (slender-tufted sedge, slim sedge),
Carex grayi (morning star sedge)
Carex pseudocyperus (cyprus-like sedge, false bristly sedge)
Cyperus longus (common galingale)
Lysimachia nummularia (creeping jenny, moneywort)
Eleocharis palustris (common spikerush)
Iris laevigata (rabbit-ear iris, kakitsubata)
Juncus effusus (soft rush)
Mentha aquatica (water mint)
Acorus calamus (calamus)
Alisma plantago (common water plantain)
Caltha palustris (yellow marsh marigold, kingcup)
Equisetum fluviatile (water horsetail)
Menyanthes trifoliata (buckbean, bogbean)
Iris pseudacorus (pale yellow iris)
Pontederia cordata (pickerelweed)
Sparganium erectum (branched bur-reed)
Typha minima (dwarf bulrush)
Butomus umbellatus (flowering rush)
Hippuris vulgaris (common mare's tail)
Sagittaria sagittifolia (arrowhead)
Callitriche palustris (spiny water starwort)
Typha latifolia (broadleaf cattail, great reedmace)
Phragmites australis (reed)
Typha angustifolia (narrowleaf cattail, lesser bulrush)
Polygonum amphibium (water knotweed)
Schoenoplectus lacustris (lakeshore bulrush, club rush)
Hottonia palustris (water violet, featherfoil)
Nymphoides peltata (yellow floatingheart)
Ceratophyllum demersum (coon's tail, hornwort)
Elodea canadensis (Canadian waterweed, Canadian pondweed)
Equisetum fluviatile (water horsetail)
Hydrocharis morsus-ranae (common frogbit)
Trapa natans (water chestnut)
Nuphar lutea (yellow pond lily, yellow water lily)
Potamogeton natans (floating pondweed)
Nymphaea alba (European white water lily)
Ranunculus aquatilis (white water crowfoot, common water crowfoot)
0 cm
−20 cm
−40 cm
−60 cm
−80 cm
−100 cm
−120 cm
−140 cm
−150 cm

Figure 3.9.2 Habitats of aquatic plants

Water Overflow Device

To maintain a regulated flow of water in water basins and ponds, and to prevent water from flowing out onto peripheral areas after rainfalls and causing them to become waterlogged, a water overflow device must be provided. An overflow device for small ponds or basins can be a simple seepage pit, provided that its only intended purpose is to collect excess stormwater. If greater amounts of water are expected – or if designing a well installation or a water feature that can be expected to have overflowing water at regular intervals – an overflow device that feeds the water into a drainage system or a water circuit must be provided.

Water Depths

When designing basins without plants, the size and dimensions can be chosen relatively freely. Regular maintenance work is still required all the same.

Once it is intended to include plants, certain minimum dimensions should not be exceeded. The water depth depends on the type of planting and can therefore vary. → **Figure 3.9.4** Terraced steps on the bottom of the pool or pond allow for different water zones in a relatively small space.

If a lasting ecological balance is sought, however, the depth should be no less than 80 cm and preferably 100–120 cm. To enable aquatic life to survive in the water over the winter, the pond should not freeze fully and, depending on the region, the water depth that is required can vary accordingly; it is roughly 100 cm in Central Europe.

For seminatural designs and the creation of a peripheral flat shore or terracing, a minimum size of 10 m² should be expected. The larger the facility, the more likely it is that a stable ecosystem will develop.

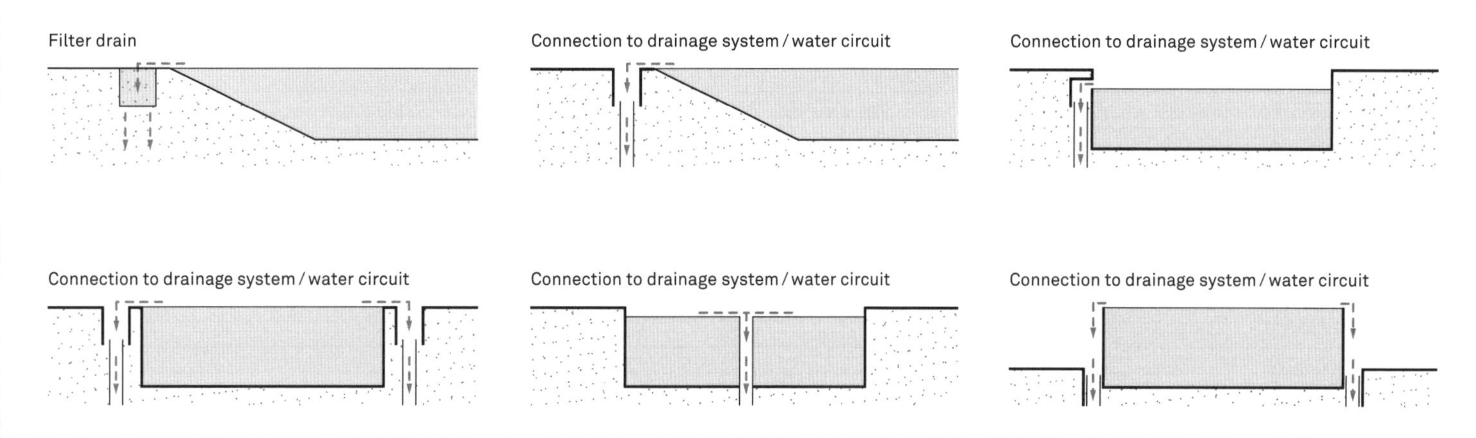

Figure 3.9.3 Overflows for ponds and water basins

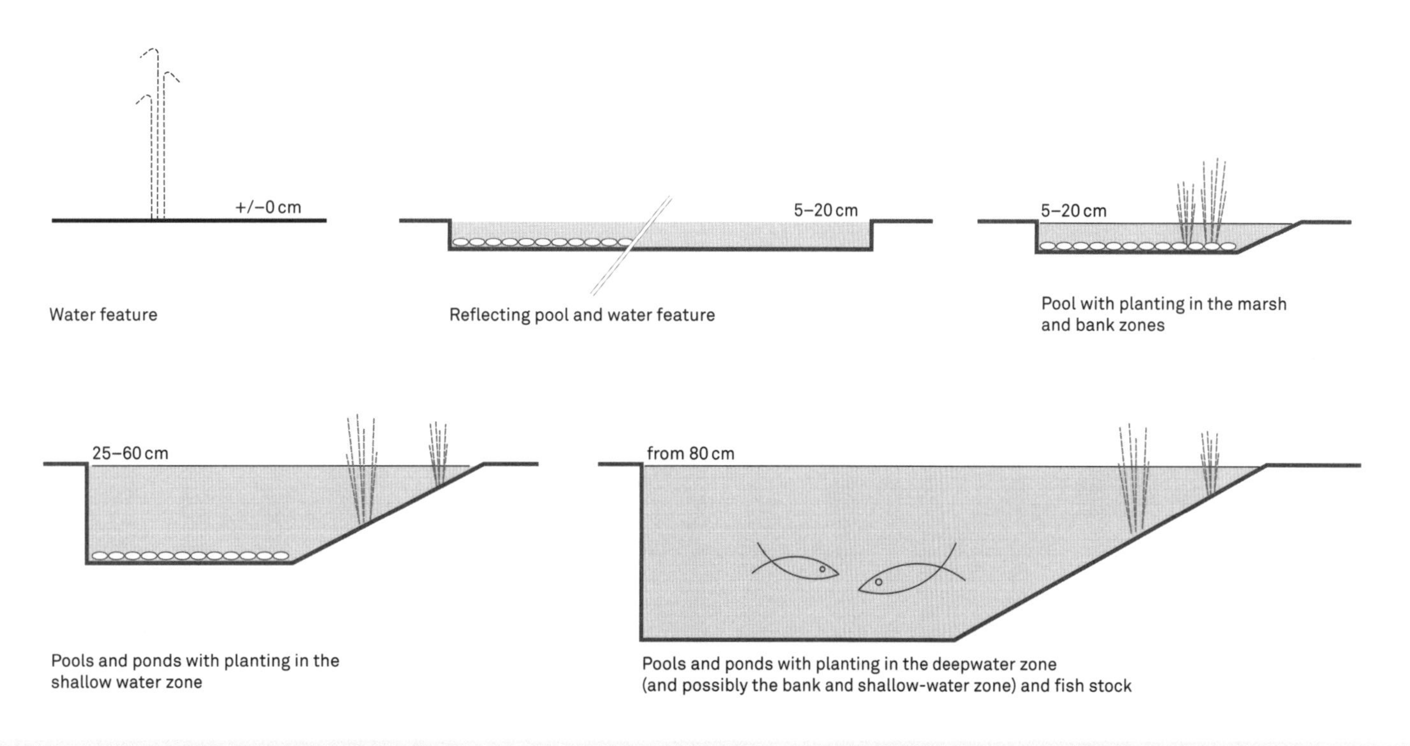

Figure 3.9.4 Water depths for different uses and plant zones

Planted Facilities

	Planted pools	Seminatural ponds
Site		
Location	Freely selectable	At a low point in the natural terrain
Exposure to sunlight	Optimal: 6–7 hours, more for lily hybrids	
	Alternative: Use of floating-leaved plants, as long as they do not take up more than 50 % of the water surface	
	Avoid direct proximity to deciduous trees	
Dimensions		
Minimum size	None	Minimum 6–10 m²
Minimum size with fish stock	6 m²	
Minimum size for swimming ponds	35–60 m²	
Minimum depth	None	80 cm, preferably 100–120 cm
Minimum depth with fish stock	Depending on the freezing depth: 80 cm in Central Europe, preferably 100–120 cm	
Minimum depth for swimming ponds	1.35 cm	

Table 3.9.1 Local conditions and minimum sizes of pools and ponds

Site Requirements for Stormwater Infiltration

The infiltration of stormwater is only an option if the pollution level of the surface runoff does not give reason to expect it would cause significant contamination of the soil and the groundwater. For certain special areas, such as truck parking lots, yards, and streets in commercial and industrial areas, as well as unroofed storage areas for recyclable materials (organic compost, paper, refuse), stormwater infiltration is fundamentally not an option or may only be considered in exceptional cases. Rainwater draining from metal roofs made of uncoated copper, zinc, or lead and the runoff from car parking spaces are not suitable for all types of infiltration, because the harmful substances occurring there could contaminate the soil and the groundwater. Uncontaminated water can percolate through every system. → **Table 3.9.2**

The following conditions are to be reviewed prior to proceeding with the planning:

- The soil must be sufficiently permeable to water. → **Table 3.9.3 and 3.9.4**
- The appropriate infiltration system must be selected according to the potential contamination of the surface runoff. → **Table 3.9.2 and Table 3.9.4**
- The conditions for permit-free use of groundwater treated by infiltration must be met or authorization must be granted under water law.
- An adequately sized site must exist on the property in a location that is appropriate for an infiltration system. → **Figure 3.9.6**
- Near buildings, minimum clearances are to be maintained between any building and the infiltration system. → **Figure 3.9.5**
- It must be possible to conduct the stormwater to the location of the infiltration system without undue effort.

Infiltration System Selection

Stormwater usually infiltrates through the active soil layer. If insufficient space is available for surface infiltration, subsurface facilities such as French drains or infiltration shaft systems are used in addition, since their storage capacity accommodates larger volumes of stormwater until the water is later discharged to the subsoil. The following options are available for stormwater infiltration:

- Infiltration field
- Infiltration swale
- Infiltration trench (French drain)
- Swales with underdrainage
- Infiltration basin / perforated pipe
- Infiltration shaft

When choosing the infiltration system, in addition to the quality of the runoff water infiltrating the ground, the geological conditions – and thus the infiltration capacity of the subsoil – play a crucial role, as does the availability of open areas. → **Figure 3.9.6**

Area			Surface infiltration systems			Subsurface infiltration systems	
	Pollutant content	Qualitative assessment	$A_u : A_s \leq 5$ Usually wide-area infiltration	$5 < A_u : A_s \leq 15$ Usually remote infiltration fields and swales, individual swales with underdrainage	$A_u : A_s > 15$ Usually centralized swales and infiltration basins	French drains and perforated pipe systems	Infiltration shaft
Green roofs; meadows and cultivated land with stormwater runoff into the drainage system possible	Low		+	+	+	+	+
Roofs with no uncoated metals (copper, zinc or lead); terrace / patio areas in residential districts and comparable commercial zones		Harmless	+	+	+	+	(+)
Roofs with typical amounts of uncoated metals (copper, zinc, or lead)			+	+	+	(+)	(+)
Bikeways and walkways in residential districts; bikeways and walkways beyond the splash-and-spray zone of roads, traffic-calmed areas			+	+	(+)	(–)	(–)
Yards, car parking lots without frequent movement of vehicles, and roadways with little traffic (maximum ADT: 300 vehicles) in residential districts and comparable commercial zones			+	+	(+)	(–)	–
Roads with 300–5,000 vehicles per day (ADT), e.g., residential streets, connecting roads, county roads	Increasing ↓		+	+	(+)	(–)	–
Runways and taxiways of airfields, airport taxiways		Tolerable	+	+	(+)	(–)	–
Roofs in commercial and industrial zones with significant air pollution			+	+	(+)	(–)	–
Roads with 5,000–15,000 vehicles per day (ADT), e.g., major roads; airport runways			+	+	(+)	–	–
Car parking lots with frequent movement of vehicles, e.g., at shopping centers			+	(+)	(+)	–	–
Roofs with uncoated roofing made of copper, zinc, or lead; roads and open spaces with heavy pollution, e.g., from agriculture, trucking companies, riding stables, markets			+	(+)	(+)	–	–
Roads with more than 15,000 vehicles per day (ADT), e.g., main arterial roads, highways			+	(+)	(+)	–	–
Yards and roads in commercial and industrial zones with significant air pollution			(–)	(–)	(–)	–	–
Special areas, e.g., truck parking lots and parking spaces; Aircraft position areas at airports	Very high	Intolerable	–	–	–	–	–

+ Usually permitted (+) Usually permitted after removal of substances through pretreatment measures; e.g., as per ATV-DVWK-M 153
(–) Only permitted in exceptional cases – Not permitted

Table 3.9.2 Suitability of infiltration systems according to the potential impact of surface runoff, outside drinking water protection zones I and II

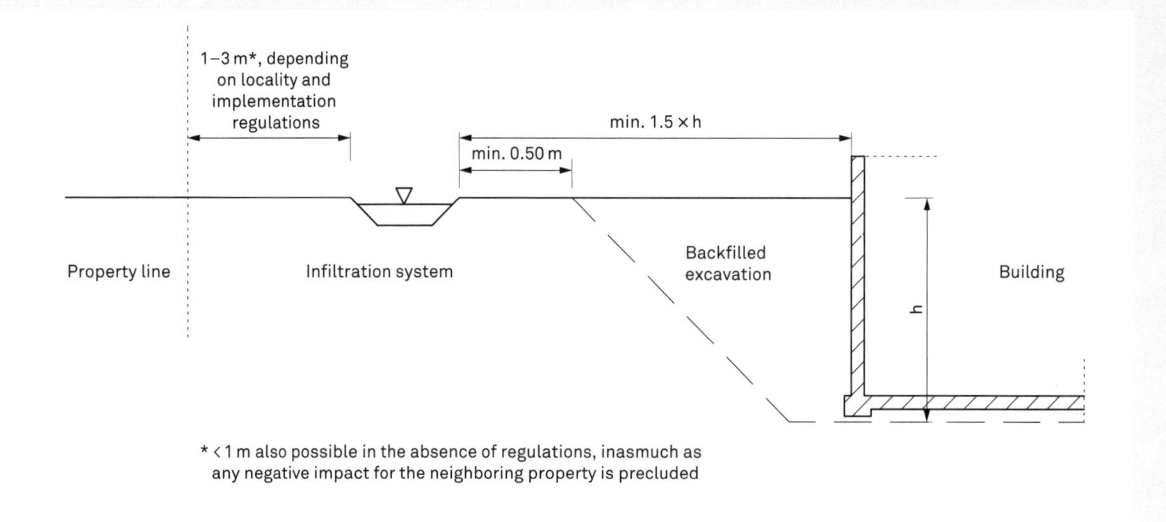

Figure 3.9.5 Minimum distance between decentralized infiltration systems and buildings without hydrostatic pressure resistant waterproofing

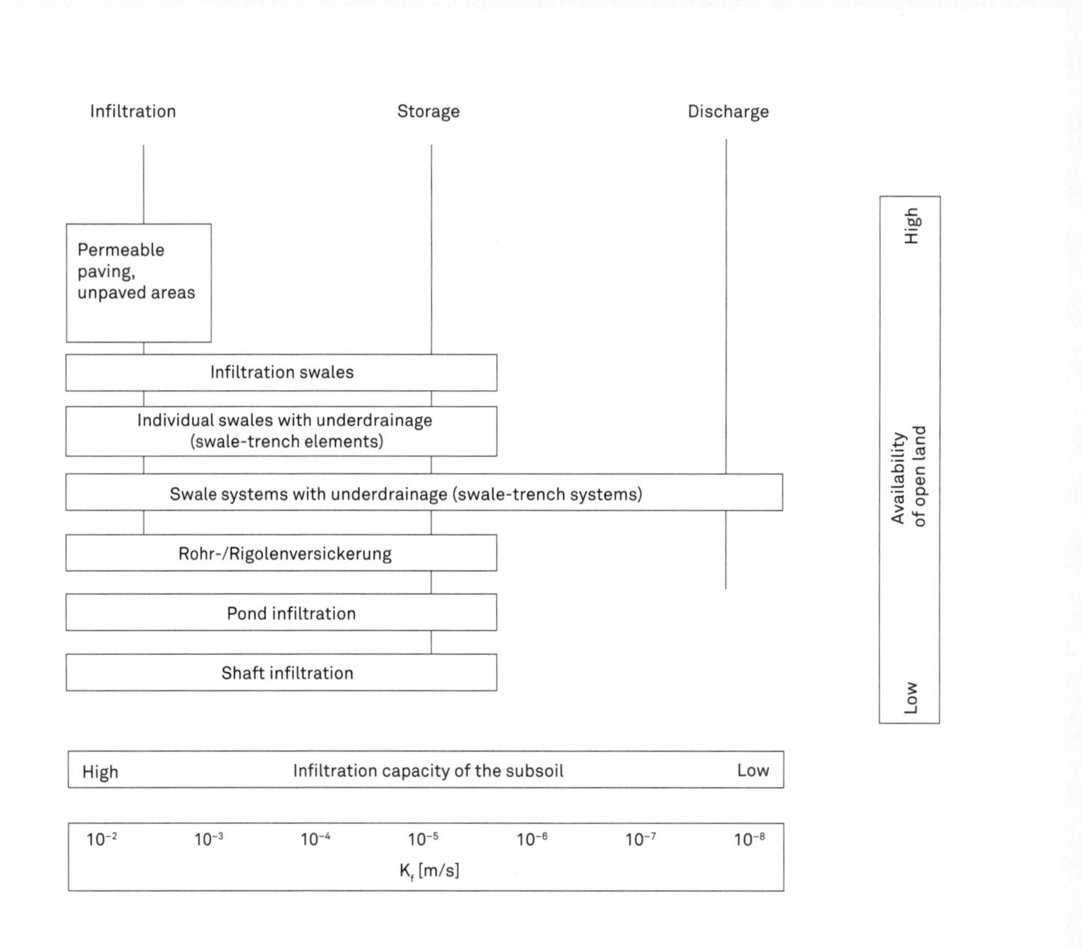

Figure 3.9.6 Selection of the infiltration system depends on subsoil and land availability

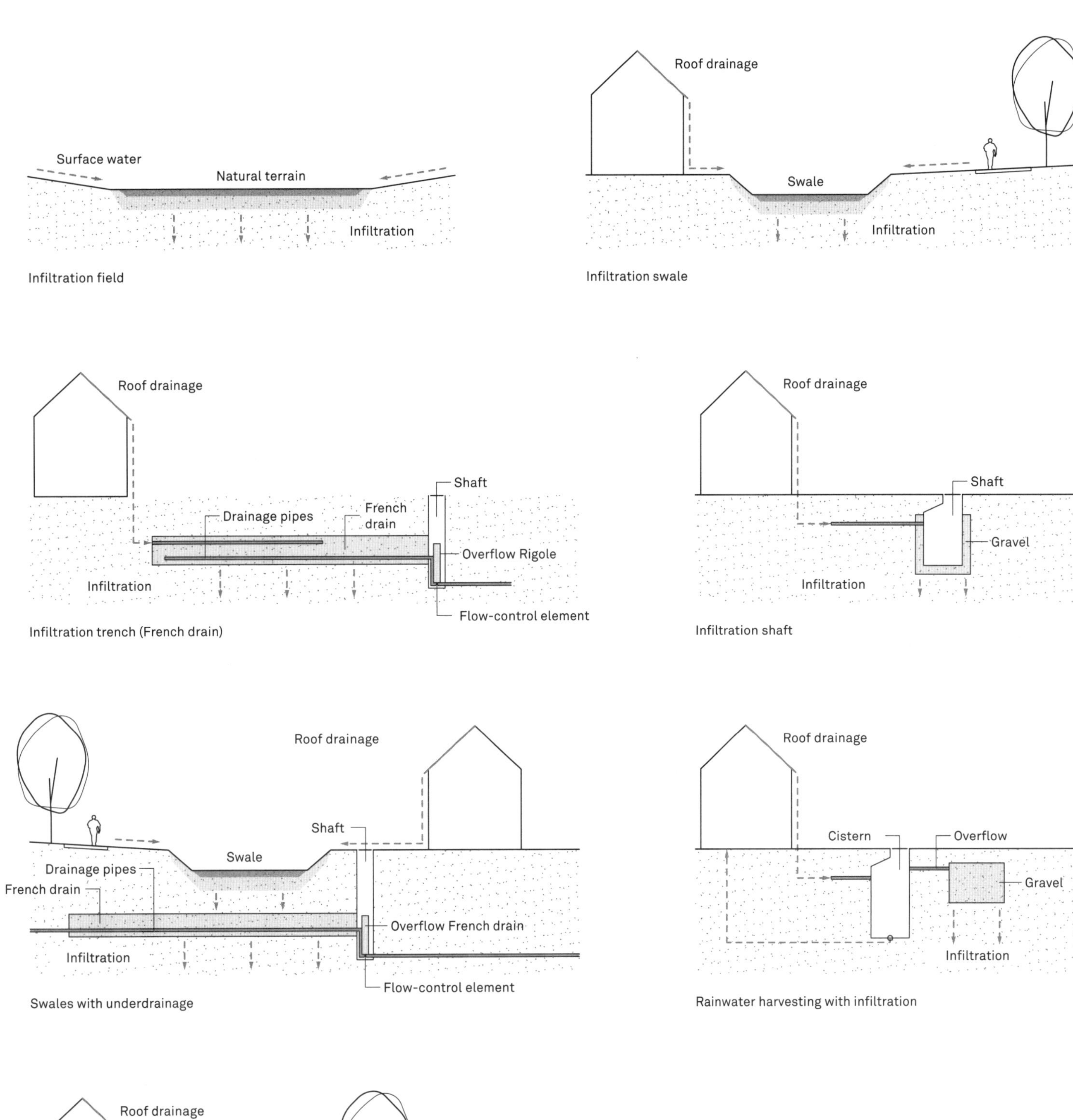

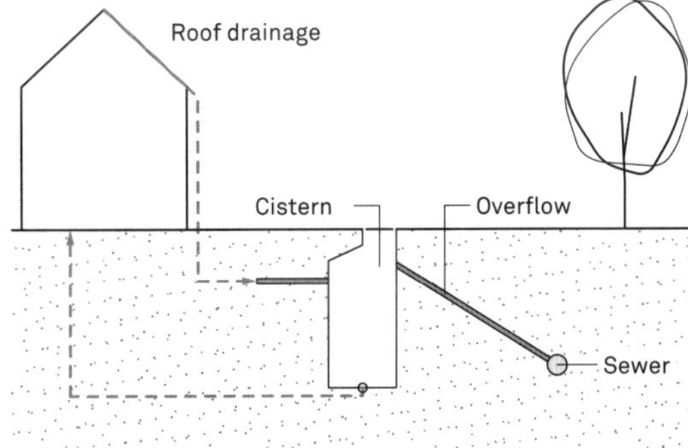

Rainwater harvesting with discharge

Figure 3.9.7 Schematic representations of various infiltration systems

Dimensions and Characteristics

Permeability of the Paving

In order to minimize the quantities of stormwater that must infiltrate the ground via remote facilities, paved areas should be permeable where possible, and adjacent roof areas should be vegetated. In so doing, the effort expended to construct infiltration systems and the space needed for them can be reduced. → Table 3.9.2

Permeability can be expressed with the runoff coefficient (Ψ). This is the quotient of the amount of precipitation that directly drains off (effective precipitation) in relation to the total precipitation. Thus a value of Ψ = 0.7 means that from the total amount of precipitation, only 70 % is runoff that must infiltrate the ground or be carried away.

Infiltration Capacity

To determine whether infiltration is possible, the local conditions must be checked in advance. The permeability of the soil is expressed by the kf value, which reflects the infiltration capacity. Soils with a high clay content and a k_f value of 10^{-7} have a high retention effect and are less suitable than sandy soils with a k_f value of 10^{-4}. But even very good permeability can have negative impact. Pure gravel, for example, percolates water too quickly, with the result that the stormwater is not cleansed sufficiently by the soil filter.

Design Rainfall

Since rain events are dependent on the local climatic and topographic conditions and also differ in duration and intensity, individual values must be used for each location and each application.

The locally relevant precipitation intensity can be obtained from the local building authorities or – at cost – from the German Weather Service (DWD). The DWD regularly compiles a summary of heavy precipitation totals for Germany, so even extreme rainfall events that have frequently occurred recently are represented in their data (see KOSTRA-DWD-2000 → **KO**ordinierte **ST**arkniederschlags-**R**egionalisierungs-**A**uswertungen [Coordinated heavy precipitation regionalization evaluations]).

For dimensioning a stormwater drainage facility (drainage gutter, drain line, or drain) the following rain event is used as a basis, in accordance with DIN 1986-100:

- For draining roof areas: calculated rainfall intensity = $r_{5,5}$ i.e., rainfall duration D = 5 minutes and the rainfall frequency is at least once every 5 years (T = 5)
- For draining ground areas (without planned stormwater detention): calculated rainfall intensity = $r_{5,2}$ i.e., rainfall duration D = 5 minutes and the rainfall frequency is at least once every 2 years (T = 2)

Calculation of the Stormwater Runoff

The runoff coefficient is used to determine the accumulated volume of water that is decisive for subsequent dimensioning of the drainage facilities and infiltration systems.

The formula for calculating stormwater runoff is as follows:

$$Qr = r(D,T) \cdot \Psi \cdot A\,y$$

Qr = stormwater runoff [L/s]
A = effective catchment surface area (horizontal projection) [m²]
Ψ = runoff coefficient according to Table 3.9.3
r(D,T) = calculated rainfall intensity [L / (s · ha)], where D denotes the duration and T denotes the frequency

Dimensioning of Infiltration Facilities

For determining the dimensions of infiltration facilities, the following formulas are used: → Table 3.9.5

Clearances

The following minimum distances from infiltration facilities should be maintained:

- 3 m to property lines
- 1.5 m between decentralized infiltration systems and buildings without waterproofing resistant to hydrostatic pressure (DWA)
- 6 m to buildings (or 1.5 m × basement depth), 10 m to other infiltration systems

Catchment Area of Drainage Facilities

The drainage capacity of a channel or a drain is particularly dependent on the inlet cross section and the local rainfall intensity. Therefore, an individual calculation should be made in each and every case for definitive dimensioning of the facilities. For the purposes of preliminary design, however, rough calculations can offer a basic estimate of the dimensions needed by appropriate facilities.

The catchment area for street drains should be approximately 400 m² and yard drains should be 200 m², although the actual capacity of the inlet cross section is often higher for standardized covers.

The following standard value can be used for a rough calculation of the capacity: 1 cm² inlet cross section corresponds to about 1 m² of surface to be drained. In order to ensure that stormwater is quickly discharged, the drain or channel size and the pipe cross sections must be dimensioned accordingly. In addition, the path the water must take should not be too long.

For steep slopes, on the ramps leading to parking garages, for example, significantly larger inlet cross sections are required because otherwise the water can possibly flow past the channel. Wider channels with heavy-duty grating covers should be used.

Surface	Runoff coefficient γ	
	as per DIN 1986-100	as per DWA-A 117
Paved surfaces		
Asphalt and concrete surfaces	1	(0.9)
Paving stones with sealed joints	1	
Paving stones and slabs on sand/gravel bedding	0.7	(0.75)
Paving stones with > 15 % joints	0.6	(0.5)
Synthetic surfacing and artificial turf	0.6	
Packed earth on sports fields	0.4	
Water-bound surfaces	0.3	
Grass paving blocks	0 (small areas, e.g., individual parking spaces and their approaches)	(0.15)
Garden paths made of water-bound paving	0.0	
Roof surfaces		
Asphalt or tile roofing	1	(0.9–1)
Gravel roofs	0.5	(0.7)
Extensive green roofs < 10 cm thick	0.5	(0.5)
Extensive green roofs ≥ 10 cm thick	0.3	(0.3)
Intensive green roofs	0.3	(0.3)
Unpaved surfaces		
Lawns	0.3	
Lawns and vegetated areas in gardens and parks	0	(0–0.3) Depending on slope
Round gravel and crushed stone surfaces	0	(0.3)

Table 3.9.3 Runoff coefficients of various surfaces

Soil types	Sand	Silt	Clay
K_f value (average values; exact value of the soil type according to soil investigation report)	10^{-4}	10^{-6}	10^{-7}
Infiltration time for a hydrostatic head of 1,000 mm	3 hours	12 days	115 days
Infiltration time for a hydraulic load of 5,000 mm (equivalent to A_s to A_{red} 1:10.645 mm precipitation, 0.8 runoff coefficient for sealed surface)	15 hours	60 days	575 days
Management options	Infiltration possible with no additional measures	Buffer storage necessary	Buffer storage and greater surface area or reduced discharge necessary
Preferred means of infiltration	IF, SW, IT, IS	ST, STS	STS

IF Infiltration field IS Infiltration shaft SW Infiltration swale ST Swale-trench element IT Infiltration trench STS Swale-trench system

Table 3.9.4 Infiltration capacity of different soil types

Infiltration system	Formula	Variables
Infiltration field	Calculation of the infiltration area (horizontal projection) A_S $A_s = \frac{A_u}{(k_f \cdot 10^{-7} / 2 \cdot r_{D(5)}) - 1}$	A_s = infiltration area (horizontal projection) A_u = surface area to be drained (AE) k_f = permeability coefficient $2 \cdot r_{D(0.2)} \cdot 10^{-7}$ $r_{D(0.2)}$= rainfall frequency, where T = 5a D = 10–15 min.
Infiltration swale	Volume of the swale V_M in m³ $V_M = \left[(A_u + \text{erf.}\, A_S)\, 10^{-7} \cdot r_{D(0,2)} = \text{erf.}\, A_S \cdot \frac{k_f}{2}\right] \cdot D \cdot 60 \cdot f_Z$	V_M = volume of the swale in m³ erf. $A_S = 0.1 \cdot A_u$ (soil types MSa, FSa), $0.2 \cdot A_u$ (soil types siSa, saSi, Si) $r_{D(0.2)}$ = rainfall frequency, where T = 5a D = variable* k_f = permeability coefficient f_z = safety factor (generally 1.2)
Infiltration trench (French drain)	Calculation of the trench length: $L_R = \frac{(A_u \cdot 10^{-7} \cdot r_{D(0,2)}}{\frac{b_R \cdot h \cdot S_{RR}}{D \cdot 60 \cdot f_Z} + \left(b_r + \frac{h}{2}\right) \cdot \frac{k_f}{2}}$	$r_{D(n)}$ = rainfall frequency, where n = 0.2 b_R = trench width h = height of the trench D = variable* S_{RR} = total storage coefficient > for trenches A S_R, for trenches with perforated pipe > formula for S_{RR}
	Calculation of the storage coefficient S_{RR}: $S_{RR} = \frac{S_R}{b_R \cdot h}\left[b_R \cdot h + \frac{\pi \cdot d^2}{4}\left(\frac{1}{S_R - 1}\right)\right]$	S_R = storage coefficient of the fill material > porosity of the fill material (e.g., 8/32 gravel > $S_R = 0.35$) b_R = trench width h = height of the trench d = pipe diameter (for thin-walled pipes)
Swales with underdrainage	Calculation of the swale and trench length: $L = \frac{(A_u + A_{s,M}) \cdot 10^{-7} \cdot r_{D(0,2)} - \frac{Q_{dr} - V_M}{D \cdot 60 \cdot f_Z}}{\frac{b_R \cdot h \cdot S_{RR}}{D \cdot 60 \cdot f_Z} + \left(b_r + \frac{h}{2}\right) \cdot \frac{k_f}{2}}$ The result must correspond to the following equation: existing $A_{s,M} = L \cdot b_R < A_{s,M} (0{,}1 \cdot A_u)$	A_s,M = infiltration area of the swale (estimated) = $0.1 \cdot A_u$ r_{DT} = rainfall frequency, where T'' = 5a Q_{dr} = regulated outflow in m³/s (for trenches without outlet = 0) V_M = swale volume (see above for calculation)
Infiltration shaft	Calculation of the shaft detention depth z: $Z = \frac{(A_u \cdot 10^{-7} \cdot r_{D(n)} - \left(\frac{\pi \cdot d^2}{4^a} \cdot \frac{k_f}{2}\right)}{\frac{d_i^2 \cdot \pi}{4 \cdot D \cdot 60 \cdot f_z} + \frac{d_a \cdot \pi \cdot k_f}{4}}$	$r_{D(0.2)}$ = rainfall frequency, where T = 5a d_a = outside diameter of the shaft d_i = inside diameter of the shaft

* Determination of the maximum value for varying rainfall duration D (> change to runoff velocity with increasing duration of rainfall)

Table 3.9.5 Fundamentals for calculating the dimensions of facilities with catchment areas of no more than 200 hectares, per worksheet DWA-A 138E – Planning, Construction, and Operation of Facilities for the Percolation of Precipitation Water

Irrigation Quantities

Rainwater can be stored temporarily and used for irrigating vegetated areas. The amount of water required and the needed frequency of watering is highly dependent on the type of planting, the water retention capacity of the soil / soil type, and the climatic conditions. Plantings that are appropriate to the location require no additional watering under normal circumstances.

But certain planted areas – especially high-maintenance grassy areas, such as ornamental lawns and heavy-duty turf (sports fields), trees and shrubs planted along roads, roses, and bedding perennials – cannot do without additional irrigation in dry periods.

Generally, 30–40 L/m² are needed to achieve effective moisture penetration of the soil that ensures the water penetrates to sufficient depths. With only 10 L/m², the water penetrates only about 10 cm deep into the soil, so the deeper root zones are not reached. Since grass has a shallower rooting depth than other plants, average quantities of 15–20 L/m²are sufficient.

Type of vegetation	Average irrigation quantities*	Frequency*	Remarks
Ornamental lawns Heavy-duty turf	Approx. 15–20 L/m²	On average every 3–7 days, or depending on the temperature: <20°C: max. every 15 days, >20–25°C: every 8–10 days, >25–30°C: every 6–8 days, >30°C: every 4–5 days	Up to 1,000 L/m² per year can be necessary in the Mediterranean region
Utility lawns	(approx. 15–20 L/m²)	as needed, 0.5 to 1× per week	Grass is capable of regeneration, so irrigation can be omitted if the lawn is not used extensively and the visual impression is not disturbing
Natural lawns Meadows	Generally not required		
Wild perennials Rock gardens	Generally not required		
Bedding perennials	30–40 L/m²	In dry periods	
Roses	30–40 L/m²	In dry periods	
Hedge plantings, especially trimmed hedges and topiary, but also flowering hedges	30–40 L/m²	In dry periods	Evergreens also need to be kept sufficiently moist in the winter
Large trees, 30–50 cm trunk circumference	200–500 L/tree	Up to 10×/year	(8×/year min. 300 L/tree)
Large trees, 50–80 cm trunk circumference	300–1,000 L/tree	Up to 10×/year	
Large trees, ≥80 cm trunk circumference	400–1,500 L/tree	Up to 10×/year	
Plants in tubs			
1 m balcony boxes Potted plants in 10 L containers	1–5 L/day		
Large potted plants	up to 20 L/day		

* The values given are for the period from mid-March to the end of September; in warmer climates and in areas with very permeable soils, larger amounts or more frequent watering can be necessary; in colder climates, the irrigation period may be shortened.

Table 3.9.6 Amounts of water potentially needed for irrigating green areas for routine maintenance care (Source: Lomer/Koppen 2001, Niesel 2006, Hansen/Stahl)

Water Requirements for Sports Fields

Maximum daily temperature °C	Water consumption mm/day (equivalent to L/m²)	
	Grassy sports areas	Packed-earth areas
>30	>5	Approximately 4
25–30	3–4	Approximately 3
20–25	2–3	Approximately 2
15–20	<2	<2

These consumption figures pertain to periods of daily maximum temperatures lasting several hours. They are tempered by humidity and air movement.

Table 3.9.7 Water consumption for sports areas (as per DIN 18035-2)

Precipitation occurrence	Precipitation amount mm/year	Water requirements for sprinklering mm/year				
		Grass sports fields	Packed earth areas	Golf courses		
				Greens/aprons	Tees	Fairways
Frequent	>900	0–75	0–60	100–200	50–100	0–100
Average	700–900	75–150	60–120	200–300	100–200	100–150
Seldom	500–700	150–250	120–180	300–400	200–250	150–200
Very seldom	<500	>250	>180	400–600	250–400	200–300

Table 3.9.8 Water requirements for sprinklering (as per DIN 18035-2)

Technical Devices

Water Connection

A water connection for supplying fresh water should be within easy access at every pond, to enable initial filling and to facilitate refilling after cleaning or repair work and for the compensation of evaporated water.

Water Pumps

Especially when continuous water circulation is planned, as is the case for moving water surfaces, artificial streams, and fountains, pumps are utilized. These can be submersible pumps located directly within the water basin, or they can be placed in a separate shaft outside the basin. → Figure 3.9.8

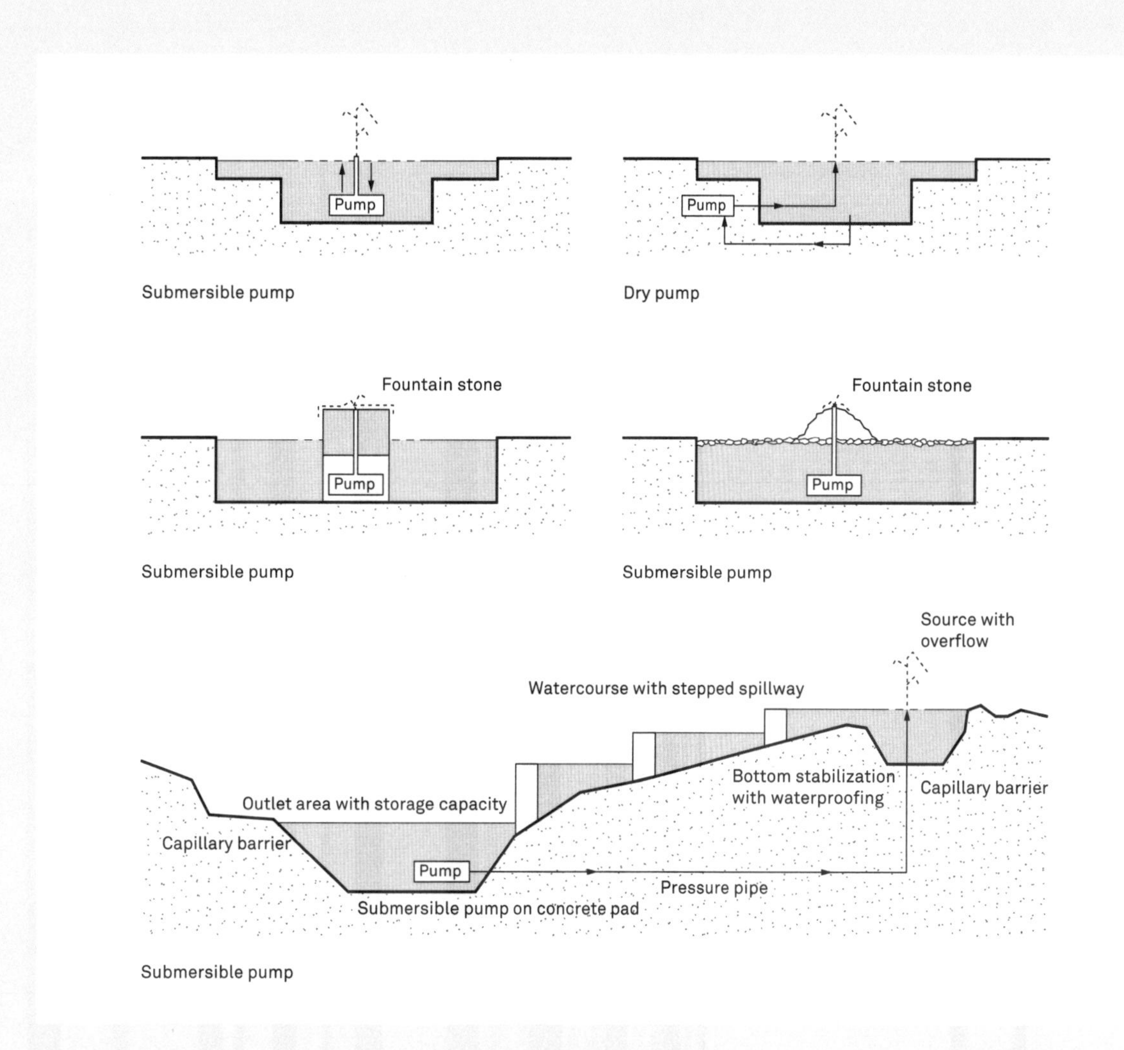

Figure 3.9.8 Principle of water circulation and pump location for fountains and artificial streams

Remarks on Building Law and Regulatory Approval

In Germany, authorization must be granted for the introduction of stormwater into a body of water or for infiltration on an industrial or commercial property or when infiltration is desired within the protective zones of a water protection area, so the necessary application should be made at an early stage.

National or state building regulations stipulate threshold values. Under normal circumstances, pools up to a size of 100 m³ are exempt from procedural requirements. In undeveloped open areas (beyond built-up areas), different regulations may apply.

The withdrawal of water for filling pools and ponds and the discharge of excess water into public bodies of water is subject to authorization.

3 Elements
3.10 Woody Plants

3.10 Woody Plants

Temperature equalization, shading, dust control, oxygen production, and carbon dioxide reduction are some of the positive benefits for the surroundings that can be expected from woody plants. They also increase humidity and can provide protection from the wind, and hence they play an important role in designs for open spaces. Efforts should be made to use them wherever possible – even in situations where it can be difficult to use woody plants, such as along urban streets.

Aside from choosing the right tree species for a particular location, it is also important to take account of functional constraints, such as clearance distances from piping and cable routes as well as neighboring properties.

Site

Spatial Requirements for Tree Locations

In its natural habitat, a tree develops a root zone whose volume amounts to as much as 0.75 m³ per square meter of crown projection surface (see Bakker and Kopinga). → Figure 3.10.1 This illustrates the enormous amount of space that is ordinarily required for a tree location. Especially along streets or on paved plazas in an urban context, this volume can rarely be made available. Minimum requirements for a sufficiently large root zone must nevertheless be observed, and in addition, sufficient water supply and adequate aeration needed for healthy tree growth must be ensured.

For planting trees in street spaces and on or around paved plazas and squares in a manner that is appropriate to the species and their functional needs, the following requirements and instructions should be fulfilled or observed:

A root zone of 12 m³ with a minimum depth of 1.5 m should be provided for each tree (these minimums must not be met for trees with small crowns). The city of Munich's technical specifications for root zone layers actually call for 36 m³. → Figure 3.10.2

- Depending on the tree pit size, a ventilation system may be necessary for aerating the soil beneath open tree pit surfaces → Figures 3.10.2 and 3.10.3.
- In areas subject to high loading pressures where high compaction of the root zone can thus be expected, the drip-line area must be protected with grating over the tree pit surface (covered tree pit) → Figure 3.10.4.
- Use of (reduced humus) single-layer substrates that direct roots downward.
- The adjacent areas should preferably be constructed using permeable paving materials, such as unit pavers with wide joints or water-bound materials, in order to improve the local conditions for the tree.
- Clearance distances from piping and cable routes, buildings, and traffic areas are to be observed (→ Table 3.10.1), bearing in mind that single-sided wind loads, e.g., in street corridors, can lead to asymmetric root development that results in disproportionately more roots to one side, which makes greater clearances a necessity on one side.

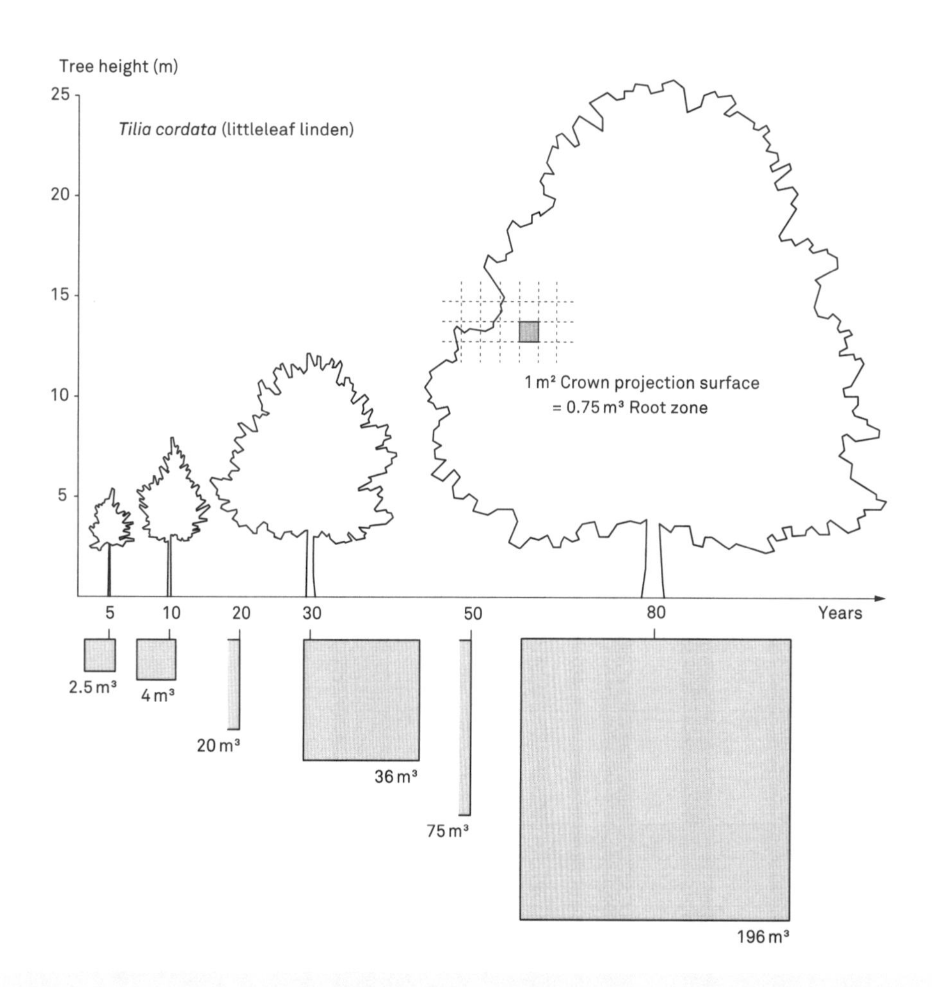

Figure 3.10.1 Relationship between crown projection surface and the root-permeable space of trees under natural conditions, as exemplified by *Tilia cordata*

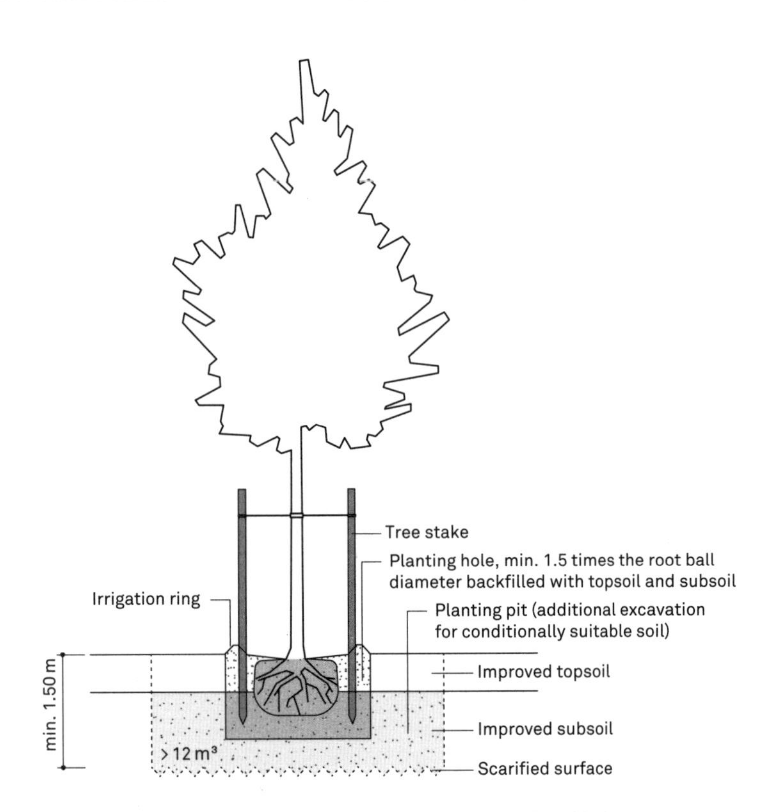

Planting in suitable and conditionally suitable soil per DIN 18916

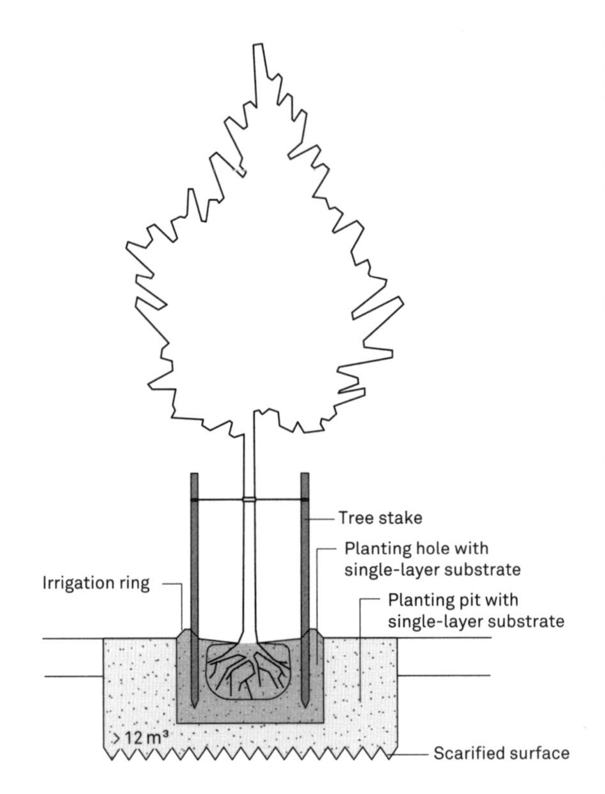

Planting in unsuitable soil – FLL planting pit type 1

Figure 3.10.2 Planting pits for locations within planted areas and in paved areas with open or covered tree pit surface

Traffic areas, buildings, and technical equipment and facilities (as per RASt 06)	Clearance
Traffic space for bicycle traffic	≥0.75 m
Traffic space for motorized traffic	≥1 m
Traffic space for rail transport	≥2 m
Buildings, for trees with small crowns	≥3 m
Buildings, for trees with large crowns	≥7 m
Cable tunnel with internal access	≥1.5 m
Underground piping and cable routes (minimum clearance of up to 5 m, depending on the type and size of utility lines)	≥2 m
Luminaires	≥3 m
Water lines, associated manholes, and attendant accessories (control cables, markers, etc.) (as per DVGW W400 Part 1)	
Dia. ≤DN 150	≥2 m
Dia. DN 150–400	≥3 m
Dia. >DN 400/≤DN 600	≥4 m
Dia. >DN 600	≥5 m

Table 3.10.1 Minimum clearance distances for tree plantings

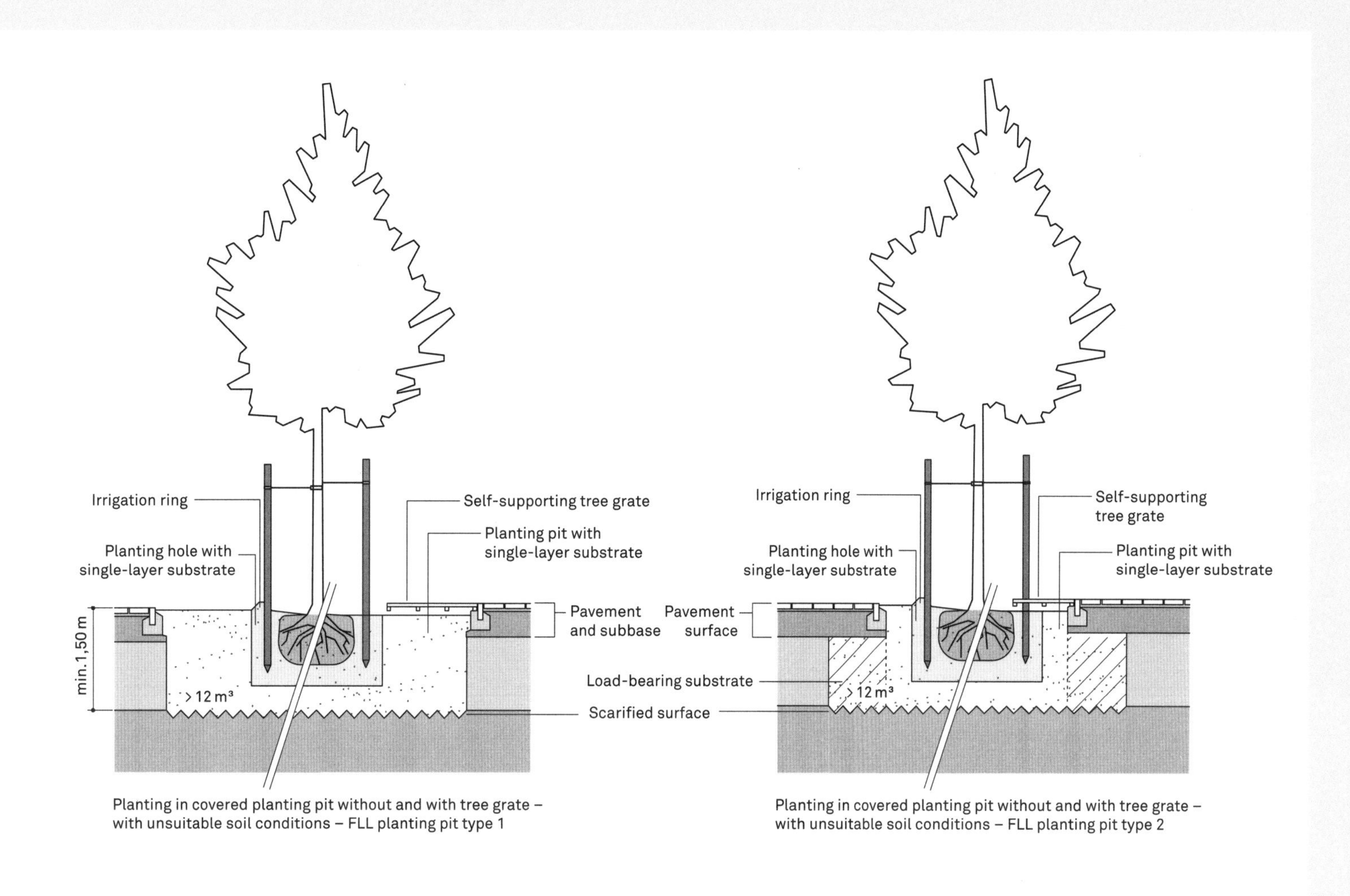

Figure 3.10.2 Planting pits at locations within planted areas and in paved areas with open or covered tree pit surface

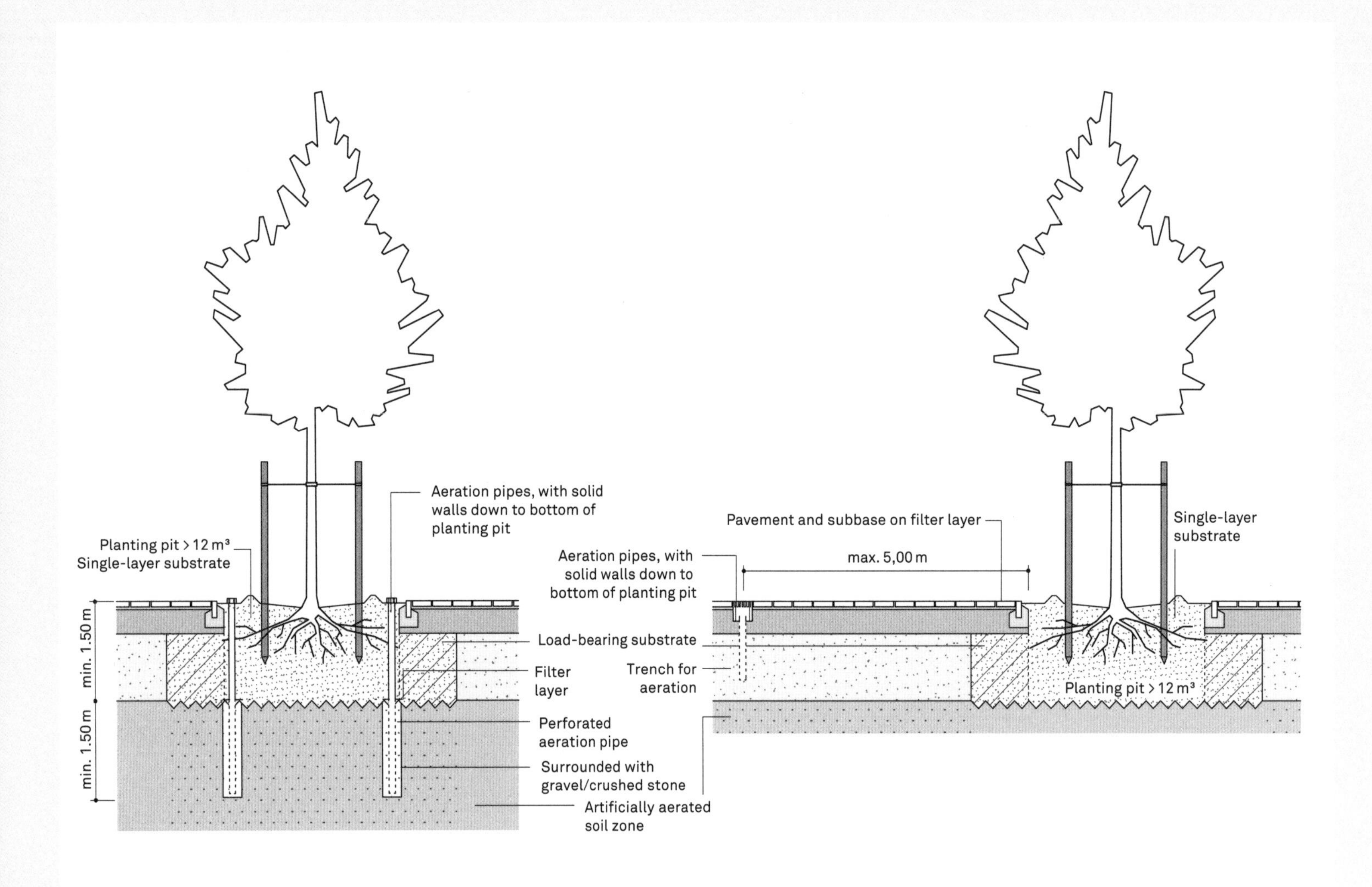

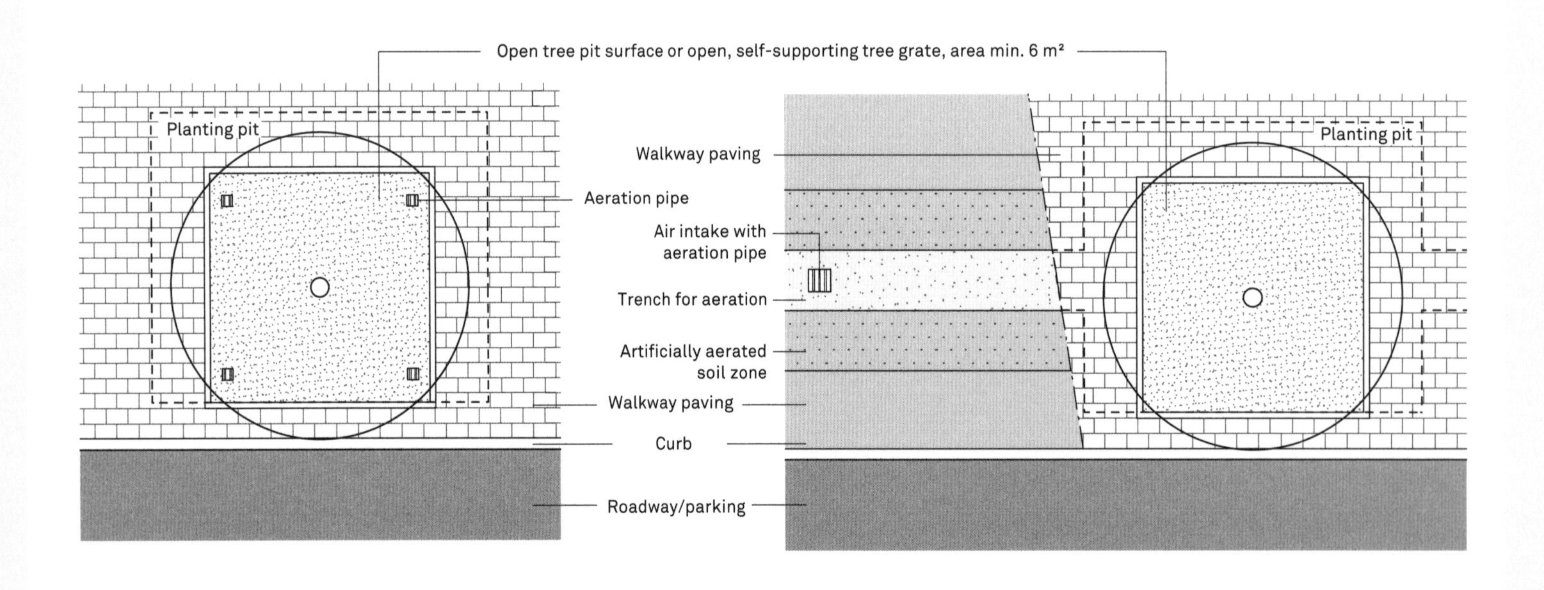

Figure 3.10.3 Requirements for tree locations with coverable tree pit surface ≥ 6 m²: size of planting pit (root zone) ≥ 12 m³

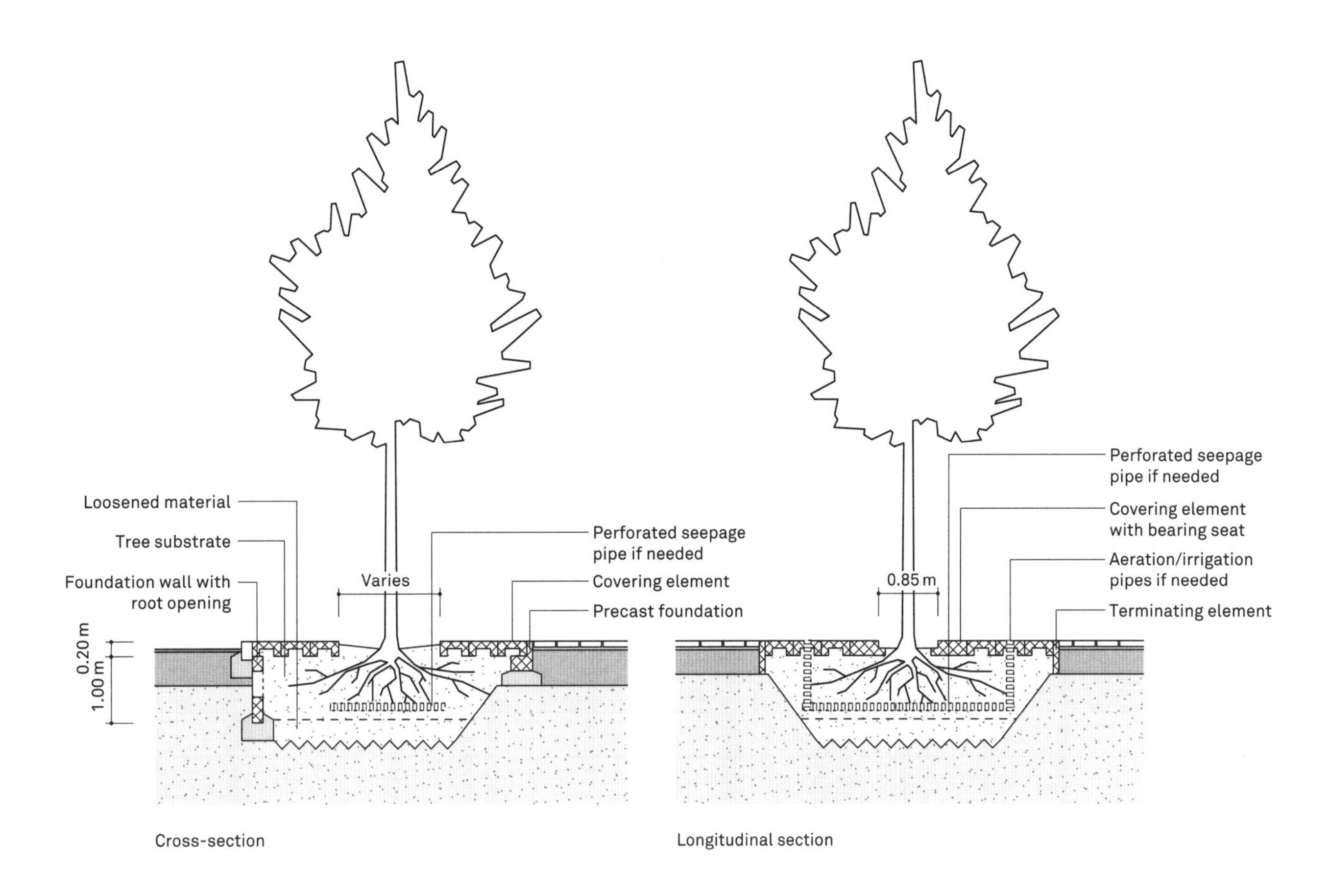

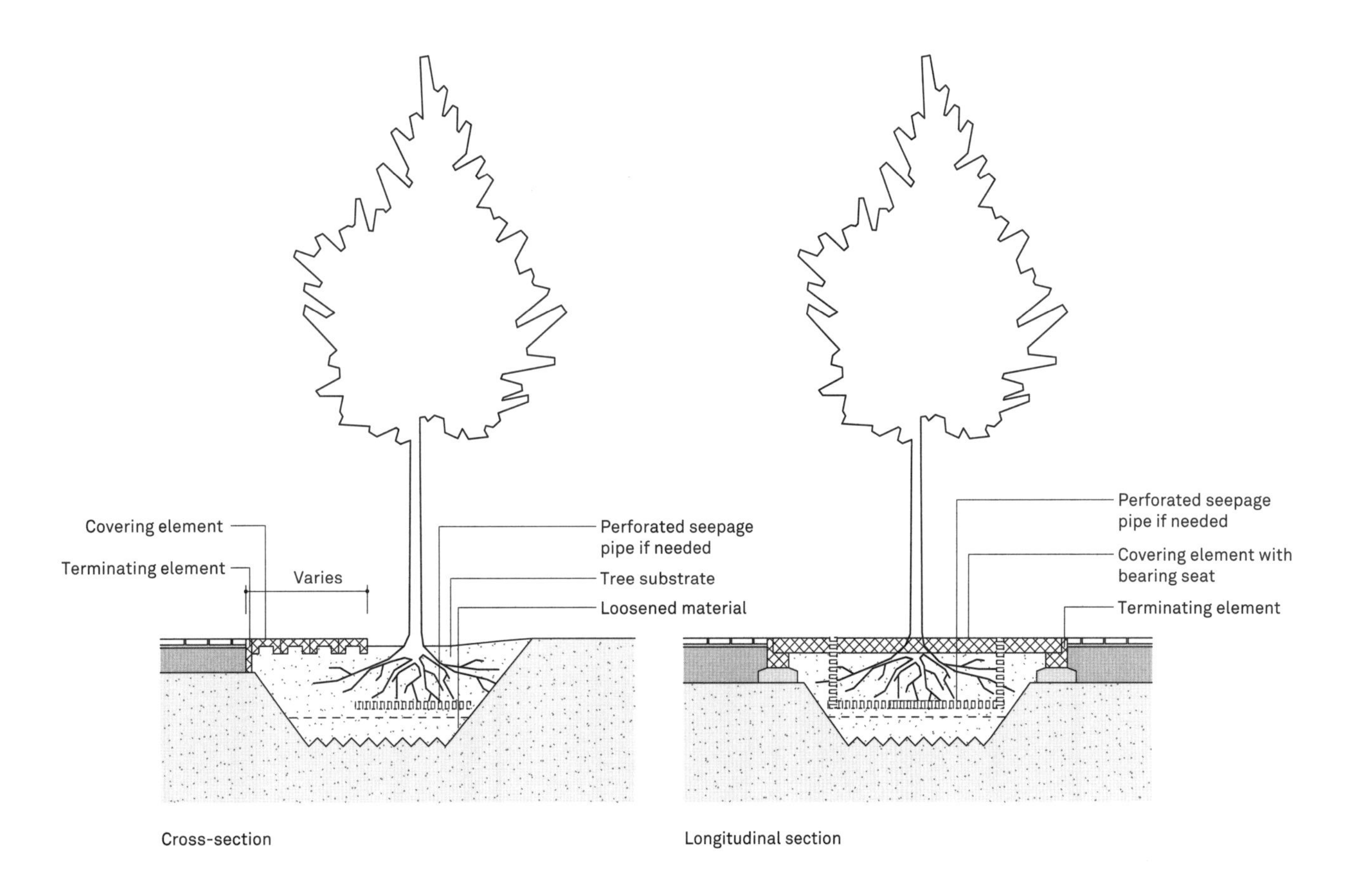

Figure 3.10.4 Requirements for tree locations with covered tree pit surface/root protection bridges in confined streetside locations

Existing Trees

Whether the integration of existing trees into a new installation is functionally necessary or desired from a design standpoint, the objective is to provide optimum protection for the tree's habitat. In so doing, the utmost attention must be given to the tree's root zone. As a rule, the following measures must be taken into account:

- It is essential to maintain the original ground level within the area beneath the tree canopy. Neither the filling nor the removal of soil is permitted in this area, as most woody plants react very sensitively and their long-term existence would thereby be endangered.
- The area beneath the tree canopy plus 1.5 m (5 m for columnar-shaped trees) must be kept free of built structures and surfacing. → **Figure 3.10.5**

Everyday situations do not always permit these fundamental conditions to be observed and road construction or other built obstructions may be unavoidable beneath the canopy.

With the proper choice of materials and means of execution, however, any impacts to the root zone can be reduced to a bare minimum. The use of permeable surfaces, minimal base course thicknesses, and minimal compaction can reduce the adverse effects, as can raising the pavement level above the existing ground level. Impermeable pavement surfaces should not cover more than 30 %, and permeable pavement surfaces no more than 50 % of the root zone of the fully grown tree. For changes to existing paving, these values should represent an absolute limit. Additional measures, such as aeration and irrigation systems, tree grates, or tree guards, are employed as needed.

Underground Utilities within the Root Zone

Underground utilities should normally be kept at a distance of at least 2.5 m from the tree, measured as the horizontal distance from the stem axis to the outer encasement of the utility lines or equipment. Depending on the type and size of the lines, the clearance distance can vary greatly. For water pipes with nominal diameters of DN 600 or more, for example, a minimum of 5 m clearance can be required. → **Table 3.10.1** If the specified distances cannot be met, protective measures in the form of subterranean barriers must be provided. Distances of less than 1.5 m should be avoided, particularly with sanitary sewer facilities, since the restricted space would not allow maintenance work to be performed or it could only be accomplished with considerable technical effort.

The fact that roots spread out, especially in very porous soil and in areas with high levels of moisture, can be used to advantage in the planning: backfill material of low porosity should be used to fill pipe and cable trenches. This measure is supplemented by the use of root-resistant pipe fittings and the installation of membranes or rigid sheets to line the utility trench. By employing trenchless subsurface construction methods, the root zone can be protected during utility line construction activities. → **Figures 3.10.6 and 3.10.7**

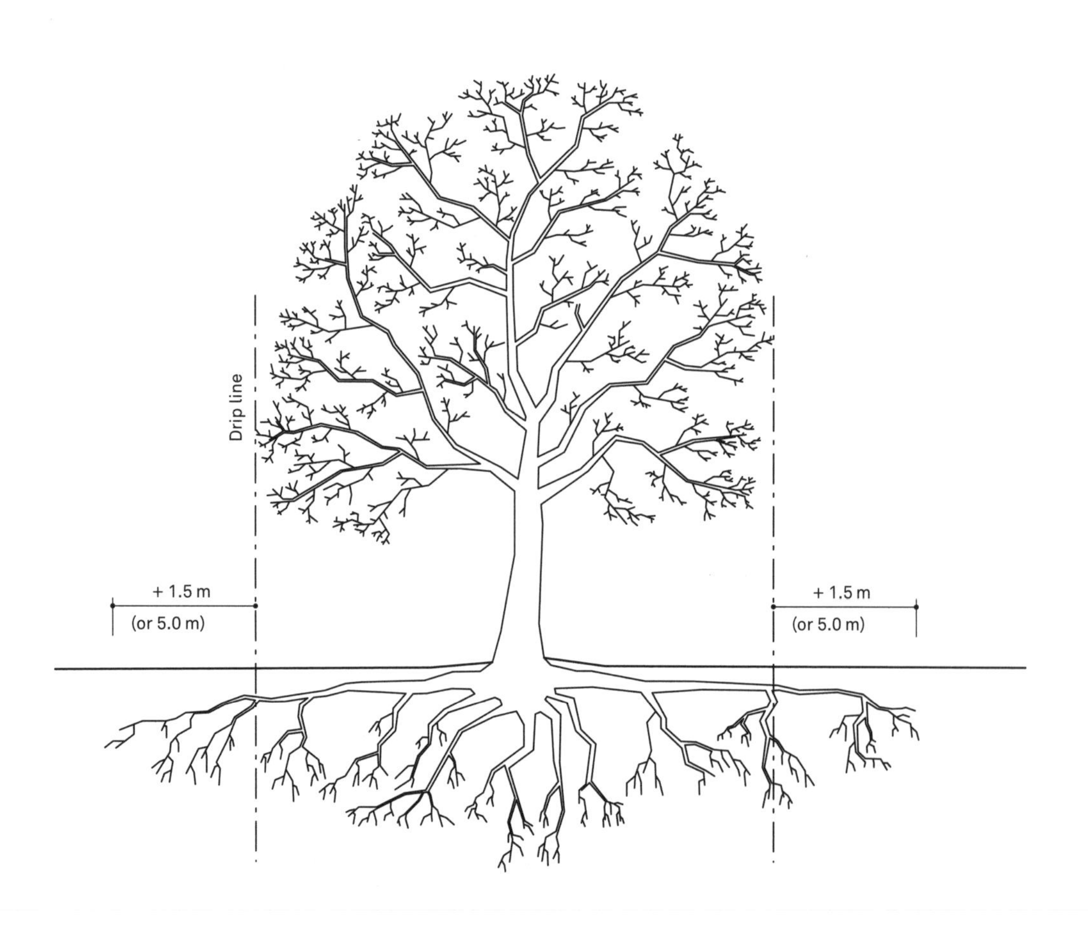

Figure 3.10.5 Protection for the root zone of existing trees (tree protection zone)

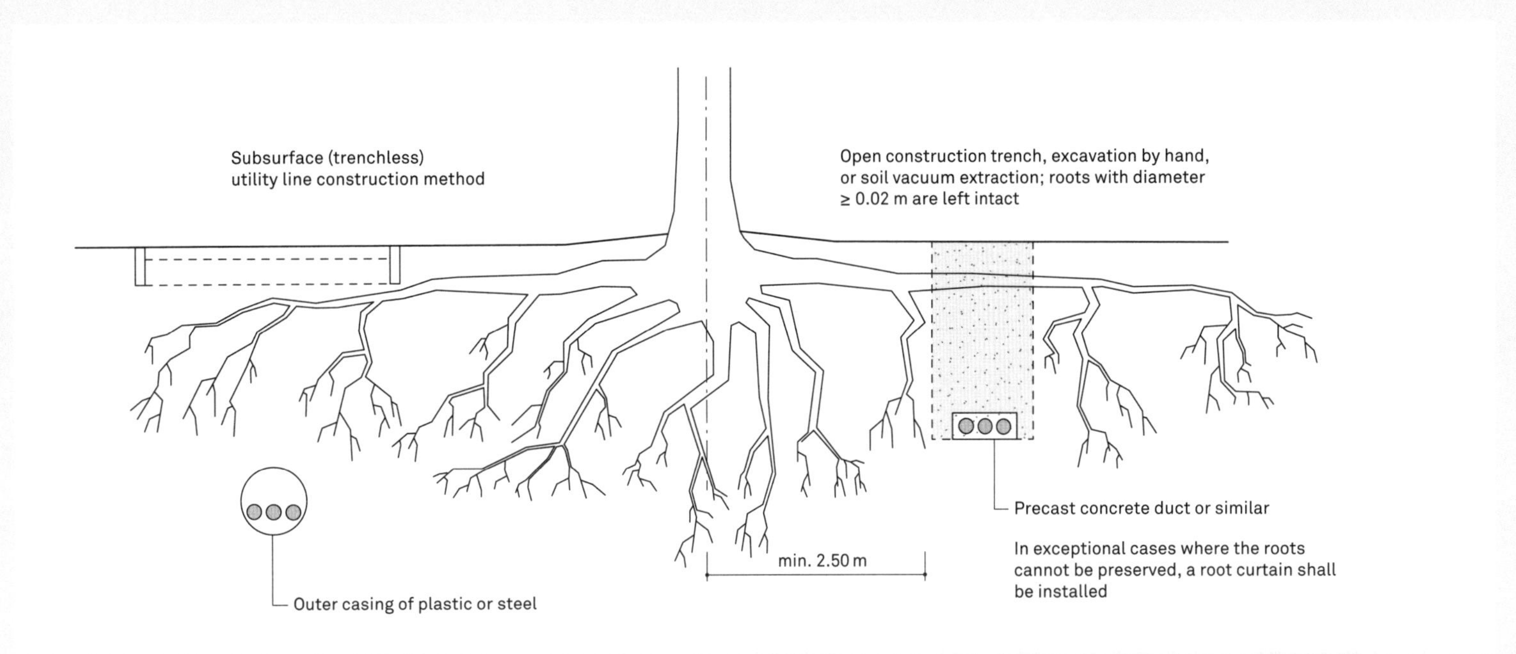

Figure 3.10.6 Protection of the root zone from underground utility lines (existing and newly planted trees)

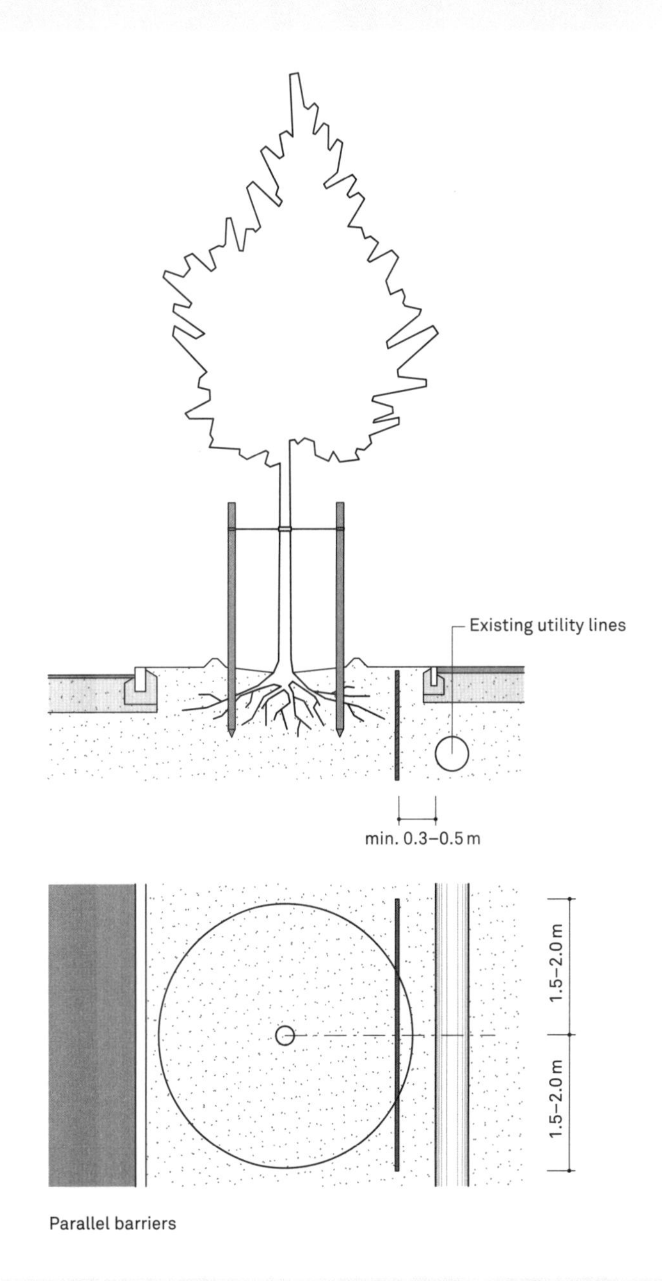

Figure 3.10.7 Protection of the root zone from underground utility lines (new plantings)

Clearance Profile

Along streets and sidewalks, adequate clearances must be observed for two main reasons: to maintain an area where the movement of traffic participants is not hindered by obstacles or hazards and to not impede the trees' tendency to spread out.

Hence all planning should observe the clearances required from the roadway or walkway, and appropriate growth forms and characteristics (high trunks, suitability for planting in rows, etc.) should be selected. The anticipated growth in the thickness of the tree's trunk must be considered.

To ensure that no branches grow into the traffic space and the tree's geometry can be conserved over the long term, young trees should be pruned in a timely and foresighted manner. Pruning measures should aim for balance in the tree geometry.

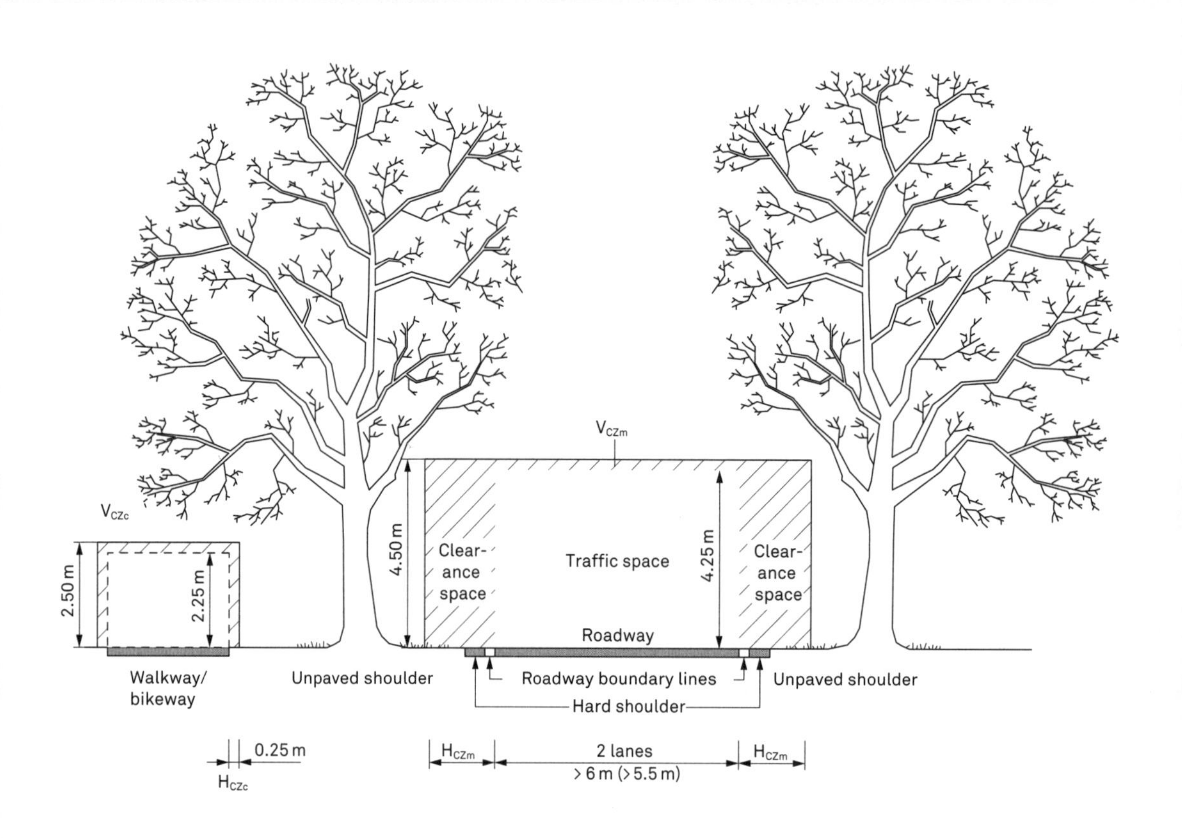

Figure 3.10.8 Clearances along roads

Dimensions and Characteristics

Crown Shapes and Growth Forms

The various species of both deciduous and coniferous trees have different characteristics with regard to the growth of their crowns. These are important aspects of design and relevant characteristics for spatial planning.

However, the crown shape of every tree only takes on its characteristic form over the course of time. This aspect illustrates once more the process-like aspect of planning with vegetation, which rarely or only after years reaches a lasting state. In addition, an unusual or extreme location has an effect on the crown shape and also changes it under certain circumstances. Moreover, pruning and years of “giving shape” to the tree can deliberately yield certain special forms.

The development of the growth form of a tree, from the juvenile crown shape to the mature (adult) and senile forms extends over a number of decades. Depending on the species of tree, these time frames can be very diverse, and changes to the size and appearance of the crown can be more or less apparent. In a close stand of trees, the growth in width is usually reduced.

Some trees grow upright and pointed at the outset, but with age they increasingly grow in width and take on more rounded shapes (e.g., *Carpinus betulus*). In some cases, the foliage and branches on lower portions grow bare over time, so the growth form increasingly assumes an umbrella-like character (e.g., pine). → **Figure 3.10.10**

Hedges

According to their structure, the intensity of care, and their application, hedges can be divided into three main groups: seminatural hedges in the open landscape, free-growing hedges, and trimmed (topiary) hedges.

Seminatural Hedges

Seminatural hedges are mostly to be found in the open landscape, particularly in rural areas. They are distinguished by the use of native woody plants. They were and are today sometimes still planted as windbreaks for shielding fields, as enclosures, and for marking boundaries. Some hedges were also able to develop atop the piles of stones gathered along the sides of fields, since these areas were not cultivated agriculturally. Their structures and the shrub species used to create them differ substantially by region. For functional purposes, hedgerows are often elevated on a small berm of earth that serves as a base. These hedgerows are known generically as hedgebanks, and the many regional variations include Devon hedges in England and "Knicks" in northern Germany. The bases of "Steinriegel" hedges [stone-row hedges] are formed with fieldstones instead of earth, as are the bases of Cornish hedges. All such formations offer better protection from the wind and a clearer demarcation of borders, and where needed, they also aid the diversion and drainage of water. Field hedges are often also planted near changes in terrain, or have been able to develop there undisturbed, because the possibilities for cultivating the adjacent fields encounter natural limits there. If hedges are not cut back regularly, a kind of double woodland margin develops with core and mantle zones of trees and shrubs, bordered with herbs along the sides. → **Figures 3.10.11**

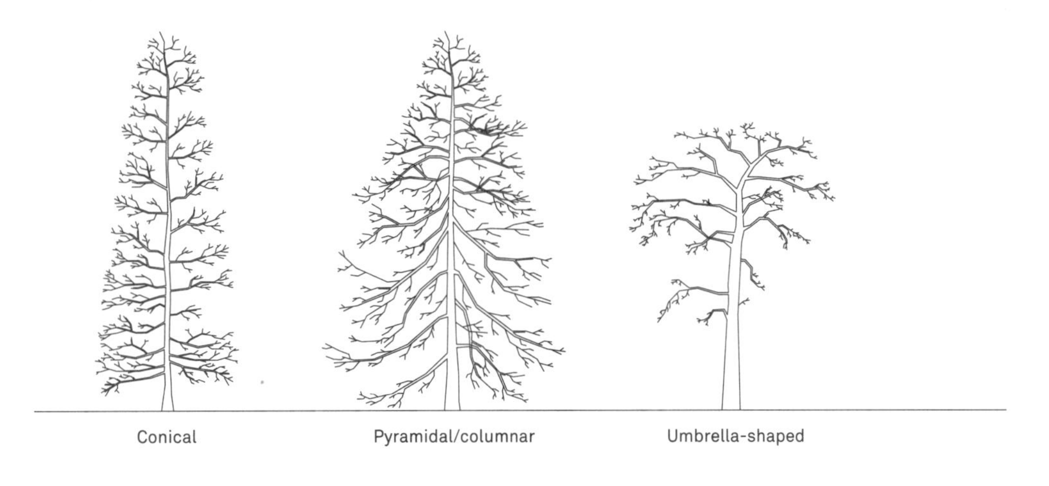

Figure 3.10.9 Basic shapes and special forms of trees

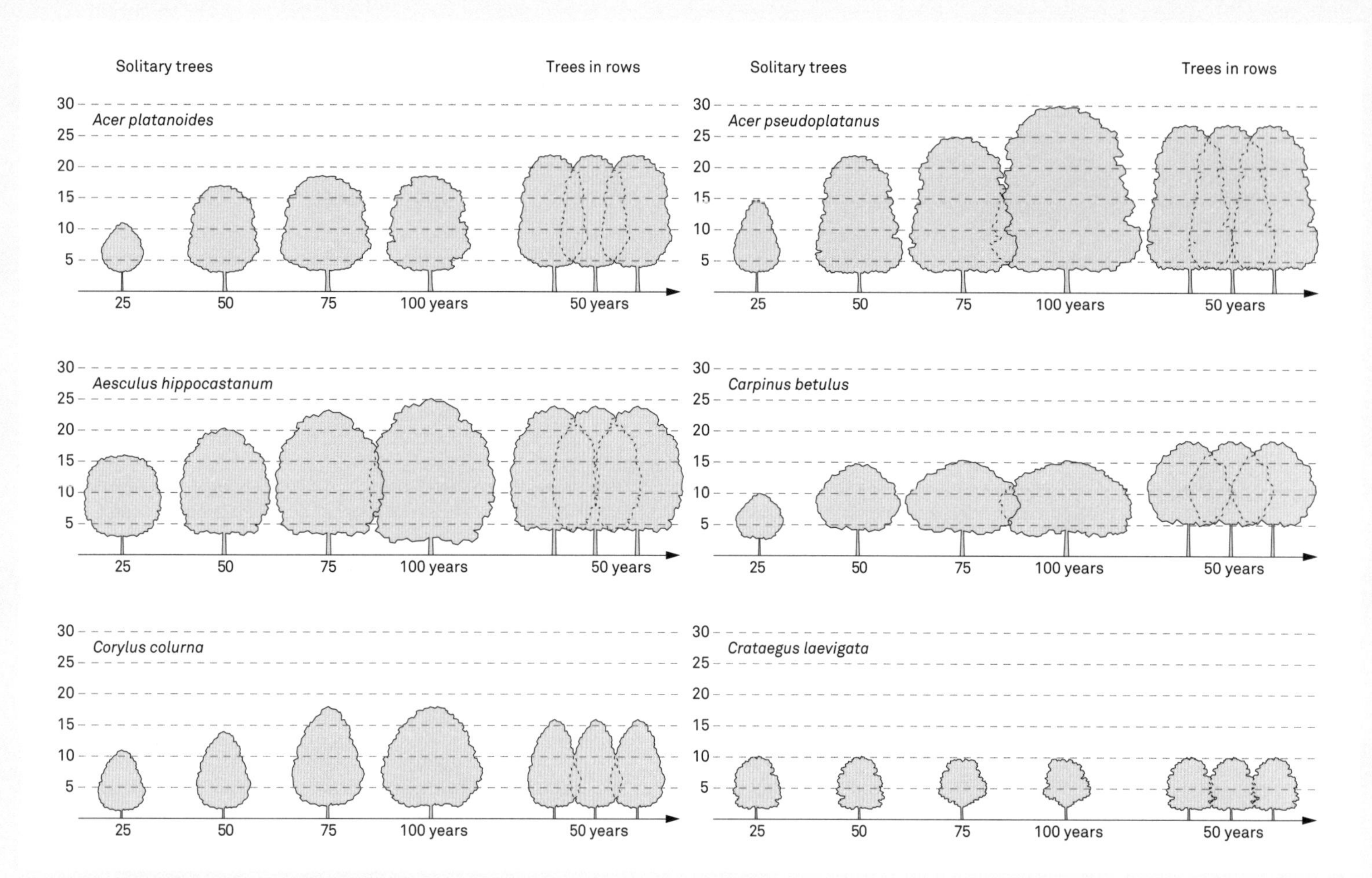

Figure 3.10.10 Typical development of various tree species from juvenile to mature form as solitary trees and in rows

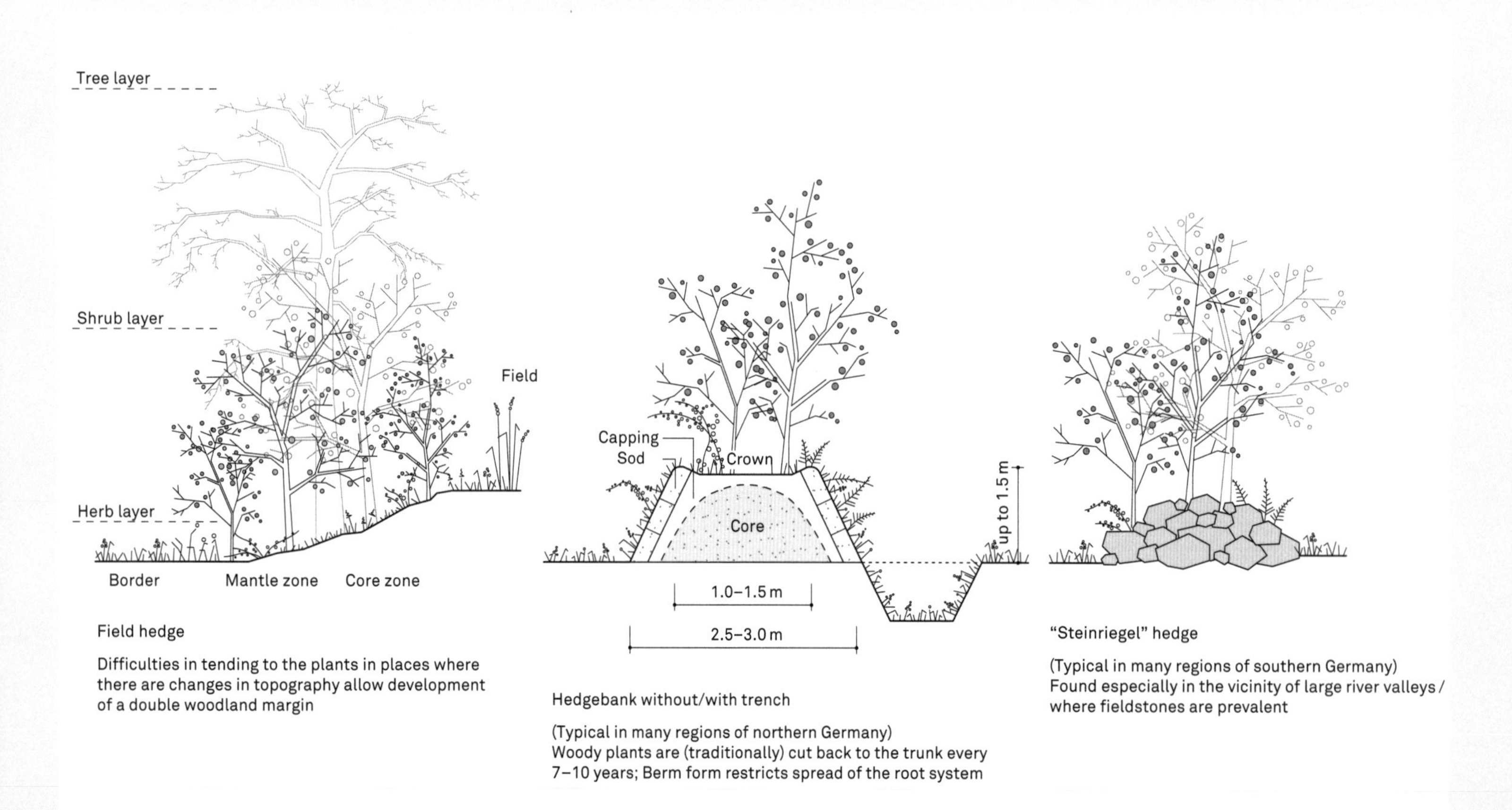

Figure 3.10.11 Various types of seminatural hedges

Free-Growing Hedges

Free-growing hedges provide decorative or functional enclosure of a property or they structure an open space as linear elements. They can be planted as flowering hedges, evergreen hedges, as mixed plantings, or as homogeneous hedgerows. Depending on the species selected, they also offer sources of nourishment and nesting opportunities for various birds, bees, and other animals. Since these hedges only receive occasional maintenance pruning, their growth is more consistent with natural conditions, generally making their space requirements relatively large. A zone 2 m wide plus swaths for future growth on both sides (1 m each) should be planned as a minimum. → **Figure 3.10.12** However, small species that are less than 1 m wide without pruning can also be used. But these species will not grow any taller than 0.5–1 m.

Trimmed Hedges

Trimmed hedges are given shape through regular and repeated pruning, so the plants which are used must be accordingly tolerant of pruning. They are more laborious to care for than free-growing hedges.

Since the growth in many woody plants is strongest at the top, the lower part can quickly grow bare. A tapered cut that gets narrower toward the top is therefore recommended. With evergreen woody plants, the edges can be trimmed more vertically than with deciduous woody plants.

Due to the trimming, which is done one to two times each year, most woody plants do not bloom or do so only to a limited degree. Some varieties, such as *Buxus sempervirens* 'BlauerHeinz,' only grow to be 0.4 m high and wide. These woody plants are well suited for low borders, and pruning back is not required.

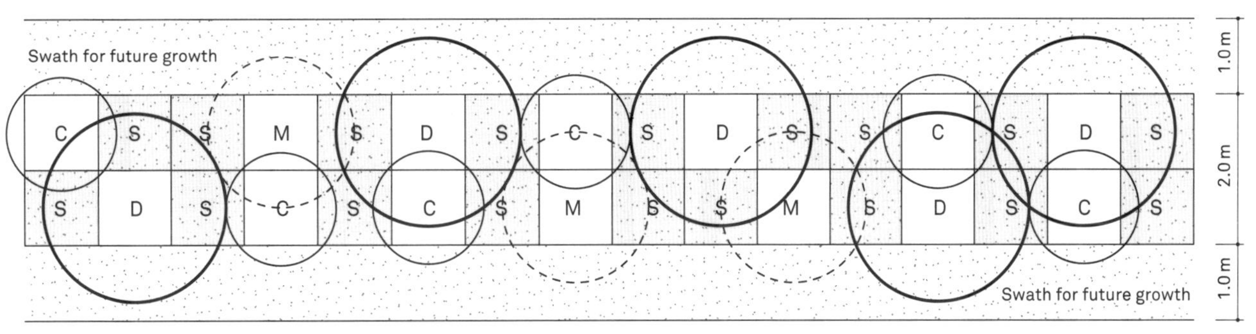

Trees and shrubs planted in two rows on a 1 × 1 m grid, with underplanting

D Dominant
M Mantle shrubs
C Companion trees and shrubs
S Perennials, herbs, and secondary woody plants

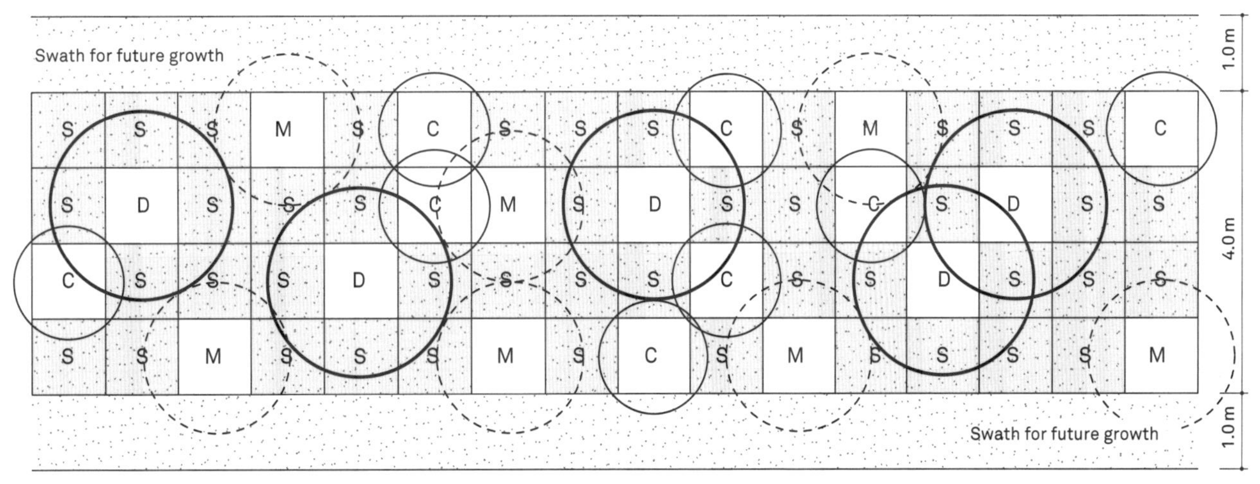

Trees and shrubs planted in four rows on a 1 × 1 m grid, with underplanting

Figure 3.10.12 Planting scheme for free-growing hedges

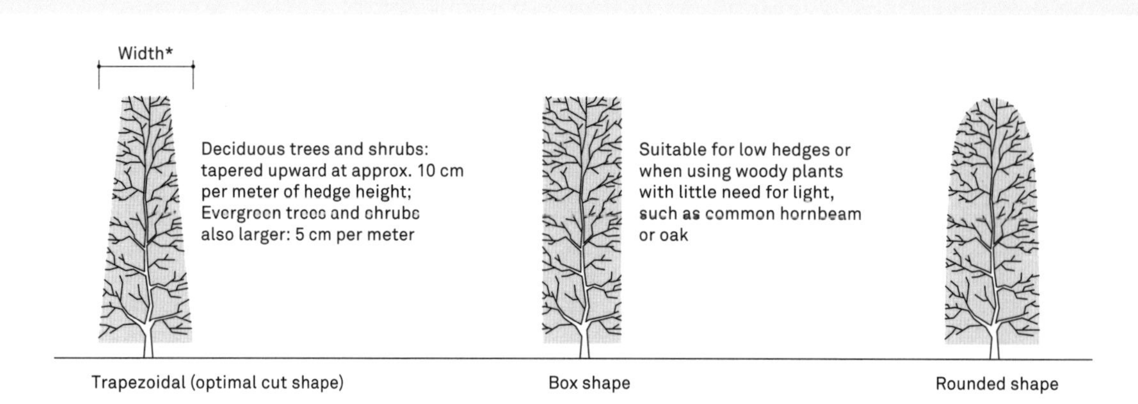

Figure 3.10.13 Trimmed hedge profiles

Species	Max. growth height	Suitable for hedge height, in m			Suitable for hedge height, in m	Plants per m, depending on initial height	Light needs	Comments
		up to 1	1–2	2–4				
Acer campestre (field maple, hedge maple)	15 m		x	x	35–40	2–3	FSu–PSh	Yellow fall foliage; bee pasture; also for hedge gateways and hedge arbors; susceptible to mildew
Berberis vulgaris (barberry)	3 m	x	x		20–50	3–4	FSu–PSh	Thorns, bright red fall foliage; insect food
Berberis thunbergii 'Atropurpurea' (Japanese, or red barberry)	1.5–2 m	x			20–40	2–4	FSu–PSh	Dark red foliage, yellow flowers; undemanding
Buxus sempervirens (common box)	2–6 m	x	x	x	10	4–5	FSu–FSh	Infestation with the fungus Cylindrocladium buxicola possible
Carpinus betulus (European, or common, hornbeam)	25 m		x	x	25–35	2,5–4	FSu–FSh	Undemanding, heat- and drought-tolerant, dry foliage persistent through winter
Cornus mas (Cornelian cherry)	3–7 m		x	x	20–40	3–4	FSu–PSh	Deciduous; yellowish-red-orange (variable) fall foliage; bee pasture; protective planting for birds
Crataegus monogyna (oneseed or common hawthorn)	up to 8 m		x	x	20–25	3–4	FSu–FSh	Protective planting for birds; also tolerates being pruned back completely; can succomb to fire blight
Crataegus prunifolia (plum-leaved thorn)	up to 7 m		x	x	20–25	2–3	FSu–PSh	Bark is very thorny
Fagus sylvatica (common beech)	up to 30 m			x	20–50	2–3	FSu–PSh	Prefers loose soil; retains dry leaves for long time
Ilex aquifolium (English holly)	4–7 m		x	x	15–40	2–4	PSh–FSh	
Juniperus communis (common juniper)	up to 10 m		x	x	10–15	1–2	FSu–PSh	Undemanding; can prune from spring to mid-September; intermediate host for pear trellis rust
Ligustrum vulgare 'Atrovirens' (privet)	2–4 m	x	x		20–50	3–4	FSu–PSh	Undemanding; tolerates heat
Ligustrum vulgare 'Lodense' (dwarf privet)	up to 0.7 m	x			5–8	3–4	FSu–PSh	
Prunus laurocerasus 'Herbergii' (cherry laurel)	2–3 m		x		20–45	2–3	FSu–FSh	Evergreen; tolerates much shade and root pressure
Pyracantha coccinea 'Red Column' (firethorn, pyracantha)	1.5–2.5 m	x	x		10–20	2–3	FSu–PSh	Evergreen; thorns; conspicuous berries
Ribes alpinum (Alpine currant)	1.5–2 m	x	x		15–25	2–3	FSu–FSh	Food source for birds and insects
Spirea japonica 'Froebeli' (Japanese spirea)	0.8–1.2 m	x	x		10–20	3–4	FSu–PSh	Deciduous; spring pruning encourages blossoms
Taxus baccata (common or European yew)	12–15 m		x	x	20–40	3–4	FSu–PSh	Very resilient; also nutrient-poor soils; tolerates radical rejuvenation pruning
Thuja occidentalis (arborvitae)	15–20 m		x	x	20–25	2–5	FSu–PSh	Very hardy, wind-resistent, high sprouting and regeneration capacity

Table 3.10.2 Woody plants for trimmed hedges: standard values for plant spacing, plant size/height, and annual growth

Boundary Setbacks for Trees and Shrubs

The boundary setbacks between hedges and neighboring properties are listed in **→ Chapter 3.6 Boundary Enclosures and Railings**

Baden-Württemberg
> Nachbarrechtsgesetz BW

When planting trees, shrubs, and other woody plants in built-up areas, the following boundary setbacks shall be observed:
- Large-growing trees: 8 m
- Medium-sized and narrow trees: 4 m
- Moderately strong fruit trees with maximum growth height >4 m: 3 m
- weak-growing trees with maximum growth height ≤4 m: 2 m
- Shrubs over 1.8 m high: 2 m
- Shrubs ≤1.8 m high: 0.5 m

Berlin
> Berliner Nachbarrecht

For trees and shrubs, the following minimum clearances shall be maintained from neighboring properties:
- Strong-growing trees: 3 m
- Trees that do not fall under categories (a) or (c): 1.5 m
- Fruit trees if not high-stemmed: 1 m
- Shrubs: 0.5 m

Brandenburg
> Bbg. Nachbarrechtsgesetz

For trees, shrubs, and hedges with regular maximum growth height >2 m, the following distances from the neighboring property shall be observed:
- Fruit trees: 2 m
- Other trees: 4 m
- Regardless, for every part of the planting, the setback shall amount to at least one third of the plant's height above the ground.

Hesse
> Hessisches Nachbarrechtsgesetz

When planting trees, shrubs, and individual vines, the following setbacks shall be maintained from neighboring properties – subject to § 40:
- Very strong-growing avenue and park trees: 4 m
- Strong-growing avenue and park trees: 2 m
- All other avenue and park trees: 1.5 m
- Fruit trees:
  - Walnut seedlings: 4 m
  - Pomaceous fruit trees, provided they are grafted onto strong-growing understock, as well as sweet cherry trees and grafted walnut trees: 2 m
  - Pomaceous fruit trees, provided they are grafted onto weak-growing understock, as well as stone fruit trees, except sweet cherry trees: 1.5 m
- Strong-growing ornamental shrubs: 1 m
- Other ornamental shrubs: 0.5 m
- Blackberry bushes: 1 m
- Other berry fruit bushes: 0.5 m

Lower Saxony
> Nachbarrechtsgesetz Nds.

With trees and shrubs, depending on their height, the following distances shall be maintained as a minimum from neighboring properties:
- maximum 1.2 m high: 0.25 m
- maximum 2 m high: 0.5 m
- maximum 3 m high: 0.75 m
- maximum 5 m high: 1.25 m
- maximum 15 m high: 3 m
- over 15 m high: 8 m

North Rhine-Westphalia
> Nachbarrechtsgesetz für NRW

With trees outside of forests, with shrubs, and with vines, the following distances shall be maintained from neighboring properties:
- Strong-growing trees: 4 m
- Other trees: 2 m
- Strong-growing ornamental shrubs: 1 m
- Other ornamental shrubs: 0.5 m
- Hedges over 2 m high: 1 m
- Hedges under 2 m high: 0.5 m

Rhineland-Palatinate
> Nachbarrechtsgesetz für RLP

With trees, shrubs, and solitary vines, the following distances shall be maintained from neighboring properties:
- Very strong-growing trees: 4 m
- Strong-growing trees: 2 m
- Other trees: 1.5 m
- Strong-growing shrubs: 1 m
- Other shrubs: 0.5 m

Saarland
> Nachbarrechtsgesetz d. Saarlands

The following boundary setbacks for plants are to be maintained in Saarland:
- Very strong-growing trees: 4 m
- Strong-growing trees: 2 m
- Other trees: 1.5 m
- Strong-growing shrubs: 1 m
- Other shrubs: 0.5 m

Exceptions for fruit trees and berry bushes: see statute on neighborly rights.

Saxony
> Sächs. Nachbarrechtsgesetz

In Saxony, the following boundary setbacks are to be maintained:
- All trees, shrubs, and hedges >2 m high: 2 m
- All trees, shrubs, and hedges ≤2 m high: 0.5 m

Saxony-Anhalt
> Nachbarrechtsgesetz Sachsen-Anhalt

All trees, shrubs, and hedges ...
- maximum 1.5 m high: 0.5 m
- maximum 3 m high: 1 m
- maximum 5 m high: 1.25 m
- maximum 15 m high: 3 m
- over 15 m high: 6 m

Schleswig-Holstein
> Nachbarrechtsgesetz SchlH

With trees, shrubs, and hedges (plantings) >1.2 m high, a setback distance from the neighboring property shall be maintained that ensures for every part of the planting, the setback shall amount to at least one third of the plant's height above the ground.

Thuringia
> Nachbarrechtsgesetz Thüringen

In Thuringia, the following boundary setbacks are to be maintained for plants:
- Very strong-growing trees: 4 m
- Strong-growing trees: 2 m
- Other trees: 1.5 m
- Strong-growing shrubs: 1 m
- Other shrubs: 0.5 m

Exceptions for berry fruit bushes and fruit trees: see statute on neighborly rights.

Switzerland
> Kantonale Regelungen im Nachbarrecht

In Aargau (for example), the following boundary setbacks are to be maintained:
- High-stemmed trees, as well as walnut and chestnut trees: 6 m
- Fruit trees: 3 m
- Dwarf trees, ornamental trees, and shrubs, which are not higher than 3 m: 1 m
- Vines: 0.5 m
- Ornamental trees, provided they do not exceed a height of 6 m: 3 m
- When opposite vineyards, these distances increase by 2 m each for trees that are not dwarf trees.
- When opposite woodlands, the distance for all plantings shall be only 0.5 m
- When opposite properties in the agricultural zone that are not vineyards: 60 cm from the planted edge

Table 3.10.3 Boundary setbacks between woody plants and neighboring properties

Classifications

Trees Suitable for Inner-City Locations and Along Streets

The street tree list issued by the German Conference of Gardening Office Directors (GALK) [Deutsche Gartenamtsleiterkonferenz] provides an overview of the suitability of tree species and varieties for use along streets. It is based on actual experiences from various cities in Germany and the Netherlands, and it is updated intermittently. In addition, a classification of the tree species can be made according to the KlimaArtenMatrix (KLAM) [climate/species matrix] for species of city trees and shrubs. This list, developed by Prof. Andreas Roloff, takes into account the predicted climate change and classifies important woody plant species with regard to drought tolerance and winter hardiness as a measure of their suitability for use in urban areas.

Botanical and common names	Height in m	Width in m	Permeability to light	Light requirements	Suitability for city streetscapes	Drough tolerance (according to KLAM)	Winter hardiness (Winter hardiness zoness) (according to KLAM)	Comments
Acer campestre (field maple, hedge maple)	10–15 (20)	10–15	Medium	○–◗	R	VG	VG	Ovoid and irregular crown, becoming more rounded with age; tolerates dry soils and high degree of surface sealing, good for holding topsoil on banks and on slopes
Acer campestre 'Elsrijk' (field maple)	6–12 (15)	4–6	Medium	○–◗	R	–	–	Like the species but with straight central leader, narrower and more uniform growth, localized frost damage in the crown, mildew-free
Acer platanoides (Norway maple)	20–30	15–22	Low	○–◗	R	S	VG (4)	Rounded, densely closed crown, blooms before leaves sprout; very frost-hardy, sensitive to soil compaction, honeydew secretion
Acer platanoides, 'Allershausen' (Norway maple)	15–20	up to 10	Low	○–◗	S	–	–	Highly branched, dense crown, well suited for locations susceptible to frost, honeydew secretion, included in Straßenbaumtest [street tree test] 2 since 2005
Acer platanoides 'Apollo' (tapered Norway maple)	14–18	10–15	Low	○–◗	R	–	–	Like the species but grows faster and more upright, frost-resistant, honeydew secretion, included in Straßenbaumtest 2 since 2005
Acer platanoides 'Cleveland' (tapered Norway maple)	10–15	7–9	Low	○–◗	S	–	–	Oval crown, broadly ovoid and regular with age; bright red shoots, good for urban environments, honeydew secretion
Acer platanoides 'Columnare' Types 1, 2, 3 (columnar Norway maple)	up to 10 (16)	2–7	Low	○–◗	S	–	–	Narrow, columnar growth, very frost-hardy, heat-tolerant, drought-tolerant, wind- and shade-tolerant, honeydew secretion, good compartmentalization of decay
Acer platanoides 'Deborah' (Norway maple)	15–20	10–15	Low	○–◗	R	–	–	Rounded to broadly rounded, straight central leader, honeydew secretion, heed results of Straßenbaumtest 1
Acer platanoides 'Emerald Queen' (Norway maple)	up to 15	8–10	Low	○–◗	R	NA	NA	Oval crown, markedly upright when young, heat- and drought-tolerant, wind-tolerant, suitable for narrow streets, honeydew secretion
Acer platanoides 'Farlake's Green' (Norway maple)	15–20	10–15	Low	○–◗	R	–	–	Symmetrical habit, heat- and drought-tolerant, wind-tolerant, scarcely susceptible to mildew, sensitive to road salt (experience from NL), heed results of Straßenbaumtest 1
Acer platanoides 'Globosum', (globe Norway maple)	up to 6	5–8	Low	○–◗	S	–	–	Densely branched, compact round crown, give regard to clearance profile, frost-hardy, heat- and drought-tolerant, wind and shade-tolerant, honeydew secretion, suitable for tubs and containers
Acer platanoides 'Olmsted' (Norway maple)	10–12 (15)	2–3	Low	○–◗	S	–	–	Narrow, columnar; suitable for restricted spaces in exposed urban locations with dry air; presumably equivalent to type 1 of *Acerplatanoides* 'Columnare,' honeydew secretion

NA = not available; R = with restrictions; VG = very good; WS = well-suited; S = suitable; P = problematic; VL = very limited suitability

Table 3.10.4 Suitability of trees for streets and inner-city locations, per GALK and KLAM

Botanical and common names	Height in m	Width in m	Permeability to light	Light requirements	Suitability for city streetscapes	Drough tolerance (according to KLAM)	Winter hardiness (Winter hardiness zoness) (according to KLAM)	Comments
Acer platanoides 'Royal Red' (red-leafed Norway maple)	up to 15 (20)	8–10	Low	○–◗	R	–	–	Leaves are bright red as buds, then consistently deep crimson and glossy until autumn, very frost-hardy, heat-tolerant, wind-tolerant, honeydew secretion
Acer platanoides 'Summershade', (Norway maple)	20–25	15–20	Low	○–◗	R	–	–	Expansive hanging branches, forms whorls, susceptible to wind breakage, good for urban environments, honeydew secretion
Acer rubrum (red maple)	10–15 (20)	6–10 (14)	Low	○–◗	R	VG	S	Deep red blossoms in advance of leaf shoots, frost-hardy, somewhat sensitive to heat, conditionally good for urban environments, shallow roots, risk of chlorosis in chalky soil
Aesculus hippo-castanum (horse chestnut)	up to 25 (30)	15–20 (25)	Low	○	R	VL	S	Sensitive to soil compaction and road salt, be mindful of fruit fall, strong crown and root pressure
Aesculus hippo-castanum 'Baumannii' (double-flowering horse chestnut)	up to 25 (30)	15–20 (25)	Low	○	R	–	–	Like the species, but blooms longer and has filled blossoms, no fruit production
Aesculus × carnea (red horse chestnut)	10–15 (20)	8–12 (16)	Low	○–◗	R	S	VG	Difficult to cut away branches, unsuitable for compact soils and high degree of surface seal-ing, minor infestation by leaf-mining moths, negligible fruit fall
Aesculus × carnea 'Briotii' (ruby red horse chestnut)	10–15	8–12	Low	○–◗	R	–	–	Like the species but more deeply colored blossoms, available in different varieties
Alnus cordata (Italian alder)	10–15 (20)	8–10	Medium	○	R	S	S	Shoots form early, so occasionally subject to frost in late spring, good for urban and industrial environments, very wind-tolerant, risk of break-age from snow due to long-lasting foliage
Alnus × spaethii (Spaeth's alder)	12–15	8–10	Medium	○	WS	S	VG	Frost-hardy, wind-tolerant, vigorous growth, straight central leader, risk of breakage from snow due to long-lasting foliage, heed results of Straßenbaumtest 1
Amelanchier arborea 'Robin Hill' (downy serviceberry)	6–8	3–5	Medium	○–◗	S	–	–	Broadly ovoid crown, blossoms early and has pleasant fragrance, suitable for tubs and con-tainers, included in Straßenbaumtest 2 since 2005
Betula papyrifera (paper birch)	18–25	7–12	High	○	R	–	–	Pyramidal crown, short-lived, not good for urban environments, do not use within paved areas, observe proper planting times
Betula pendula, syn. B. verrucosa (silver birch, European white birch)	18–25 (30)	10–15 (18)	High	○	R	S	VG	Loose, high domed crown; side branches often hang down far, frost-hardy, not good for urban environments, tends to lift up pavements; do not use within paved areas, observe proper plant-ing times
Betula utilis, syn. B. jacquemontii (Himalayan birch)	8–10 (15)	5–7	High	○	R	VL	P	Grows upright, shallow spreading roots, large percentage of fine roots in the upper soil zone, observe proper planting times
Carpinus betulus (European, or common hornbeam)	10–20 (25)	7–12 (15)	Low	◗	R	S	VG	Conical; high domed crown with age; not good for urban environments, so do not use within paved areas
Carpinus betulus 'Fastigiata' (fastigiate hornbeam)	15–20	4–6 (10)	Low	◗	S	–	–	Columnar to conical crown, spreads apart with age, less sensitive to heat and radiation than the species, suitable for tubs and containers

NA = not available; R = with restrictions; VG = very good; WS = well-suited; S = suitable; P = problematic; VL = very limited suitability

Botanical and common names	Height in m	Width in m	Permeability to light	Light requirements	Suitability for city streetscapes	Drough tolerance (according to KLAM)	Winter hardiness (Winter hardiness zones) (according to KLAM)	Comments
Carpinus betulus 'Frans Fontaine' (columnar European hornbeam)	10–15	4–5	Low	○–◗	R	–	–	Like *Carpinus betulus* 'Fastigiata', but columnar even in maturity, crown not entirely closed when young, very wind-tolerant, increased late frost damage to the trunks of young trees, suitable for tubs and containers
Catalpa bignonioides (Southern catalpa, Indian bean tree)	8–10 (15)	6–10	Medium	○–◗	R	P	P	Rounded crown and broadly spreading side branches, species-specific characteristic is no central leader; striking flowers, leaves, and fruits; heed clearance profile
Celtis australis (European hackberry or nettle tree)	10–20	10–15	Medium	○	R	VG	P	Expansive, round, umbrella-shaped crown; trunk formation better than *Celtis occidentalis*; loves warmth and suitable for dry sites (viticulture climate)
Cercis siliquastrum (Judas tree, lovetree)	4–6	4–6	Low	○	R	VG	VL	Round, wide-growing crown, loves warmth (viticulture climate), suitable for dry sites, watch for straight leading shoots
Cornus mas (Cornelian cherry, cornejo macho, cornel)	5–6 (8)	3–5	Medium	○–◗	WS	VG	VG	Small crowned, very early blooming trees for narrow streets, trunks with peeling bark, undemanding, not sensitive to frost, good for urban environments, be mindful of fruit fall, heed clearance profile
Corylus colurna (Turkish hazelnut)	15–18 (23)	8–12 (16)	Low	○–◗	S	S	S	Regular, widely conical crown; undemanding, good for urban environments, severe fruit fall in some years
Crataegus crus-galli syn. C. prunifolia 'Splendens' (cockspur hawthorn)	5–7 (9)	5–7 (9)	Medium	○–◗	R	–	–	Broadly rounded crown, especially long thorns, frost-hardy, wind-tolerant, heed clearance profile, suitable for tubs and containers
Crataegus laevigata 'Paul's Scarlet' syn. C. monogyna 'Kermesina Plena' (English or common hawthorn)	4–6 (8)	4–6 (8)	Medium	○	R	–	–	Regular, widely conical crown, has filled blossoms, undemanding, not too dry, suitable for tubs and containers
Crataegus lavallei 'Carrierei' syn. C. carrierei (Carrière's hawthorn)	5–7	5–7	Medium	○	S	VG	VG	Widely conical crown; shoots with strong thorns; long-lasting, leathery, shiny dark green foliage; suitable for tubs and containers
Crataegus monogyna 'Stricta' (upright hawthorn)	5–7 (10)	2–3	Medium	○–◗	R	–	–	Stiffly upright to columnar, spreads apart with age, shoots covered with thorns, suitable for tubs and containers
Crataegus × prunifolia syn. C. × persimilus (plumleaf hawthorn)	6–7	5–6	Medium	○	R	–	–	Like *Crataegus crus-gallii*, glossy, dark green foliage, frost-hardy, good for urban environments
Fraxinus angustifolia 'Raywood' syn. F. oxyacarpa 'Flame', F. oxyacarpa 'Raywood' (narrow-leafed ash)	10–15 (20)	10–15	High	○–◗	R	–	–	Heat-tolerant and loves warmth, sensitive to frost in some areas, good for urban environments, without fruits, striking fall foliage
Fraxinus excelsior (European or common ash)	25–35 (40)	20–25 (30)	High	○–◗	R	S	S	Rounded, light crown, widely spreading; late shoots, early leaf fall, sensitive to surface compaction
Fraxinus excelsior 'Altena' syn. F. excelsior 'Monarch' (ash)	15–20	10–12	High	○–◗	R	–	–	Like the species but more slender and regular, ascending twigs, straight central leader, sensitive to surface compaction and dryness

NA = not available; R = with restrictions; VG = very good; WS = well-suited; S = suitable; P = problematic; VL = very limited suitability

Table 3.10.4 Suitability of trees for streets and inner-city locations, per GALK and KLAM

Botanical and common names	Height in m	Width in m	Permeability to light	Light requirements	Suitability for city streetscapes	Drough tolerance (according to KLAM)	Winter hardiness (Winter hardiness zoness) (according to KLAM)	Comments
Fraxinus excelsior 'Atlas' (ash)	15–20	10–15	High	○–◗	S	–	–	Like the species but compacter and narrower crown, loves warmth, heat-tolerant, heed results of Straßenbaumtest 1
Fraxinus excelsior 'Diversifolia' syn. F. excelsior 'Monophylla' (single-leaved ash)	10–18	6–12	High	○–◗	S	–	–	Like the species but smaller and more narrow growth, good for urban environments, loose crown, upright growth, wind-tolerant, heed results of Straßenbaumtest 1
Fraxinus excelsior 'Geessink' (ash)	15–20	10–12	High	○–◗	S	–	–	Like the species but narrower and weaker grow-ing, very wind-resistant, hardly subject to late freezing
Fraxinus excelsior 'Globosa' syn. F. excelsior 'Nana' (European Globehead ash)	3–5	3–5	Medium	○–◗	S	–	–	Like the species, but small and spherical, with densely branched crown, slow-growing, heed clearance profile, suitable for tubs and containers
Fraxinus excelsior 'Westhof's Glorie' (non-fruiting ash)	20–25 (30)	12–15	High	○–◗	S	–	–	Like the species but leaves shoot very late, thus hardly subject to late freezing; straight central leader
Fraxinus ornus (flowering ash, manna ash)	8–12 (15)	6–8 (10)	High	○	S	VG	VL	Slow growing, good for urban environments, seldom with straight leading shoots, give regard to clearance profile, do not use within paved areas, attractive blossoms
Fraxinus ornus 'Rotterdam' (flowering ash, manna ash)	8–12	6–8	Medium	○	S	–	–	Like the species but with a regular and conical crown, leading shoots, tolerant of dryness and heat, suitable for tubs and containers, attractive blossoms
Ginkgo biloba (ginkgo, maidenhair tree)	15–30 (35)	10–15 (20)	High	○	WS	VG	S	Undemanding, good for urban environments, free of pests, needs plentiful light, attractive fall foliage, diocious, draw on male selections
Gleditsia triacanthos (thornless honey locust)	10–25	8–15 (20)	High	○	S	–	–	Like the species but thornless variety in which thorns can subsequently form in individual cases; sensitive to frost as young tree
Gleditsia triacanthos 'Shademaster' (thornless honey locust)	10–15 (20)	10–15	High	○	S	–	–	Like the species but thornless variety in which thorns can subsequently form in individual cases, later leaf fall
Gleditsia triacanthos 'Skyline' (thornless honey locust)	10–15 (20)	10–15	High	○	WS	–	–	Like the species but regular closed crown with ascending branches, thornless variety in which thorns can subsequently form in individual cases, forms no fruits
Gleditsia triacanthos 'Sunburst' (honey locust)	8–10	6–8	High	○	R	–	–	Like the species but thornless, light yellow shoots, later yellow-green, give regard to clearance profile
Koelreuteria paniculata (goldenrain tree, pride of India, varnish tree)	6–8	6–8	High	○	R	VG	VL	Small, slow-growing, very wide crown, striking flowers and seedpods, included in Straßen-baumtest 2 since 2005
Liquidambar styraciflua (sweetgum)	10–20 (30)	6–12	Medium	○	R	S	P	Varies significantly, open crown with age, lime-sensitive, long-lasting fall foliage if in a sunny location and exposed to cold nights
Liquidambar styraciflua 'Moraine' (sweetgum)	10–20	6–12	Medium	○–◗	R	–	–	Like the species but smaller, with more uniform crown and faster growth, attractive fall foliage
Liquidambar styraciflua 'Paarl' (sweetgum)	15–25	3–4	Medium	○	R	–	–	Like the species but with slim and pointed-conical crown, average growth vigor, early and long-lasting fall foliage, included in Straßen-baumtest 2 since 2005

NA = not available; R = with restrictions; VG = very good; WS = well-suited; S = suitable; P = problematic; VL = very limited suitability

Botanical and common names	Height in m	Width in m	Permeability to light	Light requirements	Suitability for city streetscapes	Drought tolerance (according to KLAM)	Winter hardiness (Winter hardiness zoness) (according to KLAM)	Comments
Liriodendron tulipifera (tulip tree)	25–35	15–20	Medium	○	R	P	S	Broadly conical crown, straight central leader, loves warmth but also frost-hardy, rapid-growing, older specimens are susceptible to wind breakage, attractive fall foliage
Liriodendron tulipifera 'Fastigiata' (columnar tulip tree)	15–18	4–6	Low	○	R	–	–	Like the species but with narrow crown, grows stiffly upright, attractive fall foliage
Malus spec, (crab apple varieties)	4–12	2–6	Medium	○–◗	R	–	–	Richly flowering and fruit-bearing varieties, sometimes fruits remain hanging into the winter, heed clearance profile, suitable for tubs and containers
Malus tschonoskii (Chonosuki crab, pillar apple)	8–12	2–4	Medium	○–◗	S	S	VG	Narrow conical crown, becomes wider with age, straight and continuous leading shoots; fruits yellow to red, minor susceptibility to scab, included in Straßenbaumtest 2 since 2005
Malus hybrid 'Evereste' (crab apple)	4–6	3–5	Medium	○–◗	R	–	–	Broadly upright crown, overhanging side branches with age, heed clearance profile, small orange-red fruits, minor susceptibility to scab, suitable for tubs and containers
Malus hybrid 'Red Sentinel' (crab apple)	4–5	3–4	Medium	○–◗	R	–	–	Slender crown, deeply overhanging side branches, heed clearance profile, dark red fruits, minor susceptibility to scab, suitable for tubs and containers
Malus hybrid 'Rudolph' (crab apple)	5–6	4–5	Medium	○–◗	R	–	–	Upright crown, later broadly ovoid to rounded, heed clearance profile, orange-yellow fruits; minor susceptibility to scab, tends to develop superficial cracks in the bark, suitable for tubs and containers
Malus hybrid 'Street Parade' (Siberian crabapple)	4–6	2–3	Medium	○–◗	R	–	–	Narrow ovoid crown, heed clearance profile, minor susceptibility to mildew and scab, small purple fruits; suitable for tubs and containers
Metasequoia glyptostroboides (dawn redwood)	25–35 (40)	7–10	High	○	R	P	VG	Pointedly conical crown with dense branches, straight central leader, bases of roots become wide, expansive root system, ensure sufficient distance to edges of streets, etc.
Ostrya carpinifolia (hop hornbeam)	10–15 (20)	8–12	Medium	○–◗	S	VG	VG	Conical, later rounded crown, appearance similar to common hornbeam; Fruits similar to hops, decorative, included in Straßenbaumtest 2 since 2005
Platanus acerifolia syn. P. × hybrida, P. hispanica (London plane)	20–30 (40)	15–25	Low	○	R	–	–	Broadly extended crown, striking trunks due to peeling bark, undemanding, not sensitive to frost, good for urban environments, often causes root heave, foliage rots poorly, infestation by harmful organisms has increased in recent years
Populus berolinensis (Berlin poplar)	18–25	8–10	Medium	○	R	S	VG	Broadly columnar, branches ascend diagonally upward, conical when young, irregular with age, straight central leader, forms suckering shoots
Populus simonii syn. P. brevifolia (Simon poplar)	12–15	6–8 (10)	Medium	○	R	P	S	Narrow and conical, wide and round with age, short-lived, early shoots at risk of breakage from snow
Populus simonii 'Fastigiata' (balsam poplar)	7–10	4–6	Medium	○	R	–	–	Like the species but initially narrow and columnar, later broadly conical, tolerates road salt
Prunus avium 'Plena' (double-flowering sweet cherry)	10–15	8–10	Low	○	R	–	–	Like the species but with a regularly pyramidal, dense and closed crown; has filled blossoms, no fruits; good for urban environments

NA = not available; R = with restrictions; VG = very good; WS = well-suited; S = suitable; P = problematic; VL = very limited suitability

Table 3.10.4 Suitability of trees for streets and inner-city locations, per GALK and KLAM

Botanical and common names	Height in m	Width in m	Permeability to light	Light requirements	Suitability for city streetscapes	Drough tolerance (according to KLAM)	Winter hardiness (Winter hardiness zoness) (according to KLAM)	Comments
Prunus padus 'Schloss Tiefurt' (bird cherry, hackberry)	9–12	–8	Medium	○–◗	S	–	–	Like the species but smaller and with regular, closed crown; forms strikingly beautiful and straight stems; striking, strongly fragrant blossoms; included in Straßenbaumtest 2 since 2005
Prunus sargentii (Sargent's cherry, hill cherry)	8–12	5–8	Medium	○–◗	R	P	S	Broad fan-shaped crown, funnel-shaped branches, crown spreads broadly with age, sparse fruit-bearing, striking fall foliage
Prunus sargentii 'Accolade' syn. Pr. 'Accolade' (flowering cherry)	5–8	3–5 (7)	Medium	○–◗	R	–	–	Rounded to slightly funnel-shaped crown, give regard to clearance profile, striking blossoms and fall foliage
Prunus sargentii 'Rancho' (flowering cherry)	6–8	3–4	Medium	○–◗	R	–	–	Like the species but with narrow and columnar crown and stronger coloration of blossoms, does not bear fruit
Prunus serrulata 'Kanzan' syn. Pr. 'Hisakura', Pr. 'Kwanzan' (Japanese or Oriental cherry)	7–10 (12)	5–8	Medium	○–◗	R	–	–	Wide funnel-shaped, later overhanging crown, give regard to clearance profile, striking blossoms and fall foliage, seldom bears fruit
Prunus spec. (Japanese cherry species and varietals)	3–15	1–10	Low	○	R	–	–	Different crown shapes, highly ornamental owing to blossoms; trunk or root suckers, depending on grafting method; suitable for tubs and containers
Prunus subhirtella 'Autumnalis' (winter-flowering cherry, rosebud cherry)	5–8	3–5	Medium	○	R	–	–	Small tree with striking blossoms and fall foliage, give regard to clearance profile, suitable for tubs and containers
Prunus × schmittii (flowering cherry)	8–10	3–5	Medium	○–◗	S	–	–	Closed, narrow conical crown, branches grow upright, straight central leader, only flowers for a short time
Pyrus calleryana 'Chanticleer' (flowering pear, callery pear)	8–12 (15)	4–5	Medium	○	R	–	–	Narrow conical crown, later loose and broadly pyramidal, leaf fall not until after a strong frost (risk of breakage from snow), infrequent fruit production, early aging
Pyrus caucasica (Caucasian wild pear)	8–12	3–4	Medium	○–◗	R	–	–	Columnar to conical crown, grows stiffly upright, straight central leader; very adaptable, tolerates dryness, fruit production, heed results of Straßenbaumtest 1
Pyrus communis 'Beech Hill' (common pear)	8–12	5–7	Medium	○–◗	R	–	–	Initially grows stiffly upright, later spreads apart; vulnerable to fire risk; pear trellis rust in some areas; fruit production; heed results of Straßenbaumtest 1
Pyrus regelii (wild pear, Regel's pear)	8–10	7–9	Low	○–◗	R	–	–	Ovoid to rounded loose, ungainly branching, vulnerable to fire risk, pear trellis rust in some areas, occasionally strong fruit production, heed results of Straßenbaumtest 1
Quercus cerris (European Turkey oak)	20–30	10–15 (25)	Medium	○	S	–	–	Bluntly conical, broad central leader, spreads with age; long-lasting and slowly rotting foliage; also thrives in dry soils, good for urban environments
Quercus frainetto (Hungarian, or Italian oak)	10–20 (25)	10–15	Low	○–◗	R	–	–	Regular and closed crown, oval to rounded, looser with age, good for urban environments, foliage rots slowly, included in Straßenbaumtest 2 since 2005

NA = not available; R = with restrictions; VG = very good; WS = well-suited; S = suitable; P = problematic; VL = very limited suitability

Botanical and common names	Height in m	Width in m	Permeability to light	Light requirements	Suitability for city streetscapes	Drough tolerance (according to KLAM)	Winter hardiness (Winter hardiness zoness) (according to KLAM)	Comments
Quercus palustris (pin oak)	15–20 (25)	8–15 (20)	Medium	○	S	S	S	Regular conical crown, straight central leader, also thrives in moderately dry soils, risk of chlorosis in chalky soil, foliage often long-lasting, striking fall colors
Quercus petraea (durmast or sessile oak)	20–30 (40)	15–20 (25)	Medium	○	S	S	S	Regular ovoid crown, glossy deep green leaves, better for urban environments than *Quercus robur*
Quercus robur syn. Quercus pedunculata (pedunculate, or English oak)	25–35 (40)	15–20 (25)	High	○	S	P	VG	Broad conical crown, widely spreading, long-lasting and slowly rotting foliage, may not be planted prior to December, tolerates flooding, reacts to reduced groundwater table with treetop drought; frost-hardy
Quercus robur 'Fastigiata' syn. Quercus pedunculata 'Fastigiata' (pedunculate oak, pyramid-shaped oak)	15–20	5–7	Low	○	S	–	–	Like the species but columnar crown, spreads apart with age, sowing often yields atypical growth form, long-lasting foliage; frost-hardy, undemanding
Quercus robur 'Fastigiata Koster' syn. Quercus robusta 'Koster' (upright English oak)	15–20	3–5	Medium	○–◗	S	–	–	Like *Quercus robur* 'Fastigiata' but has slender and compact growth also with age, long-lasting foliage often remains until spring; frost-hardy, undemanding
Quercus rubra syn. Quercus borealis (northern red oak)	20–25	12–18 (20)	Medium	○	R	S	S	Rounded crown, continuous central leader, less demanding than *Quercus robur*; risk of chlorosis in chalky soil, good for urban environments, long-lasting foliage, striking fall foliage
Robinia pseudoacacia (black locust, false acacia)	20–25	12–18 (22)	High	○	S	VG	VG	Loose irregular crown, rapid-growing when young, umbrella-shaped with age; undemanding, susceptible to wind breakage in nutrient-rich soils, formation of deadwood with age; flowers very fragrant
Robinia pseudoacacia 'Bessoniana' (black locust)	20–25	10–12 (15)	High	○	S	–	–	Broad, rounded, and densely branched crown with age; usually straight and continuous leading shoots, few and only small thorns, seldom flowering
Robinia pseudoacacia 'Monophylla' (syn. Robinia pseudoacacia 'Unifolia' (single-leaf black locust)	15–20 (25)	8–10	Medium	○	S	–	–	Irregular conical crown, upright growth, main branches are slender and upright,straight and continuous leading shoots, only a few small thorns
Robinia pseudoacacia 'Nyirsegi' (black locust, false acacia)	25–30	10–15	Medium	○	S	–	–	Upright and rounded ovoid, densely branched crown; straight central leader extends into the crown, few thorns, lower risk of breakage than the species
Robinia pseudoacacia 'Sandraudiga' (black locust, false acacia)	20–25	12–18 (22)	High	○	S	–	–	Widely pyramidal, strikingly loose crown, straight central leader, pink blossoms, heed results of Straßenbaumtest 1
Robinia pseudoacacia 'Semperflorens' (black locust, false acacia)	15–20	10–15 (18)	High	○	S	–	–	Upright and loose crown, broadly oval with age; few thorns, often has blossoms continuously from June to September owing to second flowering
Robinia pseudoacacia 'Umbraculifera' (umbrella black locust)	4–6	4–6	Low	○	S	–	–	Dense and spherical crown with fine shoots; more broadly oval with age, heed clearance profile, tolerates radical pruning, no blossoms, suitable for tubs and containers

NA = not available; R = with restrictions; VG = very good; WS = well-suited; S = suitable; P = problematic; VL = very limited suitability

Table 3.10.4 Suitability of trees for streets and inner-city locations, per GALK and KLAM

Botanical and common names	Height in m	Width in m	Permeability to light	Light requirements	Suitability for city streetscapes	Drough tolerance (according to KLAM)	Winter hardiness (Winter hardiness zoness) (according to KLAM)	Comments
Sophora japonica (Japanese pagoda tree)	15–20 (25)	12–18 (20)	High	○	R	VG	S	Broad and rounded, very loose and light crown spreads with age; pay heed to obtaining a straight central leader; summer pruning; young trees susceptible to frost in some areas; striking blossoms
Sophora japonica 'Regent' (Japanese pagoda tree)	15–20 (25)	10–15	High	○	R	–	–	Like the species, broad and rounded crown, spreads with age, superfluous variety since it does not represent an improvement to the species, heed results of Straßenbaumtest 1
Sorbus aria (chess-apple, whitebeam)	6–12 (18)	4–7 (12)	Medium	○	R	VG	VG	Regularly structured conical crown, wider and looser with age, slow-growing, heed clearance profile
Sorbus aria 'Magnifica' (chess-apple, hitebeam)	6–12 (18)	4–7 (12)	Medium	○	S	–	–	Like the species but smaller and narrower, with regularly structured crown, wider with age
Sorbus aria 'Majestica' syn. S. aria decaisneana (chess-apple, whitebeam)	8–10 (12)	4–7	Medium	○	R	–	–	Like the species but with narrow conical crown, umbrella-shaped with age, fruits and leaves larger
Sorbus intermedia syn. Sorbus suecica (Swedish whitebeam)	10–15 (20)	5–7	Medium	○	R	S	VG	Conical crown, round with age, heed clearance profile
Sorbus intermedia 'Brouwers' (Swedish whitebeam)	9–12	4–7	Low	○	S	–	–	Like the species but with compact pyramidal crown, straight central leader, good for urban environments, wind-tolerant, frost-hardy
Sorbus × thuringiaca 'Fastigiata' (Thuringian hybrid ash)	5–7	4–5	Medium	○	S	–	–	Narrow, conical, and compact crown; good for urban environments, wind-tolerant, frost-hardy, drought-tolerant, slow-growing
Tilia americana 'Nova' syn. T. flaccida 'Nova' (American lime, American basswood)	25–30	15–20	Low	○–◗	S	–	–	Broadly conical crown, round with age, straight central leader, comparatively large leaves, honeydew secretion, frost-hardy, heat-tolerant
Tilia cordata (littleleaf linden, small-leaved lime)	18–20 (30)	12–15 (20)	Low	○–◗	R	S	VG	Very strongly fragrant, outstanding pollen source; habits can be highly variable, resulting in a difficult crown structure, difficult to cut away branches; honeydew secretion
Tilia cordata 'Erecta' syn. T. cordata 'Böhlje' (densely crowned littleleaf linden)	15–20	10–12 (14)	Low	○–◗	S	–	–	Like the species but with smaller and more regular crown, small leaves, slow-growing as young tree, less honeydew secretion
Tilia cordata 'Greenspire' (American linden)	18–20	10–12	Low	○–◗	WS	–	–	Narrow, regular, and dense crown, wider with age; ascending branches; good for urban environments; honeydew secretion
Tilia cordata 'Rancho' (American linden)	8–12 (15)	4–6 (8)	Low	○–◗	S	–	–	Like the species but with narrow ovoid crown that becomes broadly rounder and more regular with age; slow and compact growth; less honeydew secretion, heed results of Straßenbaumtest 1
Tilia cordata 'Roelvo' (littleleaf linden, linden)	10–15	7–10	Low	○–◗	S	–	–	Like the species but with broadly conical to rounded crown, longer shoots and growth not as compact as 'Rancho,' less honeydew secretion, heed results of Straßenbaumtest 1

NA = not available; R = with restrictions; VG = very good; WS = well-suited; S = suitable; P = problematic; VL = very limited suitability

Botanical and common names	Height in m	Width in m	Permeability to light	Light requirements	Suitability for city streetscapes	Drough tolerance (according to KLAM)	Winter hardiness (Winter hardiness zoness) (according to KLAM)	Comments
Tilia tomentosa (silver linden)	25–30	15–20	Low	○	R	VG	S	Regular and broadly conical closed crown, tendency to forked growth; late profusion of flowers, not hazardous to bees or bumblebees, no honeydew secretion, the use of varieties is recommended
Tilia tomentosa 'Brabant' (Brabant silver linden)	20–25 (30)	12–18 (20)	Low	○	WS	–	–	Broad and conical, dense and regularly structured crown; selection with straight central leader, better formation of leading shoots than the species, no honeydew secretion
Tilia × euchlora syn. Tilia × europaea 'Euchlora' (Caucasian lime)	15–20 (25)	10–12	Medium	○	S	S	VG	Bluntly conical crown, straight central leader, heavily hanging branches, give regard to clearance profile, fast-growing, wind-tolerant, frost-hardy, honeydew secretion
Tilia × europaea syn. T. × intermedia, T. × vulgaris, T. × hollandica (Dutch linden)	25–35 (40)	15–20	Low	○	S	P	VG	Regularly structured conical crown, good for urban environments, drought-tolerant and loves warmth, bee pasture, honeydew secretion
Tilia × europaea 'Pallida' syn. T. × intermedia 'Pallida', T. × vulgaris 'Pallida' (Emperor's lime)	30–35 (40)	12–18 (20)	Low	○	WS	–	–	Like the species but regular conical crown, spreads widely with age; leaves remain in autumn longer than for the species, various selections available commercially; honeydew secretion
Tilia × flavescens 'Glenleven' (Glenleven linden)	15–20 (25)	12–15	Low	○	R	–	–	Closed, broadly conical crown, spreads and becomes rounder with age, straight central leader, fast-growing, good for urban environments, honeydew secretion, heed results of Straßenbaumtest 1
Ulmus × hollandica 'Lobel' (Lobel elm)	12–15	4–5	Low	○	R	–	–	Initially narrow- and upright-growing columnar crown, later becomes more conical and broader, vigorous growth, less susceptibility to Dutch elm disease
Ulmus hybrid 'Dodoens' (elm)	12–15	5–6	Low	○–◗	R	–	–	Loose and slender upright crown, broadly conical with age, less susceptibility to Dutch elm disease
Ulmus 'New Horizon' (elm)	20–25	5–6	Low	○–◗	m-E.	–	–	Columnar to conical and dense crown, slim and conical when young, later wider, presumably highly resistant to Dutch elm disease, included in Straßenbaumtest 2 since 2007/08
Ulmus hybrid 'Rebona' (Rebona elm)	15–20	10–15	Low	○–◗	R	–	–	Broadly conical crown, branches protrude horizontally, presumably resistant to Dutch elm disease
Ulmus hybrid 'Regal' (elm)	15–20	6–8	Medium	○	R	–	–	Initially slim and conical, wide and columnar with age, fast-growing, presumably resistant to Dutch elm disease, included in Straßenbaumtest 2 since 2007/08
Zelkova serrata syn. Z. acuminata, Z. keaki (Japanese zelkova)	20–25	15–25	Low	○–◗	R	S	S	Wide, round crown with broadly extended growth, watch for straight leading shoots, good for urban environments, included in Straßenbaumtest 2 since 2005

NA = not available; R = with restrictions; VG = very good; WS = well-suited; S = suitable; P = problematic; VL = very limited suitability

Table 3.10.4 Suitability of trees for streets and inner-city locations, per GALK and KLAM

Root Systems of Trees

The root systems of trees can be classified into three main groups: they can have roots that are mainly vertical and deep (taprooters), lateral and shallow (shallow rooters), or oblique (heart rooters). In some cases, there are of course hybrid forms. In correspondence to the various root systems, each particular tree species exhibits different characteristics and may be suitable for different applications. As a result, each tree species has other possibilities for use and tolerances toward intrusive actions, which affect a tree's potential use near sewer lines or its reaction to construction activity, for example. → **Table 3.10.5**

Species/variety (Latin name)	Species/variety (Common name)	Root system	Formation of runners	Heaves pavement	Adding soil depth at base	Reaction to intrusive actions	Penetrates sewer lines
Large trees (first order trees)							
Acer platanoides	Norway maple	Shallow/heart roots	–	Possible	Possible	Tolerant	Observed
Acer pseudoplatanus varieties	Sycamore	Deep	–	Seldom	Viable	Tolerant	Often
Acer saccharinum	Silver maple	Extremely shallow	–	Strong	Viable	Sensitive	Preferable
Aesculus hippocastanum	Horse chestnut	Shallow, broad	+	Strong	Sensitive	Sensitive	Preferable
Ailanthus altissima	Tree of heaven	Shallow	–	Strong	Sensitive	Sensitive	Often
Alnus glutinosa	European (or black) alder	Shallow	–	Seldom	Possible	Tolerant	Often
Betula papyrifera	Paper birch	Shallow	–	Possible	Sensitive		
Betula pendula	European white birch, silver birch	Extremely shallow	–	Strong	Impossible	Sensitive	Seldom
Castanea sativa	European (or sweet) chestnut	Deep, dense	–	Seldom	Possible		
Fagus sylvatica varieties	European (or common) beech	Shallow/heart roots	–	Possible	Impossible	Sensitive	Never
Fraxinus excelsior varieties	European (or common) ash	Deep, broad	–	Seldom	Possible	Tolerant	Often
Gleditsia triacanthos 'Inermis'	Honey locust	Shallow	–	Seldom	Possible	Tolerant	
Liriodendron tulipifera	Tulip tree	Shallow, Succulent	–	Possible	Sensitive	Sensitive	
Platanus × acerifolia	London plane	Heart roots	–	Strong	Viable	Tolerant	Often
Populus alba 'Nivea'	White (or silver) poplar	Shallow	+	Strong	Viable	Tolerant	Preferable
Populus balsamifera	Balsam poplar	Shallow	+	Strong	Viable	Tolerant	Preferable
Populus × berolinensis	Berlin poplar	Shallow	+	Possible	Possible	Tolerant	Observed
Populus × canescens	Gray poplar	Shallow	+	Possible	Possible	Tolerant	Preferable
Populus × euramericana 'Robusta'	Robusta poplar	Shallow	–	Possible	Possible	Tolerant	Observed
Populus nigra 'Italica'	Lombardy poplar, black poplar	Shallow	+	Strong	Possible	Tolerant	Preferable
Quercus cerris	Turkey oak	Deep	–	Seldom	Possible	Tolerant	Observed
Quercus frainetto	Hungarian (or Italian) oak	Deep	–				
Quercus petraea	Durmast (or sessile) oak	Deep	–	Seldom	Possible	Tolerant	Often

Table 3.10.5 Root systems and attendant characteristics of trees

Species/variety (Latin name)	Species/variety (Common name)	Root system	Formation of runners	Heaves pavement	Adding soil depth at base	Reaction to intrusive actions	Penetrates sewer lines
Quercus robur	English oak	Deep	–	Seldom	Possible	Tolerant	Often
Quercus rubra	Northern red oak	Shallow	–	Strong	Sensitive	Sensitive	Often
Robinia pseudoacacia	Black locust	Shallow, broad	+	Strong	Minimal	Tolerant	Never
Salix alba varieties	White willow	Shallow	–	Strong	Viable	Tolerant	Preferable
Tilia species and varieties	Lime, linden, or basswood	Heart roots, intensive	–	Strong	Minimal	Tolerant	Never
Ulmus laevis	European white elm	Deep	+	Seldom	Sensitive	Sensitive	Possible
Medium-sized trees							
Acer campestre varieties	Hedge maple, field maple	Heart roots	–	Seldom	Possible	Tolerant	Seldom
Acer negundo	Box elder	Shallow	–	Possible	Sensitive	Sensitive	Often
Acer platanoides varieties	Norway maple	Shallow / heart roots	–	Possible	Possible	Tolerant	Observed
Acer rubrum varieties	Red maple	Shallow	–	Possible	Sensitive	Sensitive	Observed
Acer saccharinum 'Laciniatum Wieri'	Wier maple	Extremely shallow	–	Strong	Viable	Sensitive	Preferable
Alnus cordata	Italian alder		–		Possible		
Alnus incana	Gray alder	Shallow	+	Possible	Possible	Tolerant	Preferable
Alnus × spaethii	Spaeth's alder	Shallow	–				
Betula nigra	River birch	Shallow, dense	–	Possible	Sensitive	Sensitive	Seldom
Betula pubescens	Downy birch	Shallow, Heart roots	–		Possible	Tolerant	
Betula utilis	Himalayan birch	Shallow	–	Strong	Sensitive	Sensitive	
Carpinus betulus varieties	European (or common) hornbeam	Heart roots, intensive	–	Seldom	Minimal	Sensitive	
Cercidiphyllum japonicum	Katsura tree	Shallow / heart roots	–	Strong			
Corylus colurna	Turkish hazelnut	Heart roots	–	Possible	Minimal	Sensitive	
Davidia involucrata var. *vilmoriniana*	Handkerchief (or dove) tree	Shallow	–		Impossible	Sensitive	
Fagus sylvatica varieties	European (or common) beech	Shallow / heart roots	–	Possible	Impossible	Sensitive	Never
Fraxinus excelsior varieties	European (or common) ash	Deep/broad	–	Seldom	Possible	Tolerant	Often
Juglans	Walnut	Deep	–	Seldom	Possible	Sensitive	
Liquidambar	Sweetgum	Heart roots, Succulent	Possible	Minimal	Sensitive	Observed	
Populus simonii	Simon poplar	Shallow		Strong	Possible	Tolerant	Observed
Populus tremula	European aspen	Shallow / heart roots	–	Strong	Possible	Tolerant	Preferable

Table 3.10.5 Root systems and attendant characteristics of trees

Species/variety (Latin name)	Species/variety (Common name)	Root system	Formation of runners	Heaves pavement	Adding soil depth at base	Reaction to intrusive actions	Penetrates sewer lines
Prunus avium	Sweet cherry	Shallow, broad	+	Possible	Minimal	Sensitive	Observed
Pterocarya fraxinifolia	Caucasian wingnut	Shallow	+	Strong	Possible	Tolerant	Preferable
Quercus coccinea	Scarlet oak	Deep	+	Possible	Sensitive	Sensitive	Observed
Quercus macranthera	Caucasian (or Persian) oak	Shallow	–	Seldom	Possible		
Quercus palustris	Pin oak	Shallow	–	Strong	Sensitive	Sensitive	Observed
Robinia pseudoacacia varieties	Black locust	Shallow	+	Possible	Minimal	Tolerant	Never
Salix alba varieties	White willow	Shallow	–	Strong	Viable	Tolerant	Preferable
Sophora japonica varieties	Japanese pagoda tree	Shallow	–	Strong	Minimal	Sensitive	
Sorbus aucuparia varieties	European mountain ash or rowan	Shallow / heart roots	+	Strong	Possible	Sensitive	Never
Sorbus intermedia	Swedish whitebeam	Heart roots	–	Possible	Possible	Tolerant	Never
Tilia cordata varieties	Littleleaf linden	Heart roots, intensive	–	Strong	Minimal	Tolerant	Never
Tilia × euchlora	Caucasian lime	Heart roots	–	Strong	Minimal	Sensitive	
Ulmus 'Lobel'	Lobel elm	Heart roots	–	Possible	Minimal		
Small trees							
Acer ginnala	Amur maple	Shallow	–	Possible	Minimal	Sensitive	
Acer japonicum 'Aconitifolium'	Downy Japanese maple 'Aconitifolium'	Shallow	–		Impossible	Sensitive	
Acer negundo varieties	Box elder	Shallow	–	Possible	Sensitive	Sensitive	Often
Acer palmatum varieties	Japanese Maple	Shallow	–		Impossible	Sensitive	
Acer rufinerve	Redvein maple	Shallow	–		Sensitive	Sensitive	
Acer × zoeschense 'Annae'	Zoeschen maple	Shallow / heart roots	–	Possible			
Aesculus × carnea 'Briotii'	Red horse chestnut	Shallow / heart roots	–	Strong	Sensitive	Sensitive	
Alnus cordata	Italian alder		–		Possible		
Amelanchier species	Serviceberry	Shallow	–	Possible	Sensitive	Sensitive	
Aralia elata	Japanese angelica tree	Shallow	–		Minimal	Sensitive	
Buxus sempervirens var. *arborescens*	Common box	Heart roots, intensive	–		Minimal	Tolerant	
Catalpa bignonioides	Southern catalpa, Indian bean tree	Heart roots, Succulent	–	Never	Minimal	Sensitive	
Cercis siliquastrum	Judas tree	Shallow	+	Possible			
Cornus species and varieties	Common dogwood	Shallow / heart roots	–	Seldom	Minimal	Sensitive	

Species/variety (Latin name)	Species/variety (Common name)	Root system	Formation of runners	Heaves pavement	Adding soil depth at base	Reaction to intrusive actions	Penetrates sewer lines
Crataegus laevigata 'Paul's Scarlet'	Paul's Scarlet hawthorn	Deep	–	Seldom	Sensitive	Sensitive	Never
Crataegus × lavallei	Lavallée's hawthorn	Deep	–	Seldom	Possible	Tolerant	Never
Crataegus monogyna varieties	Oneseed (or common) hawthorn	Deep	–	Seldom	Sensitive	Sensitive	Never
Crataegus pedicellata	Scarlet hawthorn	Deep	–		Possible	Tolerant	Never
Crataegus × prunifolia 'Splendens'	Hawthorn 'Splendens'	Deep	–	Seldom			
Davidia involucrata var. *vilmoriniana*	Handkerchief (or dove) tree	Shallow	–		Impossible	Sensitive	
Elaeagnus angustifolia	Russian olive, oleaster	Shallow / deep	–		Minimal		Never
Fraxinus ornus varieties	Flowering ash	Heart roots / deep	–	Possible	Possible	Sensitive	
Halesia carolina	Carolina silverbell	Shallow	–	Never	Impossible	Sensitive	
Hippophae rhamnoides	Seaberry or sea buckthorn	Shallow / deep	+	Strong	Possible	Tolerant	Never
Ilex aquifolium varieties	English (or European) holly	Heart roots	–	Seldom	Sensitive	Sensitive	Never
Koelreuteria paniculata	Goldenrain tree, pride of India	Shallow	–	Seldom	Sensitive	Sensitive	Never
Laburnum species and varieties	Goldenchain, laburnum	Shallow, with gaps	–	Possible	Sensitive	Never	
Lonicera maackii	Amur honeysuckle	Heart roots	–	Possible	Sensitive	Sensitive	Never
Magnolia species and varieties	Magnolia	Shallow	–	Possible	Impossible	Sensitive	
Malus species and varieties	Apple	Shallow / heart roots	+	Possible	Sensitive	Sensitive	Possible
Parrotia persica	Persian ironwood	Shallow	–	Possible	Sensitive	Sensitive	
Prunus species and varieties	Cherry/Laurel/Plum	Heart roots	–	Possible	Sensitive	Sensitive	Possible
Pyrus calleryana 'Chanticleer'	Callery pear 'Chanticleer'	Deep	+	Seldom	Possible	Tolerant	Possible
Pyrus salicifolia	Willow-leaved pear Pear	Deep	–		Tolerant	Possible	
Quercus pontica	Pontine (or Armenian) oak	Deep	–	Seldom			
Quercus × turneri 'Pseudoturneri'	Turner's oak 'Pseudoturneri'	Deep	–	Seldom			
Rhus typhina	Staghorn sumac	Shallow, broad	+	Strong	Sensitive	Sensitive	
Salix species and varieties	Willow	Shallow	–	Strong	Viable	Tolerant	Preferable
Sorbus species and varieties	Mountain ash	Heart roots / deep	–	Possible	Sensitive	Sensitive	Possible

Table 3.10.5 Root systems and attendant characteristics of trees

Species/variety (Latin name)	Species/variety (Common name)	Root system	Formation of runners	Heaves pavement	Adding soil depth at base	Reaction to intrusive actions	Penetrates sewer lines
Coniferous trees							
Abies species and varieties	Fir	Heart roots / deep	–	Seldom	Possible		Never
Cedrus species and varieties	Cedar	Heart roots / deep	–	Seldom	Possible	Sensitive	Never
Chamaecyparis varieties	False cypress	Shallow, intensive	–	Possible	Sensitive	Sensitive	Possible
Ginkgo biloba	Ginkgo, maidenhair tree	Heart roots	–	Seldom	Sensitive	Sensitive	
Juniperus virginiana 'Skyrocket'	Rocky Mountain juniper 'Skyrocket'	Shallow / deep	–	Seldom	Possible		
Larix species	Larch	Heart roots	–	Possible	Possible	Tolerant	
Metasequoia glyptostroboides	Dawn redwood	Shallow	–	Strong	Sensitive	Sensitive	Possible
Picea species and varieties	Spruce	Shallow	–	Possible	Sensitive	Sensitive	Never
Pinus species and varieties	Pine	Shallow / deep	–	Possible	Possible	Tolerant	Never
Pseudolarix amabilis	Golden larch	Deep	–				
Pseudotsuga menziesii var. *caesia*	Douglas fir	Heart roots	–	Seldom	Minimal		
Sciadopitys verticillata	Umbrella pine	Shallow, Succulent	–	Never	Impossible	Sensitive	Never
Sequoiadendron giganteum	Giant sequoia	Shallow / deep	–	Seldom	Impossible	Sensitive	Never

Remarks on Regulatory Approval

Stipulations and information on the use of woody plants can, for example, stem from urban green structure plans, binding land-use plans, or design statutes.

Legal requirements, such as those arising from nature conservation legislation, tree protection ordinances, neighbor law, or rights of way, must be observed.

Setback distances for hedges
→ 3.6 Boundary Enclosures and Railings

3 Elements
3.11 Vegetated Roofing

3.11 Vegetated Roofing

Vegetated roofs, also known commonly as green roofs or living roofs, constitute a broad category that encompasses the landscaped roofs of conventional buildings as well as any landscape situated on a built structure, be it a courtyard above an underground parking garage or a park running directly over a subterranean structure or even set atop a bridge. Their positive effect on the (local) climate and their abilities to trap dust and pollutants, retain stormwater, create habitats for flora and fauna, and protect the roof as well as an increase in the quality of any usable open spaces all represent good arguments for green roofs.

Since the load capacity is limited in most cases by the built structure itself, the maximum distributed load in combination with the roof slope can result in restrictions to the overall design and the planting choices available for consideration. In addition, highly exposed areas can present conditions that are too extreme for many uses or types of vegetation.

Site

Types of Green Roofs

With regard to the composition of layers and their thicknesses, distinctions are made between extensive, semi-intensive, and intensive forms of landscaping. The thickness of the vegetation layer determines the type of planting, which can range from an extensive system with a drought-resistant mixture of moss and sedum species to a semi-intensive system with perennials and grasses or an intensive system with varied woody plants. All types of green roofs are feasible on flat roof slopes, but only the extensive system is feasible for roof slopes greater than 5°. → Table 3.11.2

Both walkable and trafficable areas can be constructed with either bound or unbound material. The details and layer thicknesses are dependent on the anticipated loading from vehicles. The point loads must be distributed by suitably thick base courses, or in the case of shallower installations, load distribution plates are needed to spread the point loads. → Figure 3.11.1

Plants

Because positions of these landscapes and their exposure to the elements are generally predetermined by the building's configuration, the potential planting is sometimes subjected to extreme site-specific differences. The prevailing wind conditions on roofs are often much more harsh than on the ground or within courtyards. The exposure on the roof or location within a courtyard often yield extreme situations with intense solar radiation or complete shade. Especially on steeply sloped roofs, the conditions can become extremely dry because precipitation can barely be held in the thin substrate layers and quickly drains away.

Contingent on the building, a variety of habitats thus arise, for which appropriate choices of plants must be made.

The thickness of the root-permeable layers determines the fundamentally different types of planting. The range of these planting forms is shown in Table 3.11.1

	Root-permeable layer thickness, in cm	4	6	8	10	12	15	18	20	25	30	35	40	45	50	60	70	80	90	100	125	150	200
Extensive landscaping (≥ 45 Vol. %)*	Moss / sedum mix																						
	Sedum / moss / herb mix																						
	Sedum / grass / herb mix																						
	Grass / herb mix																						
Semi-intensive landscaping (≥ 50 Vol. %)*	Grass / herb mix																						
	Wildflowers / woody plants mix																						
	Woody plants / perennials mix																						
	Woody plants																						
Intensive landscaping (≥ 55 Vol. %)*	Grass																						
	Low perennials and woody plants																						
	Medium-height perennials and woody plants																						
	High perennials and woody plants																						
	Large shrubs and small trees																						
	Tall and medium-height trees																						
	Tall trees																						

* maximum water capacity of the vegetation substrate and drainage layer

Tab. 3.11.1 Possible types of vegetation as a function of vegetation layer thickness

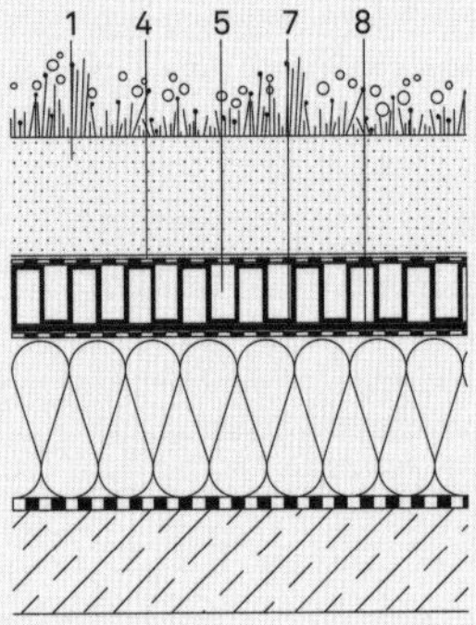

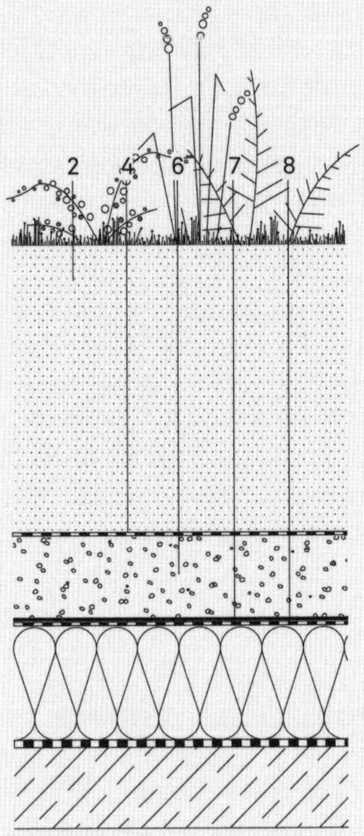

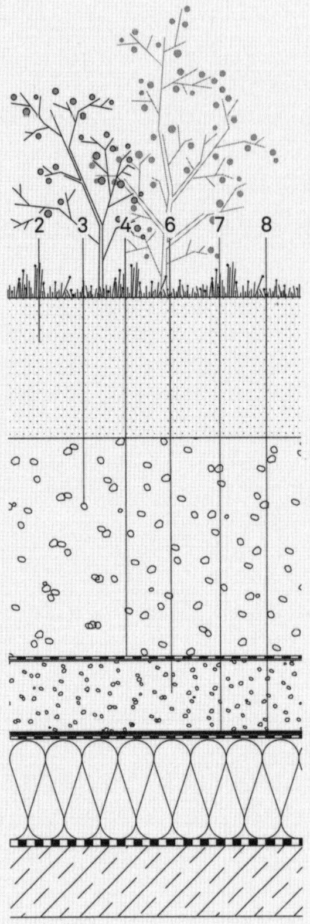

	Type of planting Extensive landscaping	Semi-intensive landscaping	Intensive landscaping
Layers 1 Extensive substrate 2 Intensive substrate 3 Inorganic substrate (growth medium) 4 Filter layer 5 Rigid drainage board 6 Drainage layer 7 Protection layer 8 Roof waterproofing (root-resistant)	1 4 5 7 8	2 4 6 7 8	2 3 4 6 7 8
Drainage layer	Approx. 3 cm (omitted for single-layer system)	3–5 cm	>10 cm
Vegetation layer	5–15 cm	10–25 cm	>25 cm
Roof load	50–150 kg/m²	150–350 kg/m²	>350 kg/m²
Type of vegetation	Mosses, some drought-tolerant grasses and perennial flowers, particularly mixtures of moss / sedum, sedum / moss / herbs, sedum / grass / herbs, and grass / herbs	Drought-tolerant perennial flowers, grasses, and woody plants	Nearly unrestricted use of plants, depending on local conditions; no wind-sensitive plants and no large woody plants
	No strongly growing climbing plants or plants with aggressive root growth, e.g., some bamboo species, which could damage the root barrier or roof waterproofing		
Maintenance	Low: no irrigation ordinarily required	Moderate: occasional irrigation when needed (dry periods); pruning back and fertilizing as required, depending on plant species	High: regular irrigation; pruning back and fertilizing as required, depending on plant species
	Inspection of the roof drains and, if necessary, removal of foreign growth – particularly from protective strips		
Roof pitch	(0) 1°–35° (up to 45° in exceptional cases) 20° pitch or greater only with protection against shear forces and slippage in order to prevent erosion due to the runoff velocity of precipitation.	(0) 1°–5° (approx. 8 %)	(0) 1°–5° (approx. 8 %)
Suitable roof types	• Simple structures such as carports, pavilions, garden sheds, etc. • Ventilated (cold) roofs	• Simple structures only after verifying specific conditions	
	• Inverted roof with thermal insulation • Nonventilated (warm) roofs, when pressure-resistant insulation is used • Watertight concrete roof with thermal insulation • Roofs without thermal insulation (e.g., underground garages, bridges, outbuildings, etc.)		

Table 3.11.2 Characteristics of the different types of green roofs (Source: State Research Institute for Horticulture Weihenstephan, amended and supplemented)

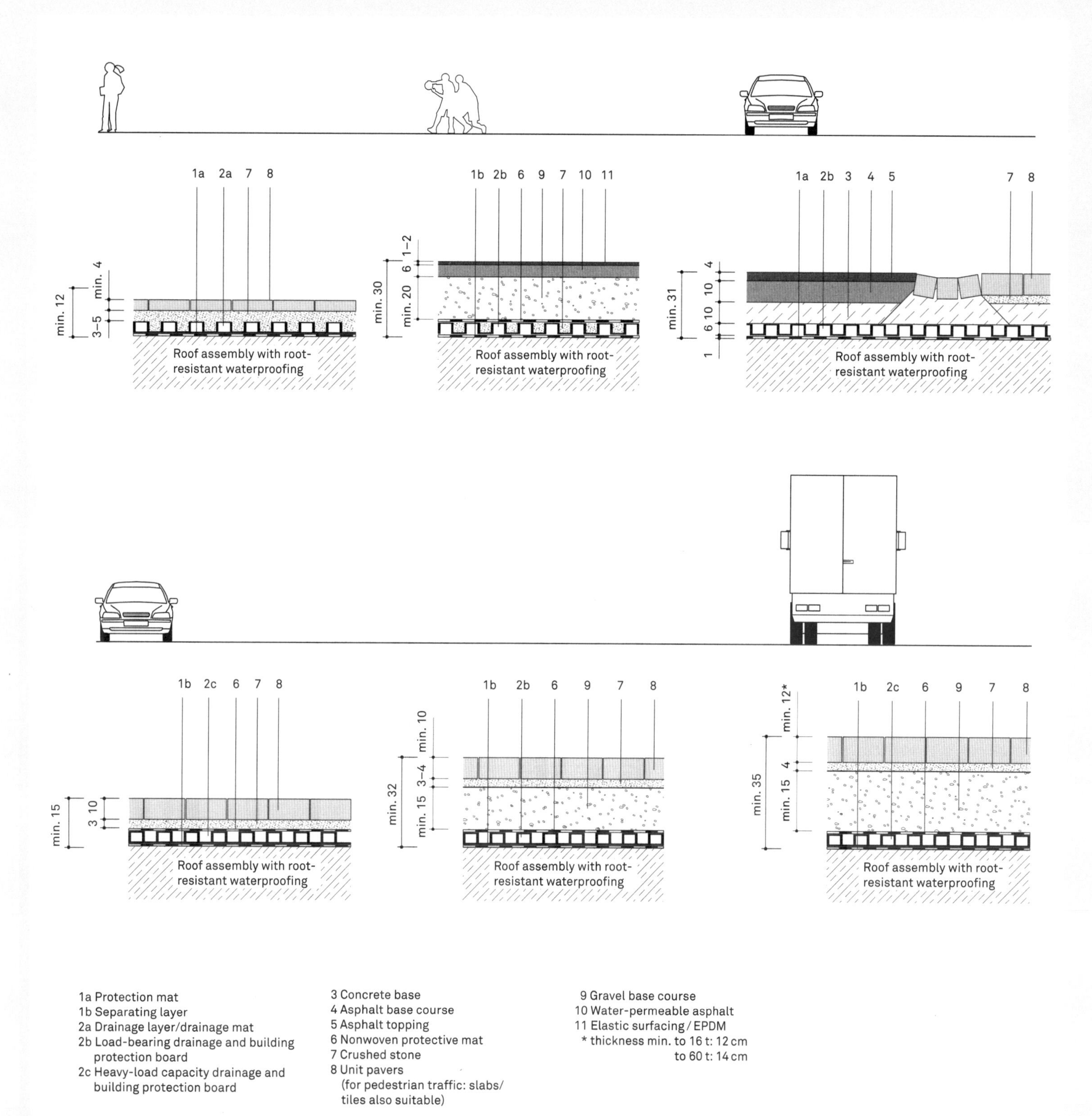
1a 2a 7 8
min. 12
min. 4
3–5
Roof assembly with root-resistant waterproofing
1b 2b 6 9 7 10 11
min. 30
1–2
6
min. 20
Roof assembly with root-resistant waterproofing
1a 2b 3 4 5 7 8
min. 31
4
10
10
6
1
Roof assembly with root-resistant waterproofing
1b 2c 6 7 8
min. 15
10
3
Roof assembly with root-resistant waterproofing
1b 2b 6 9 7 8
min. 32
min. 10
3–4
min. 15
Roof assembly with root-resistant waterproofing
1b 2c 6 9 7 8
min. 35
min. 12*
4
min. 15
Roof assembly with root-resistant waterproofing
1a Protection mat
1b Separating layer
2a Drainage layer/drainage mat
2b Load-bearing drainage and building protection board
2c Heavy-load capacity drainage and building protection board
3 Concrete base
4 Asphalt base course
5 Asphalt topping
6 Nonwoven protective mat
7 Crushed stone
8 Unit pavers (for pedestrian traffic: slabs/tiles also suitable)
9 Gravel base course
10 Water-permeable asphalt
11 Elastic surfacing / EPDM
* thickness min. to 16 t: 12 cm
to 60 t: 14 cm

Figure 3.11.1 Paving for pedestrians and vehicles on roofs and above underground structures

Dimensions and Characteristics

Load Assumptions

The constructional details of the building, especially the type of roof and its loading capacity, can restrict the options available for the type of green roof, the type of fixtures, and the type and thickness of the drainage and vegetation layers. In addition to the intrinsic weight of the roof assembly, load reserves – for snow loads, for example – must also be taken into account. For usable flat roofs, loads for built-in elements and additional imposed loads must also be factored in, as well as loads from occasional or regular pedestrian or vehicular traffic. → Table 3.11.4

Protection Against Wind Suction

For roofs in exposed locations, bulkheads and other rooftop elements must be protected against strong wind forces. These wind suction forces vary depending on the building height and roof form, and hence they must be calculated individually. At the perimeter, the wind suction forces are counteracted with a sufficient quantity of ballast (concrete pavers or the like). Dependent on the roof configuration (→ Figure 3.11.2) and the building height, the ballast required for buildings with flat roofs with a maximum 8° slope can be found in Table 3.11.3.

Erosion Control

To protect the applied substrates and the vegetation itself against wind and water erosion, additional measures are required. This can be accomplished by selecting appropriate landscaping measures and by securing the corner areas of flat roofs.

The landscaping measures for both flat and steeply pitched roofs are diverse, but include in particular:

- Erosion-control fabric
- Seeding and subsequent fixation with soil stabilizer
- Hydroseeding with binder and mulch cover
- Precultivated vegetation mats
- Substrates with bonded layers.

The measures are also dependent on the roof slope. With extensive landscaping on steeply sloped roofs, measures must be taken to prevent erosion from the runoff velocity of precipitation and the ensuing shear forces.

Minimum Clearances

Minimum clearances to vertical building components are defined for the purposes of fire safety and keep certain areas free of vegetation and water infiltration. These vegetation-free zones are indispensable and usually take the form of gravel strips or unit pavers.

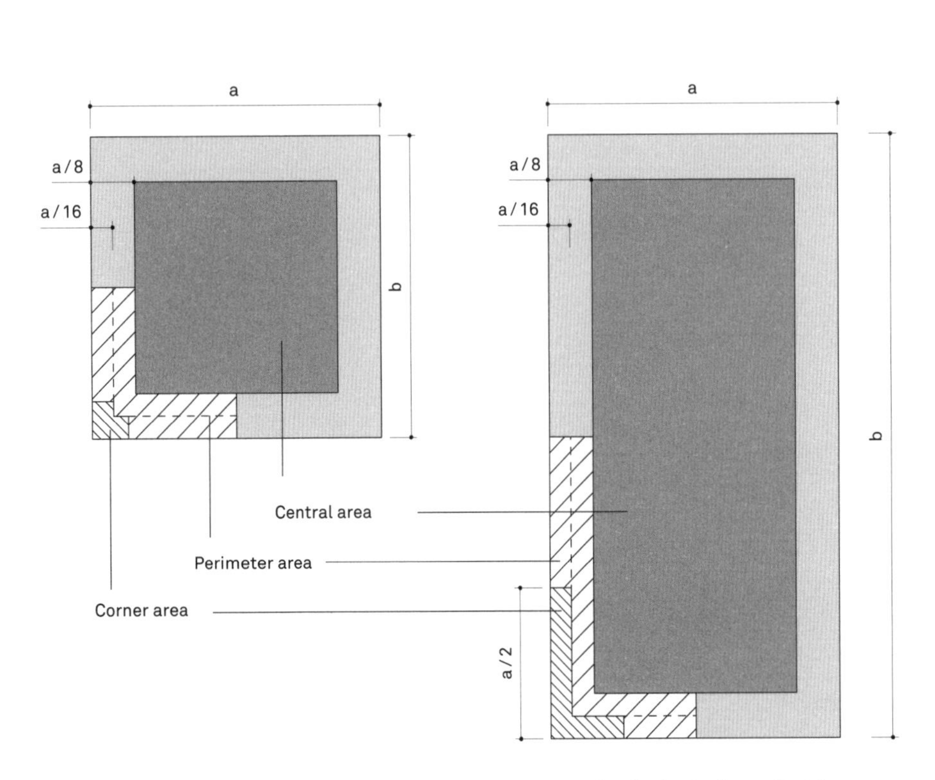

Figure 3.11.2 Area distribution for flat roofs with a maximum 8° slope for determining the required ballast

Wind suction forces and required ballast for flat roofs with max. 8° slope as a function of roof plan (a × b) and building height (h) (as per DIN 1055, Part 4)		Building height above grade					
		0–8 m		8–20 m		20–100 m	
		Dynamic pressure q					
		0.5 kN/m²		0.8 kN/m²		1.1 kN/m²	
Building type	**Roof areas and wind pressure coefficient c_p**	**Wind suction forces and required ballast (including safety factor 1.5), in [kN/m²]**					
	Dimensional proportions b / a ≤ 1.5; h / a > 0.4	Suction force	Reqd. ballast	Suction force	Reqd. ballast	Suction force	Reqd. ballast
	Corner c_p = −2.0	1.00	1.50	1.60	2.40	2.20	3.30
	Perimeter c_p = −1.0	0.50	0.75	0.80	1.20	1.10	1.65
	Center c_p = −0.6	0.30	0.45	0.48	0.72	0.66	0.99
	Dimensional proportions b / a ≤ 1.5; h / a > 0.4						
	Corner c_p = −2.8	1.40	2.10	2.24	3.36	3.08	4.62
	Perimeter c_p = −1.5	0.75	1.13	1.20	1.80	1.65	2.48
	Center c_p = −0.8	0.40	0.60	0.64	0.96	0.88	1.32
	Dimensional proportions b / a > 1.5; h / a ≤ 0.4						
	Corner c_p = −2.5	1.25	1.88	2.00	3.00	2.75	4.13
	Perimeter c_p = −1.0	0.50	0.75	0.80	1.20	1.10	1.65
	Center c_p = −0.6	0.30	0.45	0.48	0.72	0.66	0.99
	Dimensional proportions b / a > 1.5; h / a > 0.4						
	Corner c_p = −3.0	1.50	2.25	2.40	3.60	3.30	4.95
	Perimeter c_p = −1.7	0.85	1.28	1.36	2.04	1.87	2.81
	Center c_p = −0.8	0.40	0.60	0.64	0.96	0.88	1.32

* kN/m² is equivalent to 100 kg/m²

Table 3.11.3 Wind suction forces and required ballast

Type of use	Distributed load for max. water capacity, in kN/m²
Extensive landscaping	0.5–1.5
Semi-intensive landscaping	1.5–3.5
Intensive landscaping	>3.5
Supplemental loads	
Small trees up to 10 m high	0.6
Trees up to 15 m high	1.5
Load reserves	
Snow	0.75
Access for maintenance purposes	0.75
Imposed (live) loads	
Traffic loads from pedestrians/ cyclists	4
Traffic loads from vehicles – cars up to 2.5 t	3.5–5
Traffic loads from vehicles – trucks from 2.5 to 16 t	8.9

Table 3.11.4 Load assumptions for green roofs, average values

Remarks on Building Law and Regulatory Approval

Stipulations for required vegetative roofing can be part of the urban land-use planning. In Germany, green roofs for buildings can be specified in the binding land-use plan in accordance with § 9 (1) no. 25 of the German Federal Building Code (Baugesetzbuch, BauGB) or as a compensatory measure pursuant to § 31 (2) of the BauGB. Green roofs can be required for new buildings, particularly in connection with a need for the retention of stormwater.

Vegetative roofs are not subject to approval per se, but authorization may be required for usable roof areas (verification of protective barriers, roof loads, etc.). In any case, approval must be obtained from the historic preservation authority for landmarked historic buildings. The fire protection requirements (→ **Figure 3.8.5**) must be observed in all cases.

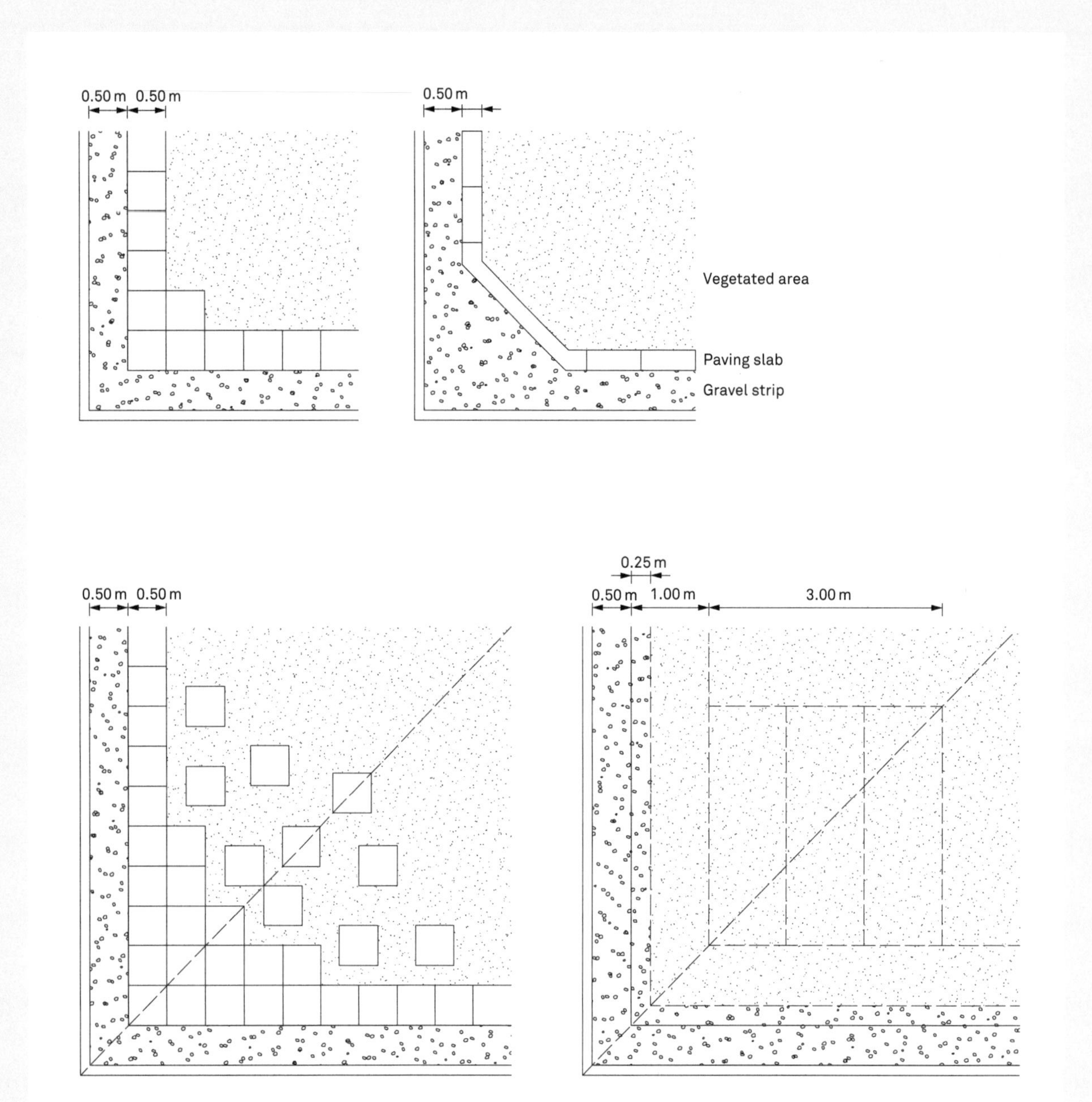

Figure 3.11.3 Measures for securing corner areas

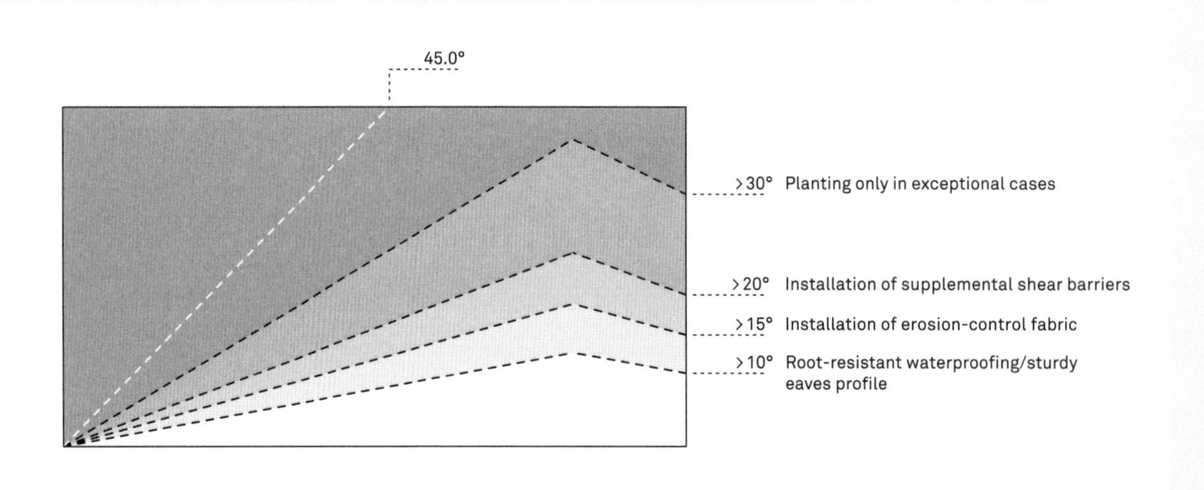

Figure 3.11.4 Safeguards needed as roof slope increases

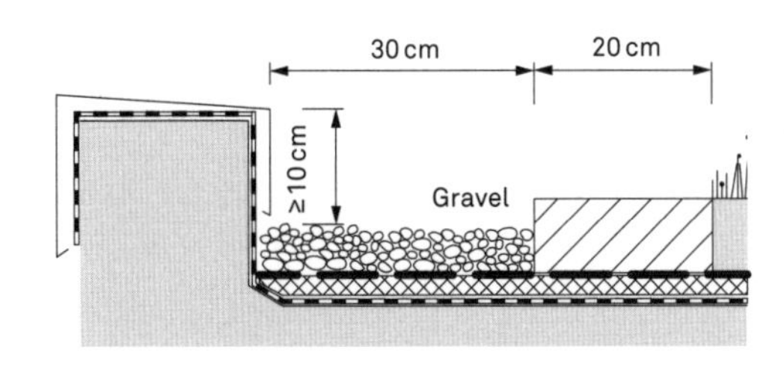

Clearance strip along roof edge

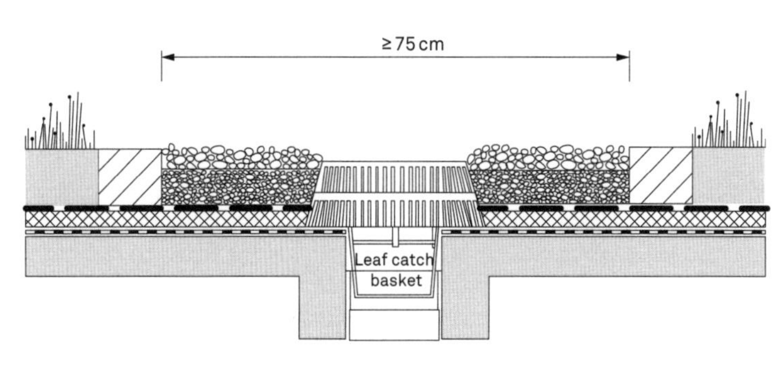

Vegetation-free zone around a roof drain

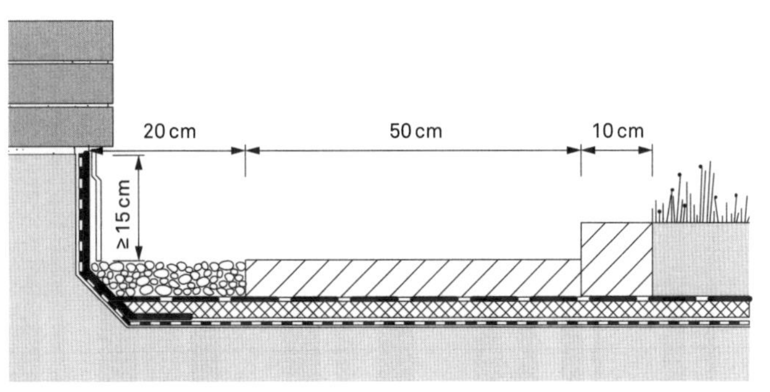

Protective strip along a masonry wall

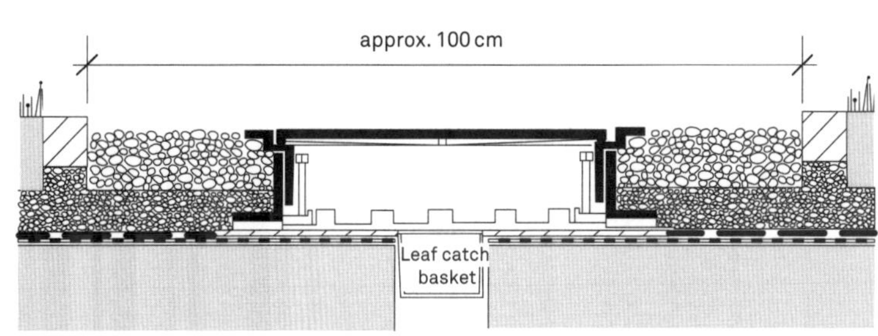

Roof drain

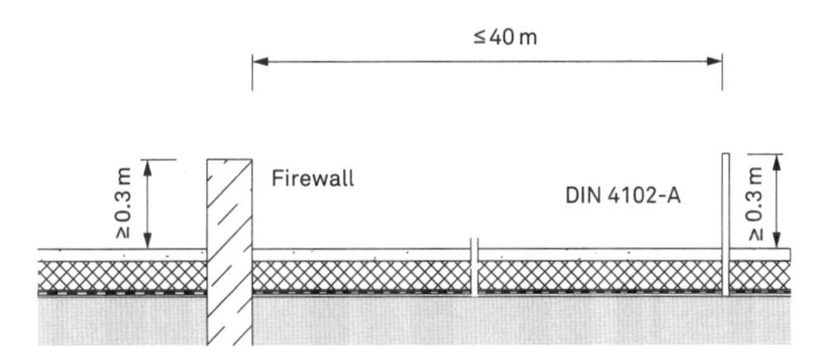

Fire compartment wall extending above roof as per DIN 4102-A

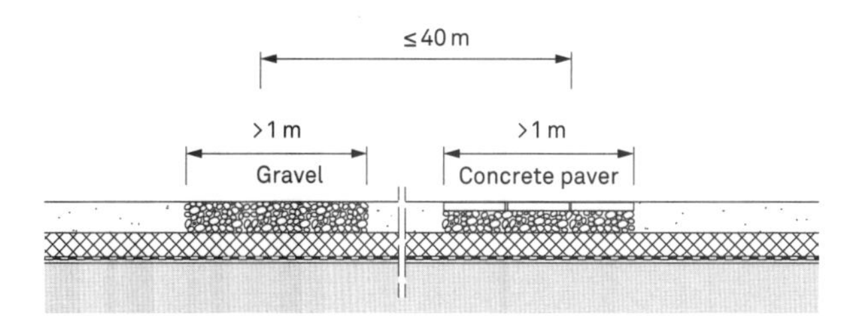

or bands of gravel or concrete pavers at a spacing of ≤ 40 m

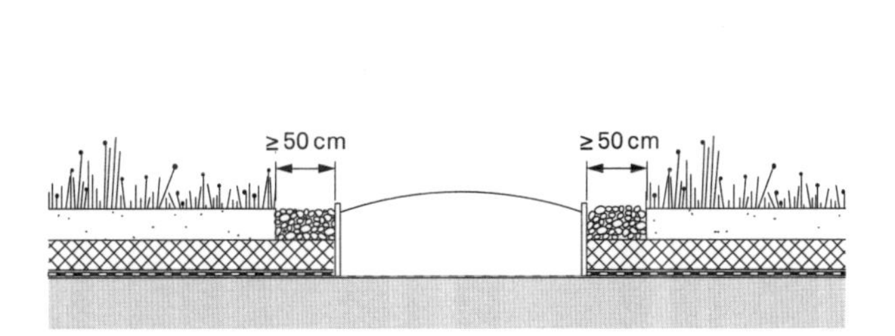

Bands of gravel or concrete pavers surrounding roof openings (e.g. domed skylights)

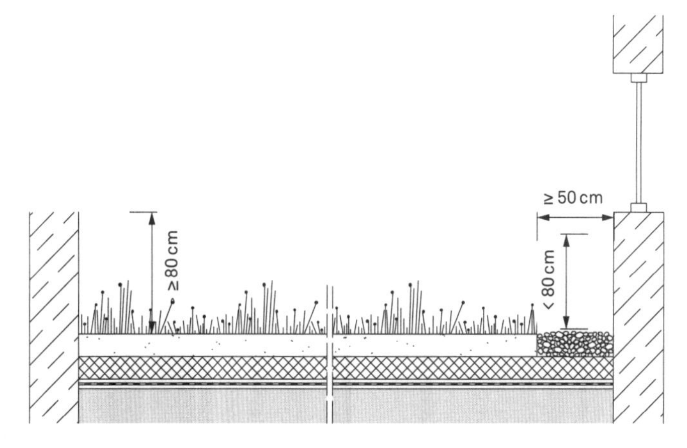

Bands of gravel or concrete pavers in front of walls with window sill height < 80 cm.

Figure 3.11.5 Minimum clearances to vertical building components and edge conditions

3 Elements
3.12 Vertical Planting

3.12 Vertical Planting

Vertical planting embraces the cultivation of climbing plants that grow along a climbing aid, such as a trellis panel or espalier, as well as self-climbing plants that can grow directly on a building or a thicket. Vegetated pots or trough systems can also be arranged along a facade. A sort of further development and synthesis of these systems is represented by facade greening systems (also called "living walls") in which plants grow on substrate mats or within bags, thus making it possible to have a landscape that grows across the entire surface of a building wall. Various proprietary systems are available.

By regularly moistening porous surfaces, a green landscape of mosses (or lichens) can be created.

For selecting a specific system and the appropriate plant materials, it is relevant to know if the design foresees partial or full greening and whether unhindered growth or a geometric arrangement and development of plants is desired.

In general, climbing plants have a very strong tendency to spread. Self-climbing plants in particular find their own way along a facade, and hence their growth often appears irregular until a surface is completely covered. But some species, such as ivy, for example, can be kept in nice form if regularly pruned. Using climbing aids, the growth of twiners, tendril climbers, and scrambling plants are specifically guided in the appropriate direction, although a certain degree of "irregularity" often remains from overhanging shoots. Climbing aids can be used for partial or full planting coverage. If certain heights are desired, specific species with corresponding growth heights are recommended, especially fast-growing species.

Facade greening systems are suitable for targeted greening of building or garden walls and provide the opportunity for creating a mostly two-dimensional ornamental design. Since mainly perennials and herbaceous plants are used for these systems, they can also be used for designing surfaces in a more precise manner than is possible with climbing plants.

The use of trained fruit represents a more formal design variation, because by pruning and tying together shoots and branches, a strongly formalistic character is created.

Site

As a general rule, wind conditions at the site must be taken into account. Especially for freestanding climbing supports, locations affected by strong winds should be avoided.

For warmth-loving species, especially numerous fruit varieties, the heat-retaining effect of walls can be exploited to good effect. First and foremost, the direct sunlight that strikes the surfaces obliquely in spring and autumn is absorbed by walls especially well, thus creating ideal conditions for growth.

To ensure an adequate supply of water and nutrients, the planting area must be of sufficient size, especially in front of walls. If the planting area is situated within a grassed area, a zone about 1 m^2 larger should be kept free of sod.

With suspended planters, the danger of frost in winter must be taken into account. Protection that needs to be individually applied in winter is very costly, hence it is advisable to apply a layer of insulation to troughs.

Any plants that are not planted in the ground require an irrigation system. Facade greening systems and planters, too, therefore have higher operating and maintenance costs. → Table 3.12.3

Classifications

Plants

A distinction can be made among the following plant groups used for vertical planting, based on their application and the corresponding properties: annual and perennial climbing plants, trained woody plants, plants for facade greening systems (perennials, herbs, and dwarf shrubs), and trimmed shrubs.

Annual climbing plants
- Plants that climb on or over a substructure
- Fast greening success
- No problem with excessive loads
- Green only for a limited time; must be renewed yearly

Perennial climbing plants
- Plants that climb on or over a substructure
- Speed of greening success depends on the species
- Long-term planting
- Can introduce high loads onto the substructure

Trained woody plants
- Trees, shrubs, and vines trained (and frequently bound) along wires, cables, and (wood or metal) frameworks
- Formation of a green wall
- Freestanding or set in front of/against masonry or other walls
- Long-term planting
- High upkeep due to need for regular pruning

Trimmed shrubs
- Narrow, trimmed hedges set in front of a facade
- Long-term planting
- Expensive upkeep due to need for regular pruning

Plants for facade greening systems
- Nonclimbing perennials, herbaceous plants, grasses, dwarf woody species, or ferns; in some cases also climbing plants
- Long-term planting
- Very high upkeep

Self-climbers
- Grow upward autonomously on masonry walls, wooden structures, or any sufficiently rough construction
- Mostly vigorous growth

For perennial climbing plants:
- Damage possible to wood surfaces, unsound masonry, nonstructural facades, and construction methods with a high proportion of open joints or small-scaled wall cladding
- Unsuitable if building maintenance is required (periodic wood preservation treatment, surface reconditioning, etc.)

Trellis climbers
- Grow upward with help of climbing aid (cables, rods, grids, slats)
- Mostly vigorous growth
- Possible damage to structures with large proportion of open joints
- Unsuitable if walls behind require building maintenance (periodic wood preservation treatment, surface reconditioning, etc.)

Climbers with clinging stem roots
- Formation of adventitious roots on the young shoots, which are used to anchor the plant autonomously on rough or uneven surfaces

Climbers with adhesive pads
- Formation of tendrils whose young shoots form adhesive pads upon contact with a surface, thus enabling the plant to anchor itself autonomously, even on smooth surfaces

Twining climbers
- Formation of winding shoots, which use circular movements to seek supports; stalks twist spirally around the supports

Tendril climbers
- Formation of filamentous transformations of leaves (leaf tendril climbers), shoots (stem tendril climbers), or, less commonly, of roots; circular searching movements of young tendril climbers respond to contact by bending and wrapping themselves around the support

Scrambling plants
- Formation of long shoots, which usually hook on to or brace themselves against other plants or a substrate by means of thorns, spines, or hook-like hairs

Figure 3.12.1 Categories of plants used for vertical planting

Dimensions and Characteristics

Climbing Aids and Espaliers

Climbing aids can be linear or planar in form. Moreover, they differ in their orientation (horizontal, vertical, or diagonal) and in the spacing between the individual struts as well as the cross-sectional diameter of those elements. Variations in the spacing of the struts and in their distance from the wall result in respective suitability for different types of trellis climbers.

The term *espalier* refers to a construction along which the plants are pulled and onto which they are generally lashed down, in order to train them and bring them into a certain shape. To this end, the plants need to be pruned regularly according to a specific procedure and their shoots must be aligned in the desired direction and tied down. In addition to fruit trees, other deciduous trees and shrubs, such as the common hornbeam, can be trained in this manner. Many nurseries also offer clear-stemmed espaliers with tall trunks.

Especially when they are used for fruit trees, espaliers are placed in front of a wall in order to take advantage of the heat radiating from the wall and thus to increase yields. Due to their differing growth characteristics, not every fruit is suitable for each type of cultivation. Depending on the choice of variety or species, a different spacing for the slats/cables and/or espalier form may be needed. The fruit trees most suitable for such training are apple, apricot, pear, and peach. → Table 3.12.2

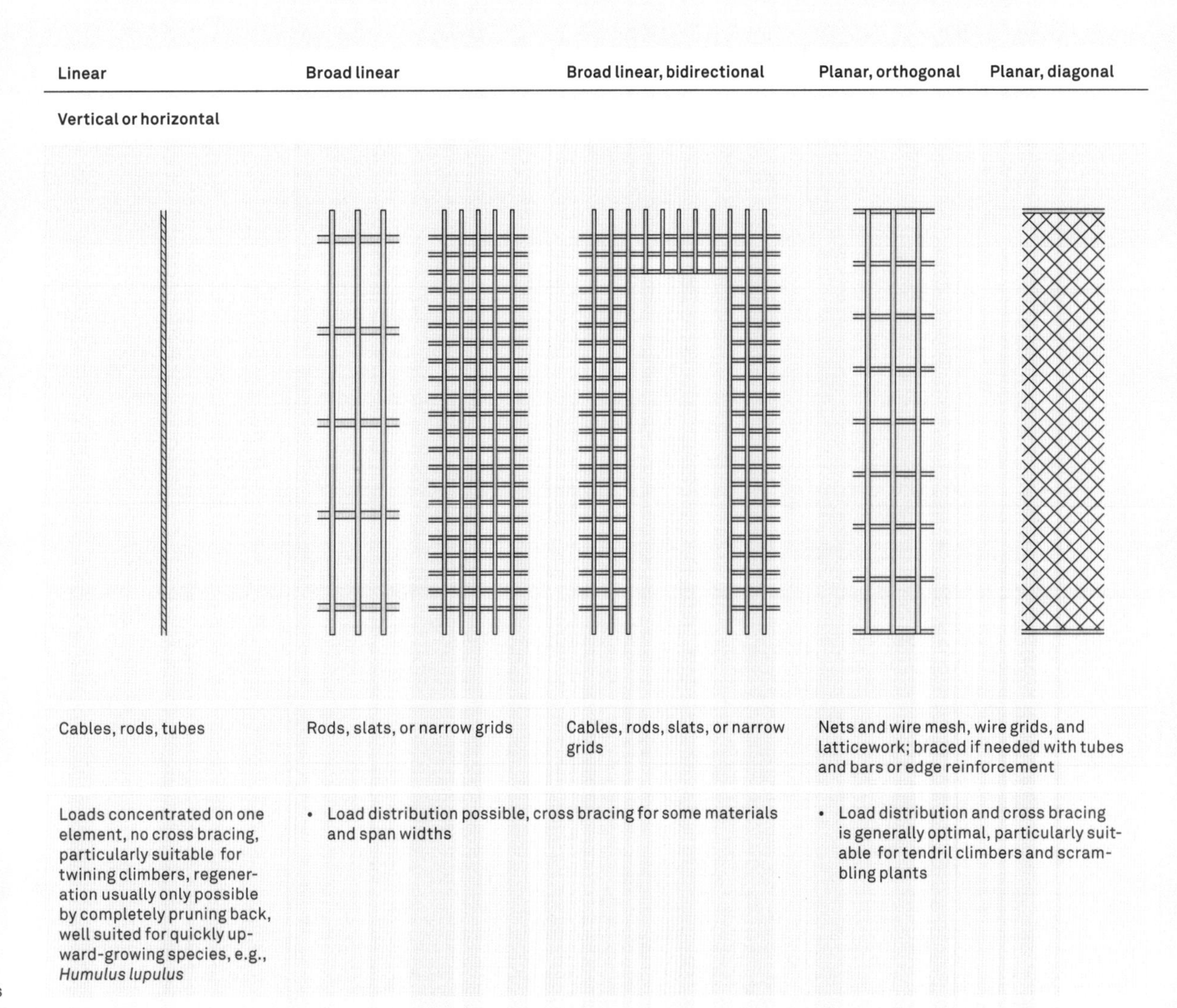

Linear
Broad linear
Broad linear, bidirectional
Planar, orthogonal
Planar, diagonal
Vertical or horizontal
Cables, rods, tubes
Rods, slats, or narrow grids
Cables, rods, slats, or narrow grids
Nets and wire mesh, wire grids, and latticework; braced if needed with tubes and bars or edge reinforcement
Loads concentrated on one element, no cross bracing, particularly suitable for twining climbers, regeneration usually only possible by completely pruning back, well suited for quickly upward-growing species, e.g., Humulus lupulus
• Load distribution possible, cross bracing for some materials and span widths
• Load distribution and cross bracing is generally optimal, particularly suitable for tendril climbers and scrambling plants

Figure 3.12.2 Basic forms of climbing aids for trellis climbers

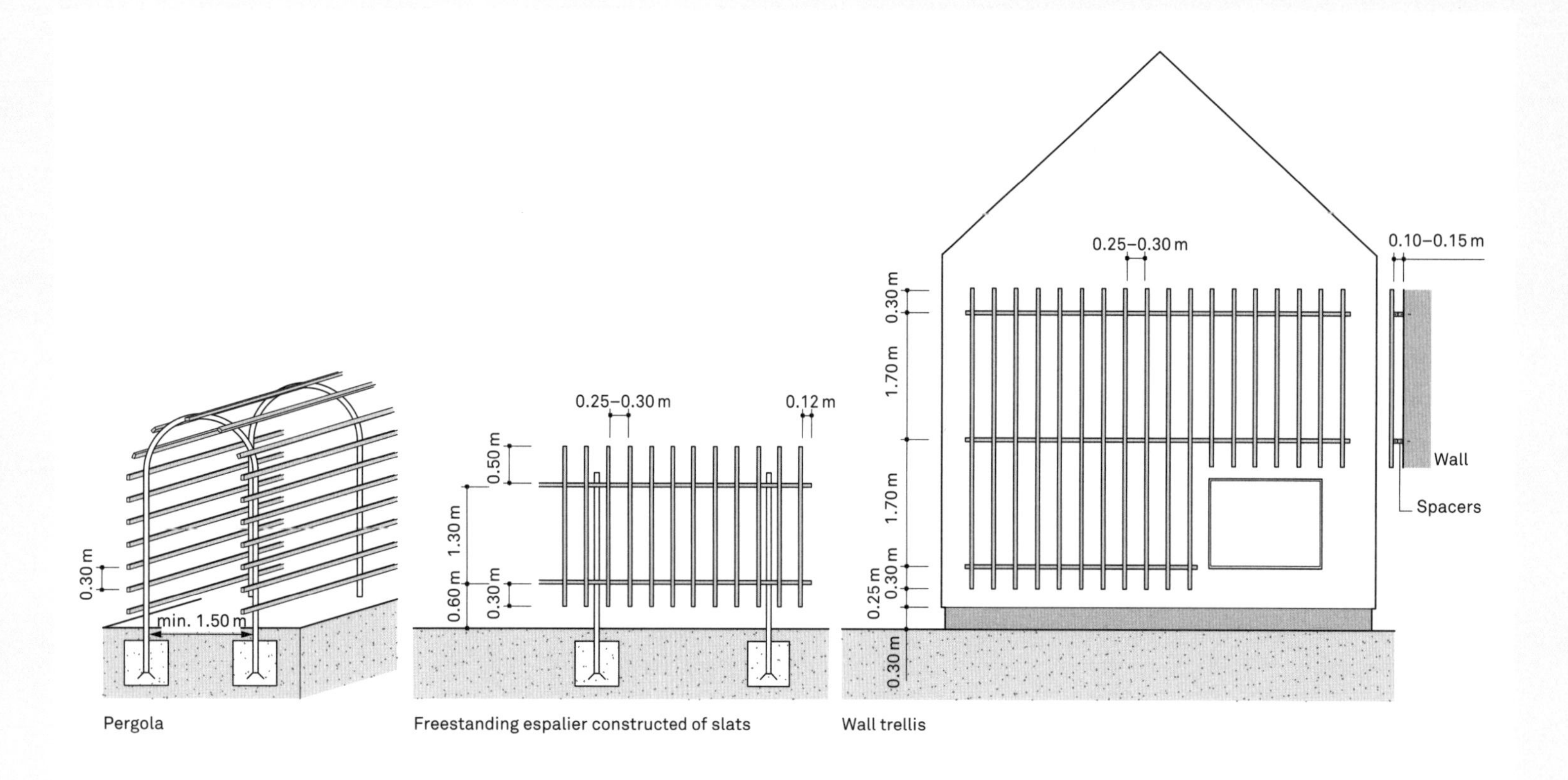

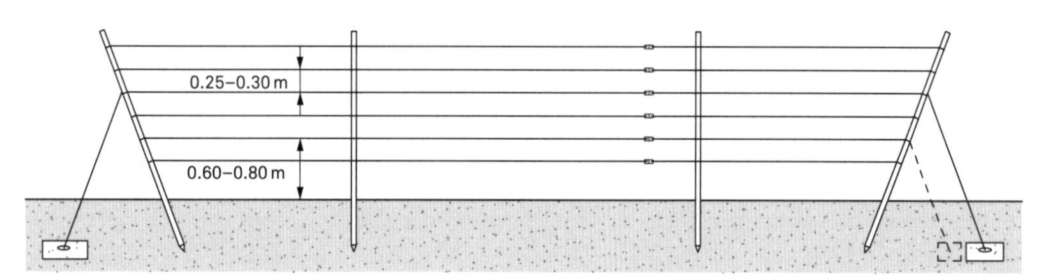

Figure 3.12.3 Wall trellises and freestanding espaliers

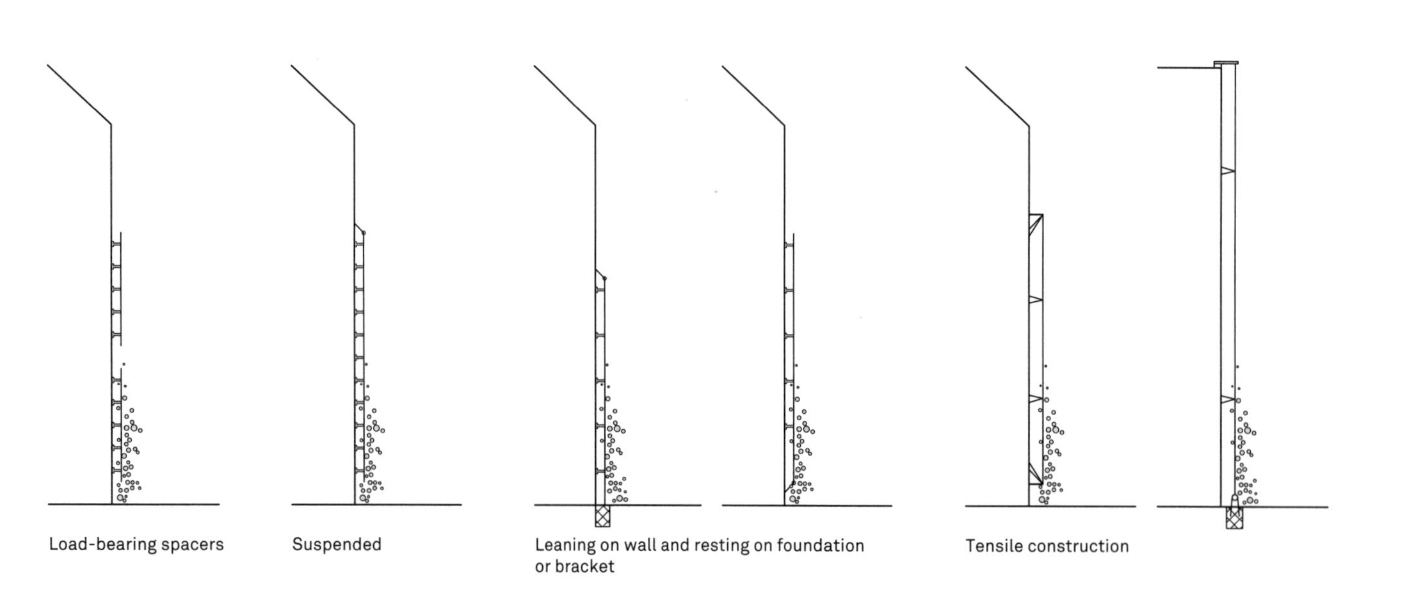

Figure 3.12.4 Anchorage of climbing aids on walls

Botanical and common name	Average growth height (climbing)	Width of growth (= sensible width of climbing aid if needed)	Growth (annual increase in height under typical conditions)				Max. shoot diameter at root collar/clearance between wall and climbing aid	Section thickness of climbing aid	Light requirement	Foliage	Special characteristics
			>200 cm	100–200 cm	50–100 cm	<50 cm			FSu = Full sun PSh = Partial shade FSh = Full shade	Deciduous (D) Evergreen (E)	
Self-climbers											
Climbers with clinging stem roots											
Campsis radicans (trumpet creeper or trumpet vine)	6–12 m	6–10 m	x	x			up to 20 cm	–	FSu	D	Initially slow-growing, fast-growing after 3–5 years; light-shunning shoots, protected location
Campsis radicans 'Flava' (yellow trumpet creeper)	4–5 m, in favorable locations up to 8 m	4 m		x			–	–	FSu	D	Dense, with overhanging branches
Campsis × tagliabuana 'Madame Galen' (Madame Galen trumpet creeper)	3–5 m	5–6 m	x		x	x	up to 10 cm	–	FSu	D	Slow-growing, shoots overhang far, clings weakly, climbing aids that let the long shoots cling to them are recommended, light-shunning shoots, protected location
Euonymus fortunei var. *radicans* (winter creeper or spindle)	0.5–0.8 m 4–6 m	0.8–1.2 m				x	up to 10 cm	–	PSh	E	
Euonymus fortunei var. *vegetus* (winter creeper or spindle)	4–6 m	1–4 m 1–1,5 m				x	up to 10 cm	–	FSu–PSh	E	
Euonymus fortunei varieties (winter creeper or spindle)	3–5 m					x	up to 10 cm	–	PSh–FSh	E	
Hedera colchica (Persian ivy)	6–8 m in favorable locations 10–20 cm	up to 10 cm		x	x		up to 15 cm	–	PSh–FSh	E	
Hedera helix (common ivy)	10–20 m (–30 m)	2–15 m		x	x			–	FSu–FSh	E	Clinging stem roots on the shaded side infiltrate even the finest cracks and pores (0.2 mm) and anchor themselves there
Hedera helix 'Woerner' (common ivy)	10–15 m	5 m and more		x				–	FSu–FSh	E	
Hedera helix 'Hibernica' (Irish ivy)	5–20 m	>5 m 4–10 m		x				–	FSu–FSh	E	Strong-growing, but prefers creeping and mat-like growth
Hydrangea petiolaris (climbing hydrangea)	10–12 m 10–20 m	2–6 m 8–12 m				x		–	FSu–FSh	D	Loosely flung, overhanging branches; older plants show some twining tendencies, very slow-growing for the first three to five years; annual growth: 5–10 cm
Climbers with adhesive pads											
Parthenocissus quinquefolia 'Engelmannii' (Engelmann's ivy)	15–18 m 10–15 m	3–4 m		x	x		up to 20 cm		FSu–FSh	D	Strong-growing, also overhangs droopily
Parthenocissus tricuspidata 'Veitchii' (Virginia creeper 'Veitchii')	15–18 m 20–25 m			x					FSu–PSh	D	Very strong-growing, mat-like and dense

Table 3.12.1 Characteristics of perennial climbing plants

Botanical and common name	Average growth height (climbing)	Width of growth (= sensible width of climbing aid if needed)	Growth (annual increase in height under typical conditions)				Max. shoot diameter at root collar/clearance between wall and climbing aid	Section thickness of climbing aid	Light requirement	Foliage	Special characteristics
			>200 cm	100–200 cm	50–100 cm	<50 cm			FSu = Full sun PSh = Partial shade FSh = Full shade	Deciduous (D) Evergreen (E)	
Trellis climbers											
Twining climbers											
Actinidia arguta (hardy kiwi)	5–12 m	5–6 m	x	x	x		up to 15 cm	up to 3.5 cm	FSu–PSh	D	Anchors very solidly
Actinidia chinensis (kiwi)	8–10 m	6–8 m	x	x	x		up to 20 cm	up to 4 cm	FSu–PSh	D	
Actinidia kolomikta (kolomikta)	2–(6) m	3–5 m		x	x		up to 3 cm	up to 3.5 cm	FSu	D	Slow-growing
Akebia quinata (chocolate vine or five-leaf akebia)	4–(10) m	2–4 m 6–8 m		x			up to 3 cm	up to 3 cm	FSu–PSh	D	Also overhangs droopily (approx. 2 m long)
Aristolochia macrophylla (Dutchman's pipe or pipevine)	8–10 m	1–8 m 4–6 m	x	x			up to 10 cm	2 (3) cm	FSu–PSh	D	Very slow-growing at the outset, strong-growing from the 3rd to 5th year onward
Celastrus orbiculatus (Oriental bittersweet)	8–12 m (15 m)	2–6 m 8–10 m	x	x			up to 16 cm	Young plants: 1–2 cm; for older plants: up to 7.5 cm	FSu–PSh	D	Entwined trees up to 20 cm in diameter can be strangled by strong growth in thickness; pendent with loosely flung branches reaching out up to 2 m, also overhangs droopily (2–3 m long)
Humulus lupulus (common hop)	3–6 m 5–6 cm	8–12 m 1–2 m	x				up to 2 cm	up to 2 cm	FSu–PSh	D	Perennial, dies back after each growing season, losing the superficial parts of the plant; growth performance during the vegetation period 0.5–1 m per week, strong tendency to spread
Lonicera japonica var. *repens* (creeping Japanese honeysuckle)	up to 3 m (10) m					x	up to 2 cm	up to 2 cm	FSu–PSh	D	
Lonicera × brownii 'Dropmore Scarlet' (Dropmore Scarlet honeysuckle)	2–5 m	0.5–1 m			x	x	up to 2 cm	0.5–1.5 cm	FSu	D	
Lonicera caprifolium (Italian or goat-leaf honeysuckle)	2–5 (8) m	0.5–2 m			x		up to 2 cm	0.5–3 cm	FSu–PSh	D	
Lonicera × heckrottii 'Gold Flame' (Gold Flame honeysuckle)	2–6 m	2–3 m branches, reaching out up to 1.5 m			x	x	up to 2 cm	0.2–1 cm	PSh	D	Only weakly twining, tends to grow loose and shrubby
Lonicera henryi (evergreen honeysuckle)	5–8 m	1–2 m		x			up to 4 cm	1–3 cm	PSh–FSh FSu–PSh	E	Also overhangs droopily (2–3 m long)
Lonicera periclymenum (common or European honeysuckle or woodbine)	1–3 (6) m				x		up to 2 cm	up to 2 cm	FSu–PSh	D	Strong-growing, strangling
Lonicera × tellmanniana (Tellmann's honeysuckle)	4–6 m	1–4 m		x			up to 3 cm	0.5–3 cm	PSh–FSh FSu–PSh		Side branches stand away horizontally

Table 3.12.1 Characteristics of perennial climbing plants

Botanical and common name	Average growth height (climbing)	Width of growth (= sensible width of climbing aid if needed)	Growth (annual increase in height under typical conditions)				Max. shoot diameter at root collar/clearance between wall and climbing aid	Section thickness of climbing aid	Light requirement	Foliage	Special characteristics
			>200 cm	100–200 cm	50–100 cm	<50 cm			FSu = Full sun PSh = Partial shade FSh = Full shade	Deciduous (D) Evergreen (E)	
Polygonum aubertii (silver lace vine)	8–15 m (20) m	5–10 m	x					1–5 cm	FSu–PSh	D	Dense and mat-like, can strangle itself on supports that are too thin
Wisteria floribunda (Japanese wisteria)	6–8 m high and more		x	x			up to 25 cm	up to 7.5 cm	FSu–PSh	D	Powerful twiners with extremely strong growth in thickness; can crush fragile supports and tear out anchorages
Wisteria sinensis (Chinese wisteria)	6–15 m	2–10 m 8–30 m	x				up to 50 cm	2–10 cm	FSu	D	Can strangle itself on supports that are too thin; strangles small trees, crimps rainwater downspouts
Tendril climbers											
Clematis alpina varieties (alpine clematis)	1.5–2 m	1–3 m				x	up to 3 cm	0.2–0.5 cm	PSh–FSh	D	Thin, cobweb-like shoots
Clematis hybrid varieties (clematis hybrids)	Depending on the variety: 2–3 m or 3–4 m	1–2 m						0.2–0.5 cm		D	Only the upper third is tightly branched and has blossoms if left untrimmed; overhangs droopily
Clematis macropetala varieties (downy clematis)	2–3 m	2–2.5 m			x			up to 0.7 cm	FSu–PSh	D	Partly dense and mat-like; thin, bowed, occasionally overhanging shoots
Clematis montana varieties (anemone clematis)	3–6 m (–11 cm)	2–4 m			x			0.2–1 cm			
Clematis montana 'Rubens' (clematis 'Rubens')	3–6 (10) m	2–4 m					up to 5 cm	0.2–1 cm	FSu–PSh	D	
Clematis orientalis 'Orange Peel' (orange peel clematis)	4–6 m (occasionally to 8 m),				x		up to 5 cm		FSu	D	Dense, mat-like growth; strong-growing in treetops
Clematis tangutica (golden clematis)	4–6 m	2–4 m		x	x		up to 5 cm	0.2–0.5 cm	FSu–FSh	D	Branched tightly and cobweb-like
Clematis texensis varieties (crimson or scarlet clematis)	1–1.5 (2.5) m									D	Tendril climbing subshrub, climbs cobweb-like over other plants
Clematis vitalba (old man's beard or traveler's joy)	5–15 (30) m	2–8 m	x				up to 15 cm	0.2–1 cm	FSu–PSh	D	Impenetrable mat-like growth, in isolation up to 500 cm
Clematis viticella varieties (virgin's bower)	2–5 m	2–3 m			x			0.2–0.5 cm	FSu–PSh	D	Also overhangs droopily (up to 2 m long)
Cobaea scandens (cathedral bells or cup-and-saucer vine)										D	
Parthenocissus quinquefolia (inserta) (Northern creeper)	6–10 (15) m	1–4 m	x		x		up to 20 cm	up to 1.3 cm	FSu–PSh	D	Also overhangs droopily, also forms adhesive pads
Vitis coignetiae (crimson glory vine)	6–8 m, climbs up to 25 m high in trees	10–12 m			x			3 cm	FSu–PSh	D	Covers up to 30 m² with no gaps; fast-growing, tendrils up to 25 cm long, clasps around supports

Botanical and common name	Average growth height (climbing)	Width of growth (= sensible width of climbing aid if needed)	Growth (annual increase in height under typical conditions)				Max. shoot diameter at root collar/clearance between wall and climbing aid	Section thickness of climbing aid	Light requirement	Foliage	Special characteristics
			>200 cm	100–200 cm	50–100 cm	<50 cm			FSu = Full sun PSh = Partial shade FSh = Full shade	Deciduous (D) Evergreen (E)	
Scrambling plants											
Jasminum nudiflorum (winter jasmine)	2–3 (5) m	2–3 m			x		up to 3 cm	–	FSu–PSh	D	Also overhangs droopily, then 2–5 m long, 2–3 m wide; tolerates pruning into hedge shape
Rosa arvensis (field rose)	0.5–2 m	1–2 m			x			–	FSu–PSh	D	Partly with thin, creeping, rooted shoots and partly climbing
Climbing roses	2–3 (6) m 2–6 m				x		up to 20 cm	–	FSu–PSh	D	Usually grows upright
Rubus fruticosus (blackberry)	0.5–3 (4) m	2–3 m		x	x		up to 4 cm	–	FSu–FSh	D	
Rubus henryi (climbing evergreen blackberry)	2–4 cm			x			up to 2 cm	–	PSh–FSh	D	Shoots tend to exhibit twining

Table 3.12.1 Characteristics of perennial climbing plants

Type	Fan espalier	Vertical cordon	Horizontal cordon	Bilateral horizontal cordon	Oblique cordon	U-shaped palmette	Double U candelabra	Spindle	Simple Palmette	Palmette Verrier	Candelabra	Kesselbaum [kettle-tree]	V-shaped hedge	Pergola	Spacing of the leading branches
Apricot	(x)	s	x	x	x	x	x	x	x	(x)	x	x	x	(x)	30 cm average
Aprikose	x					(x)									
Pear	(x)	s	s	s	x	x	x	x	x	x	x	x	x	x	30 cm average
Fig	x														
Kiwi *(Actinidia)*	x		x								x			x	50–60 cm
Peach	x					x									50–60 cm
Plum	x								(x)	(x)					
Sweet cherry	s									s					
Morello cherry	x		(x)		(x)				s						
Grape	x	x	x	x							x			x	25–35 cm

x = well-suited, (x) = conditionally suitable or only suitable for single varieties, s = suitable for slow growing varieties

Table 3.12.2 Suitability of espalier forms for various fruits

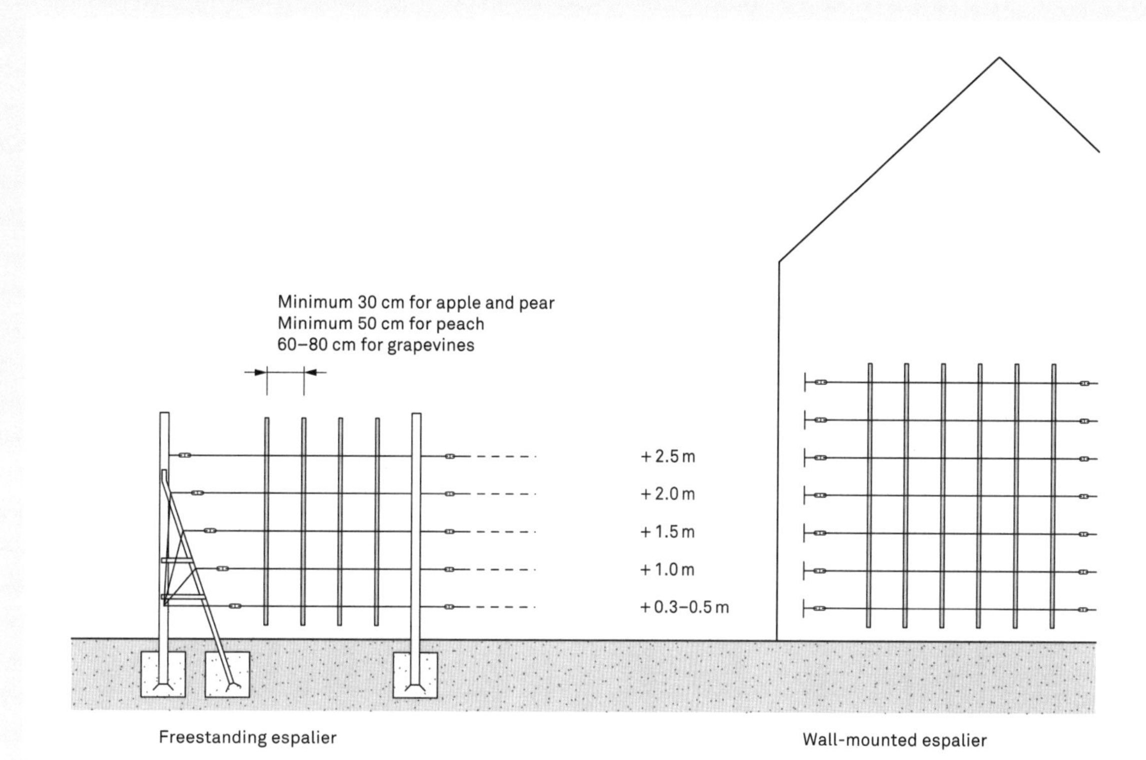

Figure 3.12.5 Freestanding and wall-mounted espaliers for fruit

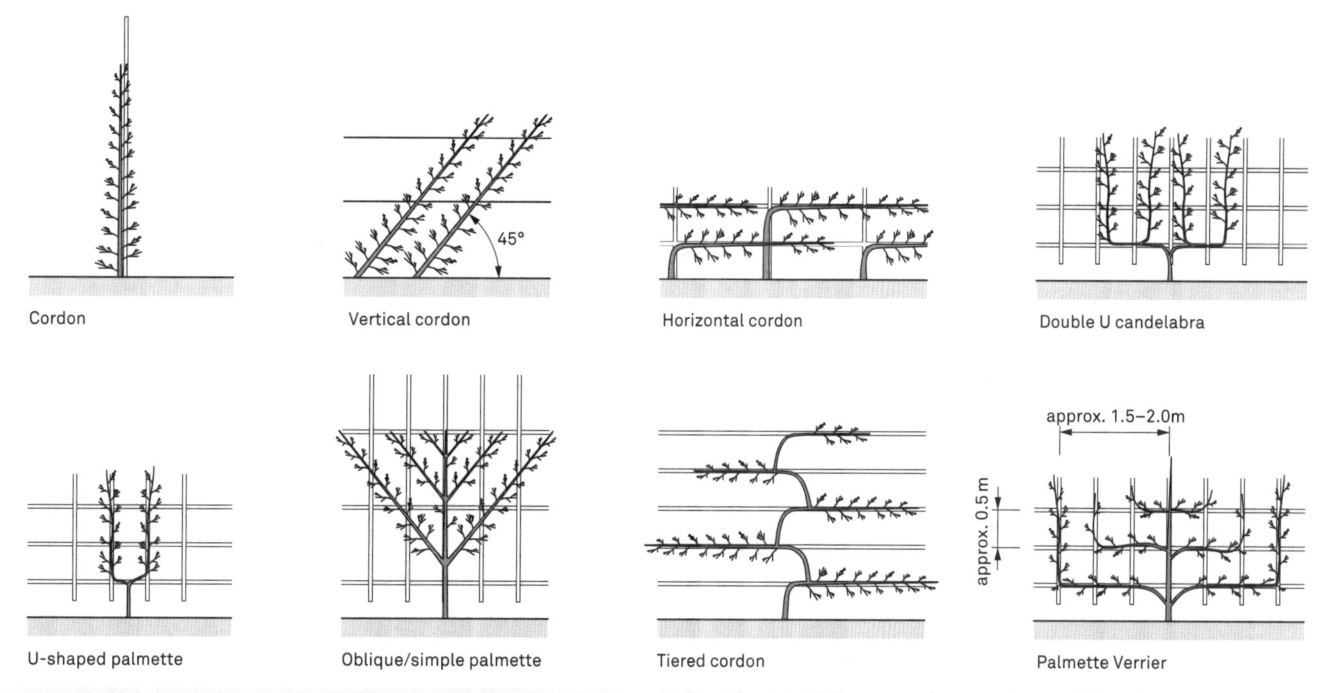

Figure 3.12.7 Selection of espalier (training) forms

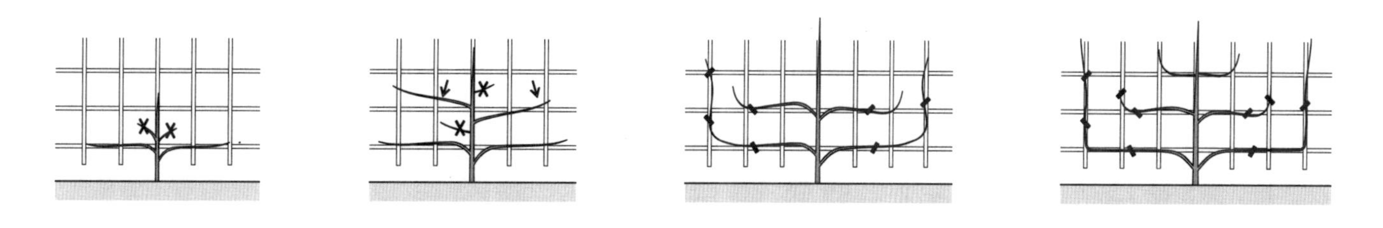

Figure 3.12.6 Steps to training a fruit tree into a palmette Verrier

Facade Greening Systems

Facade greening systems are essentially planters that are installed vertically, affixed to a more or less elaborate support system on the facade. Bags and trough-like systems are used as containers for the plants. The limited root zone makes it necessary to use substrates with a particularly high water-storage capacity and/or to install an irrigation system. No climbing plants are ordinarily used. Instead, "normal" perennials, grasses, or even small shrubs are used – and depending on the system, these are placed at angles of up to 90°. Moss walls are a special form of facade planting that does not require substrates: A rough surface (e.g., porous natural stone) serves as the supporting material for a vegetation cover of mosses and sometimes lichens.

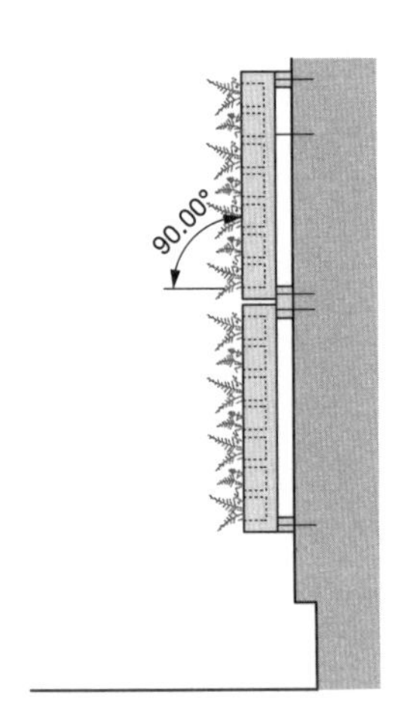

Full-surface vegetation carrier, plants oriented at 90°

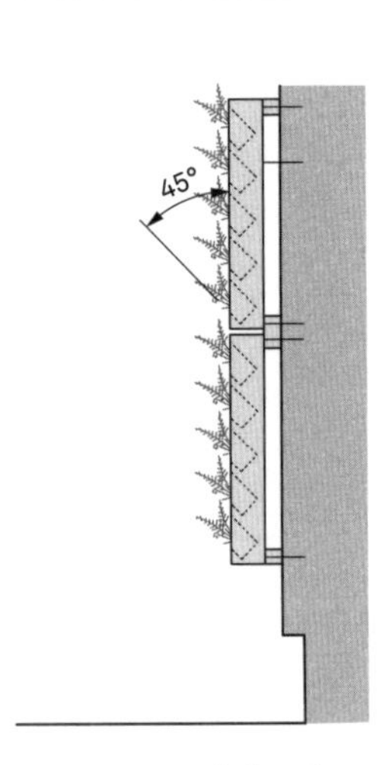

Full-surface vegetation carrier, plants oriented at <90° (e.g., 45°)

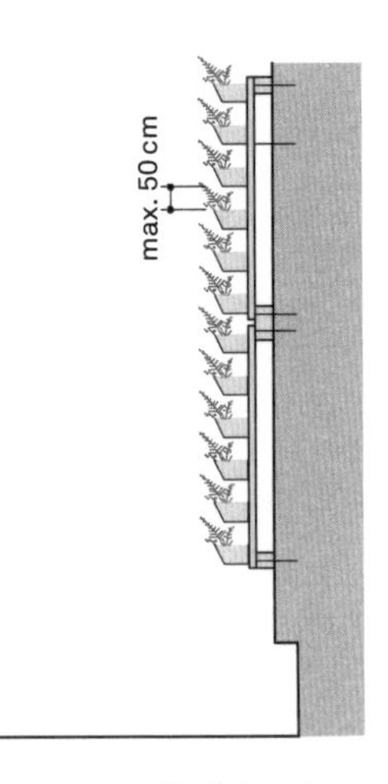

Partial-surface vegetation carrier, linear, ≤50 cm between plant levels

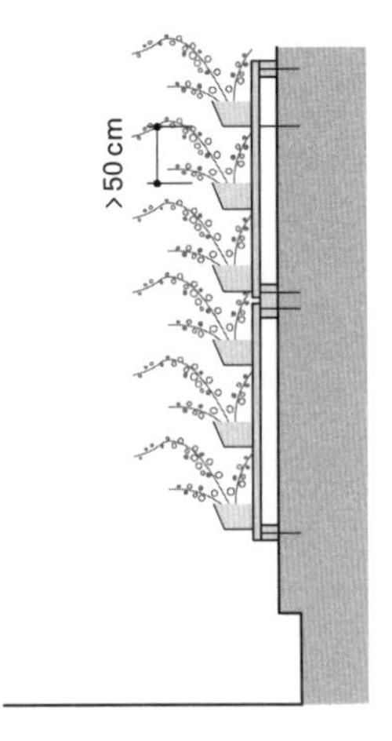

Partial-surface vegetation carrier, linear, >50 cm between plant levels

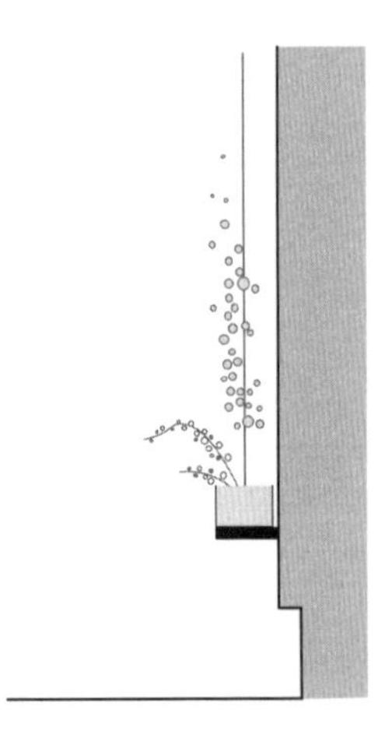
Partial-surface vegetation carrier, solitary elements

Figure 3.12.8 Components of facade greening systems

Table 3.12.3 Overview of ground-based and facade-bound vertical planting systems with regard to use of materials and need for maintenance

Type	Material/type of construction: Support systems	Material/type of construction: Suitable facades	Material/type of construction: Plant species	Upkeep: Servicing	Upkeep: Irrigation	Upkeep: Maintenance actions	Upkeep: Establishment phase
Ground-based vertical planting systems							
Rigid climbing aid, planar	Framework and grating: e.g., steel frame with steel bars, steel rod grids, wood latticework and wall trellises	Well suited: • Masonry and concrete construction • Exterior insulation and finish systems (structural suitability must be confirmed, poor workmanship can yield thermal bridges) Unsuitable: • Rear-ventilated (rainscreen) facades not suitable for plants with negative phototropism (e.g., clinging stem roots of ivy)	Trellis climbers	Average, every 5–10 years	As needed	As needed	>3 years
Rigid climbing aid, linear	Rod-like/linear elements: e.g., steel tubes or steel rods		Trellis climbers	Average, every 5–10 years	As needed	As needed	1–2 years
Flexible climbing aid, planar	(Stainless steel wire) nets and stretched cables		Trellis climbers	Average, every 5–10 years	As needed	As needed	>3 years
Flexible climbing aid, linear	(Stainless steel wire) nets and stretched cables		Trellis climbers	Average, every 5–10 years	As needed	As needed	>3 years
Without climbing aid	Building and garden walls		Self-climbers	Average, every 5–10 years	As needed	As needed	>3 years

Type	Material/type of construction			Upkeep			
	Support systems	Suitable facades	Plant species	Servicing	Irrigation	Maintenance actions	Establishment phase
Facade-bound vertical planting systems							
Full-surface vegetation carrier, 90° orientation	Vegetation carrier on mounting plate, visible surface material: Metal, non-woven fabric, geotextile and/or synthetic	Well suited: • Rear-ventilated (rainscreen) facade • With masonry and concrete walls, rear-ventilation should be retroactively installed • Exterior insulation and finish systems when structural suitability is confirmed (poor workmanship can yield thermal bridges)	Well suited: • Grasses, perennials, herbs Moderately suited: Climbing plants • (tendency to overgrow) • Woody plants (restricted root zone)	Very high, <3 years	High, daily	High, 1–2/year	Full coverage attained immediately or near-term
Full-surface vegetation carrier, <90° orientation (e.g., 45°)			Well suited: • Grasses, perennials, herbs, and sedum Moderately suited: • Climbing plants (tendency to overgrow) • Woody plants (restricted root zone)	Very high, <3 years	High-very high, daily to several times daily	Very high, >2/year	1–2 years
Partial-surface vegetation carrier, linear, ≤50 cm between plant levels			Well suited: • Grasses, perennials, herbs, and sedum Moderately suited: • Climbing plants (tendency to overgrow) • Woody plants (restricted root zone)	High, every 3–5 years	Average, 1–4 times per week	High, 1–2/year	1–2 years
Partial-surface vegetation carrier, linear, >50 cm between plant levels			Very well suited: • Climbing plants Well suited: • Surface-covering/overhanging woody plants (full coverage difficult)	Very high, <3 years	Average, 1–4 times per week	High, 1–2/year	2–3 years
Partial-surface vegetation carrier, solitary elements	Trough planters (concrete, steel, plastic) on support frame/mounting plate, with and without climbing aid	Well suited: • Masonry and concrete construction • Exterior insulation and finish systems (structural suitability must be confirmed, poor workmanship can yield thermal bridges) Conditionally suitable: • Rear-ventilated (rainscreen) facade, not suitable for plants with negative phototropism	Very well suited: Climbing plants Suitable: Ground-covering/overhanging woody plants Moderately suited: Grasses, perennials, herbs, and sedum	Very high, <3 years	High, daily	High, 1–2/year	2–3 years

Remarks on Building Law and Regulatory Approval

Stipulations that require facade planting can be made as part of the urban land-use planning.

Facade plantings are, as a rule, not subject to approval, but landmarked historic buildings are an exception.

4 Typologies
4.1 Gardens

4.1 Gardens

The gardens examined in this chapter encompass private (domestic) and semipublic (community) spaces. They may be attractive or simply utilitarian and can be divided into the following types:

- **House garden/apartment garden: private garden with a direct spatial and functional relationship to a residential house or apartment.**
- **Tenant garden: rented garden that is made available for the exclusive use of an apartment tenant or a tenant collective and which is located in the immediate vicinity; when it is an apartment garden there is direct access to the garden.**
- **Allotment garden: rented plot used for gardening and leisure, usually close to one's place of residence; under German law, a distinction is made between ordinary (temporary) and permanent allotment gardens: the latter are defined as such in a binding land-use plan, thus giving leaseholders a tenancy claim for an unlimited period of time.**
- **Recreational and weekend garden: similar to above, but with larger plot that is used mainly on weekends; buildings are permissible and utilities (power and water supply) are allowed; no requirements for areas dedicated to crops, etc.; viewed under planning law as "special zones serving recreational purposes."**
- **Ownership garden: plot owned by the users themselves; like recreational and weekend gardens, ownership gardens are used in a way similar to allotment gardens, but they are not subject to the same legal restrictions.**
- **Employee garden: generally located on company property and made available to a user under the terms of their employment contract.**
- **Temporary community garden: according to allotment garden laws, these plots may only be cultivated with annuals, may not be built upon (no shed or similar structure), and are usually leased for only one year at a time.**

Site

Spatial Configuration of House and Apartment Gardens

For residential gardens, the spatial and functional relationship to a house or apartment is of the greatest importance. The outdoor space becomes an extension of the living space and, when of an adequate size, can also be used for recreation and growing fruits and vegetables.

Placing a terrace, patio, or deck directly next to the living spaces creates an intermediary transitional zone between the house and the garden and also offers many functional benefits. Access from the house is simplified and the building walls, which offer privacy and protection from the wind, can also be used to provide thermal storage capacity. Furthermore, a roof canopy can be integrated with the building and additional circulation is unnecessary. The terrace should nevertheless be located where it has good exposure to the sun, especially for residential gardens – which usually means orienting it to the southwest if possible.

If the garden and the dwelling's floor plan present an opportunity to also have a second terrace, seating areas for different times of the day can be created. The orientation of the building and its location on the property establish the basic conditions in that regard. → Figure 4.1.4

The features of a house or apartment garden depends upon its location, the garden's size, and the user's individual needs and requirements. → See also Table 4.1.2

Spatial Configuration of Allotment Gardens

Allotment gardens generally have a summer house with an adjoining terrace. In some regions, however, the gardens are predominantly for purely horticultural use, in which case a simple tool shed is often the only built structure.

The summer house should optimally face northeast, especially if an outdoor seating area is to adjoin it, since the afternoon sun is then used to its best advantage. But under certain circumstances, this results in an unfavorable situation where the location of the summer house is too close to the path. Especially at the end of a row, this restricts the entrance area and views of the garden. This can, however, also help increase the level of privacy. The summer house can also be located in the middle of the plot, but that has the disadvantage of limiting the options available for making full use of the remaining space. → Figure 4.1.3

According to Germany's allotment garden law, a connection to the sewer system is not mandatory for allotment sites; only a water supply connection for irrigation must be provided. Thus not all sites offer the possibility of connecting a sink or a toilet in the summer house. In any case, it is necessary to provide a common room and a storage room (or closet) in the floor plan. Optimally, the layout also includes a covered outdoor seating area.

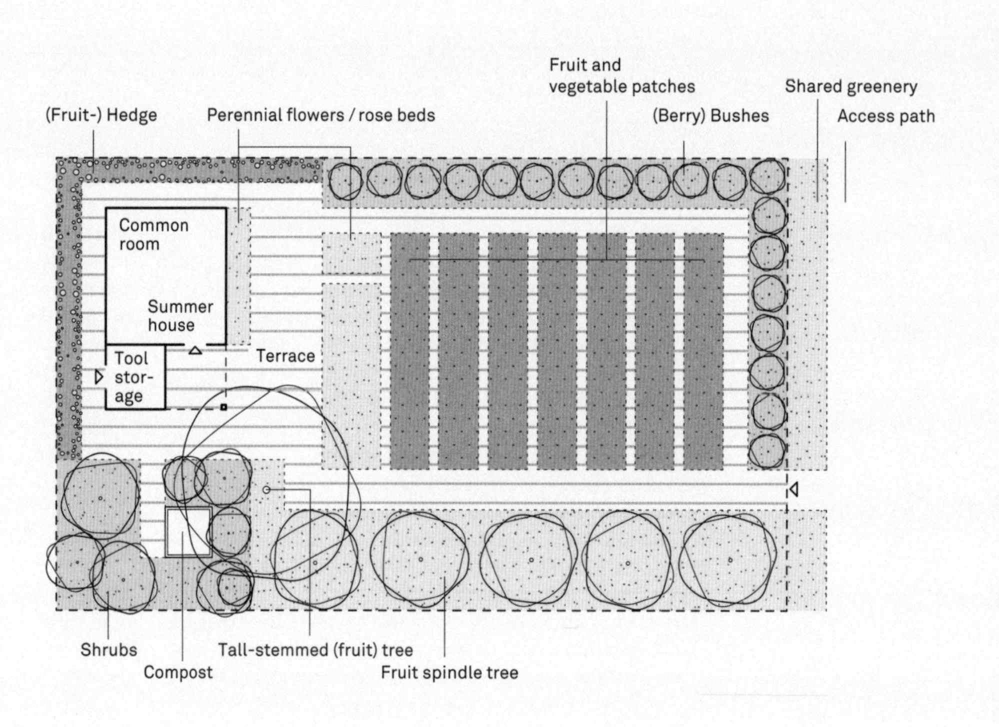

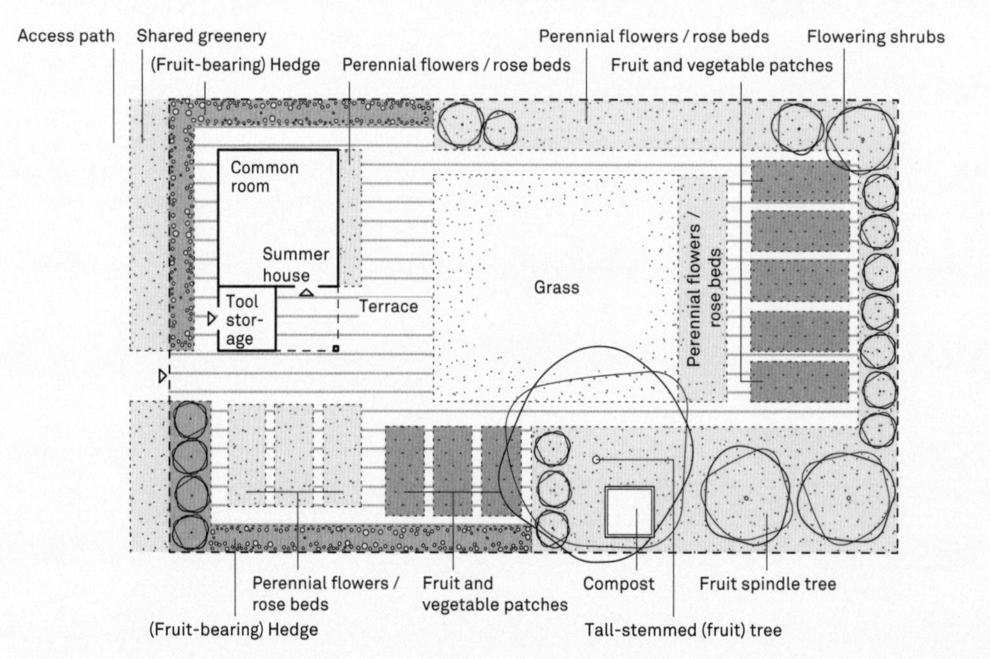

Figure 4.1.1 Exemplary layouts of allotment garden plots with summer houses (max. 24 m² floor area)

Spatial Configuration of Allotment Garden Sites

Allotment gardens and community gardens are primarily reserved for noncommercial horticultural use and for recreation. Accordingly, many laws and regulations governing allotment gardens limit other uses, the degree of impermeable surfaces, etc.

Allotment gardens are always part of a larger allotment garden site with collective infrastructure and shared open spaces and possibly a clubhouse. A publicly accessible route through the site is not always available, but should be provided. Especially with larger sites, doing so averts the creation of a barrier and better integrates the allotment gardens into their surroundings.

Allotment gardens fulfill important social, climatic, and ecological functions. In inner-city locations, they serve to significantly improve the microclimatic conditions, have a positive effect on the water balance, provide habitats for flora and fauna, and contribute to a healthy air exchange and to linking habitats.

The following communal facilities should be provided for an allotment garden site:

- Circulation paths
- Clubhouse
- Waste container area
- Storage shed and/or yard
- Bicycle parking
- Automobile parking, capacity dependent on the site's accessibility via public transport
- Play area for children (if needed)
- Boundary planting (if needed)
- Public route through the site / small green corridor

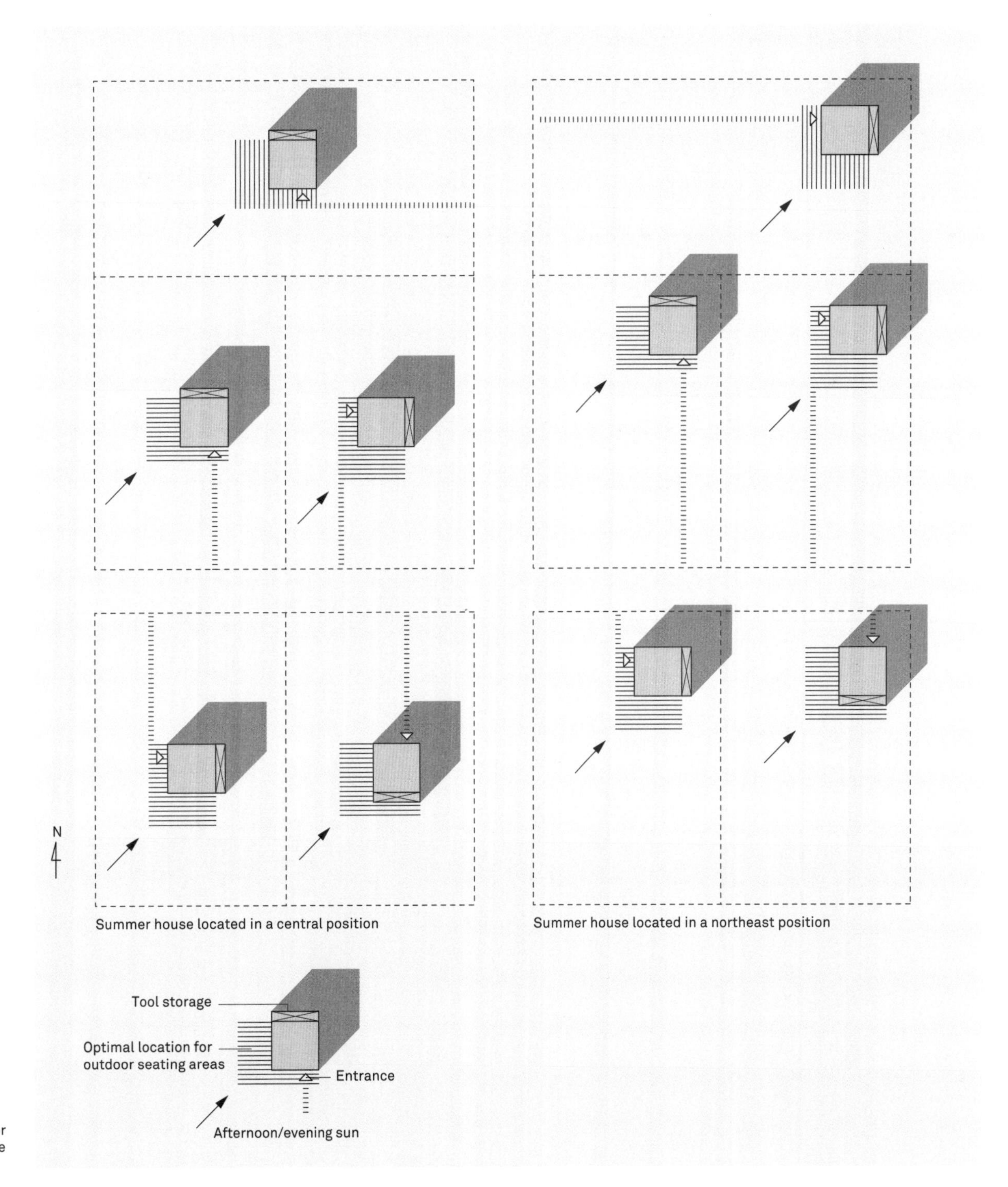

Figure 4.1.2 Location of summer house and outdoor seating on the plot

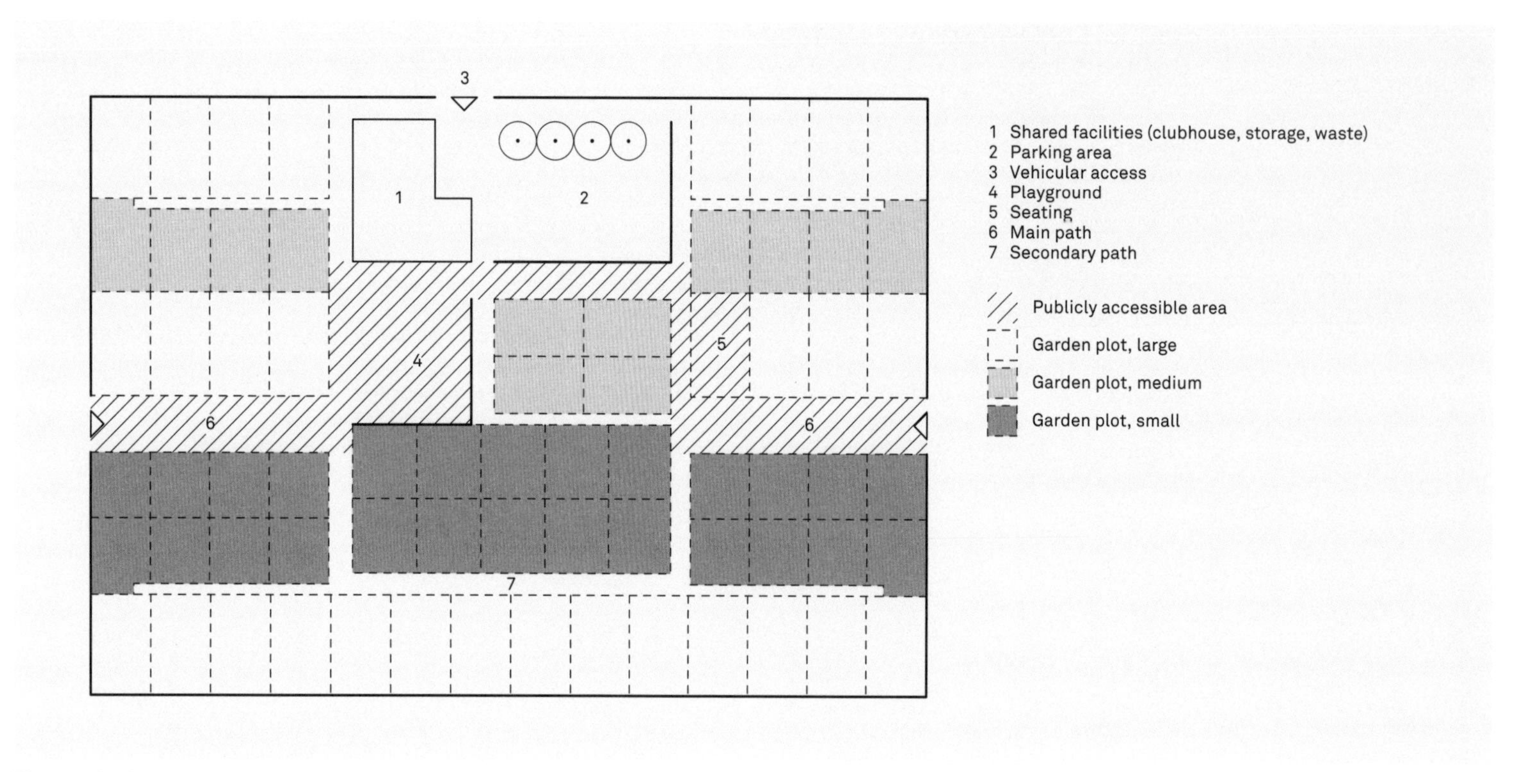

Figure 4.1.3 Functional layout of a permanent allotment site

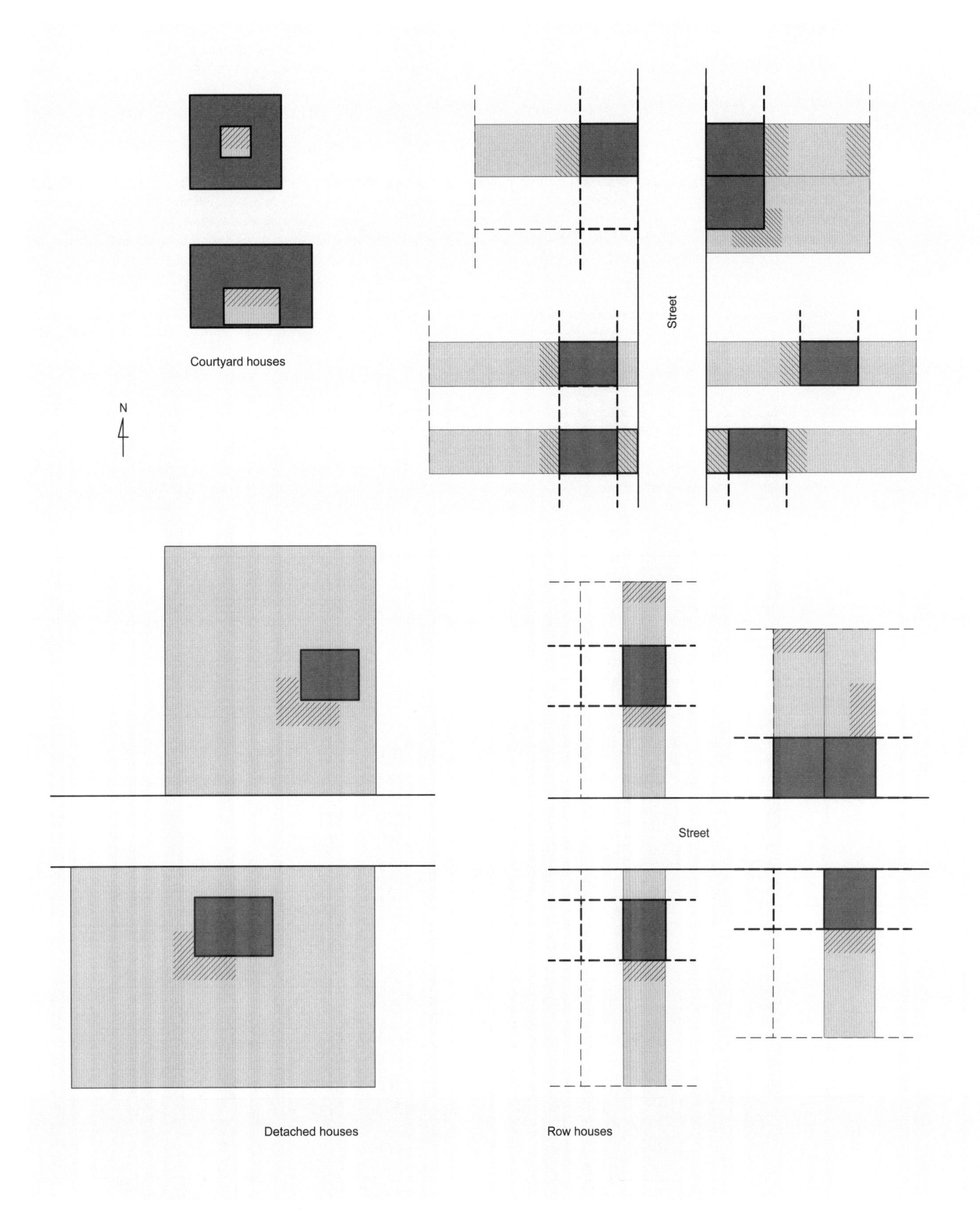

Figure 4.1.4 Locations of terraces and other outdoor seating areas (gray hatching) for different types of houses

Dimensions and Characteristics

Sizes of Residential Gardens

The size of a residential garden can vary from very small apartment gardens to expansive, park-like grounds. Even though an area that measures about 300 m^2 and/or 8–9 m wide is needed to attain sufficient privacy and offer varied design opportunities, gardens can still be created in even the smallest of spaces. Since a lawn must have a certain minimum size for it to be effective as an element of design and to justify the effort involved in its upkeep, in small gardens the creation of a lawn should be forgone in favor of a spacious terrace with planting that frames it.

The size of a garden has an influence on the design opportunities available and also on the types and range of features a garden contains. Aspects like path widths and terrace sizes must be appropriate to the scale and the possible uses which are predetermined by the building. Although the dimensions of many areas are variable, certain minimum sizes should be observed. Other measurements depend on the garden's intended use. → **Table 4.1.2**

The selection of trees and shrubs should take into account the size of the garden, so normally only trees with small to medium crowns are considered. Lots of significantly more than 1,000 m^2 are also suitable for trees with large crowns. But even in that case, choices should be made very carefully. With free-growing hedges or solitary trees and shrubs, the final growth widths must also be taken into account.

Dimensions of Allotment Gardens

The plot size varies from country to country, averaging between 250 and 400 m^2 or more. With plot sizes of less than 300 m^2, acoustical and visual privacy may be limited (see Richter, 133). This is also dependent on other factors, however, such as the overall layout, the positions of the summer house and the seating area, and the planting used on the plot.

To make good use of the area available, plot proportions of approximately 1:1.6 (golden section) should be sought. Dimensions that meet this criterion are, for example, 15 × 24 m (360 m^2) or 14 × 22.5 m (315 m^2). The summer house must have a setback of 1 to 1.5 m from the property line along a neighboring plot at the side (see Richter, 131ff). The floor area of summer houses – or more specifically, the built area per lot – is not allowed to exceed 24 m^2 in Germany, and in Vienna the size is restricted to maximums of 16–50 m^2 depending on the use.

Table 4.1.1 Typical plot and garden sizes of single-family houses

House type	Stories*	Property size*	Property dimensions (exemplary)	Floor area*	Average garden size
Detached single-family house	1	400–600 m^2	e.g., 16 × 30 m	120–140 m^2	260 m^2
Detached single-family house	2	350 m^2	e.g., 16 × 22 m	70 m^2	280 m^2
Semidetached house	2	300–350 m^2	e.g., 13 × 30 m	120 m^2	180–220 m^2
Row house, standard	2	200–250 m^2	e.g., 8 × 28 m	100 m^2	100–130 m^2
Row house, small	2–3	150 m^2	e.g., 6 × 25 m	80 m^2	70 m^2
Atrium/courtyard house	1	180 m^2	e.g., 15 × 13 m	130 m^2	50 m^2

* Reference values – specifications in binding land-use plans (e.g., floor area ratio and percentage of lot coverage), can limit the degree to which a plot can be built upon, and thus restrict the buildable area of a property.

Table 4.1.2 Dimensions and requirements for allotment gardens in various countries/cities

	Lot size	Constructed area	Circulation within allotment site	Enclosure
Germany	≤400 m^2	≤24 m^2 including covered outdoor seating	–	–
Berlin		Permissible in addition to the summer house: mobile tool box (1.5 m × 1 m and approx. 1.3 m high), greenhouse (12 m^2, h = 2.2 m), impermeable surfaces, a maximum of 6 % of the open space (excluding the summer house and a 0.8 m strip all around)	Construct using water-bound paving, crushed aggregate lawn, or grass paving blocks	≤1.25 m high (fence or hedge)
Austria	120–650 m^2	–	–	–
Vienna	≥250 m^2, ≥10 m wide	16 m^2 for summer houses on land used temporarily as allotment gardens, 35 m^2 for summer houses in declared allotment garden areas, 50 m^2 for garden houses when year-round residential use of the allotment garden areas has been sanctioned, plus 5 m^2 for covered bicycle parking	Secondary paths: 1.2 m wide; main paths: 3 m wide, 10 m curve radius	1–2 m high
Lower Austria		–	Secondary paths: 2 m wide; main paths: 3 m wide	–
France	average 250 m^2	–	–	–

Garden spaces and infrastructure	Recommended minimum size	Preferred location	Miscellaneous
Main circulation path	1.2–1.5 m wide	–	–
Path with "wheelbarrow width"	0.9 m wide	–	–
Vehicular access	2 m wide	–	–
Parking space for a passenger vehicle	2.6 × 5 m (or larger, depending on vehicle); minimum width if obstructed along the side: 2.90 m	Near public streets and entrance	Avoid locations under trees with falling fruit or secretions
Carport	3 × 5 m (overall dimensions for open construction), clear width min. 2.5 m, clear height approx. 2.15 m	–	–
Bicycle parking space	1.9 × 0.8 m	In combination with car parking space and/or near entrance	–
Waste container area	→ Chapter 3.5	Near street; observe maximum permitted distance from street → Chapter 3.5	Omitted in residential developments with a central waste container area
Terrace/patio	12 m²	Southwest/west → Figure 4.1.1	Incorporate visual screening, slope 1–2 %, avoid locations under trees with falling fruit or secretions
Additional terrace / seating area	5 m²	East/southeast	
Usable (accessible) garden courtyard / atrium	25–40 m², depending on building height and natural lighting	Bounding walls should not be too high	No lawns; only sensible for larger courtyards and with adequate maintenance
Tree plantings	–	Observe minimum setback from the neighboring property → Table 3.10.3	Select trees with small crowns, medium- to large-crowned trees only for sufficiently large gardens
Visual screening and boundary enclosures (fences/hedges)	–	Observe boundary setbacks for hedges → Table 3.6.3	Observe allowable heights for boundary enclosures → Tab. 3.6.4
Rose bed	–	Mostly sunny and airy, not beneath trees	Water tap within adequate distance
Perennial flower beds and borders	–	Sunny to shady, depending on plant selection	
Vegetable garden	50 m² / person for self-subsistence	Mostly sunny	
Fruit and vegetable garden (incl. orchard trees)	130 m² / person for self-subsistence	Mostly sunny	
Herb garden	–	Mostly sunny, proximity to the kitchen	–
Raised beds	Height and dimensions variable; wheelchair-accessible raised bed: • Roll-under clearance 52 cm: ideal for children's wheelchairs • Roll-under clearance 65 cm: ideal for ordinary wheelchairs • Roll-under clearance 78 cm: ideal for higher (electric)wheelchairs	Sunny to partial shade	–
Composting facility	4 m² (2 compost bins with approx. 1 m² surface area each, plus access)	Partial shade	One compost bin is actively filled while the compost in the other bin matures
Sandbox/play area for children	as needed	Morning sun can facilitate drying of the sand and play areas	–
Water feature/pond	→ Chapter 3.9	Mostly sunny, proximity to a terrace/patio	Water tap within sufficient distance
Garden pavilion	–	Observe required property line setback per building code	–

Table 4.1.3 Minimum sizes and requirements for the features and site infrastructure of gardens

Path widths
→ 3.3 Paths and Roads

Size of Seatings
→ 3.7 Seating

Boundary Enclosures
→ 3.6 Boundary Enclosures and Railings

Selection of trees and shrubs
→ 3.10 Woody Plants

4 Typologies

4.2 Open Spaces in Schools and Preschools

4.2 Open Spaces in Schools and Preschools

High demands are placed on the open spaces at schools and preschools in order to do justice not only to the functional requirements that arise from their daily operation, but also to address the inherent and complex needs of children and young people. Given that children typically spend several hours a day using the outdoor facilities of a preschool and/or the recess area of a school operating on a full-day schedule, the expectations placed on the outdoor space – as a counterbalance to the interior space – are great from a pedagogical perspective. Exterior spaces that are designed in a differentiated manner and which can be used in different ways help prevent or lessen the physical and social deficits of children and young people – so it should be the rule to give consideration to developmental needs for physical activity when designing outdoor spaces for children and young people.

Movement is a basic need, and especially in the interest of the healthy development of children's bodies, this need should be enjoyed freely to the greatest extent possible. Movement is what first enables children and young people to experience their physical strengths and weaknesses in full measure, to understand material and spatial situations within their environment, and to establish and to live out social contacts. Thus physical activity constitutes the basis for the development of a child's personality and his or her spiritual and intellectual understanding of the environment. To complement this, the outdoor space should have provisions to help promote the tactile, olfactory, and visual senses.

Beyond satisfying the minimum functional requirements, other facilities – such as a field for exploratory play, an outdoor classroom, a school garden, a pond area, opportunities for climbing, and additional sports fields and ball courts – can supplement the areas specifically used for recess and create new opportunities to use and enjoy the school grounds. Zones for physical activity should be clearly distinguished from quiet zones, and differences in the capabilities and interests of children in different grade levels should be addressed through age-appropriate adaptation of the respective zones. Using specifically targeted measures, various forms of sensory perception are promoted. → Table 4.2.1

Type of sensory perception	Promotional means
Touch	Different materials, different surfaces, soil structures, plant growth forms, use of water
Balance	Swinging, seesawing, sliding, swaying/rotating, balancing
Movement	Climbing, crawling, hanging/traversing hand over hand
Sight	Color contrast, color change, shapes
Smell	Scents of flowers, leaves, and fruits
Spatial perception	Height differences, sloped surfaces, hiding, plants, canopies/roofs, walls

Table 4.2.1 Selected measures for strengthening sensory perception

Site

Feature Elements and Fixtures

Feature elements and fixtures (boulders, cut segments of tree trunks laid horizontally, etc.) on school and preschool premises must be firmly installed in a stable manner. Like for playgrounds, the area surrounding play equipment must be outfitted with suitable impact-absorbing surfaces. Sharp edges (e.g., on stone blocks) must be beveled or slightly rounded. → Chapter 4.3

Waste Containers

Especially in and around preschools, a location beyond the reach of children is to be chosen for the waste containers.

Lighting

On the grounds of schools and preschools, necessary circulation paths, obstacles, and stairs shall be lit with at least 5 lux (nominal illuminance as per DIN 5035-2, 1990-09).

Bicycle and Motorized Traffic

Traffic from motor vehicles must be principally avoided on school recess areas during school hours. Thus recess areas should be spatially separated from parking lots and with the aid of signage, unavoidable traffic should be restricted to walking pace. Exits from school premises are to be segregated from street traffic, for instance with railings or planted buffer strips. These same provisions apply to preschools and their outdoor spaces.

If there are bus stops directly on the school grounds, these are to be provided with a waiting area of sufficient dimensions, allotting 0.5 m² per waiting person. Students must be able to reach the waiting area without crossing a traffic lane, and the waiting area itself shall be clearly separated from the school recess area.

Bicycle parking spaces should be located separately from or along the side of the schoolyard. Attention must be given to safe design of the bicycle racks (e.g., fabricated without sharp edges) as well as the access paths. Any necessary ramps should have a maximum slope of 25%. With a slope of more than 10%, steps must also be provided (see GUV-V S1 – Unfallverhütungsvorschrift Schulen [Accident prevention regulations for schools]).

Use of Plants

Plants should be well suited to supplying material for play and for stimulating the senses. But care must be taken that the plants are not poisonous. Absolutely no poisonous plants should be used in areas used by children. Besides highly poisonous plants, there are also some mildly poisonous plants whose fruits are tempting to eat and which can thus frequently lead to apparent symptoms of poisoning. For poisonous plants and for plants suitable for "play," see Chapter 4.3

Dimensions and Characteristics

Required Facilities and Sizes

Despite the growing importance of outdoor facilities at schools and preschools, not everywhere will planners find clear standards for area sizes, for site design in close touch with nature, or for how to appropriately satisfy children's needs for physical activity.

Basic guide values for the size of outdoor spaces for schools can be found in the school regulations applicable in the local jurisdiction. In Germany, these regulations are set at the state level and are still based in part on DIN 18031 "Hygiene in School Buildings" – meanwhile withdrawn without replacement – which can still be taken as a basis when needed. Some school regulations nevertheless require less than the 5 m² per pupil set out by that standard for recess areas. Moreover, the size of a schoolyard and the diversity it offers are dependent on the number of parallel classes per grade level as well as the duration and intensity of daily use. → Table 4.2.2

In determining the dimensions for the outdoor facilities of preschools, a recommended value of 10 m² per child is applied, although some jurisdictions require more space per child or a minimum size for the total area of the outdoor facilities. → Table 2.2.1

State/school type	General requirements	School						Preschool
		1 Classes per grade	2 Classes per grade*	3 Classes per grade**	4 Classes per grade	5 Classes per grade	6 Classes per grade	
General recommended values:								
• Grounds (including buildings but excluding outdoor sports facilities)	20 m²/child							
• Recess area	5 m²/child							
Bavaria (1994 school building regulations)								
• Schoolyard	3 m²/child							Sufficiently large
• Enclosed (indoor) recess area			0.5 m²	0.4 m²				
• Areas for indoor and outdoor sports	For mandatory physical education in close proximity							
Berlin (2010 model room schedule) Elementary schools								
• Recess area, 1st grade, min.			540 m²	810 m²	1,080 m²			
• With sand play area and playground equipment, max.			900 m²	1,350 m²	1,800 m²			
• Recess area, grades 2–6, with gymnastics and playground equipment			1,500 m²	2,250 m²	3,000 m²			
• School garden	400 m²							
• Playing field/court 27 × 45 m	1,363 m²							
• 75 m running track (95 m overall), 3 lanes	550 m²							
• Long jump with 35 m approach (overall), 3 lanes, landing pit 5.55 × 8.00 m	288 m²							
• Gymnastics field	400 m²							
Berlin Comprehensive secondary school (full-day operation)								No rqmts.
• Recess area	5 m²/child				2,400 m²	3,000 m²	3,600 m²	
• School garden (kitchen garden, biotope)					480 m²	600 m²	720 m²	
• Playing field/court 52 × 79 m (overall)	4,760 m²							
• 100 m running track (120 m overall), 4 lanes	962 m²							
• Long jump with 45 m approach (overall), 3 lanes, landing pit 5.55 × 9.00 m	350 m²							
• High jump mat 4 × 6 m (next to playing field)	40 m²							
• Shot put: 1 ring sector 34.92°, 20 m side length	approx. 200 m²							
• Gymnastics field	400 m²							
Berlin Comprehensive secondary school with upper secondary level (college prep) (full-day operation)								
• Recess area	5 m²/child				3,300 m²	4,125 m²	4,950 m²	
• School garden (kitchen garden, biotope)					480 m²	600 m²	720 m²	
• Playing field/court 52 × 79 m (overall)	4,760 m²							
• 100 m running track (120 m overall), 4 lanes	962 m²							
• Long jump with 45 m approach (overall), 3 lanes, landing pit 5.55 × 9.00 m	350 m²							
• High jump mat 4 × 6 m (next to playing field)	40 m²							
• Shot put: 1 ring sector 34.92°, 20 m side length	approx. 200 m²							
• Gymnastics field	400 m²							

Table 4.2.2 Selected requirements for size and features of outdoor facilities at schools and preschools

State/school type	General requirements	School 1 Classes per grade	 2 Classes per grade*	 3 Classes per grade**	 4 Classes per grade	 5 Classes per grade	 6 Classes per grade	Preschool
Berlin High school (regular form/full-day operation)								No rqmts.
• Recess area	5 m^2/child			2,550 m^2	3,400 m^2	4,250 m^2		
• Student garden	30 m^2/class			360 m^2	480 m^2	600 m^2		
• Playing field/court 52 × 79 m (overall)	4,760 m^2							
• 100 m running track (120 m overall), 4 lanes	962 m^2							
• Long jump with 45 m approach (overall), 3 lanes, landing pit 5.55 × 9.00 m	350 m^2							
• High jump mat 4 × 6 m (next to playing field)	40 m^2							
• Shot put: 1 ring sector 34.92°, 20 m side length	approx. 200 m^2							
• Gymnastics field	400 m^2							
Berlin: Bike racks/motor vehicle parking spaces for people with disabilities	Per implementing provisions for parking spaces							
Hesse	Individually regulated by the districts and cities with district status							6 m^2/child
Lower Saxony								200 m^2 for one group, otherwise 10 m^2/child
Mecklenburg-Vorpommern								2.5 m^2/child
Rhineland-Palatinate (2010 administrative regulation)								No rqmts.
• Schoolyard	5 m^2/child, min. 400 m^2							
Saarland								≥5 m^2/child
Saxony (1993 recommended spatial program) Elementary school								10 m^2/child
• Recess area with gymnastics and playground equipment		600 m^2	1,200 m^2	1,800 m^2	2,400 m^2			
• School garden		150 m^2	300 m^2	360 m^2	480 m^2			
• Playing field/court		1 ×	1 ×	1 ×	1 ×			
• 100 m running track, 4 lanes		–	–	600 m^2	600 m^2			
• Long jump facility, 3 lanes		–	–	300 m^2	300 m^2			
• Gymnastics field		400 m^2	400 m^2	400 m^2	400 m^2			
Saxony High schools								
• Sports playing field				1 ×	1 ×	1 ×		
• 100 m running track, 4 lanes				750 m^2	750 m^2	750 m^2		
• Long jump facility, 3 lanes				480 m^2	480 m^2	480 m^2		
• Shot put facility 10 × 15 m				150 m^2	150 m^2	150 m^2		
• Gymnastics field				400 m^2	400 m^2	400 m^2		
Schleswig-Holstein								≥300 m^2, 10 m^2/child
Thuringia								10 m^2/child
		Schools with 8 classes		Schools with 12 classes		Schools with 24 classes		
Vienna, Austria								
• Outdoor recess area		500 m^2		800 m^2		1,500 m^2		
• Play and sports area		1,700 m^2		2,000 m^2		3,500 m^2		
• Car parking, waste collection		270 m^2		370 m^2		700 m^2		
• Residual areas (setbacks, paths, etc.)		230 m^2		330 m^2		500 m^2		

No rqmts. = no requirements * ≤400 m^2 ** ≥400 m^2

Anthropometric Data

A comparison of the body measurements of children of different ages and of their caregivers illustrates the range of different requirements that are encountered when planning facilities for schoolchildren and preschoolers. The range of motion of the children as well as that of the teaching staff and caregivers must be taken into account. The goal in so doing is to provide the greatest possible range of options for movement and play. → Table 4.2.3

Stairs and Steps

Stairs must be appropriate for the particular use and safely constructed.

According to the German accident prevention regulations for schools (GUV-V S1), a rise-to-run ratio in accordance with DIN 18065-1 (2r + t = 59–65 cm) is stipulated for stairs in and at schools. In schools, however, the rise should not be more than 17 cm and the tread should be at least 28 cm. → Chapter 3.2

For exterior stairs (outside flights of steps that are separate from the building) and for stairs in preschools, risers of 14–16 cm with a tread of 32–30 cm are recommended (see GUV-I 561 and the bulletin "Sichere Schulen und Kindergärten" [Safe schools and preschools]). The openings of open steps may not exceed 11 cm – or 8.9 cm when used by children under the age of 3.

A clear distinction shall be made between the stair treads and adjoining surfaces. Besides markings and/or lighting, attention is to be drawn in particular to single steps – inasmuch as they cannot be avoided altogether – by using contrasting colors or a different texture.

Safeguards for Elevated Occupied Areas

Within school grounds, all parts of occupied areas with a height difference of 0.3 to 1 m above another area must be protected – by a barrier, benches, planted buffer strips, or raised planters, for example – or be given clear and distinct identification/markings.

For a height difference of more than 1 m, the potentially hazardous edge must be protected by a barrier with a minimum height of 1 m (see DIN 58125). Additional provisions pertaining to fall protection are, for instance, found in local building codes. → Chapter 3.6

In preschools, occupied areas are to be protected beginning with a height difference of 20 cm by using planted buffer strips or raised planters, benches, guardrails, or parapets, when children under the age of 3 use the area. → Figure 4.2.1 In other respects, the regulations for platforms and landings of play equipment apply (→ Table 4.3.5).

Water Features

When designing a water feature for a school or preschool, attention must be given to ensure that the water depth does not exceed 1.2 m. A shallow water zone with a maximum water depth of 0.4 m and a width of at least 1 m should be provided.

In preschools, water features or wetland habitats with a maximum depth of 40 cm are to be separated by a continuous shore zone that is at least 1 m wide and offers secure footing. If the water depth exceeds 40 cm, the feature or habitat must be secured by an enclosure, which must not offer the child any incentive to climb over (e.g., no crossbars permitted).

Small children can drown in water that is just a few centimeters deep. In order to guard against such risks, water features in facilities for children under three years of age should be avoided completely or made thoroughly inaccessible. Water playgrounds with rock bubblers or areas for playing in mud are feasible if no deep puddles can develop.

Enclosures

On fences, railings, and walls serving as enclosures to the grounds of schools and preschools, no "pointy, sharp-edged and protruding parts or barbed wire may be attached." Fencing or other enclosures around preschools must have a minimum height of 1 m and may not encourage anyone to climb on or over them. Openings in enclosures and railings may not be any larger than 11 cm, or 8.9 cm when the area is used by children under the age of 3.

Entries are to be designed so that they are lockable and, if there is nearby moving traffic, that they cannot be opened by children's hands.

	3 years	4 years	5 years	6 years	12 years	Women (16–60 years)	Men (16–60 years)
Height	92–111	101–118	106–126	111–129	139–168	152–176	160–189
Reach, upward	105–127	107–136	121–144	127–151	162–199	171–209	188–226
Reach, forward	42	48	52	57	–	–	–
Seat height Seat width	19–28	23–30	25–32	25–33	36–42	35–43	40–48
Eye level	85–99	87–108	96–113	98–120	126–154	139–166	150–175
Head width	12.4–14.2	12.8–14.5	13.1–15	13.2–15.2	13.6–15.5	13.7–16	14.3–16.9
Hand thickness	1.8–2.3	1.9–2.3	1.9–2.4	1.9–2.4	2.2–3.0	2.1–3.2	2.3–3.4
Hand grasp	7.5–8.3	8–8.9	8–9.4	8.1–10.3	10–13	10.7–15.9	11.9–15.6
Foot length	14.9–17.3	14.9–19	16.1–19.7	16.4–20.9	21–26.6	22.1–26.4	24–28.1
Foot width	5.8–7.1	5.9–7.5	6.5–7.6	6.5–7.9	7.8–9.9	9–10.7	9.3–10.7

Table 4.2.4 Anthropometric data for children and adults (Source: Unfallkasse Hessen) (All dimensions in cm)

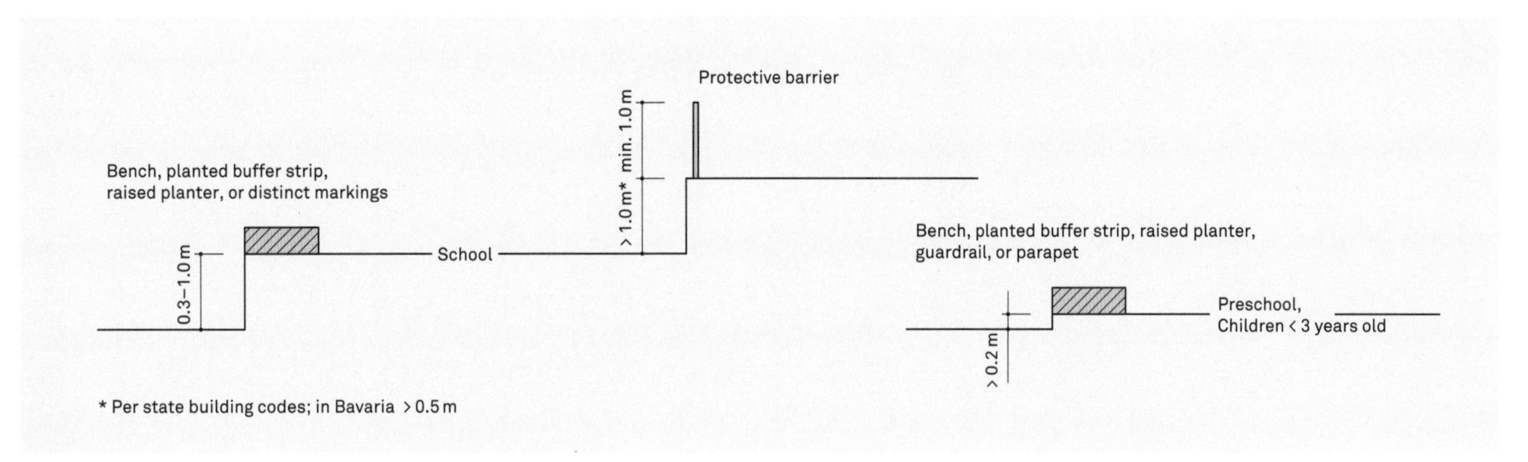

Figure 4.2.1 Fall heights and protective measures in schools (left) and preschools (right)

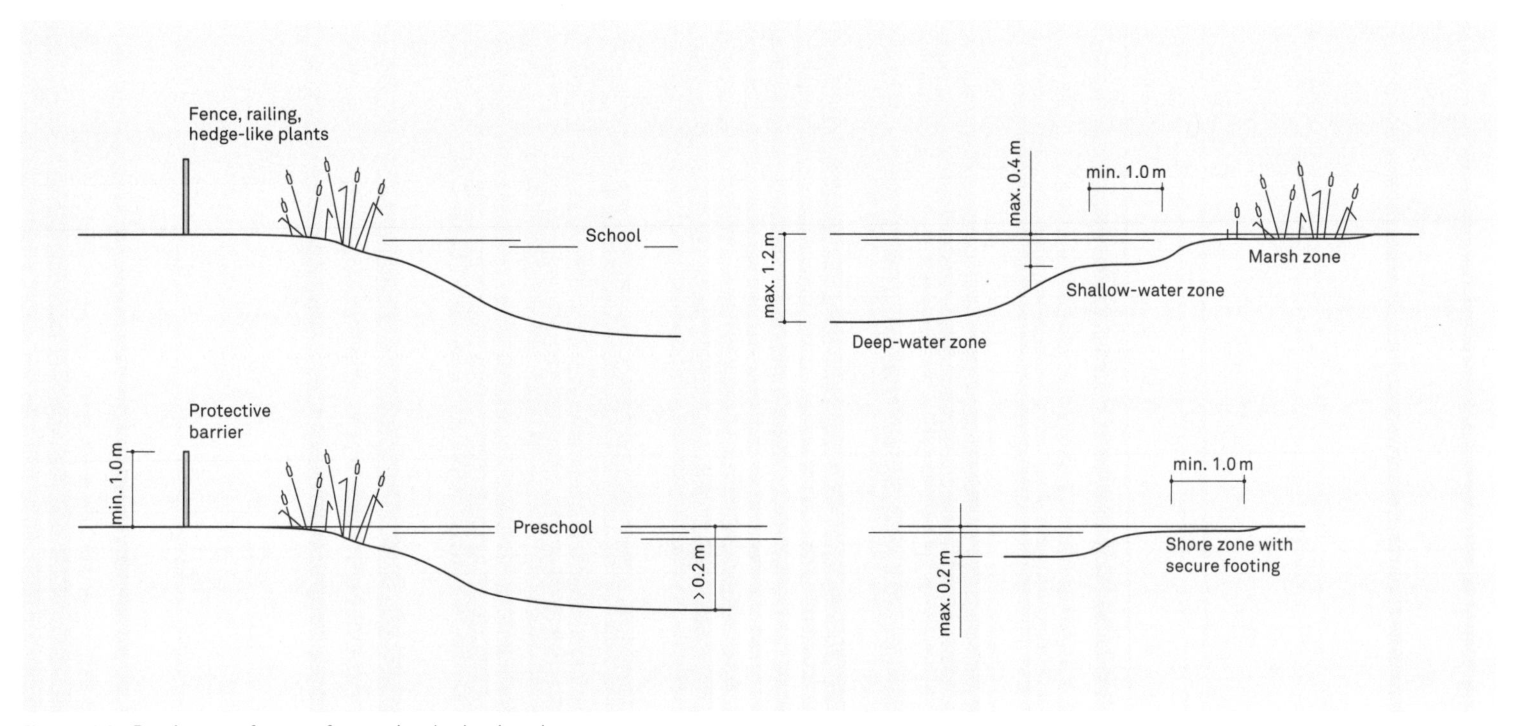

Figure 4.2.2 Requirements for water features in schoolyards and on the grounds of preschools

Requirements for Playground Equipment and Surfacing
→ 4.3 Play Areas and Playgrounds

Stairs
→ 3.2 Grading, Stairs, and Ramps

4 Typologies
4.3 Play Areas and Playgrounds

4.3 Play Areas and Playgrounds

Playgrounds promote and challenge the development phases of children and young people and beyond that, offer adults and entire families a space to move about and experience themselves and their surroundings. But play and training equipment particularly geared to the needs of older people is also becoming increasingly popular and is found in public open spaces to an increasing extent. Where possible, play equipment that is equally usable by all age groups should be installed, in order to establish the greatest possible flexibility and usability. In this respect, the universally beloved swing continues to be a popular example that is also enjoyed by adults.

As opposed to natural settings, built-up areas present fewer opportunities for self-expression and development in the open, so it is imperative to expand the opportunities for recreation in towns and cities by creating consciously designed areas for play. Beyond conventional playgrounds, play spaces should augment the available offerings, encourage free play, and fit comfortably into the urban outdoor space. Ways to accomplish this can include establishing seminatural adventure areas or increasing the opportunities for play on streets by introducing traffic-calming measures in residential areas.

New concepts for play areas are also needed because conventionally equipped playgrounds alone cannot satisfy the needs for exciting outdoor space, especially not for older children. "Creative disorder" can frequently contribute more to discover and change. And the networking of existing play areas into a coherent system can counteract the tendency toward fragmentation into isolated islands. The local pedestrian network, and especially the routes to and from school, can, for example, be linked via "patrolled spaces" and "play paths," thereby taking on supplemental functions as playable space.

Giving consideration to age-specific needs can be helpful in the development of age-appropriate playground and play space concepts.

Figure 4.3.1 Versatile and universally beloved: the swing

Location

By maintaining sufficient distance from adjacent buildings and by applying sensible zoning, any negative impact to adjacent residential development and other noise-sensitive uses (e.g., hospitals and nursing homes) can be minimized when laying out playgrounds. Requirements for minimum setbacks are often specified by local municipalities in playground regulations or bylaws. For children's playgrounds adjacent to housing, a minimum setback of 10 m from windows of occupied rooms is generally required. Vienna's playground ordinance stipulates a minimum setback of 5 meters from living and sleeping rooms for playgrounds serving small children up to age six and 15 meters for playgrounds suitable for older children and youth. Youth play areas should preferably be sited at the edge of a residential development. If skateparks or playing fields for ball sports are planned, suitably sized buffer zones should be established. → Table 4.4.2

Playgrounds should be sheltered from the wind and have a balance of sunny and semishaded areas that takes into account local climate factors. To enable sand play areas to rapidly dry out and warm up, they should receive morning sun and in any case must not be located in full shade. Especially during the midday hours, semishady places, such as under trees, are recommended.

Due to the risk of overheating, the inclined sliding surface of a slide should never be oriented to the south. Splashing and bathing areas should receive direct sun all day.

Age (in years)	Needs	Type of play	Objects	Activities
Up to 4	Gathering experiences with materials and surfaces	Functional play, imaginary play, dramatic play, simple construction play, individual and group experimental play, movement games, balancing exercises	Child's own body, all sorts of objects, and people	Shoveling, filling, emptying, digging, throwing, pouring, splashing, kneading, sledding, sliding, crawling, hiding
4–6	Gathering experiences with materials and people	Role playing, construction play, sand play, movement games, balancing exercises	Child's own person and partners-in-play, physical objects	Building castles, streets, and bridges; crawling through objects; hiding, running, sledding, sliding, climbing, swinging, etc.
6–10	Gathering experiences with materials and people, romping around, and learning rules	Cooperative play and rules games, construction play, functional play, movement games, role playing, artistic and quiet play	Other people, objects, and situations; social games	Handicrafts, building, hammering, carving, taking things apart, assembling things, building dams, playing cowboys and Indians, painting, board games
10–14	Gathering experiences with materials and people, constructing and designing	Group play, acquisition of social roles, functional play, construction play, movement games, rules games	Expansion of the group of people identified for 6- to 10-year-olds and the situations listed for them	Expansion of the activities identified for the 6- to 10-year-olds

Table 4.3.1 Age-specific needs of children and youth (Source: Gerhard Dittrich (ed.), *Kinderspielplätze: Analysen, empirische Befunde und Planungsempfehlungen* [Children's playgrounds: Analyses, empirical findings and planning recommendations], Stuttgart 1974)

Dimensions and Characteristics

Orientation Values for Play Areas

Details about the necessary areas for playgrounds within towns and cities vary according to the country, state, and municipality, but in some cases there are no set requirements. In any case, the pertinent building codes and regulations must be observed. For aspects pertaining to the overall urban design, orientation values are based in Germany on DIN 18034-1 and trace back to guidelines for the provision of recreation, play, and sports facilities that were issued by the German Olympic Society (DOG) in 1976. Particularly for the construction of new residential developments, many countries or municipalities have regulations governing playgrounds near housing. → Table 4.3.2

The space needed for different play areas and pieces of playground equipment determines the necessary playground size – or, in other cases, the space available will only permit certain play areas to be created and certain playground equipment to be used. → Table 4.3.3

Type/main user group	Guideline value for urban design	Recommended sizes per playground	Location
Playgrounds in public spaces			
Close to housing/small children up to 6 years	0.5 m²/inhabitant usable play area, 0.75 m²/inhabitant gross area	40–50 m² usable play area, 60–225 m² gross area	Max. walking distance from the dwellings: 100 m
Neighborhood playground/children 6–12 years	2 m²/inhabitant (ÖNORM 2607)	450–800 m² usable play area, 675–1,200 m² gross area	Max. walking distance from the dwellings: 400 m
Village, borough, or district playground/children and youth 12 years and older		600–3,000 m² usable play area, 800–3,750 m² gross area	Max. walking distance from the dwellings: 800–1,000 m
Families/adults	1.5 m²/inhabitant (gross area)	≥ 1,500 m² usable area, ≥ 2,250 m² gross area	Max. walking distance from the dwellings: 800–1,000 m
Playgrounds in residential developments (refer to building code or community statutes and bylaws for applicable local regulations)			
Play areas for small children; in Berlin, when serving 75 or more dwellings: also suitable for older children	Provide 4–6 m² usable play area per dwelling unit for 3 or more dwellings	Minimum 25 m²; Berlin: 50 m², Upper Austria: 100 m²	Max. walking distance from the dwellings: 100 (50) m

Table 4.3.2 Orientation values: minimum requirements for playground areas (relevant directives and building regulations must be observed) (Sources: German Olympic Society (DOG) guidelines, DIN 18034-1, state building codes, ÖNORM B 2607)

Play area	Minimum size including safety and movement area	Equipment
Sand play	20–35 m²	Sandbox, sandpit, game table
Stand-alone equipment	6–20 m²	Spring rocker; seesaw; playhouse; balance beam
Stand-alone equipment	20–30 m²	Swing; slide; balance station; climbing net, water feature
Composite structures	70–100 m²	Themed play structure; climber-slide combination; water feature combination
Play on multiple elements	150–500 m²	Slides, seesaws, swings, climbers and upper body equipment (overhead ladders, rings, etc.), balance beam
Adventure playground	600–800 m²	Play combination (themed) with surrounding wooded areas
Ball games, running and mobility games	800–1,300 m²	Small courts; terrain modeling and climbing wall; fitness course
Played with and in water	200–500 m²	Wading pool; water features
Skate parks	250–400 m²	Pools, half-pipes, quarter-pipes, etc.

Table 4.3.3 Minimum sizes for different play areas in public spaces (Source: Gälzer, 2001), supplemented)

Falling Space and Free Space

Elements of playground equipment must be positioned to avoid any overlap of the main circulation routes and equipment play areas as well as obstructions in areas of swinging movement. According to EN 1176-1 this free space encompasses all areas with action that is caused by the play movements or involuntary movements during play. In addition to these safety areas, the falling space that could be occupied by a user when falling from an elevated part of the equipment must also be taken into consideration.

For fall heights up to 1.5 m, the falling space width (width of impact area) shall be at least 1.5 m, whereas for fall heights of up to 0.6 m, there are no requirements for impact-absorbing surfacing.

With fall heights between 1.5 and 3 m, the falling space is calculated according to the following formula, up to a max. of 2.5 m:

Falling space = free height of fall
(= height of the play level) × 2/3 + 0.5 m

For swings, the falling space is calculated as the suspended length of the swing (distance between swivel joint and top of swing seat) × 0.867 + 2.25 m. For merry-go-rounds, the falling space shall be at least 2 m.

The clearance beneath swing seats must be at least 35 cm when at rest. For tire (and bird's nest) seats, the clearance must be at least 40 cm.

Free height of fall	Falling space width/ width of impact area	Surfacing
≤0.6 m	1.5 m	No impact absorption required
≤1.5 m	1.5 m	Protection from falling → Table 4.3.5
Formula for calculating the falling space = free height of fall × 2/3 + 0.5 m		
1.65 m	1.6 m	Protection from falling → Table 4.3.5
1.8 m	1.7 m	
2 m	1.83 m	
2.5 m	2.16 m	
3 m	2.5 m	

Table 4.3.4 Width of falling space as a function of fall height

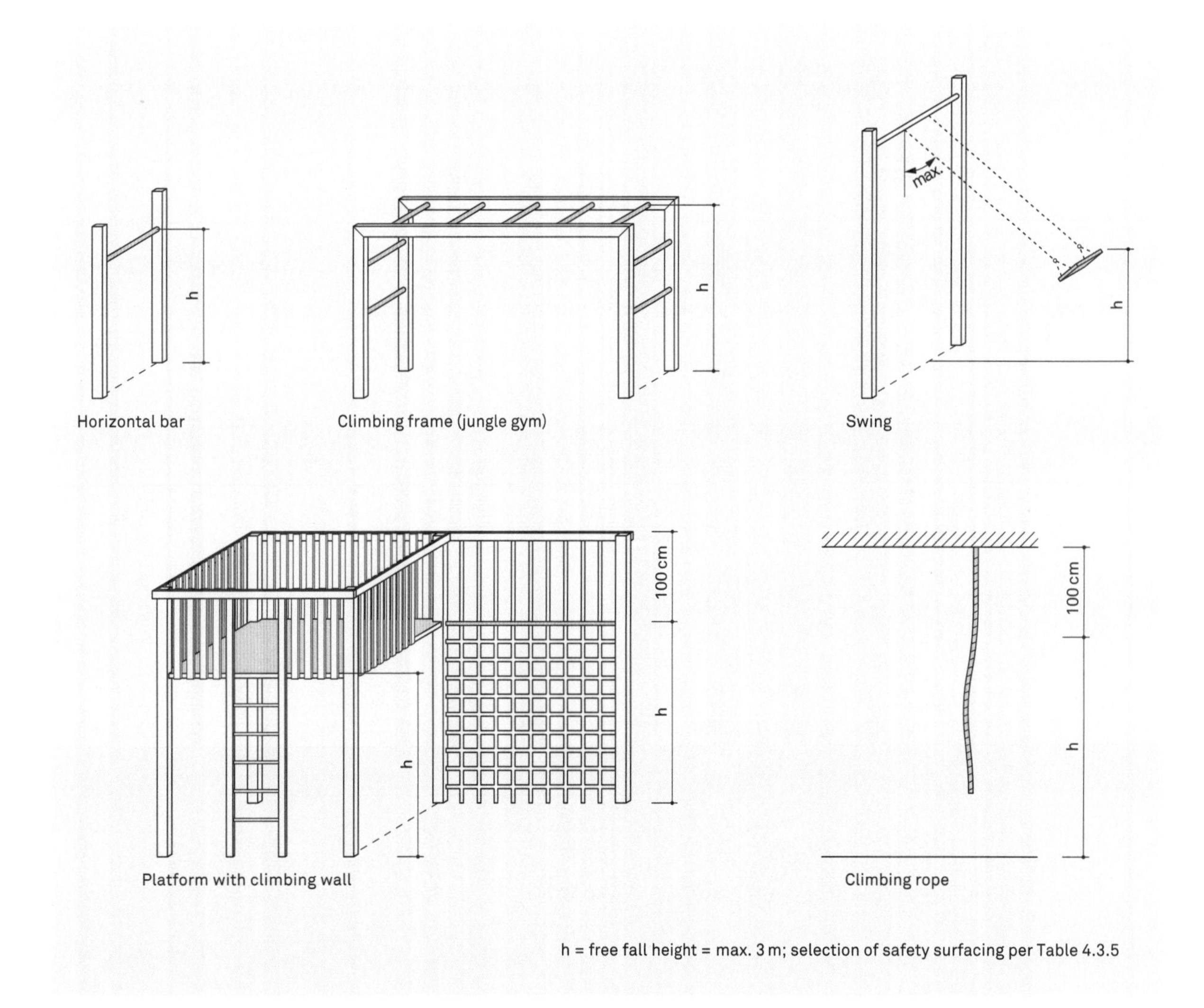

Figure 4.3.2 Examples for defining fall heights (h) for typical playground equipment per EN 1176-1

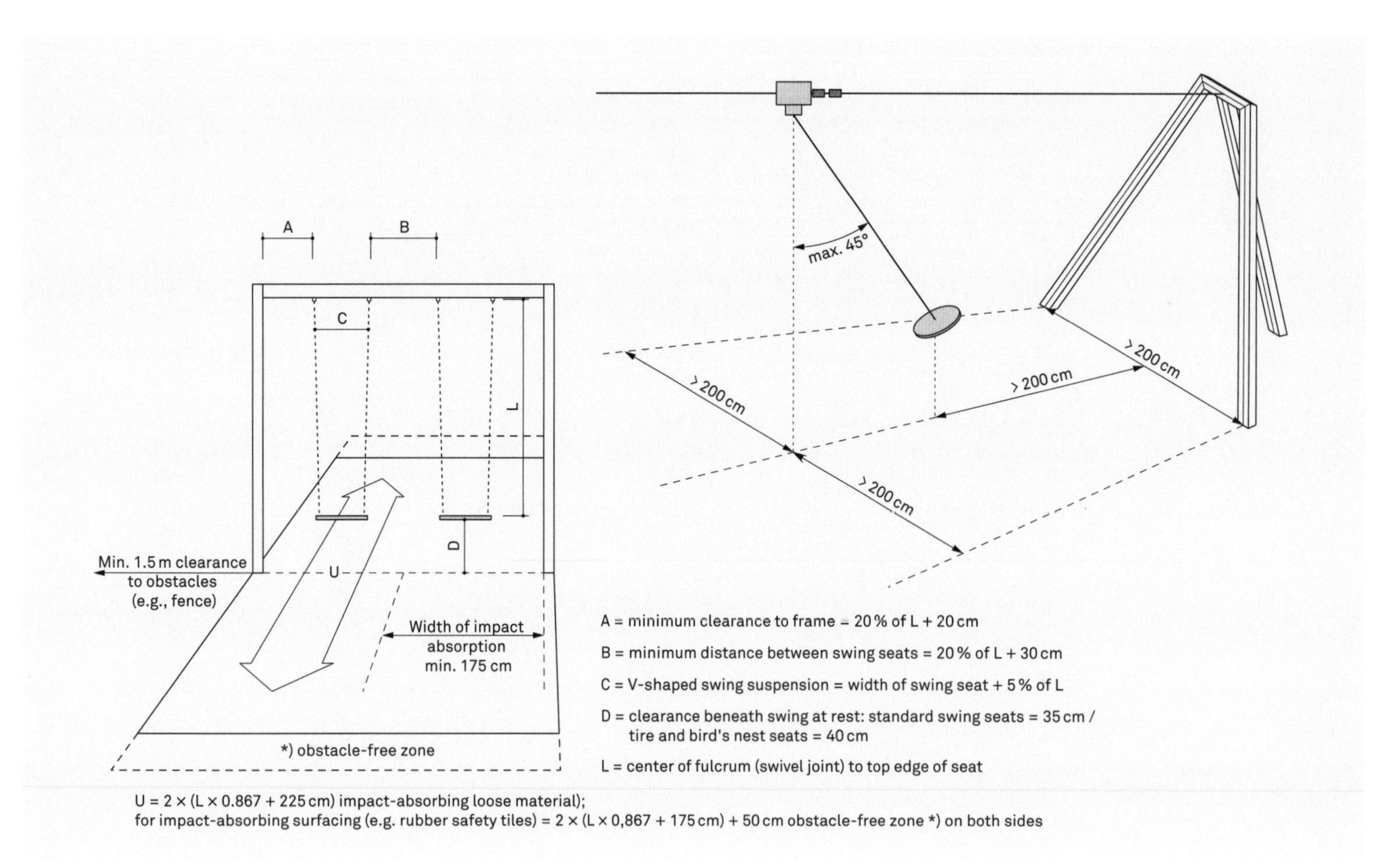

Figure 4.3.3 Examples for minimum clearances at swings and cableways per EN 1176-1

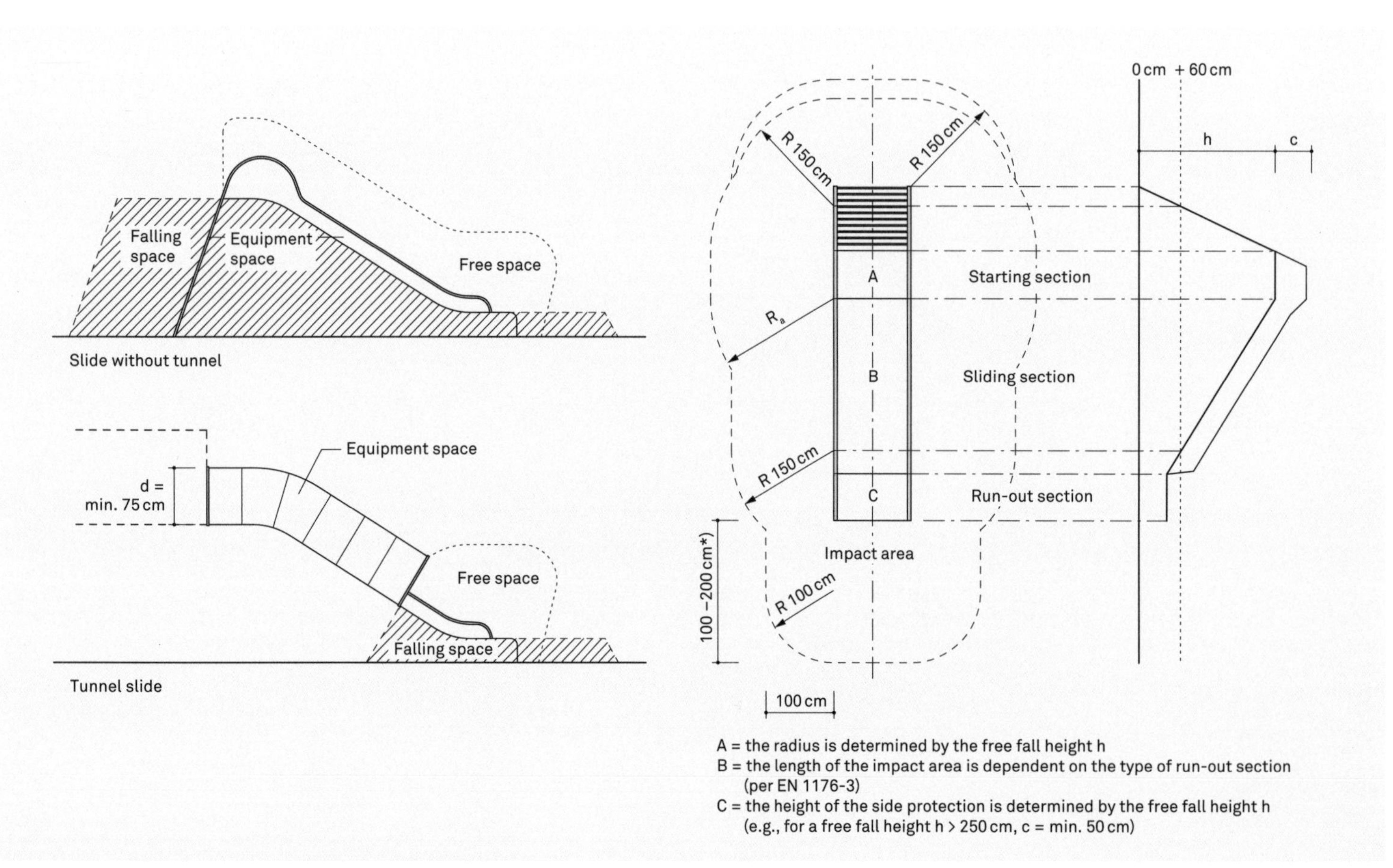

Figure 4.3.4 Examples of falling spaces and free spaces for slides

Fall Prevention and Impact Attenuation

On platforms and landings on playground equipment, measures for preventing falls shall be provided in the form of guardrails or protective barriers, depending on the potential height of fall. Care must be taken in designing and building these guardrails and protective barriers do not encourage or enable children to climb or sit on them. Playground equipment is subject to the specifications in Table 4.3.5. On playgrounds in Vienna, places that present a risk of falling must generally have a guardrail with a minimum height of 1.10 m. If the guardrail is mounted on a base that is higher than 0.25 m, the height including base must be at least 1.25 m.

Depending on the free-fall height, different demands are made regarding the ground beneath playground equipment. For all items of equipment where the user carries out a forced movement (e.g., swings, slides, seesaws, cable runways, carousels, etc.), an impact-absorbing surface is required over the entire impact area. These requirements apply to both stationary as well as portable children's play equipment.

Due to their nonslip surface, rubber safety tiles act as a stopper. Hence with falls that are oblique or largely horizontal, joint and ligament injuries can easily result. Loose materials such as gravel or bark mulch allow the foot of a falling person to assume a more optimal position. Fall protection areas with loose materials should be bordered and sunken to form pond-like pits so that the impact-absorbing material remains in the pit, thus reducing maintenance needs. The periphery should be compacted. It is important for the bottom of the depressed area to have good drainage so that rainwater does not collect in the pit.

Table 4.3.5 Required protection against falling from platforms and landings of playground equipment

Platform or landing height	Fall prevention on play equipment		Surfacing
	Easily accessible for all ages (EU)	Not easily accessible for children under 3 years old / accessible for all ages in DE*	
<0.6 m	No requirements	No requirements	No requirements (in DE)
0.6 to <1 m		No requirements	Loose material
1 to <2 m	Protective barrier (to prevent unintentional falls or climbing over or through) required, height ≥0.7 m	Guardrail required, with a height of ≥0.6 m to 0.85 m	Impact-absorbing surface (up to 1.5 m grass allowed) → Table 4.3.6
2 m to <3 m		Protective barrier required, height ≥0.7 m	Impact-absorbing surface → Table 4.3.6

* Deviating rule in Germany due to the legal duty of supervision for children up to 3 years of age

Table 4.3.6 Fall heights as a function of the ground material

Surface material	Maximum fall height per EN 1176-1:2008-08					Comments
	≤60 cm	≤100 cm	≤150 cm	≤200 cm	≤300 cm	
Concrete, stone, bitumen-bound materials	Only permitted in DE					Should only be used in exceptional cases, and not for equipment that causes a forced movement of the user's body, such as slides, swings, or carousels
Topsoil	×	×				No compacted or dried-out earth; not barrier-free
Grass	×	×	Permitted in DE (assuming sod is well maintained)			National regulations and regional climatic conditions must be observed; areas must be protected from drying out; not barrier-free
Wood chips (particle size 5–30 mm)	Layer thickness ≥20 cm, plus 10 cm to counteract the material's tendency to scatter				Layer thickness ≥30 cm, plus 10 cm to counteract the material's tendency to scatter	Must be placed on a well-drained substrate; not barrier-free
Bark mulch (particle size 20–80 mm)						Must be placed on a well-drained substrate; not barrier-free
Sand (particle size 0.2–2 mm)						Should not contain any silt or clay, recommended particle size: 1–5 mm, not barrier-free
Gravel (particle size 2–8 mm)						
Other materials (e.g., rubber safety tiles, synthetic surfacing)	With adequate HIC test value as per EN 1177					HIC = Head Injury Criterion

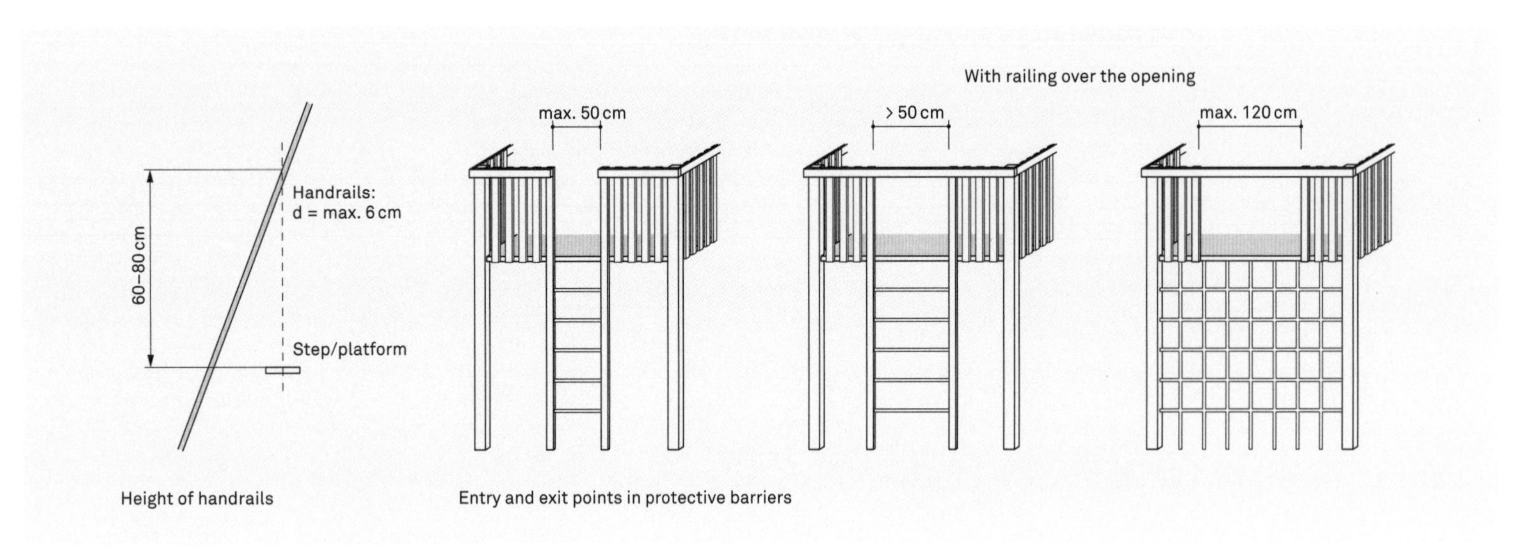

Figure 4.3.5 Requirements for handrails and guardrails

Construction Details

European Standard EN 1176-1 (Playground equipment and surfacing – Part 1: General safety requirements and test methods) stipulates, among other things, a series of safety requirements pertaining to the construction of playground equipment. Some – with relevance for the planning phase – are mentioned here:

- The materials for children's play equipment must generally have a smooth surface without splinters. Equipment made of wood cannot be produced completely free of splinters due to the natural character of the material. So care must be taken to ensure that surfaces in areas where users play come in contact with the wood are as free of splinters as possible. Swing seats made of wood are not permitted!
- Openings (on ladders, climbing nets, etc.) shall either be < 8.9 cm or > 23 cm.
- Tunnels and tunnel slides shall have an inside diameter of ≥ 75 cm, and in tunnels with an incline steeper than 15°, a means for internal climbing (e.g., steps or handles) shall be provided.
- Sharp edges and protruding connectors on fasteners at head or leg height shall be precluded.
- Corners and edges that protrude more than 8 mm must be rounded with a radius of at least 3 mm (also applies to the edges of natural stone blocks within playgrounds). All edges on projecting parts that protrude less than 8 mm must also be rounded off.
- To minimize impact injuries from contact with swinging elements or other moving parts as much as possible, the following conditions must be satisfied when selecting and forming the material: all pertinent components shall be heavily rounded off and materials with cushioning properties (e.g., car tires) or other forms of padding shall be used.

For playground equipment and facilities for small children up to 3 years of age, further measures should be taken (see Unfallkasse Baden-Württemberg: *Kinder unter drei Jahren sicher betreuen* [Safe care of children under the age of three]):

- Openings and gaps that can be reached by a user's fingers may not, when measured from any position, have a space between 4 mm and 25 mm (to avoid risk of entrapment!).
- Head entrapments are not allowable, so openings are not permitted to exceed 89 mm (use small test probes with 89 mm diameter!) unless they are greater than 230 mm.
- Protective barriers shall be provided where fall heights are greater than 60 cm.
- Stairs are to be provided with handrails beginning with the first step.

To also hinder children up to the age of three from gaining access to playground equipment intended for older children, a variety of measures are available:

- The first rung of a ladder is more than 40 cm above the ground.
- There are no stairs or level access to the equipment.
- There are no ramps with a slope of less than 38°.
- There is a height difference of at least 60 cm to terraced platforms so they cannot be climbed upon by young children.

Classifications

Poisonous Plants

No poisonous plants should be used in the vicinity of playgrounds and public areas that are frequented by children. → Tables 4.3.7 and 4.3.8 Even mildly poisonous plants can lead to symptoms of poisoning if they are consumed in large amounts. Especially in the vicinity of play areas and other public spaces visited by small children, these species should be avoided. → Tables 4.3.9

Botanical name	Common name	Poisonous parts of plant	Toxicity	Remarks	Source
Ailanthus altissima	Tree of heaven	Bark, seeds	*	Bitter	5
Andromeda polifolia	Bog rosemary	Leaves, flowers	**		2, 3
Aralia elata	Japanese angelica tree	Bark, seeds	*	Repugnantly bittersweet	5
Aristolochia macrophylla	Dutchman's pipe, or pipevine	Entire plant	*		5
Berberis species and varieties	Berberis	Roots, bark	*	Leaves and types with red berries are harmless	5
Buxus sempervirens varieties	Common box	Leaves, fruit	**		5
Celastrus orbiculatus	Oriental (or round-leaved) bittersweet	Entire plant	*	Bittersweet berries	5
Chamaecyparis species and varieties	False cypress	Entire plant	*	Bitter-aromatic	5
Clematis species and varieties	Clematis	Entire plant	*		5
Colutea arborescens	Bladder senna	Leaves, seeds	*	Bitter	5
Cytisus scoparius	Scotch (or common) broom	Leaves, seeds (entire plant)	*	Seed pods are slightly bean-like	1, 2, 5
Daphne mezereum	Paradise plant	All parts (including seeds of the red berries)	***	All *Daphne* species are poisonous; DIN 18034 prohibits planting in the vicinity of areas designated for play; peppery hot	1, 2, 3, 5, 6
Euonymus europaeus	European (or common) spindle	All parts, especially the red fruits	**	Applies to all *Euonymus* species except those not bearing fruit; DIN 18034 prohibits planting in the vicinity of areas designated for play	1, 2, 3, 6
Genista tinctoria	Dyer's broom	Seeds	**–*	Applies to all *Genista* species; bitter	3, 5
Gleditsia triacanthos varieties	Honey locust	Only the leaves	*	Seeds and fruits are edible	5
Hedera helix	Common ivy	Leaves and especially the (ripe) berries	**–*	Berries are dry like paper, bitter-burning	1, 2, 3, 5
Ilex aquifolium	English (or European) holly	Red berries	**	Berries are bitter	1, 2, 3, 5, 6
Juniperus × media	Pfitzer juniper	Entire plant	***!	Berries are aromatic and peppery hot	5
Juniperus chinensis	Chinese juniper	Entire plant	**	Entire plant	1, 2, 3
Juniperus sabina	Savin juniper	Entire plant, especially the young shoots	**–***!)	Berries are bitter-aromatic	1, 2, 3, 5

Toxicity: *** = extremely poisonous ** = very poisonous * = poisonous (*) = mildly poisonous
Sources: **1** *Giftpflanzen – Beschauen, nicht kauen* [Poisonous plants: Look, don't chew] (Bundesverband der Unfallkassen, 2001). **2** *Giftige Pflanzen an Kinderspielplätzen* [Poisonous plants on children's playgrounds] (Verband Garten- und Landschaftsbau Rheinland, 1974). **3** List of toxic plant species (Federal Ministry for the Environment, Nature Conservation and Nuclear Safety, 2000). **4** *Wege zum Naturverständnis: Pflanzenverwendung in Kindergärten und kinderfreundlichen Anlagen* [Paths toward understanding nature] (Landwirtschaftskammer Nordrhein-Westfalen, 2002). **5** Lorenz von Ehren, Nursery catalogue (CD): *Planning Tips for Trees and Shrubs*, ed. Peter Kiermeier, n.d. **6** Per DIN 18034.

Table 4.3.7 Woody plants with poisonous and very poisonous substances, which should not be planted near areas occupied by children

Botanical name	Common name	Poisonous parts of plant	Toxicity	Remarks	Source
Juniperus virginiana	Eastern red cedar	Entire plant	***!	Berries are bitter-aromatic	1, 2, 3, 5
Laburnum anagyroides	Golden rain, or common laburnum	Entire plant, especially the seeds	**–***!	Sweet roots, bean-like fruit; DIN 18034 prohibits planting in the vicinity of areas designated for play	1, 2, 3, 5, 6
Ligustrum vulgare	European (or common) privet	Entire plant	*	Fruits are persistently repugnant, bittersweet	1, 2, 5
Liriodendron tulipifera	Tulip tree	Entire plant	*	Fruits are slightly aromatic-bitter	5
Lonicera nigra	Black-berried honeysuckle	Black berries	(*)	Other berry-producing *Lonicera* species are okay	1, 2, 5
Lonicera xylosteum	European fly honeysuckle	Red berries	(*)	Other berry-producing *Lonicera* species are okay	1, 2, 5
Lycium barbarum	Matrimony vine	Entire plant	**	Often grows wild in southern Germany	2, 5
Mahonia aquifolium	Oregon grape	Entire plant, except berries	*		1, 5
Nerium oleander	Oleander	Entire plant	**		1, 3
Pachysandra terminalis	Japanese pachysandra	Entire plant	*		
Prunus laurocerasus	Cherry laurel	Entire plant, especially the seeds and leaves	**–*	Flesh of fruit is nontoxic	
Prunus serotina	Black cherry	Entire plant, except cherries	*		5
Rhamnus frangula	Glossy (or alder) buckthorn	Bark, berries	**–*	Berries are bittersweet	1, 2, 3, 5
Robinia pseudoacacia	Black locust (false Acacia, Robinia)	Entire plant	**	Bark and roots pleasantly sweetish	1, 2, 5
Sambucus racemosa	Red elderberry	Fruits	(*)	Seldom planted	2, 5
Taxus baccata species and varieties	Common (or European) yew	Needles, bitten seeds (kernel)	***!	Also other *Taxus* species; *Taxus media* produces many berries	1, 2, 3, 5
Thuja occidentalis	Arborvitae (white cedar)	Entire plant, especially the plant tips and cones	***!		1, 2, 3, 5
Thuja orientalis	Oriental arborvitae	Entire plant, especially the plant tips and cones	***!		1, 2, 3, 5

Toxicity: *** = extremely poisonous ** = very poisonous * = poisonous (*) = mildly poisonous

Sources: **1** *Giftpflanzen – Beschauen, nicht kauen* [Poisonous plants: Look, don't chew] (Bundesverband der Unfallkassen, 2001). **2** *Giftige Pflanzen an Kinderspielplätzen* [Poisonous plants on children's playgrounds] (Verband Garten- und Landschaftsbau Rheinland, 1974). **3** List of toxic plant species (Federal Ministry for the Environment, Nature Conservation and Nuclear Safety, 2000). **4** *Wege zum Naturverständnis: Pflanzenverwendung in Kindergärten und kinderfreundlichen Anlagen* [Paths toward understanding nature] (Landwirtschaftskammer Nordrhein-Westfalen, 2002). **5** Lorenz von Ehren, Nursery catalogue (CD): *Planning Tips for Trees and Shrubs*, ed. Peter Kiermeier, n.d. **6** Per DIN 18034.

Table 4.3.7 Woody plants with poisonous and very poisonous substances, which should not be planted near areas occupied by children

Botanical name	Common name	Poisonous parts of plant	Toxicity	Remarks	Source
Aconitum napellus	Monkshood	Entire plant, especially the roots, seeds	***		1, 2, 3
Aconitum vulparia	Wolfsbane, foxbane	Entire plant, especially the roots, seeds	***		1, 2
Arum maculatum	Cuckoo pint, wild arum	All fresh parts of plant, fruit	**		1, 2, 3
Atropa belladonna	Belladonna, deadly nightshade	Entire plant, especially the roots, seeds	***		1, 3
Brugmansia species	Angel's trumpet – all species	Entire plant, especially in bloom	***		3
Bryonia alba	White bryony	Entire plant, including berries	**		1, 2, 3
Bryonia dioica	Cretan bryony, red (or white) bryony	Entire plant, including berries	**		1, 2, 3
Cicuta virosa	Water hemlock, cowbane	All fresh parts of plant, especially the seeds and roots	***		1, 3
Colchicum autumnale	Autumn crocus, meadow saffron	Entire plant, especially the seeds	***		1, 2, 3
Conium maculatum	Hemlock, poison hemlock	Entire plant, especially the fruits	***		1, 3
Convallaria majalis	lily of the valley	Entire plants + berries	**		1, 2, 3
Datura stramonium	Jimsonweed, datura, thorn apple	Entire plant, especially the roots, seeds	***		1, 2, 3
Digitalis lanata	Grecian (or woolly) foxglove	Leaves, flowers, seeds	**		2, 3
Digitalis purpurea	Purple (or common) foxglove	Entire plant	**		1, 2, 3
Euphorbia cyparissias	Cypress spurge, Bonaparte's crown	Entire plant (through milky sap)	**		1
Euphorbia peplus	Petty spurge, milkweed	Entire plant (through milky sap)	**		1
Euphorbia species	Spurge species	Milky sap	**	Irritation to eyes, skin, and mucous membranes	3
Fritillaria imperialis	Imperial fritillary, crown imperial, kaiser's crown	Bulb	**		3
Helleborus niger	Christmas rose, black hellebore	Entire plant			1, 2
Heracleum mantegazzianum	Giant hogweed	Stem juice	**	Combines with sunlight to cause skin burns	1, 3
Heracleum sphondylium	Common hogweed	Stem juice	**	Combines with sunlight to cause skin burns	1, 3
Hyoscyamus niger	Black henbane, henbane	Entire plant, especially the seeds	***		1, 3
Lactuca virosa	Bitter lettuce, great lettuce	Milky sap	**		3
Lantana camara	Lantana, yellow sage	Berries, leaves	**		3
Lupinus angustifolius	Narrowleaf lupine, blue lupin	Seeds			1
Lupinus luteus	European yellow lupine	Seeds			1
Nicotiana tabacum	Cultivated tobacco	Entire plant, seeds	***		1
Nicotiana species	tobacco species	Entire plant	***		3
Papaver somniferum	Opium poppy	Unripe capsules (seed pods), milky sap	**		3
Phaseolus coccineus	Scarlet runner, multiflora bean	Raw beans	**		1, 2, 3
Phaseolus vulgaris	Common bean	Raw beans	**		1, 2

Toxicity: *** = extremely poisonous ** = very poisonous * = poisonous (*) = mildly poisonous

Sources: **1** *Giftpflanzen – Beschauen, nicht kauen* (Bundesverband der Unfallkassen, 2001). **2** *Giftige Pflanzen an Kinderspielplätzen* (Verband Garten- und Landschaftsbau Rheinland, 1974). **3** List of toxic plant species (Federal Ministry for the Environment, Nature Conservation and Nuclear Safety, 2000). **4** *Wege zum Naturverständnis: Pflanzenverwendung in Kindergärten und kinderfreundlichen Anlagen*, Landwirtschaftskammer Nordrhein-Westfalen, 2002. **5** Lorenz von Ehren, Nursery catalogue (CD): *Planning Tips for Trees and Shrubs*, ed. Peter Kiermeier, n.d.

Table 4.3.8 Herbaceous plants with poisonous and very poisonous substances, which should not be planted near areas occupied by children

Botanical name	Common name	Poisonous parts of plant	Toxicity	Remarks	Source
Phytolacca americana	American pokeweed	Entire plant	**		3
Ranunculus acris	Tall buttercup, meadow buttercup	Entire plant			1
Ranunculus sceleratus	Cursed buttercup, celery-leaved buttercup	Entire plant	**		3
Sambucus ebulus	Dwarf elderberry, dwarf elder, danewort	Especially the fruit			2
Solanum dulcamara	Climbing nightshade, bittersweet	Entire plant, unripe berries	**	Ripe berries have only traces of toxic substances	1, 2, 3
Solanum nigrum	Black nightshade	Entire plant including unripe berries	**	Ripe berries contain only traces of toxic substances	1, 2, 3
Solanum tuberosum	Potato	All above-ground parts of plant, including the green berries, as well as potato sprouts and green parts of the tubers	**		1,3
Urginea maritima	Sea onion or sea squill	Bulb	**		3
Veratrum album	White (or false) hellebore	Entire plant	**		3

Toxicity: *** = extremely poisonous ** = very poisonous * = poisonous (*) = mildly poisonous
Sources: **1** *Giftpflanzen – Beschauen, nicht kauen* (Bundesverband der Unfallkassen, 2001). **2** *Giftige Pflanzen an Kinderspielplätzen* (Verband Garten- und Landschaftsbau Rheinland, 1974). **3** List of toxic plant species (Federal Ministry for the Environment, Nature Conservation and Nuclear Safety, 2000). **4** *Wege zum Naturverständnis: Pflanzenverwendung in Kindergärten und kinderfreundlichen Anlagen*, Landwirtschaftskammer Nordrhein-Westfalen, 2002. **5** Lorenz von Ehren, Nursery catalogue (CD): *Planning Tips for Trees and Shrubs*, ed. Peter Kiermeier, n.d.

Table 4.3.8 Herbaceous plants with poisonous and very poisonous substances, which should not be planted near areas occupied by children

Botanical name	Common name	Poisonous parts of plant	Remarks	Source
Aesculus hippocastanum	Horse chestnut, conker	Chestnuts, especially unripe fruits	Tart, bitter	1,3
Cotoneaster species	Cotoneaster	Entire plant		1
Pyracantha coccinea	Firethorn, pyracantha	Mildly poisonous – nontoxic: Fruits		1
Sorbus aucuparia	European mountain ash, rowan	Mildly poisonous: only the fresh fruits	The 'Edulis' variety = edible rowan berries – can also be eaten raw	1
Symphoricarpos albus	Common snowberry	Berries		1, 2, 3
Viburnum lantana	Wayfaring tree, cotton tree	Bark, leaves, black berries	Berries are bittersweet, harmless when cooked	1, 2, 3
Viburnum opulus	Guelder rose, European cranberry bush	Bark, leaves, red berries	Berries are bittersweet, harmless when cooked	1, 2, 3

Sources: **1** *Giftpflanzen – Beschauen, nicht kauen* (Bundesverband der Unfallkassen, 2001). **2** *Giftige Pflanzen an Kinderspielplätzen* (Verband Garten- und Landschaftsbau Rheinland, 1974). **3** Lorenz von Ehren, Nursery catalogue (CD): *Planning Tips for Trees and Shrubs*, ed. Peter Kiermeier, n.d.

Table 4.3.9 Mildly poisonous woody plants that often lead to cases of poisoning

Particularly Well-Suited Plants

The quality of play spaces can be increased through the selective use of plants. Berry plants, fruit and nut trees, fragrant plants, or even plants with special leaf colors and shapes can stimulate the senses and serve as play material. In addition, the parts of some woody plants, such as willow withes, are particularly good for use in making handicrafts or building simple structures. As a border surrounding play areas, hardy plant species are especially suitable. However, shrubs with prickles and thorns should not be used. → **Table 4.3.10**

Botanical name	Common name	Suitability as play material	Robust species
Acer campestre	Hedge maple, field maple	Fruit as "nose pincher," "helicopter"	xx
Amelanchier ovalis	Snowy mespilus		x
Buddleja alternifolia	Butterfly bush		x (potentially invasive species – not to be planted along the edges of residential development or in the open landscape)
Carpinus betulus	European (or common) hornbeam		x
Cornus mas	Cornelian cherry		x
Cornus sanguinea	Bloodtwig dogwood, common dogwood		xx
Corylus avellana	Common filbert, (common) hazel	Material for bows and arrows; nuts can be eaten	xx
Fraxinus excelsior	European ash, common ash	Suitable for making whistles	
Rosa species	Wild roses	Fine hairs from inside the rose hips as itching powder	
Salix caprea	Goat willow	Dormant cuttings for making willow tunnels, willow tents, and similar living willow structures	xx
Salix purpurea	Purple willow, purple osier		
Salix repens	Basket willow, common osier		
Salix viminalis	Creeping willow		
Sambucus nigra	Black elderberry, elder	Suitable for making whistles and blow pipes as well as arrowheads for archery; *because the berries are mildly poisonous when raw, can only be recommended with restrictions*	x
Staphylea pinnata	European (or common) bladdernut		
Symphoricarpos albus	Common snowberry	Fruits used as "bang snaps"; *because the berries are mildly poisonous, can only be recommended with restrictions*	
Syringa vulgaris	Common lilac		x
Tilia cordata / Tilia *platyphyllos*	Little-leaf linden (small-leaved lime) / large-leaf linden (large-leaved lime)	Good wood for carving	
Viburnum lantana	Wayfaring tree		

Table 4.3.10 Woody plants for use in play areas (Source: Landwirtschaftskammer Nordrhein-Westfalen: *Wege zum Naturverständnis: Pflanzenverwendung in Kindergärten und kinderfreundlichen Anlagen,* 2002)

Remarks on Building Law and Regulatory Approval

When building residential developments, the necessity and required size of playgrounds are primarily governed by the (state) building codes.

Children's play equipment is subject to equipment safety laws. It must be regularly inspected, maintained, and repaired. This is especially true for equipment that remains outdoors all year round or is exposed to heavy wear conditions. In addition to routine visual inspections, inspections of functional operation and structural stability must be regularly carried out as specified by the manufacturer. In addition, an annual general inspection is made by a qualified person.

Dimensions of sports facilities

→ 4.4 Sports Facilities – for Specialized Facilities such as Skating Rinks, Climbing Walls, etc.

4 Typologies
4.4 Sports Facilities

4.4 Sports Facilities

The type of sports facility being planned and issues related to how it will be used form the basis for its design: the required dimensions and features vary, depending on whether the premises is for public recreation or will be used by a school or a club.

When the competition rules of the respective sports associations are used to set the dimensions, it will be feasible to use the premises for competitions. For purely recreational sport facilities or facilities used for school sports, this is not absolutely necessary. In such cases, it can make sense to utilize dimensions that deviate from the competition rules – in order to increase the diversity of offerings, for example, or due to insufficient space. Combined facilities, in which fields for different types of sports are juxtaposed and often superimposed in a minimum amount of space, are particularly attractive for recreational and school sports. These facilities are usually combined with track-and-field facilities for sports like the high jump and long jump.

Location

Orientation

A north-south orientation generally represents the optimal alignment of playing fields and running tracks. The impact of glare on the athletes from high sun angles from the south is significantly lower than it would be in an east-west orientation when the sun is lower in the sky. If the spatial conditions do not permit alignment in the preferred direction, other orientations can be feasible, but due regard should preferably be given to the position of the sun during the main period of use. For sports facilities that are expected to frequently welcome spectators, the orientation should also give consideration to the prime times of day when competitions will be held, so that the majority of spectators will not be subjected to undue glare.

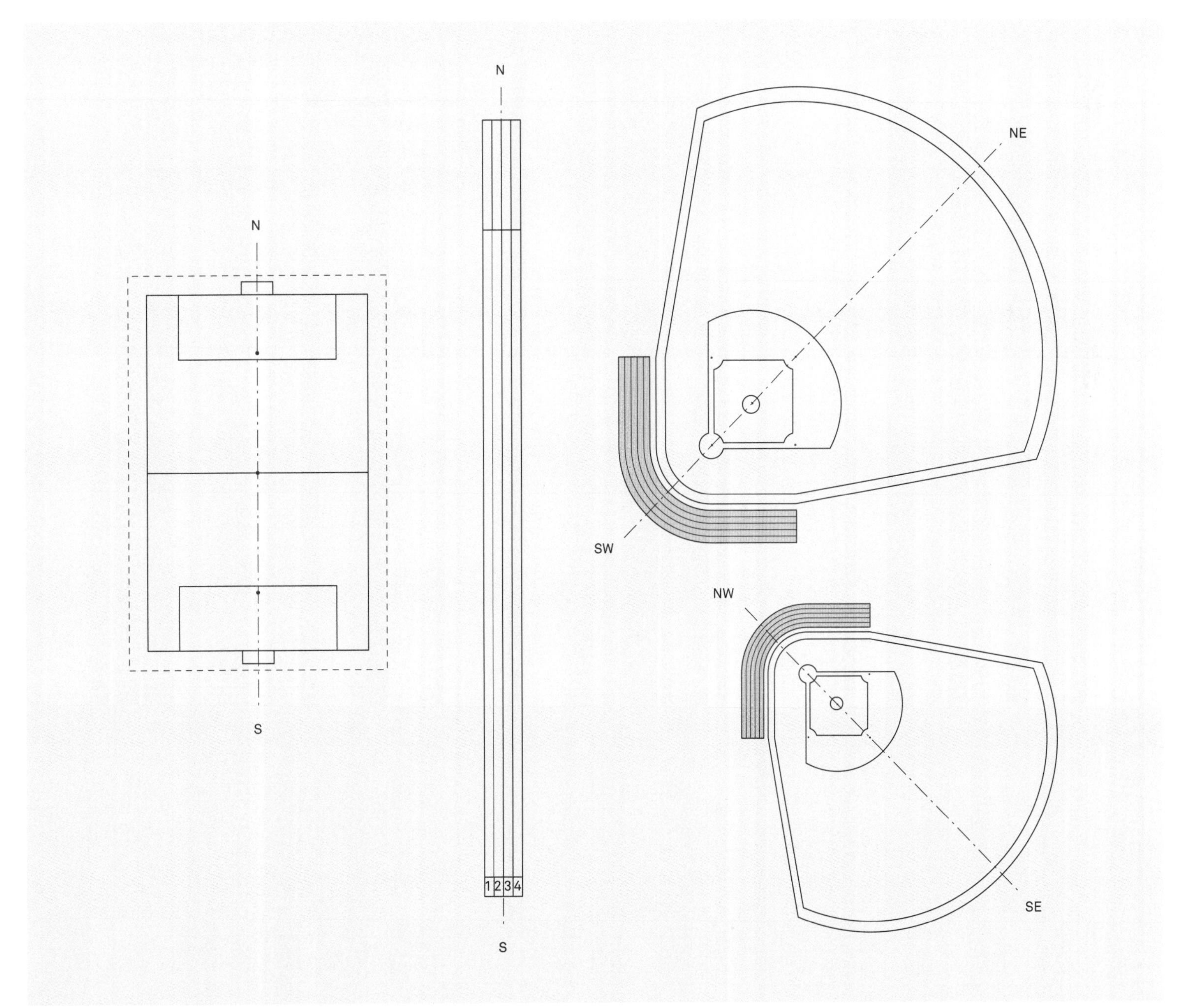

Figure 4.4.1 Orientation of sports facilities

Enclosure

The necessity for a fence depends on the local conditions and the way the site will be used. Especially if high-flying balls can be anticipated, as is the case with soccer, volleyball, or tennis, ball stop fencing should be installed. Depending on the situation, ball stop fencing behind the goals or along the full width of the field's ends may be sufficient for recreational facilities. If the playing field is situated in confined conditions, such as on a hillside or in the immediate vicinity of roads or areas used by other groups, ball stop fencing is always required. The height should be not less than 4 m (3 m in exceptional cases) along the sides and not less than 6 m at the ends and near any goals. Boundaries along busy thoroughfares and highways as well as main roads used by public transit (or which are otherwise heavily traveled) should generally be provided with ball stop fencing to a height of 6 m. In order to minimize the hazard potential and any potential for conflicts, consideration should be given to generally providing an enclosure of suitable height along adjacent traffic areas of any kind and along directly adjoining private property.

A full perimeter enclosure is necessary if regulated entry to competitions is desired, or if the facility should be protected against unauthorized access.

Sport/playing field	Color*	Line width In mm
Soccer (football)	White	120
Hockey	Yellow, white	75
American football	Blue, white	50
Badminton	Green	40
Basketball	Black	50
Five-a-side football	Orange	50
Handball	White	50
Five-a-side hockey	White	50
Volleyball	Blue	50
Tennis	White	50
Track-and-field	White	50

* can vary depending on the color of the sports flooring

Table 4.4.1 Recommendations for marking playing fields on artificial turf and all-weather fields / combined facilities as per DIN 18035-1, augmented

Dimensions and Characteristics

Playing Field Markings

The colors of the playing field markings are defined by the respective sports associations. Markings on grass are generally white. Other colors are also used for some sports that are not played outside on grass (or not done so exclusively) – and when multiple markings are needed. In this way, the different (and sometimes overlapping) playing fields at combined facilities can be easily distinguished. Recommendations for the marking of sports facilities are given in Table 4.4.1.

Noise Abatement Measures

Tremendous noise emissions can emanate from sports facilities. Therefore adequate minimum distances from adjacent places of impact must be maintained.

Sport	Times of use	Minimum setback (measured from the edge of the field to the area in need of protection)		
		Purely residential	Predominantly residential	Mixed use (residential and commercial)
Beach volleyball	All day	75 m	50 m	35 m
	Daytime, outside of mandatory quiet times	50 m	35 m	20 m
	Daytime, maximum 6 hrs outside of mandatory quiet times	45 m	25 m	15 m
Beach volleyball with referee	All day	105 m	70 m	45 m
	Daytime, outside of mandatory quiet times	70 m	45 m	30 m
	Daytime, maximum 6 hrs outside of mandatory quiet times	60 m	40 m	25 m
Kickabout area	All day	155 m	100 m	65 m
	Daytime, outside of mandatory quiet times	100 m	65 m	45 m
	Daytime, maximum 6 hrs outside of mandatory quiet times	80 m	55 m	40 m
Inline skater hockey	All day	290 m	175 m	105 m
	Daytime, outside of mandatory quiet times	175 m	105 m	70 m
	Daytime, maximum 6 hrs outside of mandatory quiet times	145 m	90 m	60 m
Streetball (Half-court)	All day	75 m	50 m	35 m
	Daytime, outside of mandatory quiet times	50 m	35 m	20 m
	Daytime, maximum 6 hrs outside of mandatory quiet times	45 m	25 m	15 m
Halfpipe or minipipe	All day	260 m	160 m	100 m
	Daytime, outside of mandatory quiet times	160 m	100 m	70 m
Small skatepark (features: bank, funbox, coping ramp, flatland)	All day	210 m	130 m	80 m
	Daytime, outside of mandatory quiet times	130 m	80 m	60 m
Large skatepark (features: bank, funbox, coping ramp, minipipe, rail, curb, ollie box, flat-land)	All day	360 m	210 m	130 m
	Daytime, outside of mandatory quiet times	210 m	130 m	80 m

Table 4.4.2 Minimum separation of sports facilities from places of impact (Sources: Bayerisches Landesamt für Umwelt (LfU): *Geräusche von Trendsportanlagen Teile 1 und 2* (2005).)

Ball Sports

American Football

Course type	Playing field	Safety zone		Overall	Lines	Surface
		Side	End		Width/Color	
American football	53.33 × 120 yd 48,46 × 109,73 m	12 ft 3,66 m	12 ft 3,66 m	61 × 127 yd 55,78 × 117,04 m	White	Lawn

Table 4.4.3 American Football

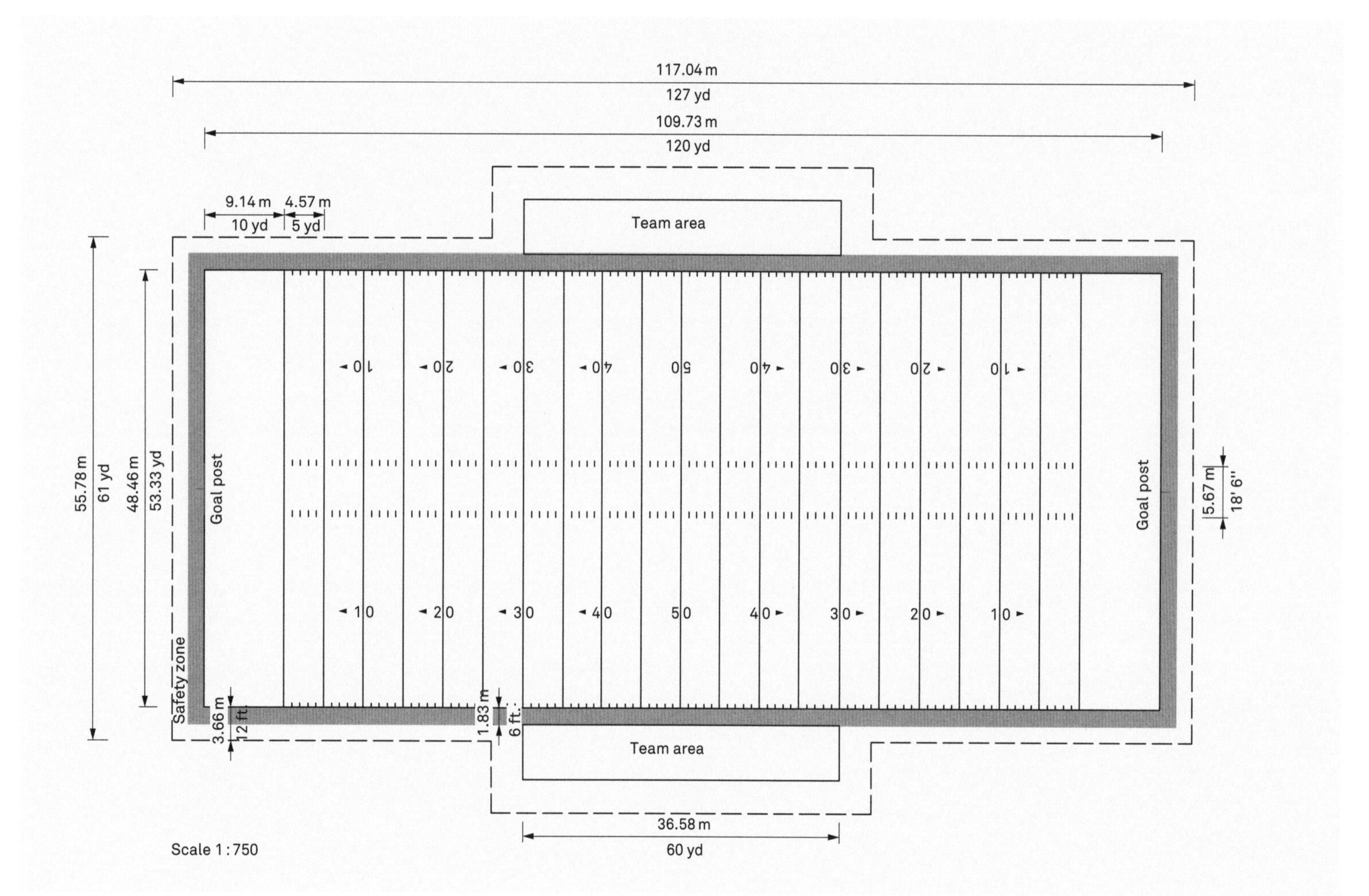

Figure 4.4.2 American Football

Baseball and Softball

Since baseball fields do not have orthogonal perimeters, the overall size only provides an approximate value. The length of the foul line at the sides is a minimum value. The length along the side is specified to be at least 98 m when a field is desired that is suitable for competitions in compliance with the rules of the International Baseball Federation (IBAF). Since this distance can also be greater (up to about 120 m), the overall size may vary significantly. The preferred orientation of the playing field is for the central axis (though home plate and center field) to run from southwest to northeast. In exceptional cases, an orientation from northwest to southeast may also be considered.

Softball is a variant of baseball that is played on a smaller field with a larger ball.

Course type	Playing field	Overall	Lines Width/Color	Surface
Baseball	Length of side lines (foul lines): minimum 98 m; distance from home plate to deep center field: minimum 122 m	approx. 132 × 132 m	7.62 cm (3 inches)/ White	Grass and water-bound sand/clay mixture (dirt)
Softball	Length of the side lines (foul lines) and distance between home plate and far end of the outfield at center field: minimum 67.06 m	approx. 4,800 m²	7.62 cm (3 inches)/ White	Grass and water-bound sand/clay mixture (dirt)

Table 4.4.4 Baseball and Softball

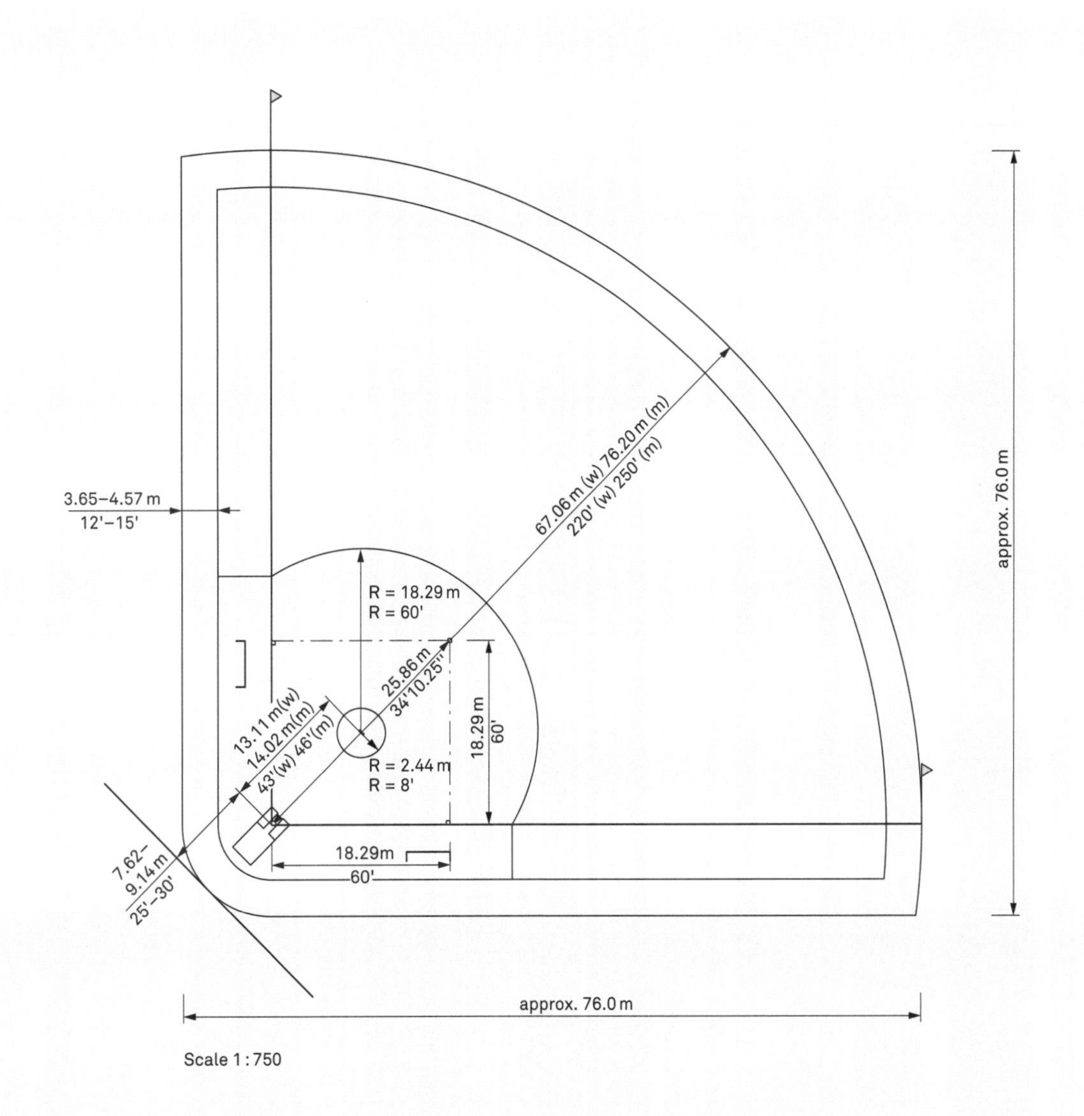

Figure 4.4.3 Softball

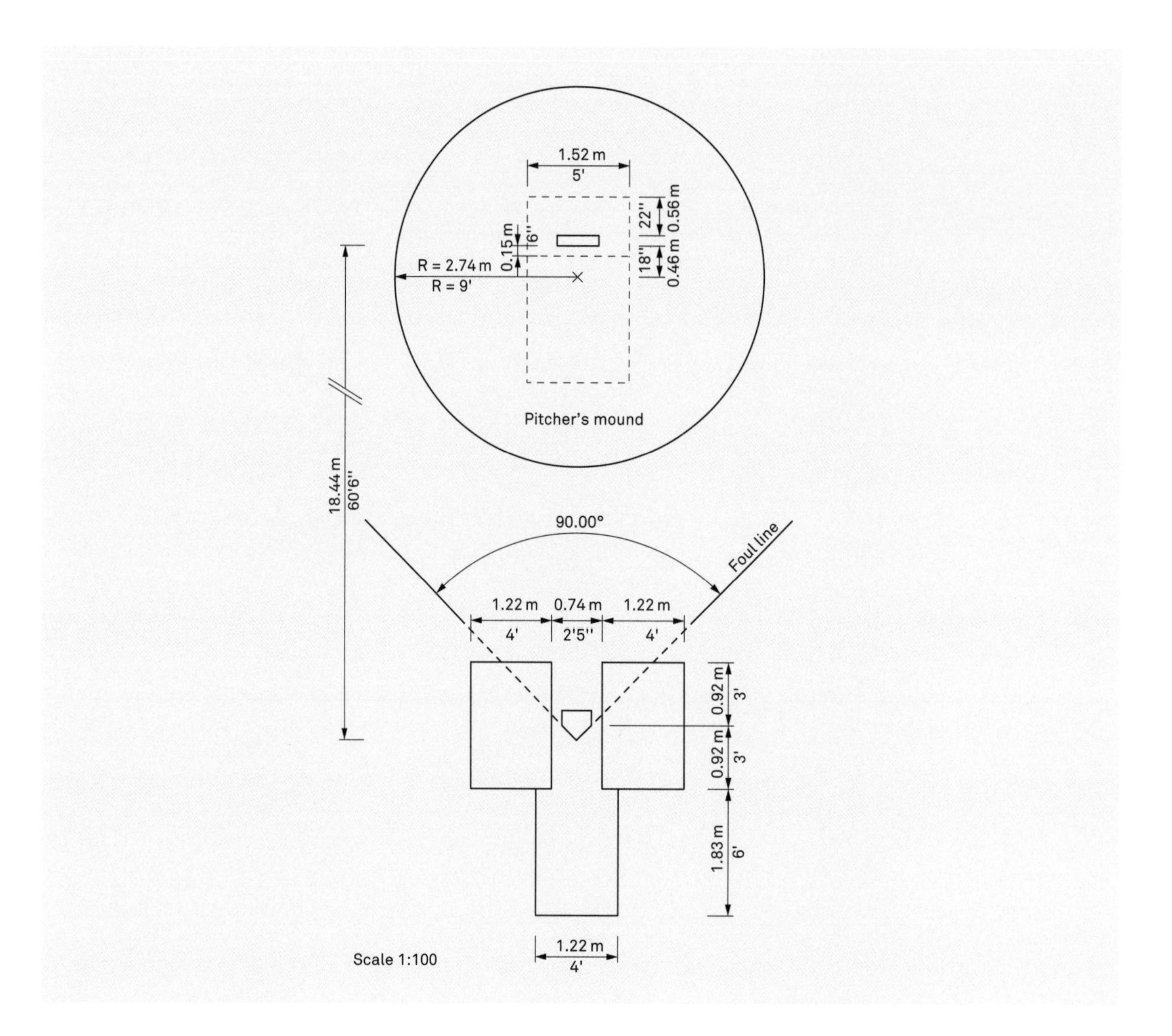

Figure 4.4.4 Baseball details

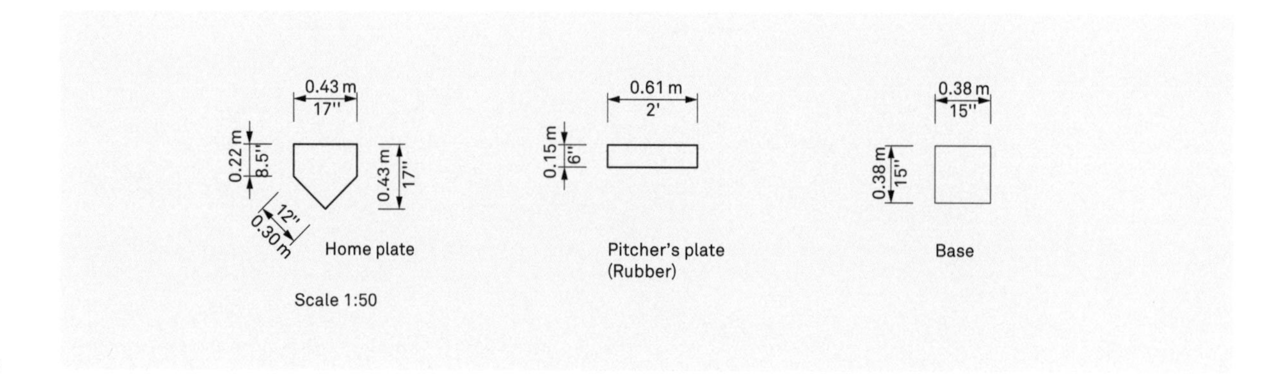

Figure 4.4.5 Baseball details

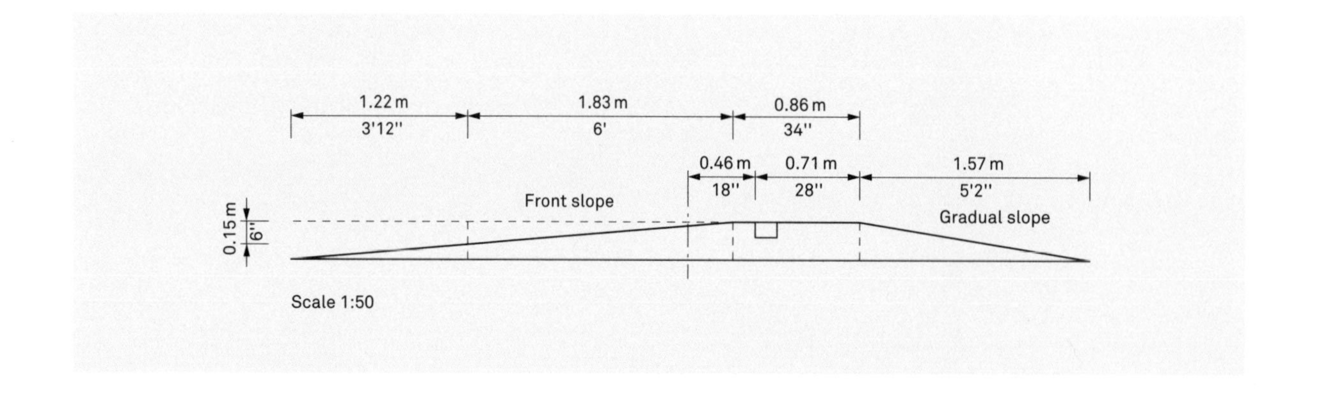

Figure 4.4.6 Baseball detail – Pitcher's mound (cross section)

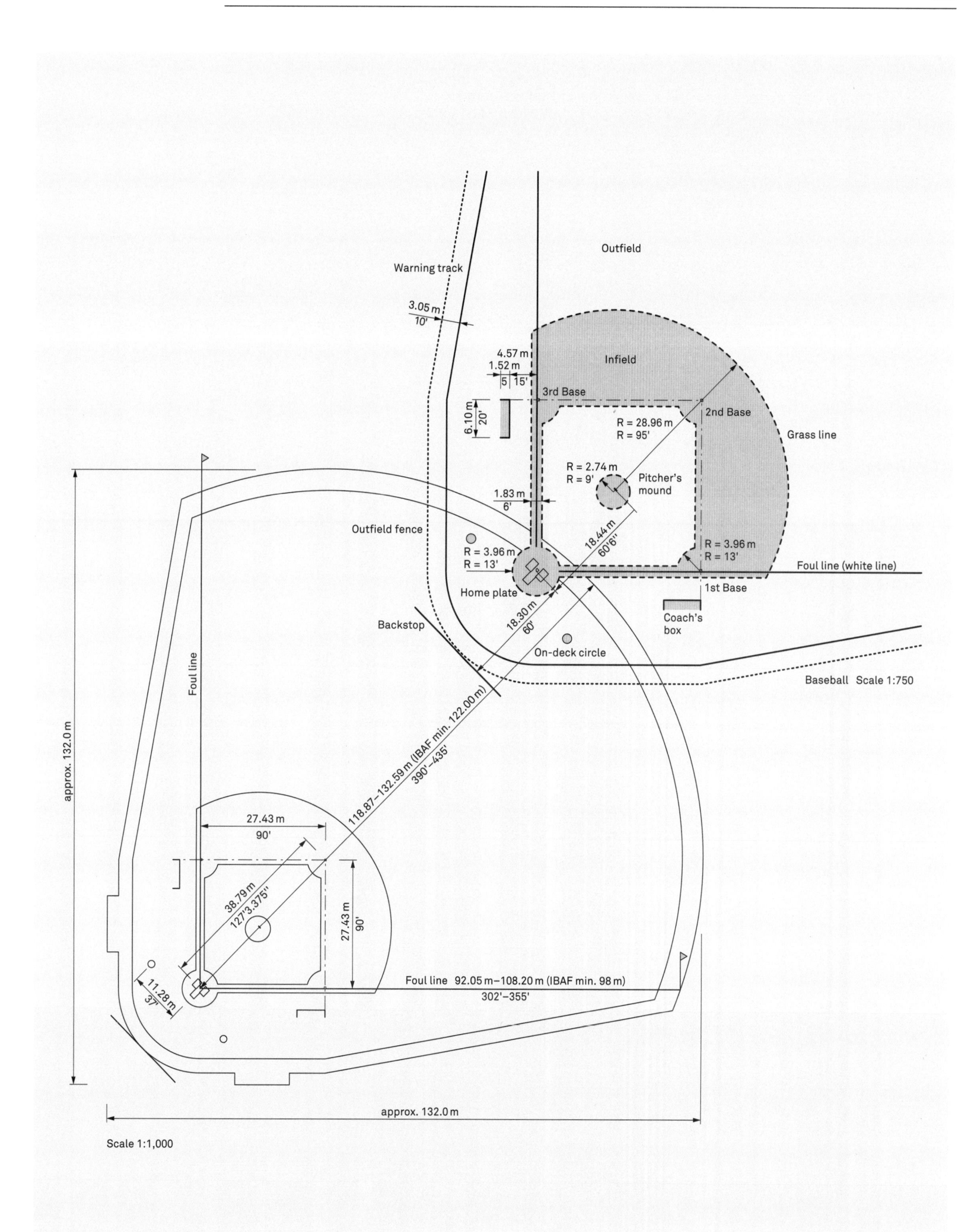
Outfield
Warning track
3.05 m
10'
4.57 m
1.52 m
5
15'
Infield
3rd Base
2nd Base
6.10 m
20'
R = 28.96 m
R = 95'
Grass line
R = 2.74 m
R = 9'
Pitcher's mound
1.83 m
6'
Outfield fence
18.44 m
60'6"
R = 3.96 m
R = 13'
R = 3.96 m
R = 13'
Foul line (white line)
Home plate
1st Base
Coach's box
Backstop
18.30 m
60'
On-deck circle
Baseball Scale 1:750
Foul line
approx. 132.0 m
118.87–132.59 m (IBAF min. 122.00 m)
390'–435'
27.43 m
90'
38.79 m
127'3.375"
27.43 m
90'
11.28 m
37'
Foul line 92.05 m–108.20 m (IBAF min. 98 m)
302'–355'
approx. 132.0 m
Scale 1:1,000

Figure 4.4.7 Baseball

Basketball

Basketball is predominantly played indoors, and that is solely the case for competitions. Outdoors, basketball is primarily a recreational sport or part of physical education at school. Streetball is a variant of basketball that is typically played outside. The game has fewer codified rules and the court dimensions are more flexible. Since it is played with only one basket, the dimensions of the court are also smaller.

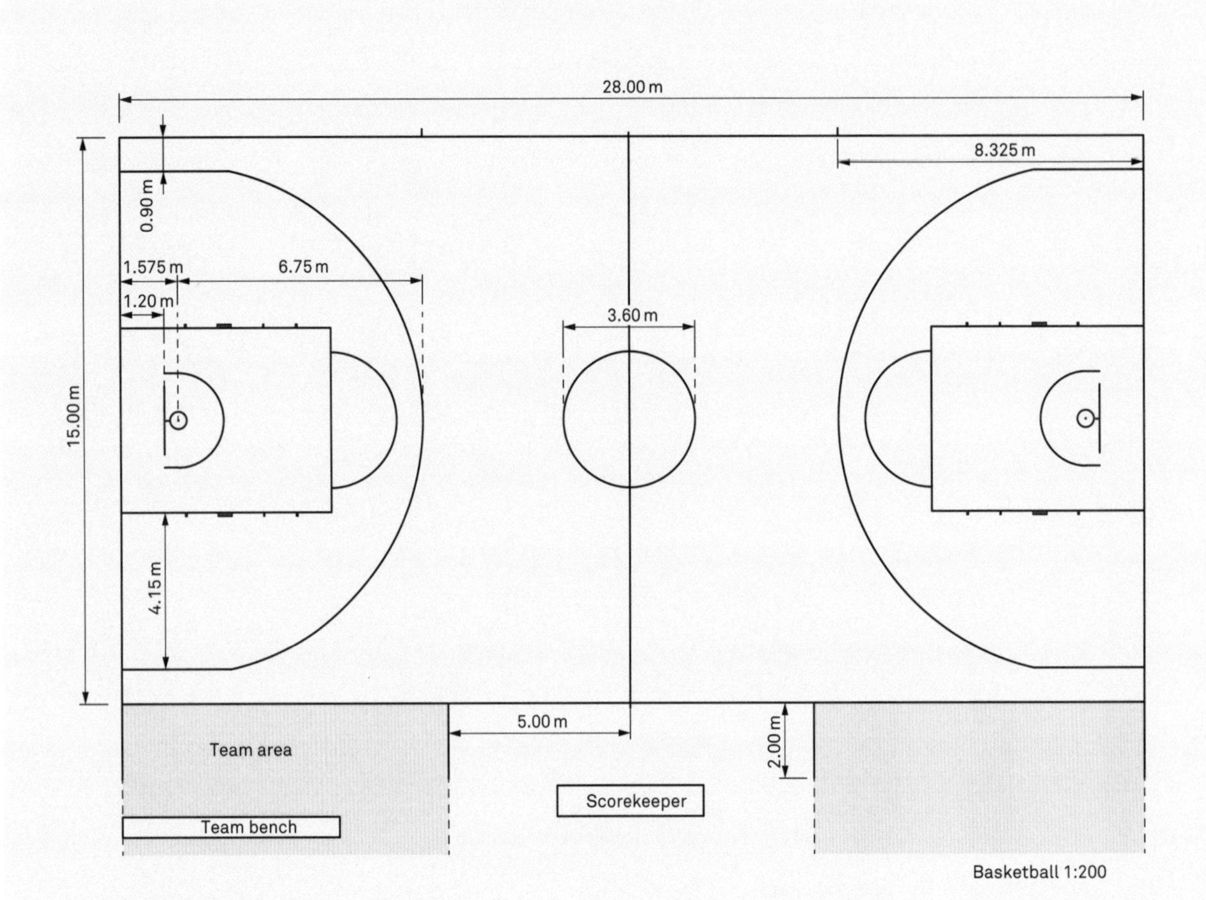

Figure 4.4.8 Basketball and Streetball

Course type	Playing court	Safety zone		Overall	Lines	Basket	Surface
		Side	End		Width/Color		
Basketball	28 × 15 m	2 m	2 m	32 × 19 m	–	Ø 0.45 m H 3.05 m	Synthetic
Streetball (Half-court)	10 × 10 m 13 × 13 m 15 × 15 m	≥ 1 m	≥ 1 m	12 × 12 m 15 × 15 m 17 × 17 m	–	Ø 0.45 m H 3.05 m	Asphalt, concrete, polyurethane, (unit pavers)

Table 4.4.5 Basketball and Streetball

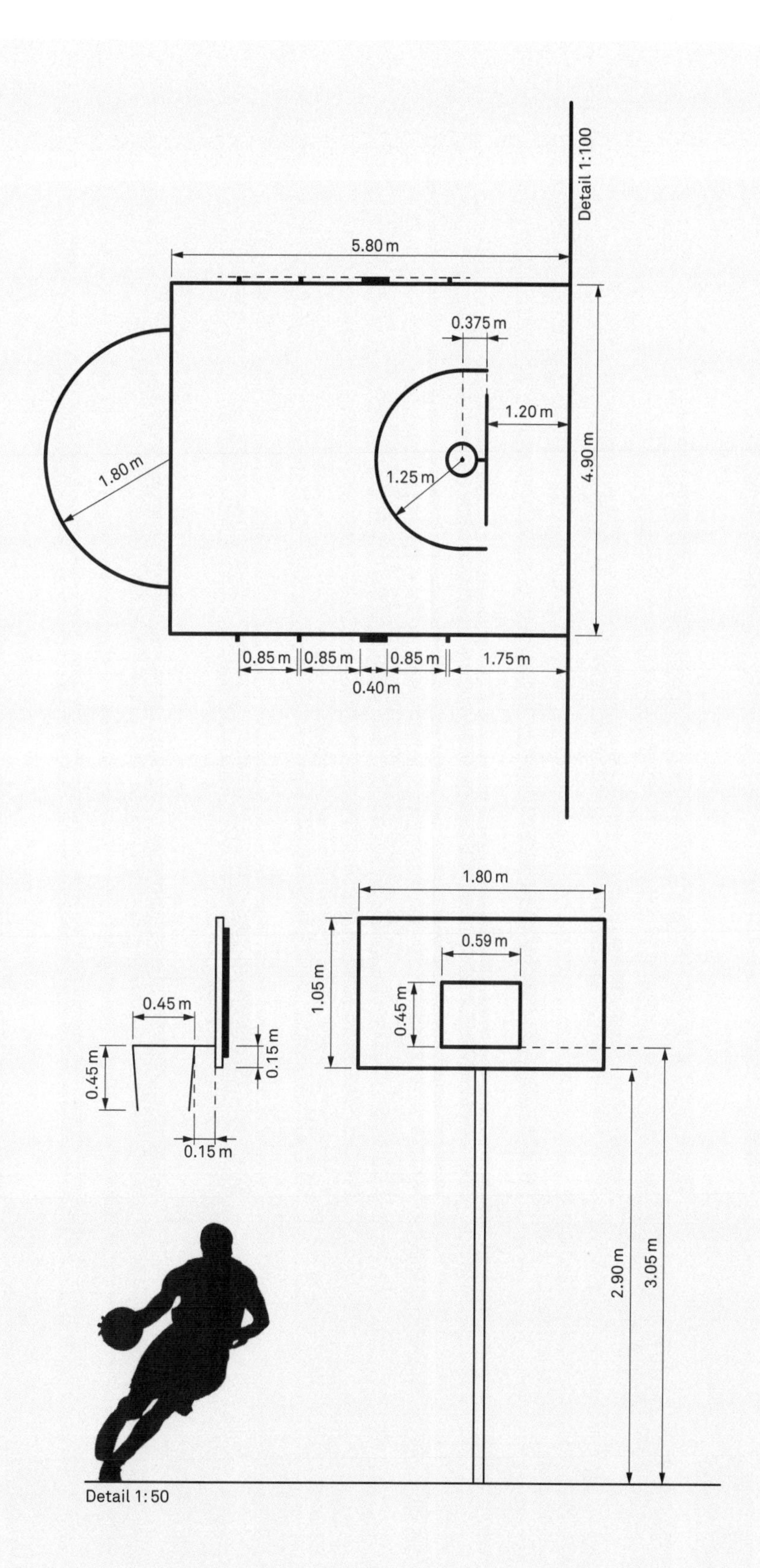

Soccer (Association Football)

Sport	Playing field	Safety zone		Overall	Line	Goal	Surface
		Side	End		Width/Color	Width/Height	
Competition (FIFA)	90–120 m × 45–90 m	3 m	3 m	96–126 × 51–96 m	12 cm/White	7.32 m/2.44 m	Grass Artificial turf*
International competition (FIFA)	100–110 m × 64–75 m	3 m	3 m	106–116 × 70–81 m		7.32 m/2.44 m	Grass Artificial turf*
Leisure sport/ standard for surrounding 400 m track	105 × 68(–70) m	1 m	2 m	109 × 70 (–72) m		7.32 m/2.44 m	Grass Artificial turf Polyurethane Sand/clay mixture
Compact sports field	30–60 m × 15–30 m	3 m	3 m	61 × 41 m		5.00 m/2.00 m	Grass Artificial turf Polyurethane Sand/clay mixture
Mini playing field (recreation)	20 × 13 m	Boundary line is formed by a tape; circulation space should be provided around the entire perimeter		20 × 13 m	–		Artificial turf with rubber granulate infill
Kickabout area	No specifications	–	–	–	–	Depends on playing field size	Grass Artificial turf Polyurethane Sand/clay mixture Sand

Table 4.4.6 Soccer

* in accordance with the FIFA quality requirements

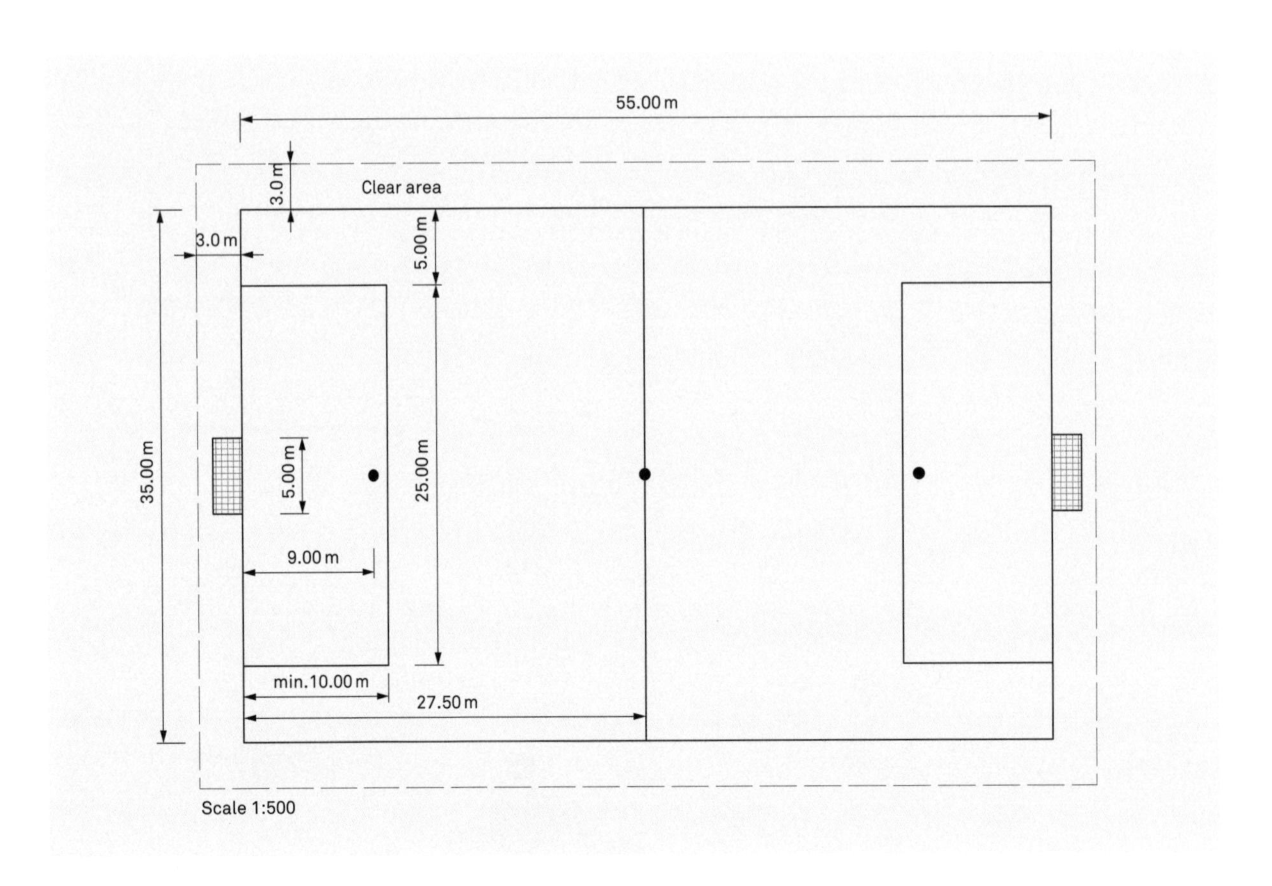

Figure 4.4.9 Soccer (compact sports field)

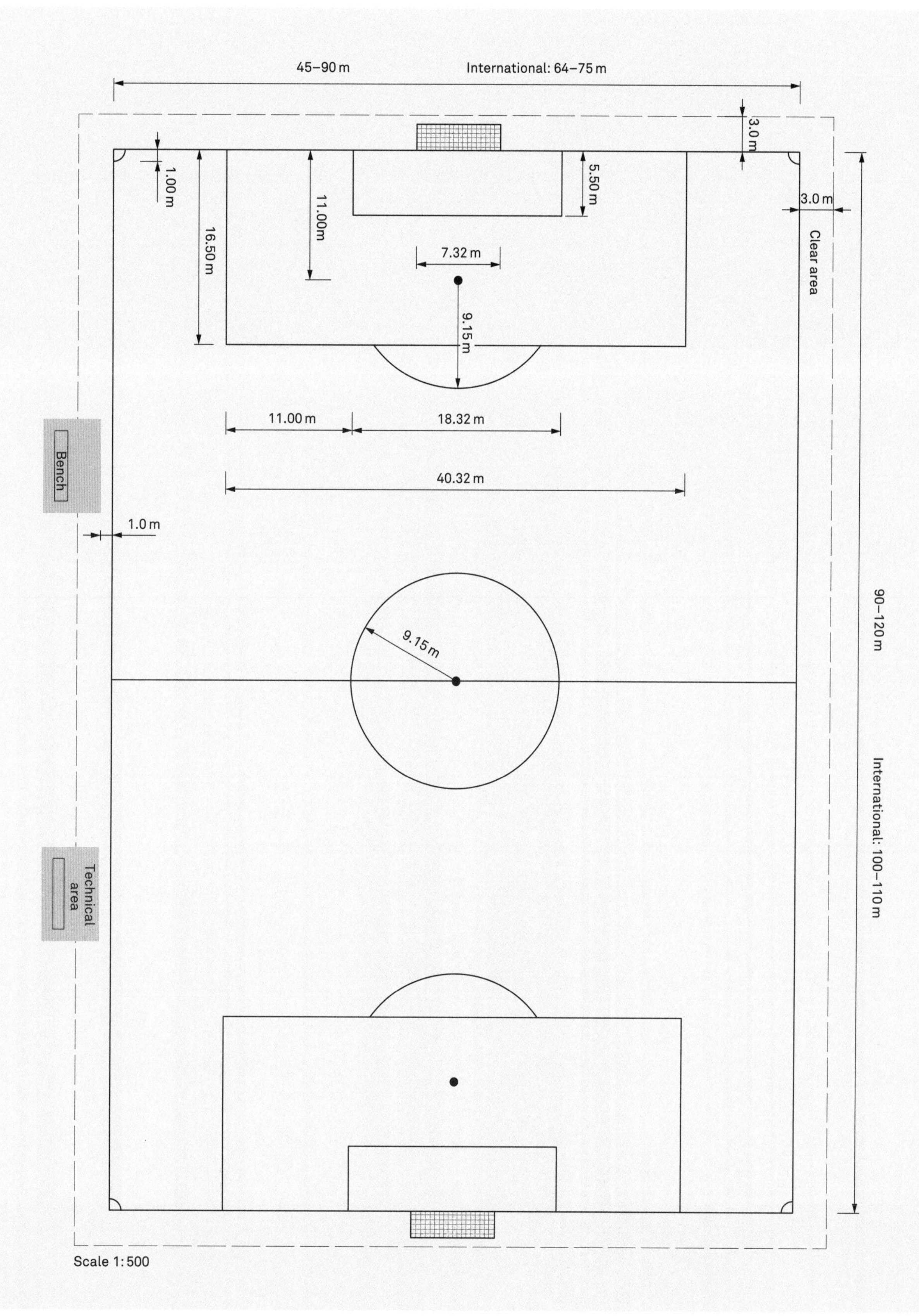

Figure 4.4.10 Soccer (international competition (FIFA))

Handball (Team Handball)

Handball is played competitively only indoors. Playing fields can, however, also be provided outdoors for school physical education, training purposes, and/or recreation.

Course type	Playing field	Safety zone		Overall	Lines	Goal	Surface
		Side	End		Width/Color	Width × Height	
Competition (IHF)	40 × 20 m	≥1 m	≥2 m	44 × 22 m	5 cm/White	3 × 2 m	Plastic, artificial turf without rubber granulate infill

Table 4.4.7 Handball

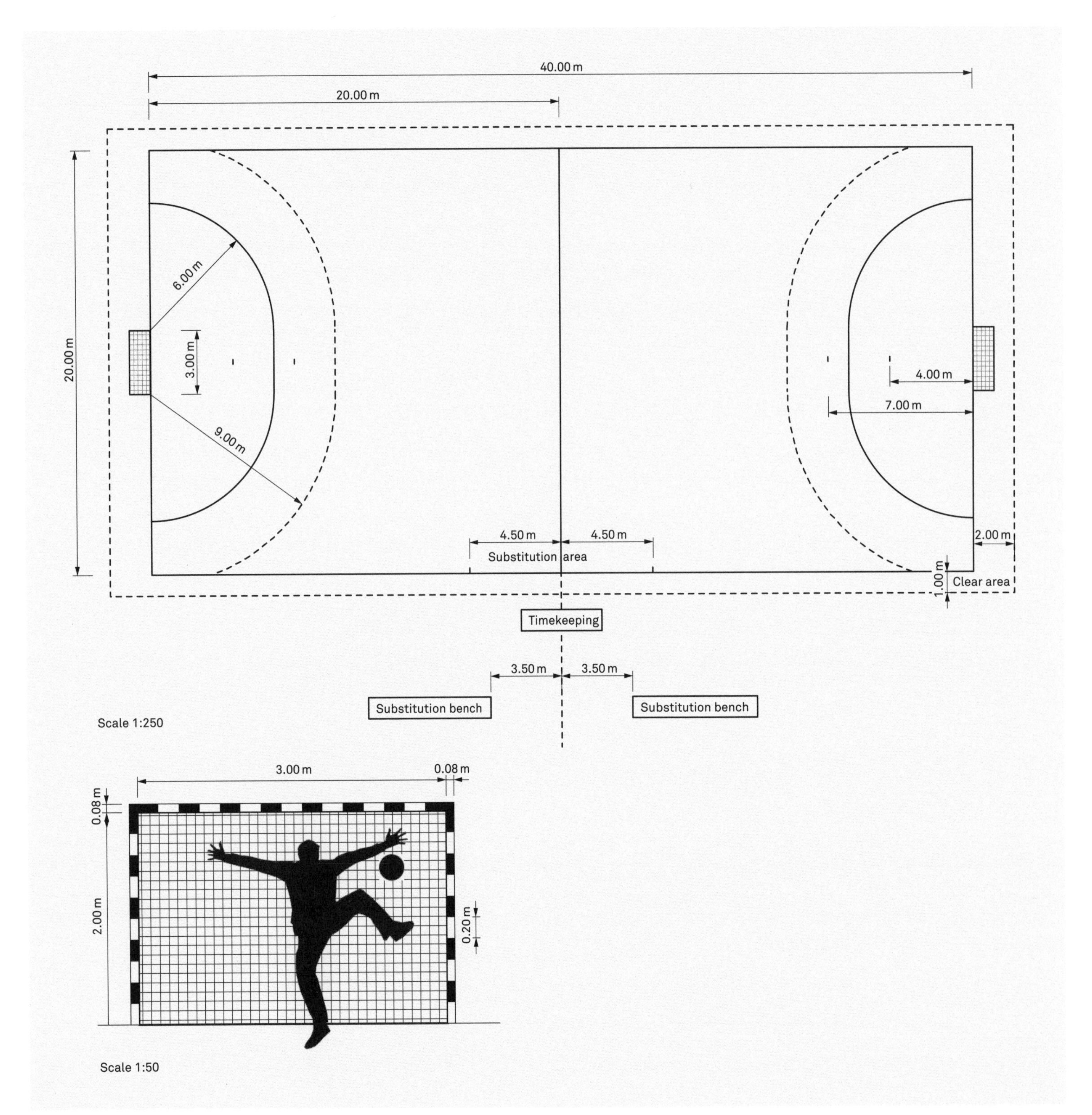

Figure 4.4.11 Handball

Hockey

Course type	Playing field	Safety zone		Overall	Lines	Goal	Surface
		Side	End		Width/Color	Width × Height (Inside measurements)	
Field hockey	91.4 m × 55 m	2 m	4 m	99.4 × 59 m	7.5 cm / Yellow or white	3.66 × 2.14 m	Grass, artificial turf
Inline hockey (roller hockey)	60–40 m × 30–20 m (2:1 ratio)	– none – Perimeter enclosure (boards): 1.2–1.22 m high, with safety glass above to height of 1.6–2 m		–	4–10 cm	1.7 × 1.05 (maximum 1.83 × 1.22) m	Concrete, asphalt
Ice hockey (IIHF)	60–61 m × 29–30 m	– none – Perimeter enclosure (boards): 0.8–1.22 m		–	30 cm lines in Blue (blue line) and red (center line), 5 cm line in blue (center ice spot and circle) and red (other)	1.83 × 1.22 m	Ice

Table 4.4.8 Hockey

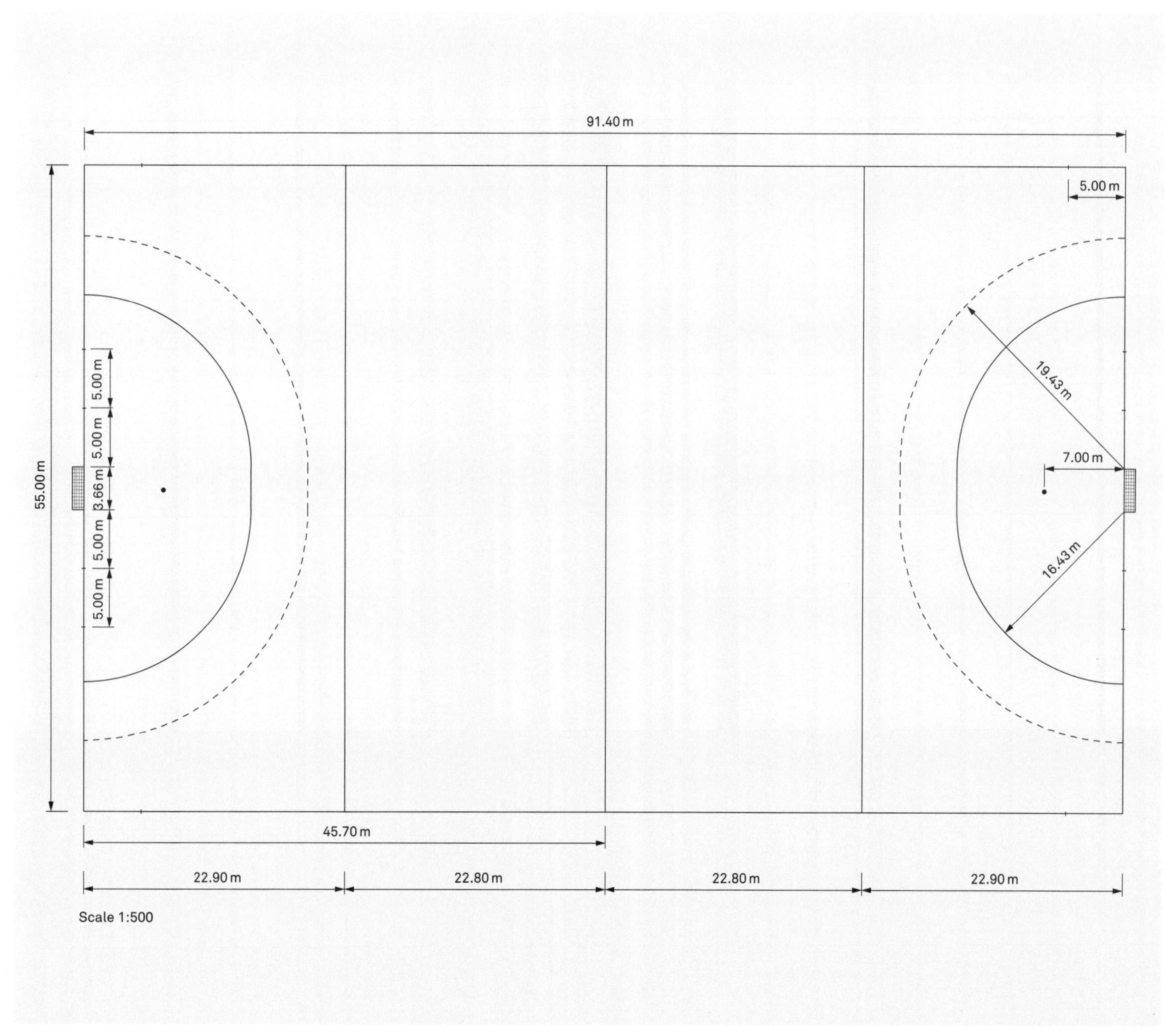

Figure 4.4.12 Field hockey

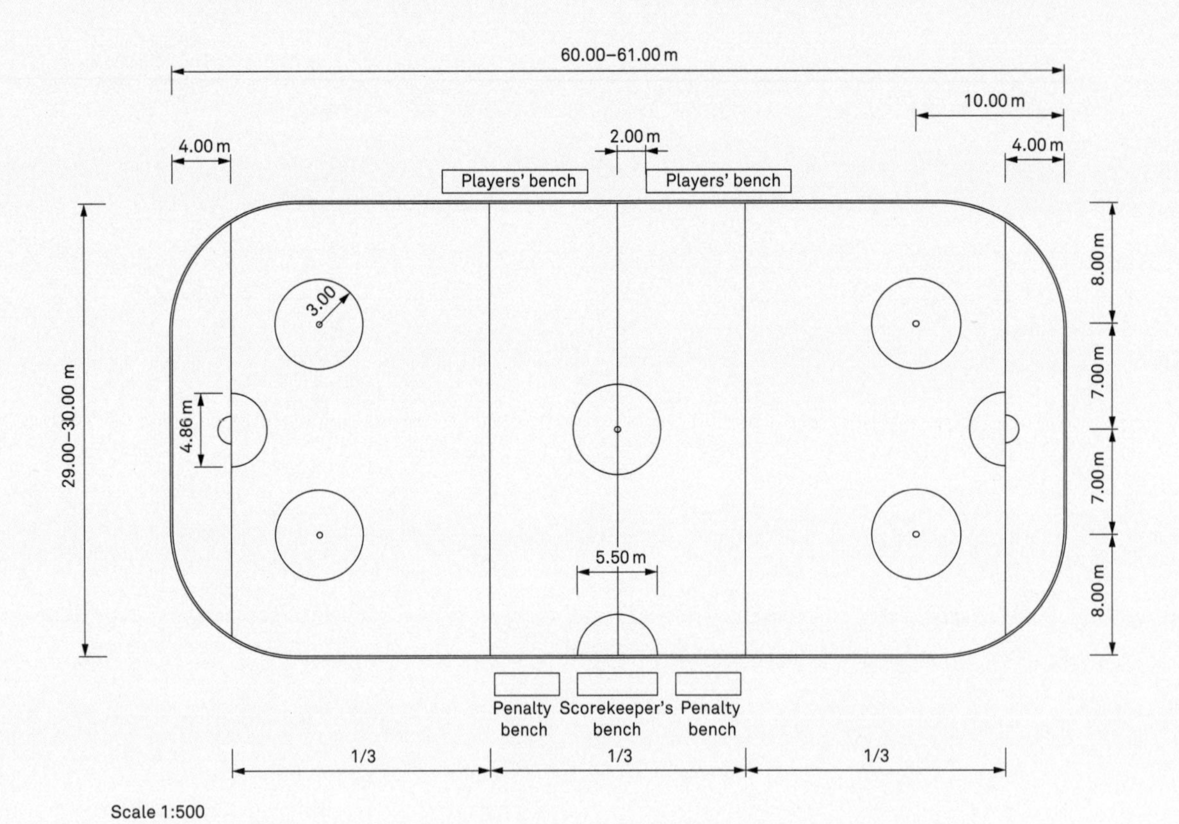

Neutral zone

End zone

Red line 0.3 m width

Blue line 0.3 m width

Referee crease

Scale 1:250

Figure 4.4.13 Ice hockey

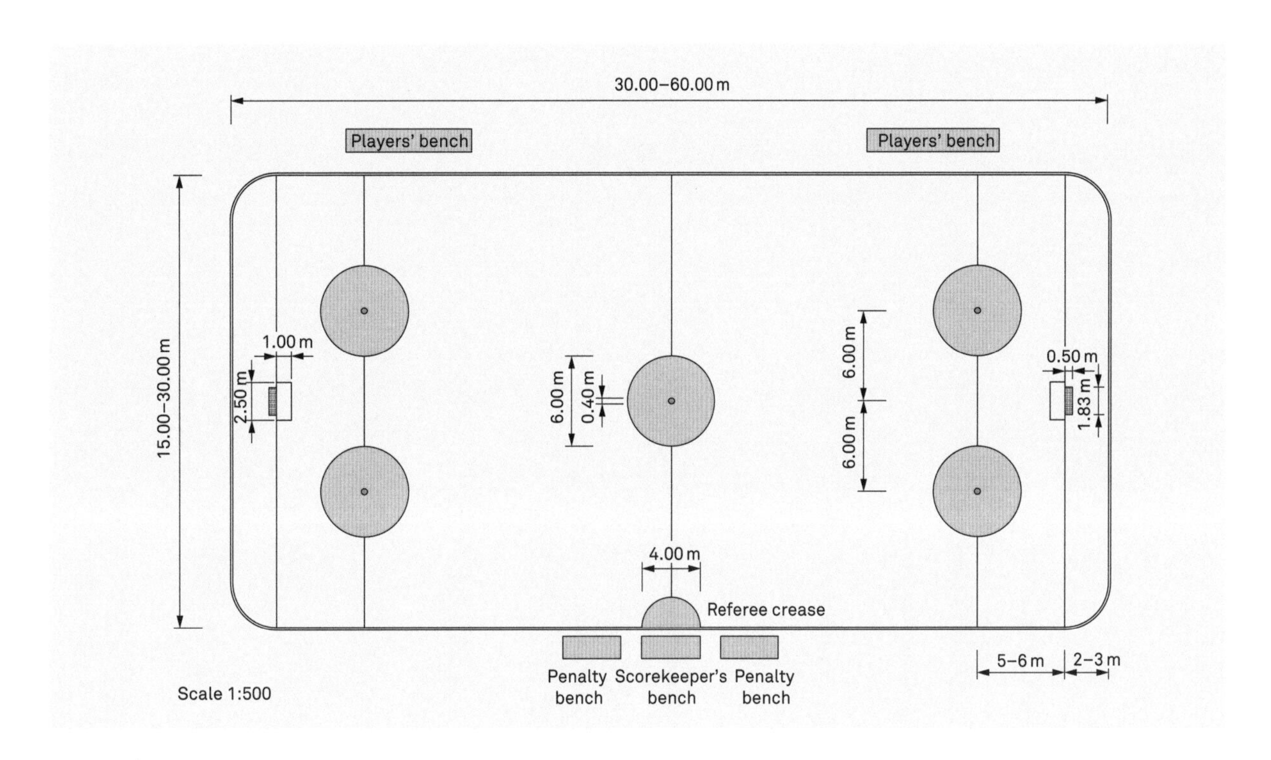

Figure 4.4.14 Inline hockey

Netball

Table 4.4.9 Netball

Course type	Playing court	Safety clearance		Overall	Lines	Basket/Goal	Surface
		Side	End		Width	Width/Height	
Competition/Leisure sport Feldkorbball*	25 × 50 m (per DIN 18035-1 25 × 60 m)	1 m	2 m	27 × 54 m	3–5 cm	Ø 0.55/2.50	Grass
Competition Netball**	15.25 × 30.5 m	3.05 m	3.05 m	21.35 × 36.60 m	max. 5 cm	Ø 0.38/3.05	Hard court (such as asphalt, concrete)
Leisure sport Netball**		1 m	2 m	18.25 × 34.5 m			

* Standard dimensions of the German state leagues; playing field and playing field dimensions can vary in other countries
** Ball sport derived from basketball and played worldwide; most popular in Australia, Great Britain, and New Zealand

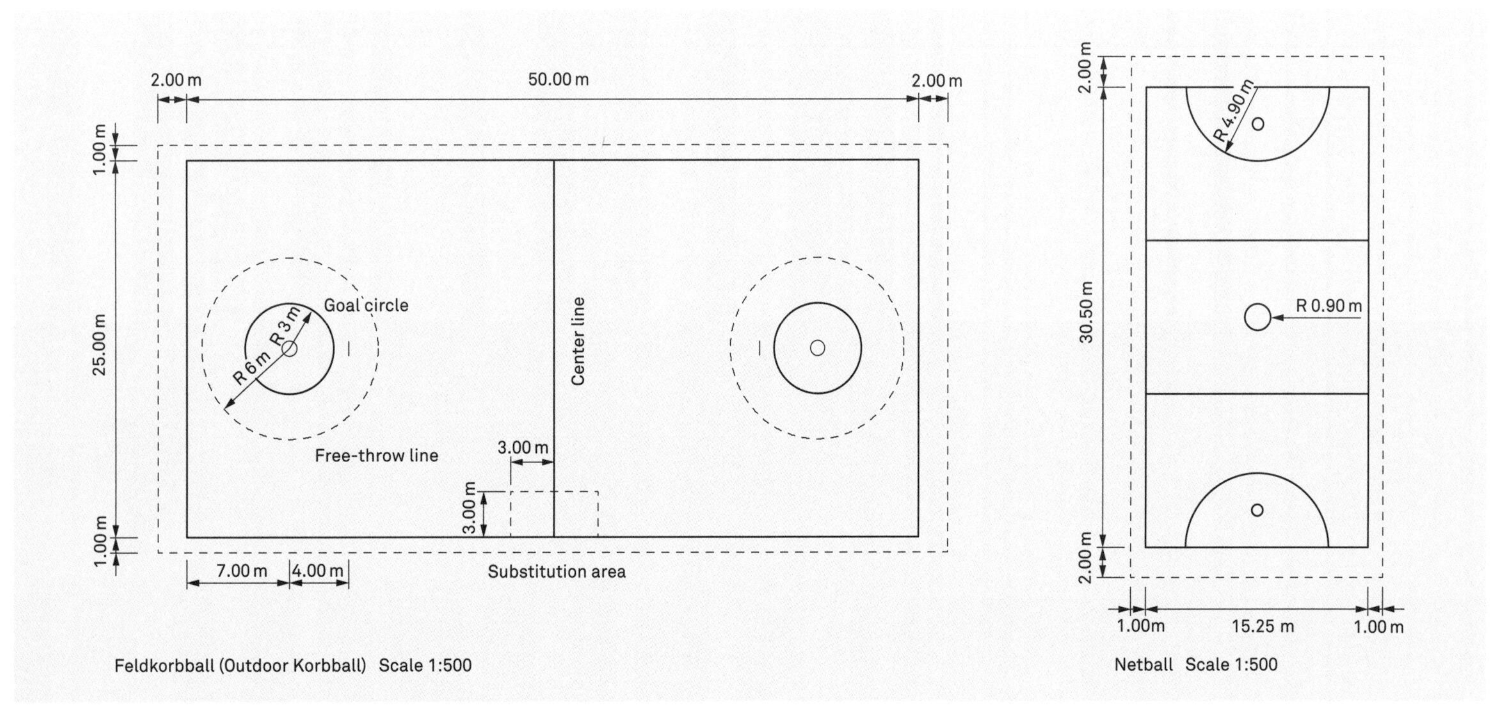

Abb. 4.4.15 Feldkorbball (standard playing field of the German state leagues), Netball

Course type	Playing field	Safety zone		Overall	Goal	Surface
		Side	End		Width/Height	
Rugby union	Max. 69 × 100 m	2 m	12–22 m (depth of the in-goal areas)	74 × 144 m	5.6 m / 3 m	Grass as well as clay, artificial turf, or snow (sanctioned by IRB)

Table 4.4.10 Rubgy

Rugby

The term rugby encompasses a group of different rugby sports. The most common versions of rugby are rugby union and rugby league.

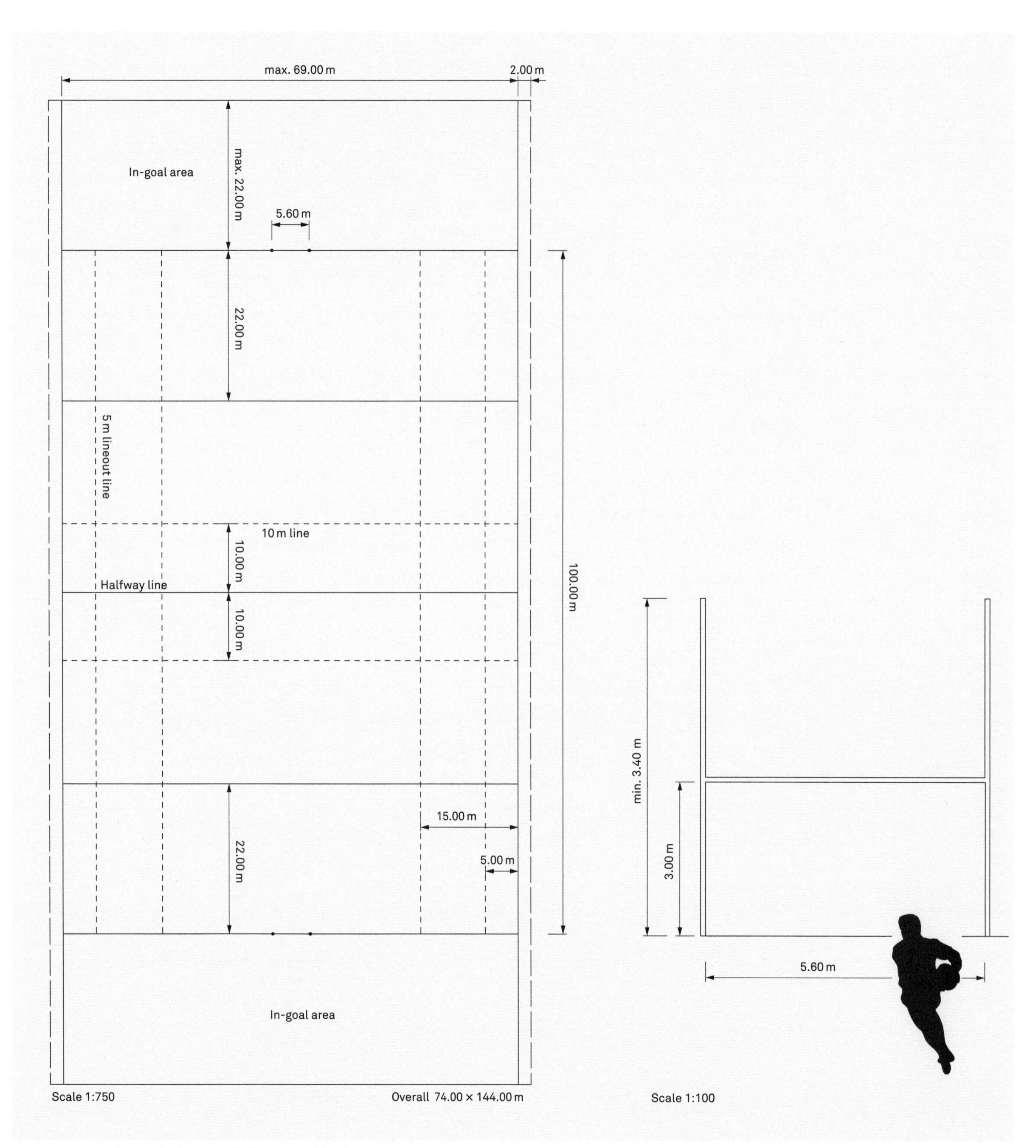

Figure 4.4.16 Rugby field (left) and detail of rugby goal (right)

Racquet/Net Sports

Badminton

Badminton is played competitively only indoors. Playing fields can, however, also be provided outdoors for school physical education, training purposes, and/or recreation.

Course type	Playing court	Safety clearance		Overall	Lines	Net height	Surface
		Side	End		Width/Color	Women/Men	
Badminton	6.1 × 13.4 m	0.3 m	1.3 m	Single court: 6.7 × 16 m Paired courts: 14 × 16 m	4 cm/White, yellow, or green (on combination courts)	1.52 m	Plastic (concrete, asphalt)

Table 4.4.11 Badminton

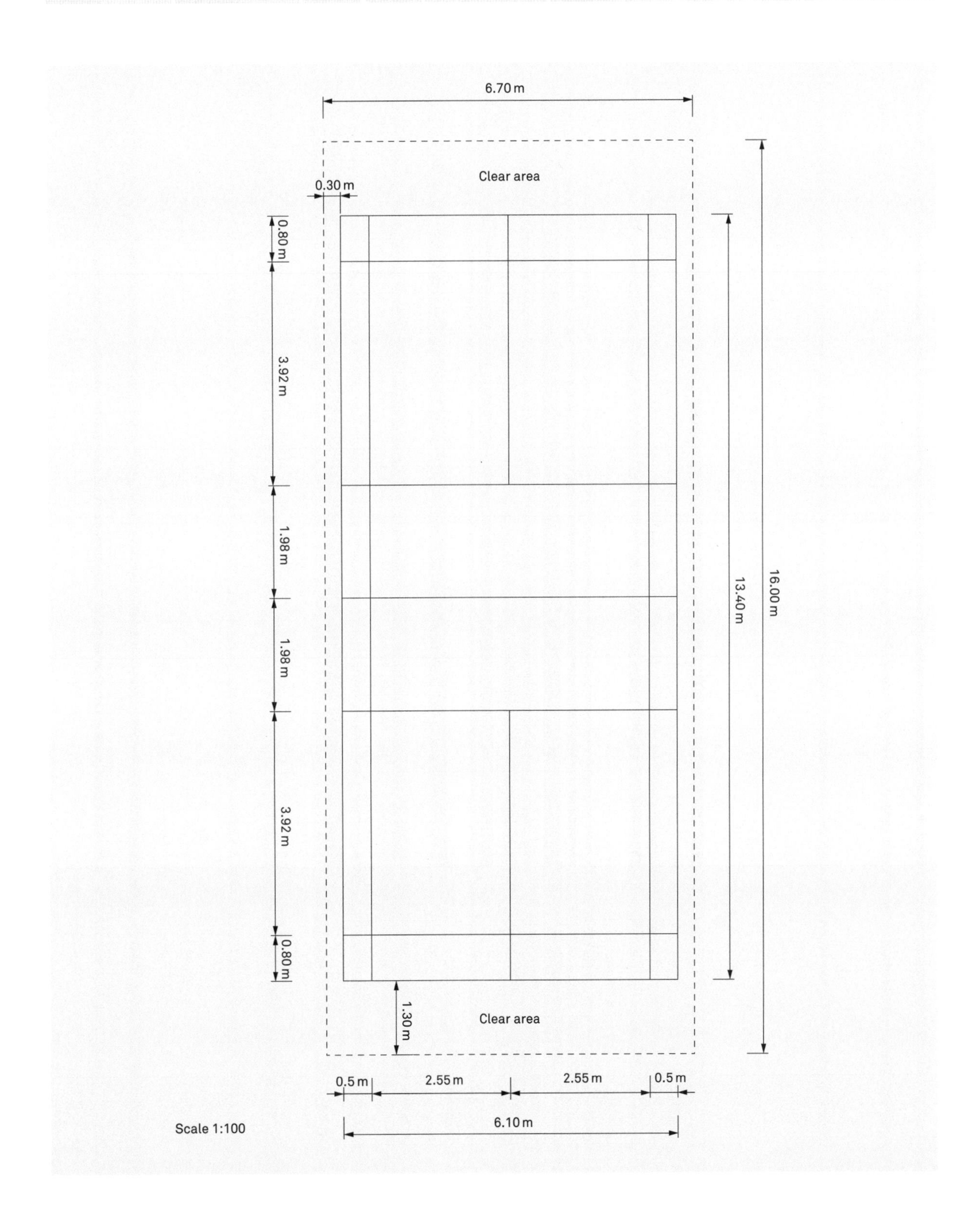

Figure 4.4.17 Badminton

Tennis

Table 4.4.12 Tennis

Course type	Playing court	Safety clearance		Overall	Lines	Net height	Surface
		Side	End		Width/Color	Women/Men	
Tennis	10.97 × 23.77 m	3.65 m	6.4–8 m	Single court: 18.27 × 36.57–39.77 m Paired courts: 33.82 × 36.57–39.77 m	5 cm/White	0.91 m	Grass, polyurethane, clay, artificial turf

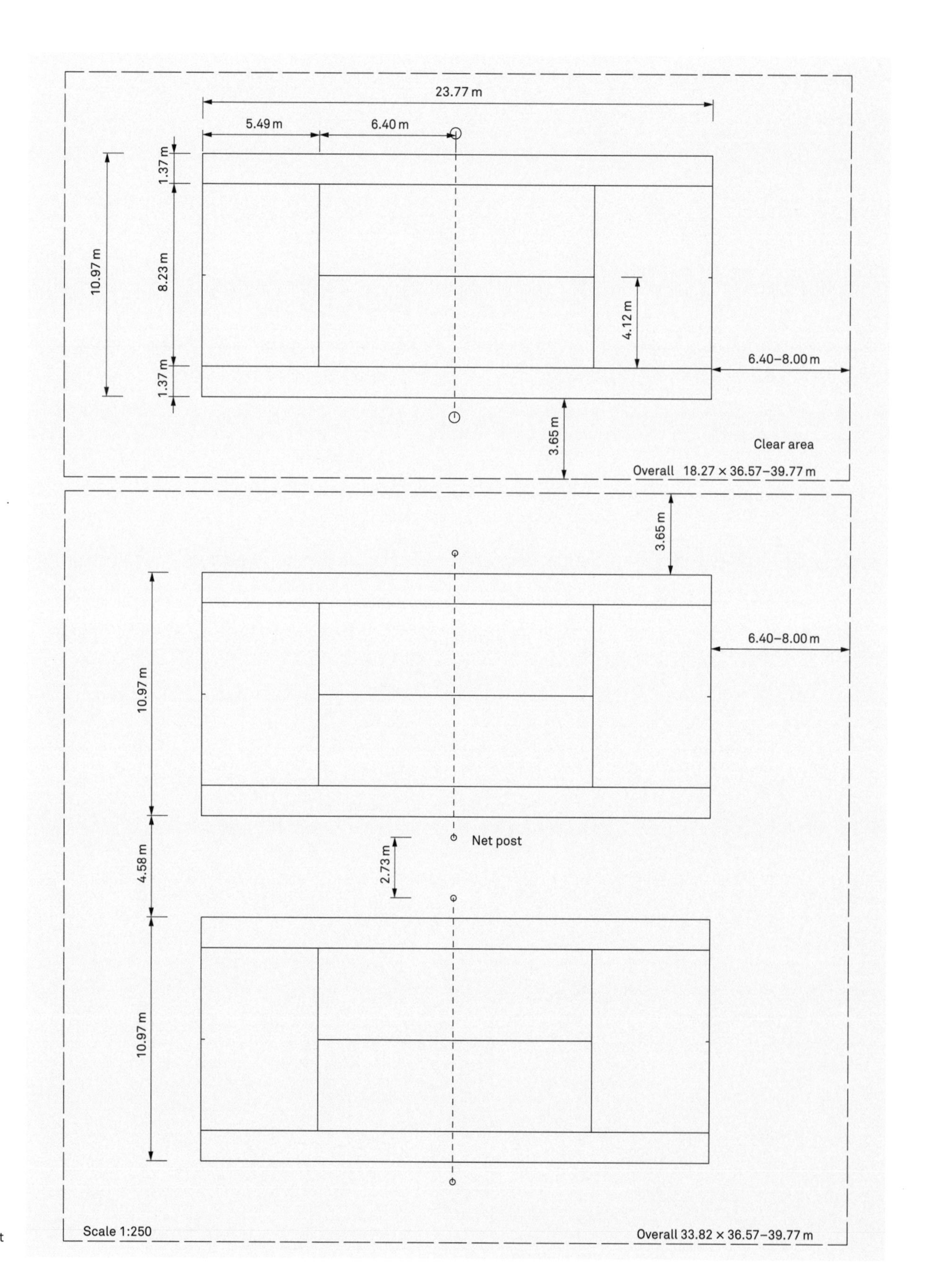

Figure 4.4.18 Tennis: single court and paired courts

Table Tennis

Table tennis is played competitively only indoors. Therefore game tables are only used outdoors for recreational purposes or in schoolyards. So there is also no need for the play area to fulfill the conditions for competitions (international: 14 × 7 m; regional: e.g., 10 × 5 m). There are no set values for required safety clearances.

Table 4.4.13 Table tennis

Course type	Playing surface	Safety clearance		Overall	Net height	Surface
	L × W × H	Side	End		Women/Men	
Leisure sport	2.74 × 1.52 × 0.76 m (table tennis table)	2 m	3 m	5.52 × 6.8 m (two tables: 9.04 × 8.74 m)	15.25 cm	Asphalt, stone paving (natural soil)

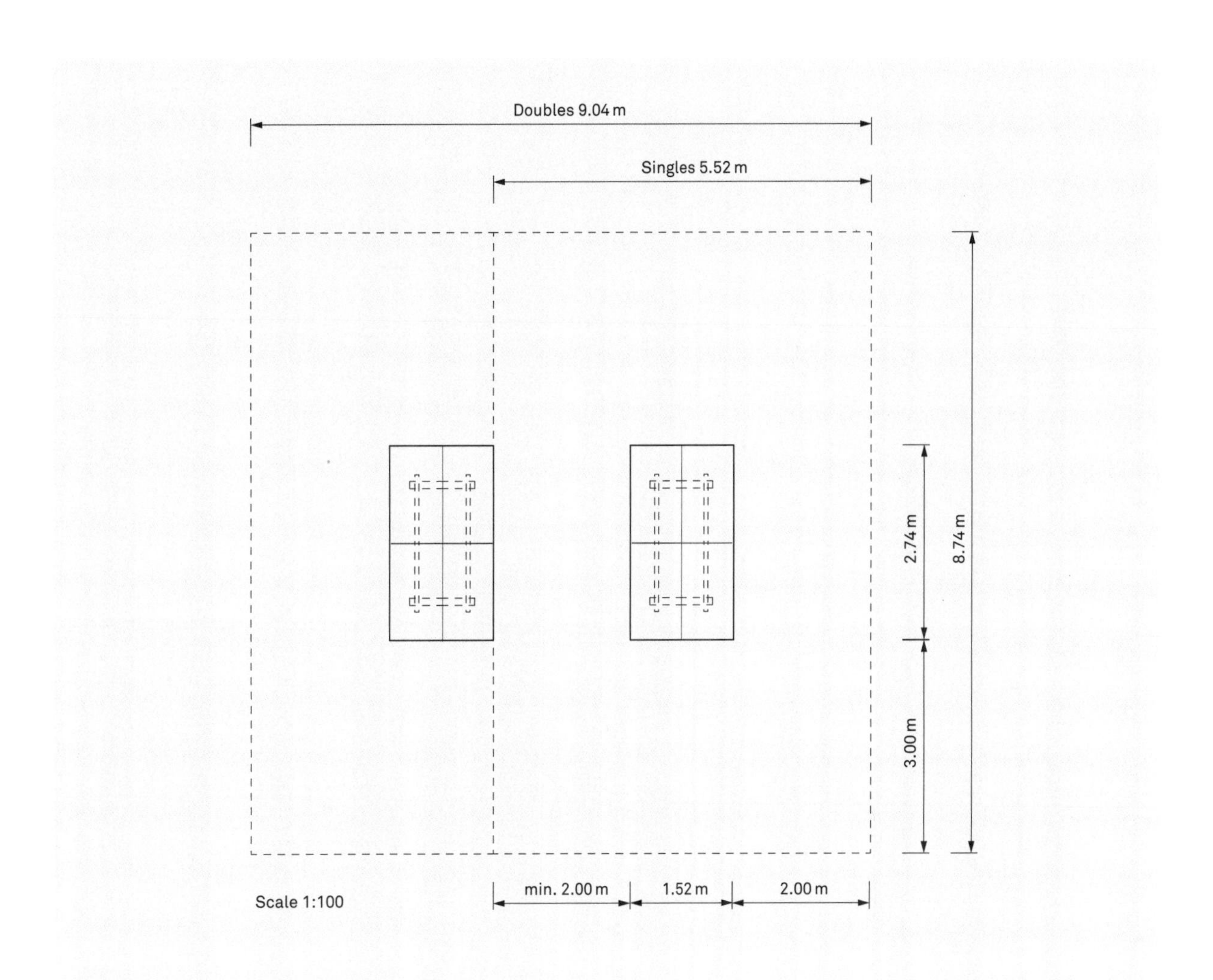

Figure 4.4.19 Table tennis

Fistball

Table 4.4.14 Fistball

Course type	Playing court	Safety clearance		Overall	Lines	Tape/net height	Surface
		Side	End		Width/Color	Women/Men	
Competition/leisure sport	50 × 20	6m	8m	66 × 32m	5cm/free	1.9m/2m	Grass
"Small court" fistball	18 × 9m	–	–	–	5cm/free	1.6m/2m	Grass

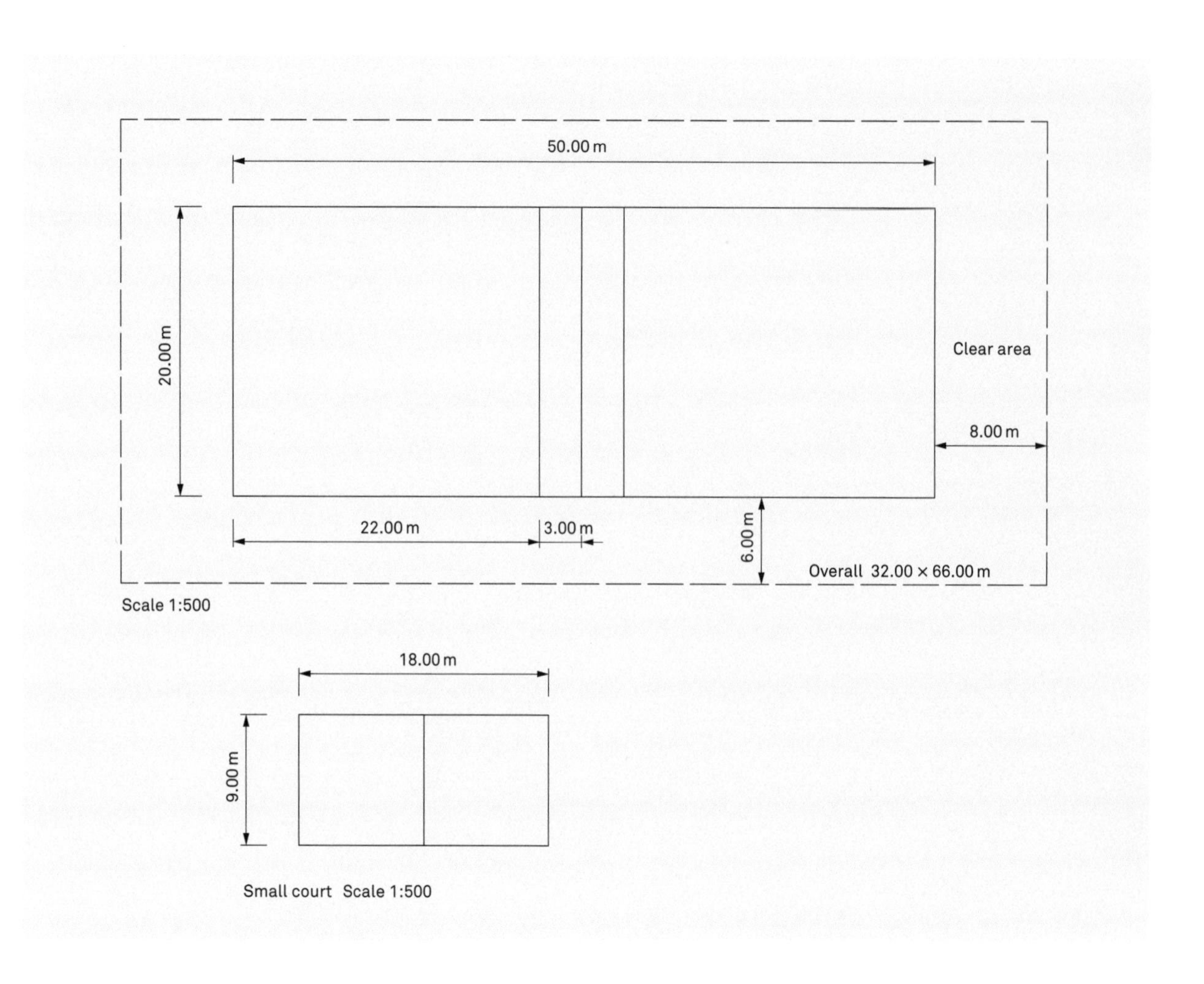

Figure 4.4.20 Fistball

Tennikoit (Ring Tennis)

Table 4.4.15 Tennikoit

Course type	Playing court	Safety clearance		Overall	Net height	Surface
		Side	End		Women/Men	
International	5.5 × 12.2 m	2 m	2 m	9.5 × 16.2 m	1.55 m	–

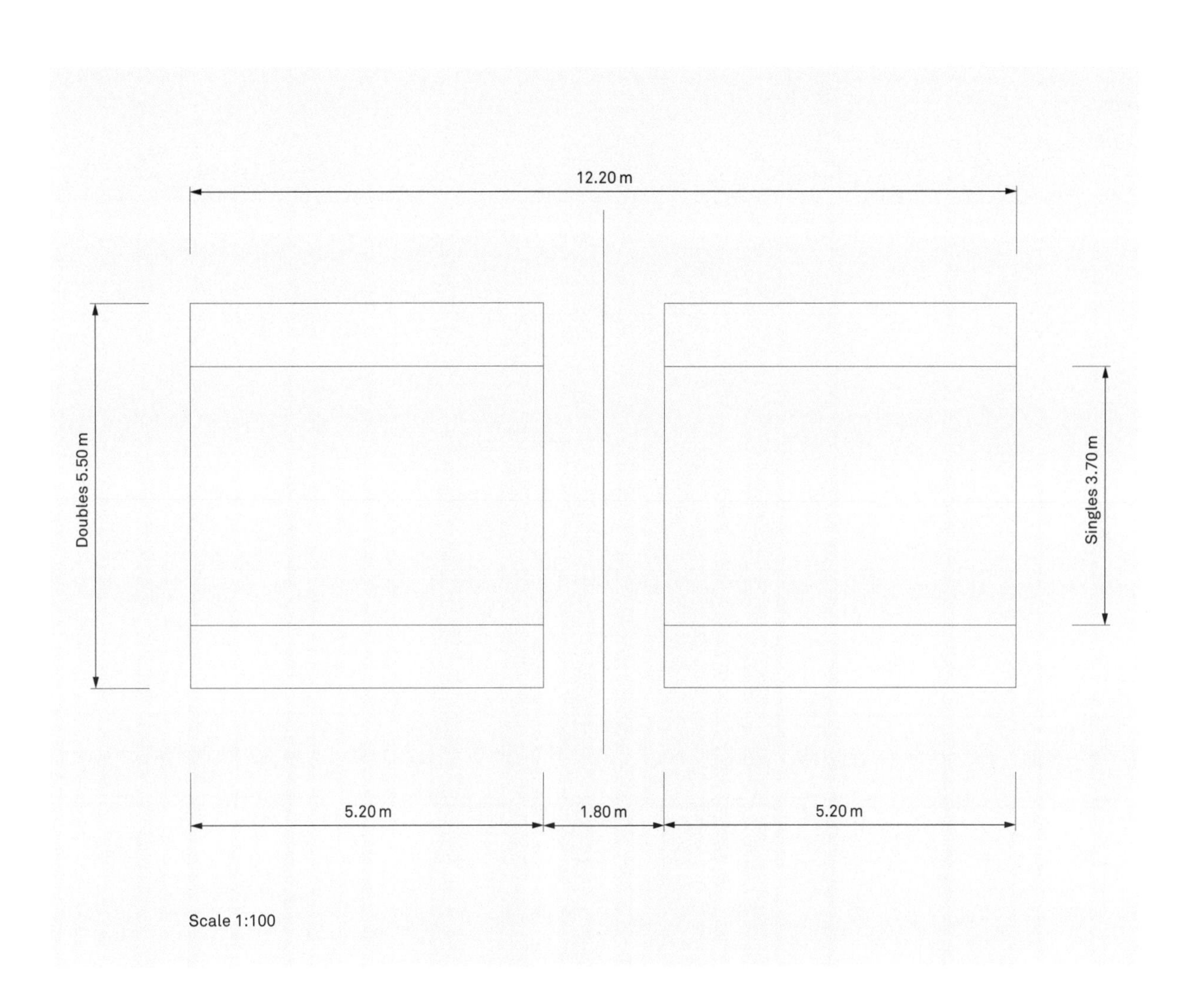

Figure 4.4.21 Tennikoit

Volleyball

Volleyball is played competitively only indoors. Courts can, however, also be provided outdoors for school physical education, training purposes, and/or recreation.

Course type	Playing court	Safety clearance		Overall	Net height	Net length	Surface
		Side	End		Women/Men		
Competition	18 × 9 m	≥5 m	≥8 m	34 × 19 m	2.24 m/2.43 m	9.5–10 m	Synthetic
Leisure sport	18 × 9 m	≥3 m	≥3 m	24 × 15 m	2.24 m/2.43 m	9.5–10 m	Synthetic

Table 4.4.16 Volleyball

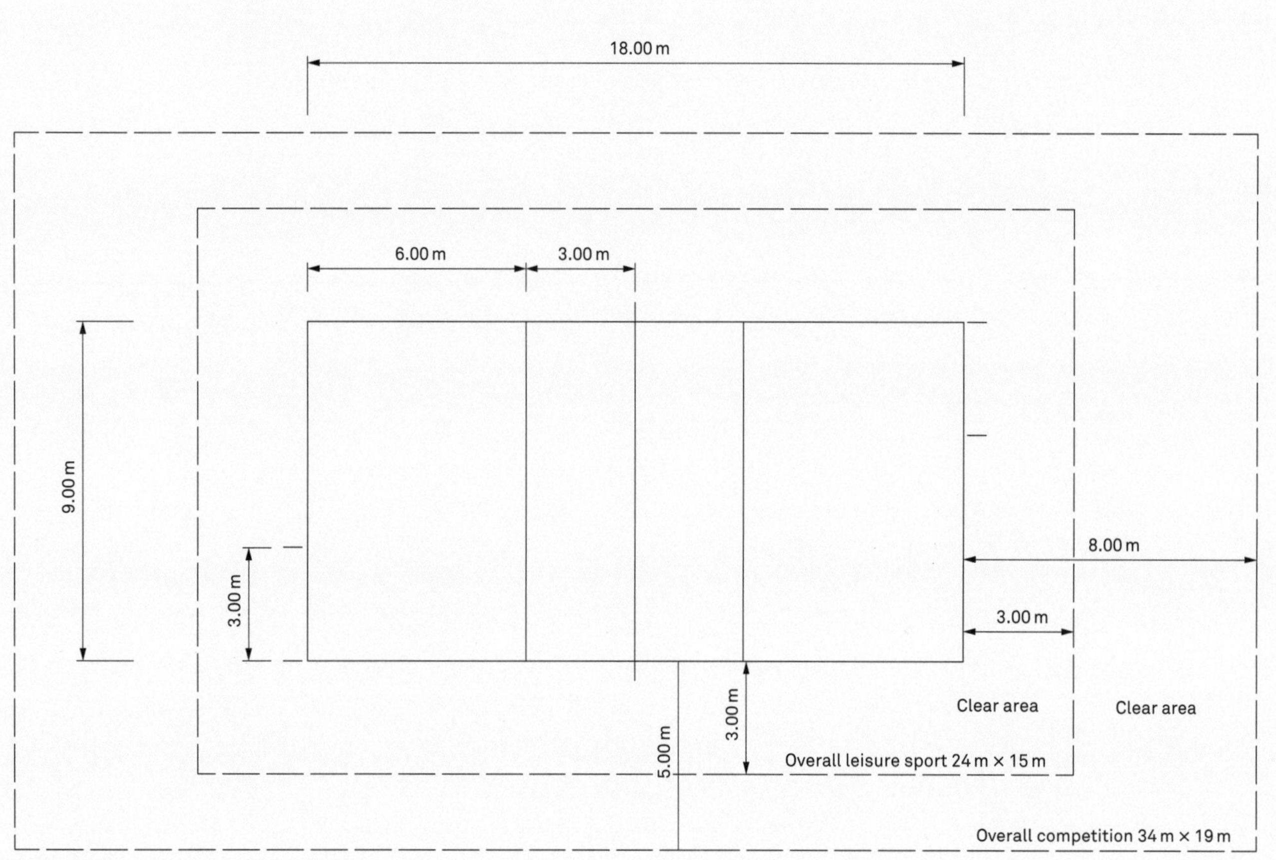

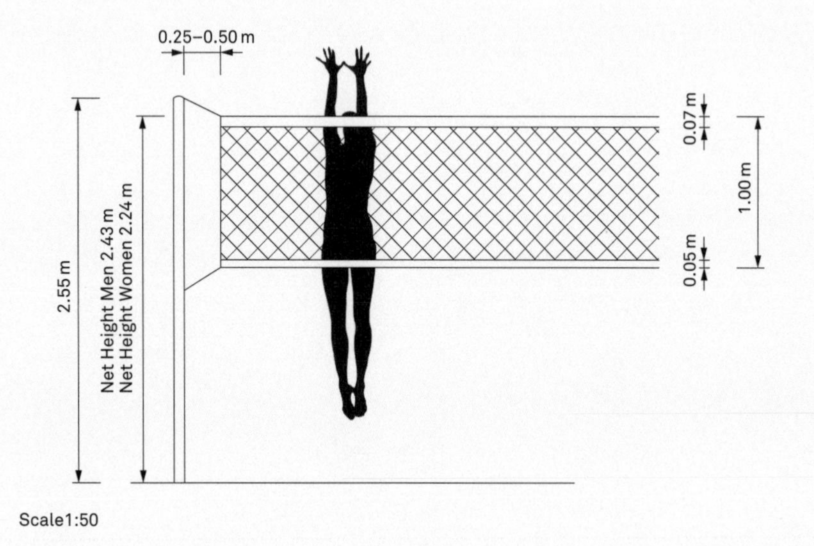

Figure 4.4.22 Volleyball

Beach Sports

The court markings are made of brightly colored tape or ribbons 5 cm wide.

The recommended particle size of the sand is 0.063 to 2 mm (grading from 0.1 to 1.25 mm) with an overall layer thickness of 40 cm – although at least 45 cm is to be provided under the net and at least 35 cm around the perimeter.

If the subsoil is impermeable, drainage must be integrated.

A water connection close to the court is useful for moistening the sand during dry periods and is absolutely necessary for competition facilities.

Course type	Playing court	Safety clearance		Overall	Goal	Net height	Surface
		Side	End		Width × Height		
Beach badminton							
Competition	12 × 5 m (Beachminton: 12.3 × 3.8 m)	1 m	2 m	16 × 7 m		1.55 m	Sand
Leisure sport	12 × 5 m	1 m	2 m	16 × 7 m		1.55 m	Sand
German beach basketball							
Competition	12 m between backboards	–	–	–		3.05 m	Sand*
Leisure sport	15 × 8 m	1 m	–	15 × 10 m		3.05 m	Sand*
Beach handball (sandball)							
Competition	27 × 12 m	3 m	3 m	33 × 18 m	3 m × 2 m		Sand
Leisure sport	27 × 12 m	1.5 m	1 m	29 × 15 m	3 m × 2 m		Sand
Beach paletta (beach ball)	5.5 × 6 m	–	–	5.5 × 6 m		1.85 m	Sand
Beach rugby	30–50 × 20–35 m	...	...	...	...		Sand
Beach soccer							
Competition	35–37 × 26–28 m	2 m	2 m	41–32 m	5.5 m × 2.2 m		Sand
Leisure sport	26–28 m × 35–37 m	1–2 m	1–2 m	27 × 20 m – 39 × 30 m	5 m × 2 m (youth)		Sand
Beach tennis	Singles: 18 × 6 m Doubles: 18 × 9 m	3 m	3 m	24 × 12 m 24 × 15 m		1.5 m	Sand
With paddles	16–20 × 8–9 m					Net: 1.7–1.85 m Sideline width 2.5–5 cm Baseline width up to 10 cm	Sand
With racquets	18 × 6 m (singles) 18 × 9 m (doubles)	–	–	–		1.6 m	Sand
Beach volleyball							
Competition • international	16 × 8 m	5–6 m	5–6 m	26–28 m × 18–20 m		2.24 m Women 2.43 m Men (8.5 m long)	Sand
Leisure sport	16 × 8 m	3 m	3 m	22 × 14 m 22 × 26 m (Doubles)		2.24 m Women 2.43 m Men (8.5 m long)	Sand

* tamped, smoothed, and (if necessary) dampened

Table 4.4.17 Beach sports

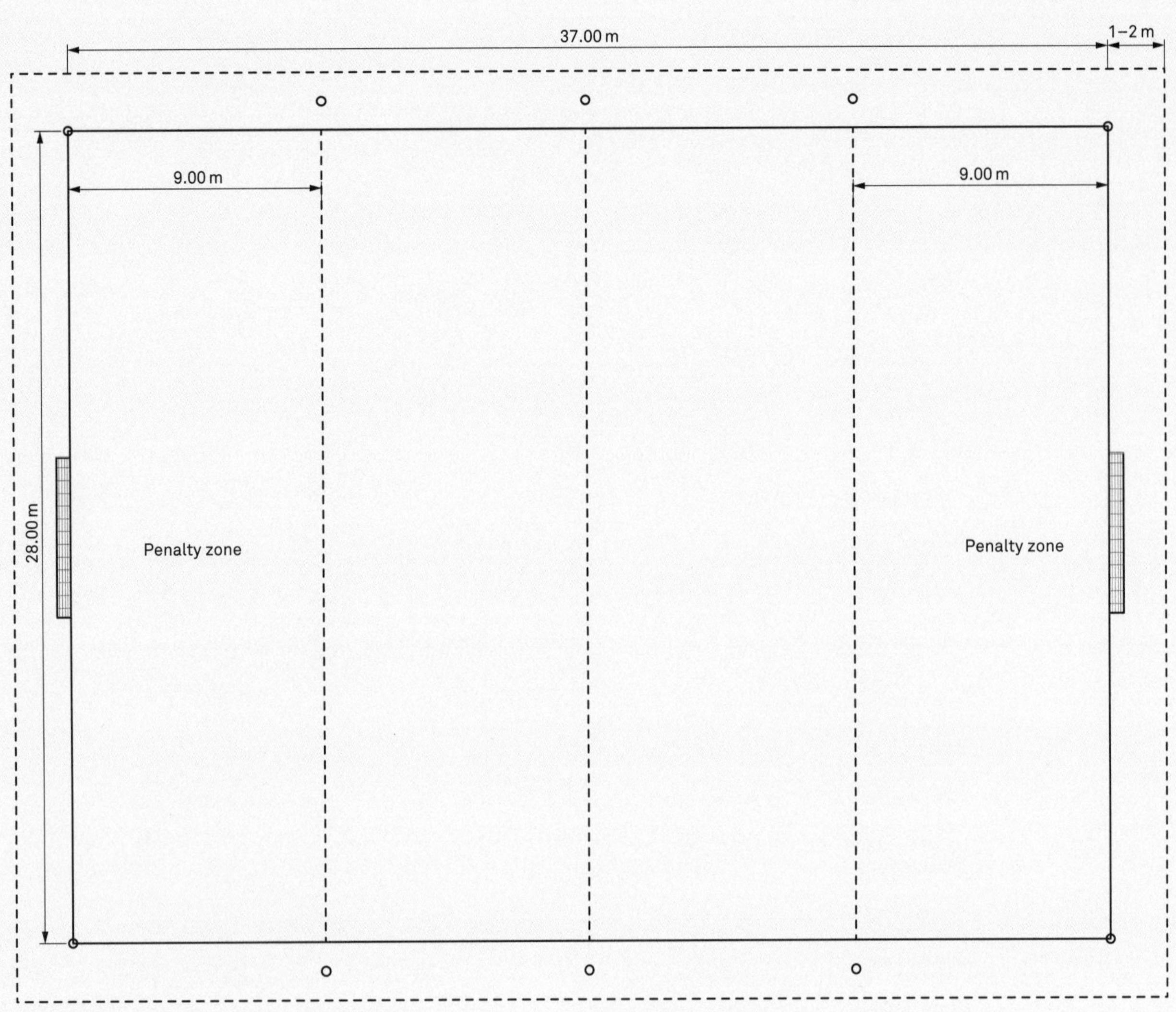

Beachsoccer competition Scale 1:250

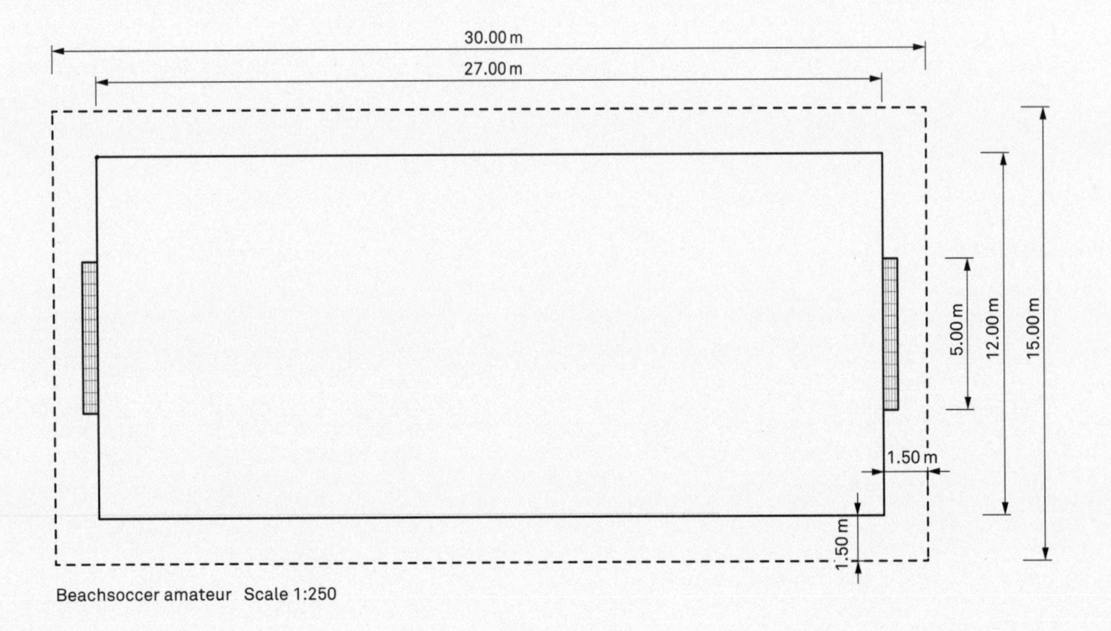

Beachsoccer amateur Scale 1:250

Figure 4.4.23 Beach sports

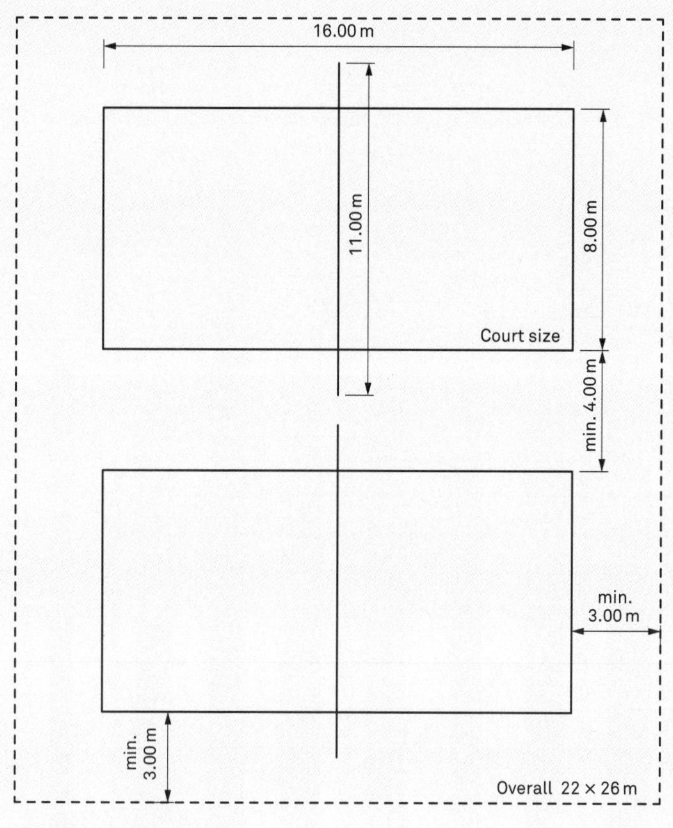

Beachvolleyball doubles
Leisure sports Scale 1:200

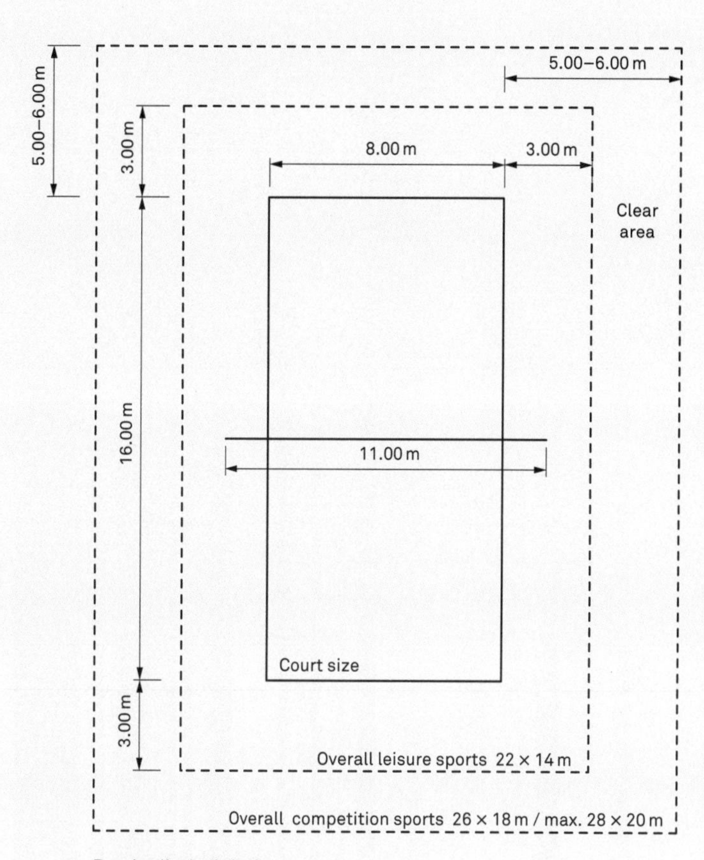

Beachvolleyball singles
Competition/leisure Sports Scale 1:200

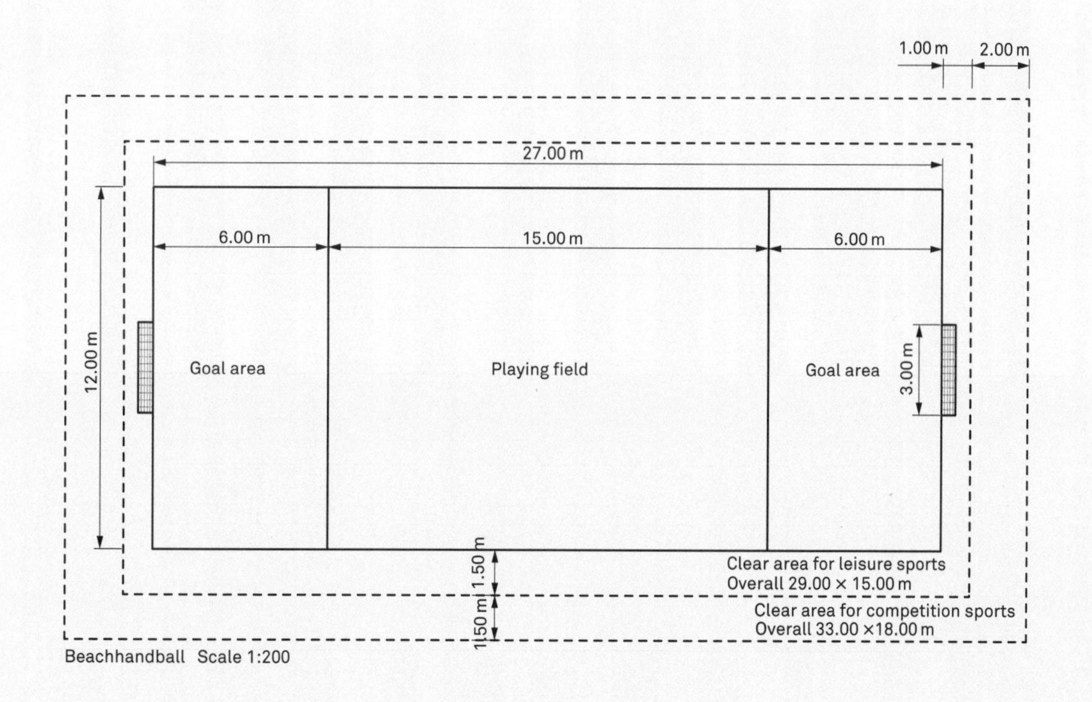

Beachhandball Scale 1:200

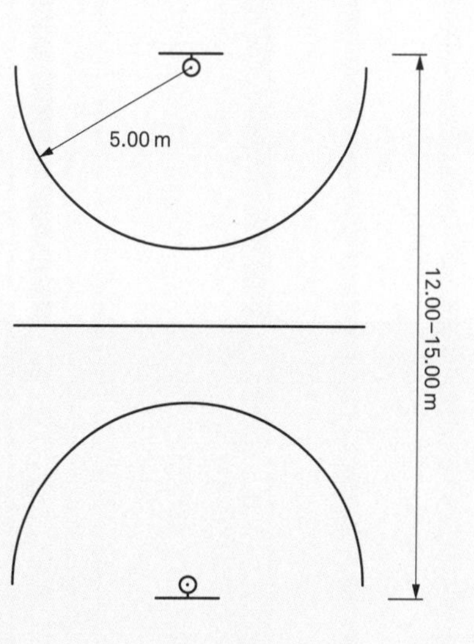

Beachbasketball Scale 1:200

Track-and-Field

Running Tracks

Sport	Length			Width of individual lane	Safety zone along outer lane
	Start area	Distance	Run-out		
Sprint track	3 m	110 m	17 m	1.22 m	0.28 m
Standard track	–	400 m	17 m	1.22 m	0.28 m

Table 4.4.18 Running Tracks

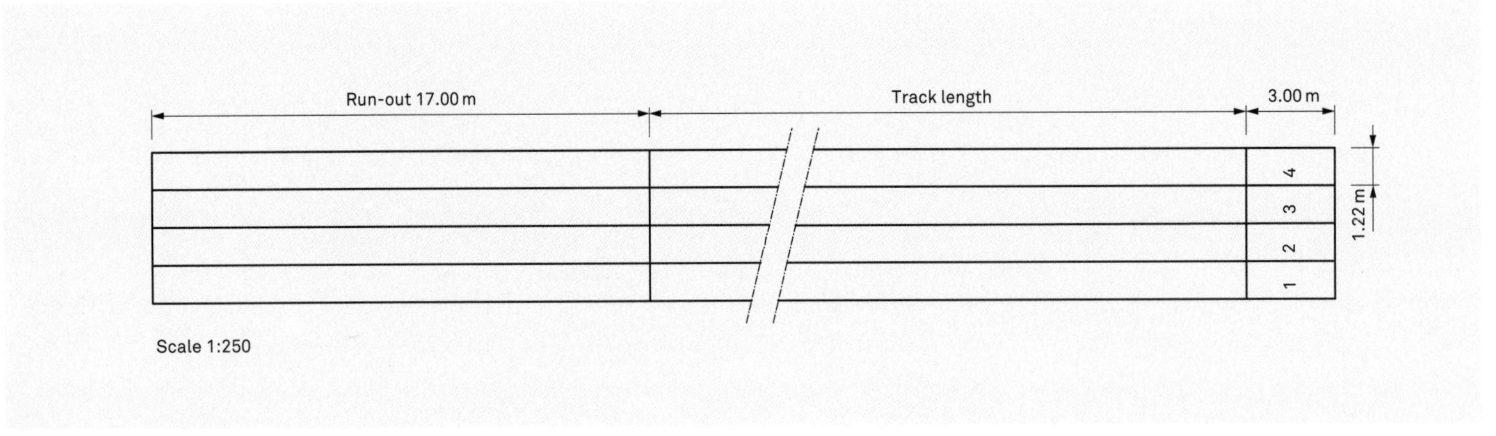

Figure 4.4.24 Running Tracks

Facilities for Jumping Events

Jumping event	Runway		Landing area	
	Length	Width of single/multiple facilities	Length	Width
Long jump	≥45 m, take-off board ≥2 m in front of the landing area (1 m for top-level competitive sports)	1.22 m / 2 m	Landing area ≥8 m (9 m for top-level competitive sports)	2.75 m
Triple jump	≥45 m, take-off board ≥11 m in front of the landing area	1.22 m / 2 m	Landing area ≥8 m (for youth ≥9 m, for top-ranking athletes ≥13 m)	2.75 m
Pole vault	≥45 m	1.22 m / 2 m	Cushion ≥5 m	≥5 m
High jump	Semicircle with r ≥ 18 m		Cushion ≥4 m	5–6 m

Table 4.4.19 Jumping Event

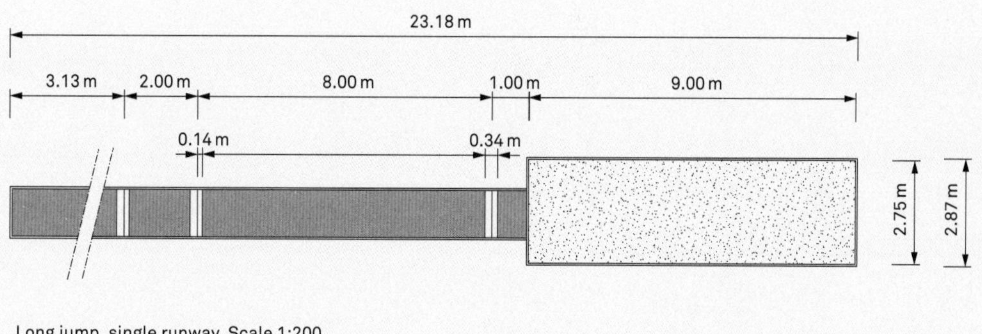

Long jump, single runway Scale 1:200

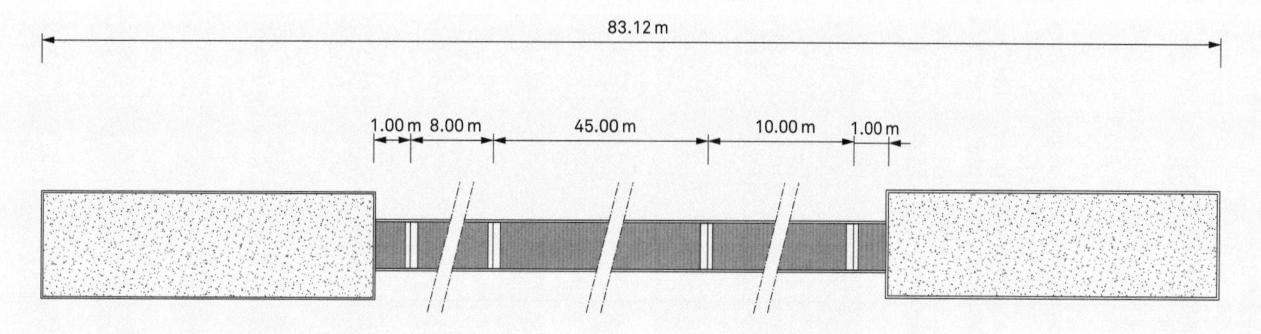

Long jump, bidirectional single runway Scale 1:200

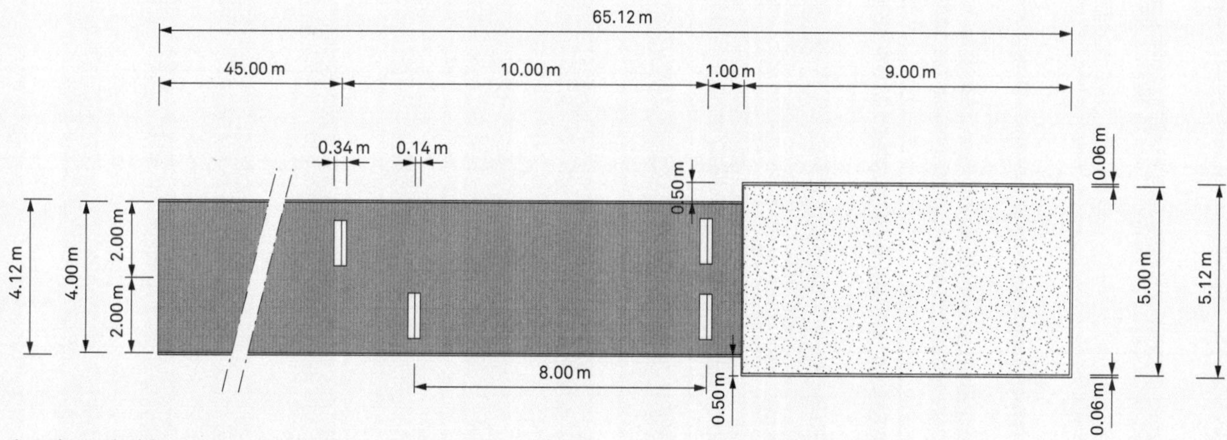

Long jump, dual-lane runway Scale 1:200

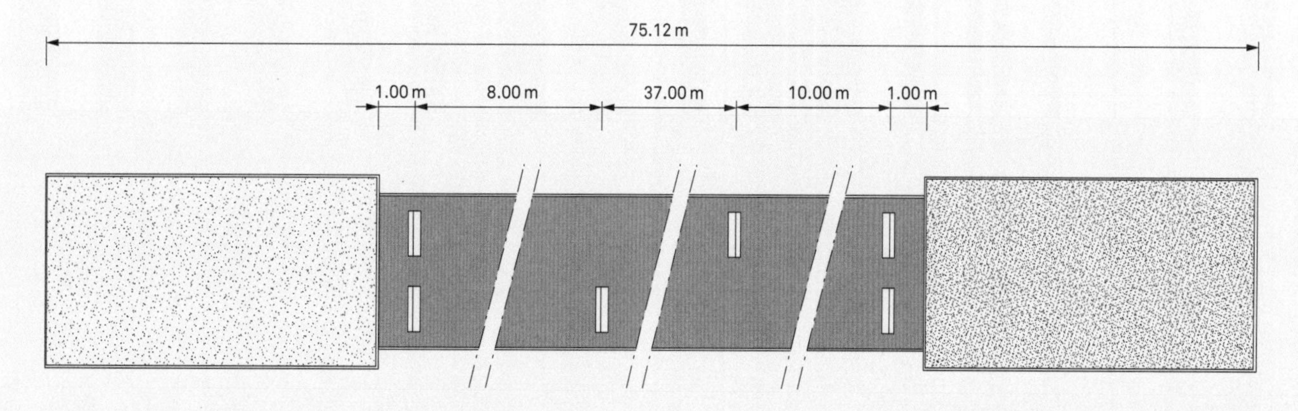

Long jump, bidirectional dual-lane runway Scale 1:200

Figure 4.4.25 Long jump

Facilities for Throwing Events

Throwing event	Throwing area	Landing sector	
		Angle	Length
Discus throw	Throwing circle d = 2.5 m	40°	80 m
Hammer throw	Throwing circle d = 2.5 m	40°	80 m
Javelin throw	Runway length = 36.5 m (minimum 30 m) Runway width = 4 m	29°	100 m
Shot put	Throwing circle d = 2.135 m	40°	25 m

Table 4.4.20 Throwing events

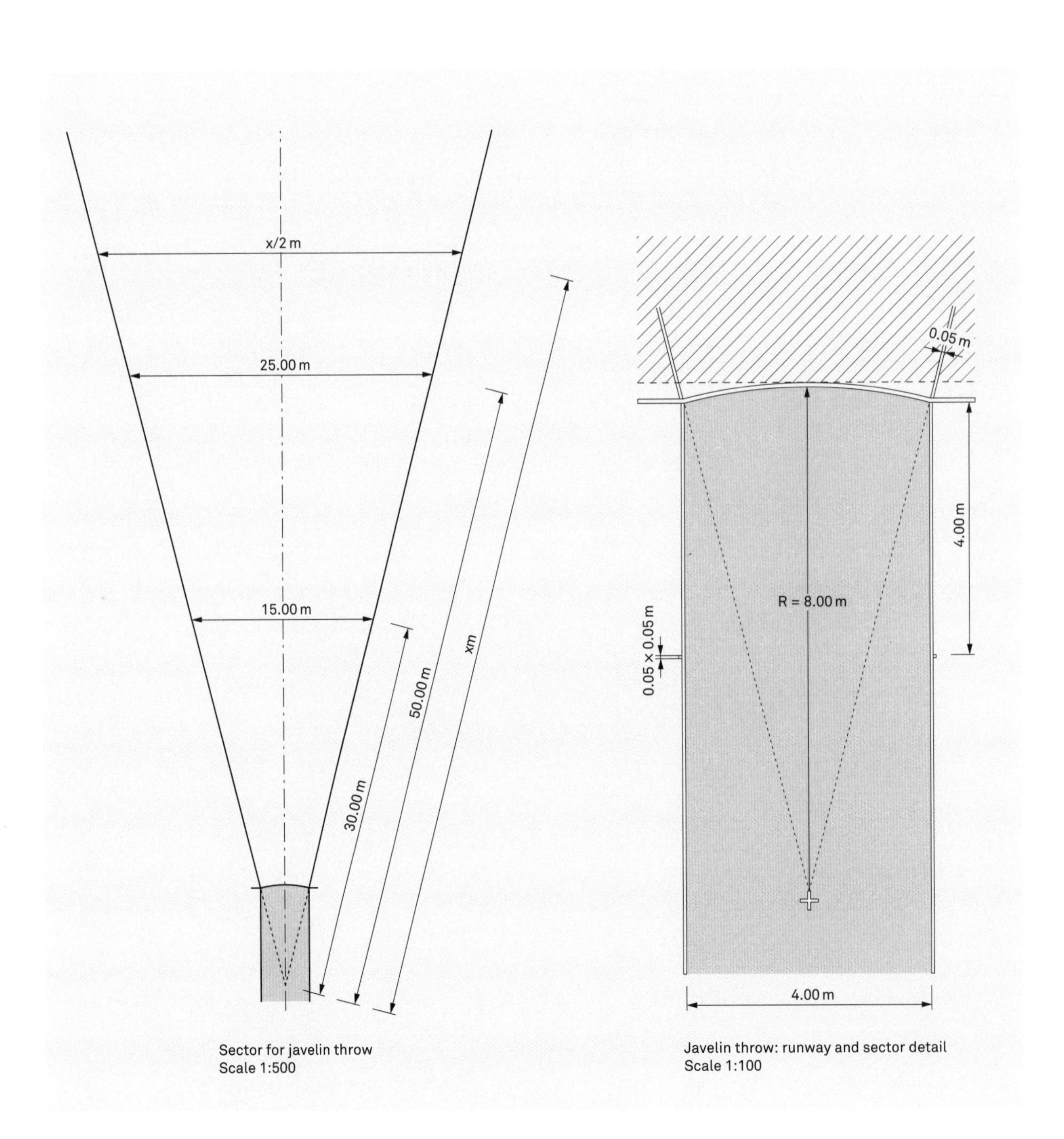

Sector for javelin throw
Scale 1:500

Javelin throw: runway and sector detail
Scale 1:100

Figure 4.4.26 Throwing event: Javelin

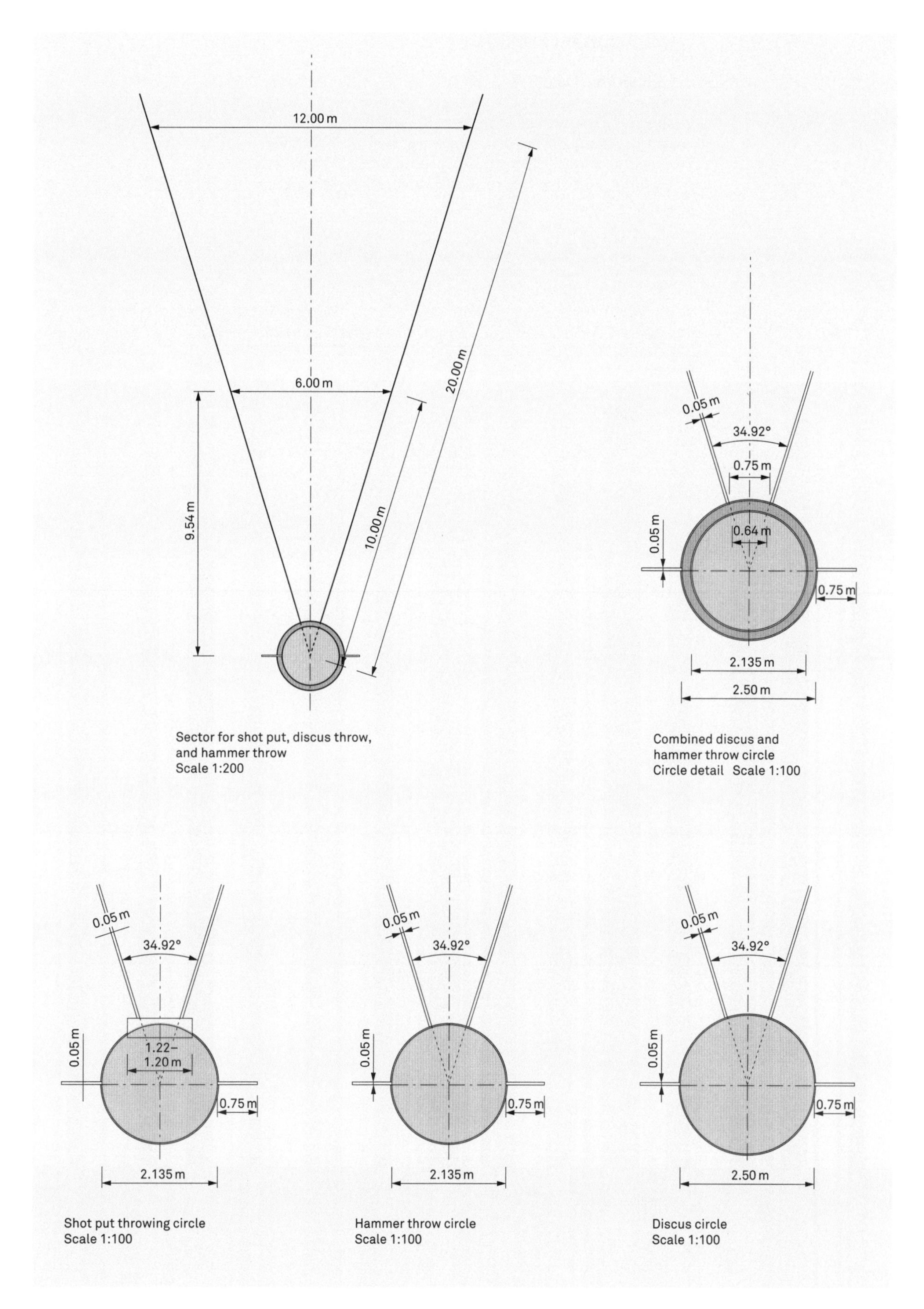

Figure 4.4.27 Throwing events: Shot put, hammer throw, and discus

Combination Facilities

Competition Facilities

Running tracks and provisions for jumping and throwing events are frequently consolidated into multisport competition facilities that also feature a large playing field. These are categorized into 4 types (according to DIN 18035-1). Facilities that meet the requirements as listed below are suitable to use for competitions.

	Type A	B	C	D
Suitability	National championships, major national and international events, international competitions	Regional championships, certain international matches, local events	Local events (up to district level), regional school sports	Smaller catchment areas, local school sports
Facilities				
Large playing field	73 × 109 m 68 × 105 m	73 × 109 m	73 × 109 m	73 × 109 m 68 × 109 m
Small playing field				27 × 45 m with added landing pit
Standard track	8 lanes	6 lanes	4 lanes	–
Sprint track	8 lanes	6–7	6	6
Steeplechase with water jump pit	x	x	–	–
Javelin runway	2	2	1	1
Combined discus/hammer throw circle	x	x	1	optional
High jump facilities	2 (5 m × 3 m cushions)	2	1	1
Shot put circle	2	1	–	1
Javelin runway	2	2	1	1
Long and triple jump	Two lanes	Three lanes	Three lanes	Three lanes
Pole vault facility with runway from both sides	1 (40 m + 5 m runway; 5 × 5 m cushion)	–	–	–
Pole vault facility	2 (ea. 40 m + 5 m runway; 5 × 5 m cushion)	1	1	–
Shot put circle	2	1	3	2
Combined discus/hammer throw circle	2	1	1	1

Table 4.4.21 Competition facilities

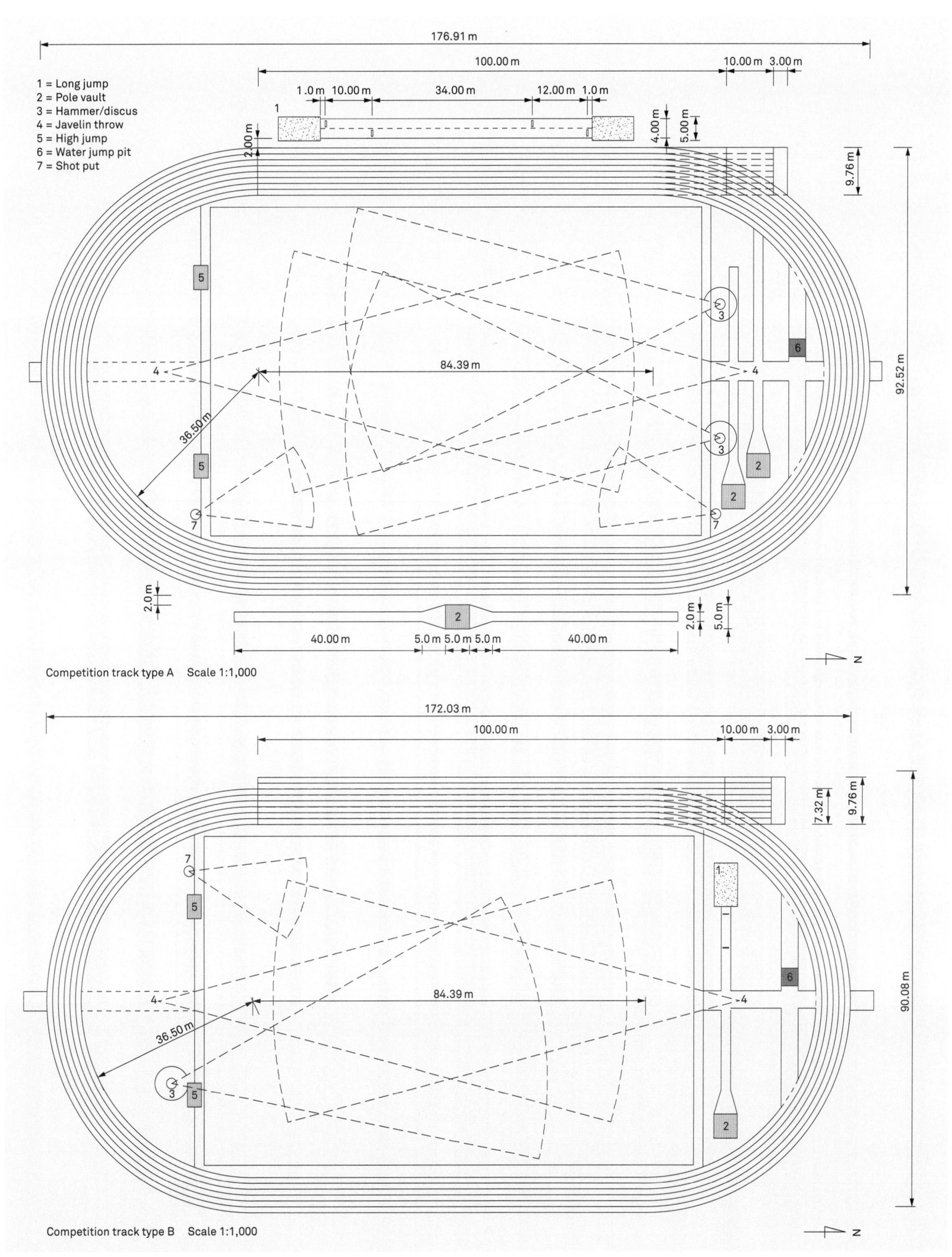

Figure 4.4.28 Competition track type A and B

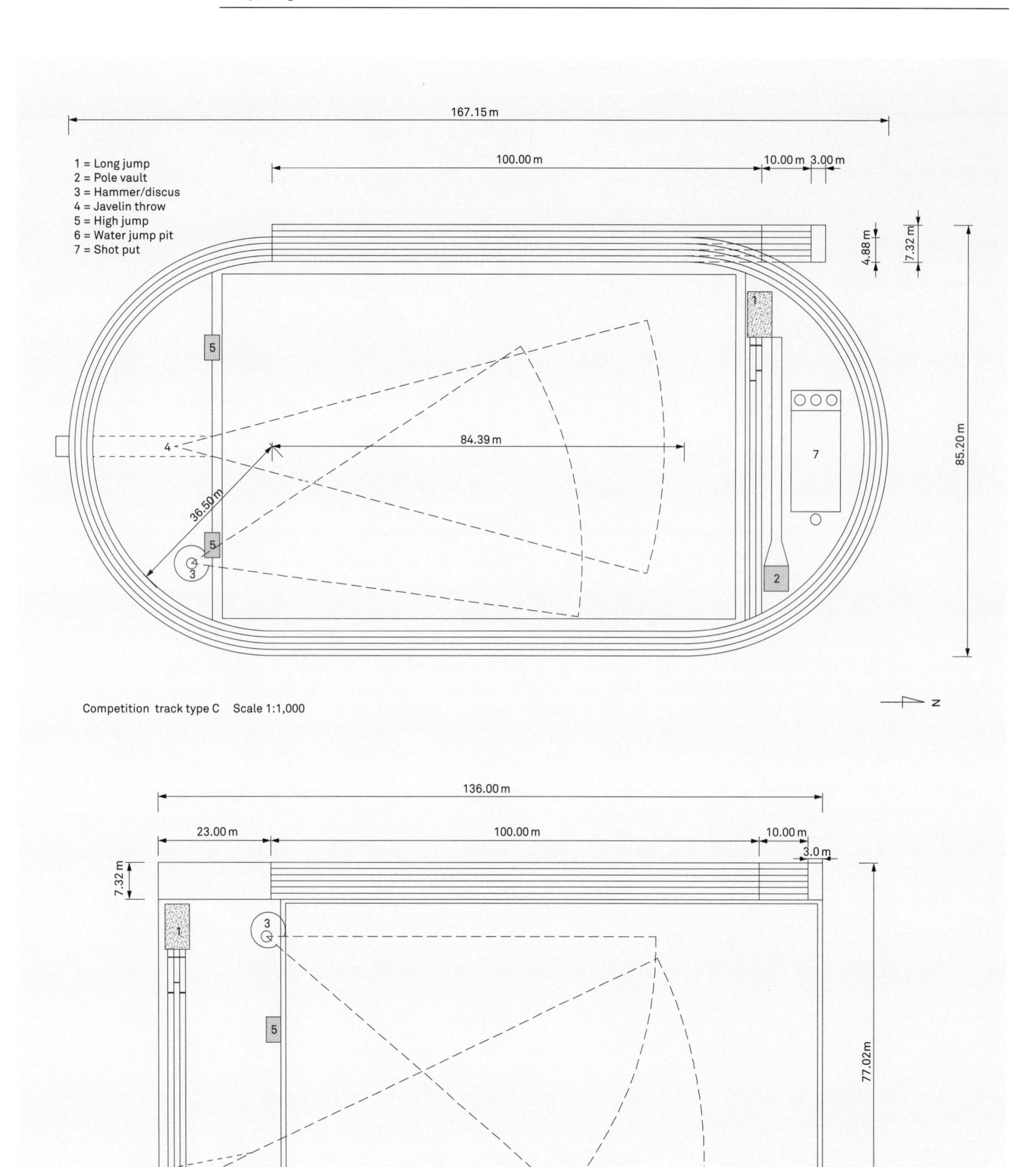

Figure 4.4.29 Competition track types C and D

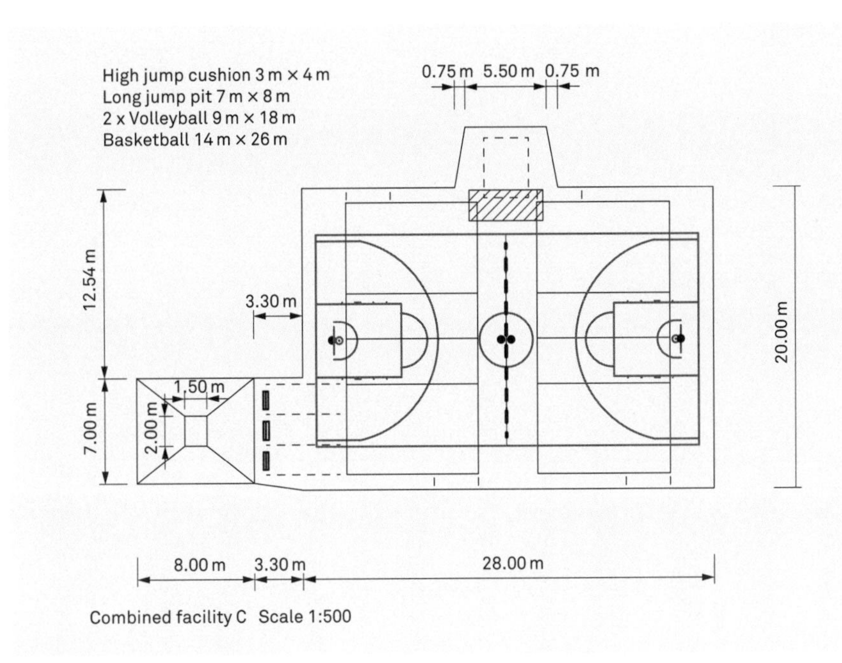

Figure 4.4.30 Combined facility C

Small Playing Fields and Combined Facilities / All-Weather Fields

Especially for school sports or recreational purposes, playing field combinations can offer the greatest possible range of use and contribute a high degree of flexibility. The individual playing fields or courts and the track-and-field facilities are, for the most part, unsuitable for competitions but can be used for training purposes and physical education.

Combination facility	Area requirements for all-weather field + facilities for high jump and long jump, including clearances	Area requirements, total (outer dimensions)
A	27 × 45 m + high jump 8 × 5 m + long jump 10 × 7 m = 1,325 m²	32 × 55 m = 1,760 m²
B	28 × 44 m + high jump 8 × 4 m + long jump 10 × 7 m = 1,334 m²	32 × 54 m = 1,728 m²
C	20 × 28 m + high jump 8 × 4 m + long jump 10 × 7 m = 662 m²	20 × 39.3 m = 786 m²

Table 4.4.22 Combined Facilities

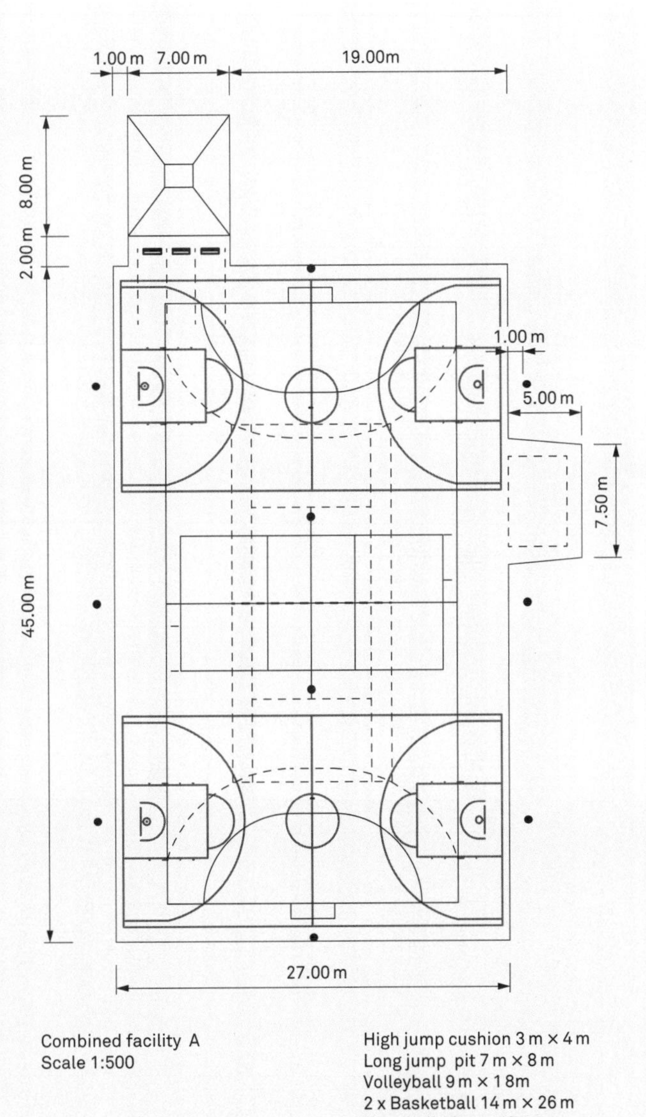

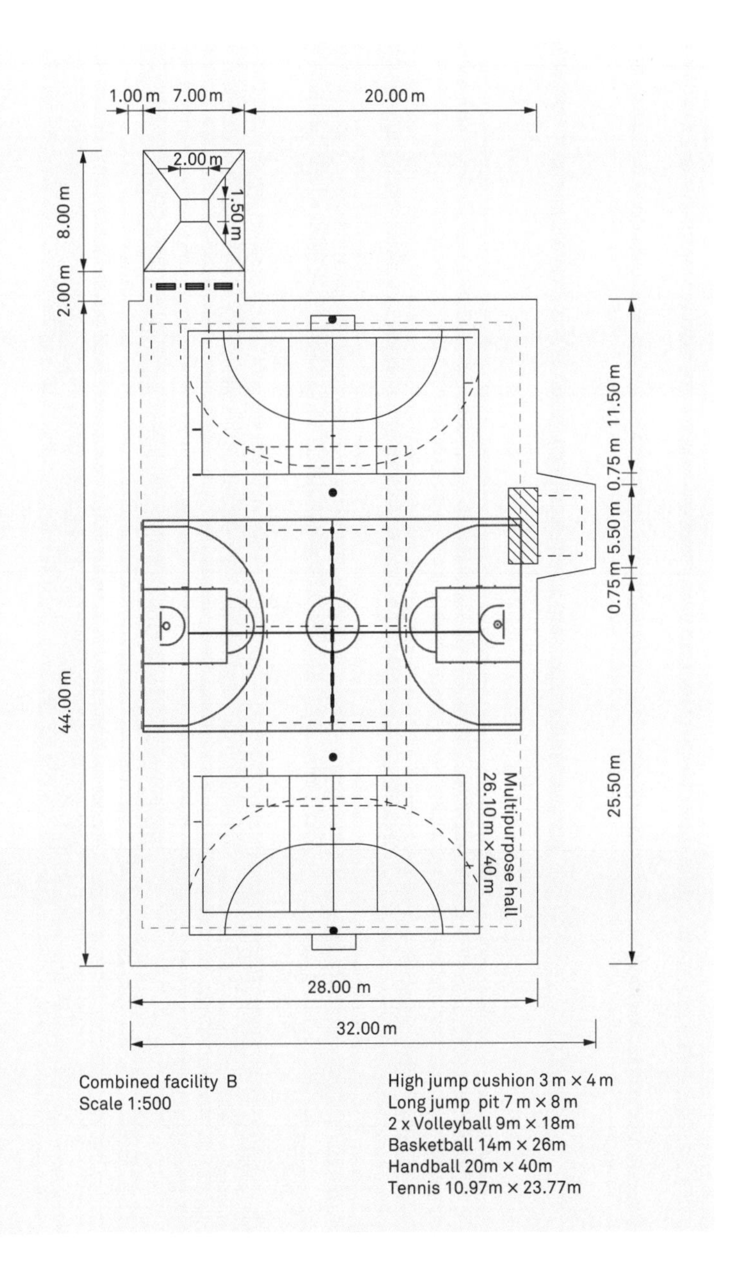

Figure 4.4.31 Combined facilities A and B

Precision Sports/Games of Skill

Putting Courses (Miniature Golf)

There are five different types of standardized miniature golf courses recognized by the sport's international governing body, the World Minigolfsport Federation (WMF): beton, Eternit, Swedish felt, cobigolf, and stargolf. These types differ especially in terms of the materials used and the dimensions of the lanes. In cobigolf, which itself has two variants (small- and large-format), each hole has one or two gates that a player also needs to get past before encountering the actual obstacle.

Course type	Lanes		Total area required	Surface
	Quantity	Length × Width		
Eternit ("miniature golf")	18 (from 28 standardized configurations)	6.25 × 0.9 m, target circle Ø: 1.4 m	≥800 m²	Fiber cement panels
Beton ("minigolf")	18 (from 18 standardized configurations)	12 × 1.25 m, target circle Ø: 2.5 m; one long hole (25 m)	≥1,200 m²	Concrete
Cobigolf *large-format*	16–17	Standardized lanes, each 12.5 m long; 1 or 2 holes without obstacles, each approximately 27 m long	≥1,200 m²	Concrete
Cobigolf *small-format*	16–17	Length 6.25 m each; 1 or 2 holes without obstacles, each approximately 14 m long	≥800 m²	Fiber cement panels
Stargolf	18	8 × 1 m, target circle Ø: 2.00 m	≥800 m²	Concrete
Swedish felt	18	6–(16 m–)18 m, 0.9 m wide, target circle (octagonal): Ø 1.6–2.4 m	≥1,200 m²	Weatherproof felt

Table 4.4.23 Putting courses

Miniature Golf (Eternit course)

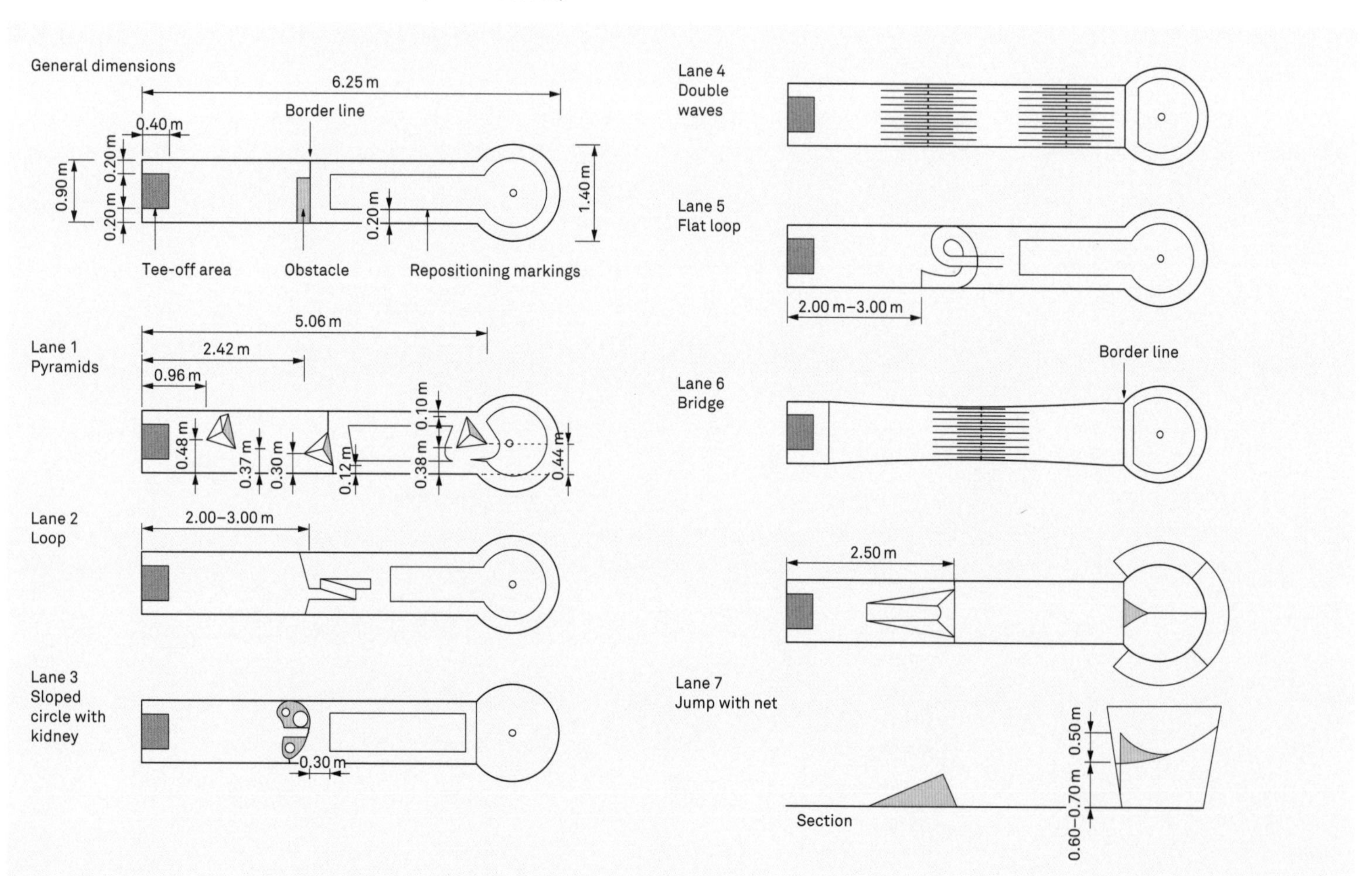

Figure 4.4.32 Miniature golf (Eternit course)

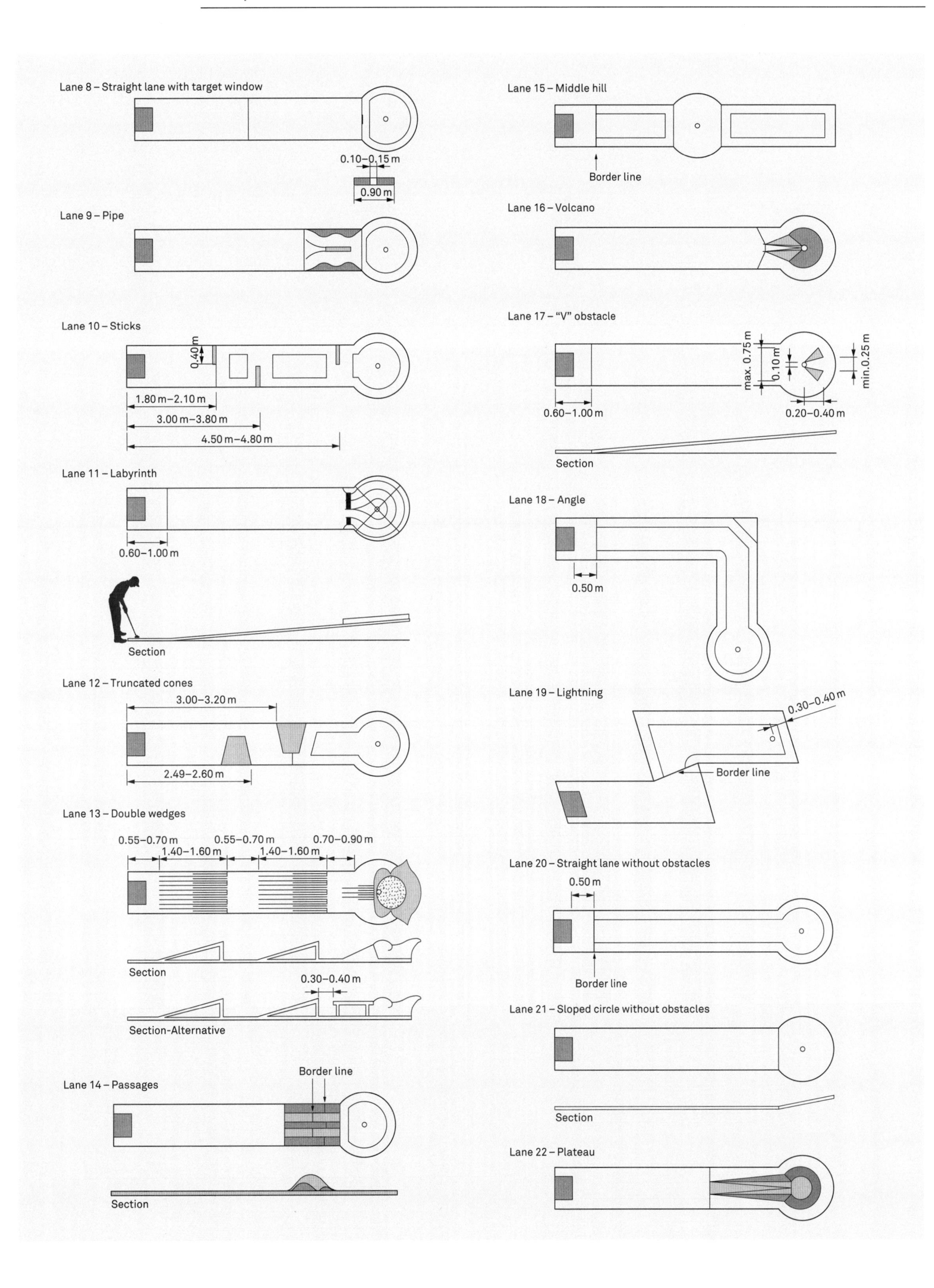

Lane 8 – Straight lane with target window
0.10–0.15 m
0.90 m
Lane 9 – Pipe
Lane 10 – Sticks
0.40 m
1.80 m–2.10 m
3.00 m–3.80 m
4.50 m–4.80 m
Lane 11 – Labyrinth
0.60–1.00 m
Section
Lane 12 – Truncated cones
3.00–3.20 m
2.49–2.60 m
Lane 13 – Double wedges
0.55–0.70 m
0.55–0.70 m
0.70–0.90 m
1.40–1.60 m
1.40–1.60 m
Section
0.30–0.40 m
Section-Alternative
Lane 14 – Passages
Border line
Section
Lane 15 – Middle hill
Border line
Lane 16 – Volcano
Lane 17 – "V" obstacle
max. 0.75 m
0.10 m
min. 0.25 m
0.60–1.00 m
0.20–0.40 m
Section
Lane 18 – Angle
0.50 m
Lane 19 – Lightning
0.30–0.40 m
Border line
Lane 20 – Straight lane without obstacles
0.50 m
Border line
Lane 21 – Sloped circle without obstacles
Section
Lane 22 – Plateau

Minigolf

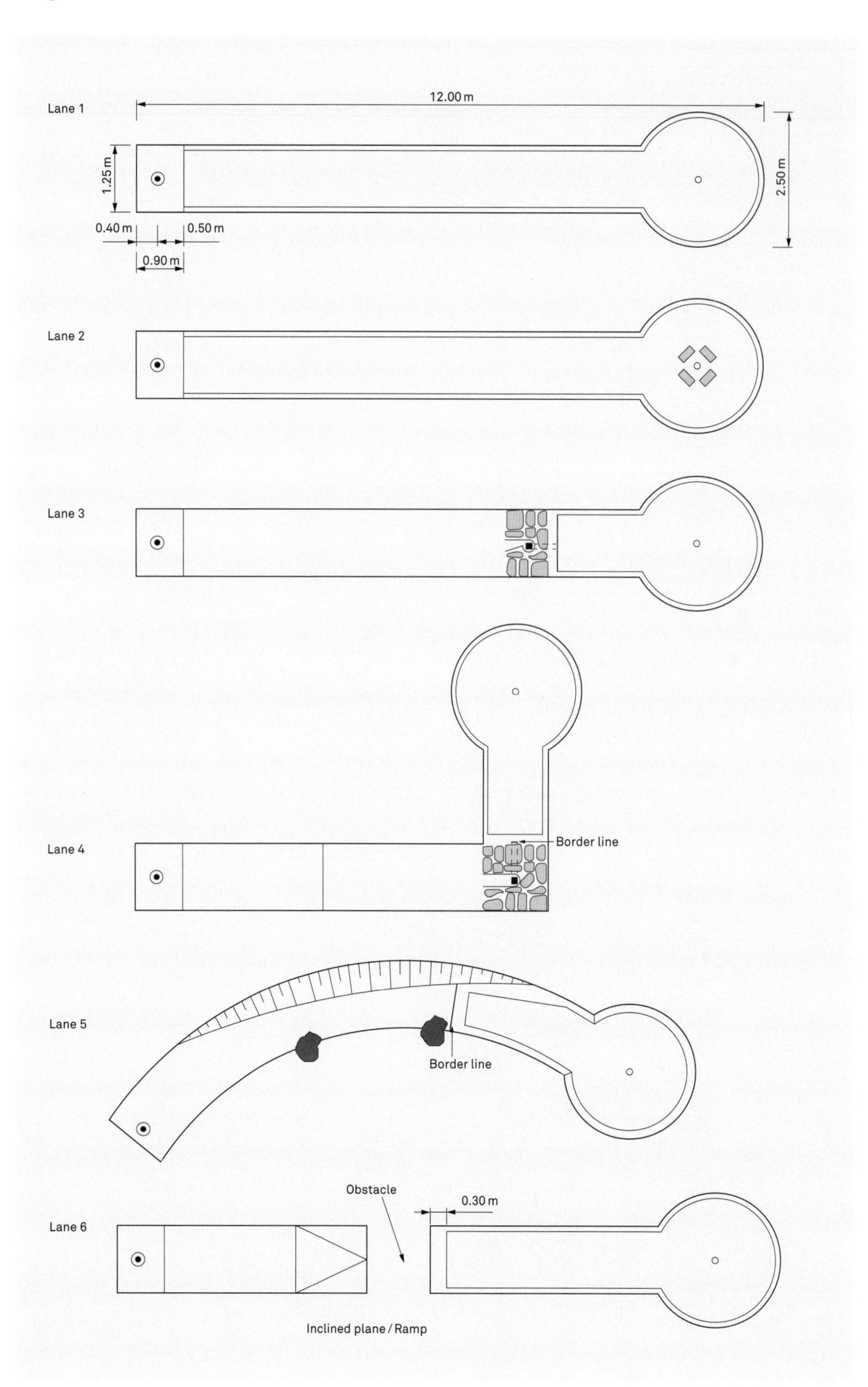

Figure 4.4.33 Minigolf (Beton course)

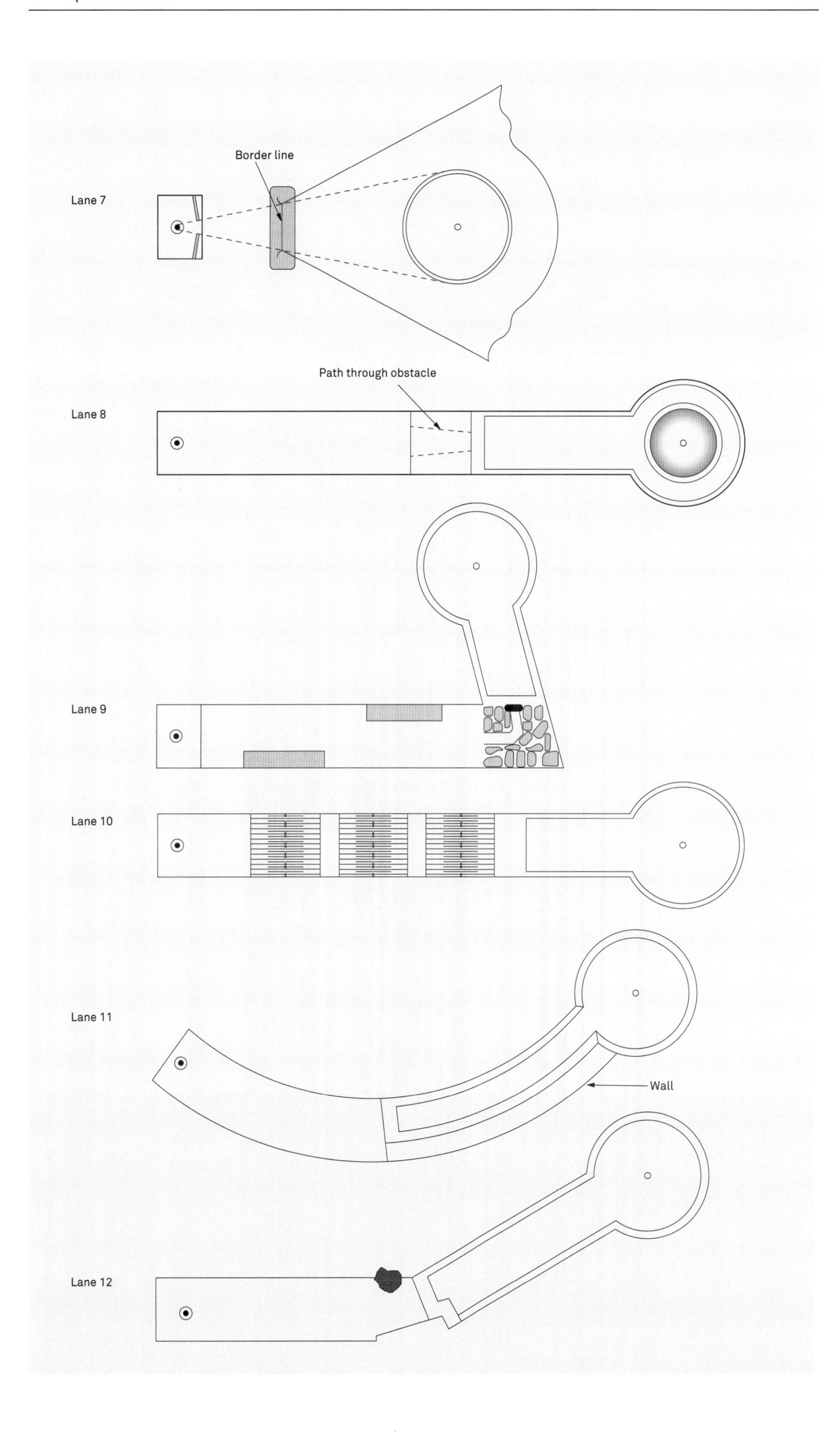
Lane 7
Border line
Path through obstacle
Lane 8
Lane 9
Lane 10
Lane 11
Wall
Lane 12

Minigolf

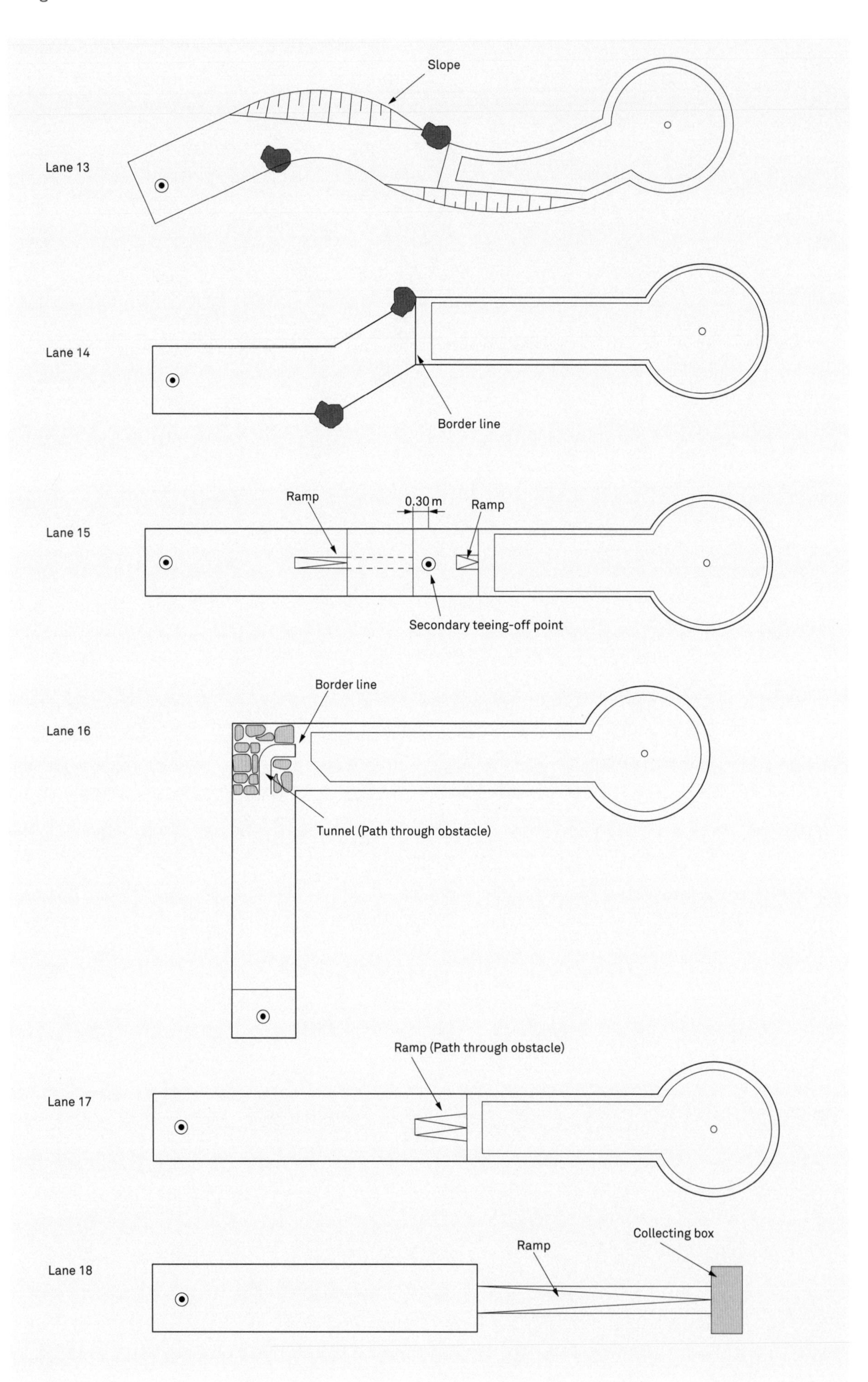

Figure 4.4.33 Minigolf (Beton course)

Croquet

Table 4.4.24 Croquet

Sport	Playing field	Safety clearance		Surface
		Side	End	
Full-size croquet	25.6 × 32 m (28 × 35 yards)	–	–	Grass
Short croquet (6-wicket)	15 × 22 m*	–	–	Grass

* Per Deutschem Krocketbund

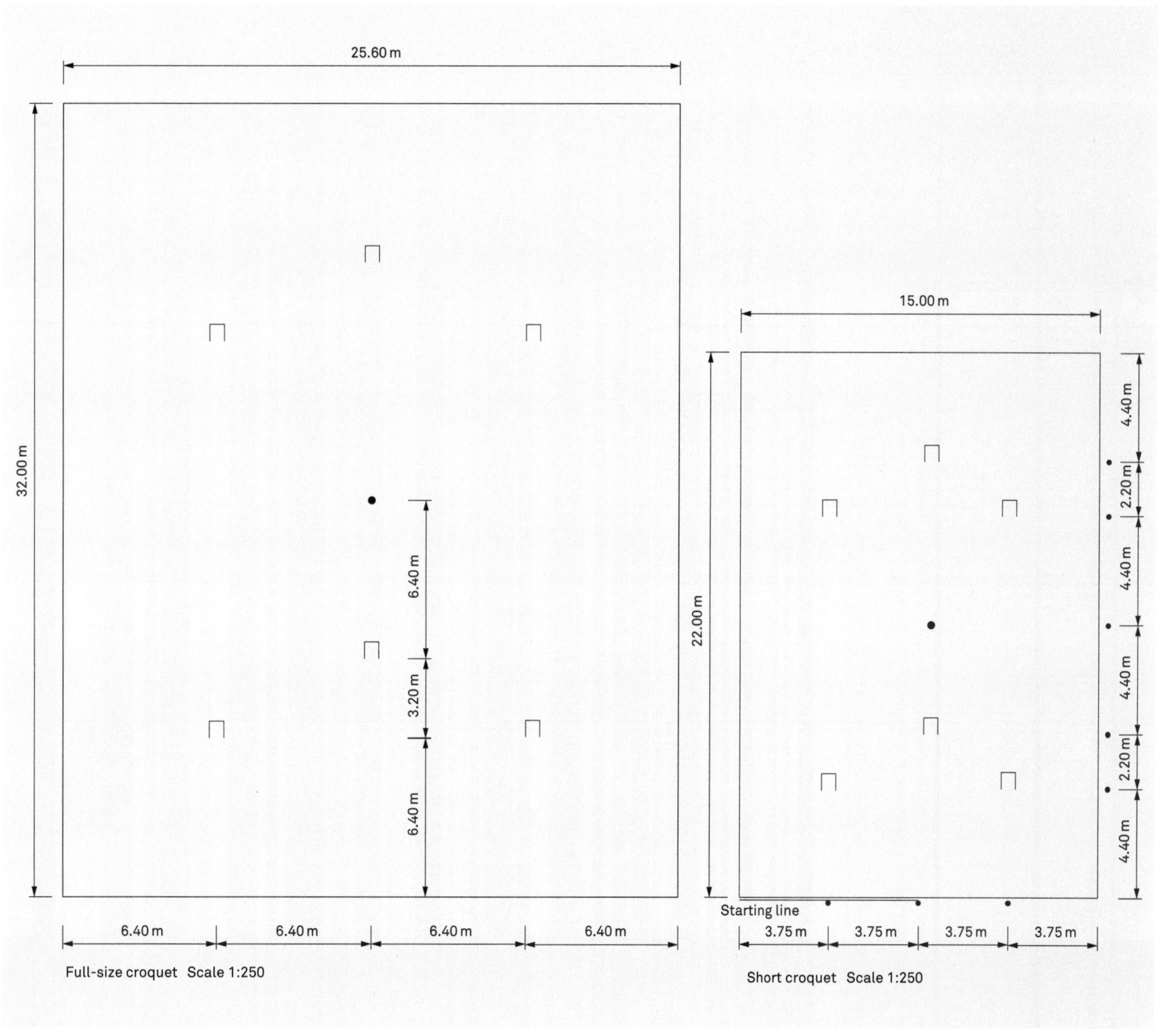

Figure 4.4.34 Croquet

Boules

The various boules games are closely related. Their basic principles are similar and they differ particularly in the material and weight of the balls (*boule* is French for "ball") and in differences in some of the rules. Both boule lyonnaise and jeu Provençal, for instance, are played with a run up to the throw.

Among the most popular, however, is pétanque, which is often called "boule" in Germany. Like jeu Provençal, it is a modified variant of the game of boule lyonnaise. The games can be played on expressly staked-out areas or even in any open space or public square, regardless of any irregularities in the ground surface or the presence of obstructions ("terrain libre"). Barriers – if necessary – are located at least 1 m outside the area marked for play. Pétanque can be played on any ground surface, but particularly suitable surfaces include, for example, water-bound paving and compacted sand and crushed stone mixtures.

Sport		Playing field/lane	Clearance to side barriers	Surface
Pétanque	International/national competition	Minimum 15 × 4 m		Any ground surface, preferably water-bound paving or a compacted sand/crushed stone mixture
	Leisure sports and other competitions	Minimum 12 × 3 m (12 × 5 m double lane) or terrain libre		
Boule lyonnaise		27.5 × 4 (2.5) m		Any ground surface
Jeu Provençal		24 × 4 m or terrain libre	1.5 m	Any ground surface
Boccia		26.5 m × 4.5 m		Special surface, typically on natural sand lanes
Bowls (lawn bowling)		31–40 m × 4.3–5.8 m		Grass

Table 4.4.25 Boules

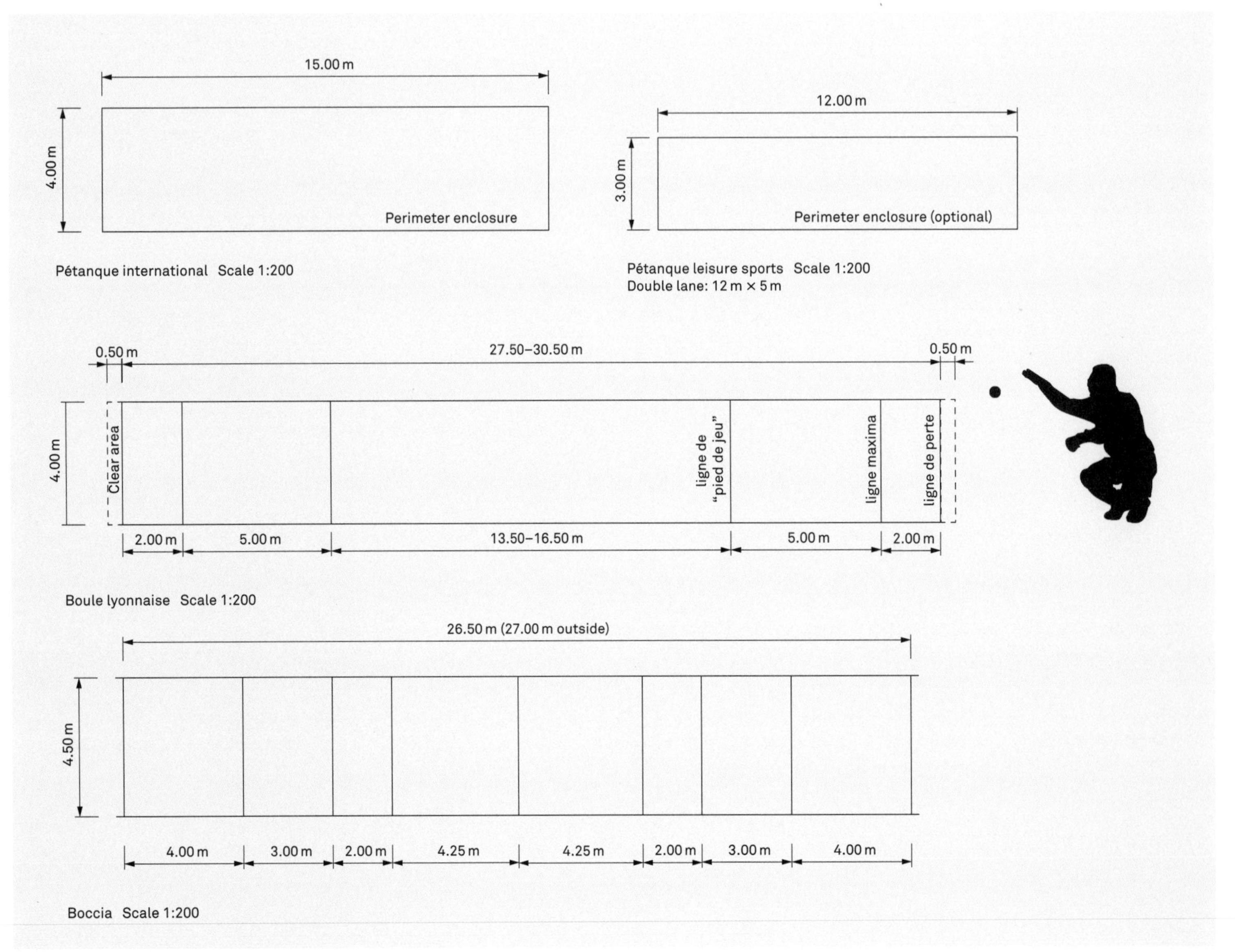

Figure 4.4.35 Boules

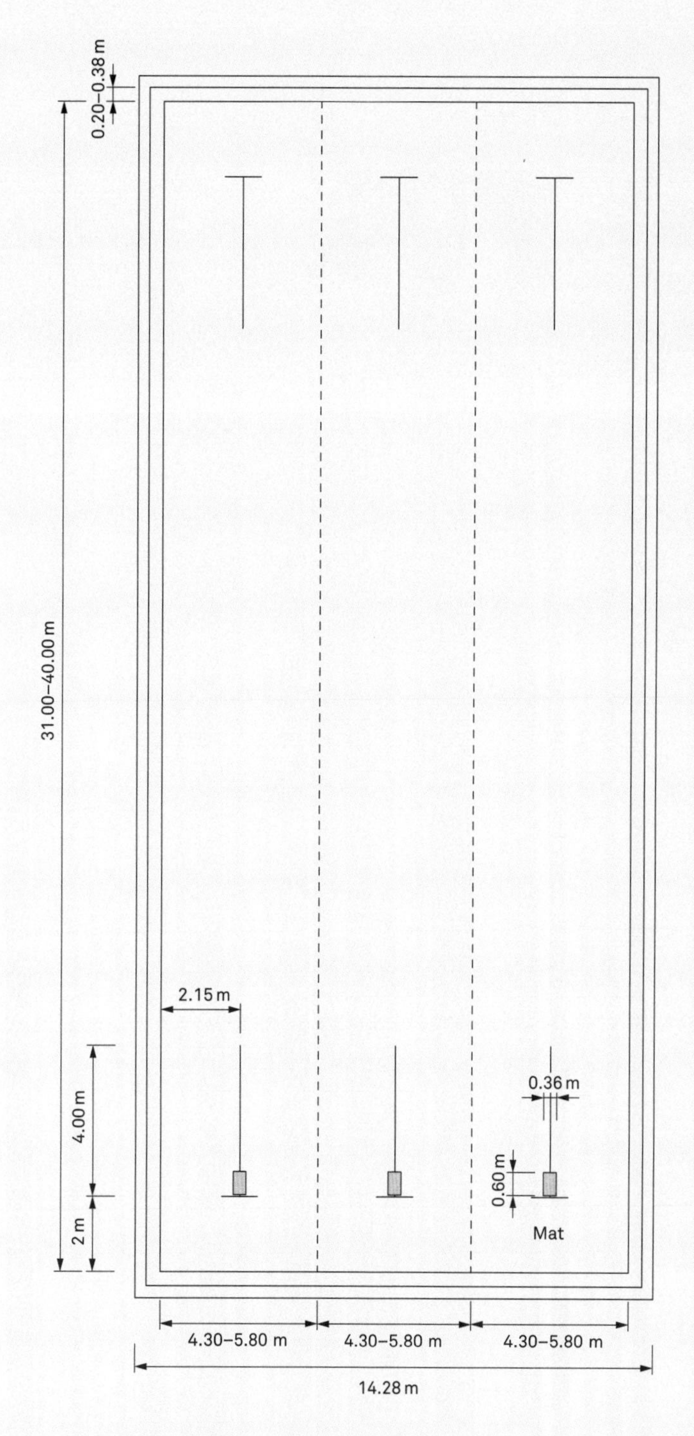

Figure 4.4.36 Lawn bowls with three lanes (rinks)

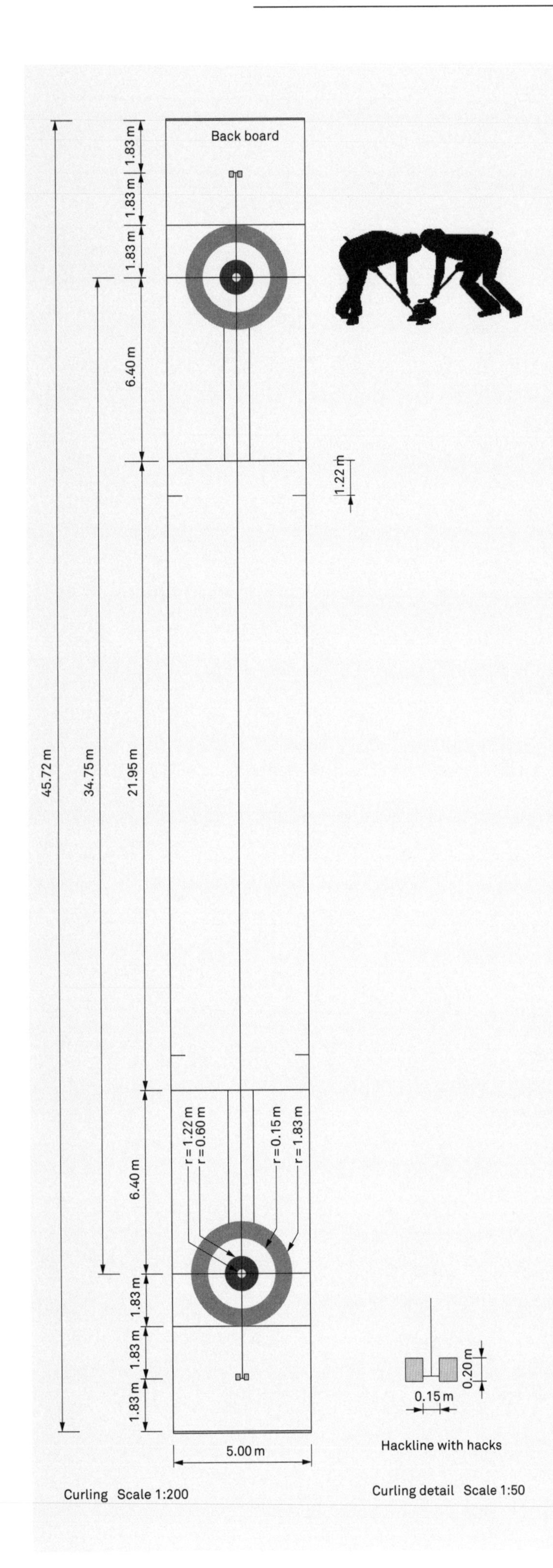

Curling Scale 1:200

Curling detail Scale 1:50

Curling

Course type	Playing court	Safety clearance		Overall	Surface
		Side	End		
Curling	45.72 m × 5 m (minimum 44.5 m × 4.42 m)	–	–	45.72 m × 5 m (minimum 44.5 m × 4.42 m)	Ice

Table 4.4.26 Curling

Figure 4.4.37 Curling

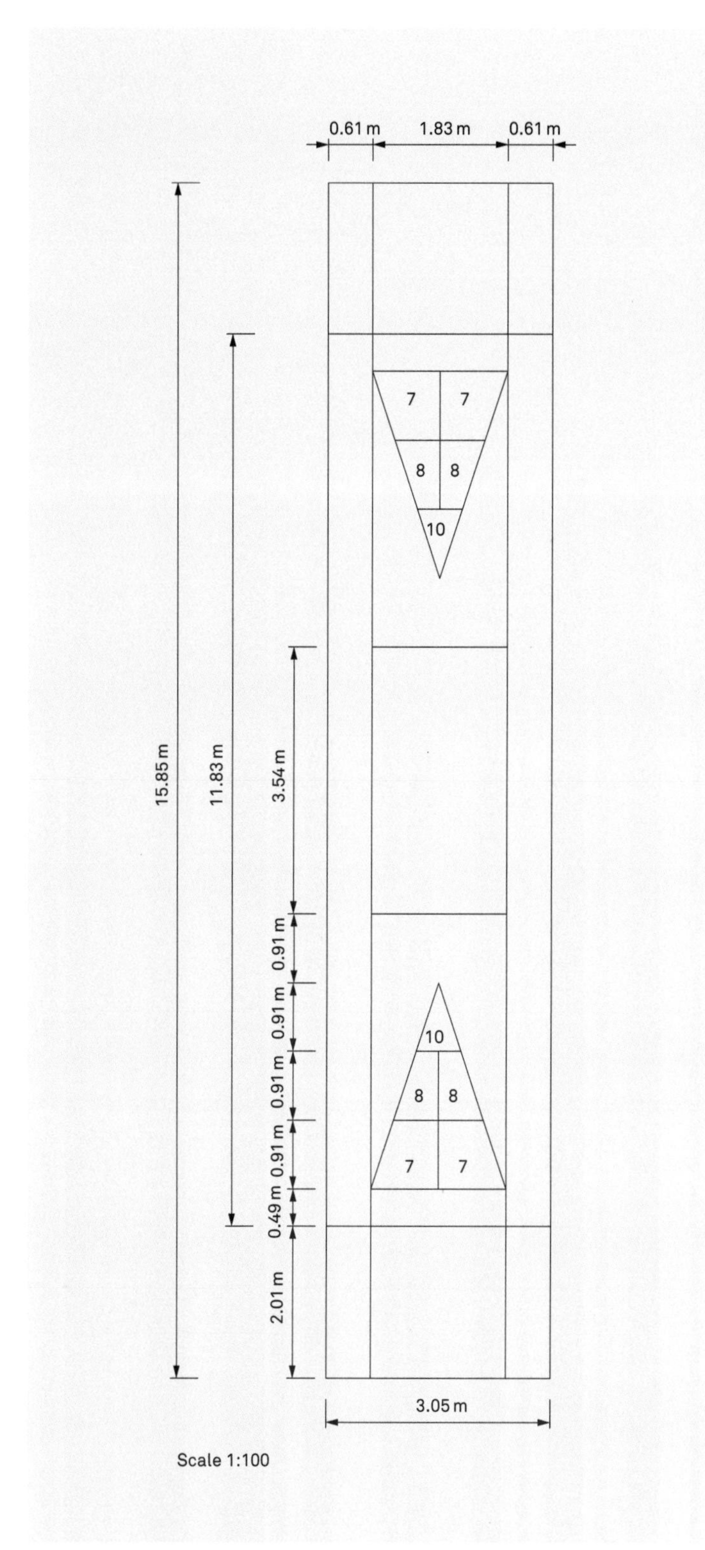

Figure 4.4.38 Shuffleboard

Shuffleboard

Sport	Playing court	Safety clearance		Overall	Surface
		Side	End		
Team game	15.85 × 1.83 m	–	–	–	Concrete, removable plastic mats

Table 4.4.27 Shuffleboard

Bavarian Curling (Ice Stock Sport)

Table 4.4.28 Bavarian Curling (Ice Stock Sport)

Course type	Playing field	Safety clearance		Overall	Surface
		Side	End		
Team competition (target shooting)	28 × 3 m	0.6 m	≥1 m	30 × 4.2 m	Ice, asphalt, concrete
Distance shooting	Length = 150 m, 300 m, or more	–	–	–	Ice, asphalt, concrete

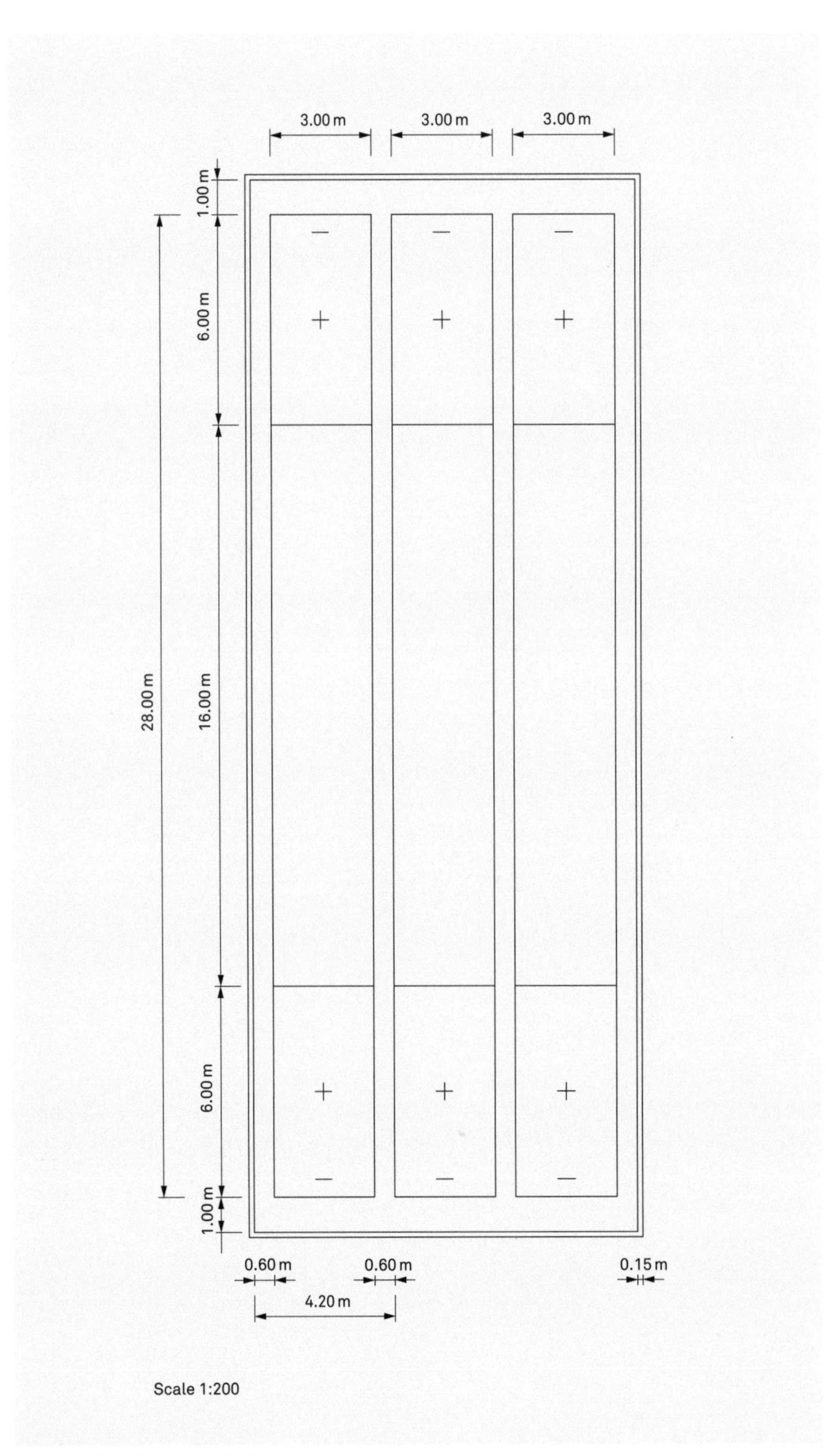

Figure 4.4.39 Bavarian Curling in summer, team competition

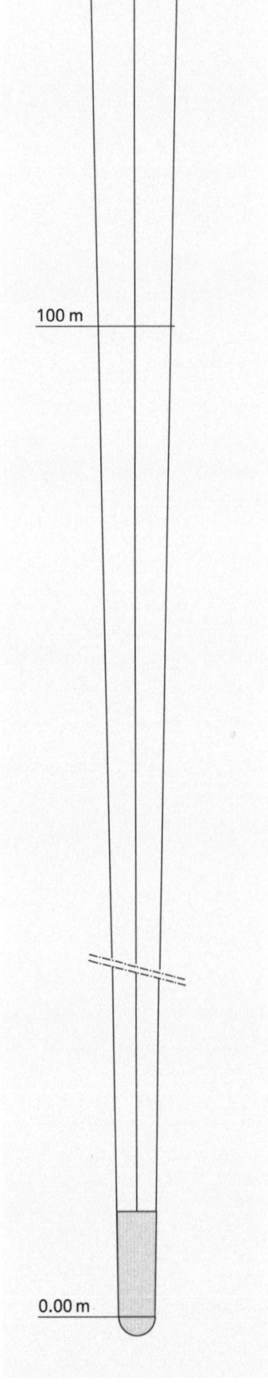

Figure 4.4.40 Bavarian Curling in summer, distance shooting

Trend Sports / Fun Sports

Flying Disc Sports

Sport	Playing field / hole	Clearance / end zone	Overall	Goal Width/height	Surface
Disc golf	40–250 m hole length	–	18 holes (course segments)	–	Played on natural terrain / on grass
Ultimate	37 × 64 m	End: 18 m (15–20 m)	37 × 100 m	–	Grass
Goaltimate	Ø 55	–	–	5.5 m / maximum 3.4 m semicircular	Grass
Double Disc Court (DDC)	2 × 13 × 13 m	Space between courts 17 m	13 × 43 m		
Discathon	–	–	1 km circuit	–	...

Table 4.4.29 Flying Disc Sports

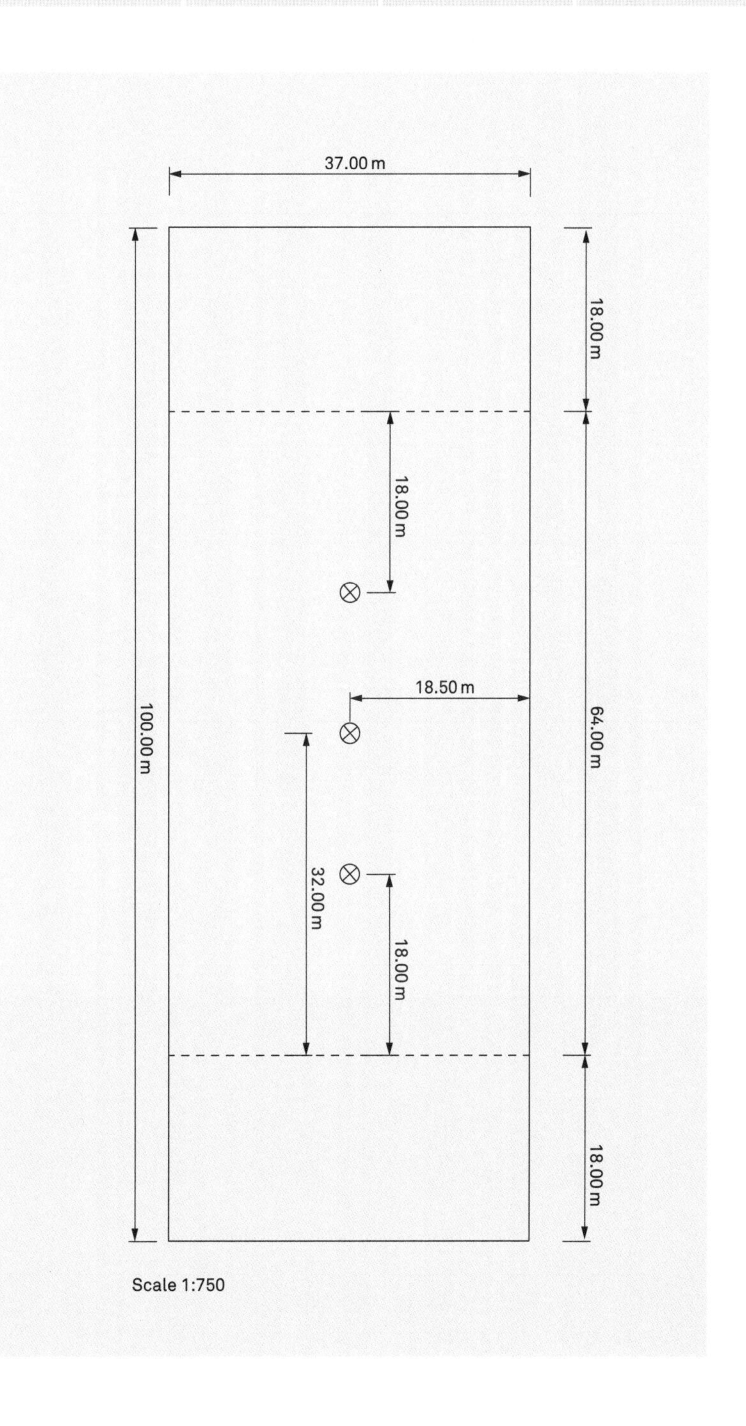

Figure 4.4.41 Ultimate

Skateparks

Skateparks can be used and enjoyed equally with skateboards, BMX bikes, and inline skates. Depending on the primary use, however, there may be different requirements for dimensions and proportions within the facility, so that if desired, skateparks with different characters and priorities can be created.

With its specific features, a "plaza" is reminiscent of an urban space and its elements, including basic fixtures such as rails, ledges, curbs, and benches, as well as funboxes, single ramps, miniramps, or float ramps. The individual items can be ridden in succession, thus resulting in so-called lines.

Minipipes and halfpipes, by contrast, constitute independent elements in a skatepark, which are ridden alone and not in combination with other elements.

A special form of the sport is pool skating, which came about when some inventive skaters in the US decided to skate in empty swimming pools. The pools (also called bowls) in a skatepark are modeled on these swimming pools, which have a curve where the wall meets the floor. Pools are supplemented by hips, elevators, volcanoes, or mellows. As self-contained elements, they can comprise a facility of their own or they can be part of a larger skatepark.

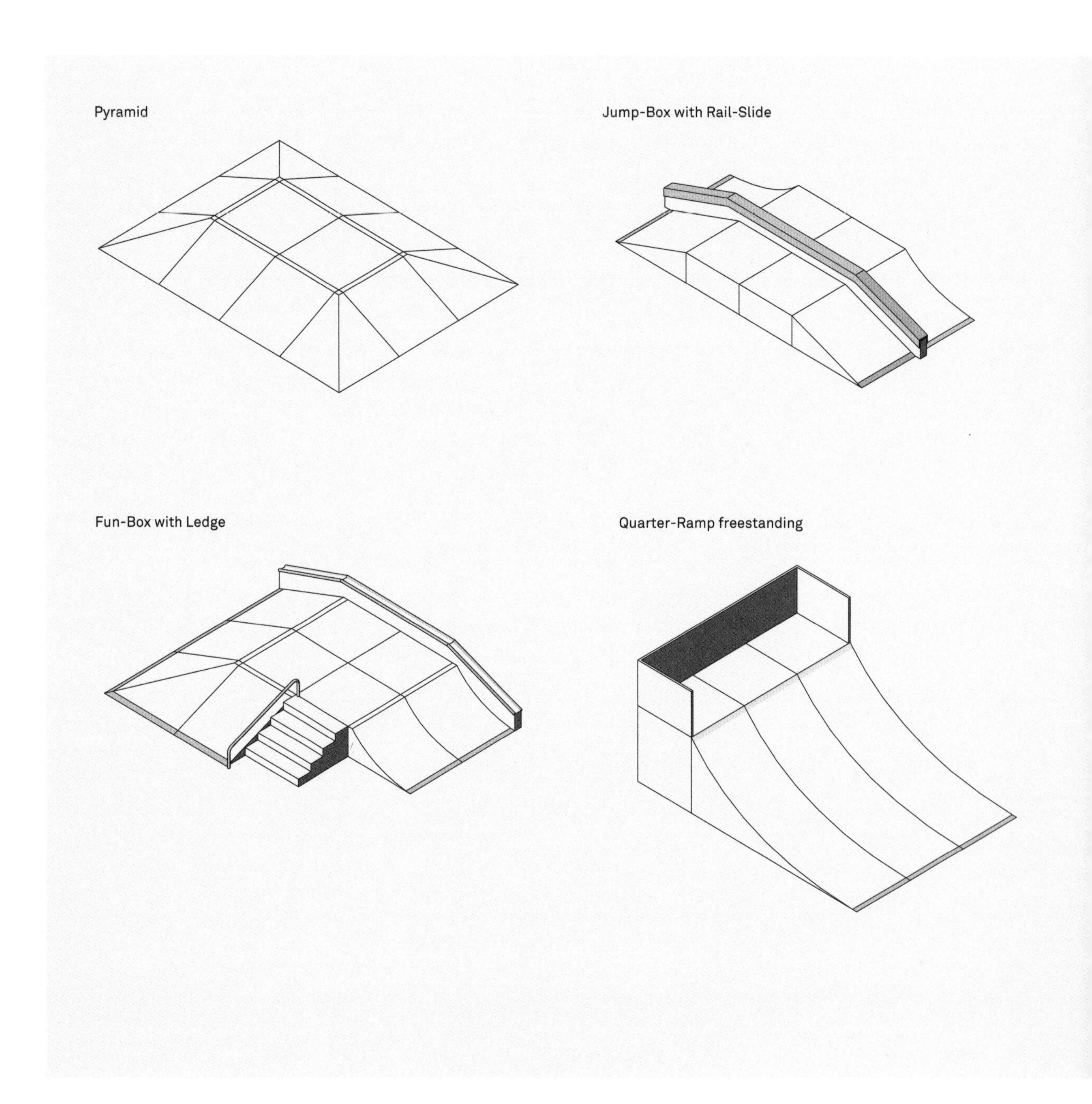

Figure 4.4.42 Skating facility

Skating facility	Minimum size	Average size
Skatepark	Approximately 350 m^2	1,000 m^2
Pools/bowls	Approximately 100 m^2 (without table)	400 m^2
BMX competition track	Length: 300–400 m Width: 5–10 m Distance between parallel tracks min. 0.5 m	–

Table 4.4.30 Skating facility

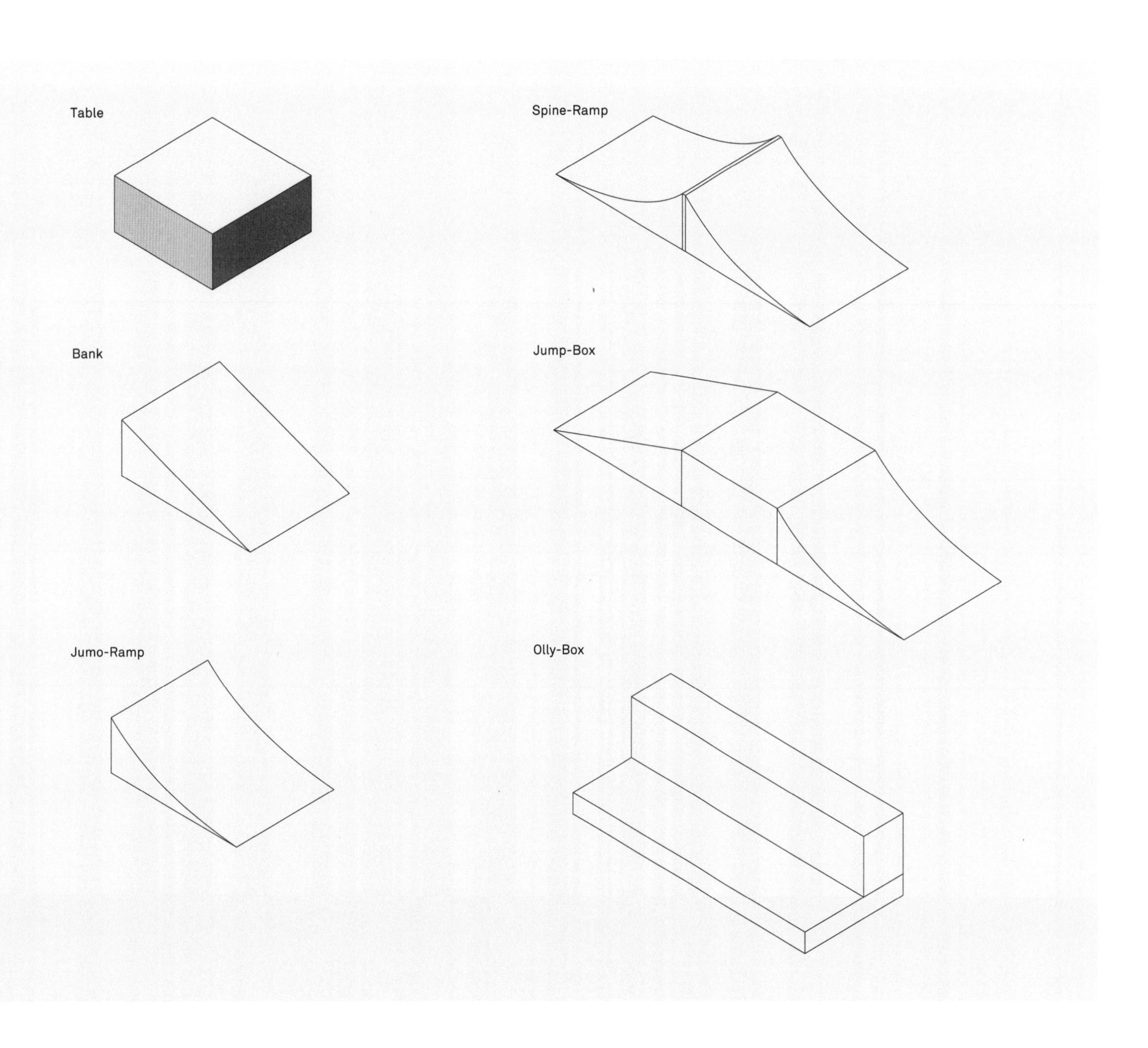

Sport Climbing

In sport climbing, a distinction is made between free climbing without using safety ropes (bouldering) and climbing with the aid of ropes. As a general rule, safety ropes are not needed for a person to climb heights of up to 3 m (measured at the foothold).

Foothold height (height of fall to the ground)	Safety area	Surfacing In safety area	Additional requirements
Boulder walls			
≤0.6 m	–	–	–
>0.6–1 m	2 m	Unbound (grass/topsoil)	–
>1 m–3 m	2 m	Noncohesive sand, water-worn gravel (4–8 mm), wood shavings, bark mulch, or rubber safety tiles	–
Climbing wall with safety rope			
>3 m			Minimum 2 m high fenced enclosure around the grounds or the climbing wall (to prevent unauthorized entry) or, alternatively, no climbing holds (grips) below a height of 2.50 m.

Table 4.4.31 Sport climbing

Equestrian Sports

In equestrian sports, also commonly known as horseback riding, various disciplines can be distinguished. Dressage, show jumping, eventing (formerly called combined training or The Military) and western riding are the best known. In order to keep the potential uses of the riding arena flexible, it is recommended to provide a size of 20 × 40 meters where possible (also required for conducting riding badge tests). For private training use, an area of 15 × 30 meters is ordinarily adequate, assuming reining will not be performed and no jumping parcours planned. In either of those cases, more space must be made available.
Riding arenas are suitable only to a limited extent for dressage driving competitions or obstacle driving competitions because the surfacing is usually too soft for horses teamed with carriages or carts. For reasons of safety, flat grassy fields or areas with a compacted surface are to be outfitted with a fenced enclosure and barrier-free access. Consideration should also be given to whether the riding or driving arena is to be used solely for training or also for competitions, since bleacher seating and spectator areas may then need to be incorporated and, in addition, it will be necessary to fulfill special requirements for the various disciplines that ordinarily take place on the arena floor. For horse racing and competitions in Icelandic horse riding, separate facilities are required.

Type of sport / riding arena	Dimensions	Surface
Riding arenas in general	Min. 20 × 40 m	
Dressage	Dressage arena for classes A-L: 20 × 40 m International competitions for classes M-S: 20 × 60 m	Quartz sand, sand mixtures (e.g. mixture of sand and sawdust/fleece shreds
Show jumping	Training: Overall size: ≥3000 m² Jumping competition: 25 × 50 m	
Western riding	Min. 20 x 40 m, optimal = 30 × 60 m	
Longeing circle	Diameter: minimum 12 m, better 15 m	
Round pen	Diameter: minimum 15 m, better 18–20 m	
Driving	Competition arena: 40 × 80 m	
Icelandic horse riding	Track: 6 × 250 m Oval track: 46 × 79.44 m / 46 × 110.70 m	

Table 4.4.32 Equestrian sports

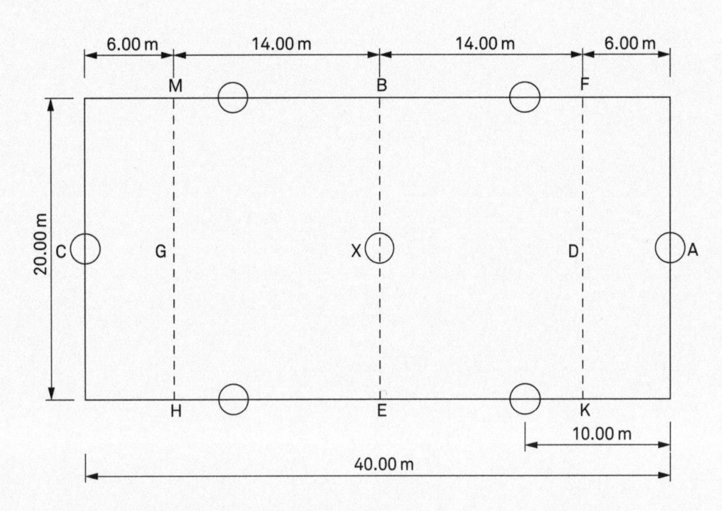

Dressage arena 20 × 40 m Scale 1:250

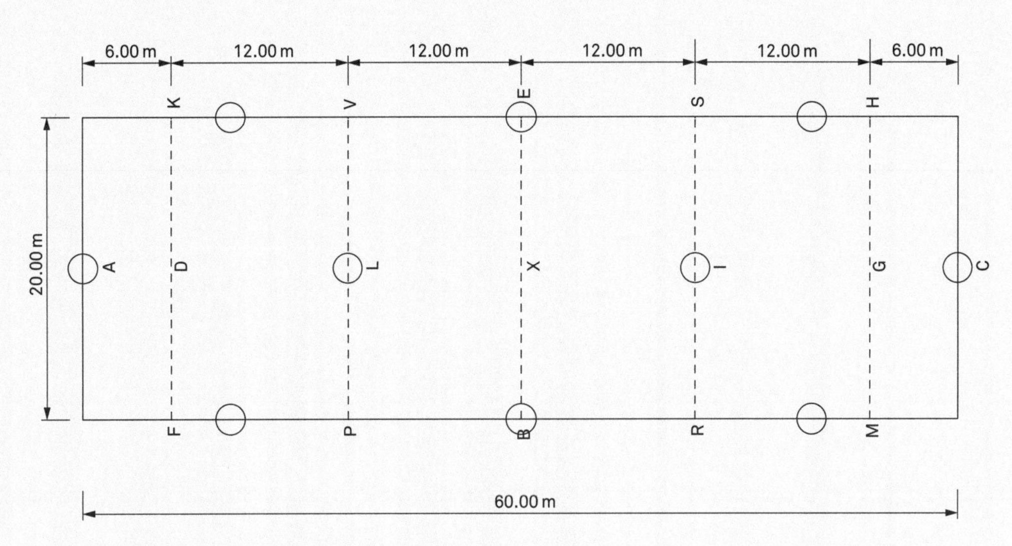

Dressage arena 20 × 60 m Scale 1:500

Abb. 4.4.43 Equestrian sports

4 Typologies
4.5 Swimming Pools, Bathing Ponds, Water-Treading Pools

4.5 Swimming Pools, Bathing Ponds, Water-Treading Pools

Outdoor swimming pools can be built either as conventional (chlorinated) pools or in the form of swimming and bathing ponds – commonly known as natural swimming pools (NSPs). A significant difference is the means of water purification, or rather, water treatment. → Figures 4.5.1 and 4.5.2 In chlorinated pools, this is accomplished primarily by means of chemical processing techniques. Along with various stages of treatment, the key action in this process is the chlorination of the water, usually by injecting chlorine gas. The goal of every type of procedure is to clean the water and achieve a maximum degree of sterility. In Germany, the basis for this is DIN 19643, which also defines allowable threshold values for the pool water. Modern practices seek to use environmentally friendly methods of water treatment and also to minimize the use of chlorine.

In swimming and bathing ponds, too, the goal of the water treatment is to yield water in a condition that is as germ-free as possible. By emphasizing biotechnological treatment and dispensing with disinfection of the water, an ecological balance is established that is able to produce a satisfactory level of water quality. Immediate and complete sterility cannot be guaranteed by this means, however, because the degradation processes naturally involve time lags. The threshold values for the water in swimming and bathing ponds are therefore higher than for chlorinated pools. → Table 4.5.11

The biotechnological purification process takes place, for one thing, with plant-based methods that exploit a range of plants with a pronounced capability for decontamination, which are located outside the utilization area in a separate basin or – for small facilities – in a separate area within the same basin (single chamber system). In addition, ground-based methods are employed, which involve a special substrate (gravel and sand filter) that is used to support microbial communities that contribute to water purification. The two techniques are usually combined.

A bathing pond can only make do entirely without technology if it is a single-chamber system for private use. For public facilities, the general rule is for there to be forced circulation of water between the swimming area and the treatment area. Sump pits and sometimes equipment rooms for the pumps and filter systems then become necessary.

Water-treading pools, as a form of Kneipp (naturopathic) hydrotherapy treatment, are found in spa parks as well as along natural stream courses beside the edges of hiking paths. They expand the range of healthy recreational opportunities offered in public open spaces. These facilities usually do not get by without a program of regular maintenance, however, so it only makes sense to build one if that is ensured. Two cleaning operations per week can typically be expected. But along stream courses, the natural flow of water is often sufficient to forgo regular conventional cleaning.

Kneipp therapy stimulates the circulation and blood flow, purportedly strengthening veins, stimulating the metabolism, and building up a person's resistance. To do so, it is important for a maximum water temperature of 15–17°C to be maintained.

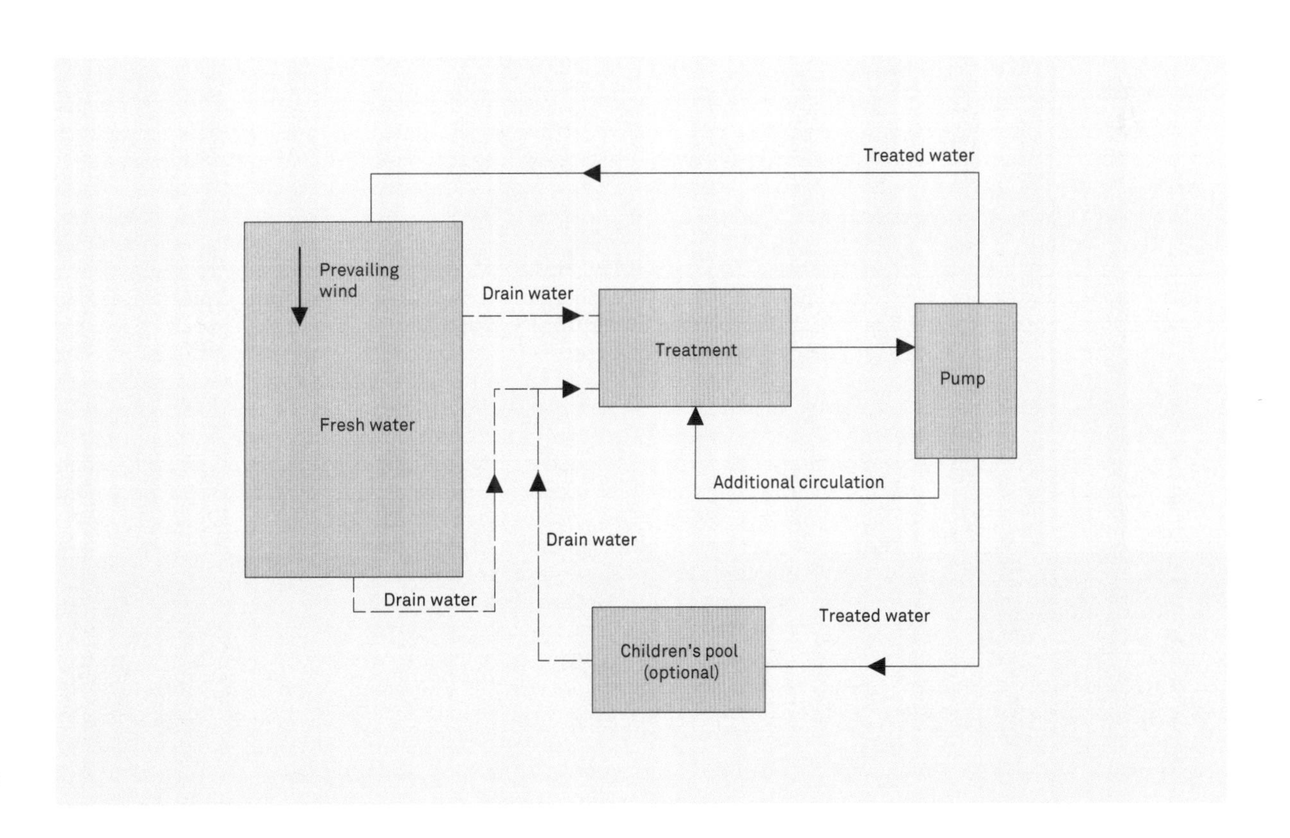

Figure 4.5.1 Water circulation principle for bathing ponds

Location

Outdoor Swimming Pools and Swimming Ponds

When selecting a site, not only should the location be easily accessible but the availability of utilities such as electricity, fresh water, and wastewater connections should also be given. Further criteria are the slope of the terrain – whereby a slight slope is preferred and large height differences involve extra construction and technical effort – and subsoil with a good load-bearing capacity. Sites in floodplain areas and wetlands are not suitable.

The immediate vicinity of cemeteries or hospitals should be avoided and the proximity to residential neighborhoods or other noise-sensitive areas must be scrutinized critically. For the premises themselves, issues of barrier-free accessibility must be taken into account.

A site sheltered from the wind and a predominantly sunny location are ideal for all types of pools. Nevertheless, light wind has a positive impact on the flow performance of bathing ponds. Additionally, trees should generally be kept away from close proximity to the water surface in order to minimize the introduction of organic matter such as leaves, blossoms, or fruit into the water – and any such problem can be expected to be worse in the direction of the prevailing wind.

Water-Treading Pools

The maximum temperature of 15–17 °C needed for Kneipp therapy is usually ensured by the natural flow of water along a watercourse. Especially when exposed to strong sunshine, this can usually only be achieved in standing bodies of water and in artificial pools by providing a (continuous) supply of fresh water. The choice of location consequently also determines the type of construction and a facility's technical complexity.

To avert health risks caused by misuse, it is necessary to create appropriate instructions for use (e.g., the need to sufficiently warm up the body beforehand, especially the feet and legs) and to post these in plain sight at the facility.

Dimensions and Characteristics

Area Requirements and Space Allocation for Outdoor Swimming Pools

The size needed for a public outdoor swimming pool is determined by the municipality's analysis of requirements, the quantity and size of any nearby existing (outdoor) pools, the way the pool will primarily be used (e.g., recreational swimming or waterpark or nature adventure pool), and the partially resultant catchment area. As a basis for calculation, the required water surface area can be taken to be 0.05–0.15 m² per inhabitant, depending on the population of the catchment area.

As a rule of thumb, the site must have roughly 10–16 m² for each square meter of usable water surface area. An area of 5–15 m² is also considered sufficient for swimming and bathing pond facilities.

For swimming and bathing ponds, the nominal number of visitors represents another important threshold value. It defines the maximum allowable number of visitors for an average day. This limit may only be exceeded on individual days, and only as long as the maximum values for hygienic and microbiological parameters are not exceeded.

The nominal number of visitors is determined according to the formula below (as per FLL guidelines from 2006). It should be noted, however, that this calculation is dependent on various factors that have influence on the water quality.

The following explanations pertain to the respective variables:

$$N = 1/k\,(V_T + V_F + A \cdot q)\ \text{[person/d]}$$

N = nominal number of visitors
k = 10
V_T = pool volume, including filter volume inasmuch as it exists within the swimming area
V_F = supply of fresh water to compensate for water losses, such as evaporation (10–50 m³/day) and discharge induced by bathers (0.75 l per guest and bathing session), as well as for cooling the water on hot days
A = the size (surface area) of the treatment area is equivalent to all areas of biological, physical, and physical-chemical treatment that are inaccessible for bathing activities.
q = volume of water from the utilization area that is circulated per day via pumps into the treatment area

Public swimming ponds should not be less than 500 m² in size. The minimum size for a private natural swimming pool depends on the swimming pond type. → **Table 4.5.11**.

When planning public facilities, requirements for the various functional zones and areas of use must be adopted as specified in **Table 4.5.1**. In the open areas or in the vicinity of the ancillary building, areas with canopies should be provided to give shelter at times of inclement weather. The area needed for the ancillary building is determined based on the space requirements listed in **Tables 4.5.2 and 4.5.3**.

For the main circulation paths within public facilities, a minimum width of 2.5 m should be provided.

Circulation areas must be provided around the entire perimeter of conventional pools – and at all points of access to bathing ponds – in order to minimize the introduction of soil material or grass into the water. For chlorinated pools, entry to the swimming area itself is generally gained by passing through a foot bath with shower. With bathing ponds, this can also be replaced by showers near points of access to the water, but the shower water may not drain into the main pool (regulated discharge via floor drains). Required minimum dimensions and other stipulations are found in **Table 4.5.4 and Figure 4.5.3**.

Function	Area/portion
Areas for sunbathing, children's play, and recreational sports	50% of the site area
Ratio between sunbathing and play areas	2:1 to 3:1
	Per 1,000 m² utilization area
Entry court	100 m²
Covered entry zone, including ticket desk and entry control	50 m²
Sand play/sandbox	≥ 100 m²
Play area	≥ 300 m²
Water play area	≥ 100 m²

Table 4.5.1 Area requirements for outdoor facilities – reference values (based on German KOK guidelines)

Function	Area
Management office (if needed)	≥ 10 m²
First-aid room	≥ 8 m²
Or: Pool supervisor and first-aid room	≥ 14 m²
Storage and equipment rooms (as needed)	20–30 m² (50–80 m² recommended)

Table 4.5.2 Area requirements inside building

	Per 1,000 m² utilization area	
Changing places (cubicles)	≥ 5, of which 4 are to be changing cubicles, including 1 cubicle for families and people with disabilities, plus 1 screened changing place near the sunbathing area	± 20%
Changing places in communal changing rooms	Minimum 2, each with 10 m bench length	
Clothing lockers	50	
Lockers for valuables	10	
Foot-washing stations	2 spigots	
Warm-up space and lounge	30–100 m²	
Toilets	Women: 3 toilets Men: 1 toilet and 3 urinals, of which 1 is to be suitable for use by children	
Showers	Minimum 2 hot water showers each for men and women	

Table 4.5.3 Infrastructural amenities for swimming pond facilities (Source: FLL, 2003)

Area	Required minimum width/clearance
General circulation areas	Width ≥ 2.5 m
Pools with foot baths	
at access points	Width ≥ 3 m
at the starting block side	Width ≥ 3 m
behind pool steps to the nonswimmer area/water slides	Width ≥ 3 m
at the diving facilities	Width ≥ 5 m
Between two pool sections	Sum of the individual dimensions
Pools without foot baths, showers at the entrance (variant for bathing ponds)	
Location of showers	Distance from access to pond ≤ 2 m Hard-surfaced area surrounding the showers ≥ 2 m in all directions
Entries	Fan-like widening toward the adjoining functional areas

Table 4.5.4 Requirements for entrances and circulation areas

Total water surface	Site area without parking spaces	Pool types	Examples of pool sizes	Water surface areas	Diving facilities
Maximum 1,500 m²	15,000–24,000 m²	Swimmer pool Diving pool Nonswimmer pool Wading pool	16.66 × 25 m 12.5 × 11.75 m 750 m' Approximately 100 m²	417 m² 147 m² 750 m² 100 m²	1 m board + 1 m platform + 3 m platform + 5 m platform
Maximum 3,000 m²	30,000–48,000 m²	Swimmer pool Diving pool Nonswimmer pool Wading pool	25 × 50 m 18.35 × 15 m 1,500 m² Approximately 200 m²	1,250 m² 275 m² 1,500 m² 200 m²	1 m board + 3 m board + 1 m, 3 m, 5 m, 7.5 m, and 10 m platforms

Table 4.5.5 Exemplary division of the water surface area into separate areas of use

Pool type	Size Length × width	Water depth	Swimming lanes: quantity and misc.	Water temperature in °C*	Remarks
Swimmer pool	25 × 12.5 m 25 × 16.66 m 50 × 16.66 m 50 × 21 m 50 × 25 m	Minimum 1.80 m (per DIN 19643, pools with water depths > 1.35 m are considered swimmer pools)	5 6 6 8 10	23°–25°	Pool rest ledge 0.1–0.15 m wide, at 1.2–1.35 m below the highest possible water level
Nonswimmer pool	Shape as desired 600–1,500 m²	0.5/0.6–1.35 m 0.5–1.1 m 0.9–1.35 m Maximum floor slope: 10 %	For school swimming: 2 m wide with two parallel sides	23°–25°	
Wading pool	Shape as desired 80–200 m²	0–0.3/0.5/0.6 m or 0.1/0.2/0.3–0.6 m	Floor slope: 5 %–10 %	24°–26°	
Wave pool	As desired, but minimum 12.5 × 33 m or 16.66 × 33 m 21 × 33 m	Tapers out toward the end: 0 or 0.15/0.3 m in the deep area: 2 m or dependent on use: 1.8 m; 1.35 m	Wave height: 0.6–1 m	23°–25°	
Diving pool	Dependent on diving facilities provided	3.4–5 m	Training possible with 20 or 25 m width	23°–25°	
Teaching pool (special type of nonswimmer pool)	12.5 × 8 m 16.66 × 10 m	0.5/0.6–1.35 m Recommended: 0.8–1.2 m	Maximum floor slope: 10 %	23°–25°	
Foot bath	6 × 3–4 m approximately 3 × 3 m	0.15 at the center, 0.1 at entry/exit	Trough shape, box shape	–	For swimming ponds, can be replaced by showers when located less than 2 m from the access point
Minimum sizes for private swimming pool facilities	2.25 × 5.25 4.25 × 8–9				Smallest one-lane swimming pool (2 strokes, 1–2 people) Mid-sized two-lane swimming pool (3–4 strokes) shortest pool for starting dive from the end

* Water temperature: for swimming ponds, the maximum temperature is 23°C.

Table 4.5.6 Reference values for pools according to type of use

Dimensions of diving pools

Width × Length	Water Depth	Diving Facilities (boards/platforms)
10.6 × 12.5 m	3.8 m	1 m and 3 m boards; 5 m platform
12.5 × 11.75 m	3.8 m	1 m and 3 m boards; 1 m, 3 m, and 5 m platforms
16.9 × 11.75 m	3.8 m	2 × 1 m and close up space: 2 × 3 m boards; 1 m, 3 m, and 5 m platforms
18.35 × 15 m	4.5–5 m	1 m and 3 m boards; 1 m, 3 m, 5 m, 7.5 m, and 10 m platforms
22,40 × 15 m	4.5–5 m	2× 1 m and 2× 3 m boards; 1 m, 3 m, 5 m, 7.5 m, and 10 m platforms

Table 4.5.7 Dimensions of diving pools

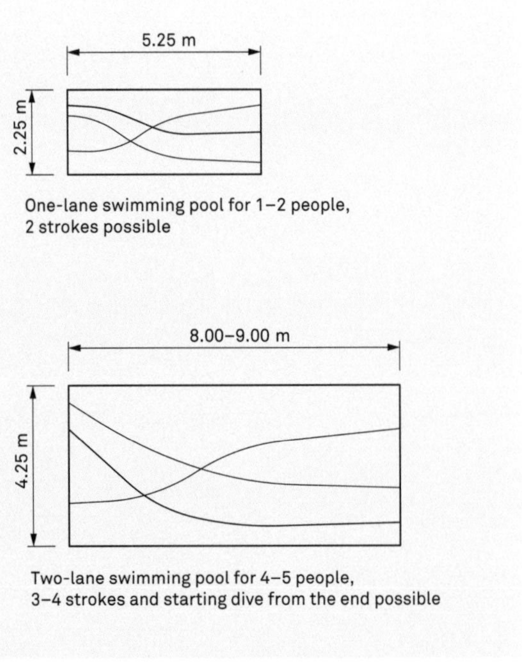

5.25 m
2.25 m
One-lane swimming pool for 1–2 people, 2 strokes possible
8.00–9.00 m
4.25 m
Two-lane swimming pool for 4–5 people, 3–4 strokes and starting dive from the end possible

Figure 4.5.2 Space required for private swimming pool facilities

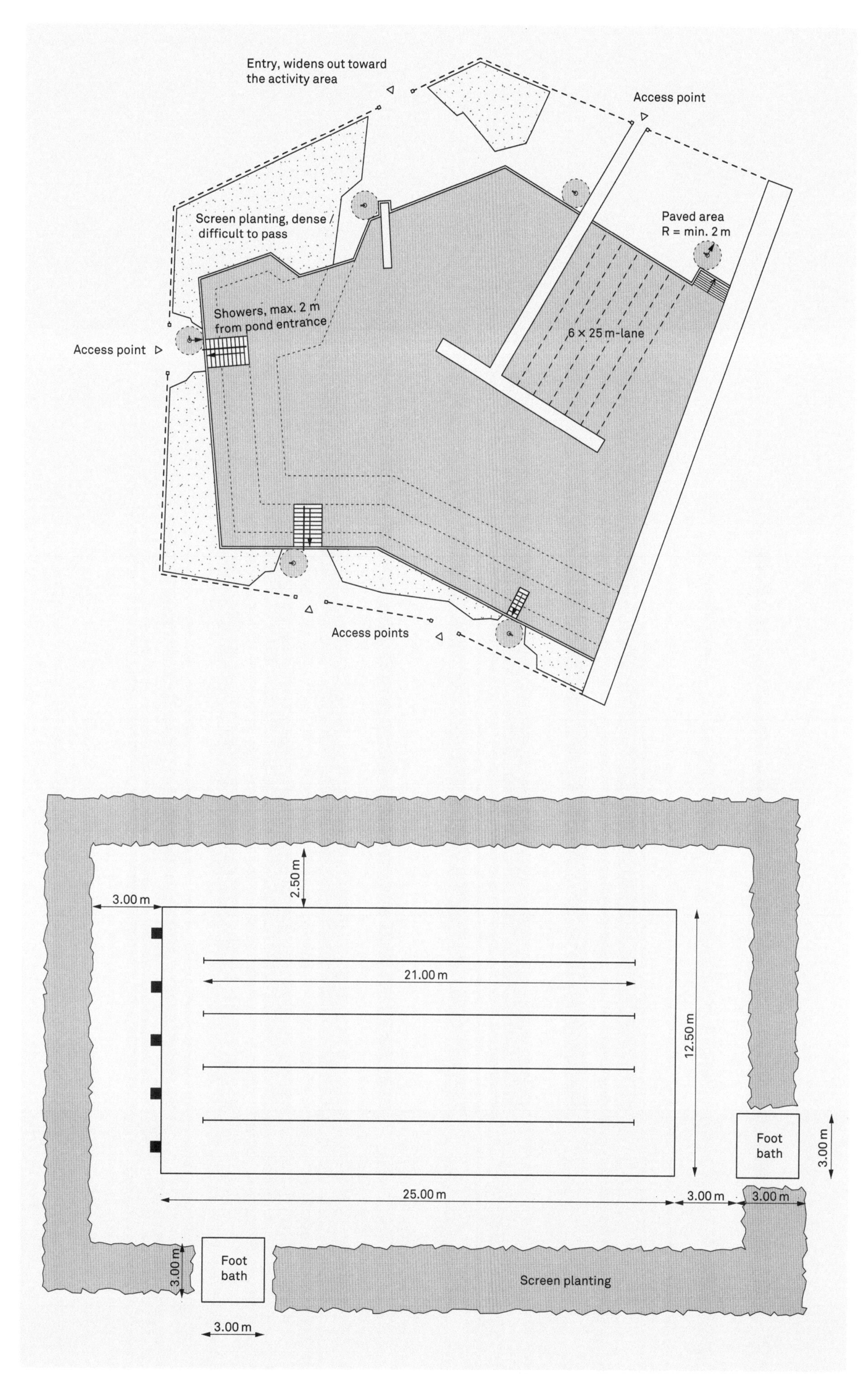

Figure 4.5.3 Dimensions for swimming pools and ponds, including circulation areas – example with 25 m lane (dimensions based on German KOK guidelines)

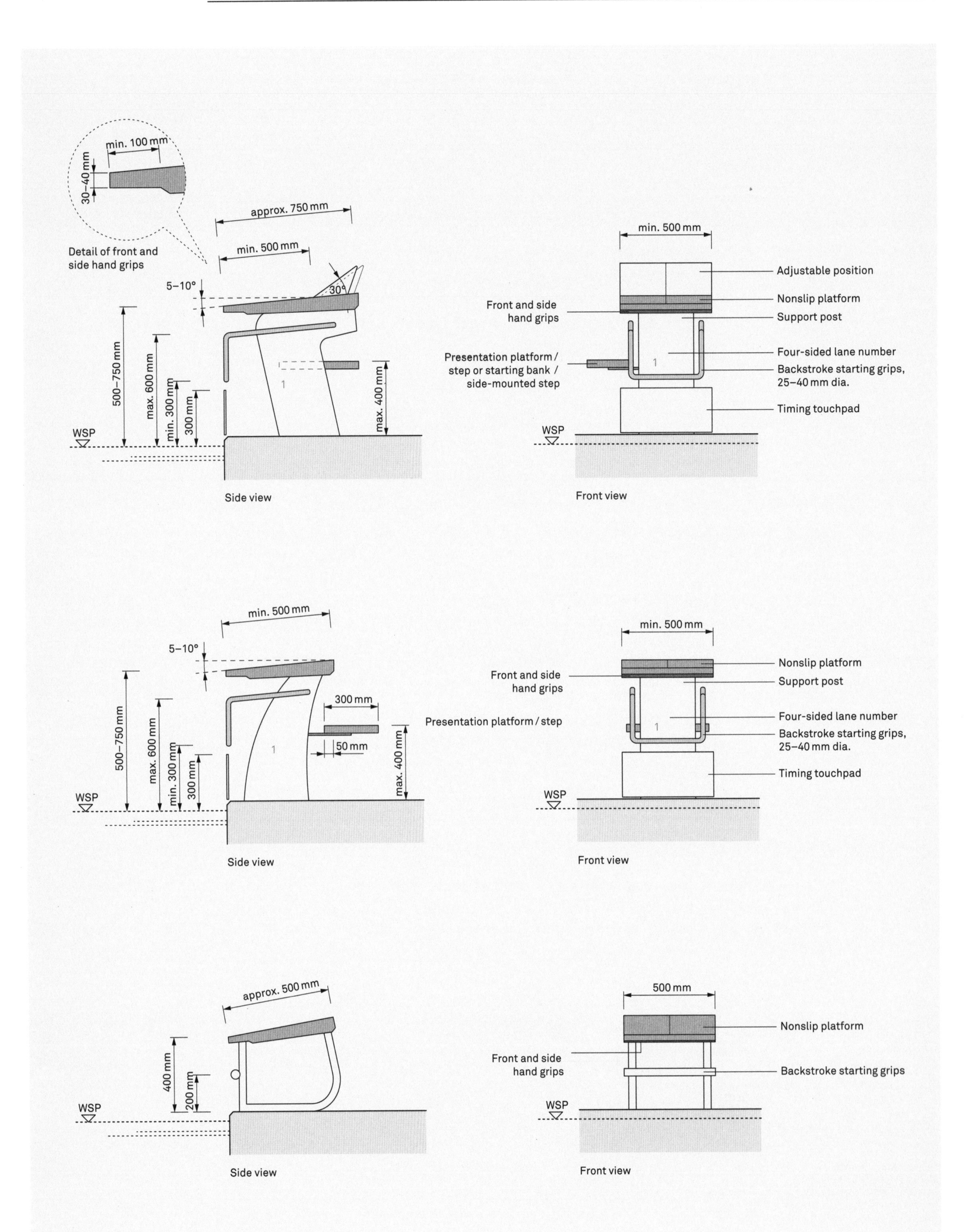

Figure 4.5.4 Dimensions of starting block for competitions

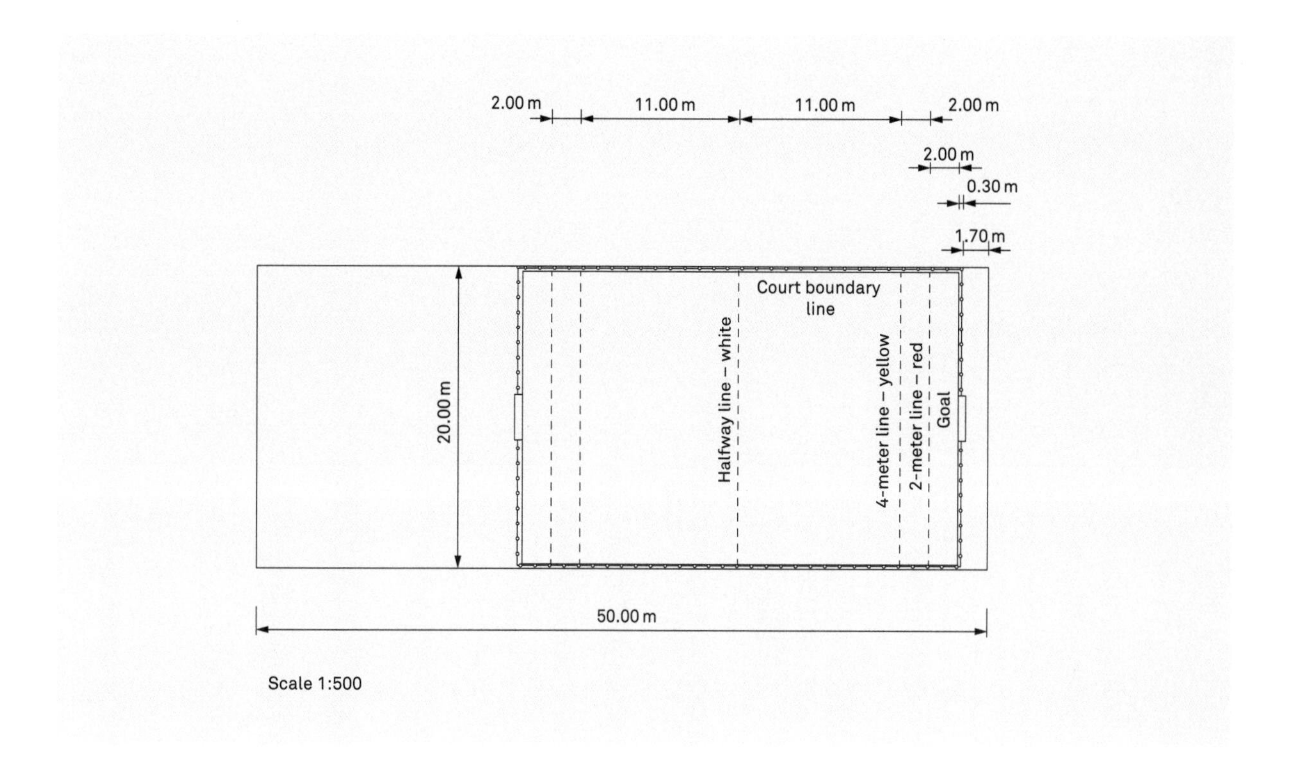

Figure 4.5.5 Dimensions of water polo court

Dimensions of Diving Area

For springboards and diving platforms, the safety clearances defined in standard EN 13451-10 apply. For the boulders commonly used as diving-off points at swimming ponds, the safety clearances for diving platforms apply correspondingly. The threshold overhead clearances must also be observed when, for example, trees are in close proximity.

Table 4.5.8 Minimum dimensions of springboard facilities and platforms

Minimum dimensions of springboard facilities as per DIN EN 13451-10

Type	Height of the springboard above water level*	Minimum usable width	Length reserved for the diver**	Perpendicular to the pool wall minimum
1	1 m ≤ h ≤ 1.05 m	0.5 m	Entire length of the springboard	1.5 m
1	3 m	0.5 m	Entire length of the springboard	1.5 m
2	<1 m	0.48–0.6 m	Entire length of the springboard	= Height above water level

* Limiting dimension for the height, as measured from the water surface ** Minimum distance from the vertical

Table 4.5.9 Minimum dimensions of springboard facilities and platforms

Minimum dimensions of platforms as per DIN EN 13451-10

Height of the platform above water level*	Minimum usable width	Length reserved for the diver**	Perpendicular to the pool wall minimum
1 m	0.6 m	0.75 m	0.75 m
3 m	0.6 m	1.25 m	1.25 m
5 m	1.5 m	1.25 m	1.25 m
7.5 m	1.5 m	1.5 m	1.5 m
10 m	2 m	1.5 m	1.5 m

* Limiting dimension for the height, as measured from the water surface ** Minimum distance from the vertical

	Dimensions of diving facilities	1-meter board 4.8 x 0.5 m	3-meter board 4.8 x 0.5 m	1-meter platform 4.5 x 0.6 m	3-meter platform 5 x 0.6 m	5-meter platform 6 x 1.5 m	7.50-meter platform 6 x 1.5 m	10-meter platform 6 x 2 m
A	6 m	5 m	6 m	6 m	8 m	12 m	1.5 m	1.5 m
A-A	From front edge of platform back to front edge of platform directly below	–	–	–	–	1.25 m	1.25 m	1.25 m
B	From plummet to pool wall at the side	2.5 m	3.5 m	2.3 m	2.8 m	4.25 m	4.5 m	5.25 m
C	From plummet to adjacent plummet	1.9 m	1.9 m	–	–	2.1 m	2.1 m or 2.45 m	3.13 m or 2.65 m
D	From front edge of board/platform to pool wall ahead	9 m	10.25 m	8 m	9.5 m	10.25 m	11 m	13.5 m
E	From board/platform to bottom of ceiling above	5 m	5 m	3 m	3 m	3 m	3.2 m	3.4 m
F	Clear overhead space behind and to each side of plummet ("E" dimension maintained)	3.4 m	3.8 m	3.4 m	3.4 m	3.8 m	4.1 m	4.5 m
G	Clear overhead space ahead of plummet ("E" dimension maintained)	5 m	5 m	5 m	5 m	5 m	5 m	6 m
H	Depth of water at plummet	3.4 m	3.8 m	3.4 m	3.4 m	3.8 m	4.1 m	4.5 m
J	Clearance ahead of front edge of board/platform	6 m	6 m	5 m	6 m	6 m	8 m	12 m
K	Water depth up to distance "J"	3.3 m	3.7 m	3.3 m	3.3 m	3.7 m	4 m	4.25 m
L	Clearance to each side of plummet	2.25 m	3.25 m	2.05 m	2.55 m	3.75 m	3.75 m	4.5 m
M	Water depth up to distance "L"	3.3 m	3.7 m	3.3 m	3.3 m	3.7 m	4 m	4.25 m

Table 4.5.10 Minimum dimensions of springboard facilities and platforms

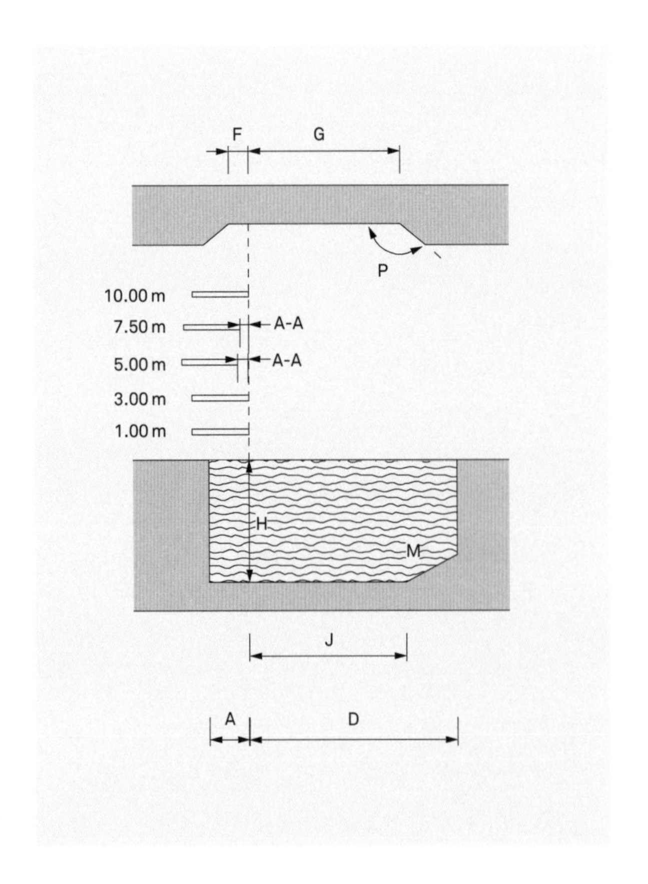

Figure 4.5.6 Safety clearances for diving facilities, key to dimensioning

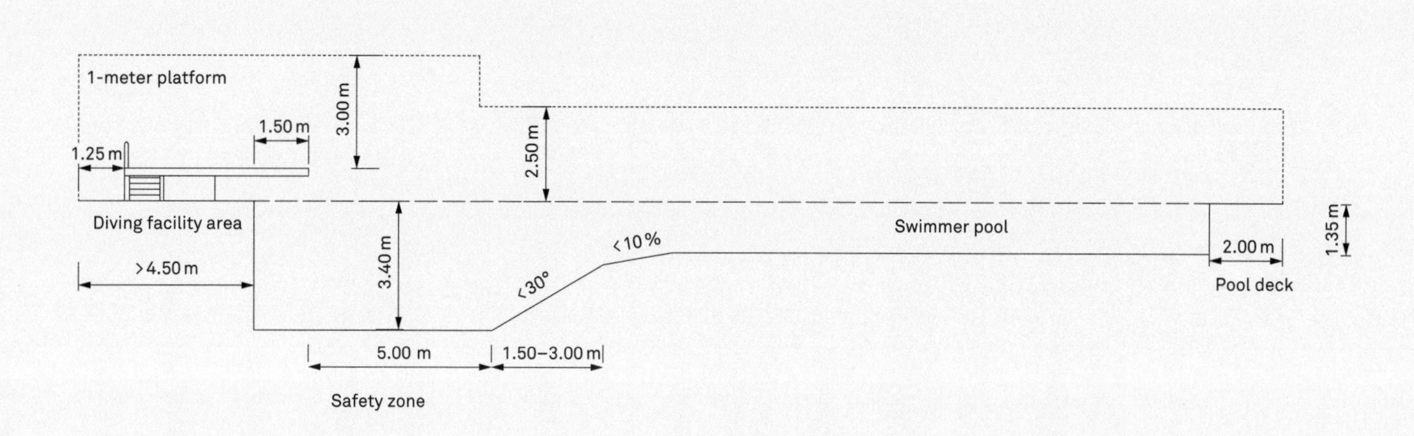

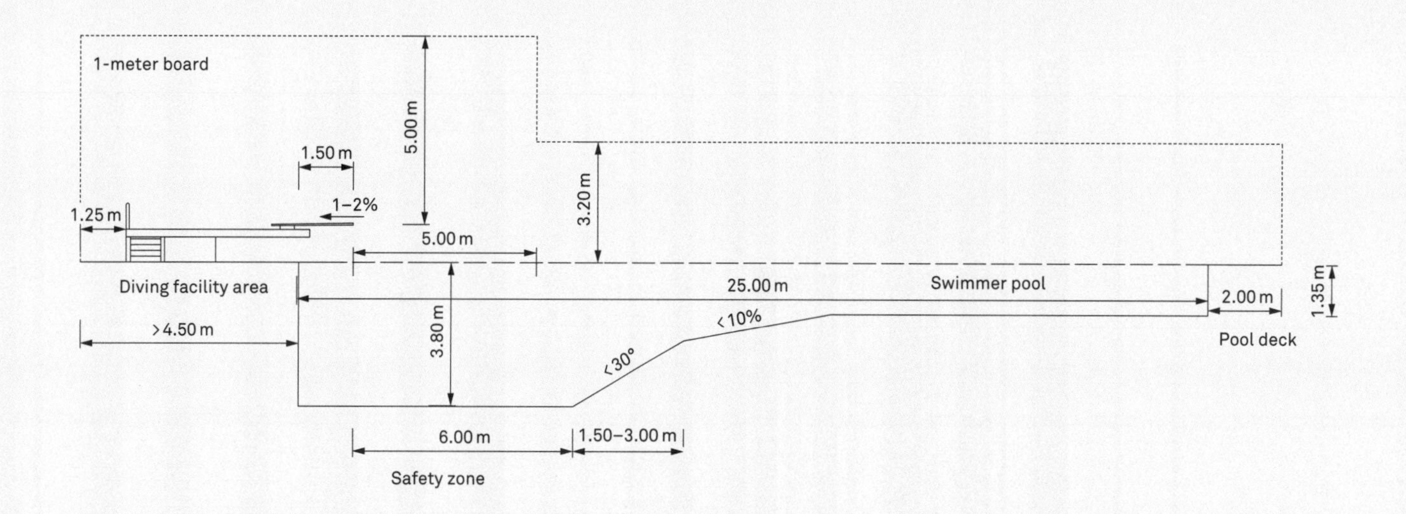

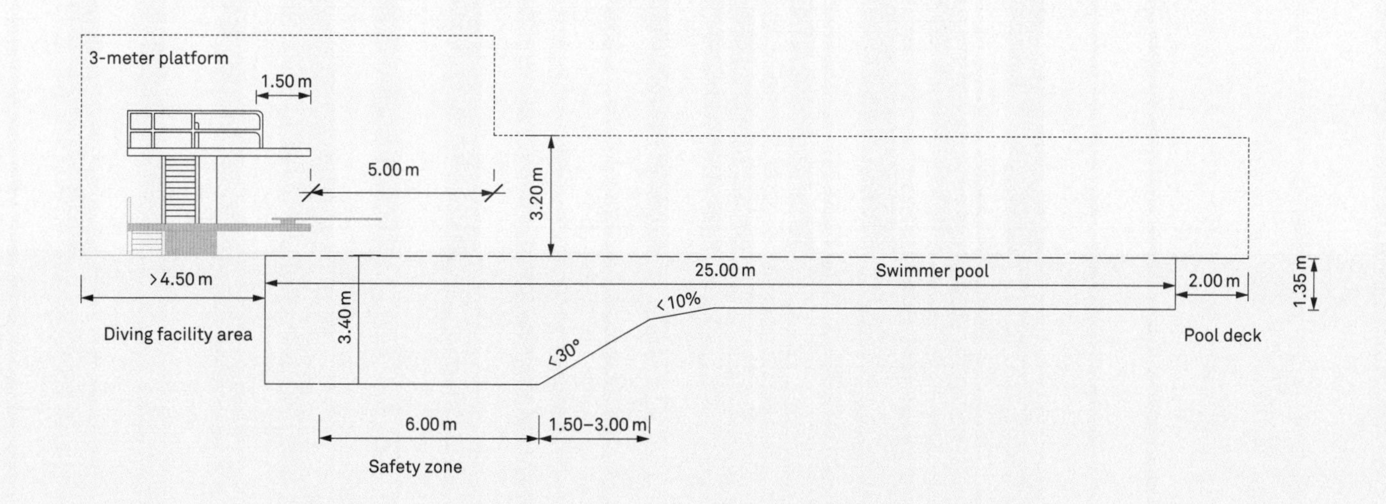

Figure 4.5.6 Safety clearances for diving facilities, key to dimensioning

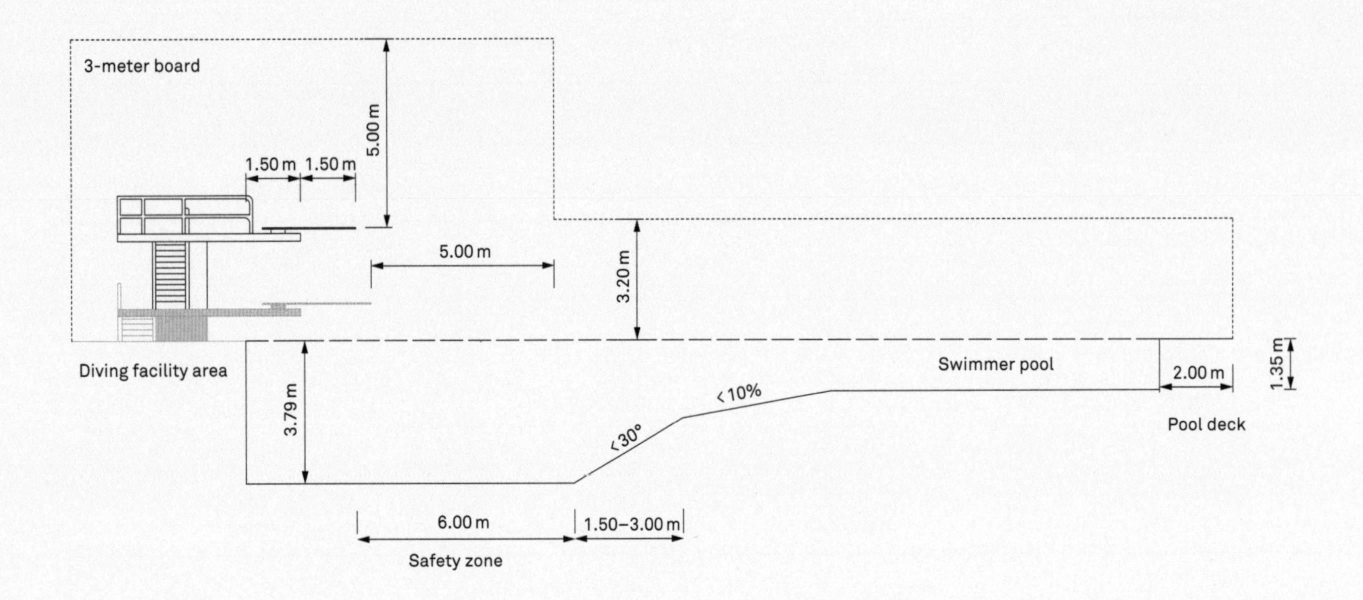

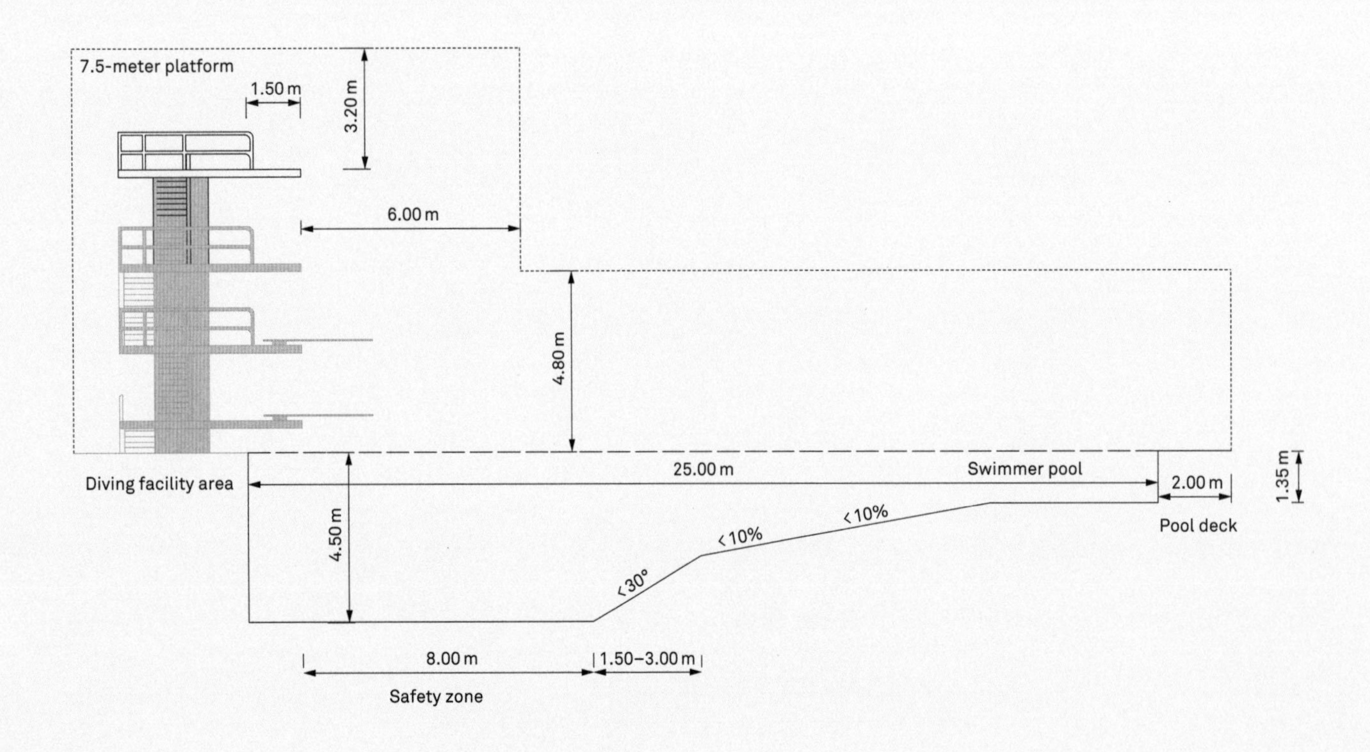

Figure 4.5.6 Safety clearances for diving facilities, key to dimensioning

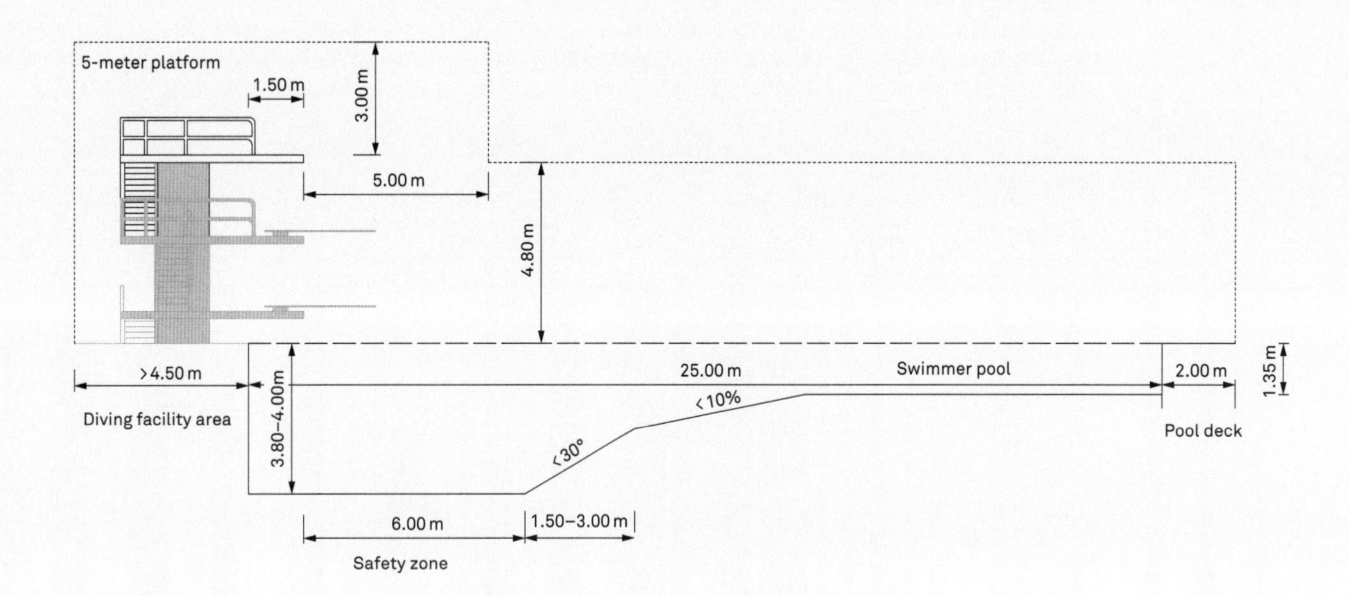
5-meter platform
1.50 m
3.00 m
5.00 m
4.80 m
>4.50 m
Diving facility area
3.80–4.00 m
25.00 m
Swimmer pool
2.00 m
1.35 m
<10%
<30°
Pool deck
6.00 m
1.50–3.00 m
Safety zone

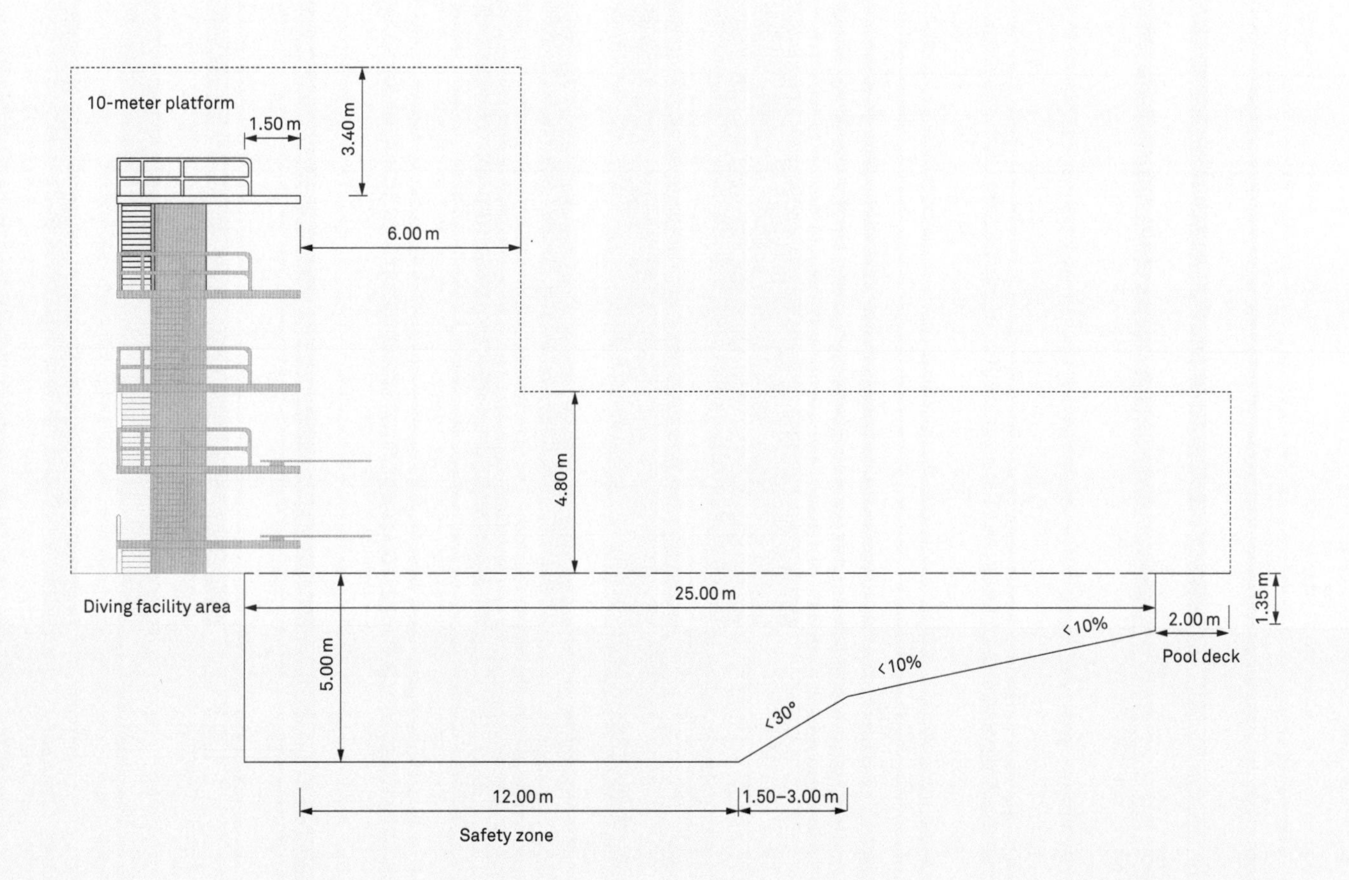
10-meter platform
1.50 m
3.40 m
6.00 m
4.80 m
Diving facility area
25.00 m
2.00 m
1.35 m
5.00 m
<10%
<10%
<30°
Pool deck
12.00 m
1.50–3.00 m
Safety zone

Construction of Swimming and Bathing Ponds

In swimming and bathing ponds, a distinction is made between the utilization (swimming) area and the treatment (regeneration) area. The two areas must be fundamentally separated from each other. For small ponds in private yards, the areas can be located in the same pool, but even in such cases, the treatment areas should not be entered. With larger facilities or when the intensity of use is greater, a physical separation should even be made for private ponds. The separation of both areas from one another enables more effective water purification and thus saves space. For public facilities, the treatment zone must definitely be separated from the utilization area in all cases. This can be achieved through built means within a pond or by spatially dividing the two pool areas in separate ponds – which is more advantageous, particularly for larger facilities.

	Swimming pond type*				
Attribute	Type I	Type II	Type III	Type IV	Type V
Aim of the technique	–	Ease of maintenance	Improve conditioning, optimize water quality, and stabilize its functional behavior, ease of maintenance		
Treatment area – standard design	• No controlled flow through plant zone • Open water		• (Planted) controlled flow through filter zone • Open water, possibly without controlled flow through plant zone		• (Planted) controlled flow through filter zone • open water • and possibly without controlled flow through plant zone
Operation of technical equipment					
Flow	Natural circulation	Surface flow	Surface flow and forced flow through treatment area		
Water purification	Plants Zooplankton Microorganisms	Plants, zooplankton, microorganisms. Increasing support by means of hydraulic/technical devices			
Recommended standard values for minimum sizes, according to use					
Private swimming ponds (3–4 people)	≥120 m²	≥100 m²	≥80 m²	≥60 m²	≥50 m²
Public swimming ponds	Unsuitable				≥500 m² (Size in accord with nominal number of visitors)
Portion reserved for regeneration	≥60%	≥50%	≥40%	≥40%	≥40% (with optimized treatment, ≥30%)
Water depth in utilization area	≥65% with a minimum 2 m depth		≥60% with a minimum 2 m depth (can be reduced to ≥40% with appropriate technical effort)	≥40% with a minimum 2 m depth	Depending on the situation; for public pools: ≥40% with a minimum 2 m depth
Care and maintenance expenditures					
Maintenance of structural and technical facilities	Low	→	→	→	High
Care of vegetation and water areas	High	←	←	←	Low

Table 4.5.11 Attributes of swimming pond types illustrated in Figure 4.5.7 (Source: FLL 2006, amended and supplemented)

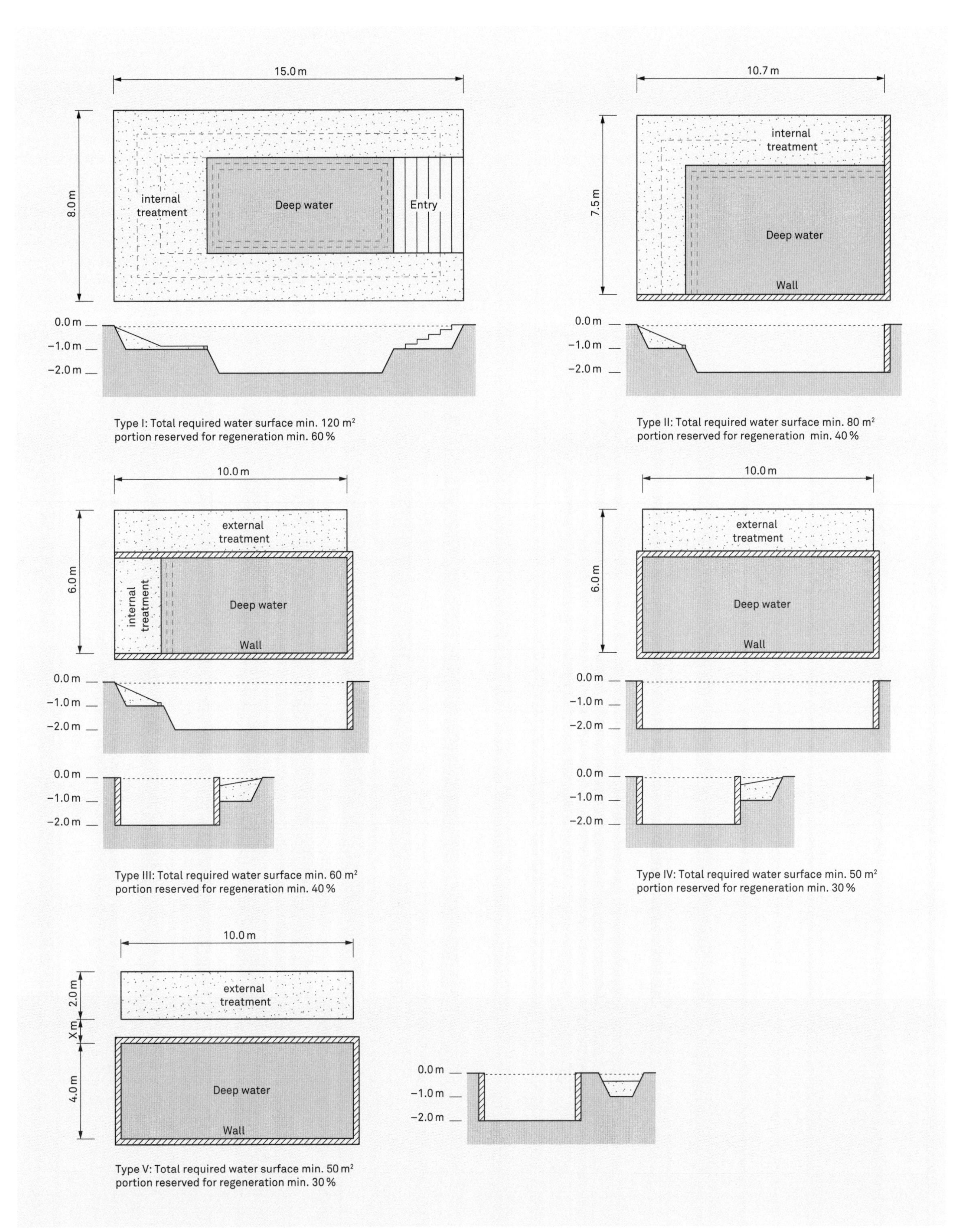

Figure 4.5.7 Principle of swimming and bathing ponds with integrated/separate regeneration area (based on FLL 2003, amended)

Parameter	Value
pH value	6–9
Acid capacity (carbonate hardness) $K_{S4.4}$	≥2 mmol/l
Total phosphorus	≤0.01 mg/l P
Conductance	≤1,000 µS/cm at 20°C
Nitrate	<50 mg/l
Ammonium	<0.5 mg/l
Iron	<0.2 mg/l
Manganese	<0.05 mg/l
Hardness	>1 mmol/l

Table 4.5.12 Chemical specifications for the fill water used for public swimming ponds

Water Quality

The quality of the fill water, which is used for the initial filling as well as for compensation of water losses and for cooling in summer, is subject to specific requirements. Even when of drinking-water quality, it is possible that the water's phosphorus content is too high, thus making it unsuitable for the biological balance in a swimming pond. Then the water must be conditioned beforehand, inasmuch as possible.

Threshold values also apply to the pool water itself, and these must not be exceeded while the pool is in use. → Table 4.5.12

To minimize the introduction of foreign matter into the pool water by bathers, walk-through foot baths and showers must be provided. → Figures 4.5.3 and 4.5.8

Parameter	Maximum value for pool water in chlorinated pools*	Maximum value for pool water in swimming ponds**
Hygienic and microbiological parameters		
Escherichia coli (E. coli) CFU/100 ml	Not detectable in 100 ml	100
Enterococci CFU/100 ml		50
Pseudomonas aeruginosa CFU/100 ml	Not detectable in 100 ml	10
Chemical reference values		
pH value	6.5–7.6	6–8.5 (also 9 in exceptional cases)
Nitrate concentration	≤20 mg/l	≤30 mg/l

* In accordance with DIN 19643 ** In accordance with Austrian pool hygiene regulations and the FLL guideline for public swimming and bathing pond facilities

Table 4.5.13 Comparison of the threshold values for selected parameters pertaining to chlorinated pools and swimming and bathing ponds

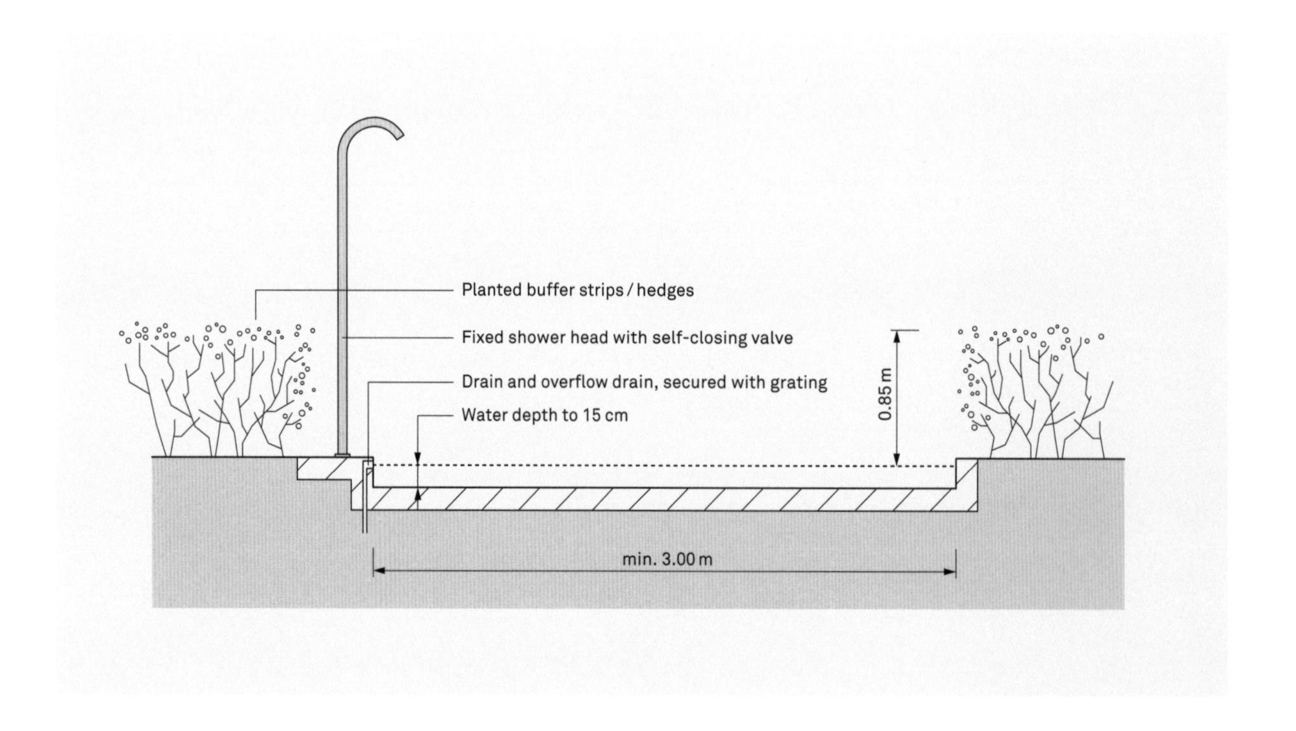

Figure 4.5.8 Dimensions of a foot bath

Pool Edge

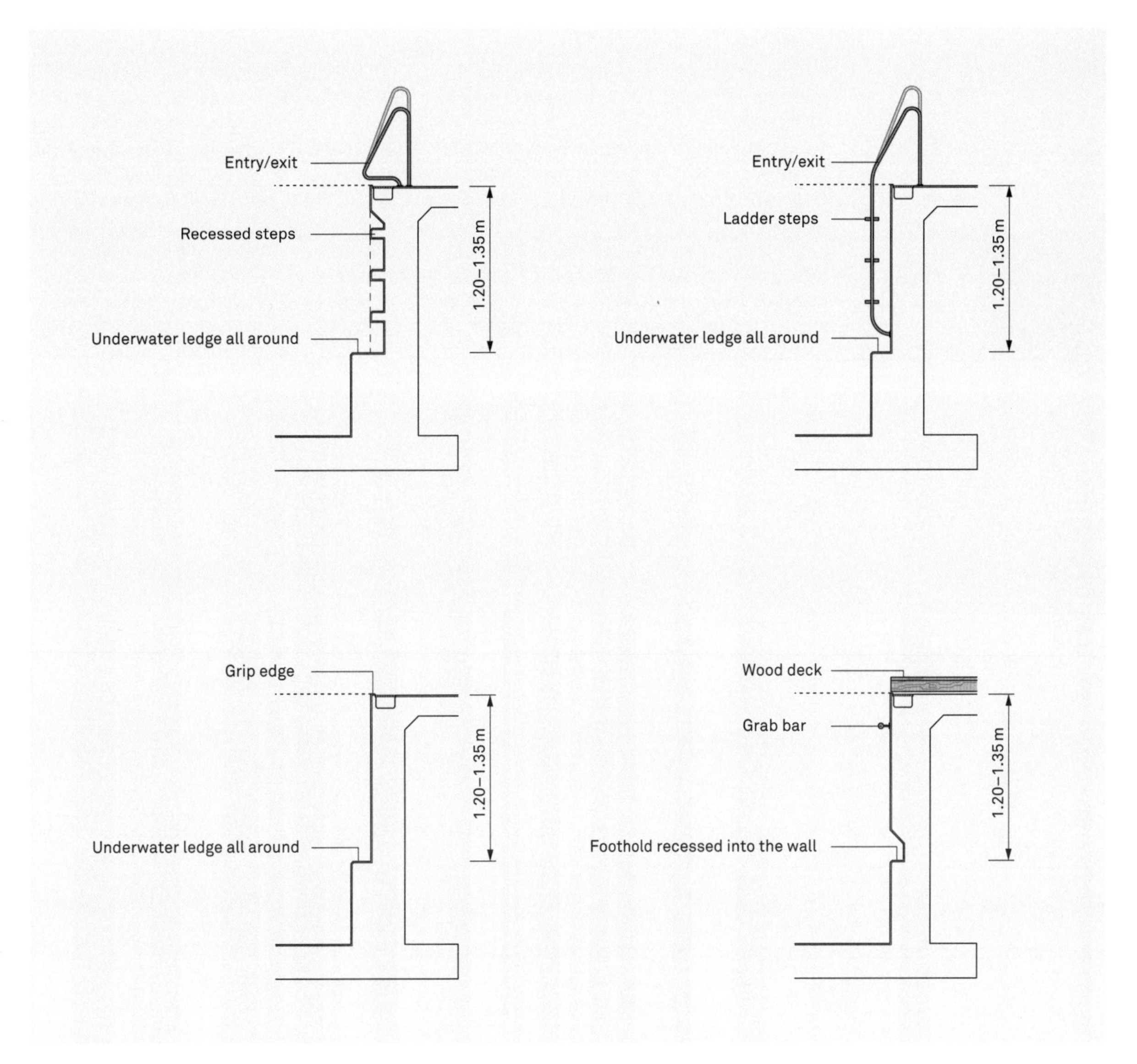

Figure 4.5.9 Pool ledge with and without entry/exit

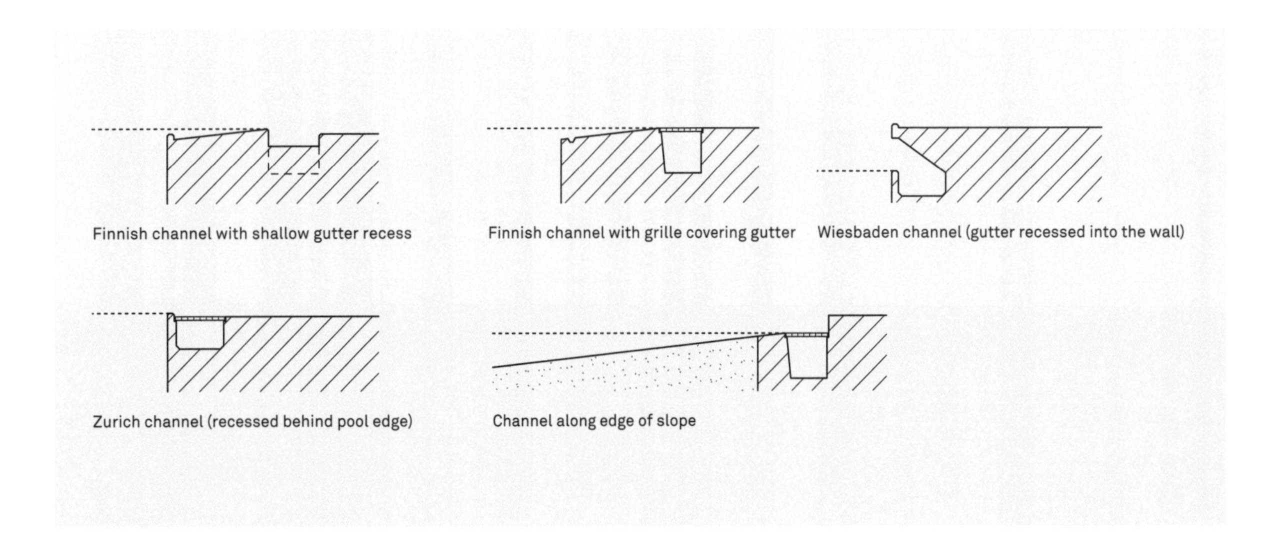

Figure 4.5.10 Pool edges with perimeter overflow channels

Dimensions and Characteristics of Water-Treading Pools

Water-treading pools have an average volume of 7 m³. The minimum dimensions in plan are 1.3 × 3.6 meters with a depth of 0.6 meter. The actual water depth should be 0.4–0.45 meter.

If heavy use is anticipated, parallel paths with a combined width of 2.2 m should be planned, and if entry/exit steps can be provided at both ends, the length should be at least 6 m.

The floor should have a slope of 0.5 %–1 % and all walking surfaces should have a nonslip finish, for example rough (sandblasted) concrete, rough-sawn natural stone, or nonslip floor tiles. The entry/exit steps should not exceed a rise-to-run ratio of 15 × 30 cm.

The average area required for the pool itself is approximately 20–60 m². With ancillary areas, such as an access path, benches, temporary storage surfaces, a relaxation area, and planted areas for spatially integrating the facility into the landscape, 300 m² or more should be available.

Pools on private property or pools that make use of existing underground springs or natural stream courses, for example along a hiking path, will need less area.

The required inflow volume varies, depending on the inlet water temperature and whether the pool is located in the sun or the shade. A flow rate of 0.5 to 5 liters per minute are necessary to remain below the maximum temperature of 15–17 °C.

The drain water can be discharged as residual water to the nearest receiving stream.

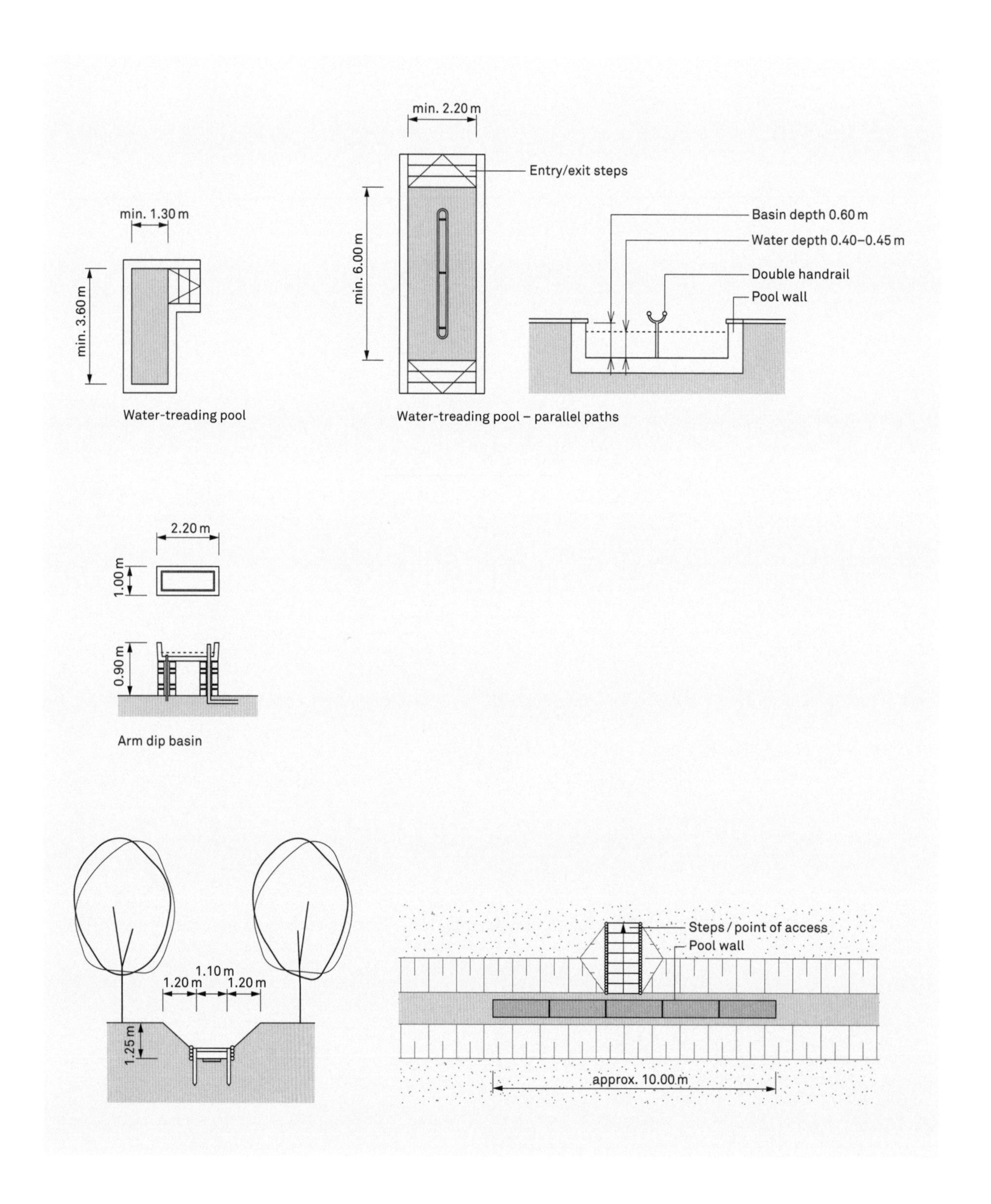

Figure 4.5.11 Dimensions of water-treading pools and arm dip basins

Remarks on Building Law and Regulatory Approval

For the use of springwater or groundwater to fill the pool with fresh water, a permit is required under water law. The same holds true for the introduction of water into a natural receiving stream.

In Germany, pools with a volume of more than 100 m^3 are subject to regulatory approval. In undeveloped open areas in rural outskirts, different regulations may apply.

4 Typologies
4.6 Campgrounds

4.6 Campgrounds

Campgrounds can be separated into short-stay (short visit), vacation, and extended-stay (long-term or seasonal stay) facilities, where the type is mainly characterized by the length of stay of the majority of the guests. Extended-stay campgrounds are distinguished by larger and separated individual campsites, whereas vacation and short-stay campgrounds have open sites on camping fields. In the majority of cases, both campsite types are combined. Separated campsite lots are suitable for recreational vehicles (RVs) and larger tents, and usually have integrated parking space for a passenger car. Areas without separation are particularly suitable for tents without an accompanying car. In this case, separate collective parking areas are designated on the periphery of the campground. Camping fields on the whole require less circulation space.

Spatial Configuration and Location

The terrain must satisfy general requirements for it to be suitable for use as a campground. A level or slightly sloping ground surface presents the ideal conditions. In the mountains, there must be terraced level areas of sufficient size. The subgrade should exhibit good drainage capacity and have no depressions or waterlogging. Locations with loamy soil are unsuitable. In any case, regulated drainage of the campsites must be ensured.

Especially on sloping sites, hazards from surface water runoff must be considered and pertinent measures evaluated. Waterfront locations are only feasible when a risk from flooding can be ruled out.

In the mountains, areas vulnerable to landslides or avalanches must also be considered unsuitable.

Near major roads, noise abatement measures are to be provided as needed.

Depending on the prevailing climate, the requirements for the site can indeed vary but as a basic principle, a sunny location is favored; shady slopes or similar situations are to be avoided. In the summer months and especially in southern countries and warm climates, sufficient shade from tree cover or sunshade devices should be available. Morning sun can be advantageous for accelerating the evaporation of morning dew.

The site should preferably be sheltered from the wind. Furthermore, hedgerows can be planted as a visual and wind protection measure.

The site should be functionally and structurally divided into two areas: The area at the entrance should accommodate all the noise-intensive use areas such as vehicle access, car parking spaces, reception, eating facilities and business premises, playgrounds and other leisure facilities, waste collection area, and sanitary facilities. The remaining area should be reserved for the campsites themselves.

Campsites for both camping vehicles and tents are to be subdivided into individual fire compartments by means of fire lanes at least 5 m wide. Depending on the country, a fire lane is to be provided after every ten consecutive individual campsites or 2000 m² total area and also along adjoining built properties. The areas are to be kept clear of built structures, objects, and undergrowth.

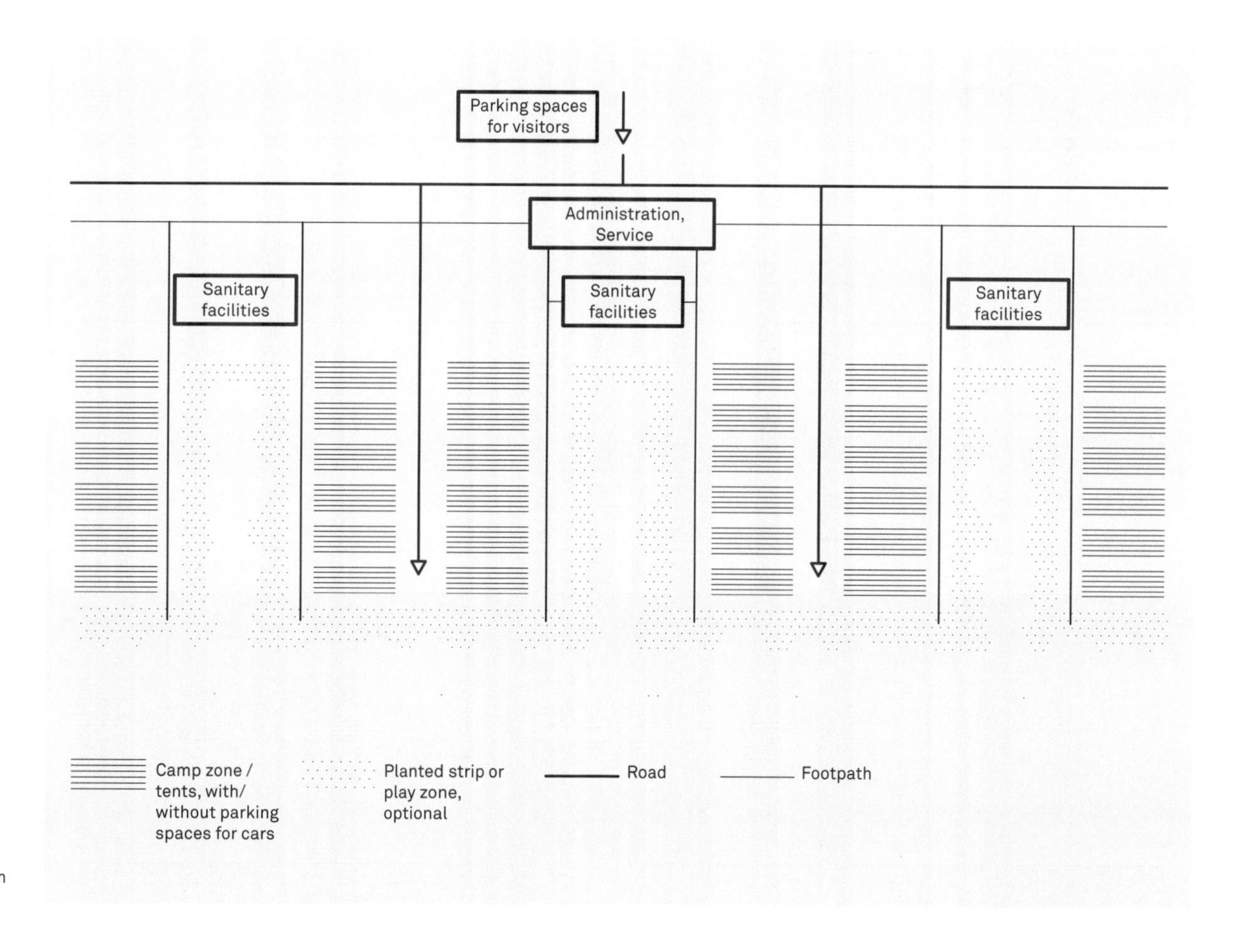

Figure 4.6.1 Functional diagram of a campground

Dimensions and Characteristics

The following areas per tent or camping vehicle, including usable areas, clearances, and access, can be assumed as a basis for calculations. For the service and circulation areas as a whole, 50–100 % of the total area of the actual campsites can be added. → **Table 4.6.1**

Type of use	Space needs / dimensions
Campsites	
Small tents on open field	40 m²
Large tents	80 m²
Average space needed per campsite on open field	60–80 m²
Separated campsite lot for RV or large tent with integrated parking for passenger car	100–120 m² (min. 75 m² *)
Separated campsite lot with passenger car in a remote parking area	min. 65 m² *
Separated campsite lot, including ancillary areas (paths and screen planting)	140 m²
Circulation	
Vehicular access and main paths	5.5 m wide
Secondary paths	3–4 m wide
Roadways with one-way traffic	3 m wide
Dead ends not longer than 100 m	3 m wide
Circulation space, total	
Service and circulation areas	50–100 % of the actual campsites

* as per Bavarian campground regulations

Table 4.6.1 Recommended values for the space needs of campgrounds

		Per 100 campsites	Per 200 campsites
Washing facilities	Washbasins, men	8 washbasins, including 2 in private compartments	Additionally: 1 washbasin and 1 shower, both accessible, suitable for wheelchair users
		4 individual showers	
	Washbasins, women	8 washbasins, including 2 in private compartments	
		4 individual showers	
	Toilets, men	4 toilets and 4 urinals	Additionally: 1 accessible toilet, suitable for wheelchair users
	Toilets, women	8 toilets	
Dishwashing and laundry facilities		2 dishwashing sinks and 1 laundry sink or washing machine	The facilities must be accessible for the disabled
Drinking water taps		4, distributed pragmatically on the site	

Table 4.6.2 Sanitary facilities at campgrounds (recommended values based on the campground regulations of Baden-Württemberg/Bavaria)

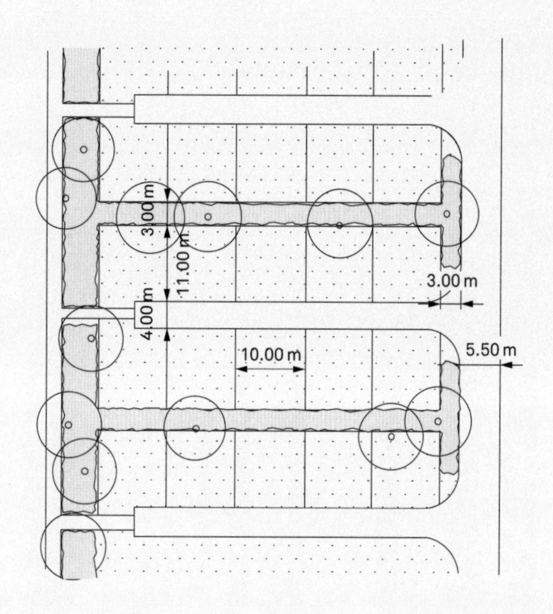

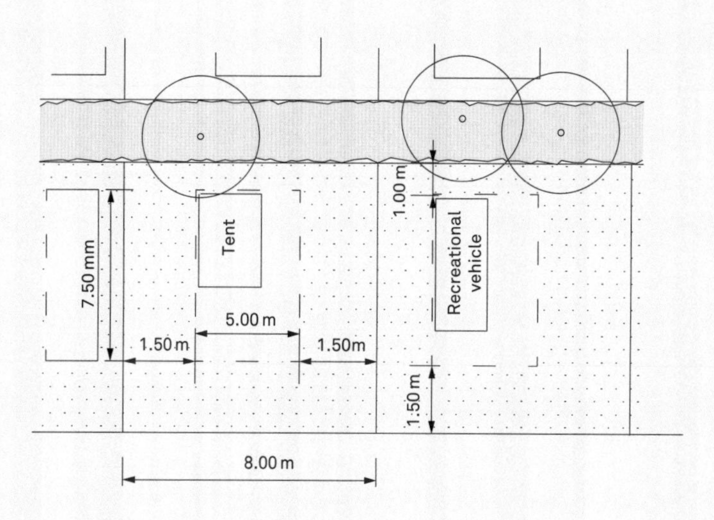

80 m² area for tent / recreational vehicle

Figure 4.6.2 Dimensions of separated campsite lots

4 Typologies
4.7 Outdoor Theaters and Tiered Seating

4.7 Outdoor Theaters and Tiered Seating

Outdoor theaters and straight or semicircular arrangements of tiered seating can be constructed in outdoor facilities for various purposes. Stepped constructions alone often serve as seating areas that can be used as outdoor classrooms in schools, for instance, or as simple gathering places in parks. Larger constructions are often established for specific uses and then possibly also furnished with a covered or open stage (also known as a performance area). For outdoor stages that are to serve as event venues (theaters, open-air cinemas, etc.) or for tiered seating at sports facilities, specific requirements must be observed. These aspects are generally governed by regulations on places of assembly. Special provisions set forth by national, state, or local governing bodies as well as use-specific regulations must thereby be taken into account. Ordinarily, requirements for places of assembly must be observed when the visitor area accommodates more than 1,000 persons.

For smaller facilities, which allow appreciably more design freedom, only generally applicable requirements must be adhered to, such as those for fall protection.

Spatial Configuration and Location

The alignment of an outdoor theater on the site is dependent in part on whether it will be chiefly used during the day or in the evening hours. In general, a north-south orientation – with seating in the south that faces north – yields the best results. This arrangement can be adapted to fit with the terrain as needed, depending on the topographic situation and possibilities for site development.

Since the type and extent of infrastructure and facilities needed are dependent on the size and use of the complex, these can vary substantially. Toilets and vending stalls can be replaced with temporary or mobile facilities if they will only be used for limited periods of time or when a permanent facility is not feasible.

The ability to provide the following infrastructure and functional elements must be examined and consideration given to their type and scope:

Minimum requirements
- Toilets/toilet trailers (quantity → **Table 4.7.1**)
- Escape routes, fire department staging area if required
- Electric power supply/lighting

Additional requirements
- Vehicular access for delivery of stage equipment, required loading
- FOH space for sound and stage equipment
- Ticket booth
- Catering facilities, vendor areas
- Bicycle parking and car parking spaces, including designated parking spaces for disabled people
- Roofing over the stage and the spectator area
- Noise abatement/trees and shrubs planted as enclosure at the sides
- Standing areas in addition to the seating area
- Type of boundary fence
- Secondary entrances
- Administration building, including dressing rooms, customer service areas, and sanitary facilities

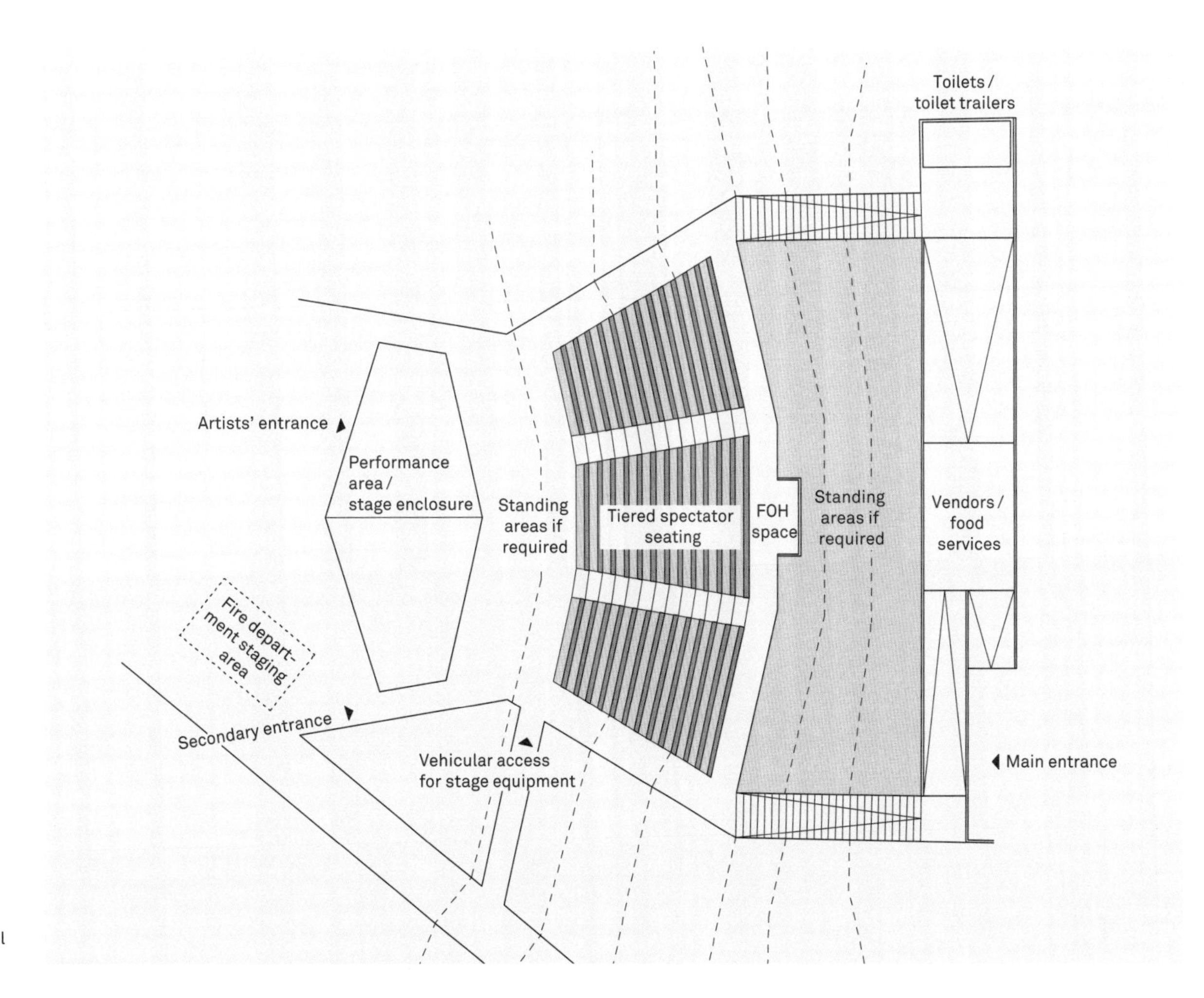

Fig. 4.7.1 Functional and spatial program for an outdoor theater

Dimensions and Characteristics

Tiered Seating and Rows of Seats

For the design of outdoor theaters and tiered seating that incorporate a performance area (stage) of more than 20 m² and a visitor area accommodating more than 1,000 persons and for sports stadiums with more than 5,000 spectators, the Versammlungsstättenverordnung [Ordinance Governing Places of Assembly] applies in Germany. It specifies limits and orientation values that can be used as initial guidelines for such facilities. For specific provisions, refer to the applicable regulations that are valid in the particular locations concerned. Additional requirements could be specified therein.

A rough estimate for the number of persons visiting a place of assembly can be made as follows:

- For seats at tables: one person per square meter of ground area
- For seats in rows: two persons per square meter
- For standing areas: two persons per running meter of a tier

If the regulations on places of assembly apply, the following requirements pertain to the seats and their physical dimensions:

- Seating arranged in rows must be securely fixed in place
- Chairs used on a temporary basis must be firmly connected to one another
- The rows of tiered seating in places of assembly for more than 5,000 persons must have individual seats securely fixed in place
- Seats must be at least 0.5 m wide and should be at least 0.4 m deep and max. 0.45 m high
- There must be a clear width of at least 0.4 m (Bavaria: 0.45 m) between the rows (total depth of tier 0.80/0.85 m)

The resulting space requirement for tiered seating is 0.5 × 0.8 m = 0.4 m² per seat area. In the VIP area of sports facilities, these values can be increased to a clearance of 0.55–0.6 m and a tier depth of 1 m. For more comfort, particularly with tiered seating that does not require individual fixed seats (capacity under 5,000 persons), larger dimensions can be provided. → **Figure 4.7.2**

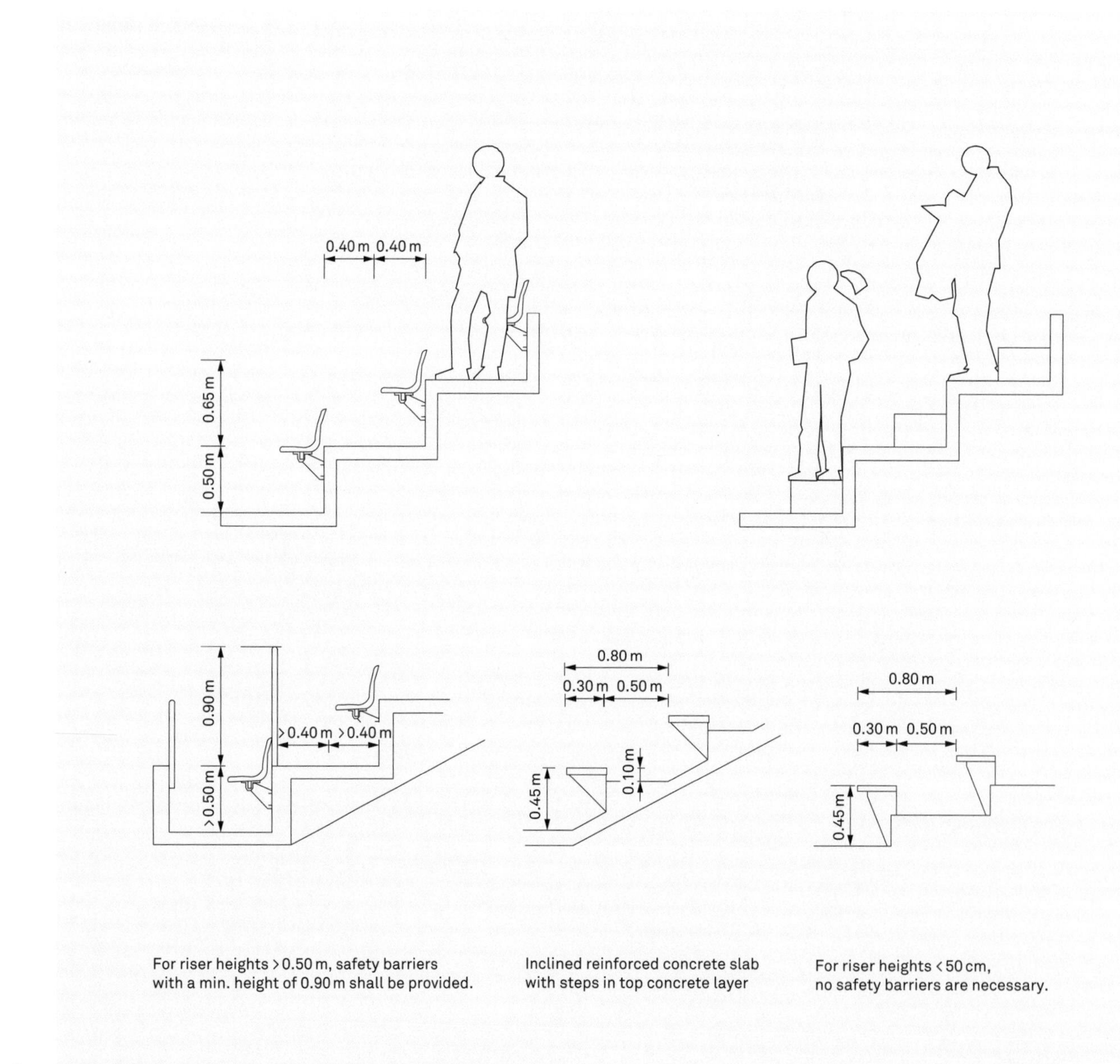

Figure 4.7.2 Fall protection and dimensions of seating rows and standing areas for outdoor places of assembly

Outdoor seating may be arranged in a maximum of 30 consecutive rows and there may be a maximum of 20 seats to a side aisle. Seating blocks with aisles on both sides can thus have a maximum of 40 seats per row.

Paths behind and to the sides of the blocks must be at least 1.2 m wide. The width of the escape routes shall be 1.2 m per 600 visitors. From every side aisle, a maximum of 20 seats may be located on each side. This results in a maximum of 40 seats between two side aisles. (see Muster-Versammlungsstättenverordnung (MVStättV) [Model ordinance governing places of assembly]) → **Figure 4.7.4**

For escape routes from roofless tiered seating, a maximum distance of 60 m applies from any seat to an exit; a maximum distance of 30 m applies from a stage or when the tiered seating is roofed over with a clear height of 5 m or less. With headroom of more than 5 m, the distance can be extended by 5 m for every 2.5 m of additional height, up to a maximum distance of 60 m to an exit. The presence of a roof automatically means that additional requirements for fire safety must be taken into account.

Places of assembly that regularly host multiple events in succession must establish a waiting area for at least half of the maximum number of visitors. This area shall be dimensioned on the basis of four people per 1 m².

For tiered seating levels that accommodate more than 800 persons, each level shall be provided with its own escape routes that extend no more than 30 m from any seat to the exit.

The quantity of spectator restrooms results from Table 4.7.1. The facilities can be permanently housed in buildings as needed or made available on a temporary basis with mobile toilet trailers.

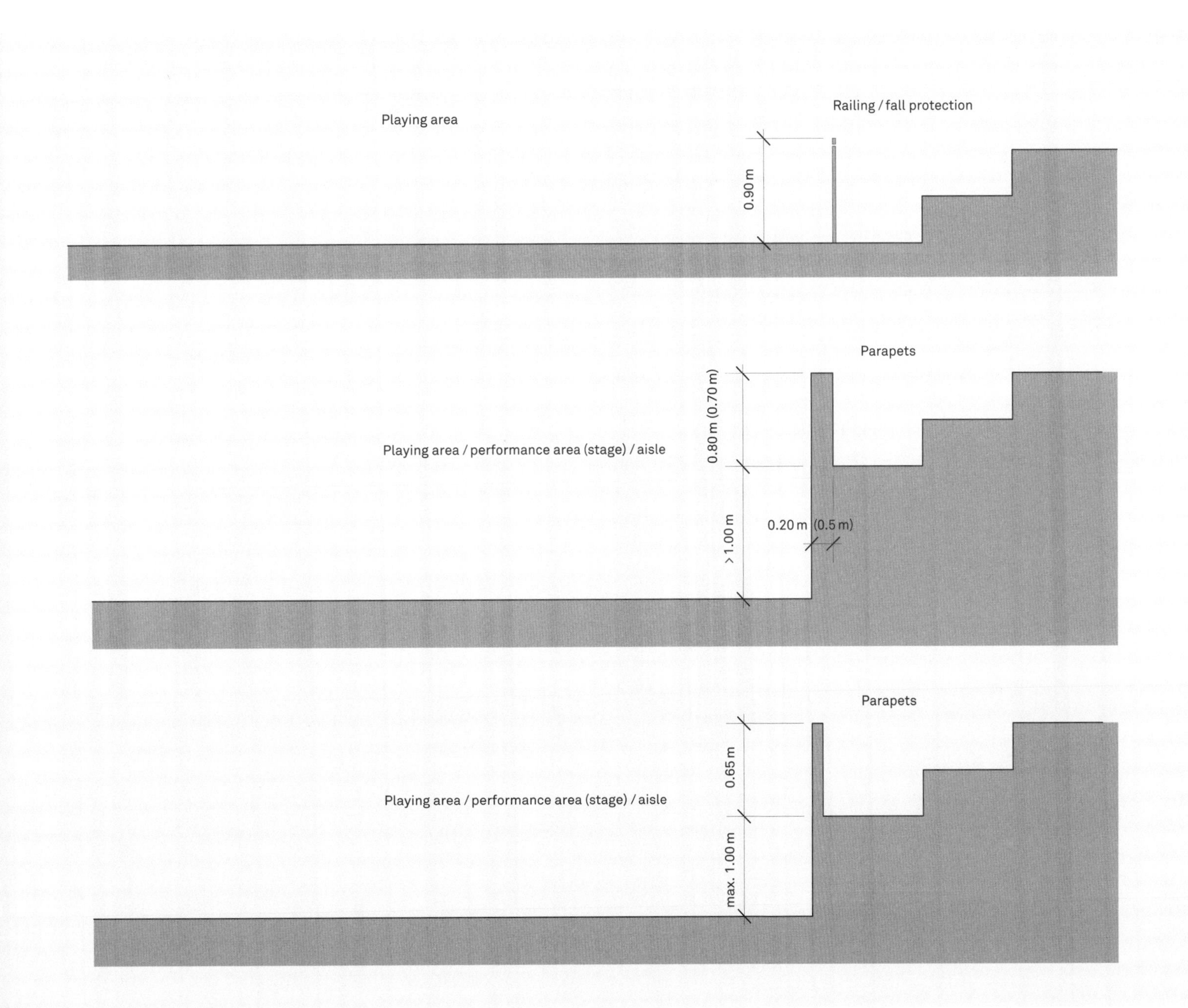

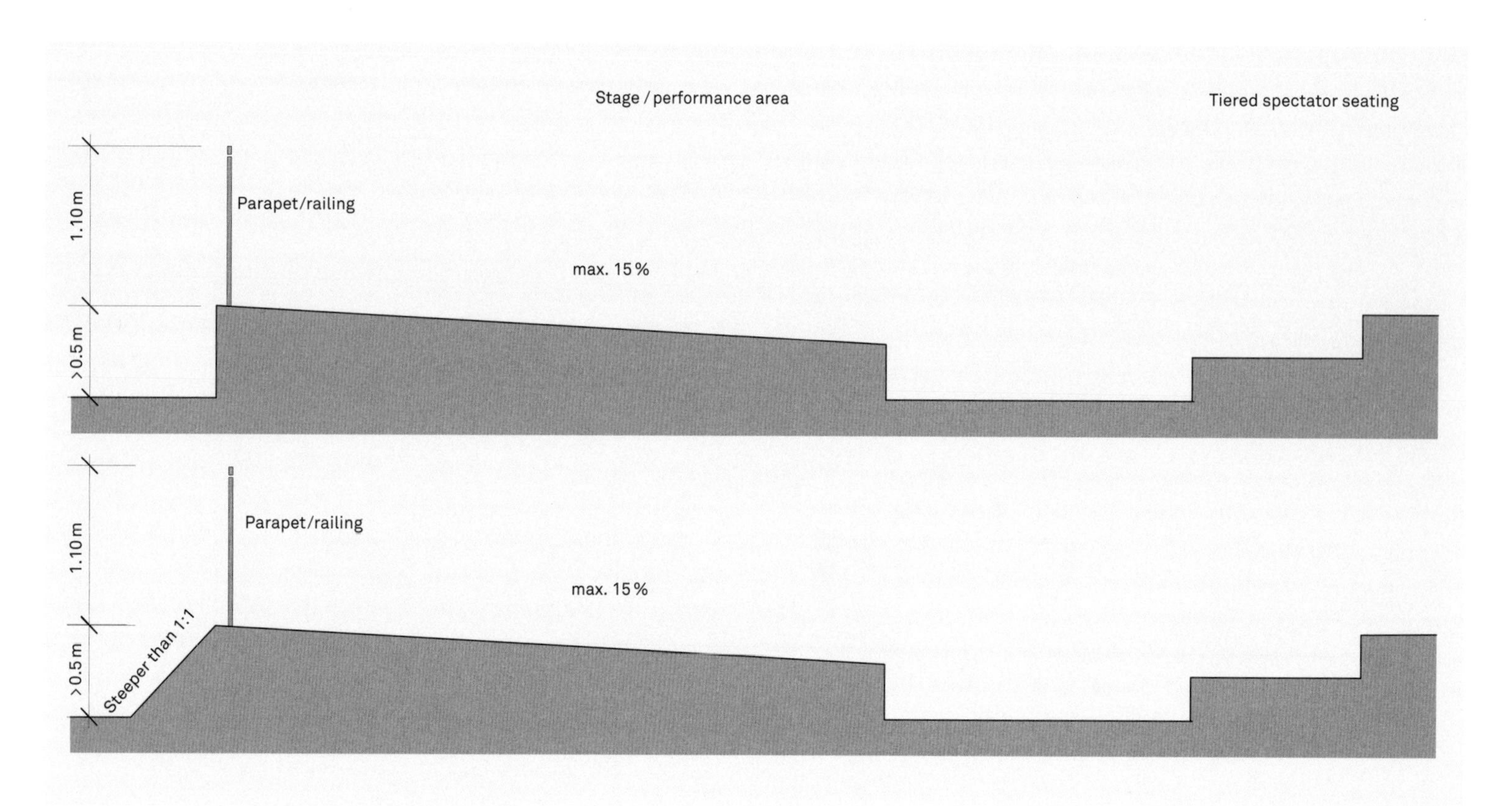

Figure 4.7.3 Fall protection for performance and playing areas

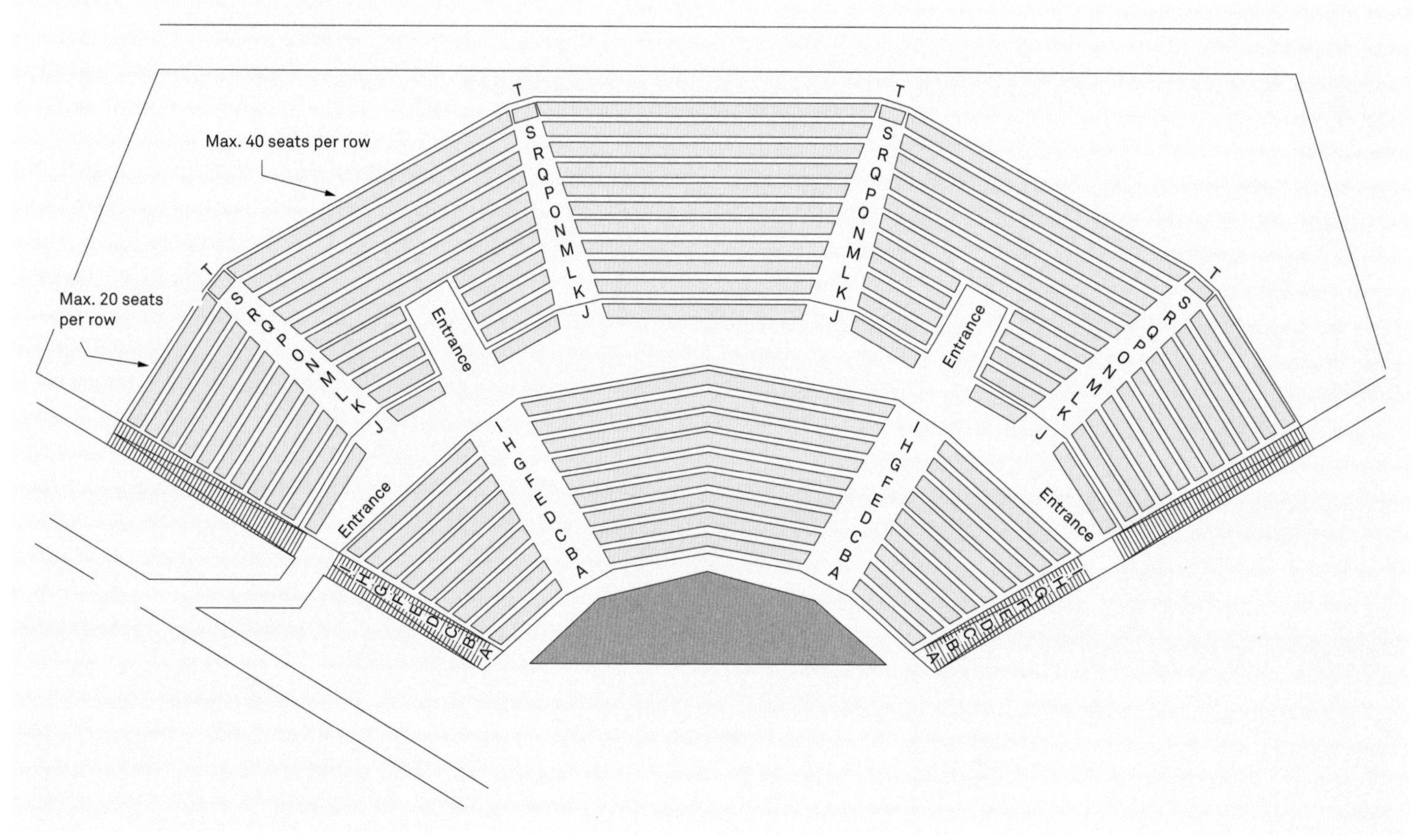

Figure 4.7.4 Exemplary layout of seating blocks and aisles

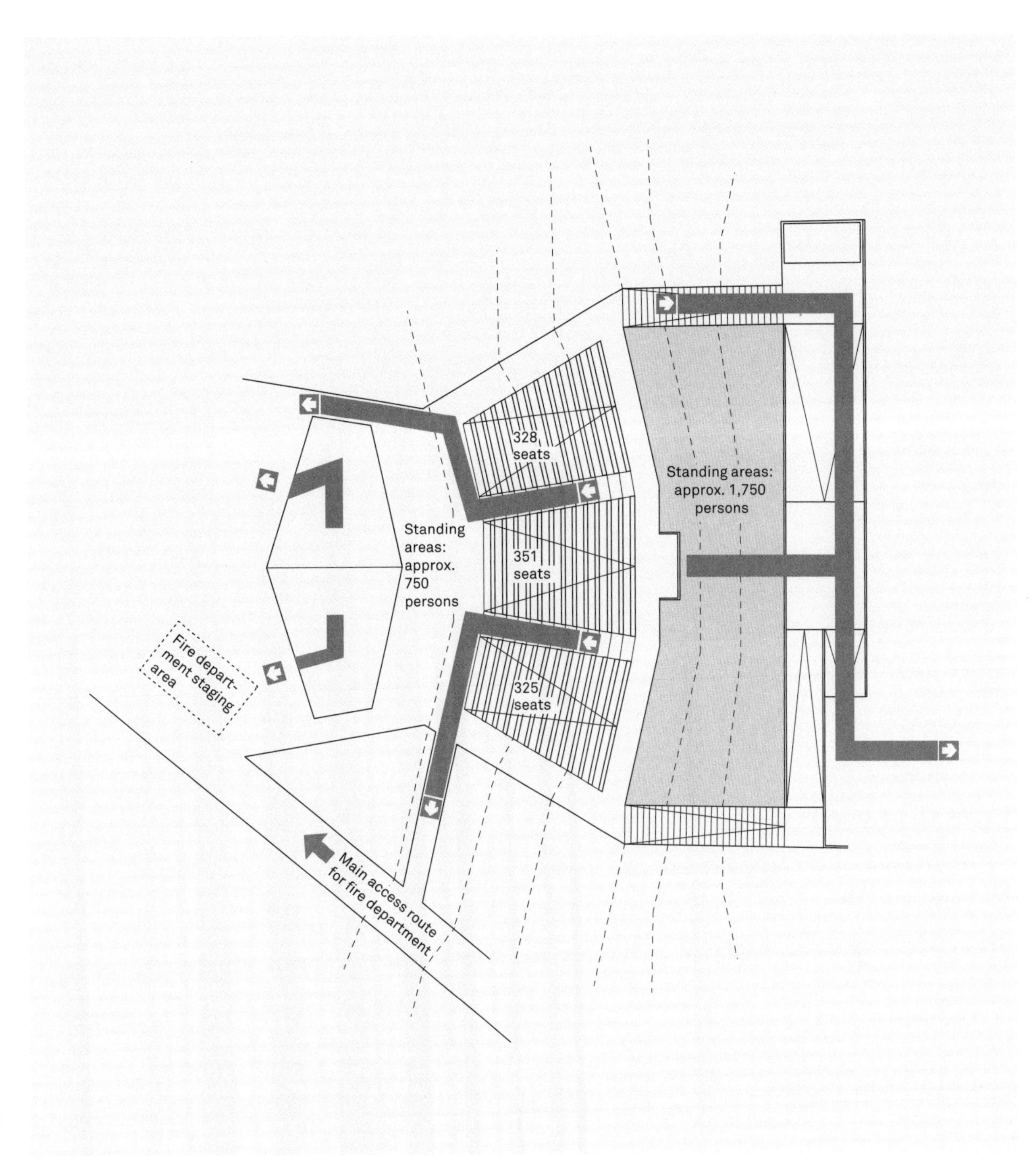

Figure 4.7.5 Example for an escape route plan, as exemplified by the outdoor theater in Spremberg

Table 4.7.1 Quantity of spectator restrooms (per MVStättV)

Visitor seating	Women	Men		Wheelchair-accessible toilets
	Water closets	Water closets	Urinals	
Up to 1,000 visitors				Min. 1 toilet per 10 wheelchair user spaces
Per 100	1.2	0.8	1.2	
More than 1,000 visitors				
Per additional 100	0.8	0.4	0.6	
More than 20,000 visitors				
Per additional 100	0.4	0.3	0.6	

5 Reference Guide

5.1 Dimensions and Units

Units of Length

In order to be able to directly compare and communicate distances or the dimensions of objects, the use of a (uniform) system of measurement is required. For open spaces, buildings, and physical objects created for people or according to their requirements, it is quite natural for there to be a relation to the human body. Thus for many years, human limbs were used as the standards for linear measure. The lengths of a finger, a palm, a forearm, an instep, a foot, etc., were all used as units of measurement. And even in those days, note was made of the comparative sizes of the limbs, such as: instep = ½ ell, ell = 2 feet, etc. Because a confusing variety of measurement systems were in use, the body-related units of measure were replaced in the nineteenth century by an artificially developed system of measurement. The so-called metric system of units was derived from one ten-millionth of the distance from the North Pole to the equator. The metric system of units is part of the Système International d'Unités [International System of Units], which is abbreviated throughout the world as SI; it was introduced in France in 1799. Today it is valid worldwide, with the sole exceptions of Liberia, Myanmar, and the USA, where it has not yet been established as binding and has only found use to date in certain sectors. Anglo-American units of length trace back to the English measurement system that had evolved over the course of centuries, and the current inch, foot, yard, and mile were uniformly defined in 1959. → **Table 5.1.1 and Figure 5.1.1**

Gray-shaded areas indicate the current Anglo-American measurement system and the metric system of units.

Over and above every measurement system, the human point of reference gains in importance, especially when working in different scales. The magnitude of a tree or a building, the distance between two posts, or the height of a jungle gym, for instance, only first becomes clearly recognizable when placed in comparison to the human body.

Area Sizes

To describe the area of a surface, a multiple or portion of the basic unit of a square meter (1 m²) is employed. One square meter corresponds to the area of a square with sides that each measure 1 m long. Depending on the application, larger or smaller area units are used (mm² dm² m², km², etc.). Other area dimensions that are common in certain areas include the are (100 m²) and hectare (10,000 m²).

Angular Measures

When planning and constructing built facilities, not only linear measures are used, but also angular measures and ratios. Using degree measure (°), a full circle has 360°, so a quarter circle has 90°. Using geodetic angular measurement (gon), which is used for surveying, a full circle is 400 gon and a quarter circle is 100 gon. → **Figure 5.1.3**

For slopes, the inclination of a surface is often specified in percent (%). The slope, or gradient, is calculated from the ratio of the height to the distance traveled. A slope of 100 % means a gradient angle of 45°. Percentages above 45 % are less common, however. → **Figure 5.1.4**

Unit English	German	Abbr.	Size	Meters
inch*	Zoll	in., "	–	0.0254
foot*	Fuß	ft., '	12 inches	0.3048
yard*	Schritt	yd.	3 feet	0.9144
mile (statute mile)*	Meile	mi., m.	8 furlongs 1,760 yards 5,280 feet	1,609.344
league	Wegstunde	lea., l.	3 miles	4,828.032
link	Kettenglied	li., l., lnk.	0.04 rods 7.92 inches	0.201168
rod, pole, perch	Rute	rd., p.	198 inches	5.0292
chain	Kette(nlänge)	ch.	4 rods	20.1168
furlong	Achtelmeile, Furchenlänge	fur.	10 chains	201.168

* contemporary Anglo-American measures of length

Table 5.1.1 Linear measures of the English measurement system and their equivalents in meters

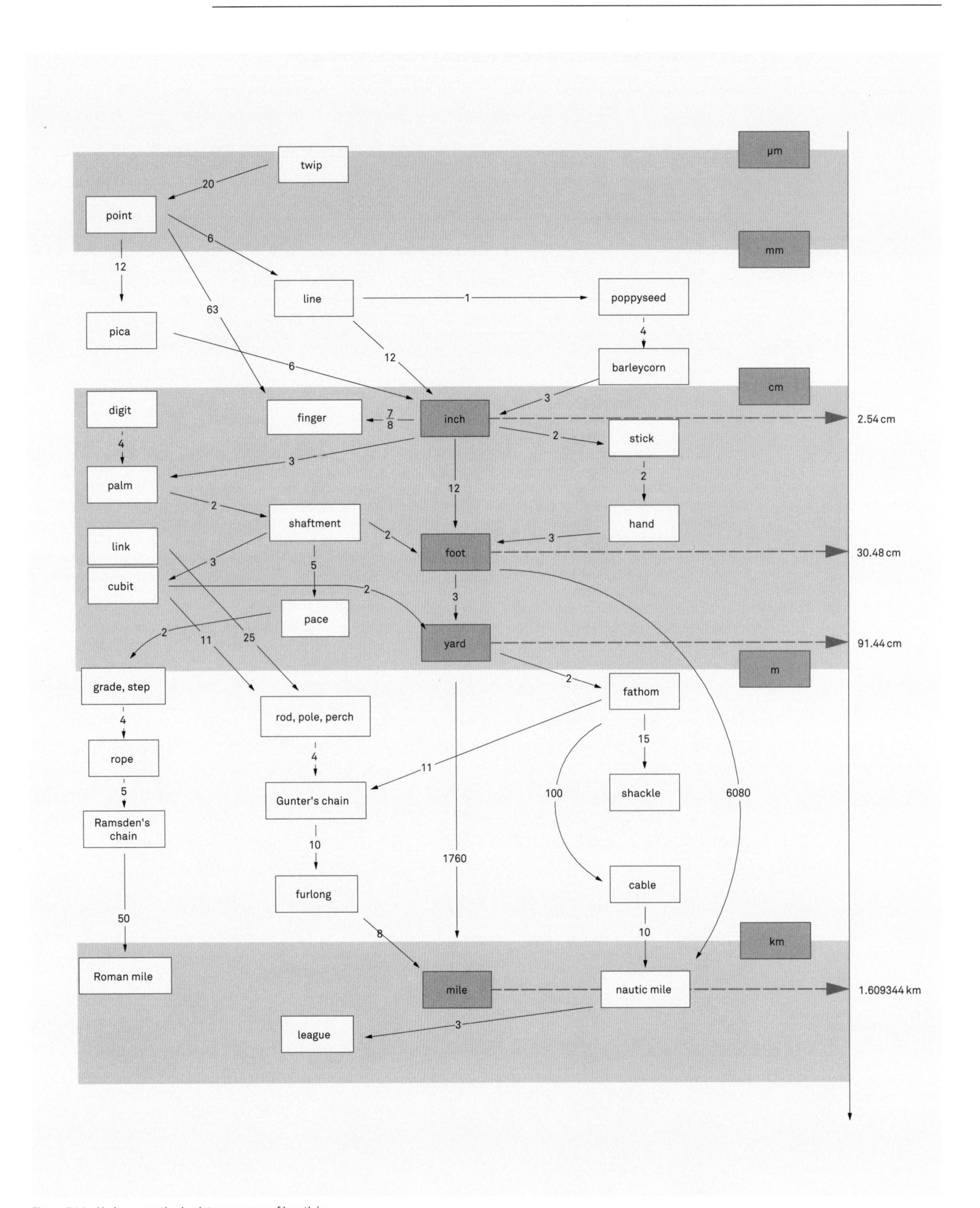

Figure 5.1.1 Various, mostly obsolete measures of length in the Anglo-American (English) measurement system and the metric system of units

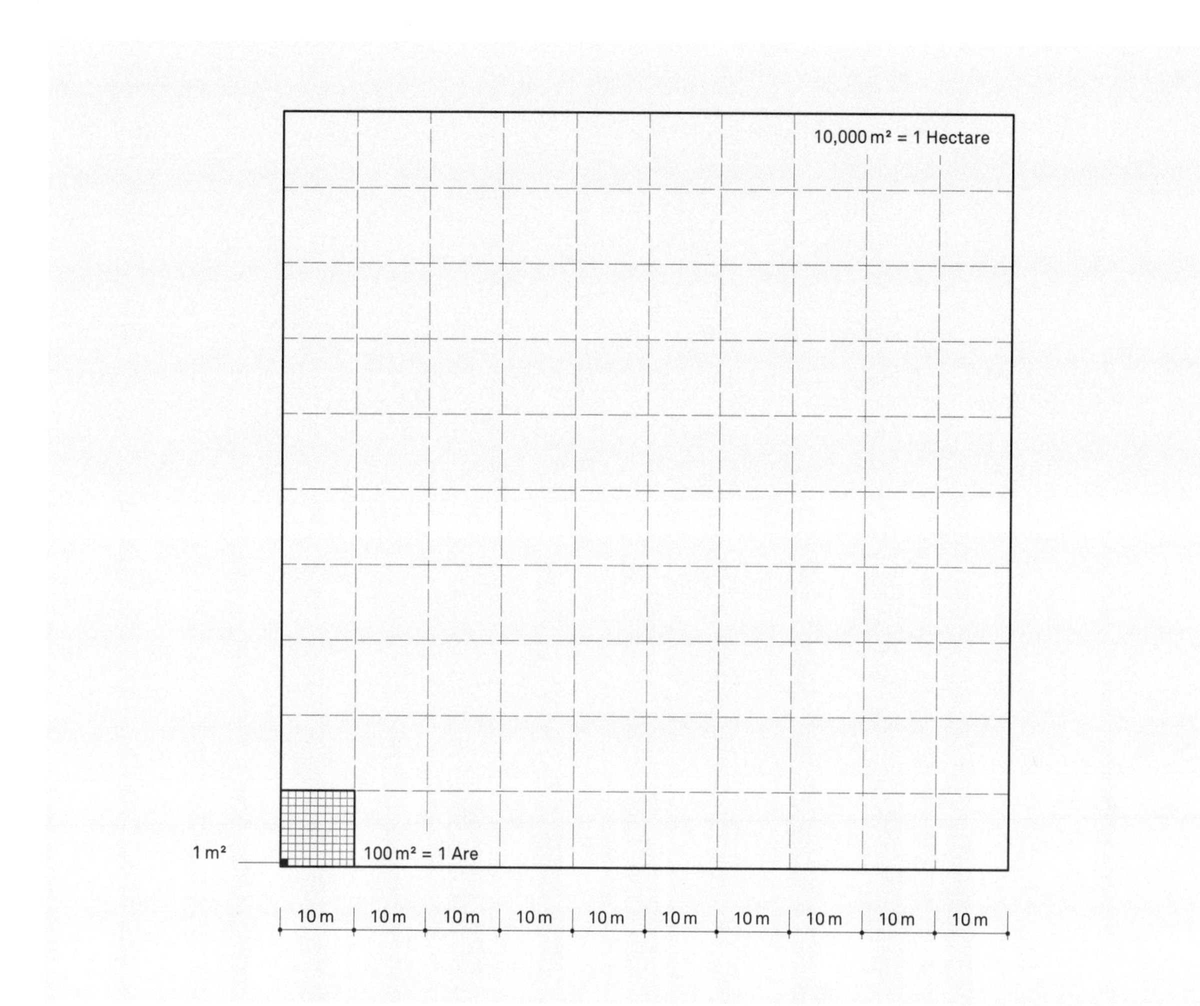

Figure 5.1.2 Area sizes

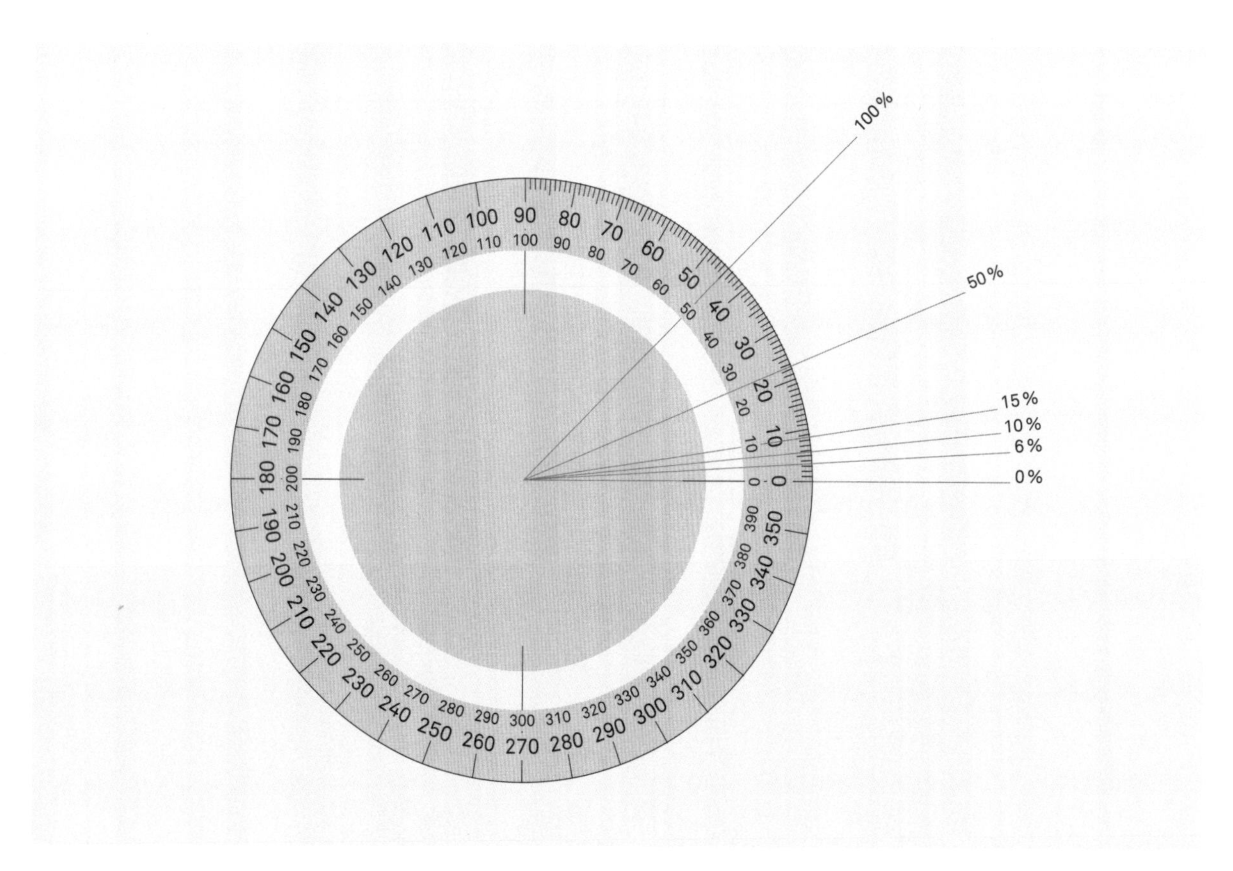

Figure 5.1.3 Degree measure (outer), geodetic angular measure (inner), and slope percentages

Degree measure	Geodetic angular measure
0°	0 gon
1°	1.111 gon
2°	2.222 gon
3°	3.333 gon
4°	4.444 gon
5°	5.555 gon
6°	6.666 gon
8°	8.888 gon
10°	11.111 gon
15°	16.666 gon
20°	22.222 gon
30°	33.333 gon
40°	44.444 gon
45°	50 gon
50°	55.555 gon
60°	66.666 gon
70°	77.777 gon
80°	88.888 gon
90°	100 gon
100°	111.111 gon
180°	200 gon
270°	300 gon
360°	400 gon

Geodetic angular measure	Degree measure
1 gon	1.8°
2 gon	2.7°
3 gon	3.6°
4 gon	4.5°
5 gon	5.4°
6 gon	6.3°
8 gon	7.2°
10 gon	9°
15 gon	13.5°
20 gon	18°
30 gon	27°
40 gon	36°
60 gon	54°
70 gon	63°
80 gon	72°
90 gon	81°
150 gon	135°
175 gon	157.5°
250 gon	225°
275 gon	247.5°
350 gon	315°
375 gon	337.5°
400 gon	360°

Table 5.1.2 Comparison of angular measures – degrees and geodetic units (grads)

Degree measure	Percent	Ratio
0°	0%	0
3.4°	6%	1:16.6
5.7°	10%	1:10
8.53°	15%	1:6.6
11.31°	20%	1:5
15°	26.795%	1:4
18.42°	33.3%	1:3
24.22°	40%	1:2.5
26.6°	50%	1:2
33.66°	66.6%	1:1.5
45°	100%	1:1

Table 5.1.3 Comparison of slopes expressed in degrees, in percent, and as a ratio

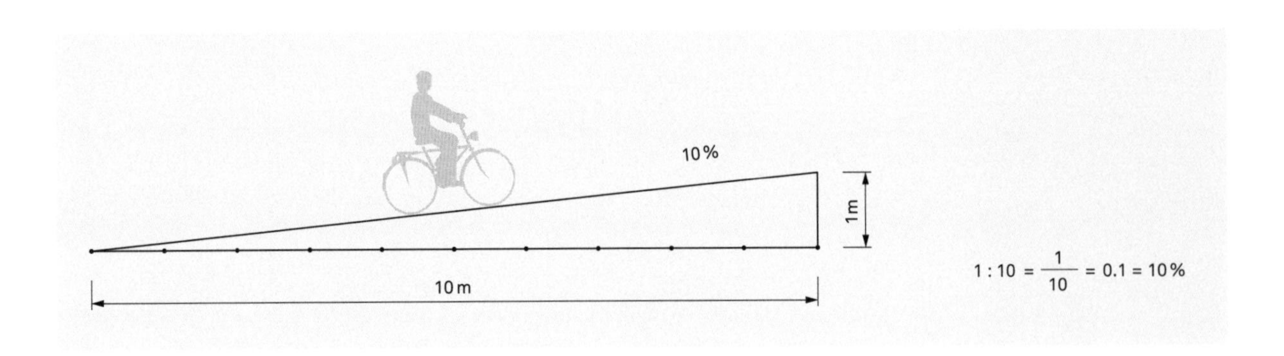

Figure 5.1.4 Determination of the incline/slope

Aesthetic Basis for Design

Even early on, measures and numerical proportions were viewed as an aesthetic reference for humans and as a basis for the design of their creations. Examples like the Pythagorean rectangle, the geometric forms of the circle, square, and equilateral triangle, or the proportion of the golden section found great appeal in architecture. Their formal application to built structures and surfaces were meant to evoke perfection, beauty, and harmony. With a proportional system based on the golden section and human proportions, in the mid–twentieth century Le Corbusier also sought to develop a harmonious measurement system that is mindful of human needs: the "Modulor."

The golden section is obtained when a line segment is divided such that the ratio of the larger part to the smaller part is the same as that of the entire line segment to the larger part. The division into parts can be accomplished by calculation or by using geometric means. The relationship between the segments can be expressed as Φ = 1.6180339 or with an approximate ratio of 8:5. The proportions of the golden section are reflected in various geometric shapes.

An approximately similar result is obtained by using the Fibonacci sequence. Beginning with the numbers 0, 1, and 2, each additional number in the series is formed by the sum of its two predecessors. This results in the following sequence:

0 – 1 – 2 – 3 – 5 – 8 – 13 – 21 – 34 – 55 – 89 – 144 – 233 – 377 – 610 – 987 – 1.597 ...).

Following the sequence in ascending order, the quotient of a number divided by its respective predecessor continually approaches a value of Φ = 1.61803.

When this relation is illustrated as a drawing, what we see is a two-dimensional space divided by the golden section. Such a division ratio or numerical sequence like the Fibonacci series is often found in nature.

Le Corbusier attributed the numerical sequence of the Fibonacci series to human proportions, which he adapted many times. Starting from a height of 1.83 m–2.26 m with an outstretched arm – he ultimately developed two numerical series (red and blue), which were meant to constitute the basis of a system of measurement that can be practically applied. → Table 5.1.4 and Figure 2.1.1

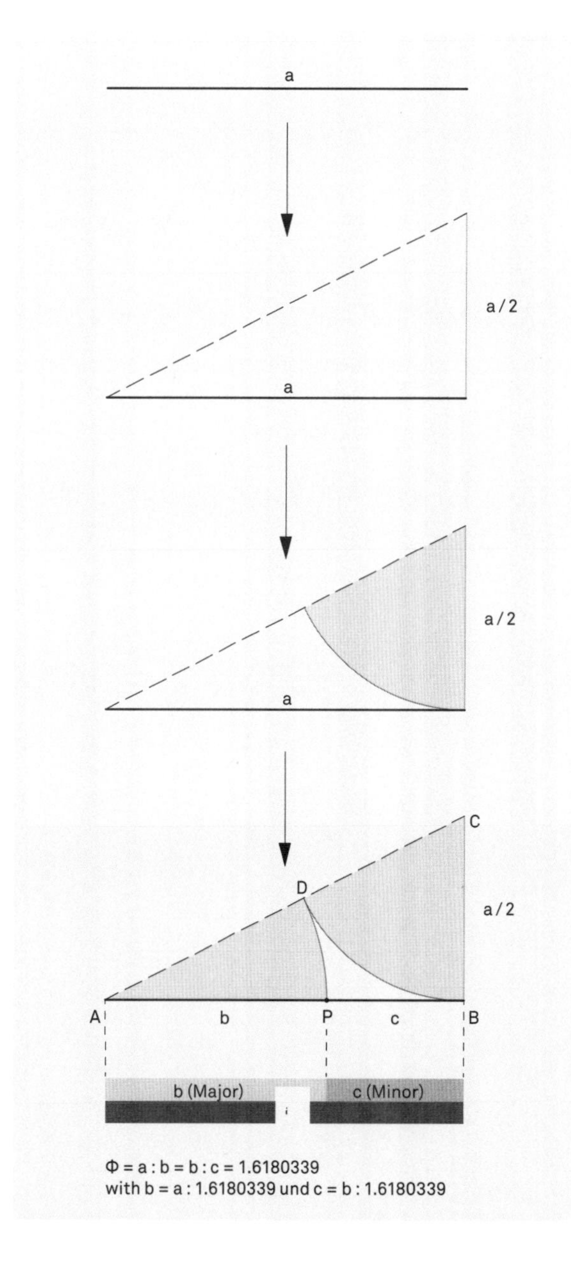

Figure 5.1.5 Golden section: determination of the aspect ratio, beginning with the known dimension "a"; determination of the "golden" intersection "P" by constructing a vertical a/2 and circular arcs at C with radius |CB| and at A with radius |AD|

Figure 5.1.6 Relationship between the geometric shapes of square, triangle, and circle

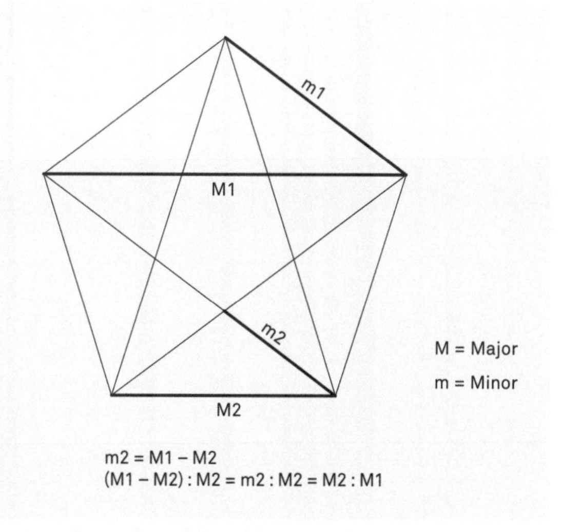

Figure 5.1.7 Proportions of the golden section in a pentagon and a decagon

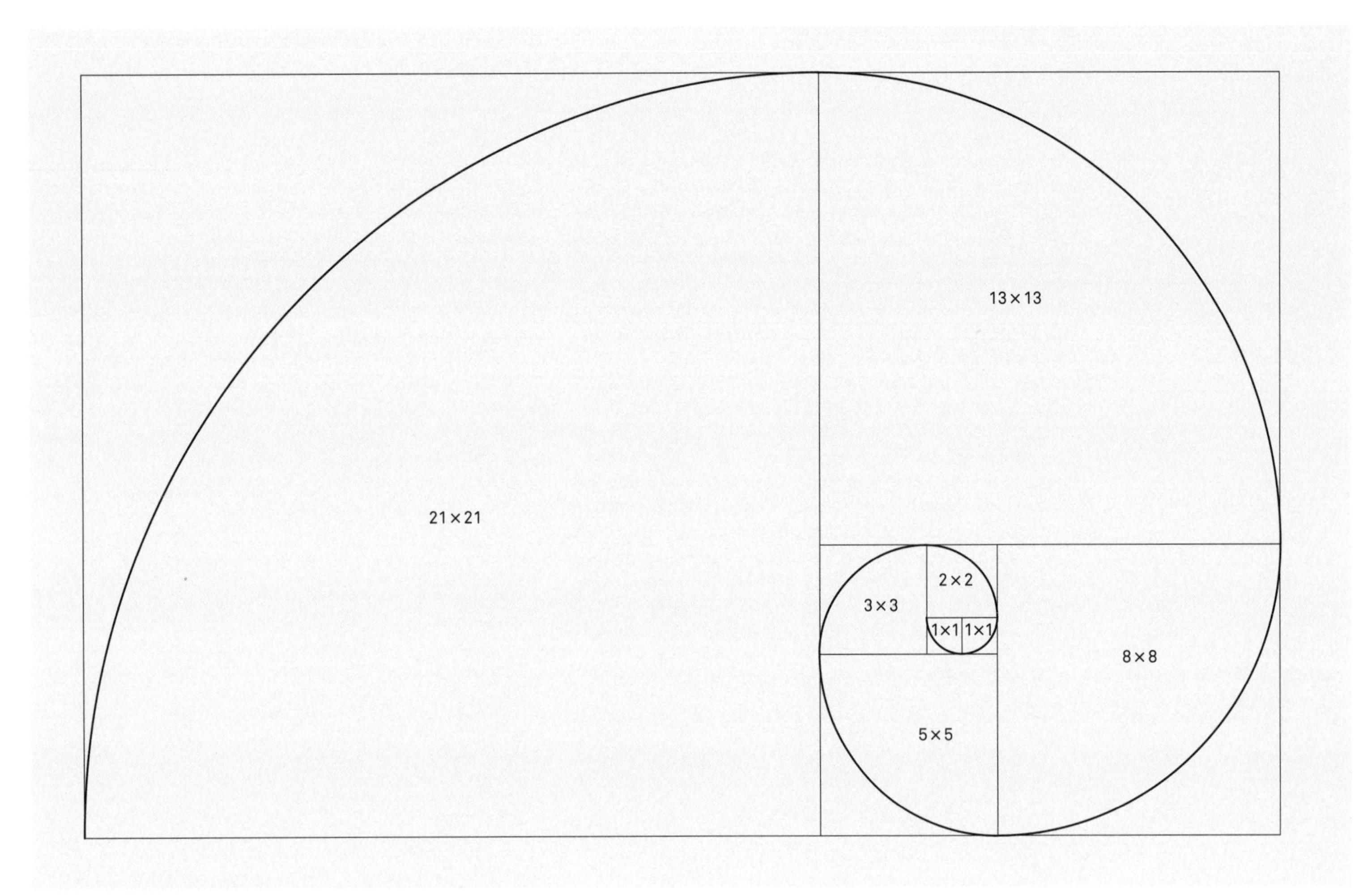

Figure 5.1.8 Two-dimensional depiction of the Fibonacci series

Red series (m)	952.80	588.86	363.94	224.92	139.01	85.91	53.10	32.81	20.28	12.53	7.74	4.79	2.96	1.83	1.13	0.70	0.43	0.26	0.16	0.10	0.06	0.04	0.02	0.01
Blue series (m)	1177.73	727.88	449.85	278.02	171.83	106.19	65.63	40.56	25.07	15.49	9.57	5.92	3.66	2.26	1.40	0.86	0.53	0.33	0.20	0.12	0.08	0.04	0.03	0.01

Table 5.1.4 Red and blue series of Le Corbusier's Modulor. When multiplied by a factor of 1.618, each value yields the next higher value. The highlighted numbers represent typical values for sitting (0.26 and 0.43 m), the height of arm supports for sitting or standing (0.7, 0.86, 1.13 and 1.4 m), and the reference height while standing, with and without an outstretched hand.

Urban Design Parameters

Urban design parameters describe the nature and extent of building use within a development zone or a redevelopment area. They define the planned or necessary public traffic areas and open spaces as well as the extent of areas for public use. For an individual lot, they indicate the nature and extent of the possible built use, whereby the percentage of lot coverage (lot coverage) specifies the maximum percentage of the lot area that can be built upon and the floor area ratio (FAR) – also known as the floor space index (FSI) – specifies the proportion of total gross floor area to the lot area. → **Table 5.1.5**

In Germany, the different types of building use are assigned according to Federal Land Utilization Ordinance § 1 (2). For these parameters, certain threshold values are defined that must be complied with under normal circumstances. → **Table 5.1.6**

In addition to specifying the type of building use, lot coverage, and FAR, the binding land-use plan may include additional stipulations that define the available alternatives further. For instance, mandatory building lines and building setback lines can specify the limits within which a lot can be built upon at all. Whereas a building may not extend beyond a building setback line but is likewise not obliged to align with it, a mandatory building line represents a boundary that must be built upon. The building alignment thereby often defines a street facade. Stipulations regarding roof pitch, the number of full stories, or whether attached or detached building development is required can also be included. With detached development (identified with "o" for "offene Bauweise") individual, duplex, or row houses that do not exceed a total (continuous) length of 50 meters may be built. With attached building development (identified with "g" for "geschlossene Bauweise"), the exterior walls at the sides of the buildings are built directly along the property line, so that the walls of the adjacent buildings touch. → **Figure 5.1.10**

Term	Abbreviation	Description
Gross development area	GDA	Sum of all building lot areas, including the associated (public) green spaces, traffic areas, and bodies of water.
Net development area	NDA	Identifies the lot areas (building sites) remaining after subtracting all public areas.
Gross residential development area	–	Sum of all residential lot areas (net residential development area) and the sum of all the areas for community use in a given designated residential zoning district, whereby only land is included for community facilities that are necessary for serving vital functions within the urban unit (e.g., residential group, neighborhood, community, district, etc., depending on the scale) under consideration itself.
Net residential development area	–	Gross residential zoning district minus deductible areas such as traffic areas, public parks, and miscellaneous areas for public use
Percentage of lot coverage		Indicates the buildable percentage of area on a building lot (net development area). Depending on the local character, this parameter fluctuates between 0.1 (10 %) and 1.0 (100 %). → Table 5.1.6 Due to building law provisions that significantly affect the buildable land area (mandatory building line, building setback line, building depth, space between buildings, allowable floor-to-floor height → Figure 5.1.10), it is possible that the permissible lot coverage percentage cannot be achieved.
Floor area ratio	FAR	Indicates the relation between the total gross floor area of all full stories (without basement or attic, provided these are not full stories) to the lot area (net [residential] development area) (BauNVO § 20). NDA × FAR = allowable total floor area. Auxiliary structures (balconies, loggias, and terraces as well as other built structures, inasmuch as they are permissible or could be permitted in the setback areas – side boundary setbacks and other mandated clearances – under state or local law) remain disregarded. The total floor area may be distributed as desired on the individual floors, although the allowable lot coverage may not be exceeded.
Cubic content ratio	CCR	Volume (m³) of built space per m² of lot area (BauNVO § 21).
Public traffic areas	–	Includes all the streets, sidewalks, and parking areas designed, built, and maintained by the community. Generally includes a 10 % to 20 % share of the gross development area.
Public open spaces	–	Includes all the parks, green spaces, and plazas designed, built, and maintained by the community. Generally includes a 10 % to 20 % share of the gross development area.
Public areas for community use	–	Identifies sites that are designated for schools, daycare centers, etc.

Table 5.1.5 Terminology for urban design parameters

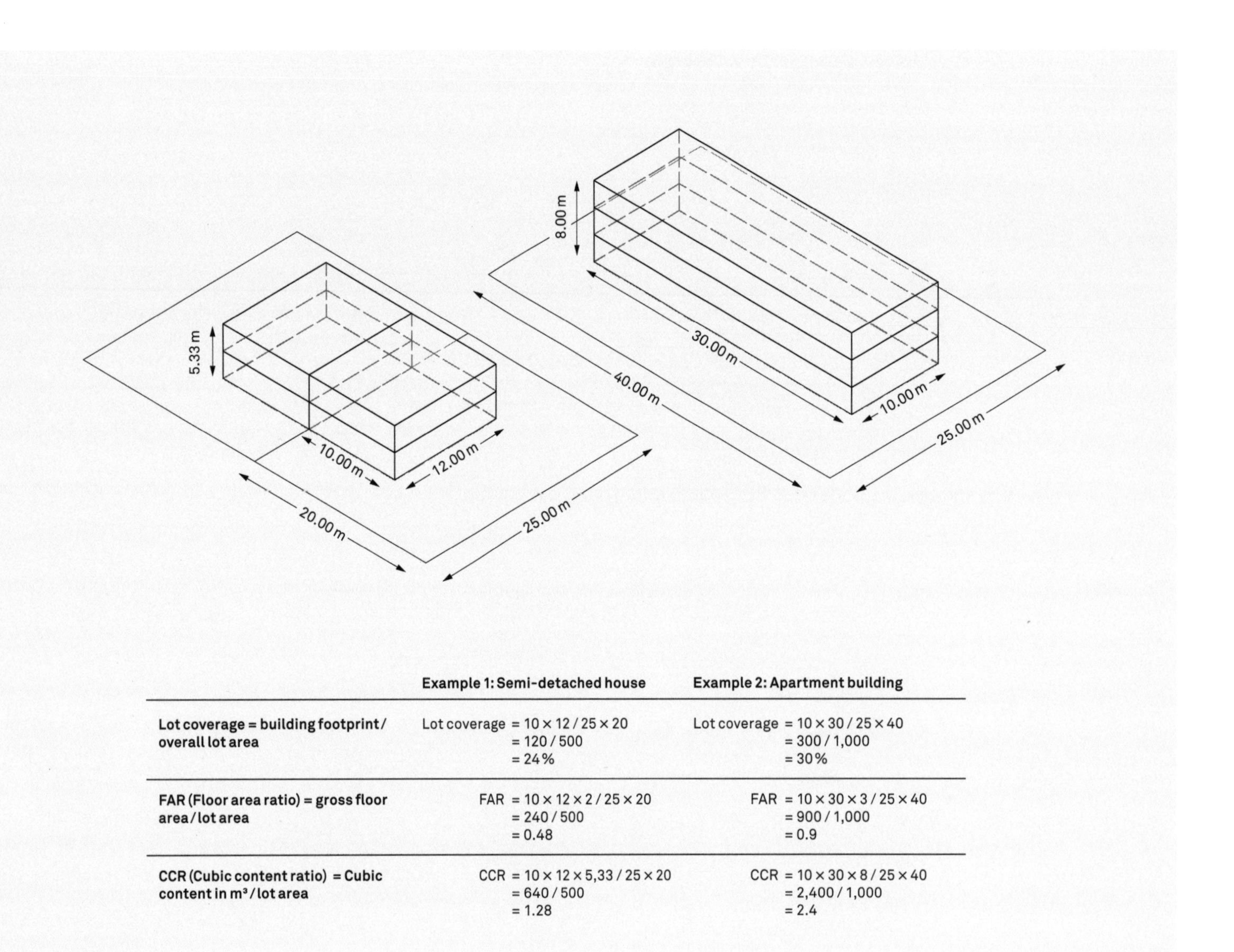

	Example 1: Semi-detached house	Example 2: Apartment building
Lot coverage = building footprint/ overall lot area	Lot coverage = 10 × 12 / 25 × 20 = 120 / 500 = 24%	Lot coverage = 10 × 30 / 25 × 40 = 300 / 1,000 = 30%
FAR (Floor area ratio) = gross floor area/lot area	FAR = 10 × 12 × 2 / 25 × 20 = 240 / 500 = 0.48	FAR = 10 × 30 × 3 / 25 × 40 = 900 / 1,000 = 0.9
CCR (Cubic content ratio) = Cubic content in m³/lot area	CCR = 10 × 12 × 5,33 / 25 × 20 = 640 / 500 = 1.28	CCR = 10 × 30 × 8 / 25 × 40 = 2,400 / 1,000 = 2.4

Figure 5.1.9 Two examples illustrating lot coverage, FAR, and CCR

Table 5.1.6 Upper limits to the dimensions of the built use (as per German Federal Land Utilization Ordinance § 17)

1 **Zoning district**	2 **Percentage of lot coverage**	3 **Floor area ratio (FAR)**	4 **Cubic content ratio (CCR)**
in Areas of small residential estates (WS)	0.2	0.4	–
in Purely residential areas (WR) General residential areas (WA) Vacation home areas	0.4	1.2	–
in Special residential areas (WB)	0.6	1.6	–
in Village areas (MD) Mixed-use areas (MI)	0.6	1.2	–
in Core areas (MK)	1.0	3.0	–
in Commercial areas (GE) Industrial areas (GI) Other special-use areas	0.8	2.4	10.0
in Weekend cottage areas	0.2	0.2	–

The threshold values "can be exceeded for urbanistic reasons if the exceedance is counterbalanced by local circumstances or it is compensated by measures which ensure that the general requirements for healthy living and working conditions are not impaired and that detrimental effects to the environment are prevented" (except weekend cottage areas and vacation home areas). (cf. BauNVO § 17)

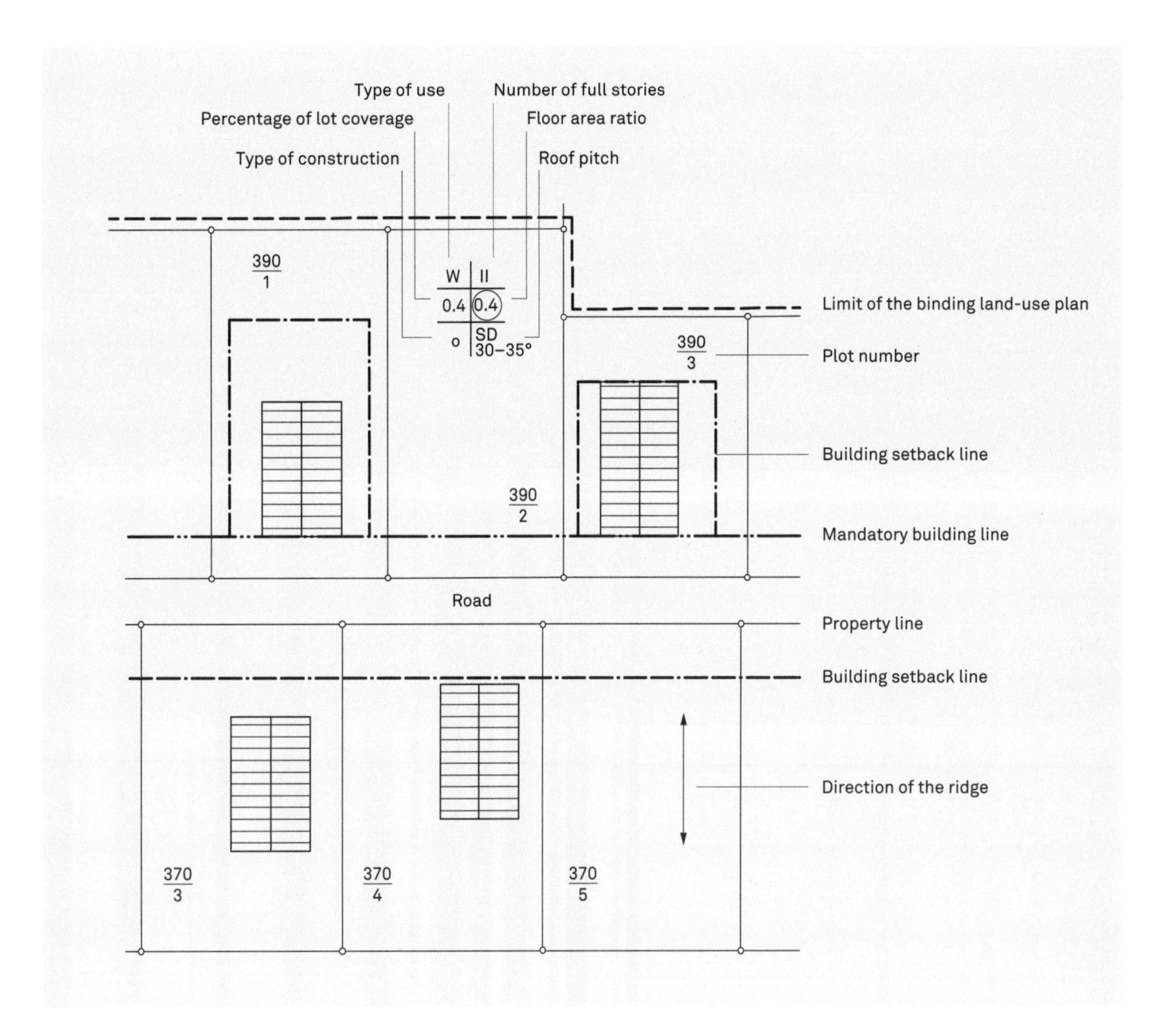

Figure 5.1.10 Illustration of building code limits and units

5.2 Regulations

Readers should be advised that although DIN standards generally also have English titles, which are used here, that is no indication of whether a particular standard has been published in English – and hence it may be solely available in German. Many but not all of the standards listed below are available as official English translations.

Chapter 2.1 Basic Human Measurements

Document	Title	Edition
Standards / technical regulations		
DIN 18040-3	Construction of accessible buildings – Design principles – Part 3: Public circulation areas and open spaces	Draft: 2013–05
DIN 33402-2	Ergonomics – Human body dimensions – Part 2: Values	2005-12

Chapter 2.2 Quantifying Need

Document	Title	Edition
Standards / technical regulations		
DIN 18034	Playgrounds and outdoor play areas – Requirements on planning, building and operation	2012–09

Chapter 3.2 Grading, Stairs, and Ramps

Document	Title	Edition
Standards / technical regulations		
DIN EN 1433	Drainage channels for vehicular and pedestrian areas – Classification, design and testing requirements, marking and evaluation of conformity; German version EN 1433:2002 + AC:2004 + A1:2005	2005–09
DIN 18024-1	Barrier-free built environment – Part 1: Streets, squares, paths, public transport, recreation areas and playgrounds – Design principles	1998–01
DIN 18035-4	Sports grounds – Part 4: Sports turf areas	2012–01
DIN 18035-5	Sports grounds – Part 5: Tamped areas	2007–08
DIN 18040-1	Construction of accessible buildings – Design principles – Part 1: Publicly accessible buildings	2010–10
DIN 18065	Stairs in buildings – Terminology, measuring rules, main dimensions	2011–06
DIN 18318	Road construction – Dry jointed sett and slab pavements, and surrounds	2010–04
DIN 32984	Ground surface indicators in public areas	2011–11
ÖNORM B 5371 (AT)	Treppen, Geländer und Brüstungen in Gebäuden und von Außenanlagen – Abmessungen	2010–09
DBSU (ES)	Documento Básico de Seguridad de Utilización	2006
Accident insurance funds / advisory centers for accident prevention		
BGI / GUV-I 561	Deutsche Gesetzliche Unfallversicherung (DGUV): Treppen	2010
bfu (CH)	Beratungsstelle für Unfallverhütung: Treppen	2009
Forschungsgesellschaft für Straßen- und Verkehrswesen (FGSV)		
ERA 10	Empfehlungen für Radverkehrsanlagen	2010
RAS-EW	Richtlinien für die Anlage von Straßen, Teil: Entwässerung	2005
RASt 06	Richtlinien für die Anlage von Stadtstraßen	2006

Chapter 3.3 Paths and Roads

Document	Title	Edition
Standards/technical regulations		
DIN EN 1433	Drainage channels for vehicular and pedestrian areas – Classification, design and testing requirements, marking and evaluation of conformity; German version EN 1433:2002 + AC:2004 + A1:2005	2005–09
DIN 14090	Areas for the fire brigade on premises	2003–05
DIN 18024-1	Barrier-free built environment – Part 1: Streets, squares, paths, public transport, recreation areas and playgrounds – Design principles	1998–01
DIN 18040-1	Construction of accessible buildings – Design principles – Part 1: Publicly accessible buildings	2010–10
DIN 18318	Road construction – Dry jointed sett and slab pavements and surrounds	2010–04
DIN 32984	Ground surface indicators in public areas	2011–11
DIN 51130	Testing of floor coverings – Determination of the anti-slip property – Workrooms and fields of activities with slip danger – Walking method – Ramp test	2010–10
Forschungsgesellschaft für Straßen- und Verkehrswesen (FGSV)		
EFA	Empfehlungen für Fußgängerverkehrsanlagen	2008
ERA 10	Empfehlungen für Radverkehrsanlagen	2010
RAS-EW	Richtlinien für die Anlage von Straßen, Teil: Entwässerung	2005
RASt 06	Richtlinien für die Anlage von Stadtstraßen	2006
Forschungsgesellschaft Landschaftsentwicklung Landschaftsbau e.V. (FLL)		
FLL	Empfehlungen für Planung, Bau und Instandhaltung von Reitplätzen im Freien	2007
FLL	Begrünbare Flächenbefestigungen	2008
Occupational and accident insurers/advisory centers for accident prevention		
BGR 181	Fußböden in Arbeitsräumen und Arbeitsbereichen mit Rutschgefahr	2003
bfu-Fachdoku 2.032 (CH)	Anforderungsliste Bodenbeläge	2012
bfu-Fachdoku 2.027 (CH)	Bodenbeläge	2011
GUV-I 8527	Bodenbeläge für nassbelastete Barfußbereiche	1999–07, updated 2010–10
Conference of Building Ministers – ARGEBAU		
MRFlFw	Richtlinien über Flächen für die Feuerwehr	2007–02, modified 2009–10

Chapter 3.4 Parking Lots for Motor Vehicles and Bicycles

Document	Title	Edition
Standards/technical regulations		
DIN 18024-1	Barrier-free built environment – Part 1: Streets, squares, paths, public transport, recreation areas and playgrounds – Design principles	1998–01
Forschungsgesellschaft für Straßen- und Verkehrswesen (FGSV)		
EAR 05	Empfehlungen für Anlagen des ruhenden Verkehrs	2005
ERA 10	Empfehlungen für Radverkehrsanlagen	2010
–	Hinweise zum Fahrradparken	2012
RASt 06	Richtlinien für die Anlage von Stadtstraßen	2006

Chapter 3.5 Waste Container Areas

Document	Title	Edition
Standards/technical regulations		
ÖNORM S 2025 (AT)	Aufstellplätze für Abfallsammelbehälter, Abmessungen	2010
VDI 2160	Waste management in buildings and on ground – Requirement[s] for bins, locations and transportation routes	2010
Occupational and accident insurers/advisory centers for accident prevention		
GUV-V C 27	Unfallverhütungsvorschrift – Müllbeseitigung	Revised version, 1997/1999

Chapter 3.6 Boundary Enclosures and Railings

Document	Title	Edition
Standards/technical regulations		
DIN 18040-1	Construction of accessible buildings – Design principles – Part 1: Publicly accessible buildings	2010–10
DIN 18065	Stairs in buildings – Terminology, measuring rules, main dimensions	2011–06
ÖNORM B 5371 (AT)	Treppen, Geländer und Brüstungen in Gebäuden und von Außenanlagen – Abmessungen	2010–09
SIA 358 (CH)	Geländer und Brüstungen	2010
Im 4.1.1	Sechste Allgemeine Verwaltungsvorschrift zum Bundes-Immissionsschutzgesetz (Technische Anleitung zum Schutz gegen Lärm – TA Lärm)	1998
VDI 3770	Characteristic noise emission values of sound sources – Facilities for recreational and sporting activities	2012–09
ZTV-ING	Zusätzliche Technische Vertragsbedingungen und Richtlinien für Ingenieurbauten, Teil 8: Bauwerksausstattung	2010–04
Occupational and accident insurers/advisory centers for accident prevention		
BGI/GUV-I 561	Deutsche Gesetzliche Unfallversicherung (DGUV): Treppen	2010
bfu (CH)	Fachbroschüre – Geländer und Brüstungen	2010
bfu 9401 (CH)	Geländer und Brüstungen	2004–03
Forschungsgesellschaft für Straßen- und Verkehrswesen (FGSV)		
ERA 10	Empfehlungen für Radverkehrsanlagen	2010
RAS-EW	Richtlinien für die Anlage von Straßen, Teil: Entwässerung	2005
RASt 06	Richtlinien für die Anlage von Stadtstraßen	2006

Chapter 3.7 Seating

Document	Title	Edition
Standards/technical regulations		
DIN 33402-2	Ergonomics – Human body dimensions – Part 2: Values	2005–12
Conference of Building Ministers – ARGEBAU		
MVStättV	Versammlungsstättenverordnung	2005–06

Chapter 3.8 Lighting

Document	Title	Edition
Standards/technical regulations		
CEN/TR 13201-1	Road lighting – Part 1: Selection of lighting classes	2004–07
DIN EN 12193	Light and lighting – Sports lighting	2008–04
DIN 13201-1	Road lighting – Part 1: Selection of lighting classes	2005–11
DIN EN 13201-2	Road lighting – Part 2: Performance requirements	2004–04
DIN EN 13201-3	Road lighting – Part 3: Calculation of performance	2004–04
ÖNORM CEN/TR 13201-1 (AT)	Road lighting – Part 1: Selection of lighting classes	2005–09
ÖNORM CEN/TR 13201-2 (AT)	Road lighting – Part 2: Performance requirements	2004–02
ÖNORM EN 13201-3 (AT)	Road lighting – Part 3: Calculation of performance	2004–02
ÖNORM EN 12193 (AT)	Light and lighting – Sports lighting	2008–04
ÖNORM O-1051 (AT)	Road lighting – Lighting of conflict areas	2007–07
SN EN 13201-2	Road lighting – Part 2: Performance requirements	2004–03
SN EN 13201-3	Road lighting – Part 3: Calculation of performance	2004–01
SLG 202 (CH)	Öffentliche Beleuchtung: Strassenbeleuchtung. Supplements to SN TR 13201-1 and SN EN 13201-2 thru -4	2005
SLG 301 (CH)	Beleuchtung von Sportanlagen/Eclairage des installations sportives: Grundlagen	2009
SLG 302 (CH)	Beleuchtung von Sportanlagen/Eclairage des installations sportives: Fussballplätze und Stadien für Fussball und Leichtathletik/Eclairage des terrains de football et des stades de football et d'athlétisme	2011
SLG 303 (CH)	Beleuchtung von Sportanlagen/Eclairage des installations sportives: Freianlagen (Rasen-, Allwetterplätze, Leichtathletik u. ä.)/Installations de plein-air (gazon, places tous temps, athlétisme léger etc)	2005

Chapter 3.9 Water Features and Stormwater Infiltration

Document	Title	Edition
Standards/technical regulations		
DIN 1986-100	Drainage systems on private ground – Part 100: Specifications in relation to DIN EN 752 and DIN EN 12056	2008–05
DIN 18035-2	Sports grounds – Part 2: Irrigation	2003–07
DWA guidelines		
DWA-A 117E	Dimensioning of Stormwater Holding Facilities	2006–04; latest German version 2013–12, rectified: 2014–02
DWA-A 138E	Planning, Construction and Operation of Facilities for the Percolation of Precipitation Water	2005–04
DWA-Kommentar zu DWA-A 138	Commentary (in German) to: Planning, Construction and Operation of Facilities for the Percolation of Precipitation Water	2008–08

Chapter 3.10 Woody Plants

Document	Title	Edition
Standards/technical regulations		
DIN 18915	Vegetation technology in landscaping – Soil working	2002–08
DIN 18916	Vegetation technology in landscaping – Plants and plant care	2002–08
DIN 18920	Vegetation technology in landscaping – Protection of trees, plantations and vegetation areas during construction work	2002-08; draft standard from 2013-10
ZTV-Vegtra-Mü	Zusätzliche Technische Vorschriften für die Herstellung und Anwendung verbesserter Vegetationstragschichten (ed.: Landeshauptstadt München, Baureferat HA Gartenbau)	2008
Forschungsgesellschaft für Straßen- und Verkehrswesen (FGSV)		
RAS-LP 4	Richtlinien für die Anlage von Straßen, Teil: Landschaftspflege, Abschnitt 4: Schutz von Bäumen, Vegetationsbeständen und Tieren bei Baumaßnahmen	1999
RASt 06	Richtlinien für die Anlage von Stadtstraßen	2006
FLL – Forschungsgesellschaft Landschaftsentwicklung Landschaftsbau e.V.		
FLL	Empfehlungen für Baumpflanzungen, Teil 2: Standortvorbereitungen für Neupflanzungen, Pflanzgruben und Wurzelraumerweiterung, Bauweisen und Substrate	2010
DVGW – Deutscher Verein des Gas- und Wasserfaches e.V.		
W 400-1; TRWV	Technische Regeln Wasserverteilungsanlagen (TRWV), Teil 1: Planung	2004–10
GW 125	Bäume, unterirdische Leitungen und Kanäle	2013–02

Chapter 3.11 Vegetated Roofing

Document	Title	Edition
Standards/technical regulations		
DIN 18195	Waterproofing of buildings	2011–12
DIN 18195 – Supplement 1	Waterproofing of buildings – Supplement 1: Examples of positioning of sealants	2011–03
DIN 18531-1	Waterproofing of roofs – Sealings for non-utilized roofs – Part 1: Terms and definitions, requirements, design principles	2010–05
DIN 1055-4	Actions on structures – Part 4: Wind actions	Withdrawn
DIN EN 1991-1 / NA	National Annex – Nationally determined parameters – Eurocode 1: Actions on structures – Part 1–4: General actions – Wind actions	2010–12 Replacement for DIN 1055-4
ÖNORM L 1131	Horticulture and landscaping – Green area on buildings – Directives for planning, building and maintenance	2010–06
FLL – Forschungsgesellschaft Landschaftsentwicklung Landschaftsbau e.V.		
FLL	Richtlinie für die Planung, Ausführung und Pflege von Dachbegrünungen – Dachbegrünungsrichtlinie	2008
FLL	Empfehlungen zu Planung und Bau von Verkehrsflächen auf Bauwerken	2005

Chapter 3.12 Vertical Planting

Document	Title	Edition
FLL – Forschungsgesellschaft Landschaftsentwicklung Landschaftsbau e.V.		
FLL	Fassadenbegrünungsrichtlinie – Richtlinie für die Planung, Ausführung und Pflege von Fassadenbegrünungen mit Kletterpflanzen	2000

Chapter 4.2 Open Spaces in Schools and Preschools

Document	Title	Edition
Standards/technical regulations		
DIN 18024-1	Barrier-free built environment – Part 1: Streets, squares, paths, public transport, recreation areas and playgrounds – Design principles	1998–01
DIN 18040-1	Construction of accessible buildings – Design principles – Part 1: Publicly accessible buildings	2010–10
DIN 18318	Road construction – Dry jointed sett and slab pavements, and surrounds	2010–04
DIN 33402-2	Ergonomics – Human body dimensions – Part 2: Values	2005–12
ÖNORM B 5371	Treppen, Geländer und Brüstungen in Gebäuden und von Außenanlagen – Abmessungen	2010–09
Occupational and accident insurers/advisory centers for accident prevention		
GUV-SI 8011	Richtig sitzen in der Schule – Mindestanforderungen an Tische und Stühle in allgemein bildenden Schulen	1999
GUV-SI 8018	Giftpflanzen – Beschauen, nicht kauen	2003
GUV-SR 2001	Richtlinien für Schulen – Bau und Ausrüstung	1987
GUV-V S 1	Unfallverhütungsvorschrift – Schulen	2002
GUV-V S 2	Unfallverhütungsvorschrift – Kindertageseinrichtungen	2009
BG/GUV-SR S2	Regel – Kindertageseinrichtungen	2009
Schriftenreihe der Unfallkasse Hessen, Band 8	Kindertagesstätten sicher gestalten – Leitfaden für Bauherren, Architekten und Planungsämter zur sicherheitsgerechten Gestaltung von Kindertageseinrichtungen	2013
Prävention in NRW 51	Die sichere Kindertageseinrichtung – Arbeitshilfe zur Planung und Gestaltung	2013
Prävention in NRW 40	Sicher bilden und betreuen – Gestaltung von Bewegungs- und Bildungsräumen für Kinder unter drei Jahren	2011
BGI/GUV-I 561	Deutsche Gesetzliche Unfallversicherung (DGUV): Treppen	2010
Unfallkasse BW	Kinder unter drei Jahren sicher betreuen – Sichere und kindgerechte Gestaltung von Kinderkrippen	
bfu (CH)	Beratungsstelle für Unfallverhütung: Treppen	2009
Forschungsgesellschaft für Straßen- und Verkehrswesen (FGSV)		
ERA 10	Empfehlungen für Radverkehrsanlagen	2010
RAS-EW	Richtlinien für die Anlage von Straßen, Teil: Entwässerung	2005
RASt 06	Richtlinien für die Anlage von Stadtstraßen	2006

Chapter 4.3 Playgrounds

Document	Title	Edition
Standards/technical regulations		
DIN 18024-1	Barrier-free built environment – Part 1: Streets, squares, paths, public transport, recreation areas and playgrounds – Design principles	1998–01
DIN EN 1176-1 Ber 1 and 2	Playground equipment and surfacing – Part 1: General safety requirements and test methods (Corrigenda 1 and 2)	2008–10 2008–12
DIN EN 1176-2 Ber 1	Playground equipment and surfacing – Part 2: Additional specific safety requirements and test methods for swings (Corrigendum 1)	2008–08 2008–12
DIN EN 1176-3 Ber 1	Playground equipment and surfacing – Part 3: Additional specific safety requirements and test methods for slides (Corrigendum 1)	2008–08 2008–12
DIN EN 1176-4 Ber 1	Playground equipment and surfacing – Part 4: Additional specific safety requirements and test methods for cableways (Corrigendum 1)	2008–10 2008–12
DIN EN 1176-5 Ber 1	Playground equipment and surfacing – Part 5: Additional specific safety requirements and test methods for carousels (Corrigendum 1)	2008–08 2008–12
DIN EN 1176-6 Ber 1	Playground equipment and surfacing – Part 6: Additional specific safety requirements and test methods for rocking equipment (Corrigendum 1)	2008–08 2008–12
DIN EN 1176-7 Ber 1	Playground equipment and surfacing – Part 7: Guidance on installation, inspection, maintenance and operation (Corrigendum 1)	2008–08 2008–12
DIN EN 1176-10	Playground equipment and surfacing – Part 10: Additional specific safety requirements and test methods for fully enclosed play equipment	2008–10
DIN EN 1176-11	Playground equipment and surfacing – Part 11: Additional specific safety requirements and test methods for spatial network[s]	2008–08
DIN EN 1176 Supplement 1	Playground equipment and surfacing – Safety requirements and test methods; Supplement 1: Explanations	2009–01
DIN EN 1177 Ber 1	Impact attenuating playground surfacing – Determination of critical fall height (Corrigendum 1)	2008–08 2008–12
DIN 18034	Playgrounds and outdoor play areas – Requirements on planning, building and operation	1999–12
DIN 33942	Barrier-free accessible playground equipment – Safety requirements and test methods	2002–08
ÖNORM B 5371	Treppen, Geländer und Brüstungen in Gebäuden und von Außenanlagen – Abmessungen	2010-09
Occupational and accident insurers/advisory centers for accident prevention		
GUV-SI 8018	Giftpflanzen – Beschauen, nicht kauen	2003
BGI/GUV-I 561	Deutsche Gesetzliche Unfallversicherung (DGUV): Treppen	2010
bfu (CH)	Beratungsstelle für Unfallverhütung: Treppen	2009
Forschungsgesellschaft für Straßen- und Verkehrswesen (FGSV)		
ERA 10	Empfehlungen für Radverkehrsanlagen	2010
RAS-EW	Richtlinien für die Anlage von Straßen, Teil: Entwässerung	2005
RASt 06	Richtlinien für die Anlage von Stadtstraßen	2006

Chapter 4.4 Sports Facilities

Document	Title	Edition
Standards/technical regulations		
DIN 18035-1	Sports grounds – Part 1: Outdoor play and athletics areas, planning and dimensions	2003–02
DIN 18035-2	Sports grounds – Part 2: Irrigation	2003–07
DIN 18035-3	Sports grounds – Part 3: Drainage	2006–09
DIN 18035-4	Sports grounds – Part 4: Sports turf areas	2012–01
DIN 18035-5	Sports grounds – Part 5: Tamped areas	2007–08
Miscellaneous		
	Rules and regulations of the respective sports associations	

Chapter 4.5 Outdoor Swimming Pools, Bathing Ponds, Water-Treading Pools

Document	Title	Edition
Standards/technical regulations		
DIN EN 15288-1	Swimming pools – Part 1: Safety requirements for design	2008/a1:2010
DIN EN 13451-1	Swimming pool equipment – Part 1: General safety requirements and test methods	2011–01
DIN EN 13451-2	Swimming pool equipment – Part 2: Additional specific safety requirements and test methods for ladders, stepladders and handle bends	2013–10
DIN EN 13451-3	Swimming pool equipment – Part 3: Additional specific safety requirements and test methods for inlets and outlets and water/air based water leisure features	2013–09
DIN EN 13451-4	Swimming pool equipment – Part 4: Additional specific safety requirements and test methods for starting platforms	2001–07
DIN EN 13451-5	Swimming pool equipment – Part 5: Additional specific safety requirements and test methods for lane lines	2001–07
DIN EN 13451-6	Swimming pool equipment – Part 6: Additional specific safety requirements and test methods for turning boards	2001–07
DIN EN 13451-7	Swimming pool equipment – Part 7: Additional specific safety requirements and test methods for water polo goals	2001–07
DIN EN 13451-10	Swimming pool equipment – Part 10: Additional specific safety requirements and test methods for diving platforms, diving springboards and associated equipment	2004–08 New as of: 2014–05
DIN EN 13451-11	Swimming pool equipment – Part 11: Additional specific safety requirements and test methods for moveable pool floors and moveable bulkheads	2004–04 New as of: 2014–05
DIN EN 1069 Ber 1	Water slides, Part 1: Safety requirements and test methods (Corrigendum)	2010–12 2012–06
DIN 19643	Treatment of water of swimming pools and baths – Part 1: General requirements	2012–11
Occupational and accident insurers/advisory centers for accident prevention		
GUV-R 1/111	Sicherheitsregeln für Bäder	Revised version, June 2005
GUV-I 8527	Bodenbeläge für nassbelastete Barfußbereiche	1999–07, updated 2010–10
FLL – Forschungsgesellschaft Landschaftsentwicklung Landschaftsbau e.V.		
FLL-Richtlinie	Richtlinien für Planung, Bau, Instandhaltung und Betrieb von Freibädern mit biologischer Wasseraufbereitung	2011
FLL	Empfehlungen für Planung, Bau und Instandhaltung von privaten Schwimm- und Badeteiche	2006

Document	Title	Edition
Miscellaneous		
BHygV 2012	Österreichische Bäderhygieneverordnung 2012 – Verordnung des Bundesministers für Gesundheit über Hygiene in Bädern, Warmsprudelwannen (Whirlwannen), Saunaanlagen, Warmluft- und Dampfbädern und Kleinbadeteichen	2012

Chapter 4.6 Campgrounds

Document	Title	Edition
Standards/technical regulations		
DIN 18024-1	Barrier-free built environment – Part 1: Streets, squares, paths, public transport, recreation areas and playgrounds – Design principles	1998-01

Chapter 4.7 Outdoor Theaters and Tiered Seating

Document	Title	Edition
Standards/technical regulations		
DIN 14090	Areas for the fire brigade on premises	2003–05
DIN 18024-1	Barrier-free built environment – Part 1: Streets, squares, paths, public transport, recreation areas and playgrounds – Design principles	1998–01
DIN 18040-1	Construction of accessible buildings – Design principles – Part 1: Publicly accessible buildings	2010–10
DIN EN 13200-1	Spectator facilities – Part 1: General characteristics for spectator viewing area	2012–11
DIN EN 13200-3	Spectator facilities – Part 3: Separating elements – Requirements	2006–03
Conference of Building Ministers – ARGEBAU		
MVStättV	Versammlungsstättenverordnung	2005–06

5.3 Selected Reference Books

In addition to the companion volume to this book – Astrid Zimmermann, ed., *Constructing Landscape: Materials, Techniques, Structural Components*, 2nd rev. and updated ed. (Basel: Birkhäuser Verlag, 2011 – there are a great many published resources that provide valuable additional information on the many facets of landscape planning and design covered here.

The list that follows, although not exhaustive, is intended to point the reader of this book – student and practitioner alike – to some of the many useful resources available.

Abbey, Buck. *U.S. Landscape Ordinances: An Annotated Reference Handbook.* Hoboken: John Wiley & Sons, 1998.

American Planning Association (APA). *Planning and Urban Design Standards.* Hoboken: John Wiley & Sons, 2006.

Beer, Anne, and Cathy Higgins. *Environmental Planning for Site Development: A Manual for Sustainable Local Planning and Design.* 2nd ed. London: E & FN Spon, 2000.

Bielefeld, Bert and Skiba, Isabella. *Basics Technical Drawing*, 2nd rev. ed. Basel: Birkhäuser Verlag, 2009

Blake, James. *An Introduction to Landscape and Garden Design and Practice.* Burlington, VT: Ashgate, 2012.

Booth, Norman K. *Basic Elements of Landscape Architectural Design.* Long Grove, IL: Waveland Press, 1990.

Buchanan, Rita and Roger Holmes, eds. *Taylor's Master Guide to Gardening.* New York: Houghton Mifflin Harcourt, 1994.

Calkins, Meg. *Materials for Sustainable Sites: A Complete Guide to the Evaluation, Selection, and Use of Sustainable Construction Materials.* Hoboken: John Wiley & Sons, 2009.

Campbell, Craig S., Michael Ogden *Constructed Wetlands in the Sustainable Landscape.* New York: Wiley, 1999.

Ching, Francis D. K., and Steven R. Winkel, *Building Codes Illustrated: A Guide to Understanding the International Building Code.* 4th ed. Hoboken: John Wiley & Sons, 2012.

Church, Thomas, Grace Hall, and Michael Laurie. *Gardens are For People.* 3rd. ed. Berkeley: Univ. of California Press, 1993.

Clouston, Brian. *Landscape Design with Plants.* 2nd ed. Boca Raton: CRC Press, 1990.

DiLaura, David L. Kevin W. Houser, Richard G. Mistrick, and Gary Steffy, eds. *The Lighting Handbook: Reference and Application.* 10th ed. New York: Illuminating Engineering Society of North America, 2011.

Dines, Nicholas, and Kyle Brown. *Landscape Architect's Portable Handbook.* McGraw-Hill, 2001. Compact abridged version of Harris and Dines's *Time-Saver Standards for Landscape Architecture* (listed below).

Dirr, Michael A. *Dirr's Encyclopedia of Trees and Shrubs.* Portland, OR: Timber Press, 2011

Dreiseitl, Herbert, and Dieter Grau, eds. *Recent Waterscapes: Planning, Building and Designing with Water.* 3rd rev. ed. Basel: Birkhäuser Verlag, 2009.

Faludi, Andreas, ed. *European Spatial Planning.* Cambridge, MA: Lincoln Institute of Land Policy, 2002.

Ferguson, Bruce K. *Introduction to Stormwater: Concept, Purpose, Design.* Hoboken: John Wiley & Sons, 1998.

Ferguson, Bruce K. *Porous Pavements*, Boca Raton: CRC Press, 2005.

Harris, Charles, and Nicholas Dines. *Time-Saver Standards for Landscape Architecture: Design and Construction Data.* 2nd ed. New York: McGraw-Hill, 1998.

Heiss, Oliver, Christine Degenhart, and Johann Ebe. *Barrier-Free Design: Principles, Planning, Examples.* Detail Practice. Basel: Edition Detail/Birkhäuser Verlag, 2010.

Holden, Robert, and Jamie Liversedge. *Construction for Landscape Architecture: Portfolio Skills.* London: Laurence King Publishing, 2010.

Hopper, Leonard J., ed. *Landscape Architectural Graphic Standards.* Hoboken: John Wiley & Sons, 2007.

Hudak, Joseph. *Gardening with Perennials Month by Month.* 2nd rev. and expanded ed. Portland, OR: Timber Press, 1993.

International Code Council. *International Building Code.* 2015 edition. Clifton Park, NY: ICC/Cengage Learning, 2014. The 2012 edition is avail. online at http://publicecodes.cyberregs.com/icod/ (last accessed July 15, 2014).

Kotzen, Benz, and Colin English. *Environmental Noise Barriers- A Guide to Their Acoustic and Visual Design.* 2nd ed. New York: Taylor & Francis, 2009.

Leopold, Donald J. *Native Plants of the Northeast: A Guide for Gardening & Conservation.* Portland, OR: Timber Press, 2005.

Littlefield, David, ed. *Metric Handbook: Planning and Design Data.* 4th ed. Abingdon and New York: Routledge, 2012.

Lohrer, Axel. Basics Designing with Water. Basel: Birkhäuser Verlag, 2008

Loidl, Hans and Bernard, Stefan. Open(ing) Spaces: design as Landscape Architecture. Basel: Birkhäuser Verlag, 2014

Lynch, Kevin and Gary Hack. *Site Planning, 3rd Edition.* Cambridge, MA: MIT Press, 1984.

Marcus, Clare Cooper, and Carolyn Francis, eds. *People Places: Design Guidelines for Urban Open Space.* 2nd ed. New York: Van Nostrand Reinhold, 1998.

Margolis, Liat and Alexander Robinson. *Living Systems: Innovative Materials and Technologies for Landscape Architecture.* Basel: Birkhäuser Verlag, 2007.

Marsh, William M. *Landscape Planning: Environmental Applications.* 5th ed. Hoboken: John Wiley & Sons, 2010.

Motloch, John L. *An Introduction to Landscape Design.* 2nd ed. New York: John Wiley & Sons, 2001.

Neufert, Ernst and Peter. *Neufert Architects' Data.* 4th ed. Updated by Johannes Kister et al. Chichester: Wiley-Blackwell, 2012.

Panero, Julius, and Martin Zelnik. *Human Dimension & Interior Space: A Source Book of Design Reference Standards.* New York: Whitney Library of Design, 1979.

Petschek, Peter. *Grading: LandscapingSMART, 3D-Machine Control, Stormwater Management.* 2nd rev. and updated ed. Basel: Birkhäuser Verlag, 2014.

Petschek, Peter, and Siegfried Gass, eds. *Constructing Shadows: Pergolas, Pavilions, Tents, Cables, and Plants.* Basel: Birkhäuser Verlag, 2011.

Reid, Grant W. *From Concept to Form in Landscape Design.* 2nd ed. Hoboken: John Wiley & Sons, 2007.

Robinson, Nick. *The Planting Design Handbook.* Rev. 2nd ed. Burlington, VT: Ashgate, 2011.

Russ, Thomas H. *Site Planning and Design Handbook.* 2nd ed. New York: McGraw-Hill. 2009.

Ryan, Tom R., Edward Allen, and Patrick J. Rand. *Detailing for Landscape Architects: Aesthetics, Function, Constructibility.* Hoboken: John Wiley & Sons, 2011
Sharky, Bruce G. *Grading With Design in Mind: Landscape Site Grading Principles*. Hoboken: John Wiley & Sons, 2014.
Skiba, Isabella and Züger, Rahel. Basics Barrier-Free Planning. Basel: Birkhäuser Verlag, 2009
Snodgrass, Edmund C., McIntyre, Linda. *The Green Roof Manual A Professional Guide to Design, Installation, and Maintenance*. Portland, OR: Timber Press, 2010.
Starke, Barry W., John Ormsbee Simonds. *Landscape Architecture: A Manual of Environmental Planning and Design*. 5th ed. New York: McGraw-Hill, 2013.
Steenbergen, Clemens. *Composing Landscapes: Analysis, Typology and Experiments for Design*. Basel: Birkhäuser Verlag, 2009
Strom, Steven, Kurt Nathan, and Jake Woland. *Site Engineering for Landscape Architects*. 6th ed. Hoboken: John Wiley & Sons, 2013.
Stürzebecher, Peter, and Sigrid Ulrich. *Architecture for Sport: New Concepts and International Projects for Sport and Leisure*. Chichester: Wiley-Academy, 2002.
Thompson, J. William and Kim Sorvig. *Sustainable Landscape Construction: A Guide to Green Building Outdoors*. 2nd ed. Washington, DC: Island Press, 2007.
Watson, Donald, and Michael J. Crosbie, eds. *Time-Saver Standards for Architectural Design: Technical Data for Professional Practice*. 8th ed. New York: McGraw-Hill, 2004.
Watson, Donald, and Kenneth Labs. *Climatic Building Design: Energy-Efficient Building Principles and Practices*. New York: McGraw-Hill, 1993.
Watson, Donald, Alan Plattus, and Robert G. Shibley, eds. *Time-Saver Standards for Urban Design*. New York: McGraw-Hill, 2003.
Winterbottom, Daniel M. *Wood in the Landscape: A Practical Guide to Specification and Design*. Hoboken: John Wiley & Sons, 2000.
Wöhrle, Regine Ellen and Wöhrle, Hans-Jörg. Basics Designing with Plants. Basel: Birkhäuser Verlag, 2008
Wylie, John. *Landscape*. Key Ideas in Geography. Abingdon and New York: Routledge, 2007.

Chapter 2.1 Basic Human Measurements

Bogardus, Emory S. "Measuring Social Distances," *Journal of Applied Sociology* 9 (1925): 299–308.
Bundesministerium für Gesundheit. *Handbuch für Planer und Praktiker.* Bad Homburg, 1996.
Gehl, Jan. *Life Between Buildings: Using Public Space*, translated by Jo Koch. New York, 1987. Originally published as *Livet mellem husene*, Copenhagen, 1971.
Hall, Edward T. *The Hidden Dimension*. New York, 1966.
Hansestadt Hamburg. *Landschaftsprogramm einschließlich Artenschutzprogramm*. Hamburg, 1997.
Hansestadt Hamburg. *Musterflächenprogramm für allgemeinbildende Schulen in Hamburg*. Hamburg, 2011.
Le Corbusier. *Le Modulor: Essai sur une mesure harmonique, à L'échelle humaine applicable universellement, à l'architecture et à la mécanique*. Boulogne (Seine), 1952.
Stolzenberg, Heribert, Heidrun Kahl, and Karl E. Bergmann. "Körpermaße bei Kindern und Jugendlichen in Deutschland," *Bundesgesundheitsblatt – Gesundheitsforschung – Gesundheitsschutz* 50, nos. 5/6 (2007): 659–669.

Chapter 2.2 Quantifying Need

Gälzer, Ralph. *Grünplanung für Städte*. Stuttgart, 2001.
Richter, Gerhard. *Handbuch Stadtgrün. Landschaftsarchitektur im städtischen Freiraum*. Munich, 1981.

Chapter 3.1 Climate and Exposure

Flemming, Günther. *Wald – Wetter – Klima*. Berlin, 1987.
Häckel, Hans. *Das Gartenklima*. Stuttgart, 1989.
Horbert, Manfred. *Klimatologische Aspekte der Stadt- und Landschaftsplanung*. TU Berlin journal series Landschaftsentwicklung und Umweltforschung 113. Berlin, 2000.
Twarowski, Mieczyslaw. *Sonne und Architektur*. Munich, 1962.
Wirtschaftsministerium Baden-Württemberg in collaboration with the Amt für Umweltschutz, Abt. Stadtklimatologie, der Landeshauptstadt Stuttgart. *Städtebauliche Klimafibel*. Stuttgart, 2007.

Chapter 3.2 Grading, Stairs, and Ramps

Deutsche Verkehrswacht e.V. *Skate & Roll – Inline-Skaten – aber sicher*. Meckenheim, 2002.
Harris, Charles, and Nicholas Dines. *Time-Saver Standards for Landscape Architecture: Design and Construction Data*. New York, 1998.
Land Salzburg, Abteilung Soziales. *Barrierefrei Bauen*. Salzburg, 2008.
Mader, Günter. *Freiraumplanung: Hausgärten, Grünanlagen, Stadtlandschaften*. Munich, 2004.
Mader, Günter. "Treppenbau, Teil 1: Kleine Mathematik des Treppenbaus," *DEGA GaLaBau* 45 (2002): 10–12.
Ministerium für Bau und Verkehr des Landes Sachsen-Anhalt. *Empfehlungen für den Bau und die Unterhaltung von straßenbegleitenden Radverkehrsanlagen in Sachsen-Anhalt*. Magdeburg, 1998.

Chapter 3.3 Paths and Roads

De Groot, Rik. *Ontwerpwijzer fietsverkeer*. Publicatie 230. Ede, 2006.
Deutsche Verkehrswacht e.V. *Skate & Roll – Inline-Skaten – aber sicher*. Meckenheim, 2002.
Deutscher Blinden- und Sehbehindertenverband e.V. *Erkennbarkeit des unteren Aufmerksamkeitsfeldes und der letzten Trittstufenmarkierung bei Treppen*. Planning commentary from July 1, 2013. www.dbsv.org (last accessed: Apr. 7, 2014).
Gerlach, Jürgen, Dirk Boenke, Jens Leven, and Rob Methorst. "Sinn und Unsinn von Shared Space – Zur Versachlichung einer populären Gestaltungsphilosophie," *Straßenverkehrstechnik* 52, no. 2 (2008): 61–65 (part 1) and *Straßenverkehrstechnik* 52, no. 3 (2008): 140–149 (part 2).
Kalwitzki, Klaus-Peter. "Shared Space – Den Raum miteinander teilen. Von einer Exkursion nach Drachten und Haren/NL," *Verkehrszeichen* 23, no. 3 (2007): 10–12.
Robatsch, Klaus. "Geschwindigkeiten, Bremsweg und Breitenbedarf von Inline-Skatern," *Zeitschrift für Verkehrssicherheit* 44, no. 1 (1998): 25–33.
Senatsverwaltung für Stadtentwicklung Berlin. *Fußverkehrsstrategie für Berlin – Ziele, Maßnahmen, Modellprojekte*. Berlin, 2011.

Chapter 3.4 Parking Lots for Motor Vehicles and Bicycles

The Danish Cyclists Federation. *Bicycle Parking Manual.* Copenhagen, 2008.
Schuster, Andreas, Josef Sattler, and Stephan Hoffmann. "Benötigen wir ein neues Pkw-Bemessungsfahrzeug für den Entwurf von Anlagen des ruhenden Verkehrs?" *Straßenverkehrstechnik* 56, no. 1 (2012): 5–10.
Senatsverwaltung für Stadtentwicklung Berlin. *Fahrradparken in Berlin – Leitfaden für die Planung.* Berlin, 2008.

Chapter 3.5 Waste Container Areas

Abfallwirtschaftsbetrieb München. *Müllräume und Müllbehälter-Standplätze – Vorschriften und Hinweise.* Munich, 2011.
Bauordnung Wien [Vienna building code], LGBl. Nr. 11/1930, last amended by LGBl. Nr. 46/2013.
Berliner Stadtreinigung. *Grundlagen für die Gestaltung von Standorten und Transportwegen für Abfallbehälter.* Berlin, 2011.
Gesetz über die Vermeidung und Behandlung von Abfällen und die Einhebung einer hierfür erforderlichen Abgabe im Gebiete des Landes Wien (Wiener Abfallwirtschaftsgesetz) [Vienna waste management act], LGBl. für Wien Nr. 13/1994, last amended by LGBl. für Wien Nr. 31/2013.
Stadt Zürich, ERZ Entsorgung + Recycling Zürich. *Wegleitung II: Kostenloser, neuer Kunststoffcontainer.* Zurich, 2008.

Chapter 3.6 Boundary Enclosures and Railings

Bayerisches Landesamt für Umwelt / Dr. Katharina Stroh (LfU), eds. *Lärm – Straße und Schiene.* http://www.lfu.bayern.de/umweltwissen/index.htm (last accessed: Apr. 7, 2014).
Wirtschaftsministerium Baden-Württemberg. *Städtebauliche Lärmfibel Online*, Stuttgart 2007: http://www.staedtebauliche-laermfibel.de (last accessed: Apr. 7, 2014).

Chapter 3.7 Seating

Beucker, Nicolas and Monika Zurnatzis. *Stadtmobiliar für Senioren – Ausstattungskriterien für eine altengerechte Stadt.* Study report, 2011, http://socialdesign.hs-niederrhein.de (last accessed: Apr. 7, 2014).

Chapter 3.8 Lighting

Eckert, Martin, and Hans-Hubert Meseberg, eds. *Straßenbeleuchtung und Sicherheit.* LiTG publication 17. Berlin, 1998.
Ris, Hans Rudolf. *Beleuchtungstechnik für Praktiker.* Berlin, 2008.
Steck, Bernhard, ed. *Zur Einwirkung von Außenbeleuchtungsanlagen auf nachtaktive Insekten.* LiTG publication 15. Berlin, 1997.
TRILUX-LENZE GmbH + Co KG. *Licht für Europas Straßen – Beleuchtung von Straßen, Wegen und Plätzen nach DIN EN 13 201.* Arnsberg, 2005.

Chapter 3.9 Water Facilities

Deutscher Wetterdienst – Institut für Technisch-Wissenschaftliche Hydrologie, ed. *KOSTRA-DWD 2000: Koordinierte Starkniederschlags-Regionalisierungs-Auswertungen.* Offenbach, 2006.
Hansen, Richard, and Friedrich Stahl. *Perennials and Their Garden Habitats*, translated by Richard Ward. Portland, 1993. Originally published as *Die Stauden und ihre Lebensbereiche in Gärten und Grünanlagen.* Stuttgart, 1991.
Lomer, Wolfgang, ed. *Garten- und Landschaftsbau.* Der Gärtner 4. Stuttgart, 2001.
Niesel, Alfred, ed. *Grünflächen-Pflegemanagement – dynamische Pflege von Grün.* Stuttgart, 2006.

Chapter 3.10 Woody Plants

Deutsche Gartenamtsleiterkonferenz (GALK), and Arbeitskreis Stadtbäume. *GALK-Straßenbaumliste.* Revised October 29, 2013. Routinely updated list available online (in German only): http://www.galk.de/
Florineth, Florin. *Pflanzen statt Beton.* Berlin, 2012.
Gaida, Wolfgang, and Helmut Grothe. *Gehölze: Handbuch für Planung und Ausführung.* Berlin, 2000.
Roloff, Andreas. *Bäume in der Stadt: Besonderheiten, Funktion, Nutzen, Arten, Risiken.* Stuttgart, 2013.

Chapter 3.11 Vegetated Roofing

Kaltenbach, Frank. "Lebende Wände, vertikale Gärten – vom Blumentopf zur grünen Systemfassade," *Detail* 48, no. 12 (2008): 1454–1466.
Köhler, Manfred, Georg Barth, Thorwald Brandwein, and Dagmar Gast. *Fassaden- und Dachbegrünung.* Stuttgart, 1993.
Krupka, Bernd. *Dachbegrünung. Pflanzen- und Vegetationsanwendung an Bauwerken.* Stuttgart, 1992.
Zentralverband des Deutschen Dachdeckerhandwerks – ZVDH, ed. *Fachregel für Abdichtungen – Flachdachrichtlinien.* Cologne, Oct. 2008, revised Dec. 2011.
ZinCo GmbH, ed. *Planungshilfe: Das grüne Dach; Standardwerk für Planung und Ausführung genutzter Dachflächen.* Untersingen, 1998.
ZinCo GmbH, ed. *Planungshilfe: Walkways and Driveways on Roofs and Decks.* Untersingen, 2013.

Chapter 3.12 Vertical Planting

Beccaletto, Jacques, and Denis Retournard. *Obstgehölze erziehen und formen: Spaliere, Kordons, Palmetten.* Stuttgart, 2007.
Beltz, Heinrich. *Spalierobst im Garten – Sorten, Pflege, Schnitt.* Munich, 2012.
Großmann, Gerd, and Wolf-Dietmar Wackwitz. *Spalierobst.* Stuttgart, 1998.
Gunkel, Rita. *Fassadenbegrünung: Kletterpflanzen und Klettergerüste.* Stuttgart, 2004.
Köhler, Manfred, Georg Barth, Thorwald Brandwein, and Dagmar Gast. *Fassaden- und Dachbegrünung.* Stuttgart, 1993.
Magistrat der Stadt Wien, and Programm für umweltgerechte Leistungen "ÖkoKauf Wien," eds. *Leitfaden Fassadenbegrünung.* Vienna, 2013.
Petschek, Peter, and Siegfried Gass. *Schatten konstruieren: Zelte, Pergolen, Seile, Pflanzen.* Basel, 2011.

Chapter 4.1 Gardens

Bundesgesetz über die Regelung des Kleingartenwesens (Kleingartengesetz). [Federal law on the regulation of allotment gardening] (Austria), December 16, 1958, last amended by BGBl. I Nr. 98/2001.
Bundeskleingartengesetz [Federal law on allotment gardens] (Germany), February 28, 1983, last amended September 19, 2006.
Gälzer, Ralph. *Grünplanung für Städte.* Stuttgart, 2001.
Prinz, Dieter. *Städtebau – Band 1: Städtebauliches Entwerfen.* Stuttgart, 1995.
Richter, Gerhard. *Handbuch Stadtgrün. Landschaftsarchitektur im städtischen Freiraum.* Munich, 1981.
Senatsverwaltung für Stadtentwicklung Berlin. *Das bunte Grün: Kleingärten in Berlin.* Berlin, 2010.
Wiener Kleingartengesetz [Vienna allotment garden act]. LGBl. für Wien Nr. 57/1996, last amended by LGBl. für Wien Nr. 35/2013.

Chapter 4.2 Open Spaces in Schools and Preschools

ILA – Institut für Landschaftsarchitektur, Universität für Bodenkultur Wien. *Schul:FREI – Empfehlungen für die Gestaltung von Schulfreiräumen.* Vienna, 2004, http://www.schulfreiraum.com/ (last accessed: Apr. 7, 2014).
Sekretariat der Kultusministerkonferenz, Zentralstelle für Normungsfragen und Wirtschaftlichkeit im Bildungswesen (ZNWB). *Arbeitshilfen zum Schulbau.* Berlin, 2008.

Chapter 4.3 Playgrounds

Bundesministerium für Umwelt, Naturschutz und Reaktorsicherheit. *Liste giftiger Pflanzenarten.* 2000.
Dittrich, Gerhard, ed. *Kinderspielplätze. Analysen, empirische Befunde und Planungsempfehlungen.* Stuttgart, 1974.
Landwirtschaftskammer Nordrhein-Westfalen. *Wege zum Naturverständnis – Pflanzenverwendung in Kindergärten und kinderfreundlichen Anlagen.* 2002.
Lorenz von Ehren Nursery. *Planning Tips Trees and Shrubs.* http://lve-baumschule.de/en > Planning tips
Natur- und Umweltschutzakademie des Landes NRW, ed. *Naturspielräume für Kinder – eine Arbeitshilfe zur Gestaltung naturnaher Spielräume an Kindergärten und anderswo.* Recklinghausen, 1999.
Satzung über die Beschaffenheit und Größe privater Spielplätze für Kleinkinder (Spielplatzsatzung), Jan. 14, 1986.
Verband Garten- und Landschaftsbau Rheinland. *Giftige Pflanzen an Kinderspielplätzen.* 1974.
Verordnung der Wiener Landesregierung, mit der nähere Vorschriften für Kleinkinderspielplätze, Kinder- und Jugendspielplätze und Kinder- und Jugendspielräume erlassen werden (Spielplatzverordnung) [Playground ordinance]. 1993.

Chapter 4.4 Sports Facilities

Bayerisches Landesamt für Umwelt (LfU). *Geräusche von Trendsportanlagen.* Parts 1 and 2, 2005.

Chapter 4.5 Outdoor Swimming Pools, Bathing Ponds, Water-Treading Pools

Baumhauer, Jörg, and Carsten Schmidt. *Schwimmteichbau: Handbuch für Planung, Technik und Betrieb.* Berlin, 2008.
Deutsche Gesellschaft für das Badewesen. *Merkblatt 94.05 Verkehrssicherungs- und Aufsichtspflicht in öffentlichen Bädern während des Badebetriebs.* 2008.
Deutsche Gesellschaft für das Badewesen. *Merkblatt 94.12 Verkehrssicherungs- und Aufsichtspflicht in öffentlichen Naturbädern während des Badebetrieb.* 2014.
Deutscher Schwimm-Verband e.V. *Bau- und Ausstattungsanforderungen für wettkampfgerechte Schwimmsportstätten.* 2012.
Koordinierungskreis Bäder. *Richtlinien für den Bäderbau* [KOK guidelines]. 2013.
Mahabadi, Mehdi, and Inés M. Rohlfing. *Schwimm- und Badeteichanlagen: Planungs- und Baugrundsätze.* Stuttgart, 2008.

Chapter 4.6 Campgrounds

Gälzer, Ralph. *Grünplanung für Städte.* Stuttgart, 2001.
Richter, Gerhard. *Handbuch Stadtgrün. Landschaftsarchitektur im städtischen Freiraum.* Munich, 1981.

5.4 Index

H

I

J

K

L

M

N

O

P

R

S

T

U

V

W

Picture credits

The excerpts of the German and international standards are quoted with the permission by DIN Deutschen Institut für Normung e. V. It is essential when using the DIN standards to consult the version of most recent date, available from Beuth Verlag GmbH, Burgrafenstraße 6, 10787 Berlin.

All photographies: Astrid Zimmermann, unless indicated otherwise in the following. All drawings were done for this publication, based on drawings by Astrid Zimmermann or after the following authors/publications:

Cover: Annette Gref
Tab. 1.1 ECA for Administrations, 2008 (EuCAN – European Concept
for Accessibility Network)
Fig. 2.1.5 and fig. 2.1.6 based on Gehl, Jan: *Life Between Buildings*, 1987, p. 62 ff.
Fig. 2.1.3 L. Michow & Sohn GmbH, Hamburg
Fig. 2.1.9 based on Hall, Edward: *The Hidden Dimension*, 1966, p. 126
Fig. 2.1.10 based on Gehl, Jan: *Life Between Buildings*, 1987, p. 62 ff.
Fig. 2.1.12 based on Stadt Graz: *Barrierefreies Bauen für alle*, 2006, p. 7
Tab. 2.1.1 Bundesministerium für Gesundheit: *Verbesserung von visuellen Informationen im öffentlichen Raum,* 1996, p. 32
Fig. 3.1.2 based on Heinze, W. / Schreiber, D.: *Eine neue Kartierung der Winterhärtezonen für Gehölze* in Mitteleuropa. In: Mitteilungen der Deutschen Dendrologischen Gesellschaft 75, 1984, p. 11–56
Fig. 3.1.5 based on Ministere de l'Equipement: L'Amenagement des espaces verts, 1992, S. 104 and Flemming, Günther: Wald – Wetter – Klima, 1987, p. 73
Fig. 3.1.6 Flemming, Günther: *Wald – Wetter – Klima*, 1987, p. 45/54
Fig. 3.1.7 based on Gehl, Jan: *Life Between Buildings*, 1987, p. 176; Gandemer, J.: *Wind Environment around Buildings: Aerodynamic Concepts Proceedings, 4. International Conference on Wind Effects on Buildings and Structures*, 1977, p. 423–432; Häckel, Hans: *Das Gartenklima*, 1989, p. 94
Fig. 3.1.8 Häckel, Hans: *Das Gartenklima*, 1989, p. 25
Tab. 3.1.1 Hackel, Hans: *Das Gartenklima*, 1989, p. 36
Tab. 3.1.2 Twarowski, Mieczyslaw: *Sonne und Architektur*, 1962, p. 143 ff.
Fig. 3.1.15 and Abb. 3.1.17 Häckel, Hans: *Das Gartenklima*, 1989, p. 20
Fig. 3.2.13 DIN 32984: 2011-10 and Ingenieurbüro – Barrierefreies Planen und Bauen Fulda: www.barrierefrei-mobilitaet.de
Fig. 3.2.9 Land Salzburg: *barrierefrei bauen*, 2008, p. 45
Fig. 3.2.15 and Fig. 3.2.16: DIN 18040-1:2010-10 (changed)
Fig. 3.2.18 EAR 05, p. 40
Fig. 3.3.3 RASt 06
Tab. 3.3.5 RASt 06
Fig. 3.3.5 RASt 06 and DIN 32984:2011-10
Fig. 3.3.11 ERA 10
Fig. 3.3.14 ERA 10
Fig. 3.3.15 DIN 32984:2011-10
Fig. 3.3.17 RASt 06
Tab. 3.3.12 RASt 06
Tab. 3.3.14 RASt 06
Tab. 3.3.15 Ingenieurbüro – Barrierefreies Planen und Bauen Fulda: www.barrierefrei-mobilitaet.de
Fig. 3.3.23–25 RASt 06
Fig. 3.3.29–31 Muster-Richtlinien über Flachen für die Feuerwehr, 2007 / DIN 14090:2003-05
Fig. 3.4.1 Danish Cycling Federation: Bicycle Parking Manual, 2008 (changed)
Fig. 3.4.5–7 EAR 05
Fig. 3.4.8–9 EAR 05
Tab. 3.4.3–4 EAR 05
Fig. 3.4.11–16 EAR 05
Fig. 3.5.2–3 RASt 06
Fig. 3.6.5–6 Bayerisches Landesamt für Umwelt 2008: *Lärm – Straße und Schiene, 2008 and Wirtschaftsministerium Baden-Württemberg: Städtebauliche Lärmfibel Online,* date: 26.11.2007
Fig. 3.6.7 DIN 18065:2011-06 (expanded)
Fig. 3.8.4–12 DIN 13201-1:2005-11 (German version of DIN 13201-1:2005-11)
Tab. 3.8.13 EN 12464-2
Fig. 3.8.4–12 DIN 13201-1:2005-11 (German version of DIN 13201-1:2005-11)
Tab. 3.8.16 EN 13201-2:2003
Tab. 3.8.17 DIN EN 12193: 2008-04
Tab. 3.9.2 DWA-A 138 – Planning, Construction and Operation of Facilities for the Percolation of Precipitation Water
Fig. 3.9.5–6 DWA-A 138 – Planning, Construction and Operation of Facilities for the Percolation of Precipitation Water
Tab. 3.9.7 DIN 18035-2:2003-07
Fig. 3.10.2–3 FLL – Empfehlungen für Baumpflanzungen – Teil 2, 2010
Tab. 3.10.4 Straßenbaumliste der Deutschen Gartenamtsleiterkonferenz (GALK) und KLimaArtenMatrix für Stadtbaumarten
Tab. 3.10.5 Wurzelwuchsverhalten der Straßenbäume (expanded), www.greenmax.eu; last accessed: Aug. 18, 2014
Fig. 3.10.5–6 RAS-LP 4 Richtlinie für die Anlage von Straßen, part: Landschaftspflege, chapter 4: Schutz von Bäumen, Vegetationsbestanden und Tieren bei Baumaßnahmen, 1999
Fig. 3.10.8 FLL – Empfehlungen für Baumpflanzungen – part 2, 2010
Tab. 3.11.1 ZinCo GmbH (ed.): *Planungshilfe „Das grüne Dach". Standardwerk für Planung und Ausführung genutzter Dachflächen*, Untersingen 1998
Tab. 3.11.1 ZinCo GmbH (ed.): *Planungshilfe „Das grüne Dach". Standardwerk für Planung und Ausführung genutzter Dachflächen*, Untersingen 1998
Fig. 3.11.2 and Tab. 3.11.3 ZinCo GmbH (ed.): *Planungshilfe „Das grüne Dach". Standardwerk für Planung und Ausführung genutzter Dachflächen*, Untersingen 1998
Fig. 3.11.3 Krupka, Bernd: *Dachbegrünung. Pflanzen- und Vegetationsanwendung an Bauwerken,* Stuttgart 1992
Fig. 3.11.5 ZinCo GmbH (ed.): *Planungshilfe „Das grüne Dach". Standardwerk für Planung und Ausführung genutzter Dachflächen* Untersingen 1998
Fig. 4.3.2–3, EN 1176-1:2008
Fig. 4.3.4 EN 1176-3:2008
Fig. 4.3.5, EN 1176-1:2008
Tab. 4.3.5–6 EN 1176-1:2008
Tab. 4.4.1 gem. DIN 18035-1: 2003-02, (expanded)
Tab. 4.5.9–10 DIN EN 13451-10
Fig. 4.5.6 DIN EN 13451-10
Fig. 4.5.8 FLL – FLL-Richtlinie Richtlinien für Planung, Bau, Instandhaltung und Betrieb von Freibädern mit biologischer Wasseraufbereitung, 2010

Sitting heights: after Stadt Graz: *Barrierefreies Bauen für alle,* 2006, p. 24, 47

Author
Dipl.-Ing. Astrid Zimmermann

Contributors
Research/conception: Rike Kirstein
Drawings: Rike Kirstein, Andreas Konig, Stefan Wolf, Christian Zimmermann, Christian Schellhorn

Picture editor
Astrid Zimmermann

Book concept, editing, project coordination
Annette Gref, Katharina Kulke

Translation
David Koralek/ArchiTrans

Copyediting
Keonaona Peterson

Layout concept and cover design
Hug & Eberlein

Composition
Sven Schrape

All CAD drawings were produced and laid out using the Vectorworks program Vectorworks LANDSCHAFT

The technical recommendations contained in this book reflect the current state of technology but expressly require explicit coordination by the responsible specialist planners to ensure compliance with the applicable and current laws, regulations, and standards of the country concerned. Neither the author nor the publisher can be held in any way accountable for the design, planning or execution of faulty work.

Acknowledgements: Here I would like to thank all the institutions and individuals who have contributed to the success of this publication.
Special thanks go to Annette Gref and Katharina Kulke for their support with the book's concept and its content. For technical discussions, research work, and other valued assistance, I also wish to express special thanks to Thilo Folkerts, Ulrike Zimmermann, Inge Zimmermann, Gabriele Schneider, and the Chair of Landscaping and Construction at TU Berlin/Prof. Cordula Loidl-Reisch.

Library of Congress Cataloging-in-Publication Data
A CIP catalog record for this book has been applied for at the Library of Congress.

Bibliographic information published by the German National Library
The German National Library lists this publication in the Deutsche Nationalbibliografie; detailed bibliographic data are available on the Internet at http://dnb.dnb.de.

This publication is also available in a German language edition (ISBN 978-3-0346-0758-2, Hardcover; 978-3-0346-0759-9, Softcover).

P.O. Box 44, 4009 Basel, Switzerland
Part of Walter de Gruyter GmbH, Berlin/Munich/Boston

Printed on acid-free paper produced from chlorine-free pulp. TCF ∞

Printed in Germany

ISBN 978-3-0346-0760-5 Hardcover
ISBN 978-3-0346-0761-2 Softcover

9 8 7 6 5 4 3 2 1

www.birkhauser.com